THE CALIFORNIA
HIGHWAY 1 BOOK

THE CALIFORNIA HIGHWAY 1 BOOK

CALIFORNIA 1

An Odology of America's Most Romantic Road

Rick Adams / Louise McCorkle

BALLANTINE BOOKS · NEW YORK

Library of Congress Catalog Card Number: 85-90559
ISBN: 0-345-31855-2

Cover design by Georgia Morrissey.
Photo: H. Wendler 1981/*The Image Bank.*

Design and Production: Jon Goodchild/*Triad.*

The authors also extend their grateful thanks to the production team for their individual contributions: Jon Goodchild, Mark Shepard, Jayne Osgood, Craig DuMonte, Sara Schrom, Michele Thomas, Jay Daniels, John Wong, and TBD Typography.

Copy editing: Amy Einsohn.
Cartography: Michael Hinshaw, Mindy Richter and Michael Trip.

And special thanks to the California Historial Society, San Francisco and Los Angeles, and the Fred Hill for help and encouragement.

Manufactured in the United States of America

First Edition: October 1985

10 9 8 7 6 5 4 3 2 1

The authors wish to thank the following individuals for their contributions to *The California Highway 1 Book.*

Charles Acker, Albion Adams, Miranda Adams, Linda Aherns, Wick Aherns, John Ashbaugh, Ann Banning, Ed Bauer, Susan Bensen, Grey Brechin, Betty Boatwright, Julia Bott, Barbara J. Blankman, M. Alan Born, Rudolph Brandt, Sala Burton, Ralph Buchsbaum, Jane Craven Caldwell, Anne S. Calvert, Carney Campion, Earl Carpenter, Manuel Castells, Nancy Cave, Carol Champion, Bill Chase, Maxine Chelini, Raymond H. Clary, Justin A. Cohen, Ken Comello, Steve Cooper, Joseph J. Corn, Virginia Crook, Greg Cummings, Richard Dalsemer, Jack Davis, Harry Dean, Roy Gregory DeGiere, Jeff Divine, Peter Douglas, Mark Duino, Kathie Eaton, Dean Echenberg, Rebecca Evens, Lois Ewing, Lorraine Faber, Phylis Faber, Dick Felty, Lawrence Ferlinghetti, Michael Fischer, Norma Flanery, Steven Fletcher, John Frankel, James Gandre, Ed Gardien, Susa Gates, Irene Gausch, Jennie Gerard, Tom Golden, Charles Gordon, Patrick K. Griffith, Ruth Gravanis, Bob Halligan, Gary Halloway, Douglas Haller, Norman Hammond, Gladys Hanson, Steve Harris, Pat Hathaway, William Hendricks, Dennis Herman, Richard G. Hildreth, J. S. Holliday, Marion Holmes, Joan Jackson, Bruce Johnson, Kathleen Goddard Jones, Bob Katz, Barry Keene, David J. Kennedy, T. J. Kent, John King, Sherry King, Jerry Keonig, Margaret Koch, Diane Landry, Eugene Lee, Barbara Lekisch, Henri LeNoir, Warren Littlefield, Dewey Livingston, Bruce McCorkle, Carolyn McCorkle, Sallie McCorkle, Bud McCrary, Paula Mabry, Robert C. Mahoney, Bill Majoue, Steven Maki, Jack Mason, William Masters, Elizabeth Max, Paul Maxwell, Phil Mese, Amy Meyer, Dave Mitchell, Anne Moore, Susana Montaña, Roger Montgomery, Cara Moore, Ken Moore, June Morrall, Donald B. Neuwirth, Alfred Newman, Ted Odza, Kevin O'Connell, Julie Packard, Thomas Parkinson, Dorothy Perloff, Phillip Perloff, Nancy Peters, Charles Peterson, Joseph E. Petrillo, David Plumb, Bill Prout, David Prowler, Lura Rawlson, Michael Redmon, R. A. Reinstedt, Leo Riegler, Tom Roberts, Elpidio Roache, Don Rolph, Joan Rummelsburg, Stanley Saitowitz, Dorothea Sallee, Bert Schwartzschild, Stanley Scott, Will Shaw, Judy Sheldon, Ellen Sidenberg, Mark Silberstein, Shirwin Smith, Brian Steen, Dugald Stermer, Laura Stevens, Zack Stewart, George Sumner, Paul Sussman, David Tabor, Marcia Tacus, Rita Templeman, Dough Thompson, Frances Thompson, Marc Treib, Tamara Tremaine, Michael Wade, Norman L. De Vall, Doris Walker, Joan Ward, Susan Weeks, Emil White, Betty Wiechec, Ken Winston, Baron Wolman, Sally Woodbridge, John Woolfenden, Lisa Young.

Further, many thanks to all the following organizations and institutions for their valued cooperation and contributions:

Abalone Alliance, Academy of Motion Picture Arts and Sciences Library, Amigos de Bolsa Chica, Association of Bay Area Governments, Audubon Canyon Ranch, Audubon Society, Bancroft Library, Bay Conservation and Development Commission, Big Sur Foundation, Big Sur Land Trust, Caltrans, California Coastal Commission, California Conservation Corps, California Native Plant Society, California State Parks Foundation, Canessa Park, Carmel Chamber of Commerce, Community Resources Trust of the Southern Mendocino Coast, Esalen Institute, Fort Ross Historical Park, Friends of Ballona Wetlands, Friends of the Earth, Friends of Recreation and Parks, Friends of Santa Monica Pier, Get Oil Out, Golden Gate Bridge District, Golden Gate National Recreation Area, Green Gulch Farm, Greenpeace, Half Moon Bay Chamber of Commerce, Land Trust of Santa Cruz County, League for Coastal Protection, League of Women Voters, Lompoc Historical Society, *Lompoc Record,* Lompoc Valley Chamber of Commerce, Los Angeles County Department of Beaches and Harbors, Los Angeles County Department of Planning, Malibu Chamber of Commerce, Marin Agriculture Land Trust, Marin Coast Chamber of Commerce, Marin County Chamber of Commerce, Marin County Planning Department, Memory Shop West, Mendocino County Planning Department, Monterey County Library, Monterey County Planning Department, Moss Landing Marine Lab, Mountains Restoration Trust, National Parks Service, North Coast Redwood Interpretive Association, Pacific Film Archive, Pismo Beach Chamber of Commerce, *Peninsula Times Tribune,* Peninsula Open Space Trust, People for Open Space, Point Reyes Bird Observatory, *Point Reyes Light,* Point Reyes National Seashore, Redwood Empire Association, *San Francisco Bay Guardian,* San Francisco Maritime Museum, San Francisco Mime Troup, San Francisco Muni, San Luis Obispo Environmental Center, San Luis Obispo City Library, San Luis Obispo County Planning Department, Natural History Association of the San Luis Obispo Coast, San Luis Obispo Historical Society Museum, San Luis Obispo Land Conservancy, *San Luis Obispo Telegraph Tribune,* Santa Barbara Department of City Planning, Santa Barbara Zoological Gardens, Santa Cruz County Planning Department, City of Santa Cruz Planning Department, Santa Monica Convention and Visitors Bureau, Santa Monica Mountains Conservancy, Santa Monica Mountains Trail Council, Seaside Corp., Sempervirens Fund, Sherman Library, Sierra Club, Sonoma County Parks Department, Sonoma County Planning Department, State Coastal Conservancy, State Department of Parks and Recreation, *Surfer Magazine,* The Nature Conservancy, Tor House Foundation, Trust for Public Land, University of California Berkeley College of Environmental Design Library, University of California Santa Barbara Special Collections, University of California Santa Cruz Special Collections, Vendata Society, Ventura County Chamber of Commerce, Ventura County Historical Society, Ventura County Planning Department, Alan Watts Society for Comparative Philosophy, Zoetrope Studios.

I just wanta ride man. I gotta go.

Dean Moriarity in Jack Kerouac's *On the Road*

What Is An *Odology*?

O DOLOGY is the science or study of roads. Coined by J. B. Jackson, a contemporary land use architect, the word derives from the Greek *hodos,* signifying road or journey, and often implying aspiration toward a chosen end. (*Exodus* and *method* share the same root and the same implication of movement toward something.)

This odology of California Highway 1 is meant to give the most complete possible depiction of America's most romantic road by approaching it from six perspectives: its origins, land uses, environment, attractions, location and resources. And it is meant to impart some of the exaltation of the journey that the ancient Greeks implied when they spoke of the road as being the handiwork of the gods and the traveler as an aspirant of marvels unimaginable.

I just wanta ride man. I gotta go.

Dean Moriarity in Jack Kerouac's *On the Road*

THE CALIFORNIA HIGHWAY 1 Book describes the road from six different perspectives. Each category has its own column, which appears on every two-page spread. The Book runs in geographic sequence by county from south to north.

THE CALIFORNIA HIGHWAY 1 BOOK can be read from front to back, by specific location, or from any of the six individual

Origins	Land Use	Environment	Roadside Attractions	Resources

Maps Highway 1's route through each county and shows individual points referred to in adjacent columns on each two-page spread.

Tells what the area was like before Highway 1 was constructed and how the road was built. **Examples:** doghole ports in Mendocino County, amusement piers in Los Angeles County, and convict labor road crews on the cliffs of Big Sur.

Explains the current uses of roadside land areas and their impacts. **Examples:** drive-in movies, coastal subdivisions, offshore oil development, and open space preservation.

Describes elements of the natural environment along the road. **Examples:** how beaches are made, ecological systems, whales, redwoods, and poppies.

Calls attention to unique points of interest along the highway. **Examples:** the surfing capital of the world, roadside waterfalls, and where the fortune cookie was invented.

Lists and briefly describes important information resources for each Highway 1 area. **Examples:** public transit information, guidebooks, and materials about specific places, events, and issues.

perspectives. For example, reading the Origins column by itself will provide a comprehensive historical perspective of the coast road in each county. Two sections may also be read in conjunction: the Environmental section, for instance, with the Land Use section, to amplify the significance of impacts to the natural environment from current or planned uses of the land along the road. The Resources column supplements these sections (or any others) by directing readers to further pertinent materials. If you are planning a drive along the coast, the Roadside Attractions section will be of value to draw your attention to points of interest not usually covered in guidebooks. The County maps show where everything is and how to get there.

Enjoy the book. But above all enjoy the road.

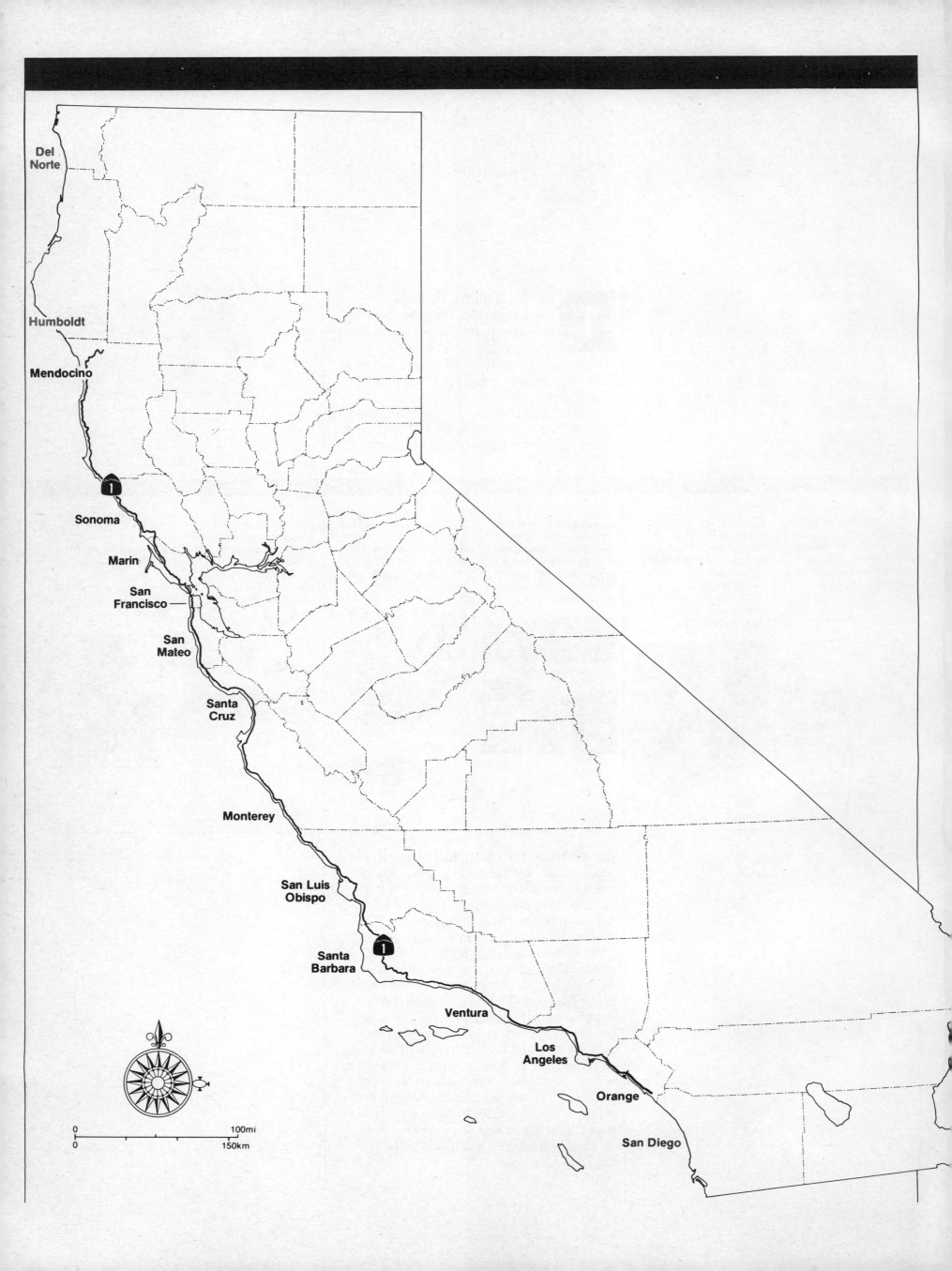

HERE WE GO: This is California's Coastal Highway 1, the mainline to the nation's most richly varied coast that transports us along the edge of the blue Pacific while we fish, swim, surf, stare, investigate, and dream. See the sites that advertise for enchantment.

The coast highway distinguishes itself from other roads as romance divides from reality. Its make-believe character is confirmed by implausible conformance to unsettled topography. Watch it dance upon the cliffs, trapeze-style, without a net, without a care; see it race astride sand flats, through redwood forests, exhilarated by undreamed possibilities beyond the next turn. Always is there the air of the miraculous.

"The road is better than the inn," said Cervantes. Drive it, cycle it, walk it, imagine it. Take the road. Use this book.

ORANGE

CALIFORNIA 1 BEGINS its journey up the coast at Dana Point, near the southern end of Orange County. From here to Ventura, State Route 1 is referred to as Pacific Coast Highway (PCH) and holds a course as near to the coast as possible.

On its route through Orange County, PCH travels through the heart of some of California's finest beach towns. Just north of Dana Point is Laguna Beach, pretty and pleasant, with enchanting small beaches south and north of town. Laguna's Main Beach is a model of masterful urban beach design.

At Newport Beach, the PCH traveler is confronted with coastal California's most upscale consumer environment. Newport offers a variety of peculiar attractions that range from John Wayne's boat—a converted minesweeper—to a shopping center catering to the richest of the rich, Fashion Island.

North of Newport, PCH streaks toward Huntington Beach, where California beach culture exuberantly conducts itself along one of the world's most popular surfing beaches. Next door is Bolsa Chica wetland, one of Southern California's most significant ecological habitats.

Few counties outpace coastal Orange County for sheer ebullience, color, and shine. PCH is its main concourse.

County Profile

Geographic

Land Area (acres)	500,480
Land Area (sq. miles)	782.0
Water Area (acres)	1,960
Water Area (sq. miles)	3.1
Acres in Public Ownership	114,897.99
Percent in Public Ownership	22.96
Miles of Public Roads	5,339
County Seat	Santa Ana

Demographic

Population	2,036,400
State Rank by Population	2
Projected 1990 Population	2,154,900
Unemployment Rate (state avg. = 9.9)	6.6
Per Capita Personal Income	$13,027
State Rank by Income	7
Total Assessed Property Value	$67,984,004,465

Origins

Richard Henry Dana's California

It is as it should be that California's Coast Highway 1 begins at Dana Point—named after Richard Henry Dana, whose *Two Years Before the Mast* (1840) was the first American book to idealize California. Like Highway 1, Dana's tale of a seaman's journey up the coast combines the two enduring preoccupations of California the dream state: travel and romance.

"This is the most romantic spot along the

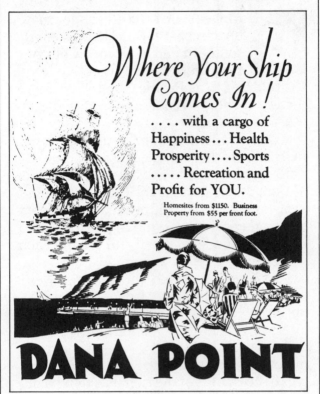

coast," said Dana of the area near San Juan Capistrano that now bears his name. Despite its beauty, almost 90 years passed before any settlement was drawn to the area. Dana garnered his impressions while loading hides and tallow from the cliffs onto his offshore ship, *The Pilgrim.* The work was backbreaking—the tallow was loaded in 500-pound bags—but it was profitable, at least for the East Coast ship owners who sailed up and down California's coast avoiding Mexican customs and trading copperware, pewter, and jewelry for the valuable hides. Each voyage assured a ship owner a net profit of $40,000 to $65,000.

California Alchemy

Soon Dana sailed on to other worlds—a law practice in Boston and a settled life on land. Dana Point would not begin to be shaped as a town until 1925, when the government-owned coastal land was sold to W. H. Woodruff, who purchased much of the area with Los Angeles capital for development of a new resort town. Woodruff put his faith into a new California alchemy that seemed to turn subdivided land into gold.

Woodruff expected riches to be delivered along the newly paved streets that were decorated with colorful lanterns. Street of the Blue Lantern. Street of the Ruby Lantern. Street of the Golden Lantern. He patterned a resort after hotels that hung on the cliffs of Sorrento, Italy. The Dana Point Inn was even more elaborately conceived, with outdoor elevators to the beach. Unfortunately, most of Woodruff's dream failed to materialize because of the advent of the Depression. But a town was begun.

Land Use

The Romance of the Road

Afoot and Lighthearted I take to the Open Road.
Walt Whitman

The romance of travel has always influenced the dreams and aspirations of Californians. The passionate desire for discovery that filled the hearts of the first white settlers, bringing them here, inaugurated a spirit with which contemporary Californians continue to explore the Golden State's magnificent treasures. "Ocean in view," recorded the Lewis and Clark expedition after crossing America on foot, "O the joy."

The arrival of the automobile expanded Californians' dreams of local exploration at the same time it opened the state to a new four-wheeled migration fueled by visions of a paradise at the end of the road. The image of the open road, always a frequent presence in American literature, gained new vibrancy with the automobile. By the end of the 1950s, Jack Kerouac combined the romance of the quest with the dream of complete mobility to stir the hearts of a generation and put them on the road, generally in the direction of California.

Imbued with desire and hope, the automobile has become the California dream machine, capable of producing complete illusions of freedom, mobility, and control, and strengthening the image of the road as a means of more than literal deliverance. No one speaks more ably of the contemporary significance of the road than Joan Didion, who describes freeway driving in California as "the only secular communion we have," which sometimes produces, as it did for Maria Wyeth in *Play It As It Lays,* a romantic "rapture" that gives purpose, if not meaning, to life.

So ingrained is the romance of the road within California culture that it is often interchangeable

with that elusive Pacific Coast grail, the California dream. All of us are, in fact, a little like Thomas Pynchon's Oedipa Maas, whose quest for the California dream in *The Crying of Lot 49* leads her directionlessly down the coast highway, certain only of the location of her desire—beside the roadside at the land's edge.

A Terrestrial Paradise

Know ye that on the right hand of the Indies there is an island called California, very close to the side of the Terrestrial Paradise.
Garcia Rodríguez Ordóñez de Montalvo, circa 1510

California 1, Pacific Coast Highway, travels through a natural environment of such splendorous diversity that even to this day portions might pass for a terrestrial paradise.

Fertile plains and valleys stretch to the east along the 1,100 mile-long California coast, which contain some of the most productive agricultural land in the world. Major mountain ranges with peaks higher than 14,000 feet loom far on the horizon, or march relentlessly west to dip their toes into the vibrant Pacific, their canyons and valleys forested by virgin stands of redwood trees that have kept a coastal watch since before the time of Christ.

Continental plates meet, rub, and collide with seismic regularity along the road's path. Underneath the surface of sea, shore, and highway lie some of America's most unstable geological mixtures, criss-crossed by earthquake faults that are constantly uplifting, folding, and rearranging the continent's edge. Valuable minerals, oil, and gas exist in uncharted supply. Jade is scattered on the beaches and gold veins the coastal mountains.

In some places, the coast highway races alongside sand dunes that stretch for miles; in others, crescent beaches with pearly white sand and perfect breakers caress a jade green sea. There are rocky shores whose tidepools harbor galaxies of sea stars, and marshes and estuaries that give birth to the microscopic life forms that are the foundation for life on this planet.

Offshore, gray whales travel thousands of miles in their annual migrations, joined along the way by seals, sea lions, porpoises, and dolphins. Forests of the world's largest kelp extend hundreds of feet underwater, hovering above submarine canyons that would easily hold several of the land-locked Grand Canyon. Between the fronds of the waving kelp swims the playful sea otter, and its major predator, the great white shark.

Above Highway 1 soars the eagle and falcon and thousands of other birds flying along the north/south migratory Pacific flyway. Surrounding all this is the famous California coastal climate, of Mediterranean moderation brightened by seasonal rains, fogs, and thrilling coastal storms.

Highway 1 begins at Dana Point in the County of Orange. Glimpses of the Terrestrial Paradise ahead.

Where the Road Begins

Less like a highway than an expression of the heart's desire, Pacific Coast Highway, (PCH), begins at Dana Point adjacent to the state's most adamant freeway, Interstate 5. From here north, America's most romantic road runs a course aside an adoring Pacific. At the roadside are attractions aplenty.

PCH is Dana Point's main street, a thoroughfare lined with familiar elements of roadside commercial activity. Gas stations, offices, shops, fast-food franchises, and small markets jumble together in a mix of loud and quiet styles that compete for the passing motorist's attention. Signs bearing advertisements, directions, and routes are stacked in front and behind one another, above and below in a hodgepodge of attention-getting images. Welcome to Dana Point.

Dana Point is enjoying a near boom in economic activity since the completion of its $20 million marina complex, which has changed the image of the town from a quiet backwater to an aspiring Newport Beach. Owners of the 2,500 pleasure boats docked at the marina graciously patronize a number of new restaurants and shops, and many have bought second homes in the already hot local real estate market.

Dana Point's most enduring attraction is Doheny Park, where people of diverse backgrounds are attracted to a tree-shaded park that adjoins the beach. Doheny features a small interpretive center, a popular campground with 115 campsites, and a fine beach. But the most exceptional aspect of this socially vital open space is the 5-acre green area next to the beach, where tall palms and eucalyptus create a pleasurable setting for games, picnics, and human contact.

North of Doheny State Park is the Dana Point Harbor, which represents the new Dana Point but still carries interesting artifacts from its past. At the center of the marina is a monument to Richard Henry Dana.

At Dana Point Harbor there are numerous waterfront restaurants, scuba diving, bike rentals, skiffs for hire, and all-day fishing and whale-watching excursions, as well as a full-scale replica of *The Pilgrim,* the ship Richard Henry Dana sailed in 1834. Next to *The Pilgrim* is the Orange County Marine Institute, with some of the best programs and activities on the coast.

AREA CODE: 714

Rules of the Road

Pacific Coast Highway in Orange County offers a classic Southern California driving experience. Traffic either zooms or creeps. Shoulders are often occupied by parked cars, especially near beach areas. Expect the sudden appearance of surfers and beach goers as they flee from car to shore, often through moving PCH traffic.

Public Transportation

636-RIDE Orange County Transit District
626-4455 Southern California Rapid Transit District (213)

Orange County Marine Institute

35502 Del Obispo
Dana Point 92629
496-2274.

The Orange County Marine Institute presents an outstanding introduction to California's southern coastline. The science of the oceans is a dominant theme at the Institute where one will find aquariums, a skeleton of a gray whale, tidal touch tanks, onshore labs, floating labs, and one of California's best public marine educational programs. Each year the Institute offers classes and tours designed to entertain and inform people of all ages, including 4-hour and over programs on the life of a sailor aboard the *Pilgrim,* whale watch expeditions, and lectures and classes. Call or write for the current schedule.

DANA POINT HARBOR: HOME PORT FOR ROMANCE
Doris Walker
To-the-Point Press
Dana Point. 1983.

The award-winning journalist and author speaks of geology, wildlife, native inhabitants, explorers, boaters, developers, and engineers. This book is an enjoyable example of California local coastal history at its best.

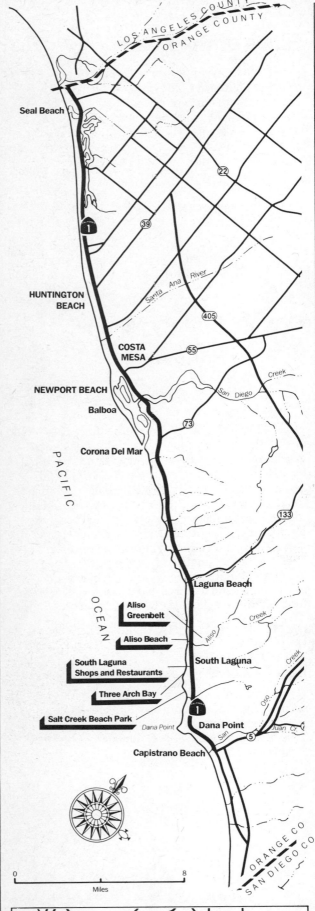

A Remote Seaside Paradise

There was no such thing as a through coast road along the Orange County shore until modern times brought sufficient economic pressure to loosen the grasp of private ownership and permit a public road. The owners of the big ranchos—San Joaquin and Niguel, later combined into the Irvine Ranch—held onto the Orange coast with an iron hand. Only one narrow section around what later became Laguna Beach was exempt from the total domination of the land barons.

Laguna was begun as a campground. By the 1870s it existed only as a remote seaside paradise known only to a few people. Entry to the clear-water coves was from the east, not along the coast, over rough trails barely able to accommodate wagons that ran through Aliso and Laguna canyons.

The first white settlers came through canyons to the coast, as if to Valhalla, drawn by the cool seawinds, visions of a better life, and an opportunity to own land. In 1871, the passage of the Timber-Culture Act opened up uninhabited government-controlled areas like Laguna Beach for homesteading. The law granted 160-acre parcels to claimants if they improved the land by planting trees. When the Thurston family arrived shortly after passage of the act, they planted 10 acres of eucalyptus in Aliso Canyon, close by what is today the third tee of the Laguna Beach Country Club, and laid claim to 60 acres of pristine Pacific coastline.

The Aliso Greenbelt: Protecting Urban Open Space

How can environmentally sensitive and important recreational land be protected in high-growth, high-cost urban areas? In Orange County a land-use plan focuses profitable private development into appropriate areas and ties the development into a public preservation program.

Orange County's Aliso Greenbelt Plan covers

5,300 acres in land from Aliso Beach. About 85% of the land (4,500 acres) is designated for habitat preservation and open space or public use. The remaining 800 acres are zoned for commercial development. The Greenbelt Plan was drafted by the County with assistance from the State Coastal Conservancy and the California Coastal Commission. As property owners design building projects, they work closely with these agencies to devise projects that will both be profitable and protect the greenbelt areas. The county can buy land, accept required offers of land associated with development, and help with land trade to focus development into allowable areas.

The Aliso Greenbelt Plan has gained national attention as a creative and successful public-private solution to the problem of maintaining open space in populated areas. The favorable result in Orange County is that one of the last large undeveloped open spaces is being protected and will be able to serve a variety of recreational needs.

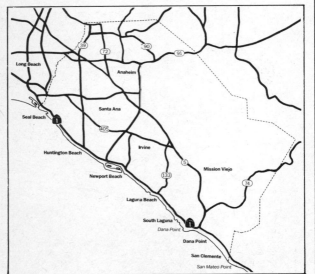

Who Came First

The first whites settled in Laguna Beach in 1871. The Thurston family set up a homestead in Eugene Salter's abandoned cabin, and a small community of Mormons built a schoolhouse in Laguna Canyon near the present cutoff of El Toro Road. But other residents had preceded them.

For hundreds of years, the Shoshone tribe inhabited the coastal area of Orange County, maintaining a relatively easy life amid the abundance of land and sea in a comfortable climate. Their tranquility was dashed by the arrival of the Spanish, who killed many Shoshone and drove the rest away.

But the Shoshone were not the first either. In 1933, the skull of a woman was discovered in Laguna Beach near Annie Springs Road. She'd been there since 15,000 BC.

Environment

California Landforms

California's topography is unmatched for landform diversity. The state's mountains, plateaus, basins, and tidal edges set the stage for an environmental spectacle as varied as it is distinctive.

Along the coast highway's route, three mountain ranges produce sometimes subtle and more often stunning environmental effects. PCH's southern endpoint lies within the granitic Peninsular Ranges. A little further north, around Malibu, the road begins to cut across the unusual east-west Transverse Ranges. From northern Santa Barbara County to the highway's end near Mendocino's Lost Coast, the sedimentary 400-mile-long Coast Ranges are responsible for the existence of Big Sur, Monterey Bay, San Francisco Bay, the San Andreas Fault, and the giant redwood forests of the north.

The Peninsular Ranges

The Peninsular Ranges are actually a northward extension of the Baja California peninsula. The Ranges stretch 1,000 miles from Baja's southern tip to Los Angeles. In Orange County, the Santa Ana Mountains are the dominant range.

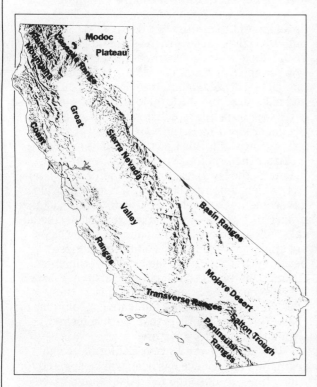

These are massive, granitic-fault block mountains, having dramatic uplifts on the eastern side (the scarpside) and more gentle sloping on the western coastal side (the dip side). The western slopes of the Santa Anas phase into a steplike pattern of marine terraces that antedate the ice ages of the Pleistocene epoch, when the Pacific Ocean retreated from a higher level. Each step in the terrace marks the spot where the receding ocean stopped for hundreds of years.

The Pacific's retreat and the later waterflows from melting ice caps cut the many canyons in Orange County. Sometimes almost vertical in slope, these canyons are to coastal Orange and Los Angeles residents what hills are to San Franciscans, both landmarks and residential status symbols.

Roadside Attractions

South Laguna Beach

Pacific Coast Highway climbs to an ocean terrace north of Dana Point where excellent views of the harbor are visible from the end of the street of the Blue Lantern. At night the harbor lights shine like diamonds.

Beyond the Chelsea Pointe subdivision ("guard-gate residences") lies Salt Creek Beach Park with a wide, gently sloping sandy beach. The shallow offshore waters produce favorable wave-refraction patterns that create large breaking swells

excellent for surfing. Above the beach is the Ritz Carlton Hotel, which attempts to recreate exotic early California glamour and sophistication.

At Three Arch Bay the shape of the landscape changes as the shoreline terrace narrows. Denser vegetation and development create a more interesting panorama. North of Crown Valley Road, the roadside architecture becomes more varied, reflecting a greater mix of periods and styles united by the frequent use of large windows and open decks. Suddenly, the landscape displays the certain charm that has seduced travelers since the opening of the coast road.

Along this part of the Orange coast are strings of magnificent coves and beaches whose deep-blue waters and shining white sands overwhelm the senses: Three Arches Cove, Tenth Avenue, Tortuga, Coast Royale, and Table Rock beaches. Access is gained by sometimes elusive walkways adjacent to Pacific Coast Highway. Persevere.

At South Laguna a number of shops and stores have escaped the more intense commercialization of Laguna Beach, a few miles to the north. A diving shop, a tropical fish store, a pharmacy, a deli, and a French restaurant sit quietly astride PCH. The most appealing attraction is the Cove Restau-

rant, which serves inexpensive breakfasts, lunches, and dinner with an ocean view.

Aliso Beach is the most popular beach area south of Laguna. Order and cleanliness characterize this county-run beach facility, which has a pleasant picnic area, bike trail, .75-mile fishing pier, snack bar, and cold showers. The surf at Aliso is superb for body surfing, and the area is a favorite for families whose youngest kids enjoy playing in the warm gentle waters of Aliso Creek.

Resources

The California Land

A consummate geography text describes the physical environment and tells the story of how landforms, climate, and natural resources function within the social, economic, and cultural evolution of a place. Here are five basic geographic resources that do this and more.

CALIFORNIA PATTERNS: A GEOGRAPHICAL AND HISTORICAL ATLAS
David Hornbeck
David L. Fuller, Design & Cartography
Mayfield Publishing Company
Palo Alto. 1983.

CALIFORNIA: THE GEOGRAPHY OF DIVERSITY
Crane S. Miller and Richard S. Hyslop
Mayfield Publishing Company
Palo Alto. 1983.

CALIFORNIA, LAND OF CONTRAST
Davis W. Lantis
Kendall/Hunt Publishing Company
Toronto. 1981.

FIELD GUIDE: COASTAL SOUTHERN CALIFORNIA
Robert P. Sharp
Kendall/Hunt Publishing Company
Dubuque. 1978.

ATLAS OF CALIFORNIA
Donley, Allan, Caro, Patton
Academic Book Center
Portland. 1979.

ATLAS of CALIFORNIA

California Geologic Time Scale

Eras	Periods / Epochs	Duration in Million Years before Present	Orogenies	Major Geologic Events in California (read from bottom to top)
CENOZOIC	**Quaternary**		Coast Ranges	Continued tectonics in all provinces
	Holocene	present to 0.01		
	Pleistocene	0.01–3		Glaciation; major building of Coast Ranges, Transverse Ranges, and Cascade volcanoes; major block faulting in Basin and Range
	Tertiary			
	Pliocene	3–11		Early building of Coast and Transverse Ranges. Origins of present San Andreas fault system
	Miocene	11–25		
	Oligocene	25–40		
	Eocene	40–60		
	Paleocene	60–70		Continued emergence of major mountain ranges
MESOZOIC	**Cretaceous**	70–135	Sonoma Nevada	Major building of Sierra Nevada, Klamath Mountains, and Peninsula Ranges
	Jurassic	135–180		
	Triassic	180–225		Continued volcanism and mountain building in shallow seas
PALEOZOIC	**Permian**	225–270	Antler	Shallow seas over much of California (Cambrian to Permian); island arc terrain
	Pennsylvanian	270–305		
	Mississippian	305–350		
	Devonian	350–400		
	Silurian	400–440		
	Ordovician	440–500		
	Cambrian	500–600		
PRE-CAMBRIAN	Late	600–1800		Some mountain building in southern California
	Early	1800–2700		

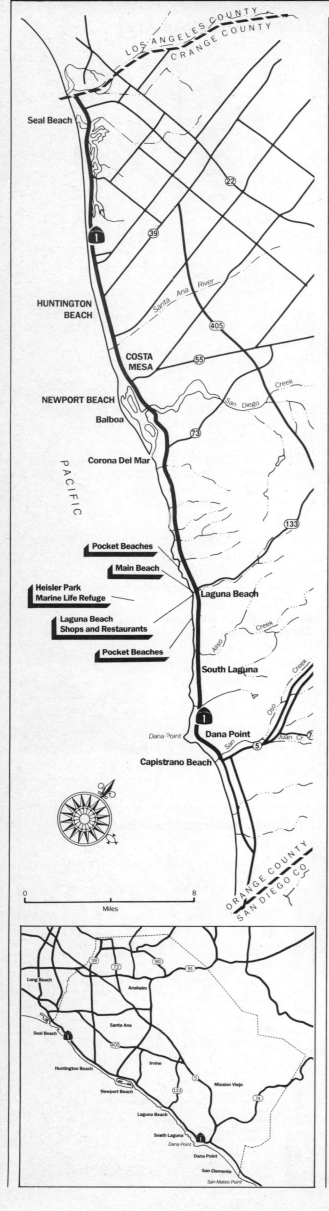
When Laguna Was Lagona and Stagecoaches Stuck in the Mud

By the mid 1880s Laguna Beach was rapidly being converted to a resort area by a community of people who soon capitalized on the seafront's most evident natural resource—its beauty—by setting up campgrounds and stores.

Travelers from Santa Ana and Riverside pitched tents on the beach and camped in the canyons. To reach Laguna—called "Lagona" until 1904 when confusion with Long Beach required the change—they came over the narrow hellish road from El Toro by carriage, wagon, and eventually by stagecoach. The stage was driven by the gregarious Mrs. Treffern, known for her skill with the whip and her footwork with heavy boots, which she demonstrated whenever the wagon wheels became mired in mud.

The Boom of the 80s

The boom of the 1880s brought more visitors to the remote Shangri-la, and more elaborate tourist facilities sprung up, with hotels at Arch Beach and Laguna. Soon a road was graded south of Laguna along the coast to connect the disparate settlements springing up along the Laguna shore. The road was the idea of Nate Brooks, who envisioned shorefront homesites in Laguna when he laid out a subdivision around Arch Beach.

Catalina On the Main

Soon Nate Brooks's subdivision at Arch Beach was matched by another a few miles south. In 1887 the Raymond Whitcomb Company bought Hubbard Goff's homesteads on each side of Aliso Canyon and introduced plans for a great new city to be known as Catalina on the Main. The company intended to build a hotel, wharves, and a depot for the Santa Fe, which was expected to pass through Arch Beach. But the project was abandoned when an armed cowboy and an injunction stopped a Southern Pacific track-laying crew

from crossing the Irvine Ranch, dead-ending the railroad's plans for a coastal extension and foreclosing the dreams of many land speculators.

Despite the booms and busts of real estate, Laguna Beach continued to grow as a summer resort. By the 1890s hotels and taverns dotted Arch Beach and Laguna. In 1897 Joseph Yoch bought Goff's Arch Beach Hotel, cut it into three sections and dragged it over "humps and gullies" to add on to the Hotel Laguna. Yoch's Hotel Laguna, with room for 500 guests and "wide verandas where you can almost catch the spray from the beaches" was the focal point of activity for 30 years.

California Coastal Land Use Regulation

In 1972, the voters of California overwhelmingly passed Proposition 20, a unique ballot initiative that gave the state regulatory contol of the 1,100 mile California coast, an area that embraces California's most precious resources and its most valuable real estate.

The electorate's approval of Proposition 20 was considered a landmark event in coastal regulation, both in California and the nation. It reflected growing public alarm over unchecked development that often failed to consider the public's right of access to the state tidelands, visual impacts of development projects, or protection of sensitive resources. "Prop 20" halted this unchecked development, transferring regulation and planning from the local level, which was perceived as too self-interested to meet the needs of the general public, to the state by way of a new agency, the California Coastal Commission.

After the first four years of state regulation planning, the legislature passed the 1976 Coastal Act, which, among other things, required local governments to develop their own "local coastal programs," which consist of land use plans, technical studies, and zoning ordinances. As the "lcps" are approved by the state commission, most permit power reverts to the local governments. Accompanying legislation in 1976 also established a new agency, the State Coastal Conservancy, whose function is to seek innovative resolutions to coastal land use conflicts that are deadlocked within the regulatory system.

How effective the 13 year California coastal regulation experience has been will be debated for a long time. In 1981, the *LA Times* summarized the Commission's accomplishments since passage of the 1972 initiative: "There has been no new subdividing of coastal farmlands in rural areas; virtually no marshlands have been filled or diked for development, even in the midst of cities; California 1 has been preserved as a scenic, winding, two-lane road; far fewer high-rise buildings are being allowed along the beaches; no new power plant sites threaten scenic spots, and no new locked-gate residential developments have been built at the shore. The commission has also created a sweeping beach access program that over the years will open dozens of miles of sand and rock outcroppings to the public."

Others are less glowing in their praise, citing the dominance of so-called "state interests" over more immediate local community needs like jobs and growth. At the same time, a new leadership in Sacramento has declared the state commission unnecessary, attacking it in a most effective manner by cutting program budgets and staffing while chipping away at its legal mandate. And many activists now predict a revival of the "Save Our Coast" movement that first gave rise to Prop 20.

Tropical Trees

In Southern California much of the roadside landscape is ornamented by the ubiquitous palm tree. A multitude of species adorn the southland, often suggesting images of paradises lost or found. There are hair palms (the only palm native to Europe), plume palms (tall, feathery creatures from Brazil), Pindo Palms (Paragua), Erythea (named for one of the Hesperides, Daughter of Evening), the Blue Palm (a California native), and Washington palms (named for George). Two of the most common palm trees are the date palm and the fan palm.

Date Palm

The Canary Island date palm, also known as the pineapple palm, is a popular street tree in Southern California, although it is also cultivated for its fruit in southeastern California and other parts of the world.

The nickname "pineapple palm" comes from the trunk's resemblance to a pineapple, and that is the easiest way to distinguish this species from others. Look also for the shape and direction of the leaves: extending upright and spreading around the top of the tree, with very narrow, long-pointed leaflets extending from green-spined stalks. Live leaves are dull green and extend in a leathery, straight line without drooping. The dead brown leaves hang down toward the stout trunk, which is often wider at the top than at the bottom.

Fan Palm

The California palm, or fan palm, usually grows taller then the date palm, reaching heights of up to 60 feet. The largest native palm in the continental United States, it is the only native western species. Fan palms are also called desert palms or petticoat palms from the shaggy mass of dead leaves hanging against the trunk.

The fan palms you see in Orange County and throughout southern California are not native stands, but ornamental plantings. The trunk of the fan palm is gray and smooth with horizontal lines broken by vertical crosses. Its leaves are very large and—not surprisingly—shaped like fans.

Laguna Beach

The town of Laguna Beach is one of the rare places in the world where in a day's stroll one may not see a single shred of garbage or refuse, encounter a solitary unattractive person, or witness one hint of evidence that the world is not always pleasant, orderly, and affluent. There are few rough edges in Laguna.

Laguna Beach exudes decorum and good taste, qualities that give it an image of dignity and set it apart from many California beach towns. Laguna is

one of California's prettiest towns, and beneath its proper exterior, it knows how to have a good time.

Between Dizz's As Is (a fine place for food and music with an informal atmosphere) and central Laguna are a number of exquisite beaches and kingly homes. At Wood's Cove stands the $11.5 million Jeffries residence; at nearby Victoria Beach a residence known as the Castle sports a 60-foot Norman tower. Beach access to a series of small pocket coves may be gained by walkways at the following street ends: Dumond Drive, Victoria Drive, Diamond Street, Pearl Street, Agate Street, Bluebird Canyon Road, Mountain Road, Cress Street, Brooks Street, Oak Street, Anita Street, Thalia Street, St. Ann's Street, Cleo Street, and Sleepy Hollow.

Bluebird Canyon is the site of what was once called Olympic Village, a community of small bungalows relocated from the 1932 Olympics, and the present location of the Surf and Sand Hotel, which features a dazzling mirrored ceiling that reflects the rolling ocean waves hundreds of feet below. The Hotel Firenze, nearby, the Hotel San Maarten, and the Hotel Laguna provide fine accommodations with lush landscaping and unsurpassed examples of the civilized travelers' tabernacle, the hotel bar.

Close by is Fahrenheit 451, a fine bookstore; its outdoor mural, which depicts a life-sized gray whale and its young, is known as the "whaling wall." See too Tippe Canoe's (clothes) and Laguna Tattoo.

Across from Main Beach, the historic White House Tavern has hosted celebrity wining and dining since 1918, when Laguna was an artists' colony. For years the White House was famous for its jazz, serving as the southern point of the LA jazz circuit. But a change of ownership in 1983 brought tepid musical fare and Sizzler Steakhouse decor.

Coastal Land Use Information

California Coastal Commission
631 Howard Street, 4th Floor
San Francisco 94105.
(415) 543-8555

The California State Coastal Conservancy
1330 Broadway, Suite 1100
Oakland 95612.
(415) 464-1015

The Commission and the Conservancy are California's two most important coastal agencies. The Commission plans and regulates through local coastal programs and permit power. The Conservancy mitigates land-use conflicts through special projects and programs. Contact these agencies for program descriptions, meeting agendas, annual reports, publication lists, and assistance on any issue concerning California coastal land use or resource protection.

GOVERNING CALIFORNIA'S COAST
Stanley Scott
Institute of Governmental Studies
University of California
Berkeley. 1975

PROTECTING THE GOLDEN SHORE: LESSONS FROM THE CALIFORNIA COASTAL COMMISSIONS
Robert G. Healy, Editor
The Conservation Foundation
Washington, D. C. 1978.

THE CALIFORNIA COASTAL COMMISSION: AT THE CROSSROADS
Richard O'Reilly
The Los Angeles Times/Reprinted by the CCC
Los Angeles. 1981.

The state of coastal regulation in California is extremely fluid, dependent on budgets and politics. Nevertheless, these two books and the series of *LA Times* articles provide an excellent introduction to the challenges facing California residents regarding their coast.

Proposition 20

27001. The people of the State of California hereby find and declare that the California coastal zone is a distinct and valuable natural resource belonging to all the people and existing as a delicately balanced ecosystem; that the permanent protection of the remaining natural and scenic resources of the coastal zone is a paramount concern to present and future residents of the state and nation . . . and that to protect the coastal zone it is necessary. . . to create the California Coastal Zone Conservation Commission, and six regional coastal zone conservation commissions, to implement the provisions of this division.
Passed by the Voters of California in November 1972

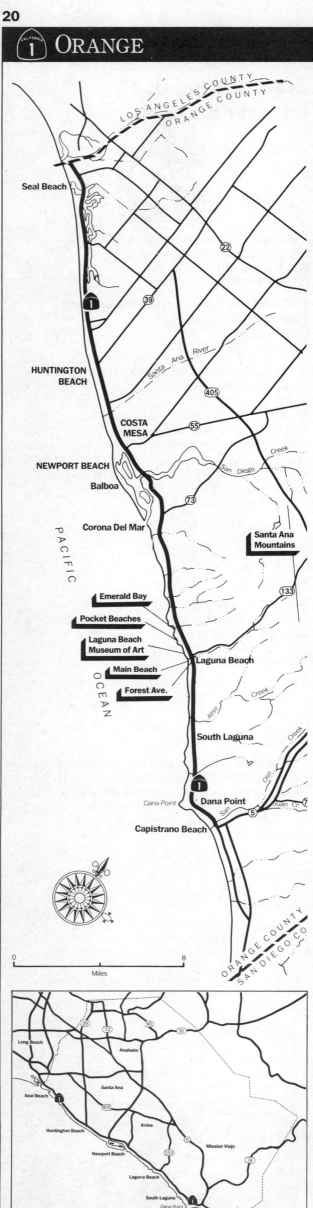

An Artists' Paradise

The serenity of Laguna's undisturbed beauty attracted numerous artists. The subtle shaded natural tableaus of surf, rock, and sandy beaches provided landscapes beautifully suited to imitation. From as early as 1890 artists came to Laguna to record its splendor. In the early 1900s Norman St. Clair moved to Laguna to paint its shoreline. Soon he was joined by Gardner Symonds, a Boston painter. Afterwards, Frank Cuprien arrived and initiated the Laguna Beach Round Table, where the likes of Erle Stanley Gardner, Hal Forest, and Boris Karloff had discussions and drinks, assisting further Laguna Beach's reputation as an art colony.

During the early 1920s hundreds of art hungry patrons made the difficult journey to the small seaside village where the Laguna Beach art gallery had been set up in a former church and dance hall. The coast highway ran only a few short miles. On the north end of town a barbed-wire fence marked the highway's end at the Irvine property; to the south it followed Nate Brooks's dusty road only to Arch Beach.

For years, Laguna Beach's isolation kept it a quiet charming enclave that prided itself on its arcadian village atmosphere. Its artists' colony reputation somehow reflected its good taste, as in a 1922 Chamber of Commerce pamphlet that veered almost to sanctimoniousness: "Because Laguna has survived so far without being forced to offer the hurdy-gurdy, hot dog, fortune teller, and other forms of artificial amusement, designed to beat the devil around a stump to eke out the semblence of a good time, it is known only to the lovers of Nature and seclusion. It is for this reason, most largely, that the famous painters of landscape subjects, particularly those who preserve for people living inland beautiful depictions of the restless Pacific, have chosen to make this an artists' paradise."

But in 1928, the artists' paradise was rudely assailed by the outside world. In an opening ceremony that starred Douglas Fairbanks as Vulcan and Mary Pickford as the Spirit of Progress, a link was forged symbolizing the completion of the coast highway through the heart of Laguna Beach from Long Beach to San Juan Capistrano. The Riviera of the Pacific would never be the same.

Locked Gates at Emerald Bay

Who owns the shoreline? In California, by constitutional law the tidelands belong to all the state's residents. The beach area from the waterline to the average high-tide line is public property. No one person can lay claim to this area or prevent others from using it.

The problem for residents and visitors is access to the public tidelands. Along California's many coves and bays, the ocean often can be reached only by passing through nonpublic land. At Emerald Bay, for example, the public hasn't been able to enjoy the tidelands for a long time. Guards and gates block the way, effectively making the entire bay the private domain of the relatively few people who live behind the gates and guards.

Other states have more liberal policies concerning public access. In Oregon, for example, the state owns all the beaches and public access is not restricted. The same is generally true in Hawaii, where anything judged to be a beach is considered public.

In 1972 the voters of California passed Proposition 20, the Coastal Conservation Act, which reflected citizens' concern over the increasing loss of public access to the beaches. As more coastal subdivisions were being built, more beaches were becoming privately controlled, like swimming pools at apartment complexes.

The establishment of the California Coastal Commission and the passage of the Coastal Act of 1976 are signs of a concerted effort to keep the state's beaches open to the public. New private developments along the coast are generally required to set aside a passageway for public access to the shoreline.

Almost every Californian would like to own a private beach, but since residents outnumber beaches the only practical solution is to keep every beach open to everyone. Fair is fair.

An Ill Wind

Southern California's winds usually blow inland off the ocean, their direction and intensity determined by the status of a clock-wise swirling high pressure cell called the Hawaiian High. At times, however (usually in the fall) an unusual combination of atmospheric conditions causes the winds in Southern California to blow in reverse.

Sometimes for a few days, sometimes for weeks, the so-called Santa Ana Winds rush across the inland mountains bringing scorching temperatures to the coast, often sweeping raging fire storms along their path. Although the Santa Anas may blow smog out to sea, the winds also flatten the near-shore surface waves of beaches, create unusually large and strangely moving waves far off shore, and damage harbors and anchorages built to provide shelter from natural forces of the sea, not inland forces.

The Desert Comes to the Coast

The source of the Santa Ana Winds is the Mojave Desert, far inland in Southern California. The winds accumulate with the simultaneous development of a strong high-pressure system in the Great Basin–Mojave Desert area, and a weakening of the usual prevailing high pressure system off the coast. The coastal low pressure system invites the hot desert air to move over the Transverse and Peninsular Ranges, moving down the mountain's coastal sides at speeds that sometimes reach hurricane strength.

As the air is forced down the western slopes of the mountains, it loses about 4,000 feet in altitude and suffers downslope compressional heating that causes the air temperature to become even hotter. When the Santa Anas blow, the normally cooler coast might have temperatures in the 90s, while

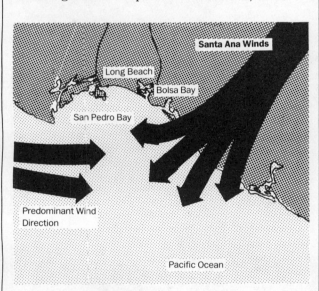

the desert communities bask in the cool 70s. Since Santa Anas also lack the humidity of coastal breezes, they also encourage fires to spread, even starting some as they demolish power lines with their force.

Main Beach

Once the site of the Cabrillo Ballroom, a pier, and numerous notorious bars, Laguna's Main Beach has been converted into the most pleasant of beach-town open spaces. The superbly designed park area between PCH and Laguna's principal commercial street, Forest Avenue, has masterfully achieved the desirable goal of integrating a number of recreational activities in a focused area, while at the same time establishing a comfortable association between the beach, the game area, and the town.

Dedicated in 1974, after a local zoning initiative prevented the construction of a convention center at the site, Main Beach provides a fine variety of amenities that attract varied age groups and interests: basketball and volleyball courts, lawns for picnicking and relaxing, game tables for Scrabble and chess players, and a wonderful children's playground that keeps them occupied in sight for hours. An appealing curved boardwalk separates the beach and park area—a nice spot to sit.

Beyond the park stretches a magnificent long beach with a landmark lifeguard tower at its center; its flag indicates surf conditions. The entire area prospers by its proximity to town, fulfilling all requirements for one of the best-designed urban beach areas in California.

Forest Avenue leads off PCH at the center of town and provides an opportunity for a stroll past an interesting series of small shops, stores, and galleries. The Vorpal Gallery is right off Forest, and the street itself has a handsome town clock and a British telephone booth.

On the way out of town, north, PCH passes by the Laguna Beach Museum of Art, famous for its early California impressionist paintings. Access to the several glorious beaches below is gained by numerous walkways off Cliff Drive.

Laguna Beach Art Festivals

Festival of Arts & Pageant of the Masters

Irvine Bowl
650 Laguna Canyon Road
Laguna Beach 92651
494-1145

Sawdust Festival

935 Laguna Canton Road
P.O. Box 1234
Laguna Beach 92651
494-3030

Art-A-Fair Festival

113 Canyon Acres Drive at Laguna Canyon Road
Laguna Beach 92651
494-5973

From early July through August $1 will gain admission to each of Laguna's three art festivals. All together over 480 artists and artisans display and sell their works at the festival, extensions of the original 1932 Festival of Arts. The highlight of the day is the Festival Pageant of the Masters, where Picassos, Goyas, and Delacroixs come to life as local volunteers pose under magical lighting in detail-accurate renditions of famous canvasses. Tickets for the Pageant performances are extra, and often sell out long in advance.

Laguna Celebrities

Laguna Beach has known its share of celebrities since the years when Douglas Fairbanks and Mary Pickford opened the coast highway and let in the new world. During the 1930s, Fred MacMurray, *My Three Sons'* dad, played a torrid saxophone at the old Cabrillo Ballroom on the beach. Charlie Chaplin and Rudolph Valentino both lived in the area at one time. As child stars, Judy Garland and Mickey Rooney attended the local school. Ozzie and Harriet Nelson with David and little Ricky were frequently seen at the local malt shop, and local resident Bette Davis once even participated in the kitschy Pageant of the Masters.

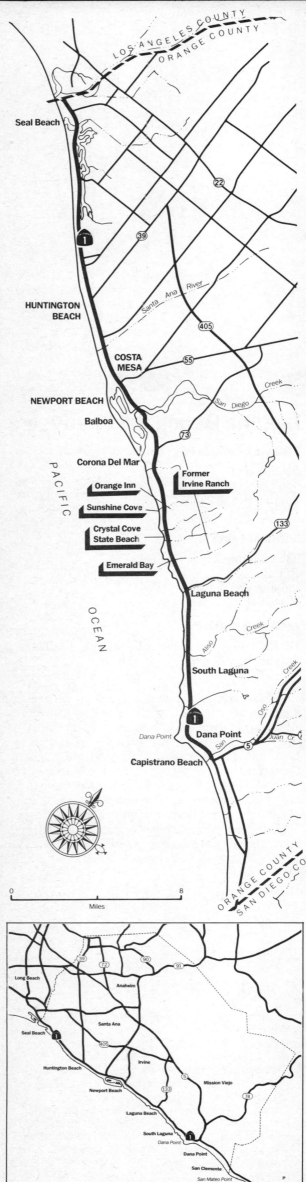

The Rise of the House of Irvine

Aside from feudal kings and Texas land barons, few people rival the dominance of the Irvine family over the land of Orange County. For more than a century the Irvines controlled land use in much of Orange County the way that dynasties control empires.

During its reign over the land, the Irvines transformed a Spanish land grant where sheep grazed into a 108,000-acre holding that served as "a plush watering hole for California new rich." In 1864 James Irvine and two partners invested $41,000 to obtain a parcel that stretched 10 miles along the coast, from the Santa Ana River to Laguna Beach, and extended 22 miles inland. Ever since, this land has been Irvine country.

Ancestry

James Irvine lived until 1886. His two most significant accomplishments were to buy out his partner, which consolidated the family holdings, and to sire James Jr. (or J.I. as he was called), who ruled over the land until 1947 and successfully held at bay the advent of the 20th century at Irvine Ranch.

Despite the arrival of the electric interurban and Henry Huntington's land company at Newport Beach, was hurled into the 20th century.

The first item on the foundation's agenda was to hire an architecture and planning firm to create a blueprint for tomorrow. William Pereira, a Los Angeles architect perhaps best known for his design of San Francisco's TransAmerica Pyramid, was chosen to transform the area into the conurbation of the future.

The Biggest and the Best

At the heart of Pereira's proposal was the Newport Center, an ostentatious megacenter more suited to the plains of Texas than to small Newport, that would have reduced the near and surrounding landscape to marginal insignificance. One aspect of the Newport Center plan was Fashion Island; another was a new freeway that would run through Newport and connect with the San Diego Freeway, transporting sufficient masses of automobile-borne consumers to make Newport Center economically feasible.

Unfortunately for the planners, in 1972 the voters of Newport voted against the Irvine-backed freeway, condemning the final build-out of Newport Center and leaving Fashion Island stranded. The Irvine Company, facing a rebuff unimaginable during the Irvine regime, decided to concentrate on other projects, such as a giant shopping and office center at the convergence of the Santa Ana and San Diego freeways and the Irvine

as well as improvements to the harbor channel by the Army Corps of Engineers, the Irvine kingdom remained secure. When James Jr. died, his son Myford assumed the throne and reigned for twelve years, until he committed suicide by, in the judgment of the county coroner, simultaneously shooting himself in the stomach with a shotgun and in the head with a rifle. When Myford shuffled off this mortal coil—or was pushed—control of the empire passed to a foundation. Newport

Industrial complex.

In 1976 the company was all but sold to Mobil Oil for $200 million when Joan Irvine Smith brought suit to prevent the purchase. Smith was successful, and in 1977 the company was sold for $337.4 million to a consortium that included Henry Ford II and Donald Bren. In April 1983 Bren became the principal owner with 86% of the stock. Smith, the last of the royal bloodline, controls the rest.

Environment

Oranges

Driving PCH in Orange County, you're more likely to see an orange on a billboard than on a tree in a roadside grove. But once it was different.

Around the turn of the century, Southern California growers gazed at the sun and saw citrus. The oranges growing at the time were "thick-skinned, sour, pithy and dry, an insult to the noblest of fruit," but innovative growers soon made amends for the insult by importing prime specimens of Tahiti oranges, Washington navel oranges from Brazil, and Valencia oranges, native to the Azores.

An industry was born. A city was called Orange, and so was a county. Virtually overnight the land blossomed with new towns surrounded by the heady, romantic fragrance and shaded beauty of orange groves.

One Orange County resident recounts the days when the county's soul was tinted orange: "When I was in college in the fifties, we all used to pile into my new Chevy and drive to the beach to spend weekends. As we'd be tooling along through miles and miles of orange groves, the trees were so close to the road we could reach out of the car and pick the oranges. It seemed as if those orange groves went on forever."

The orange perfume prevailed through the first half of this century. But then Orange County began to tool up for a new crop—quick built suburban houses all in a row. One by one orange groves were plowed under and paved over. What had once been some of the world's most productive farm land retreated beneath the foundations of single family homes in need of room to sprawl.

Roadside Attractions

North of Laguna

North of Laguna, PCH passes by two of California's most exclusive subdivisions: Emerald Bay, with a private shoreline so exquisite that the temptation to trespass is almost irresistable, and Irvine Cove, where movie stars, princes, and the ultra-rich live in Daddy Warbucks splendor.

Just ahead is Crystal Cove State Beach, a relatively new public beach on former Irvine Ranch property. This magnificent stretch of beach, which runs for about three miles from Irvine Cove to Arch Rock, has beautifully clear surf that frequently displays a complete spectrum of blue to green hues.

The Orange Inn & Sunshine Cove

Two of the Orange coast's most refreshing attractions are located on either side of PCH near Crystal Cove State Beach. The Orange Inn has been a popular coast roadside attraction since 1931, when the country was redolent with oranges, and travelers in Model A's and Studebakers motored through this section of the Irvine Ranch on their way down the coast.

Similar in character is Sunshine Cove, on the west side of PCH, which serves a comparable fare of date shakes, orange shakes, and other refreshing food with natural ingredients.

The Orange Inn and Sunshine Cove are two pleasureful landmarks from a California of yesterday. All landmarks should taste so good.

Resources

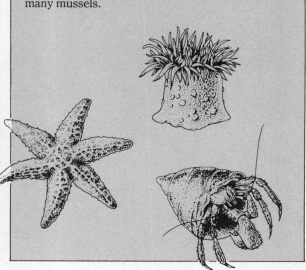

Newport Bay

Irvine Coast
Marine Life Refuge

Laguna Beach
Marine Life Refuge
and Ecological Reserve

Newport Beach
Marine Life Refuge

Niguel
Marine Life Refuge

South Laguna
Marine Life Refuge

Doheny
Marine Life Refuge

Dana Point Harbor
Marine Life Refuge

Marine Life Refuges

There are six important marine life refuges between Dana Point and Newport Beach in Orange County. The refuges were established by the State Department of Fish and Game to preserve tidepool life along the rocky areas of the south shore where massive gathering (often by well-meaning teachers or collectors) once threatened to totally eliminate tidal life here.

Even with the establishment of the refuges, scientists estimate that it may take as long as 25 years for the pools to return to the flourishing levels that used to exist here, and some may never return. Please replace any rocks that you lift in the exact position in which you found it (scores of creatures may call it home). No animals, rocks or shells may be removed from the refuge areas and even outside the refuge areas, tidepool life is protected and may be taken only with appropriate sport fishing licenses covered by California Sport Fishing Regulations.

The boundaries and major access points to Orange County refuge areas are posted with signs for their identification and protection. Contact these agencies for more information on Orange County's marine life refuges.

ORANGE COUNTY
HARBORS
Beaches and Parks District
634-7019.

CITY OF NEWPORT BEACH
MARINE DEPARTMENT
640-2156.

CITY OF LAGUNA BEACH
Lifeguard Department
494-6572.

STATE DEPARTMENT
OF FISH AND GAME
(213) 590-5177.

Common Tidepool Life

Look for these common forms of life in the tidepools of Orange County's marine life refuges: greenish brown sea anemone; brownish black sea hare; red, brown, orange, or yellow ochre starfish; spiny red or purple sea urchin; hermit crabs; and many, many mussels.

Seal Beach

HUNTINGTON
BEACH

Santa Ana
River

Newport Pier

NEWPORT BEACH

Newport Harbor   Balboa

Balboa Beach

Corona Del Mar

Corona Del
Mar Beach

Former
McFadden's Landing

Laguna Beach

South Laguna

Dana Point

Capistrano Beach

A String of Shacks on a Sandy Beach

Once Newport Beach was only a string of shacks on a sandy beach in front of a mudflat called Newport Bay. About 300 people lived in the village, their sustenance dependent on fishing. Near the middle of the cluster of shacks a pier provided the only apparent economic justification for anyone to be there at all.

The bay was created by a flood in 1825, which caused the Santa Ana River to change its course and create a new land mass. Some 38 years later Captain S. S. Dunnels sailed into the bay to pick up a cargo of hides, putting to use for the first time a New Port between San Diego and San Pedro.

It wasn't long afterward that three brothers, James, John, and Robert McFadden realized the profits to be made at Newport Landing. Besieged with offers to buy a shipment of lumber they had just received for fencing, the McFaddens decided to go into the lumber business.

The McFaddens were known for their sternness and strict Presbyterian outlook. Quite soon they became noted for their wily business acumen.

They dredged a new entrance to the bay and took control of shipments. The dock facility below the bluff, which divided the upper and lower Newport Bay, became known as McFadden's Landing. They organized the Newport Wharf and Lumber Company and in 1888 built the Newport Beach Municipal Pier, all the while earning dockloads of money. The Midas-touch McFaddens built the first coast road across the Newport Bay mudflats, and when the notion of an inland rail line held prospects for even greater profits from the shipping trade, the McFadden brothers took Orange County into the age of the locomotive.

The Santa Ana–Newport railroad line significantly expanded the McFaddens' economic domain. Within a short time a branch line was added to connect Newport and Shell Beach (Huntington Beach). Shiploads of cargo—in one year 550 of them—were unloaded at the wharf and carried on the McFaddens' railroad, but commercial use of the railroad soon became secondary.

A Real Estate Horror Story at Newport Beach

The amazing economic growth that Newport Beach has undergone in the last 20 years has not left all its citizens basking in diamonds, furs, and Maseratis. A significant number of Newport Beach citizens are being driven to the poorhouse by the booming local economy.

The problem goes back to the Irvine Company, which has always chosen to eat its cake and have it too. Their policy has been to lease land for development rather than to sell it. Thus many of Newport's homeowners are just that, *home*owners— but *land* lessees, who pay annual rents to the Irvine Company, which retains ownership of the property under the homes.

About 25 years ago, Irvine Company lots could be rented very cheaply—$400 a year for many lots, $1,200 to $1,800 a year for the best waterfront parcels. Rental fees were based on a 6% assessment of the undeveloped property's appraised market value. A typical lease ran 55 years, with the provision that rents could be raised after 25 years but only up to 6% of the parcel's appraised

value at that time.

Only recently, when the first land leases came up for the 25-year reassessment, did their tenants realize the position they were in. The market value of property in Newport Beach (once called the "City of Bonus Living") had appreciated astronomically, such that the 6% rate exceeded the budget of many seemingly well-off tenants. Harry Baker, for example, an air transportation company executive earning $80,000 a year, was one of the first to have his lease come due. When the rent skyrocketed from $1,600 a year to $67,660 a year, Baker had no choice but to default and await eviction.

In response, scared-stiff Newport leaseholders have formed the Committee of 4,000 to attempt to save their homes as their leases come due. No one is quite sure what course of action is appropriate to cope with the unexpected consequences of a boom economy. But perhaps for the first time ever in Orange County, an unfamiliar concept is being quietly contemplated. Rent control.

Environment

Newport Submarine Canyon

Newport Submarine Canyon

California's geological diversity does not end where the land slips beneath the sea. The entire underwater coastline is marked with a series of submarine canyons–some deep and wide, others less so. All the canyons have an effect on the nature of the marine life, wave action, and adjacent shorelines and beaches.

The Newport Submarine Canyon is one of three offshore formations along the Orange County/Los Angeles County coast. The canyon was formed by the Santa Ana River during ancient periods of lower sea level. Today it comes nearest shore just off the Newport Pier.

The most important and most noticeable effect of this underwater chasm is the deflecting action it exerts on waves as they approach the coast between Balboa and Newport beaches. Because of the sudden deep water, waves become more gentle, their energy absorbed downward rather than thrust upward, making the shoreline beach at Newport more stable than most Southern California beaches. The beaches south of the canyon, however, tend to have less sand since the canyons partially intercept sand as it is moved along the coast by long-shore currents.

Roadside Attractions

Newport Beach

Newport Beach is not like other places—it has more money, a lot more money. With the largest Rolls dealership in America and the richest pleasure-craft harbor in the west at their disposal, Newport citizens read their local magazine, *Gentry,* and struggle to survive on an average per capita income of $42,000 a year. Among the 62,556 who enjoy Newport's fruits of life are the town's 144 black residents, one of whom is Reggie Jackson.

In Newport Beach ("Noveau Beach" to many)

new money has bought a sense of play that places the town at the spiritual apex of the triangle it forms with Disneyland to the north and Beverly Hills to the northwest. Here, where residents fall into classes of "the prosperous, the rich, and the ridiculously rich," free enterprise is the game, yachts and high-end automobiles the toys, and million-dollor beach homes, the playhouses.

As either a preview of capitalistic heaven or an emblem of California pop art, Newport Beach is not to be missed. These attractions compel themselves to the Pacific Coast Highway adventurer:

Fashion Island. In response to a fair-housing suit, the Irvine Company once proposed to provide "affordable housing" units in Newport. At a public meeting a resident spoke out: "Do we really want this kind of element here? People already get upset when they can't join our yacht clubs. At that level of income [then about $30,000], we are talking about nonskilled labor, and they can't afford to pick up credit cards at Neiman Marcus." Neiman Marcus is located at Fashion Island. So too is Bullocks Wilshire, Buffrums, Robinsons, The Broadway, the Ritz Restaurant, and Amen Wardy—where you may browse among Galanos gowns and suits by André Lang or Brioni. How about some Cartier jewelry, a snakeskin coat, or a pair of René Caviolla gem shoes?

Newport Dunes. "Family Fun begins here" at this 14-acre lagoon adjacent to PCH. The site seems a leftover from another era but may provide an antidote to the heightened surrealism of Newport Beach. There is overnight camping, a playground and a tame swimming beach for children, plus kayaks, sea cycles, and sailboat rentals.

7-11 Rent A Car. Should you feel the need to upscale your image to better fit into the Newport scene, 7-11 rents automobiles that communicate your understanding of the game: Aston-Martins, Rolls-Royces, Clenets, Maseratis, and even lowly Mercedeses and Porsches. Not cheap, but that's the point.

Resources

On Newport Bay

Should you wish to leave solid ground behind at Newport Bay, you will find your choices are many. Here you can:
• Rent a sailboat
• Rent a skiff with motor
• Take one of several guided cruises of the bay
• Take a sport fishing trip out of the bay
• Take a whale watching cruise
• Visit Catalina on a cruise ship
• Ride the Balboa Island Auto Ferry
• Rent a sailboard for windsurfing

Festival of Lights Boat Parade

If you are in Newport Beach during the week before Christmas, you won't want to miss the sparkling Festival of Lights Boat Parade. Every year since 1908, all the yachts and sailboats light up with elaborate decorations of the season and cruise the harbor beginning at 6:30 p.m. nightly.

Cruise Information

DAVEY'S LOCKER
400 Main Street
673-1434.

MATLACK
WINDSURFING
2906 West PCH
642-1400.

NEWPORT HARBOR
SHOWBOAT CRUISES
700 Edgewater Avenue
673-0240.

NEWPORT YACHT
CHARTERS
673-3000.

PAVILION QUEEN
400 Main Street
673-5245.

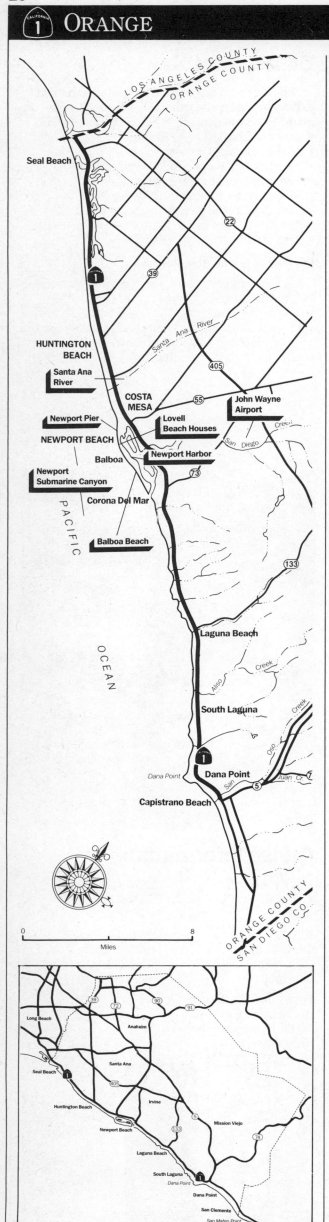

Iron Rails to the Ocean

Once the steam railroad reached Santa Ana, the distant seashore became immediately accessible to an entirely new population. At once Newport became an alluring seaside retreat that attracted Santa Ana's elite. Visitors stayed in cottages or at the Newport Hotel, which had been transported up the coast from the overnight boomtown San Juan by the Sea. Trains were packed with Santa Ana socialites who sojourned to the beach to see and be seen. Garbed in brocade and taffeta and protected by parasols, stylish young women encouraged and ignored stylish young men.

In 1904 Henry Huntington, the man who brought instant wealth to the Los Angeles basin one town at a time with his Pacific Electric Railway, came to Newport Beach, launching a real estate boom that gave instant employment to 48 real estate agents who needed 6 full-time clerks just to write the sales contracts.

Within a year Huntington had brought his electric interurban service to Newport Beach, spurring yet more growth and investment. Land values skyrocketed, and within two years the population increased sixfold.

The handsome red trolleys presented a stunning sight as they rolled down the coast from Seal Beach to Newport and (by 1906) Balboa. Festooned with flags and insignia, the colorful interurbans contrasted sharply against the sun-bleached sand and powder blue sea, inviting riders with the lure of panache.

When the first red cars rolled into Balboa on the 4th of July a celebration followed whose like had never been seen. Fireworks, picnics, an all-day concert, and all-night dancing marked the inauguration of a transportation system that meant money in the pocket for some and easy access to pleasures for others.

The Lovell Beach House

Where 13th Street ends at the beach in Newport Beach stands perhaps the most fascinating house on the California coast, the Lovell Beach House, completed in 1926 by R. A. Schindler. The concrete beach house is an early modern masterpiece, a "key work of twentieth-century architecture," designed for Dr. Lovell, a health advocate who commissioned Richard Nuetra to build another modern masterpiece near LA's Griffith Park.

The house sits atop five poured concrete forms

that elevate it above the beach in a posture of flight and seaworthiness. The abundance of fascinating angles and turns makes viewing the building a geometric pleasure, confounding expectations and eliciting spontaneous appreciation.

The outdoor sleeping porches have now been screened in, but the building retains almost all its original dignity and striking presence. Architect Charles Moore has said that this residence speaks of an architecture for people in motion. So too will it move you.

Environment

Roadside Attractions

Resources

The Newport Beach Groin Field

By the 1950s urban development in Orange County had stopped flows from the many rivers and creeks that once transported sand to the shoreline. Soon places like Newport found themselves with severely depleted beaches. Wave action continued to erode sand and to transport it south, but no new sand arrived from the north to take its place.

In 1968 the Army Corps of Engineers began a 17-mile beach restoration and shoreline protection project at Newport to correct the problem. Over a five-year period, they constructed eight groins that extended under the sand almost from the doors of shoreline homes, out several hundred feet into the ocean.

The project runs from Surfside and Sunset beaches through Newport. As soon as the first two groins were completed, sand was delivered to the site to fill the spaces between the structures. In this way, new beaches were instantly created and the natural movement of sand continued, precluding erosion of downcoast beaches.

If you think that the groins detract from the natural beauty of Newport's beaches, remember that without them, there would *be* no beaches.

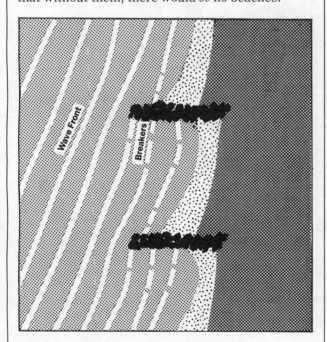

The Difference Between Jettys and Groins

Groins are beach erosion-control structures made of timber, steel, stone, or concrete and intended to impede the flow of sand along the coast. They extend into the ocean, perpendicular to the shoreline, usually rising several feet above sea level and reaching lengths of several hundred feet.

Although similar in appearance to a jetty, a groin is designed exclusively to trap materials, while a jetty is designed to stabilize a harbor entrance.

John "Duke" Wayne

The image of John Wayne still hovers over Orange County and Newport Beach, where he resided. The county airport is named for him and an 8.5-foot statue ceremonializes him. In Newport Beach, the John Wayne Tennis Club celebrates his memory with patriotic decor and a high-tech scoreboard.

Born Marion Michael Morrison in Winterset, Iowa in 1907, Wayne attended USC, played football, and "gained a reputation for prodigious alcohol consumption" before leaving school and trying Hollywood. Starting as a stuntman, then advancing to "quickie" westerns, Wayne finally found his niche when John Ford gave him the lead in *Stagecoach* (1939), followed by *Fort Apache* (1948), *She Wore a Yellow Ribbon* (1949), and *Rio Grande* (1950).

An ardent anticommunist, Wayne was for many people a symbol of a "strong America" that has little patience for protesters, welfare "cheats," or government intervention into the economy. Perhaps America's best-liked cowboy, Wayne was the very essence of the independent, western hero.

More Newport Beach

Newport's unrivaled list of attractions goes on and on:

Island: Harbor, Bay, and Linda. Here Newport's famed and fabled reside in greater-than-kingly splendor. *Harbor Island* features architecture that would stun a sheik. This is where H. R. "Bob" Haldeman sequestered himself during the Watergate revelations. *Bay Island* has been home to Roy Rogers, James Cagney, and L. Frank Baum, each of whom had to be approved—as do current residents—by a vote of the neighborhood to join this 24-member residential island, accessible only by footbridge. *Linda Isle,* site for the filming of *The Sands of Iwo Jima,* is now home to Donald Bren, lord and master of Irvine Company.

Ardell Yacht Brokerage. *The* spot to buy a yacht.

The Wild Goose. Newport's most surreal attraction, this was John Wayne's boat—a converted minesweeper.

Bobby McGhee's. Here many stylish young Newporters and aspiring young Newporters come to dance, drink, and meet others as stylish as they.

Newport Pier. Newport's most overlooked attraction with down-to-earth pleasures. Every morning of the year at about 9:30 the dory fleet arrives at the pier to sell fresh-caught fish. Stone crab, spider crab, lobster, rock cod, sand dabs, and other local catch in season may be purchased inexpensively and fresh. Along the pier a mix of nationalities and classes of people enjoy themselves without artificiality or affectation. Nearby is Scotty's Fish Fry; an array of shops sell bikinis, frozen bananas, and knickknacks; and three bars (Blackies by the Sea, the Beach Ball, Egads) offer oceanside inspiration.

The Newport Dory Fleet

The Newport Dory Fishing Fleet is the last of its kind in the United States. There are about a dozen 15½ foot Glouster dories in the fleet, which—weather willing—have been working every day of the week since 1891.

Long before dawn, the two-man crews are out more than ten miles from shore playing out trawl lines that they have baited the day before. Soon the lines team with wriggling fish, which are hailed in by the strenuous manual cranking of

winches. On a good day, the catch includes red rockfish, sea trout, snapper, kingfish, flounder, crab, and lobster.

When the dories return to shore at about 9:30 am, they are pulled onto the beach atop big rubber rollers and quickly transformed into open air shopping stalls. Weighing scales are hung from oars stuck in the sand and a piece of wood placed across the boat's stern becomes a cutting board. The fishermen are glad to oblige requests to clean and fillet their catch to the individual requests of customers lined up along the beach.

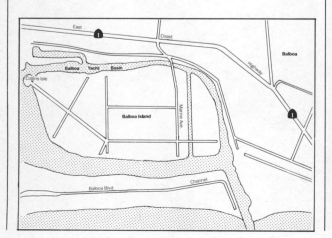

When Balboa Glittered Like Stars

After the arrival of the red cars in 1904, Balboa became one of the most exuberant pleasure spots on the entire coast. Crowds came in excited anticipation and left in gratified exhaustion. They came to swim in the ocean in the daytime and dance at the nite spots after dark. They came to dine, to drink, and—until respectability assumed a new face—they came to gamble. The center of activity was the

ornately styled pavilion, immediately adjacent to the interurban stop and ferry landing.

The pavilion was the major attraction at Balboa throughout World War I. When the pace of pleasure seeking picked up during the Roaring 20s, the Rendezvous Club opened. The Rendezvous featured dance marathons, walkathons, beauty contests, and some of the hottest music of the era.

For 40 years the Rendezvous attracted wall-to-wall crowds who traveled to Balboa (changed from Balisle in 1928) for the best of south coast high-stepping entertainment. Figures from the Big Band pantheon played regularly: Duke Ellington, Artie Shaw, Gene Krupa, Bing Crosby, Woody Herman, Benny Goodman, Nat King Cole, Glenn Miller, and the Dorsey Brothers made the Rendezvous a premier nitespot.

The Rendezvous began its adieu in the 50s, eventually being branded a "trouble spot" by the city council, which limited its hours once the surfing crowd began to supplant the hepcats and bopsters. In 1966 the Rendezvous burned to the ground after a performance by a rock-and-roll band called the Cindermen.

Semiology

In their normal roadside context, signs reliably refer to businesses, products, places, or events. Once removed from their usual environment, however, the signifier becomes the signified, and an entire range of new meaning emerges. PCH's route through Orange County displays a wealth of roadside sign art, purely entertaining in itself.

Balboa

Balboa Island is Newport's most enduring amenity, supplying its own brand of distinct waterfront pleasures. The Balboa Pavilion has stood at the center of the Orange coast's pleasure-taking activities for decades, but with old age it has become rather staid and conservative, showing less life than in its ebullient past. Next door the Fun Zone appears to have met the same unfortunate fate—most of the attractions that were fun have been removed, save a few arcade and video games. But Dillman's restaurant is still quite spry. Nearby are harbor tours and boats to Catalina. The auto ferry to the mainland remains a picturesque delight.

Balboa Pavilion and Auto Ferry

400 Main Street
Balboa, 92661
673-5245

The Balboa Auto Ferry, one of the few remaining auto ferries on the West Coast, has been operating since 1919. The small, three-car ferry shoots quickly across the harbor to Balboa Island, but it is a fine ride. The ferries leave at intervals 24 hours a day in the summer, from sunrise to midnight the rest of the year. One-way fares are 20¢ per person for pedestrians and auto passengers, 75¢ for autos and drivers. Take PCH to Balboa Blvd., and Balboa to the end of Palm Street.

The King of Surf Music

May you never hear surf music again.
Jimi Hendrix

Newport Beach is the home of Dick Dale, the creator of surf music and the person who taught Jimi Hendrix how to use tremelos and reverbs. Dale, who claims to be the first rock-and-roll performer to appear on the *Ed Sullivan Show,* brought the electric guitar out of the age of Les Paul, when echo and reverb were used sparingly, and into the era of Hendrix, from whence electric effects became the source of music once unimaginable.

With his band the Del Tones, Dale earned the title of "King of the Surf Guitar" as he filled Orange County ballrooms and armories during the early 1960s with his sustained reverberating riffs. "There was a tremendous amount of power that I felt while surfing and that feeling of power was simply transferred from myself to my guitar when I was playing surf music."

Dale's influence set the pace for the Chantays, another Orange Country group, whose hit "Pipeline" gave surf music top-of-the-charts popularity in 1961. Two years later, another California band, the Beach

Boys, added to the surf sound lyrics that celebrated the lives of California's white middle-class teenagers. Soon came Jan and Dean, the Surfaris, the Hondels, and a stream of others who followed in the wake of the King of the Surf Guitar.

How Smeltzer and Pacific City Became Huntington Beach

During the quarter century between the arrival of the Pacific Electric at Huntington Beach and the completion of the coast road in 1928, real estate promoters capitalized on the streetcars' miraculous ability to abet land sales. Free sightseeing trips brought thousands of potential buyers down the coast on the Interurban, providing close-up views of the Pacific and an opportunity to buy coastal property cheap.

Prior to July 4, 1904 when the Pacific Electric came to Huntington Beach, the place had been ungloriously known as Smeltzer—an apt name perhaps for a community where 6,000 acres of prime celery fields defined local economic existence. Smeltzer took pride in its celery, producing some of the nation's best from abundant fields.

Atlantic City West

Others saw Smeltzer more romantically and with greater potential for profits. Near the turn of the century, Philip Stanton—with visions of an Atlantic City West in his head—bought 1500 nearby acres of mostly swampland overlooking what was then called Shell Beach to establish the township of Pacific City.

Pacific City became Huntington Beach when local promoters sought to attract the attention of Henry Huntington by renaming the town after him. Two years later Huntington brought his red cars down the coast after buying up as much of the town-site as he could. To show signs of habitation, a town was fabricated from buildings hauled in from the defunct boomtown of Fairview. Streets were paved, water piped in, and the requisite oceanfront pavilion was erected.

Although it did not quite become the Atlantic City of the West, Huntington grew and prospered through the first two decades of the century as the romantic red cars continued to vitalize the region's resort economy.

In 1905 the Huntington Beach Company gave the Methodist Church four blocks in the center of town. The Methodists built a 3,000-seat revival auditorium, and for the next 10 years Huntington Beach assumed an almost pious air as thousands of Methodists made their pilgrimage to worship together and camp in a gigantic tent city.

Benefits of Open Space

The appeal of the ocean has frequently been described in romantic terms. "It keeps eternal whisperings around/desolate shores," Keats wrote. But explanations of why people go to the beach or other public open spaces have usually taken a more prosaic turn.

"Recreation is stronger than vice, and recreation alone can stifle the lust for vice," wrote Jane Addams in the 1890s, attempting to improve the nation's moral health by encouraging attendance

at outdoor recreation areas. Addams, like Whitman and Thoreau before her, presumed a positive relationship between the outdoors and psychological well-being. People should go to the beach or a park because it will be good for them.

Frederick Law Olmstead, America's most revered early park planner, maintained that open space could cleanse urban dwellers' minds and calm their nerves. Throughout the park movement during the second half of the 19th century, similar refrains were frequently heard as picturesque landscaped parks were built all over the country.

Many of the first California beachgoers who waded into the ocean did so for its "curative powers." Beaches gained the approval of "health seekers" who sought to improve their physical well-being. Eventually, California's beachgoing "health seekers" were outnumbered by the "pleasure seekers," but physical and psychological well-being still play a major part in their pleasures.

Today there are nearly as many explanations for why people to go the beach as there are people at the beach. Teenagers go to "hang out," business people to "unstress," and lots of people just to "get out of the house."

Huntington Beach, Cal.

Terns

Terns are graceful, slender seabirds with narrow wings, forked tails, and long, pointed bills. Like brown pelicans and ospreys, terns plunge-dive in midflight to capture fish beneath the ocean's surface. But the tern is too light in body-weight to submerge more than a few inches beneath the surface, so it bobs up much more quickly than do most diving birds.

Terns are as common along the shore as sea gulls. The eight distinct families of terns seen in California are Forster's, common, artic, least, royal, elegant, caspian, and black.

California Least Tern

The least tern is so named because it is the smallest of the terns. But "least" now has an unfortunate second meaning, since this bird is also the scarcest and most threatened of terns. It appears on both the state and federal endangered species lists.

The California least tern has an elegant little white body, gray wings, black outer flight feathers, black-capped head, and a black-tipped yellow bill. In flight its quick jerky wing beats and hovering motions distinguish it from the larger terns.

The Huntington Beach Least Tern Reserve

The state established the Least Tern Natural Reserve at Huntington State Beach in Orange County in 1975 as part of a statewide effort to protect nesting sites and feeding areas. The terrain at Huntington is ideal for these shorebirds: sparse vegetation, mixed sand and shell substrate, and nearby shallow water with a good supply of small fish.

The terns arrive at their breeding sites near the mouth of the Santa Ana River in April and stay through October, laying one to four buff-colored eggs in shallow depressions in the sand or dried mud. No one is sure where the birds spend the rest of the year.

The outlook for the least tern's return is cautiously optimistic. In 1973 only 20 colonies, fewer than 700 pairs of birds, remained in California. Urban development and human encroachment on their vulnerable nesting sites seemed to doom the bird to extinction. But by 1980, after an aggressive protection program, more than 900 pairs were identified in 30 colonies.

Tern Around

A nesting tern is likely to engage in a frontal attack on any intruder on its nesting territory. Watch out for a buzzing dive-bomb from above if you venture too near.

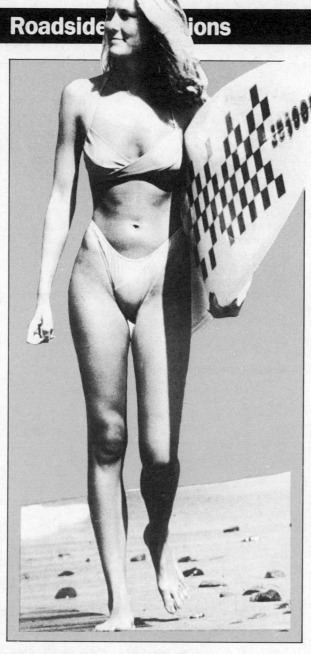

Huntington Beach

In certain parts of the world the word "California" evokes an image that is played out daily at Huntington Beach: well-tanned people in bikinis or shorts walking down the street carrying surfboards, smiling in satisfaction at having attained the perfect life (or the perfect wave), and no one older than 25 in sight.

While California by and large rejects this image of itself, Huntington Beach cultivates it. Not one, but two shrines commemorate surfing, and although Huntington is a serious-minded metropolitan area that is addressing issues related to its recent meteoric growth, the heart of the town remains the beach. The pleasure of Huntington Beach remains the pleasure of the rolling ocean at the edge of the land.

Surfing Resources

Consult *Surfers Magazine,* or these books for more on surfing in California.

SURFING CALIFORNIA
Bank Wright
Allan B. Wright, Jr., Publisher
Redondo Beach. 1982.

From Oregon to Mexico, Bank Wright has explored the California Surf. This book describes conditions at every accessible spot, including advice and comments, seasonal changes of each site, and local lore. Maps and many photos.

SURFING: THE ULTIMATE PLEASURE
Leonard Lueras
Workman Publishing
New York. 1984.

This book relates surfing's mythological beginnings, the birth of a surfside society, a worldwide quest for the perfect wave, and the soaring spirit of an ancient art form.

The Best Surf Movie Ever Made

The best surf movie ever made, hands down, is Dana Point film maker Bruce Brown's 91 minute long *The Endless Summer,* first screened in 1964. Brown's film about two California surfers who journey around the world and across the equator in search of the perfect wave earned him the reputation of the "Fellini of Foam."

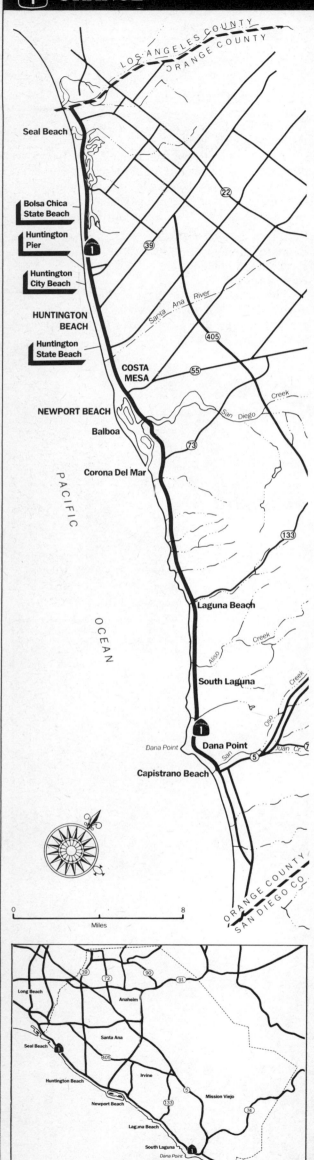

A Short History of the Art of Surfing

The origins of surfing may date back to the first time an island inhabitant contemplated a wave, recalled a particularly flat piece of wood, and thought "how bitchin." No one knows the exact genesis of surfing, but Hawaiian chants from the 15th century describe the activity as a significant part of island life that undoubtedly had persisted for generations.

Although surfing has for centuries been a part of many coastal cultures, such as those of equatorial West Africa, so many surfing myths originate in Polynesia that it was evidently a major aspect of island culture at an early date. Five hundred years ago Hawaiians made offerings and prayed to the gods to improve surfing conditions. It was believed that a demigod would, if properly summoned, intercede on behalf of the surfer.

Missing the Connection

The first description of surfing by a westerner was penned by Captain James Cooke, the explorer, who witnessed stand-up surfing in Hawaii in 1778, a year before he was killed by a group of angry Hawaiians on the Big Island's Kona Coast.

Freeth, a surfer who became the sport's first celebrity. Within the year Freeth was invited to California by Henry Huntington to conduct public exhibitions of the exotic watersport. Freeth, introduced by promoters as an "aquatic attraction," became the first known person to ride a California wave on a board.

Surfing attracted increased attention as another Hawaiian, Duke Kahanamoku, who had been a freestyle swimming hero in the 1912 Olympics, popular-

In 1866 Mark Twain visited Hawaii, witnessed the islanders surfing, and decided to try it himself: "I tried surf bathing once, subsequently, but made a failure of it. I got the board placed right, and at the right moment, too, but missed the connection myself. The board struck the shore in three-quarters of a second, without any cargo, and I struck the bottom about the same time, with a couple of bottles of water in me."

Twain's visit coincided with the height of the missionary invasion of Hawaii, during which surfing, like native cultural life in general, suffered serious decline. Intent on converting the islanders to Christianity, missionaries condemned the use of the surfboard as a "pagan activity." At the time of Cooke's arrival in 1778 the Hawaiian population was about 300,000. By 1893 diseases introduced by European visitors and immigrants had reduced the population to some 40,000. Surfing virtually disappeared.

Jack London and Duke

It was another American writer who helped revive surfing near the turn of the century. In 1907 Jack London published a travel piece in *Woman's Home Companion,* "A Royal Sport: Surfing at Waikiki," that was to do for surfing what Ernest Hemingway later did for sportfishing. Suddenly the mainland discovered this unusual Hawaiian activtiy.

While living near the beach, London met George

ized the sport on both coasts through exhibitions. At Atlantic City, New Jersey, and Corona del Mar, California, he performed for fascinated and spellbound audiences, who soon took to the waves themselves.

My Boys and I

While Kahanamoku's fame spread—he introduced surfing to Australia in 1912—he began a career in the movies, playing opposite John Wayne in the *Wake of the Red Witch.* At the 1920 Olympics he broke his own Olympic record for the 100-meter freestyle, establishing himself as the world's fastest swimmer. His legend assumed front-page notoriety in 1925, when he rescued eight people from a sinking yacht off Newport Beach, using his surfboard to bring them to safety.

At the first organized surfing competition, held at Corona del Mar in 1928, Kahanamoku gave a special exhibition. When a surfing hall of fame was created in 1965, Duke was the first member to be inducted, as 2,000 surfers stood and cheered at the Santa Monica Civic Auditorium.

A few years later, on one of his last trips to California from Honolulu, where he served as the city's elected sheriff, Duke headed a surfing entourage through Malibu from a classic Rolls Royce with surfboards on top. Said Duke as he ambled toward the surf, "My boys and I, we showed 'em how to go surfing."

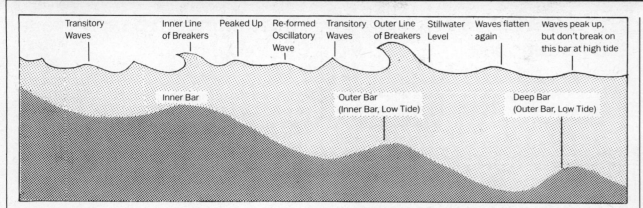

Transitory Waves | Inner Line of Breakers | Peaked Up | Re-formed Oscillatory Wave | Transitory Waves | Outer Line of Breakers | Stillwater Level | Waves flatten again | Waves peak up, but don't break on this bar at high tide

Inner Bar | Outer Bar (Inner Bar, Low Tide) | Deep Bar (Outer Bar, Low Tide)

Waves

Waves differ greatly in type and size, and their classification has always been a scientific challenge. A widely accepted system measures a wave's *period*, the time it takes to travel one *wave length* (the distance between the wave's successive peaks) past a fixed point. A swell, for example, has a fairly short period, about 10 seconds. More common surf beats measure 100 seconds, and a tsunami (tidal wave) might have a period as long as 1,000 seconds.

A wave breaks when the water depth becomes less than one-seventh of the distance between wave crests.

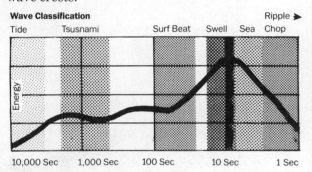

Wave Classification

Tide | Tsunami | Surf Beat | Swell | Sea | Ripple ➤ Chop

Energy

10,000 Sec | 1,000 Sec | 100 Sec | 10 Sec | 1 Sec

Beneath the Surface

The surface action of waves as they approach shore gives a clue to conditions on the ocean's floor. Offshore bars (also called long-shore bars) form underwater ridges of sand parallel to the beach. These ridges vary in height and generally slope more on the offshore side. The bars are formed as cross-shore currents release on to the ocean floor sands that were previously held in suspension by wave action.

As a wave approaches a sandy bottom shoreline, its energy dissipates according to the location and features of these offshore bars. How the wave breaks over a bar, and when, depends on the tide, the slope of the bar and the size of the waves.

The Parts of a Wave

CREST: High point of a wave
TROUGH: Low point of a wave
WAVE HEIGHT: Vertical distance from trough to crest
WAVE LENGTH: Horizontal distance between adjacent crests
WAVE PERIOD: Number of seconds it takes for a wave crest to traverse a distance equal to one wave length

The Unofficial Surfing Capital of the World

For many, Orange County represents a national bastion of conservative politics, where Richard Nixon played his first dirty tricks and retreated in exile after his last one. But to surfers of the world, Orange County is the unofficial capital of the cosmos.

Orange County is the editorial headquarters for the two most influential surfing magazines, *Surfer* and *Surfing*. Surfing's best-known filmmakers, Bruce Brown (*Endless Summer*) and Greg MacGillivray (*Five Summer Stories*), live here, as do several internationally known still photographers, and world-renowned surfboard makers Gordon "Grubby" Clark and Hobie Atler. Surfing paraphernalia and accessories form the livelihood for many residents, while others, like Phil Edwards, make or once made their living on the professional surfing circuit. Each year hordes of surfers come to Orange County beaches as if to Mecca.

The Beaches

Variously designated, the beaches at Huntington Beach run from the Santa Ana River on the south to Sunset Beach on the north. Within this preserve the beaches differ in facilities and management more than in the geophysical qualities of sand or surf. The entire stretch offers superb swimming, with fine, even rolling combers and clear, usually unvegetated water. The surfing, of course, is legendary.

Huntington State Beach. This 3-mile section of beach starting at the Santa Ana River has up-to-the-minute facilities with excellent access for the disabled. Food concessions, showers, and 2-mile bike path and promenade.

Huntington City Beach. Although surfing is limited at certain times, the nearby pier creates excellent swells for surfing. This is the site of the International Surfing Competition every spring. RV camping is available during the summer months.

Huntington Pier. A bronze statue of Duke Kahanamoku welcomes you to this 70-year-old and 1,800-foot-long pier with snack bars, a bait shop, lights for night surfing and fishing, and a parade of unusual people.

Bolsa Chica State Beach. This excellent 6-mile beach has complete facilities and is paralleled by a well-landscaped cement bike path that runs the length of Huntington Beach and connects all the beach areas, eventually joining the Santa Ana River trail.

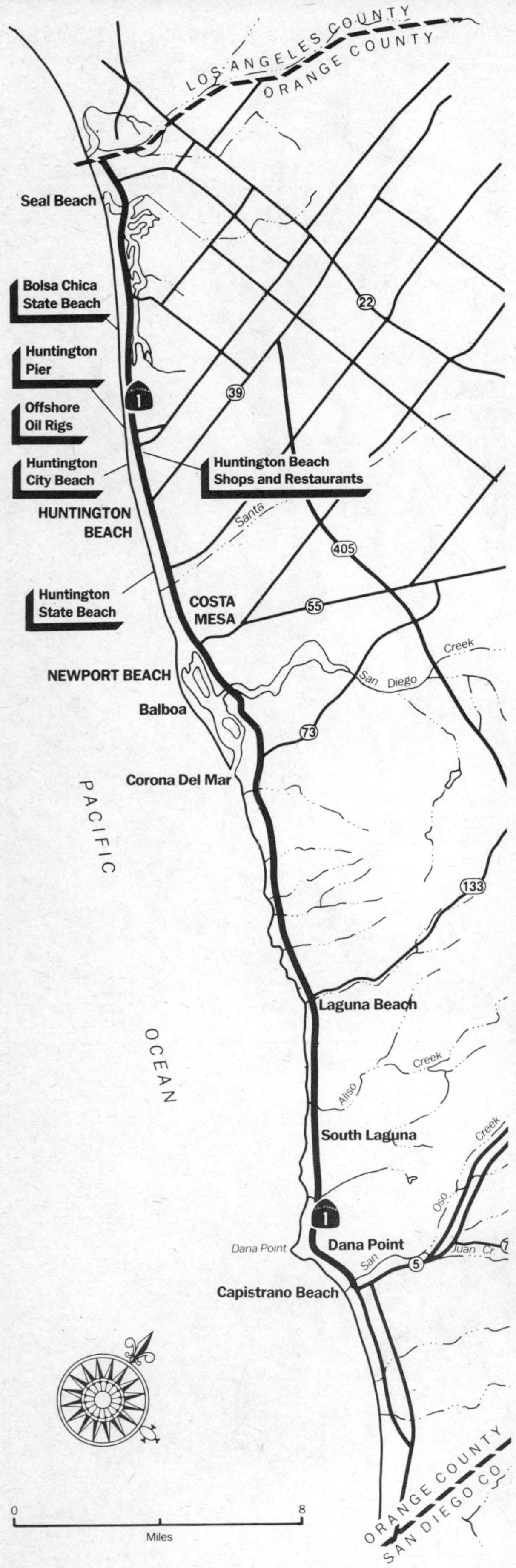

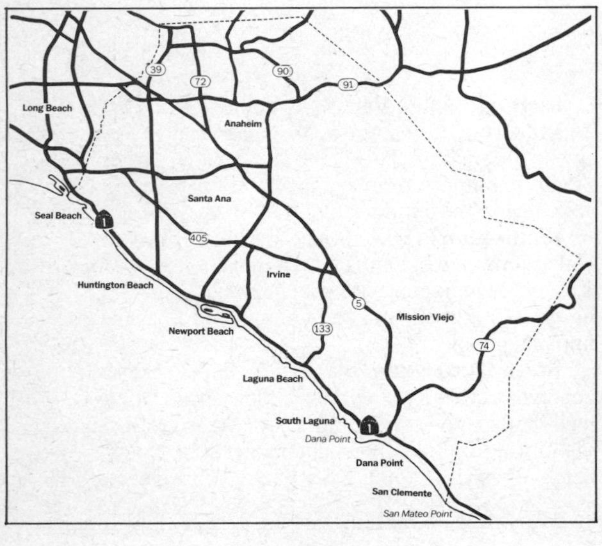

The Appearance of the Automobile

Despite torturous roads, more and more travelers to the Orange Coast arrived in automobiles. Without a through-coast road the journey was extremely indirect, but the pleasure of motoring to the sea was mesmerizing. In 1913 the South Coast Improvement Association was organized to promote and agitate for a coast highway in Orange County.

By 1920 Huntington Beach seemed to have settled into a relatively steady state of existence. Suddenly, on November 6, a rumble beneath the ground portended some unmanageable force. Earthquake? No—oil. So much oil it shot through the sky then fell to the earth blackening everything in sight. More than 500 men were rushed to the site to dyke-in the deep body of oil that ran like an overland river. For days the gusher blew uncontrolled until the crew finally stanched it.

The Huntington Beach Oil Company

For years the Huntington Beach Oil Company controlled the town with an iron hand. There was no beach, just a shoreline jungle of 120-foot-tall black oil derricks.

In 1931 the City took the oil company to court and forced it to sell the pier and the beach frontage east of the pier. As many of the oil fields tapped out, the oil company's presence became more benign and the town's economy has become more diversified.

Today Standard Oil of California owns two-thirds of Huntington Beach Oil Company, and the oil interests work with the municipal government to minimize the industry's impacts on the community.

Standard Oil Company of California

With annual corporate profits of $1.8 billion, Standard Oil Company of California (Socal) is the world's third-largest oil producer. Socal owns 27,000 oil wells and 2,000 gas wells around the globe, with reserves of 1.7 billion barrels of oil, not including their yields from Saudi Arabia and Indo-

The Unexpected Rewards of Encyclopedias

In few cases have the benefits of literature been so apparent: In 1915 the Encyclopedia Britannica gave away parcels of Huntington Beach land as an inducement to its customers. The land had been thought worthless when the company bought the inaccessible hillside acreage and divided it into 420 lots. But when oil was discovered in 1920 hundreds of people who had conscientiously invested in a set of encyclopedias to help their children with their homework, acquire added tidbits of knowledge, or settle household disputes—were suddenly rich.

Within months the resort landscape at Huntington Beach was transformed. Wooden derricks blocked the seashore and oil covered the sand. For the next 30 years Huntington Beach would be the third largest oil-producing region in California.

Excursionists on the red cars disembarked with looks of disbelief as they were greeted by the newly placed black pumping machines. All at once the notion of the red cars, carousels, and frolicking at the beach seemed to belong to another, more innocent era.

nesia ("release of such information has not been approved").

Socal's fleet of 77 ocean tankers ships to 38 refineries in 19 countries; most of the company's 14,000 gas stations are in the U.S. Socal is also one of the world's largest producers of asphalt and ranks third in the nation in the production of garden fertilizers and pesticides.

Incredibly large, Socal is also incredibly conservative. The editors of *Everybody's Business* observe: "Socal brings up the 'right wing' of the American oil industry. They have a long history of aloofness and indifference to public opinion. Socal has been known for years as a predominantly white, male, Christian company that wanted to stay that way. In a national survey of graduating business students in the early 1970s, Socal ranked 49th out of 50 corporations rated on the their social responsibility."

Map labels (left column)

LOS ANGELES COUNTY
ORANGE COUNTY

Seal Beach

Bolsa Chica State Beach

Huntington Pier

Offshore Oil Rigs

Huntington City Beach

HUNTINGTON BEACH

Huntington Beach Shops and Restaurants

Huntington State Beach

COSTA MESA

NEWPORT BEACH

Balboa

Corona Del Mar

PACIFIC OCEAN

Laguna Beach

South Laguna

Dana Point

Capistrano Beach

ORANGE COUNTY
SAN DIEGO CO.

0   8
Miles

Long Beach

Anaheim

Santa Ana

Seal Beach

Huntington Beach

Irvine

Newport Beach

Mission Viejo

Laguna Beach

South Laguna

Dana Point

San Clemente

San Mateo Point

Orange's Black Gold

Grasshoppers (pumps) on land, platforms offshore, and miles of pipeline under both shore and sea attest to the abundance and value of Southern California's oil and gas resources. Fuel production is the state's most important mineral industry and a great deal of it occurs in Orange County.

From Dana Point to Point Conception in Santa Barbara County, ages of unstable geological activity have created a complex system of underground air pockets to which oil and gas (lighter than water) migrate and cluster. The energy resources in these pockets assure major drilling activity in Orange for years to come.

Offshore Oil Rigs

There are two basic types of offshore oil-drilling facilities: fixed and mobile. Most of Southern California's rigs are of the fixed variety, attached permanently to the ocean floor and used for development drilling as well as production. Each platform can accommodate 30 or more individual wells.

Fixed platforms reached a new standard of industrial artistry in the concept of the "oil island," which is actually a platform camouflaged to look like something else. The most elaborate oil islands sprout palm trees, shrubs, and exterior structures that from a distance resemble high-rise apartment buildings instead of rigging.

Less common than fixed platforms are the mobile ones. These come in three types: the drill ship, which is most often used only in the deepest waters or for initial exploration; the semi-submersible, a large surface platform connected by columns to submerged hulls, used in waters of deeper than 1,000 feet; and the jack-up, which has legs that extend to the ocean floor in shallow depths up to about 350 feet.

Huntington Pier

Huntington Beach boasts one of the most interesting piers in Southern California. The 1,800 foot pier is a focal point of activity that defines much of the town's character. Huntington Pier has three snackbars and lights for night surfing in addition to a motley of waterfront characters. A stroll over its length will acquaint you with every assortment of humanity known to the beach scene.

Huntington Beach's roadside presence is marked by a series of surf-culture shops and night spots (The Golden Bear with name rock n roll, Cagney's By the Sea). Several shops (Jack's, Gordies) display the art of surfboard design. Talented shapers and glassers have wrought fantastic creations—double-wing pin twin fins, swallow wingers, and pintail ranch specials.

Energy Facts

California produces 400 million barrels of oil a year (4th in the nation), and 370 billion cubic feet of natural gas a year (7th in the nation).

California-produced oil meets 50% of the state's annual needs, with offshore wells producing 17% of the state's annual needs.

About 51,000 wells in California are today producing oil.

Between 3,000 and 4,000 new wells are drilled in the state each year.

In 1981, the 874 businesses involved in oil and gas extraction employed 31,000 workers on an annual payroll of $480 million.

Proven reserves of oil are estimated at over 5 billion barrels, and natural gas reserves at 4.7 trillion cubic feet. Suspected reserves could easily exceed proven ones.

The deepest offshore oil well (as of 1981) is off Ventura's coast in the Montalvo field. Drilled in 1956, it reaches a depth of 14,236 feet.

The deepest offshore gas well was drilled off Santa Barbara in 1968 to a depth of 7,810 feet.

Annual Oil and Gas Production in PCH Counties

	Oil (barrels)	Gas (thousands of cubic feet)
Orange	21,711,674	5,175,393
Los Angeles	62,021,103	22,794,164
Ventura	17,208,340	18,217,088
Santa Barbara	15,913,543	15,566,111
San Luis Obispo	1,929,290	525,046
Monterey	10,279,319	0
Santa Cruz	0	0
San Mateo	17,378	4,341
San Francisco	0	0
Marin	0	0
Sonoma	0	8,550
Mendocino	0	0

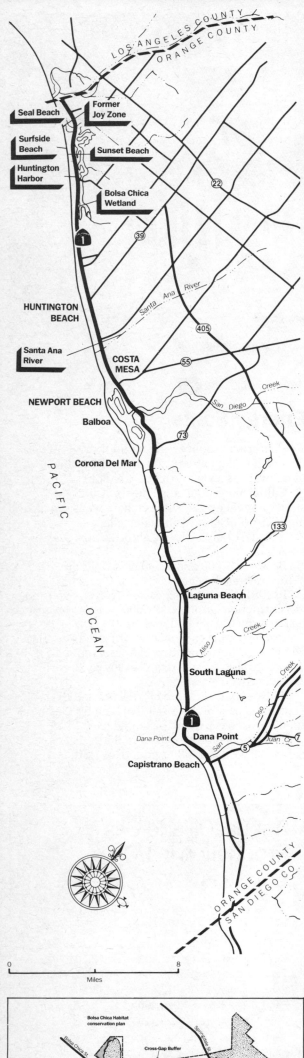

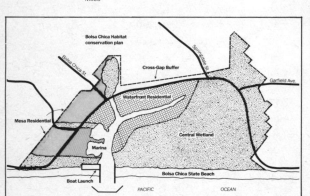

Building the Coast Highway

The popularity of the automobile and the production requirements of a booming oil industry brought rapid changes to the Orange coast. When construction began on the coast highway that would link the coastal oil fields and bring new development, the demise of the interurbans was assured.

The coast highway paralleled the route of the old red cars through Orange County, but the oceanfront dunes prevented deliveries by motor vehicle. Road crews relied on an "industrial railway" on which materials and supplies could be hauled through the sand. Fordson tractors were converted into locomotives to haul strings of dump cars to the construction site over a makeshift railway.

While the erection of oil pumping facilities continued near one part of the beach, road construction began at another, along Seal Beach, "the most most wide open town in Orange County." The first completed segment of the coast highway brought motoring tourists to the Joy Zone, a seaside amusement park that had been relocated from the 1915 Panama-Pacific International Exposition in San Francisco. Until 1937 a giant wooden roller coaster stood as a finely crafted backdrop for arcades, games, the beach, and rolling surf.

The completion of the coast highway bridge over the Santa Ana River in 1927 brought more and more tourists to the Orange coast, and a year later the Coast Highway from Newport to Laguna was completed. District fairs and regular visits by wild west shows, vaudeville acts, and balloon exhibitions created a lively atmosphere, while movie makers filmed location shots for such pictures as *All Quiet on the Western Front*. Stutzes, Studebakers, and Packards jammed into roadhouse parking lots and awaited the return of fancily dressed passengers who made the jazz-age scene and caroused through the sea-kissed night.

Bolsa Chica: An Urban Wetland

Along PCH's east side from Golden West Street to Huntington Avenue lies a narrow strip of land that represents one of Southern California's most satisfying environmental-management stories. Bolsa Chica Ecological Reserve, once almost completely robbed of natural life, is now slowly but surely recovering.

The Bolsa Chica ("little pocket") lies within Bolsa Gap, a two-mile-wide area bounded by bluffs on the northwest and southeast, which once was a 1,900-acre tidal wetland, a cradle of marine and bird life.

Bolsa Chica, however, was located in one of the state's fastest-growing areas, and its natural life was severely disrupted by human activity. In the mid 1890s the Santa Ana Gun Club built tidal gates here to create ponds for game birds. The gates constricted critical tidal flushing, and silt could not get to the ocean, so the wetland began to fill up. About the same time, the many upland rivers and creeks were dammed or rerouted, reducing freshwater flows. Discovery of oil in the Huntington Beach Oil Fields led to more dykes to protect drilling operations from salt-water intrusion and roadways.

Restoration

When Californians finally understood the environmental importance of wetlands, Bolsa Chica was almost a lost cause. Determined planning and citizen action, however, squeezed out an eleventh-hour victory.

Today the state owns 327.5 acres in Bolsa Chica and has a long-term lease on another 230 acres. The Department of Fish and Game, with help from local citizens and other agencies, has begun restoration. Tidal flushing has been restored to 100 acres. An interpretive nature trail leads from the PCH parking lot, fishing access is available on the north banks, and new accessways and restorations are planned.

The real success of the restoration of Bolsa Chica is only now becoming apparent. More than 200 species of migratory birds were counted here last season. The Bolsa Chica shelters three endangered bird species, and today 33 fish species (up from 3) live here.

Compatible Development

Because of its urban location and largely private ownership, the restoration of Bolsa Chica has had to coexist with other land uses. The wetland sits on the state's 7th largest oil field, which has about 1,899 wells on it, about 250 of them in the Bolsa Chica. Annual revenues from the oil fields are estimated at $7 million. In addition to the oil drilling, private interests plan to build up to 4,000 new shorefront homes, 1,300 boat slips, a new marina, and more. All these development projects are being carefully coordinated with future restoration and management of the Bolsa Chica, one of Southern California's most satisfying wetland protection stories.

Environment

Wetlands

Along California's coast are many shallow-water marshes, tideflats, lagoons, estuaries, and sloughs, all known by the general term of wetlands. Although some pure saltwater or fresh water wetlands do exist, most wetlands are a combination of both—fresh water arriving from inland streams and rivers, and saltwater from tidal action from the ocean.

These areas, many as ancient as 15,000 years old, are among the most ecologically important

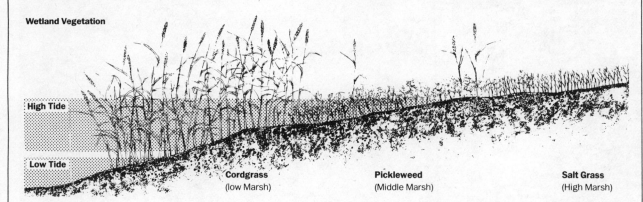

Wetland Vegetation

High Tide

Low Tide

Cordgrass (low Marsh)   **Pickleweed** (Middle Marsh)   **Salt Grass** (High Marsh)

sites on the earth. For ages, rich sediments have settled on the wetland floors, and protected sanctuary ponds have developed behind evolving berms and dunes. Highly specialized animals have evolved, including some of the lowest creatures in the food chain, upon which the rest of life depends. Wetlands are also home to unusually nutritious plants like cordgrass, which can outproduce wheat 10 to one in per acre production of nutrients and oxygen. Fish enter wetlands to spawn, birds to nest, and hundreds of sea creatures call the mudflats and tidal waterways home.

Marine scientists estimate that in the 1890s, California's coastal wetlands covered more than 380,000 acres. Today, more than three-quarters of coastal wetlands have disappeared, victims of development, fill, and mismanagement.

Bolsa Chica is the first major wetland encountered by the northbound PCH traveler. The story of its protection and partial restoration is heartening, as are the similar efforts at other major wetlands systems to the north, such as Mugu Lagoon and Elkhorn Slough.

Roadside Attractions

Seal Beach

North of Huntington, the beach strip that is PCH grows more dense with shops and commercial activity. At Sunset Beach a fine bike path accompanies the shorefront from Warner Avenue to Anderson Avenue. The virtue of Sunset Beach is its small crowds. An offshore sandbar creates dependable surf.

Seal Beach, too, has an excellent usually uncrowded beach, as well as a good pier that creates favorable conditions for surfing. But the town itself grows daily harder to recognize as it becomes more and more submerged beneath the sprawl of its LA County neighbor, Long Beach.

One attraction in Seal Beach, however, maintains its own unique identity against the tides of metropolitan expansion—the Glide'er Inn. Founded in the 1930s with an aviation motif to serve the then extant Seal Beach Airport, the Glide'er Inn has remained frozen weirdly in time like some aviator lost in flight. Stop here to enjoy fine seafood dinners with the ghosts of Charles Lindbergh, Eddie Rickenbacker, and Wiley Post, before resuming your journey

into
the wild
blue
yonder.

Resources

 TERN - TIDE

Wetlands Information

Most of California's remaining wetlands have at least one local citizen's group hard at work to ensure their continued protection. These environmental activists are usually the best source of information. The Amigos de Bolsa Chica (P.O. Box 1563, Huntington Beach, 92647, 897-7003) is one of the oldest and most successful of California's wetlands organizations. Contact the State Coastal Conservancy's Wetlands or Land Trust Program (415-464-1015) for help identifying other groups, and obtain these publications for more detail on California's wetland systems.

WETLAND RESTORATION AND ENHANCEMENT IN CALIFORNIA
Michael Josselyn, Editor
Tiburon Center for
Environmental Studies
Tiburon. 1982.

COMMON WETLAND PLANTS OF CALIFORNIA
Phylis Faber
Pickleweed Press
Inverness. 1982.

Visitor Assistance

DANA POINT HARBOR CHAMBER OF COMMERCE
33621 Del Obispo Street
Dana Point 92629
496-1555

LAGUNA BEACH CHAMBER OF COMMERCE
357 Glenneyre Street
Laguna Beach 92651
494-1018

HUNTINGTON BEACH CHAMBER OF COMMERCE
2213 Main Street, No. 32
Huntington Beach 92648
536-8888

NEWPORT BEACH CONVENTION CENTER
1470 Jamboree Road
Newport Beach 92660
644-8460

LOS ANGELES

ALTHOUGH LOS ANGELES is America's original model of a fragmented metropolis—spread out, uncentered, and "thereless"—it does not exist without a heart. LA's heart is at the beach, and PCH, California 1, is the main concourse along a string of beaches that favorably distinguishes metropolitan LA from any urban area in the world.

From Long Beach's decorated oil wells to Malibu's glittering shores, PCH connects a string of surf towns that express the best of LA's urban exuberance. North of San Pedro, PCH skirts a 50-mile stretch of world class beaches—including Redondo, Hermosa, and Manhattan beaches—that are interrupted only by a detour around LAX and Marina del Rey.

After the airport, PCH regains the coast near Venice, which heralds a landscape of seaside make-believe encompassing the Santa Monica Amusement Pier and the storied land of Malibu, where celebrities live in movie-set houses beside the reflective sea.

Malibu completes PCH's northward journey through LA county, an expedition that does not once require a freeway or detour far enough from the coast to escape the influence of one of LA's most significant contributions to the modern world—Southern California beach culture.

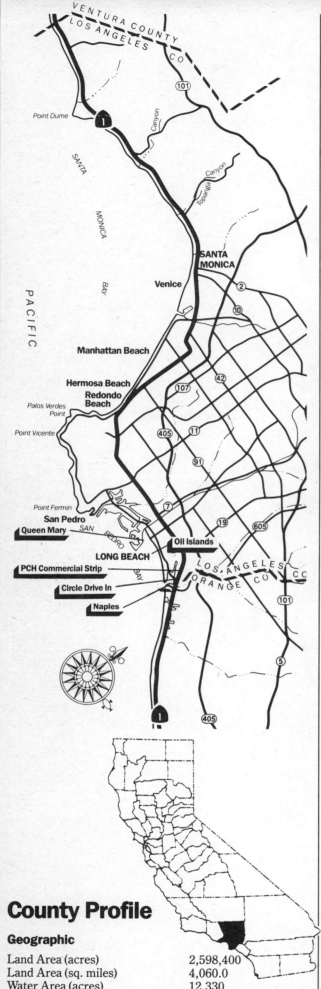

County Profile

Geographic

Land Area (acres)	2,598,400
Land Area (sq. miles)	4,060.0
Water Area (acres)	12,330
Water Area (sq. miles)	19.3
Acres in Public Ownership	1,017,378,.55
Percent in Public Ownership	39.15
Miles of Public Roads	21,012
County Seat	Los Angeles

Demographic

Population	7,763,500
State Rank by Population	1
Projected 1990 Population	8,061,000
Unemployment Rate (state avg. = 9.9)	10.1
Per Capita Personal Income	$12,544
State Rank by Income	9
Total Assessed Property Value	$199,650,802,54

Emerging Surf Cities

Actually, Los Angeles has not grown, it has been conjured into existence.

Carey McWilliams

Los Angeles did not begin as a seaside city but as an inland settlement that had to await the arrival of the railroad to begin growing toward the coast. Although regular stage routes to the sea were established in the 1870s, the journey from downtown was slow and miserable. An excursion to the

beach could take two days over harrowing trails.

Once Los Angeles began to "leapfrog to the sea," chiefly through the expansion of the Pacific Electric Railway Company, a series of shoreline cities sprung up along the coast from Long Beach to Santa Monica, each unique in character but all reliant on resort economies. The Pacific Electric provided the means to get potential land buyers to these emerging surf cities, and newly built beach parks, boardwalks, and amusement piers provided the attraction.

Willmore City

Called Willmore City until 1888, Long Beach was regarded for many years as the most straight-laced of LA County's beach towns. A strong temperance atmosphere was enforced through deed restrictions that outlawed the sale and consumption of alcoholic beverages. Tough regulations, which sometimes led to arrests, imposed severe penalties for women "immorally attired" at the beach.

The interurban railway did not arrive at Long Beach until 1901, and then it was almost refused because of opposing public sentiment. Strong objections that trolley tracks would reduce property values had to be countered by merchants, real estate promoters, and newspapers. "Wherever the [interurban] has its center," editorialized the *Long Beach Tribune*, "the town will grow."

And grow it did once the interurban was completed: zooming from a population of 2,000 to more than 17,000 within the decade, earning recognition as the fastest-growing city in the country. Long Beach, despite its conservative embrace of the status quo, was suddenly confronted with rapid change in drastic measure.

The Creature That Ate Drive-In Movies

Once drive-ins were the recreational miracles of suburbia, combining the dream of the automobile with the dream of movies for a generation of young girls in ponytails and pedal pushers and young boys in ducktails and slacks with buckles in the back. Endless evenings of incandescent adolescence were spent groping beneath starched petticoats and tight blue jeans in the backseats of '57 Chevys, while mythic stars like Sandra Dee and Troy Donahue looked on approvingly from high above on the giant outdoor screen.

But that was yesterday. Today much of the allure of the drive-in has faded like Fabian's blue jeans, and most theater owners say the drive-in is destined for extinction. In 1982, according to the National Association of Theater Owners, only 3,354 drive-ins operated in the United States—down 11% from a decade earlier and down 17% from a peak 4,063 units in 1958. Moreover, since many drive-ins have been converted to multiscreen facilities, the numbers of drive-ins that have met their demise is probably far greater.

The drive-in was born in 1934, when Richard Hollingshead pointed a 16 mm projector at an outside wall in Camden, New Jersey. But drive-ins did not become widely popular until after World War II, when suburb after suburb sprang up across the rural countryside. Suddenly whole communities emerged at once, before needed services, including entertainment facilities, could be established.

Drive-ins became a relatively cheap way for entrepreneurs to tap the suburban entertainment market. Construction was cheap—far cheaper than conventional indoor construction—and if land costs were on the rise, so much the better. No investor could go wrong with a large parcel of land that was appreciating in value.

California's climate, conducive to year-round operation, favored the drive-in, other limitations, such as the sky's refusal to darken until late in the evening during peak-use summer months, created economic inefficiencies. Competition from television didn't help, and as the land around the drive-ins was developed new problems arose—more traffic, more interfering noise, and distracting headlights.

Drive-ins never became the fantastic moneymakers that one might have expected in a culture where rampant auto-mobility conditions all things large and small. In fact, the automobile ordained the death of drive-ins by enabling so much suburban development that appreciating land values outpaced any profits to be made from showing movies.

The Maritime Fringe

PCH's route through LA County travels through the heart of a climatic zone known as the maritime fringe, which ranges inland nearly as far as the LA Civic Center, ten miles or more from water. Because of its proximity to the sea, and the effect of circulating ocean air, the maritime fringe has relatively cool summers, warmer winters, and moister air—relative humidities in early morning and later afternoon average above 60 percent. Despite more cloudy conditions, the maritime fringe is generally favored by most people for its comfortable temperature, wind, and humidity conditions—and particularly for its fresher air, which remains relatively free of smog.

Smog

Smog is a comparatively new arrival to the Los Angeles area, having not made its appearance until the end of World War II. Since its advent, however, it has become LA's most evident environmental feature. Approximately 90% of Southern California's population live in areas whose visibility is significantly impaired by smog, and the vast majority live close enough to pollution sources to suf-

> ## Pollutant Standard Index and Smog Alerts
>
> Smog forecasts are expressed in four levels of air quality by the LA area South Coast Air Quality Management District. This pollutant Standard Index (PSI) considers ozone, carbon monoxide, nitrogen dioxide, lead, sulfer dioxide, sulfates, and suspended particulate matter. *Good* is a 0-100 rating, *unhealthful* is 100-200, *very unhealthful* is 200-300, and *hazardous* is 300-500.
>
> Smog alerts are sounded in the LA Basin when the ozone levels exceed .2 of 1 part per million (PPM) of air for one hour or more (stage one alert), .35 ppm (stage two), and .5 ppm (stage 3). Alerts warn people to restrict outdoor activity, consider personal health conditions, and eliminate non-essential driving. Warnings and restrictions increase according to the severity of the alert.

fer noticeable physical effects such as occasional redness and tearing of the eyes.

Southern California's smog is the product of petroleum combustion combined with sunlight and still air. Mammoth amounts of nitrogen dioxides and hydrocarbons are released in automobile exhausts and acted upon to form ozone, the most identifiable component of smog. The ratio of ozone per million parts of air can increase by more than ten times on a smoggy day, forming huge particles that block out the sun and hinder breathing.

Once smog is created, its diffusion is seriously affected by temperature inversion, which puts a cap on smog's ability to float upward and disperse. Things are at their worst when the base of temperature inversion is only a few hundred feet above the ground. Although such conditions may persist for days, it is reassuring to know that one day's contaminated air is not piled on the previous day's. Wind studies show that the smog cycle is a daily one, with the terrain between the coastline and the mountains receiving a fresh new quantity of air to pollute at least every 24 hours.

County Line

Southern Los Angeles County begins at Long Beach, where recent growth has been so fast that even the city's outstanding collection of California curiosities—decorated oil wells, the *Queen Mary,* and Howard Hughes's flying boat—seem overshadowed. The county line marks a new Long Beach, a world of malls, marinas, condominiums, and office complexes.

Recreational living is the selling point at Spinnaker Cove, Costa del Sol, and Bixby Village, where the ubiquitous presence of boat slips and golf courses (emblems of "The California Promise," says one ad) fend off the ordinary . A few blocks west of PCH is Naples, established one year before Venice and enduringly appealing, with a circumferential canal, the Rivo Alto, a park, a fountain, and more-or-less unspectacular homes made noticeable by their waterfront locations.

Near the intersection of PCH and Bellflower, PCH turns into one of California's vaunted contributions to 20th-century civilization—the commercial strip. This is the exalted realm of the fast-passing automobile, where architectural subtlety has no place, stylistic refinement no name, and understatement no witness.

There is an art to all of this (chaos out of order?) , an "architecture without architects" with the appearance and vitality of pop art. Indeed as architect Robert Venturi has it (speaking of similar conditions in Las Vegas), "the strip shows the value of symbolism and allusion in an architecture of vast space and speed and proves that people, even architects, have fun with architecture that reminds them of something else."

The most expressive element of the commercial strip, like the pop artist's use of the found object, is the attention-getting sign. At PCH and Seventh Street, a huge brown donut with the inscription Angel Food Donuts sits atop a low building, less significant than its identifying symbol. Further north, past the Yummy Burger Stand, are carwashes, transmission clinics, and a "radiator king," all housed in undistinguished buildings, mundane except for giant heraldic signs that transform them into a particular American expression of zestful, conspicuously consumptive joy.

AREA CODE: 213

Rules of the Road

Though it travels the length of Los Angeles, the exalted realm of the freeway, Pacific Coast Highway remains a commercial boulevard or narrow highway for its entire journey through the county. Driving conditions vary most according to traffic; when PCH is not congested, drivers move at a hurried, urban pace. Parking at the beaches is a perennial challenge: lots are often filled early, and parking along PCH is subject to several restrictions. Illegally turning left across a yellow strip to sieze a parking space is a risk not often worth taking. Highway Conditions: 626-7231.

Public Transportation

626-4455 Regional Transit District (RTD)
591-2301 Long Beach Transit
723-4636 Airport Bus
451-5444 Santa Monica Municipal Bus Lines

Climate

Weather along PCH and at the beaches in California is subject to the "marine effect," benefitting from large sweeps of cool, moist sea air that keeps the coastal areas 10 to 20 degrees cooler in summer, warmer in winter, with usually cleaner air. Call 554-1212 for current weather conditions.

LA History

RIDE THE BIG RED CARS:
THE PACIFIC ELECTRIC STORY
Spencer Crump
Trans-Anglo Books
Glendale. 1983.

This book tells the story of the Pacific Railroad, the largest and most efficient interurban system in the world during the half century it served Southern California. The big red cars also ushered in a cultural and physical revolution never to be equaled in this country again.

SOUTHERN CALIFORNIA: AN ISLAND ON THE LAND
Carey McWilliams
Peregrine Smith
Salt Lake City. 1983.

Probably the best book ever written about Southern California social history, *Southern California: An Island on the Land* was written by Carey McWilliams, former editor of *The Nation,* whose interpretations of Southern California life and culture are thorough, thoughtful, and pleasureful to read.

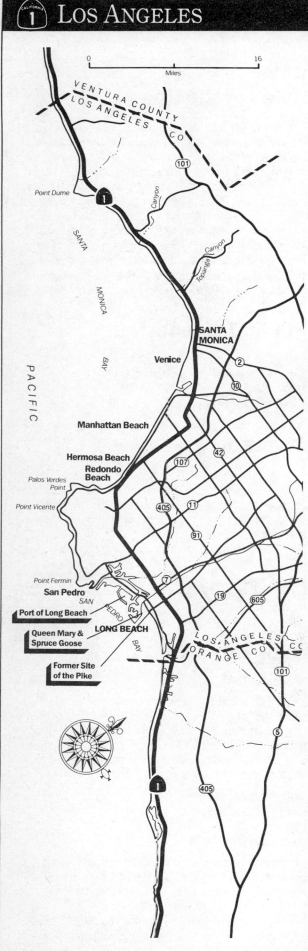

Romance and Magic on The Pike

Nobody knows how it came to be called The Pike, but by 1905 the name was permanently attached to the beach area between Pine and Chestnut Avenues, where the Pacific Electric streetcars brought thousands of people to hear concerts by Professor Meine's Band at the pavilion or to stand in lines 30 to 40 persons deep to chute the chutes! Once Long Beach's most festive and convival landmark, The Pike was a magical seafront amusement zone with few rivals on the Pacific Coast, gladdening the hearts of all who attended.

The Pike was first organized by Charles R. Drake, a former colonel and Arizona politician who turned promoter once he assessed the opportunities for economic gain in Long Beach. Drake built the original bathhouse and boardwalk along the beach, which attracted so many pleasure seekers that they overflowed the hotels and often slept on the beach in crowds. City officials concerned about the hordes of "inlanders" constructed lifelines out into the crashing surf to assist those unfamiliar with the ocean.

Soon more concessions and rides followed: the Palace Lunch Room offered homemade lemonade, popcorn, peanuts, and Crackerjack, and a roller coaster was built on the sand and high over the ocean. Sideshows offered the fat lady, the sword swallower, and the fire eater. For those who did not wish to sit on the sand, there were cabanas and gazebos.

By 1910 The Pike had expanded to include the magic ballroom, Bisley's airship, and a merry-go-round built by Arthur Loof with hand-carved horses, a Ruth organ with a xylophone, and figures of cherubs and maidens. Soon afterward Calbraith Rogers landed on the beach to a crowd cheering his completing the first sea-to-sea flight. A few months later he crashed in the surf near the Pine Avenue Pier and was killed.

Everybody liked The Pike: families and sailors, old people and young people, lovers and friends all came to

have good-natured fun at the beach. Pleasure was the basic common denominator, and it shone brightly in the eyes of those who waited impatiently to be thrilled by "Jack Rabbit the Racer," the newest roller coaster, or watch reckless Ross Millman ride a motorcycle around circular walls, appearing to defy gravity and death.

For years The Pike was Long Beach's largest industry, drawing millions of visitors to hundreds of concessions and rides. Then it was gone. The last remnants being demolished in the early 1970s so the land could serve "higher and better uses," ending an era of simple pleasures.

The Largest Port in the World

The Port of Long Beach, together with its twin, the Port of Los Angeles, forms the world's largest man-made harbor complex. The ports are bounded on the south by the Los Angeles River, and on the north by the high cliffs at Point Fermin. More than two miles offshore, the San Pedro breakwater stretches 32,000 feet, protecting the port's interior waters. Terminal island sits within the port complex, home to extensive harbor facilities, oil wells, fish canneries, a federal prison, a naval base, and a U.S. immigration and Naturalization Station. There are two outer harbor areas, two inner harbors, and an extensive system of interconnecting navigable waterways, channels, and turning basins.

Within the port, scores of terminals process more than 80 tons of cargo each year. There are giant container facilities with cranes that stand 23 stories high and move containers from ships to land transportation within 60 seconds. A supertanker terminal offloads oil from tankers that stretch to lengths of more than three football fields, accommodated by the Port of Long Beach's four mile long main channel which is 60 feet deep, by far the deepest of any in the United States.

Within this built environment, nature still thrives. There are some 83 species of birds and 100 fish species in the Port of Long Beach, including several endangered inhabitants such as the least tern and Belding's savannah sparrow.

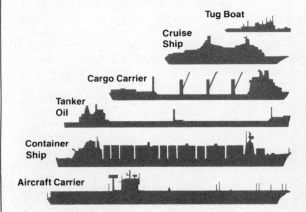

Tug Boat

Cruise Ship

Cargo Carrier

Tanker Oil

Container Ship

Aircraft Carrier

Ship Profiles

Every day a parade of ships passes through LA's harbor, often appearing as silhouettes against the bright sky. Even from a distance, passing ships are identifiable, however, by recognizing characteristics of size and shape.

The Queen Mary

Pier J
Long Beach
435-3511

For three decades the *Queen Mary* was England's pride, bespeaking a level of unmatched elegance and artful design superior to any ship that sailed the high seas. With meticulous art deco styling, the ship was the world's largest (1,019 feet long with 2,000 portholes, and a crew of 1,200) and the classiest; thirty artists created a floating museum of murals, tapestries, and hand-crafted woods, glass, marble, and shining metal. To sail the *Queen Mary* was a pinnacle of elegant living.

Since 1967 the *Queen Mary* has been docked at Long Beach in subdued and resigned retirement, an immobilized icon of mass culture that accomodates thousands of visitors each day. But although a great deal of its glory has faded and much of its splendor has tarnished, the *Queen Mary* is still an attraction like no other, available now for the pleasure of the many not the few.

The most overwhelming feature of the magnificent ship is its size: so large that its capability to speed across the sea seems impossible. Yet it was unerringly fast—fast enough to outrun German U-boats, which hunted the troop-carrying *Queen Mary* under a special bounty during World War II.

Although much of the grand ship's intricate detailing has been obliterated in its conversion from ocean liner to tourist attraction, much remains. The grand rooms still exhibit the fine high style that made sailing the *Queen Mary* an incomparable luxury. The art deco lounge still retains, unsullied, its wonderfully exotic Streamline Moderne decor.

Other fascinating features of the great ship include the bridge, with wooden ships wheels and polished brass instruments; the engine room, with gigantic ocean-churning machinery; and the upper decks, from which the true context of the *Queen Mary* as an ocean-going liner is easily and appealingly grasped. There are also numerous gift shops, restaurants, and snack bars, and a hotel that has refitted the original first class cabins.

The Spruce Goose

Pier J (Next to Queen Mary)
435-7776

The world's largest, most unusual airplane managed only one flight—aloft for one mile at an altitude of 70 feet—but its daunting size and mythic presence make it one of the most interesting flying machines anywhere.

The "Spruce Goose" contains a lot more varnished maple than spruce, but the name seemed to fit when a U.S. Senate investigating committee began inquiring into what many considered the biggest white elephant the government ever underwrote.

Howard Hughes, the plane's defiant and heroic developer, was magnificent in his creation's defense, though it remained idle until 1983, when it was granted potential immortality as a tourist curiosity in Long Beach under the world's largest clear-span aluminum dome. General operating hours for both attractions:
Summer (July 8–Labor Day) 9 a.m.–9 p.m.
General Season 10 a.m.–6 p.m.
Public Transportation: Long Beach Transit Fun Bus

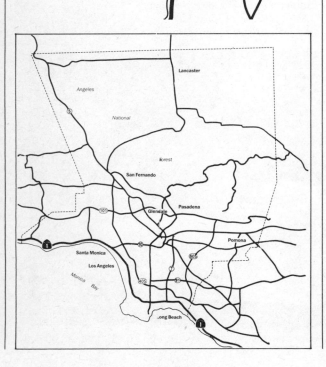

Money Made from Wind

Prior to 1880, the population of Los Angeles increased very little. Along the coast an uneven dirt road wound through an agrarian landscape, uncomfortably accommodating travelers. Most travel north and south was carried by inland El Camino Real, the major thoroughfare; along the coast an alternative, also called El Camino Real, prefigured the route of the present-day Pacific Coast Highway.

By the mid 1880s Los Angeles was transformed by an influx of immigrants that startled even the city's most enthusiastic and optimistic promoters. The arrival of the Sante Fe line initiated aggressive land promotion that relied on hyperbole and distortion. Land promoters came from all over the country to cash in on the hysteria and "make money out of wind."

Historians have observed that the only thing that prevented underwater beach land from being sold was the narrow difference between high and low tides at LA beaches.

So wild was the speculation that the number of real estate transfers doubled and tripled within a year, and prices for land exploded beyond any expectation of its productivity. So great was the population influx that between 1880 and 1890 the population increased from 11,183 to 50,395. In one 18-month period over 60 new towns were created out of air.

The Procession of Settlement

The population increases that occurred with the boom of the 1880s created the need for rapid transportation, but private developers determined where growth would take place. Practically all of LA's beach towns were begotten by the electric interurbans. Said Henry Huntington in 1904: "Railway lines have to keep ahead of the procession [of settlement]. It would never do for an electric line to wait until the demand for it came. It must anticipate the growth of communities and be there when the homebuilders arrive—or they are very likely not to arrive at all."

From the first the development of rapid transportation in LA was accompanied by direct subsidies from real estate profits, which were much more immediate and usually much more remunerative than those afforded by the transportation

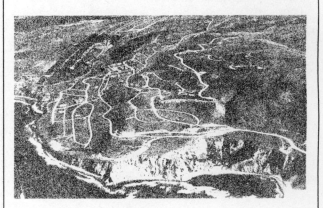

business. Small railways received subsidies in the form of cash bonuses and land grants from adjacent property owners whose land was increased in value; large railways subdivided the land and made even greater profits.

Such was the formula followed by Sherman and Clarke when they connected Santa Monica to Los Angeles with their Pasadena and Pacific Railway Company in 1895. But Sherman and Clarke lacked the immense capital needed to develop a complete transportation network and real estate empire. For that, wealth such as that held by Henry Huntington would be required.

Palos Verdes Estates

Not only did private developers determine the direction of growth in early LA, they usually shaped a town's layout, favoring the traditional American grid that facilitated the marketing of lots.

By the 1920s, however, the shape of subdivisions had changed, illustrated by the creation of Palos Verdes Estates, a 3,000-acre tract whose developer entrusted the layout of lots to Frederick Law Olmstead, Jr. and Charles H. Cheney, two of

the country's best-regarded landscape architects and city planners. Olmstead and Cheney laid out the tract according to criteria other than overt profit maximization: residential streets were separated from traffic corridors, lots were positioned to take advantage of views, and 800 acres were reserved for parks.

Even though the unusual layout did not wring every potential dollar from the land, Olmstead and Cheney's tasteful subdivision of Palos Verdes Estates was hugely profitable, achieving an exclusive residential community that has been called "the quintessence of Los Angeles."

The Man Who Made San Pedro

When Phineas Banning (1830–1885) landed at San Pedro Bay in 1851 from Philadelphia, he was shocked to find such meager harbor facilities. A ship could not even approach shore for all the mudflats and sandbars, and only a hut and warehouse defined the landing as anything more than a spot of shoreline wilderness. Los Angeles was 20 miles away, but it might as well have been 2,000.

Within a few years, Phineas Banning ("The Port Admiral") had founded a town at the site and built a railroad to Los Angeles, achieving a seaport monopoly through the sheer force of his personality at the town he named Wilmington. A colorful dresser (often decked out in red galluses and pantaloons), Banning raced horses and opened stage routes, built railroad links and purchased Catalina Island. Not until long after his death, however, was San Pedro designated Los Angeles' port of entry, after years of competition with Santa Monica in the bitter "Harbor Wars."

Environment

Subsidence

Long Beach's plentiful harvest of oil from beneath the earth's surface has not been without significant environmental consequences. During the boom days of oil extraction so much petroleum was pumped out of the ground that it caused major incidents of subsidence, or resettling of the land. Many buildings were damaged by this unfortunate repositioning of the ground.

To stabilize the ground and forestall further subsidence, salt water began being pumped into the oil drained caverns in 1959 and continues today. The solution, however, created another problem—contamination of the city's ground water supply.

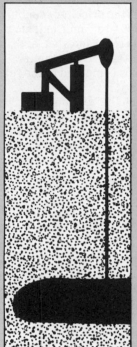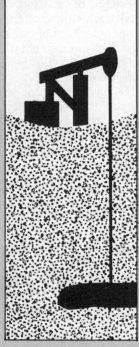

Geology

The high cliffs of the Palos Verdes Peninsula and the inland Dominguez Hills and Baldwin Hills were uplifted from the otherwise flat Los Angeles Basin eons ago. The earthquake faults that crisscross the Basin continuously fold and crush the underground formations.

The sedimentary fill of the LA Basin is a giant down fold (syncline) of basement rock that extends to depths of 31,000 feet below sea level. Folding and faulting also produces large amounts

of petroleum, including the Wilimington oil field that underlies much of Long Beach Harbor and is the first ranking oil field in California.

Roadside Attractions

San Pedro

After Pacific Coast Highway escapes the grasp of the Texaco refinery on its northward journey, a pleasant park with a white three-story Greek Revival mansion at its center comes into view. This is the Banning House and Museum, built in 1864, where Phineas Banning used to watch his ships on the harbor from an elevated cupola. Serene and simple in its white paint, green shutters, and classical lines, the house appears exactly as if designed to perform the role of "founder's house," always expecting one day to be converted to a museum surrounded by a park.

Rancho Palos Verdes

At Rancho Palos Verdes, Pacific Coast Highway comes near enough to Frank Lloyd Wright's Wayfarer's Chapel to warrant a visit. Built as a Swedenborgian memorial chapel in 1951, the Wayfarer's sits on the edge of the continent high above the sea in spiritual and architectural repose.

Nearby is Marineland, where trained dolphins and killer whales cavort in seven separate arenas. The views of the ocean to Catalina are their own show at this park perched on a cliff edge. There are plenty of dolphins and sea lions, as well as the Marine Animal Care Center, which exhibits methods of returning sick and injured birds to their natural habitats.

See, too, the Baja Reef, which provides the opportunity for visitors to don a wetsuit and mask and experience an underwater reef.

The Duck vs. the Decorated Shed

In their well-known book, *Learning from Las Vegas*, Venturi, Brown, and Izenour contemplate commercial clutter along the roadside and conclude there are "vivid lessons" to be learned from the commercial strip whose ordinary and often overlooked structures constitute "an architecture of communication."

Two types of roadside architecture are labeled "ducks" and "decorated sheds." A *duck* is a building whose shape expresses its function, such as a store that sells duck decoys housed in a building sculpted in the form of a duck. A *decorated shed,* in contrast, is a simple box structure with expressive attachments, such as billboards or ornaments plain or fancy.

In semiotic terms the duck is an *iconic* sign, in which the signifier and signified (form and content) are the same. The decorated shed is a *symbolic* sign, relying on the attachment of learned meanings expressed through billboards and decoration.

Most modern architecture, note the authors of *Learning from Las Vegas,* falls within the category of ducks—expressing itself unsuccessfully through structure and shape. The authors favor the decorated shed, which is claimed to have a much greater symbolic and expressive character and communicates more effectively.

Resources

Marine Attractions

Los Angeles Maritime Museum
Berth 84, San Pedro.
548-7618.

A fascinating place to learn more about the history and evolution of LA Harbor. Numerous exhibits, including a 16-foot scale model of the Titanic built from cardboard and matchsticks. Free.

Cabrillo Beach Maritime Museum
3720 Stephen White Dr., San Pedro.
548-7562.

A stunning array of exhibits and marine laboratories in a well-designed environment makes the Cabrillo Beach Marine Museum a wonderfully enjoyable learning environment.

Point Fermin Marine Life Refuge
Adjacent to Cabrillo Beach Marine Museum.
548-7562.

Tide pool area next to Cabrillo Beach Museum. Self-guided tour pamphlets are available at the museum.

Marineland
6600 Palos Verdes Dr. South
Rancho Palos Verdes 90274.
541-5663, 377-1571.

Marineland is a pleasureful combination of aquarium and marine circus that provides a variety of excitements and enjoyments. Cartoon characters roam the grounds and 30 aquaria display a wide-variety of marine life. There are several open air ampitheaters and plenty of theatrical sea lions, dolphins and killer whales. Baja Reef is not to be missed. Open daily 10 a.m. to 7 p.m. Admission fee.

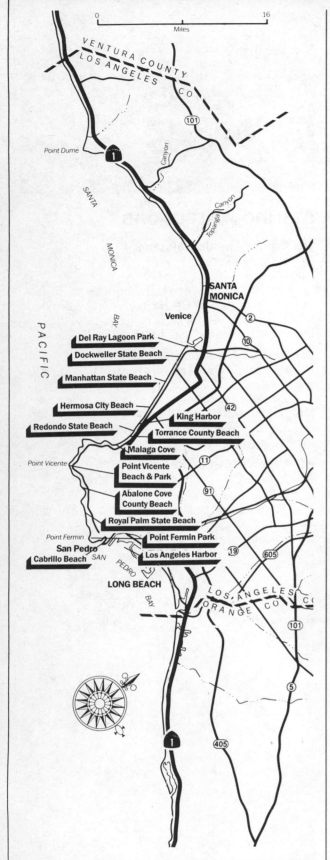

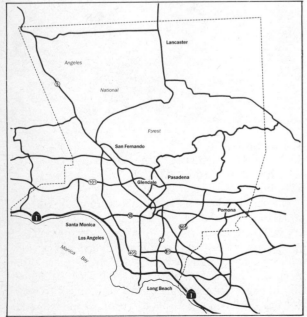

Modern Mobility

Henry Huntington's Pacific Electric represented more than a means to expand Los Angeles' boundaries and subdivide its open fields, it also supplied LA's newly arrived immigrants with a convincing symbol of an optimistic and progressive future. The bright Red Cars sped efficiently from one expanding surf town to the next, conveying a shining image of modern mobility. It was obvious things were changing fast and, in the view of hopeful immigrants, for the better.

The Pacific Electric was one of the most highly developed interurban systems of its day. Within ten years of Henry Huntington's arrival on the scene and subsequent acquisition of existing local interurbans, his $100-million corporation carried 225,000 persons 73,000 miles a day in 600 comfortable cars over a thousand miles of tracks from Los Angeles to as far as San Fernando, Riverside, and Newport Beach.

The Pacific Electric Railroad determined the route of much of the present-day Pacific Coast Highway and brought to life towns all along it. When Henry Huntington announced his purchase of the Redondo Land Company and the Los Angeles and Redondo Railway Company in 1905, the effect was to set off a boom in land sales reminiscent of the 1880s. Within three days individual parcels of land changed hand as many as six times. Progress and growth had arrived at Redondo, all generated by the utterance of a single word, as if by magic—Huntington.

Early Pleasures at Redondo Beach

We are off to gay Redondo
Fair Redondo by the sea
Where laugh and song are borne along
on breezes cool and free.

Redondo Beach flourished even before Henry Huntington purchased most of the town in 1905. The hope of a harbor and the presence of a railroad established 19th-century Redondo as a town on the move. In 1892, the town was incorporated as a sixth-class city (1,000+ inhabitants), but for two years it had already had a first-class hotel.

The Hotel Redondo was the South Bay's most exotic early attraction. Set amid a splendor of palm trees, the Redondo had 225 singular rooms that evoked Victorian country-estate elegance. English hunting scenes covered the walls, and Otis elevators sped wealthy guests from room to beach. A billiard room, 18-hole golf course, and a kingly ballroom that frequently held performances of grand opera assured guests of early Los Angeles' ultimate in refined seaside pleasure.

In 1907 Henry Huntington built the Pavilion, a white stuccoed Moorish creation with American flags and two red domes. The Pavilion became the home of the famous Mandarin Ballroom, where the best dance bands of the era played tunes for heart and soul. Redondo's most famous attraction, however, was its indoor plunge, "the largest indoor saltwater heated pool in the world." With trapezes, towers, diving boards, and a giant fountain in the center, the plunge could accommodate up to 2,000 bathers at once, a steamy indoor delight.

On the Road to Surfurbia

No more apt description fits the beach towns of Redondo, Hermosa, and Manhattan Beach than Reynor Banham's term for the seaside communities generally created by the coastal interurban railways—surfurbs. These beach strips grew up between the sand and the interurban tracks with small wooden and stucco cottages and a casual seaside character created from proximity to the beach and accessibility to the city.

Because their inhabitants commuted to work or were retired, these small towns developed as residential "urbs," usually without an autonomous economic base, much like American suburbia. The selling of small lots was the principal economic activity, which was often tied to an amusement pier or hotel to publicize the town and abet land sales. Few amusement piers turned substantial profits, certainly just pennies compared to the real estate bonanza.

The "true artery of beach life" became the concrete boardwalk that facilitated beach access and enhanced the pedestrian character of the surfurb. Most of the adjoining streets were also built tight and narrow in recognition of the main local activity,

walking to the beach. Thus, unlike suburbia—its automobile-oriented cousin—surfurbia offers a smaller-scale environment that rewards the pedestrian with pleasantly varied pathways winding among charming small bungalows.

Since World War II and the domination of the automobile, surfurbia has changed somewhat. Most towns now feature at least one busy automobile commercial strip, sprung up to attract the dollars of the passing motorist headed to or from the beach. In Redondo, Hermosa, and Manhattan Beach, PCH serves as a typical commercial strip, attached rather rudely to the less hysterical character of surfurbia

The triumph of the automobile and greater affluence has also changed the basic economy of the surfurb—stimulating a souped-up tourist economy that erases many of the distinctions between towns. Affluence, inflation, and skyrocketing real estate values have also affected the cottage character of the surfurb—property ownership is beyond all but the wealthiest purchasers, who often seek to recoup their large investments in land by demolishing the small bungalows to make way for larger, more opulent structures.

Environment

Thriving on Poison

Perhaps the darkest vision of the future is one in which the environment has become a totally polluted stink, a place where all life forms have been eliminated and the world transformed into an ecological wasteland. Most of us have faith that environmental pollution will be contained before this dark vision becomes reality. But if not, the seeds of new life forms, adaptable to the worst of polluted conditions, may be getting ready to take over to ensure than life goes on despite itself.

Recently a collection of bizarre marine life forms have been discovered off LA's coast that thrive on sulfur, which is generally a lethal substance. These poison-loving organisms include bacteria, clams, mussels, tube worms, abalone, and fish. Apparently, they are able to survive with no sunlight and no food, in an environment of highly toxic compounds.

The key to survival for these unusual marine life forms lies in their being able to establish a symbiotic relationship with sulfur-metabolizing bacteria, which use hydrogen sulfide to reproduce and grow. Clams, for example, have been found with such bacteria in their gills. The bacteria apparently live inside the clams, providing them with energy with which to make carbohydrates and proteins, thus sustaining them in an environment previously thought to be impossible for life.

Some marine life forms have adapted so well to toxic conditions that they thrive exclusively on sulfur-rich bacteria, and cases have been noted of fish with so much of the bacteria growing on them that it appeared "like white fuzz."

A great deal remains to be answered about this unusual adaptation—for example, it is still not known how the animals have adapted their outer bodies to the toxic hydrogen sulfide. But as scientists look further they are turning up a bonanza of surprising adaptations in sewage outfalls, pulpmill effluent zones, and poisonous swamps. Might these be the laboratories for the new millenium?

Roadside Attractions

Redondo Beach

For the northbound PCH traveler, Redondo Beach begins Los Angeles "surfurbia," a string of beach towns unlike any in the world, where pleasure and freedom are the main tenets of a philosophy of sun and surf. From Redondo to Venice, life is largely defined by the culture of the beach.

Redondo Beach offers a wealth of gratifying attractions, beginning with the superbly designed Veteran's Park, where an expanse of green lawns and palm trees concludes just above the beach

with a library overlooking the sea.

Adjacent is the Redondo Pier, an active place with an excellent jazz club (Concerts By the Sea), a superb restaurant (Old Tony's), and an entertaining amusement arcade (the international boardwalk) that features bumper cars, shooting galleries, skeeball, and electronic games.

George Freeth: First Surfer in the United States

Advertised as "the man who can walk on water," George Freeth brought surfing to California in 1907 as part of Henry Huntington's promotion for "the largest saltwater plunge in the world" at Redondo Beach.

Freeth, who was born November 8, 1883, revived the ancient Polynesian art of surfing while growing up in Honolulu using a solid wood 8-foot board weighing 200 pounds. He also introduced water polo to this coast and became California's first official life guard. In addition, Freeth invented the torpedo-shaped rescue buoy.

California's first surfer died in 1919 at the age of 35 from exhaustion caused by strenuous rescue work.

Resources

South LA County Beaches

Between LA Harbor and Marina del Rey are a series of highly varied beaches that strongly influence the character of adjacent communities and commercial districts. Almost all are within a few blocks of PCH or within easy reach.

LA Harbor: 28 miles of waterfront along one of the world's busiest seaports; cargo and passenger terminals, shipyards, marinas, charter boats, and fishing.

Cabrillo Beach: Actually two beaches separated by a breakwater; one protected, one with active surf.

Point Fermin Park: Located above ocean with stairway to limited beach area; lighthouse, whale watching station.

Royal Palms State Beach: Tide pools, excellent surfing, palm trees, and terraced gardens.

Abalone Cove County Beach: High cliffs and excellent surfing; popular with divers.

Point Vicente Fishing Access and County Park: Rocky beach that attracts fishermen and skin divers; lighthouse.

Malaga Cove: Also known as Rat Beach (right after Torrance); sandy beach, vista point, and gazebo.

Torrance County Beach: Start of South Bay Bicycle Trail which runs north for 19 miles to Santa Monica Beach.

Redondo State Beach: Among the best sand beaches south of Santa Monica; volleyball courts, promenade.

King Harbor: Charter Boat rentals, 1400 slips, including one which berths television's *Riptide*.

Hermosa City Beach: archetypal Southern California beach; surfing, volleyball, swimming, pedestrian walkway.

Manhattan State Beach: Similiar to Redondo and Hermosa with wide sandy beach, fine waves, pedestrian walkway.

Dockweiler State Beach: located adjacent to LAX; wide sandy beach, airplanes.

Del Rey Lagoon Park: 13 acre grassy park with complete recreational facilities; no swimming in lagoon but beach is accessible.

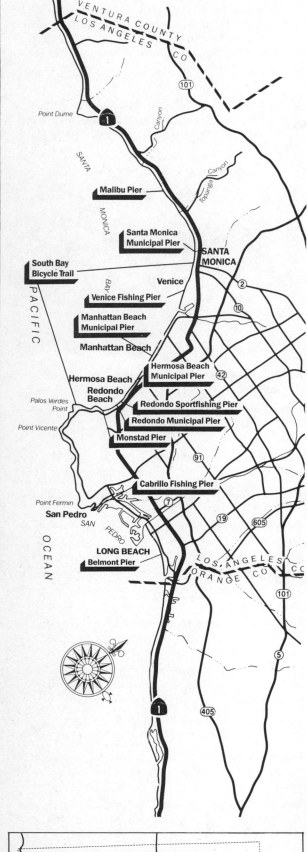

Round Trip to the Beach

Heavily used by both residents and tourists, the red car system provided pleasure and enchantment at the dawn of the new century. "It was great fun," recalls Franklin Walker, "to return from a weiner roast at Redondo on the *Mermaid*, poppies barely visible on the tracks in the moonlight, and youngsters out on the wicker seats in the open section, in the back of the car, singing 'Down Went McGinty,' and 'After the Ball.' One could always make the round trip to any of the beaches for 50 cents."

Three daily specials were available, but the grandest was surely the balloon trip, an excursion along the beach from Santa Monica to Manhattan Beach, Hermosa Beach, and Redondo, then returning via Culver City.

So wide did the interurban's popularity range that it garnered national praise and admiration. Fontaine Fox's syndicated newspaper feature, "Tooneyville Trolly," highlighted the public's anthropomorphic affection for streetcars, while "The Trolley Song" captured the rhythm and dash of the vehicles' appeal. The "Era of the Trolley" fostered fellowship and amusement as Americans were transported to expanding metropolises.

The Route to the Future

Once the red cars brought settlement, incorporation of cities soon followed. In the first decade of this century, 17 cities located on the interurban routes were incorporated, including Manhattan Beach and Hermosa Beach.

But the future was foreshadowed when "Mr. Interurban," Henry Huntington, who had become the most extensive landowner in Southern California, retired from active business affairs to assemble the most complete private library that money could buy and to amass one of the nation's most impressive art collections.

After 1914 many of the same characteristics that had favored the region's expansion through the interurbans—its favorable climate and relative affluence, as well as its "inordinate mobility and acquisitive inclinations," also favored the rise of the automobile. The automobile, which proved to be even more efficient than the streetcar at opening up isolated land for subdivision, became the interurban's inevitable successor. And though the Pacific Electric hung on for years (the last street cars were retired from service in the early 1960s), the automobile was clearly the way of future.

The Spin of the Wheel, the Roll of the Dice

Not so long ago the long arm of the law stopped just off the California coast. Offshore gambling ships with names like *Tango* and *Showboat* anchored past the three-mile limit from Long Beach to Santa Monica, providing the illicit jazz-age pleasures they advertised in theaters and by skywriting. Water taxis from shore sped excited revelers through the black night to glistening offshore ships.

Best known of the gambling ship entrepreneurs was Tony Cornero, who insisted that he was performing a valuable public service by maintaining the card games, craps, roulette, and bingo aboard his anchored barge, the *SS Rex*. The *Rex* had 300 slot machines and enough roulette wheels and dice tables to keep Lady Luck awake all night. Cornero claimed that during his best year he was able to meet the needs of more than 850,000 grateful members of the public, while earning an estimated $500,000 a month for himself.

Although Cornero in fact broke no laws in his gambling operation (there were no laws to break until 1948, when Congress passed a federal statute outlawing gambling in coastal waters), he was relentlessly harassed by the State, often with the help of local police. In 1939, Earl Warren, then the State Attorney General, placed an illegal wiretap on Cornero's telephone to gather evidence against him. But Tony was clean, and placed full ads in coastal newspapers offering $100,000 to anyone who could prove otherwise.

Cornero was never convicted of any serious crime connected to his gambling ships, although his offshore operations were shut down twice, the last time in 1945, off Long Beach. Eventually, Cornero moved to Las Vegas, where in 1955 he keeled over a crap table and died, reportedly showing snake eyes on his last roll.

Environment	Roadside Attractions	Resources

Channelized Rivers

PCH crosses many rivers and streams in Los Angeles County, but very few of them are recognizable as such. Almost all of Southern California's waterways have been channelized, victims of the demands of an urban area. The major reason for lining the rivers with concrete or rubblemound is to control devastating floods which have historically inundated surrounding land and property in Los Angeles, causing millions of dollars in property damage and sweeping vast amounts of soils and sediments to sea.

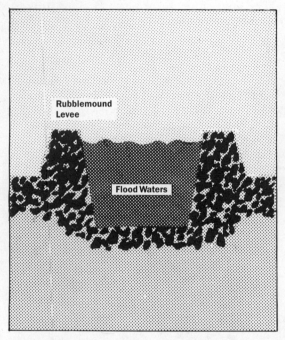

Rubblemound Levee

Flood Waters

There are other reasons as well, particularly that a channelized river is more easily kept within real estate boundaries, unable to change course like a natural waterway.

Manhattan Beach in Waikiki

In its earliest days Manhattan Beach (the "Beach" was added in 1927 to distinguish it from the nation's 14 other Manhattans) struggled for its very existence against mammoth accumulations of sand. Shifting dunes and blowing sand frequently buried major portions of the town, sometimes piling up halfway to the top of Manhattan Beach's ornamented lamposts. After years of unsuccessfully pushing the sand around with tractors, the town eventually hired a local contractor to haul away the bothersome stuff and sell it. His first customers were the Los Angeles Coliseum, which wanted sand for its floor, and Waikiki Beach in Hawaii, which wanted fill for its beach.

Hermosa Beach

At Hermosa Beach, a fine promenade and fishing pier decorate the wide beach. The splendid beachfront is enhanced by the presence of the strand, a pedestrian way that runs parallel to the South Bay Bicycle Trail. The presence of youthful blue-eyed California pleasure seekers gives the place the hue of life's golden season.

Hermosa Beach is beautiful and eager, not unlike the crowds of bronze-skinned, smiling 20-year-olds who frequent places like Steve's at the

Beach, the Lighthouse Cafe, and the Hennessy Bar. Hermosa Beach has a number of appealing cafes: Gem Cafe, Second Street Cafe, Ty's, The Spot, Le Petite Cafe, and Hoffmans. It has a popular comedy club and an excellent place for books, The Either Or Bookstore.

Manhattan Beach

Despite its late-arrived sophistication, Manhattan Beach's real charm lies in its charming realness. The town has a fine old pier that stands more nobly, for all of its creakiness, than any of the refurnished structures south of Santa Monica. The passage of time has given Manhattan Beach Pier the quality of its surrounds: it stands amid the breakers like an invited and welcome guest.

A few blocks inland a new Manhattan Beach enroaches on the true-life charm of the town, working its way toward the non-chic beachfront. Businesses sporting French names—Cafe Pierre, Le Chat (clothing), and A La Main (gifts)—harken to a more sophisticated Manhattan Beach. There is even a men and boy's clothing shop called the Young Gentry.

Manhattan Beach is a great LA beach town with all the rewarding elements that lend credence to the claim that "Los Angeles is the most magnificent seaside city in the world." In addition to its stately pier, it displays splendid examples of California vernacular beachfront architecture—a mix of enchanting old and new beach cottages that evoke a pleasant and informal way of life. The superb sandy beach unfailingly attracts people from all over the automobile metropolis, who enliven the air with eager expectations of pleasure.

LA County Piers

LA's beaches, says Reyner Banham, "are uncommonly well provided with public piers." Most of LA's piers offer fishing facilities, many have snackbars, and all are rewarding places for a stroll.

BELMONT PIER: 1300 foot municipal pier with bait shop, snack bar, 434-6781.

CABRILLO FISHING PIER: 1200 foot municipal pier; bait shop, open 7 a.m.–11 p.m., 833-1510.

MONSTAD PIER: 300 foot privately owned pier; restaurant, tackle shop, open 24 hours, parking fee.

REDONDO MUNICIPAL PIER (Horseshoe Pier): shops, restaurants, fee.

REDONDO SPORTFISHING PIER: 250 foot privately owned pier; tackle shop, snack bar, open 24 hours, parking fee.

HERMOSA BEACH MUNICIPAL PIER: 1,320 feet long; bait shop, snack bar, open 24 hours, 372-2124.

MANHATTAN BEACH MUNICIPAL PIER: 900 foot pier open 24 hours, no facilities.

VENICE FISHING PIER: 1100 foot municipal pier; snackbar, fish cleaning facilities, open 24 hours.

SANTA MONICA MUNICIPAL PIER: Amusements, restaurants, carousel; California's most pleasureable pier.

MALIBU PIER: 700 foot pier; fishing and excursion boats, restaurant, 456-8030.

Raymond Chandler's LA

Cars were parked along the sidewalk, facing out to sea, dark. The lights of the beach club were a few hundred yards away. . . . "Hold me close you beast" she said. I kissed her tightly and quickly. Then a long slow clinging kiss. Her lips opened under mine. Her body began to shake in my arms. "Killer," she said softly, her breath going into my mouth.

The Big Sleep, *1939*

Raymond Chandler wrote about LA and the tiny beach towns up and down the coast with a seedy brilliance that made heroic poetry out of the brutal darkness, sham, fakery, and hypocrisy of the Los Angeles never covered in guidebooks. The pages of *The Big Sleep* (1939), *The Lady in the Lake* (1943), and *The Long Goodbye* (1953) sing with low-down stridulation.

A former oil company executive whose bouts with the bottle cost him his job, Chandler set out to become an author of detective fiction at the age of 44 by making a systematic study of pulp fiction. He soon created one of America's most self-contained existential heroes in Philip Marlowe, a detective with a bottle of whiskey and a Smith and Wesson 38 in his desk, possessed of a heretical idealism that keeps him always at odds with the world. Said Chandler of his main character, "Marlowe and I do not despise the upper classes because they take baths and have money, we despise them because they are phony."

Chandler lived with his wife Cissy Pascal, who was 18 years older than he, until his death in 1959 in near-exile from LA film society. "To write about a place," he once acknowledged, "you have to love it or hate it or do both by turns, which is usually the way you love a woman."

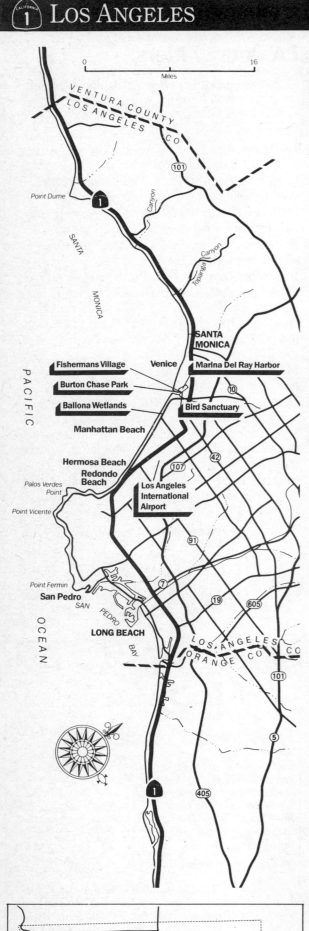

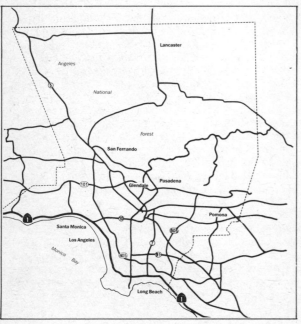

Los Angeles International Airport

Los Angeles International Airport came into being in 1925 as a small general airport known as Mines Field. Remote and infrequently used, it played an insignificant part in LA's overall transportation system.

In 1928 Mines Field became the Municipal Airport for Los Angeles. Yet it was still so inconspicuous that the adjacent neighborhood of small homes hardly noticed it. In 1929 a series of distinctive Spanish Colonial Revival hangars were built, designed by Gable and Wyant, and still visible today on LAX's south side.

Throughout the 1930s the airport remained far less busy than others at Burbank, Santa Monica, and Glendale, but in 1940-41 an extensive new passenger terminal and facility buildings were built. Plans called for increased expansion, but were interrupted by the advent of World War II.

After the war, the nation's air transportation increased significantly in concord with LA's own fantastic growth. Partly through the influence of Howard Hughes, LA's Municipal Airport became the focal point for major expansion. In 1959 William Pereira completed a "futuristic" master plan for Los Angeles International that made it one of the world's major airports, covering 3,500 acres and capable of handling more than 100 take-offs and landings per hour.

Marina Del Rey Harbor

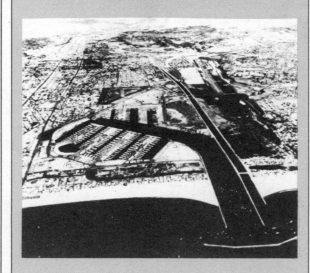

The Marina Del Rey Harbor is the largest small craft harbor in the world, home to more than 6,000 pleasure craft. Then the harbor was dredged in 1962, some three million cubic yards of sand were removed and redeposited on the beach downcoast of Ballona Creek. During dredging, a series of six moles were constructed—extensions of land lined with concrete sea walls and rubblemounds to form the interior of the harbor. The harbor is protected by two rubblemound jetties and a 2,330 foot rubblemound detached breakwater. These do an effective job in dissipating wave energy to provide calm within the huge harbor for boats as well as several beaches that offer peaceful swimming.

Ballona Wetlands

A wetland is far less glamorous than a development project, and until someone finds out how to make money from undisturbed mud, protecting wetlands from development will never be easy. Consider the case of the Ballona wetlands, one of Southern California's last wetland areas, that is slated to be the home of a $1 billion housing and commercial office complex owned by the Summa Corporation. The project has been approved by the Coastal Commission, although several environmental groups have filed suits to prevent construction.

Playa Vista

The project, called Playa Vista, would cover 926 acres of coastal plain and wetlands south of Marina Del Rey's main channel, west of Lincoln Blvd. The development is planned to include three hotels, commerical and office space, and several thousand residential units. Some 206 acres of wetlands are to be preserved in the project, an amount environmentalists insist is not enough.

Friends of the Ballona Wetlands, the state League of Women Voters, and the League of

Coastal Protection claim that the project is inconsistent with the provisions of the Coastal Act, which called for protection and restoration of wetland areas, and that the Ballona has been designated as a "critical and irreplaceable" habitat for several types of wildlife.

In response, the Coastal Commission sited the

benefits the project would bring, particularly new public access, increased visitor serving facilities, and improvements to the undeveloped wetlands. The Commission also maintained that much of the wetlands to be developed are of "low quality," and that the project, on balance, is a good compromise between competing interests. With more than 90% of the state's wetlands already destroyed, the question remains, however, whether there is room left for compromise.

Environment

Roadside Attractions

Resources

Water Wars

California's most controversial natural resource is its water. Innovation and technology has produced a water gathering and distribution system in this state that is unmatched in America. But delivery of the precious liquid to high-need agriculture and urban areas often has irreversible impacts on the environment at the source. And herein lies the base of California's great water war, documented in books like McWilliams's *Southern California* ("Water! Water! Water!") and Morrow Mayo's *Los Angeles* ("The Rape of the Owens Valley") and the movie *Chinatown*.

Supply Here; Demand There

The root of the water controversy is based in supply and demand. The state's surface streams produce about 76 million acre feet of water each year, but 75% of this supply occurs in the northern third of the state. Against this supply is a contrary demand: 80% of the annual water consumption in California occurs in the southern two-thirds of the state, and the same ratio applies to the ground water supply. Agriculture in the south accounts for the majority of the water demand; urban growth in the semi-arid LA Basin and points south, for the rest.

As early as 1913, the state began trying to level the inequities of water distribution through artificial means. That was the year that the 233 mile Los Angeles Aqueduct began operating. Today the project extends another 105 miles north into the Mono Lake Basin.

While the delivered water has allowed California's agriculture to maintain its world-competitive status, and the LA area to grow unchecked, it has also had dramatic impacts on the other end. Long ago the Owens Lake was literally sent down the drain to Los Angeles, and today the same thing is

happening to the mysteriously beautiful Mono Lake, one of the state's most important wildlife and bird sanctuaries. Salinity in the lake is increasing as the water levels lower, killing the tiny brine shrimp on which birds depend. Birds are also abandoning their nesting islands all over the lake as land bridges form when the water recedes, allowing passage for coyotes and other deadly invaders. All these impacts are acknowledged by the agencies controlling the flow through the aqueducts. Still the water flows, the perceived public benefit to the south for the time-being outweighing the documented impacts on the north.

LAX

LAX is the third busiest airport in the world, and a magnificent, if unpretty, assemblage of escalators, corridors, and confusion it is. After its recent $700 million renovation, LAX now handles 33 million passengers a year.

The theme building is surely everybody's favorite. Rising 135 feet above the ground with a restaurant, bank and observation deck, the top of the theme building looks as if it revolves, but it does not. The food is expensive and bland, but the view, particularly at night, is spectacular.

Marina Del Rey

The largest man-made small boat harbor in the world, Marina Del Rey is a wonderland of ersatz marine amenities like Fisherman's Village, a pretend Cape Cod shopping and dining area. Less cute, but more satisfying is Burton Chase Park and the nearby bird sanctuary, the last remaining elements of the original area.

LAX Information

General Information: 646-5252

RTD Airport Transfer Terminal: All area bus lines to and from LAX are centered at the transfer terminal, located at Vicksberg and 98th Street, a few blocks from the airport. To reach the transfer terminal (or the airport from the terminal), take the Shuttle—RTD Bus 206, which passes every six to eight minutes. Transportation between terminals is provided by white, green, or blue buses marked Airline Connections.

Howard Hughes

Pacific Coast Highway makes an abrupt turn from Sepulveda to Lincoln Blvd. because Howard Hughes didn't care to have a highway run through his property. Today the power of the Hughes Corporation, the major private property holder near LAX, is still immensely influential, even though its founder has passed from the scene.

Howard Hughes lived a life stranger than any fiction; indeed, stranger than perhaps any man has ever lived in California, at least among those whose efforts have been so touched with riches, glamour, and crea-

tive genius. He was the emperor of eccentricity, whose accomplishments were finally defeated only by his own madness.

During 40 years in Southern California, Hughes set world records as a pilot, owned airlines, hotels and real estate, made movies, became a powerful defense contractor who lectured to Congress, made love to the world's most beautiful women, and became the world's richest man.

Finally the world over which Hughes had such seeming mastery became his enemy in paranoia, driving him to a hermetically-sealed life as a recluse who lived a ghoulish death in life existence prior to his demise in 1976.

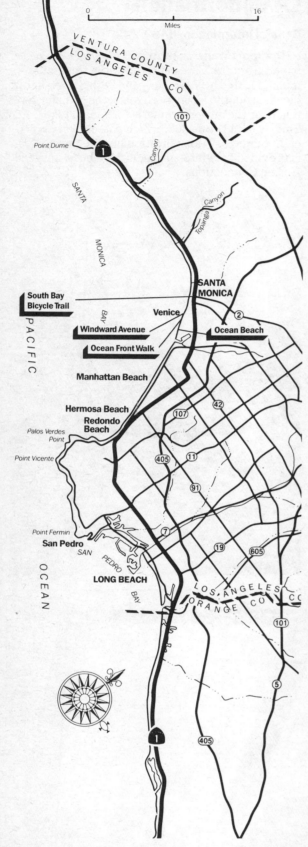

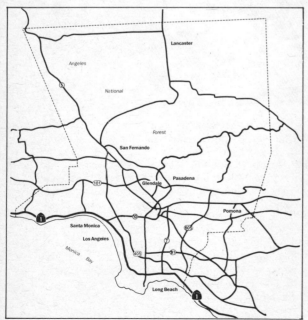

Venice of America

No California development proposal was ever more outlandish than Albert Kinney's 1904 plan to build "Venice of America," which was intended to duplicate the romantic charm of Venetian waterways and the cultural verities of Titian and Tintoretto. Though Kinney did not succeed at reproducing Venice on the California coast, at least in terms of a "cultural renaissance," he accomplished something almost as rare—a magical world of amusement and delight, purely fantastical and purely Californian.

Kinney was derided by skeptics when he announced his plan to convert the coastal swamps south of Santa Monica into a town interlaced by a network of canals and Italian Renaissance architecture. "Kinney's Folly" it was called. But Kinney's critics underestimated his pragmatic skill, and once he convinced Henry Huntington to extend an interurban line to the townsite, the creation of California's Venice was assured.

To See Venice Is to Live

At the end of June 1905, water flowed into the Venice canals and electricity illuminated the first exotic new buildings of Kinney's dream city. A few days later, on July 4, Venice of America celebrated its birth: the Venice Children's Chorus sang "Hail Columbia" while 40,000 visitors made their way amid the bedecked and bejewelled structures that decorated the seashore. They strolled, they gaped, they took gondola rides, and watched fireworks ascend against the sky. "To see Venice is to live," said Albert Kinney, choosing the words as the town's motto.

The heart of the new city was its canals: Venus, Cabrillo, Altair, Lion, Coral, Aldebaran, Grand, crossed by concrete bridges with reliefs of sea serpents and laid out to create a grid pattern with a central swimming lagoon. The canals were decorated by soft-lit Japanese lanterns and navigated by Italian gondoliers summoned from Venice to serenade young lovers beneath the yellow California moon.

Venice's main street, Windward Avenue, linked the canals with the oceanfront. Along the avenue ran a vaulted arcade with reliefs of the lion of Saint Mark's; above the arcade stood a group of ornately decorated three-story hotels that featured "therapeutic" hot saltwater piped in from the sea. In front of the hotels, a pair of camels were available for rides.

A Cultural Renaissance

Kinney's main effort to inaugurate a cultural Renaissance was the Venice Assembly, a series of lectures, music, and performances modeled after New York's Chautauqua. Readings from *Macbeth* and operatic recitals were not enough, however, to catch the fancy of Venice's earliest patrons. After one season the Venice Assembly died, and with it Albert Kinney's prospects for a high-brow Venice of America.

Honky-tonk made its entry to Venice in 1906 when the Midway-Plaisance opened next to the swimming lagoon. Barkers pitched crowds through hand-held megaphones to buy a ticket to the Temple of Mirth or Ouitta's Occult Show. Soon other amusements sprung up near the canals and along "the world's safest beach." Tom Prion's attraction, The Clouds, a roller coaster nonpareil, attracted 48,000 excited riders one July Fourth.

Despite Kinney's death in November 1920 and a disastrous fire one month later, Venice endured, hosting beauty contests and legendary music at the Venice Ballroom, where Ben Pollack and His Californians played nightly. Two of the Californians later found wider individual fame—Glenn Miller and Benny Goodman.

In 1929 the City of LA began filling the canals to create "fine new boulevards" and soon, despite local protests, all but the Shore Line Canals had been converted to city streets. In 1947 the City demolished the Kinney Company's amusement pier. The final insult came a year later when the Pacific Electric cars dropped service to California's most ambitiously conceived seaside enchantment.

Environment

Gulls

A visit to the California coast would lack authenticity without the raucous squeal and obvious presence of the sea gull. Gulls are beach scavengers and surface-feeding birds, but, given a choice, they seldom refuse a hand-out over the trying work of fishing.

All the large gulls of the Pacific Coast once belonged to the same species, having splintered into several distinct families eons ago. Their common origin makes the individual species difficult to dis-

tinguish, but it can be done if one uses the same clues that the birds themselves use to prevent inter-breeding: differences in eye, eye-ring, and foot colors.

The most common Pacific gulls are the Herring, Thayer's, Western, and California. The Thayer's and Herring gulls are almost identical in appearance, but the mantle of the Thayer's is slightly darker and the black area of the wings may be smaller with larger white "windows." About the only way to tell these two apart is that the Thayer's gulls are brown-eyes with purple-red rings around the eye. Herring gulls have a pale yellow eye, with a yellow eyelid ringing the eye. Both of these species have pink feet.

The Western gull is one of the most classic of gulls: snowy white body with dark back and wings. Its eyes and bill are yellow, and the feet are a flesh tone or light pink. The California gull is most like the Herring, but usually smaller with dark eyes and a reddish eye-ring. Its greenish legs make it a little easier to distinguish.

Roadside Attractions

Venice

A great circus without a tent.

Carey McWilliams

At Venice, Southern California beach culture takes, as it has always taken here, a decided turn toward the extra-normal. No other beach town in the world has ever dedicated itself so thoroughly to theatromania.

What sense there is to be made of Venice is made by assuming the mind of the carnival goer. All of Venice is a stage: see the man juggling chainsaws, the lady with an ocelot, the strong men at Muscle Beach. Listen to the harmonies of the festival and the songs of the dancers. Inhale the popcorn air drenched with sea salt, and attend the lure of Thalia's madness—all for fun, all for spectacle.

At Venice, amid the debris of dreams, the audition has become the show. Dada Dada.

The Disappearance of Aimee Semple McPherson

Of California's many distinguished theatrists, none had a more devoted following than Aimee Semple McPherson, who disappeared from the sands of Ocean Beach on May 18, 1926, and presumed drowned by her adoring followers.

McPherson understood show business at least as well as the religious appetite of 1920s California in her presentation of Foursquare Gospel, an idiosyncratic theosophy based on love, promises, and panache. From her red-velvet throne, McPherson appealed to her fanatical congregation accompanied by bands, orchestras, and choirs. Whether dressed as a nurse to drive out illness, or accompanied by a zoo lion to dramatize the power of faith, or broadcasting from her own radio station KFSC (Kalling Foursquare Gospel), Aimee Semple McPherson was a weaver of spells whose power and charisma gained a messianic following.

As it happened, McPherson did not drown that day near Venice—five weeks later she surfaced at a motel in the Arizona desert with her radio engineer, Kenneth Ormiston, after what appears to have been a retreat of greater passion than piety. Though the newspapers were outraged, and legal action for fraud and perjury was threatened, McPherson maintained her aplomb, even though she now seemed a changed woman, a fashionable dresser with a new bobbed hairdo, whose attention to the business matters of her organization now seemed distracted.

Resources

South Bay Bicycle Trail

The best way to tour LA's beaches may be by bicycle. Fortunately for cyclists, LA has an unsurpassed beachfront bikeway that runs from Torrance to Santa Monica. The South Bay Bicycle Trail begins just north of Palos Verdes through Redondo Beach, Hermosa Beach, Manhattan Beach, and past the refineries and power plants at El Segundo. After circling Marina Del Rey, the bikeway finds its most festive reception at Venice, where roller skaters, skateboarders and all manner of wheeled theatrics join the parade just before the trail ends north of the Santa Monica Pier.

Bike Rentals

REDONDO BEACH
Bicycle Center
1206 S. PCH.
316-5177.

HERMOSA BEACH
Hermosa Cyclery
20 13th Street.
374-7816.

PLAYA DEL REY
The Handlebar Stop
6935 Pacific Avenue.
821-5898.

VENICE
Robbie's Bike and Skate Repairs
3 Stands: At end of Rose Avenue, Venice Blvd., and Washington Street.
306-3332.

Venice Pier Bike Shop
21 Washington Street.
823-1528.

SANTA MONICA
Sea Mist Rentals
1619 Ocean Front Walk.
395-7076.

THE EROTIC OCEAN: A HANDBOOK FOR BEACHCOMBERS AND MARINE NATURALISTS
Jack Rudloe
E. P. Dutton, Inc.
New York. 1984.

THE OCEAN ALMANAC
BEING A COPIOUS COMPENDIUM ON SEA CREATURES, NAUTICAL LORE & LEGEND, MASTER MARINERS, NAVAL DISASTERS, AND MYRIAD MYSTERIES OF THE DEEP
Robert Hendrickson
Doubleday
New York. 1984.

In Search of Ocean Settings

For years Santa Monica existed in quiet reserve, settling into a position of subdued domesticity after the turn of the century. After finally losing the struggle to become LA's harbor, the town's apparent goal by the early 20th century seemed to be displacing Pasadena as the "home city" for southern California.

Since 1887 the famous Hotel Arcadia had graced Santa Monica's shoreline and drawn visitors, but after the rise of the more popular Venice

and Ocean Park, Santa Monica became content to forgo the quest for the tourist dollar and concentrate on attracting "permanent residents of the better class," seeking business and professional men and "well-to-do retirees" to buy homes beside the sundown sea.

Then the movies came to Santa Monica and upset its domestic reserve. In search of ocean backdrops for their bathing beauties, film companies came in groups to the quiet seaside town and changed the temper and tone of daily life. In 1910 Vitagraph, one of the largest early companies, set up studios on Ocean Avenue. Others, including Essanay, California's original movie makers, soon followed "and fairly took over the town." The filming of movies all over Santa Monica became a spectacle, as Santa Monicans adjusted to the serious business of make-believe.

Although by the end of 1915 the Santa Monica movie studios had moved to Hollywood, their influence had been profound. Too starstruck to yet conceive of itself as another Pasadena, Santa Monica raced toward another future, with the automobile as the means of deliverance.

Santa Monica Pier Restoration

Although the Santa Monica Pier had dispensed enchantment and romance to generations, by the 1950s it entered a serious decline. In 1974, a tragic fire seemed to seal its fate as a once-grand seaside attraction whose time had passed. But due to the concerted efforts of the City of Santa Monica and The Friends of Santa Monica Pier, the pier was not allowed to die.

In 1977 the group undertook the restoration of the carousel after the city purchased the elaborately-crafted Loof Hippodrome and its unique merry-go-round manufactured in 1922 by the Philadelphia Toboggan Company of Germantown, Pennsylvania. For four years the careful restoration of the carousel continued, as each of the 44 hand carved horses was delicately refurbished. In 1981 the carousel was re-opened to the public, as crowds of visitors streamed in to ride the individually-detailed wooden horses.

The Storms of 1983

The popularity of the carousel confirmed the wisdom of restoring the pier, but plans languished until, ironically, the western end of the pier was destroyed in the storms of 1983, which focused new attention on the pier's irreplaceable value. Shortly afterward, the City of Santa Monica formed the non-profit Pier Restoration Corporation to operate the pier and oversee its complete restoration. State and federal funds have been obtained for the project, and refurbishment of the entire pier goes on apace.

The new Santa Monica Pier has become a shining symbol for Santa Monica's tourist industry, providing a highly identifiable emblem of the city's unique pleasures. More importantly, the refurbished pier brings to life a world of enchantment and simple seaside pleasures too rare to be lost.

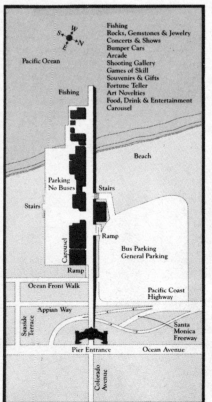

Simple Pleasures

Santa Monica Pier
End of Colorado Blvd. at Ocean Ave.
458-8964

The Santa Monica Pier is open 365 days a year and provides the most rewarding seaside amusements in Southern California; in addition to the magnificent carousel, arcade games, and bumper cars, there is a newly-completed children's park and a number of excellent cafes and restaurants. The Pier also features a number of annual special

The Fish that Breeds on Land

A tiny silvery fish called grunion comes ashore on favored Los Angeles beaches to mate and lay its eggs. This remarkable natural ritual may be observed during the months of March through September on the second, third, and fourth nights after the full moon. On those nights, about 15 minutes after each of the two highest tides of the month, female grunion float ashore on the highest waves and bury themselves in the sand where they deposit as many as 3,000 eggs. The eggs are then fertilized by the males and left protected in the sand for about ten more days. Then the next high tides activate an enzyme that causes the eggs to hatch, and the new fish are washed out to sea where they live up to four years. The Cabrillo Museum provides films, tours, and information on grunion and where and when they might be observed.

Salient Generators

Shore-parallel breakwaters like the one built off the Santa Monica Pier are of a type generally referred to as "salient generators" because their presence can drastically affect the form of the shoreline. This type of breakwater interrupts approaching waves (in this case, to protect the pier from high energy waves common in Santa Monica) and produces a wave-shadowing effect on shore. Sediment and sand builds up and the shore extends itself.

After the Santa Monica breakwater was constructed, a salient (outward projection of land) began to form in the lee of the structure. Today the salient is quite prominent and has significantly changed the contour of the entire beach area around the pier.

Santa Monica Pier

In true California splendor, Santa Monica stands next to the commodious ocean in a posture of casual urbanity and confident good looks. Pacific Coast Highway streaks between the ocean and the city beneath the sheer Palisades, always in sight of the Santa Monica Pier, the finest of California's sea-standing platforms and the emblem of a town with varied and rewarding pleasures.

The arched neon-lit Santa Monica Pier sign marks the threshold of an ebullient world of simple seaside pleasures. The world of the calliope and wooden walkway is being rehabilitated with new vitality and contemporary shine.

To walk the pier is to gain a new grasp on gladness. Starting with the best first: the 63-year-old carousel with 44 colorful hand-carved horses who leap and romp to music beneath the ceiling of the Loof Hippodrome, where the movie *The Sting* was filmed. Amid the magic of spheric motion, color, and music, delight seldom shows such an eager face.

Along the pier, other attractions fascinate and amaze: fortune-tellers, curiousity shops, and games of chance, and a bumper-car concession with a fantasy ticket booth ornamented in grandest amusement park style.

Good food can be had in several restaurants and snack stands on the pier. Enjoy, too, the pier fishing and the endless soul-satisfying sea views, often accompanied by raucous song of sea birds.

Tom and Jane in Santa Monica

At one time role models for the new millennium, Santa Monica residents Tom Hayden and Jane Fonda have tempered their radical programme for a new social and political order, accepting the lesser glories of being a state assemblyman and an exercise magnate.

As political radicals during the 1960s and 70s, when Hayden was an SDS leader and a defendant in the Chicago 7 trial, and Fonda was an ardent opponent of the Vietnam War and critic of corporate capitalism, Hayden and Fonda nettled America's political establishment. Although each has been accused by some of insincerity and opportunism during their political evolution on the California scene, others note that it is not Tom and Jane who have changed so much as the political climate, and that the effort to maintain equilibrium as a celebrity couple with children is in itself a heroic challenge.

events from Broadway shows to rock concerts. There is no admission charge, and prices for food and entertainment are low to moderate.

Film Classics

No LA pleasure is more suited to place than movie going. Film classics show regularly in several theaters near the coast. Call for a recorded message of offerings and times.

ART THEATRE
2025 E. Fourth Street
Long Beach.
438-5435.

BEVERLY CINEMA
7165 Beverly Blvd.
Los Angeles.
938-4038.

BIJOU TWIN THEATRES
1233 Hermosa Avenue
Hermosa Beach.

BIJOU TWIN CINEMAS
1233 Hermosa Avenue
Hermos Beach.
376-9988.

EL REY THEATER
5517 Wilshire Blvd.
Los Angeles.
931-1513.

FOUR STAR THEATER
5112 Wilshire Blvd.
Los Angeles.
936-3533.

FOX INTERNATIONAL
620 Lincoln Blvd.
Venice.
396-4215.

NUART THEATER
11272 Santa Monica Blvd.
West Los Angeles.
478-6379.

OLD TOWN MUSIC HALL
140 Richmond Street
El Segundo.
322-2592.

VAGABOND THEATER
2509 Wilshire Blvd.
Los Angeles.
387-2171.

VISTA THEATER
4473 Sunset Drive
Hollywood.
660-6639.

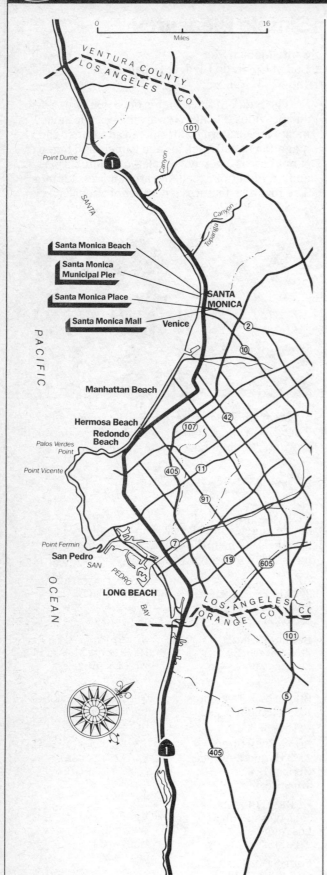

A Passion for the Automobile

There is a monster in the stable who has to be exercised, and from time to time you hear his brothers hooting to him as they rush past along the road . . . . There is no sensation so enjoyable—except that of riding a good horse in a fast run—as driving in a fast motor. The endless variety of scenery; the keen whistle of the wind in one's face; the perpetual changing sunshine and shadow create an indescribable feeling of exhilaration and excitement with the almost human consciousness of the machine; the patient, ready response which it makes to any call on its powers; the snort with which it breasts the hill; and the soft sob which dies away when it has reached the summit, make is as companionable as any living being.

Lady M. Jeune, 1904

The first long-hooded, wire-wheeled racers to roar through Santa Monica arrived on a sultry day in 1909. The completion of Wilshire Blvd. from LA had created a three-sided race course (San Vicente Blvd., Ocean Avenue, Wilshire) too enticing to be ignored by automobile enthusiasts. Santa Monica's Vanderbilt Cup and Grand Prize races soon became among the most famous in the nation.

As the smoke of the automobile acquainted Santa Monicans with the air of modernity, the town evolved into one of the main testing grounds for high-speed automobile performance. The races broadcast Santa Monica's name all across the nation as local crowds watched demons like Barney Oldfield, "The Devil Wagon Man," who drove Henry Ford's "999," often exceeding 100 mph on the straightaways. In 1912 Teddy Tetzlaff broke the world's speed record by averaging 78.7 mph over the 300-mile course.

As interest in the races grew, newspapers commented that Santa Monica "was alive with automobiles"—more than 2,200 cars among the town's 15,000 residents by 1915. All over LA County automobile registrations were rising by fantastic numbers between 1910 and 1920 (from less than 20,000 to more than 100,000) as people took to the automobile with a passion, while roadbuilding struggled—generally unsuccessfully—to keep up. Poorly designed, the average south coast road lasted only four years. Until the 1920s the only route along the coast near Santa Monica was a one-lane broken-down dirt passageway on the narrow shelf between the cliffs and the sea.

The California Bungalow

Bearing nothing if not the physical traces of dreams large and small, the Los Angeles landscape owes much of its appearance to the ubiquitous presence of the California bungalow, a type of housing that found its most receptive welcome in early Southern California suburbs, where land was cheap and the desire for inexpensive dream houses rampant.

Although the idea of the common bungalow derives from Bengal (thus "bungalow"), the appropriateness of these one-story free-standing single-family residences to California conditions was inescapable almost from the beginning.

During the first three decades of the 20th century, the bungalow's popularity was aided by an efficient and inexpensive public transportation system that easily overcame the distances between downtown and affordable suburbian land. Within the urban core higher land prices mandated multistory structures, but in the suburbs conditions were perfect for one-story homes. And the California climate both allowed economies in construction and made the bungalow's easy relationship to the outdoors desirable. Soon, California bungalows were being built all over the world.

The Dream of Home Ownership

Perhaps because of its popularity, the California bungalow was slow to garner acceptance among architectural critics and journals. Popular magazines, however, including *Good Housekeeping, Ladies Home Journal,* and *House and Garden,* saw the structures in quite another light. Like an increasing number of American homebuyers, they viewed the simple inexpensive structures as the most practical way to achieve the American Dream of homeownership.

Some of the first bungalows were built by renowned architects like the Greene brothers of Pasadena, Bernard Maybeck of Berkeley, and Frank Lloyd Wright (who also made prefabricated bungalow "kits"). But many more were built from "bungalow books," which displayed a number of floor plans and offered blueprints for $10 or $20. Several companies sold inexpensive prefabricated models that could be assembled in a matter of days.

The simplicity and practicality of the California bungalow were eminently suited to fulfilling a great many Californians' dreams, but the form also provides a model for an affordable way to address contemporary housing needs.

Environment

Firestorms

The potential for serious fire damage is greater in Southern California than anywhere else in the world. Nowhere else do climatic and land characteristics combine to create such dangerous combustable conditions.

The worst circumstances are created when the weather is the driest. High temperatures and low relative humidity create the potential for any spark to become a raging fire. High winds, such as the Santa Anas, add the extra threat of firestorms.

**Thanks, Folks,
for being careful!**

Remember—Only **you** can
PREVENT FOREST FIRES!

The Santa Anas blow strongest at the end of summer and in the fall before the rainy season, a time when the mountain chaparral and coastal vegetation is most parched. With winds that can reach up to 90 mph, a fire once started becomes almost impossible to contain.

Lives and Property

In addition to the loss of wildlife and natural habitats, Southern California wildfires take a high toll in lives and property. With the expansion of suburbs into the bush-covered hills and forested highlands, the potential continues to increase.

The Santa Monica Mountains have been the starting point for some of the worst firestorms in the state. In 1961 the second worst fire in California history started in the Santa Monica Mountains and swept westward into Bel Air when the Santa Anas fed a firestorm that caused damage in excess of $25 million. Almost 500 homes were destroyed as the winds swept over a 20 mile area, making it the fifth costliest fire in the nation's history.

The threat of firestorms is a constant reality to residents of LA's canyons and hills where slopes, wind, low humidity, and dry vegetation create a continuous fire hazard. Few victims of a firestorm's destruction remain as philosophical as Aldous Huxley, whose house was enflamed by the 1961 firestorm. "It was quite an experience," said Huxley, "it does make one feel extraordinarily clean."

Roadside Attractions

Santa Monica Mall

Once the city's principal commercial boulevard, Third Street was converted to a pedestrian mall in 1965, becoming one of the first vehicle-free outdoor shopping esplanades in the United States. Though Santa Monica Mall has had its ups and downs, it endures as one of the most interesting commercial areas on the coast, and a concerted community effort is underway to update its appeal.

In addition to its pleasing urban pedestrian atmosphere and numerous small-entrepreneur shops, Santa Monica Mall hosts many community events—art shows, folk dance festivals, and an open-air famers' market. The mall also features some of the city's best architecture. At the southern end stands the Keller Block (1456 Santa Monica Mall), a Romanesque Revival structure designed by Carrol H. Brown and the largest building in the city when it was completed in 1892. Across the mall in the same block (1441) is the 1933 art deco El Miro Theater, designed by Norman W. Allpaugh.

Between Santa Monica Blvd. and Arizona Avenue, the mall displays three treasures of 20th-century American main-street architecture: at 1349–51 is the proudly restored Kress Building, a 1924 Classical Revival structure designed by E. J. I. Hoffman; its elegant pilasters are topped by Corinthian capitals and windows with tracery arches. Nearby and facing is the 1949 Woolworth Building, with postwar Moderne styling, a luncheonette, and a handsome red sign straight out of Norman Rockwell's America. Down the mall (at 1301–13), the elegant Criterion Theater and Apartments, built in 1923 by the Venice Investment Company, show off fascinating terra-cotta flowers and stylized pilasters.

Santa Monica Place

Behind the parking garage's huge green metal screen, with 28-foot letters announcing its name, Santa Monica Place stands with full amounts of pizazz, flash, and sex appeal. Though its collection of 160 franchise shops and restaurants may seem ordinary, the mood and feel of Santa Monica Place are about as ordinary as tennis on a spaceship.

Although it adheres to all the conventions of shopping center economics with its double-anchor department stores and familiar arrangement of shops, Santa Monica Place is a dazzler of a shopping center. It is made so by its grand atrium and abundant amounts of natural light and height, which rescue it from the constricted rigidity that afflict many indoor shopping malls. Creative use of three levels of walkways also enhances Santa Monica Place, and there are plenty of pleasurable surprises—decks, viewing platforms, and imaginative uses of greenery and windows.

Resources

Santa Monica Mall and Murals

When Santa Monica was made a pedestrian mall it gave focus to some of the city's most interesting architecture as well as attracting a number of fascinating new stores and shops. Several other streets in Santa Monica, however, are also of a significant architectural interest—Fourth Street, Wilshire Blvd., Arizona Ave., Broadway, Colorado Ave., and Santa Monica Blvd. For a self-guided brochure of Santa Monica's architecture, contact:

SANTA MONICA VISITORS BUREAU
P.O. Box
Santa Monica 90405.
393-7593.

Murals

Santa Monica is California's capital of mural art. More than 20 murals add a creative dimension to the cityscape. This is a location list of most of Santa Monica's murals:

SORENTO RUINS MURALS, Jane Golden, 1978: PCH, Just north of California Incline.

FLAMINGO MOTEL MURAL, Scott Rosch, 1982: 1733 Ocean Avenue.

TROPICAL SCENE, Mike Caple: 2339 Main Street.

EARLY OCEAN PARK, Jane Golden, 1976: Ocean Park Blvd. at Main Street.

GROWTH OF SANTA MONICA, Jane Golden: Ocean Park Blvd. at 4th Street underpass.

WHALE MURAL, Daniel Alonzo, 1983: Also at Ocean Park Blvd. at 4th Street underpass.

EARLY OCEAN PARK AND VENICE SCENES, Arthur Mortimer, 1982: Joslyn Park on Kensington Road.

ELEPHANTS, A.S. Bloomfield, 1981: 702 Pier Avenue.

BIRTHDAY PARTY, Ann Thiermann, 1979: Marine Park on Marine Street.

JOHN MUIR WOODS, Jane Golden, 1976: Corner of Lincoln and Ocean Park Blvds.

WINDOWS ON ALCOHOLISM, Ann Thiermann, 1980: Corner of Pico Blvd. and 9th Street.

TRAIN STATION, Jane Golden and Peggy Edwards, 1976: 1842 14th Street.

CO-OPPORTUNITY MURAL, Ann Thiermann, 1983: 1530 Broadway.

HUGO BALLIN MURAL, Hugo Ballin, 1954: 1920 Colorado Avenue.

CROSSROADS SCHOOL, School Students, 1981: Olympic Blvd. at 21st Street.

PICO NEIGHBORHOOD, Ann Thiermann, 1982: Stewart Street underpass, Santa Monica Freeway.

HESTER STREET, Jane Golden, 1982: 2610 Santa Monica Blvd.

SANTA MONICA, Keith Tucker: 3127 Santa Monica Blvd.

FAIRY TALE, Suzanne Burke: 1227 Montana Avenue.

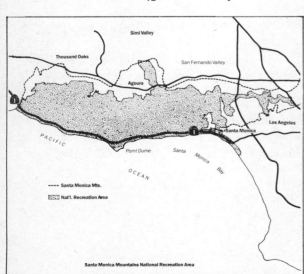

Santa Monica Mountains National Recreation Area

Surfaced Roads and Seaside Pleasures

As the nation sang along to "In My Merry Oldsmobile," a popular song by Gus Edwards, the Automobile Association of Southern California pressed for the improvement of a coast road, and when the police practice of shooting out the tires of speeders seemed to be putting the club's members in jeopardy, the organization presented the LA police with two patrol cars and speedometers to protect members from arbitrary harassment.

The early 1920s brought a spirit of familiar cordiality with the arrival of the "hail fellow, talkative, back-slapping real estate agent" whose lot it was to cheerfully assist in the town's expansion. The All Year Club's active promotion brought waves of homeseekers, and seaside summer homes sold like hotcakes. Surfaced roads to LA cut driving time from a half a day to half an hour, and Santa Monica boomed.

At the beach, the Loof Fishing Pier was sold in 1924 and converted to the Santa Monica Pleasure Pier with a roller coaster, midway, merry-go-round, and the splendorous Lamonica Ballroom

with ten spiralling domes topped with shining minarets. Next to the pier, the Santa Monica Land and Water Company constructed groins to make a beach of more useful proportions.

The newly made beach property attracted Hollywood luminaries like Marion Davies and Louis B. Mayer. With the aid of William Randolph Hearst, Davies built a Georgian-style mansion with 37 fireplaces, where for years her annual masquerade ball "was *the* social event of the Hollywood season."

SMNRA

The Congress finds that (1) there are significant scenic, recreational, educational, scientific, natural, archeological, and public health benefits provided by the Santa Monica Mountains and adjacent coastline area; (2) there is a national interest in protecting and preserving these benefits for the residents of and visitors to the area; and (3) the State of California and its local units of government have authority to prevent or minimize adverse uses of the Santa Monica Mountains and adjacent coastline area and can, to a great extent, protect the health, safety, and general welfare by the use of such authority. There is hereby established the Santa Monica Mountains National Recreation Area.

P.L. 95-625, Section 507(a)

With these words, in 1978 Congress created the Santa Monica Mountains National Recreation Area (SMNRA) with the goal of operating in a way that will "preserve and enhance its scenic, natural, and historical setting and its public health value as an airshed for the Southern California metropolitan area while providing for the recreational and educational need of the visiting public."

When Congress established a 150,000 national park area here, it did so in a manner quite different from other parks in this country. Two major exceptions were made. First, although the goal is to acquire or otherwise protect the Mountains' open spaces and environmentally sensitive lands for the public good, Congress also recognized that many people already live and work within the park, and should continue to do so. They are considered "neighbors" within the park, not "inholders" whose property rights should eventually be bought out. Further, regulation of private property within the park lies not with the federal government, but with the appropriate city, county, or state agencies.

Secondly, the land within the park boundary that is owned by public agencies is not to be transferred eventually to any one single federal agency. Rather, state, county, and local parks, beaches, landfills, reservoirs, and the like remain under local agencies' jurisdictions.

This framework acknowledged both the political and economic realities of existing land use in the mountains. But it also allowed a much larger park boundary to encompass one unified national recreation area. The structure depends on great cooperation between agencies, property owners, and the public, but so far it is considered a national model of success in protecting a unique resource in a highly-developed urban area.

Environment

The Santa Monica Mountains

The Santa Monica Mountains are part of the only east-west belt of mountains in California, the Transverse Ranges. The 46-mile long chain of peaks covers about 225,000 acres, including the tallest summit of 3,111 feet at Sandstone Peak.

The Santa Monicas are an unusually rugged mountain range, crossed with hundreds of canyons and ravines, some almost totally verticle. Only one canyon completely bisects the range— Malibu Canyon— but throughout the area are creeks, streams, waterfalls, ponds, rapids, and upland meadows that blossom with glorious wildflowers every spring.

The geology is extremely mixed, ranging in age from Precambrian gneiss (1.7 billion years p.p.) to recently deposited and faulted congolmerates. Several major earthquake faults run through the range, moving the western edge about an inch north each year. Wildlife is abundant, including the mountain lion, eagle, and the almost-extinct condor. The vegetation is beautiful if desolate in places, consisting primarily of members of the chapparal community.

Chaparral

Our Lord's Candle

California Buckwheat

California Sagebrush

Chaparral derives its name from El Chaparro, Spanish for "place of the scrub oak," and that image best describes it. This plant community consists of several types of brush growth that can be so densely intertwined so as to make the land virtually impassable for large mammals.

Chaparral covers almost 8% of the total area of California, growing only here in Southern California and five other regions of the world.

The most common chaparral shrub is chamise. It is a clumpy plant with small, needle-thin, water-conserving leaves. Chamise is often joined by other members of the chaparral community: manzanitas, scrub oak, coffeeberry, silk tassel, hollyleaf cherry, and toyon to name only a few.

Chaparral plants have developed several characteristics necessary for survival in arid places like the Santa Monica Mountains. They grow most actively in the wet winter and spring, resting the rest of the year when things get very hot and dry. (These are the months when chaparral can become some of the world's most efficient fuel for the raging fire storms that sweep over the mountains pushed on by the Santa Ana winds.) Another thing that helps the plants survive is that most have adapted a two root system, one root extending far down to seek out moisture in sub-surface rocks; and the other a lateral root system that traps surface moisture immediately when it occurs.

Roadside Attractions

Palisades Park

Perched above Pacific Coast Highway like an aerie, is one of California's most serene and beautiful open spaces, Palisades Park. A refuge of green lawns and tree-covered walkways, Palisades Park covers more than 26 acres on the edge of Santa Monica's sandstone bluffs and stretches for 14 blocks from Colorado Blvd. on the south to Santa Monica Canyon on the north.

Few cities have had the foresight to set aside a valuable portion of open space for public use.

Originally dedicated as a park in 1892 (other additions were made later), Palisades provides a pleasing green belt that softens the urban edge and celebrates Santa Monica's shorefront location with the pleasantest of settings for viewing the beach below and the sunset beyond.

Palisades Park is unsurpassed for strolling or stopping for a quiet moment. Amid the date palms and eucalyptus, several rewarding surprises await the observant stroller. There are coastal cannons and monuments to the United Nations, Cabrillo, and Santa Monica pioneers, a Northwest Indian totem pole, as well as shuffleboard courts and a sundial with a motto that expresses perfectly the mood of the place: "Count none but the happy hours."

Near the end of Idaho Avenue is The Gateway, designed by the Greene Brothers in 1912. The Senior Recreation Building, once the North Beach Station of the Pacific Electric Railway, features a fascinating camera obscura, in addition to offering a year-round program of athletic, social, and cultural activities. Nearby, strollers who turn their attention toward tree-lined Ocean Avenue are rewarded by the stunning site of the Shangri-La Hotel, designed with a wonderful mix of maritime and Streamline Moderne elements by William G. Foster in 1939.

Resources

Los Angeles Environmentalists

To learn more about the Santa Monica Mountain environment, or about any environmental issue in the Los Angeles area, contact one of these organizations.

Ecology Center of Southern California
Post Office Box 35473
Los Angeles 90035.
559-9160.

The center is a clearinghouse for all environmental groups in Southern California. Programs include *The Compendium Newsletter,* "Environmental Directions" radio show, "Special Report" weekly newspaper articles, and a comprehensive *Directory of Environmental Organizations.*

Sierra Club, Angeles Chapter
Santa Monica Mountains Task Force
Southern California Office
2410 Beverly Blvd.
Los Angeles 90057.
387-6528.

The Sierra Club has special committees dealing with all important environmental issues, as well as many recreational ones. The Mountains Task Force was an important element in establishing the National Recreation Area here, and continues to be an active and influential watchdog over land use in the mountains.

Mountains Restoration Trust
21361-b Pacific Coast Highway
Malibu 90265.
456-5625.

The Mountains Restoration Trust is among the most successful of California's coastal land trusts. Working quietly behind the scene, MRT has achieved the protection of scores of privately-held parcels in the mountains, and is responsible for many more acres being acquired by public agencies. The Trust also owns and manages the beautiful Cold Creek Canyon Preserve. Contact the Trust for the latest on their public education and special programs campaign.

National Park Service
Santa Monica Mountains National Recreation Area
23018 Ventura Boulevard
Woodland Hills 91364.

Access to Peaks and Shore

CALIFORNIA COASTAL TRAILS
VOLUME I: MEXICAN BORDER TO BIG SUR
John McKinney
Capra Press. 1983.

CALIFORNIA COASTAL ACCESS GUIDE
California Coastal Commission
University of California Press
Berkeley. 1983.

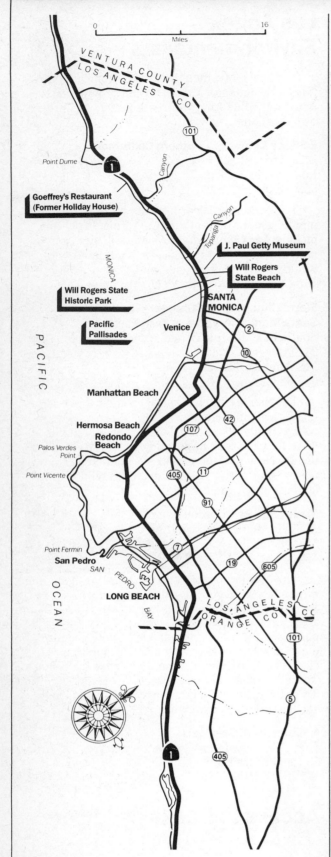

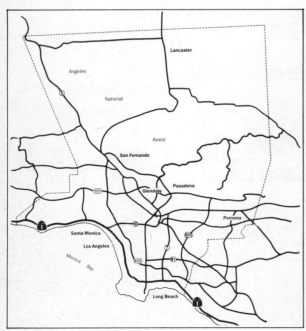

Pacific Palisades

In 1910 Pacific Palisades was the home of Thomas Ince's movie studio and not much else. Although a few years later Ince would produce the world's first westerns in Culver City while discovering some of Hollywood's original stars—Tom Mix and William S. Hart, for example—his Pacific Palisades studio merely set the stage for what was to follow.

In the 1920s a group of Methodists arrived at Pacific Palisades with visions of a Pacific coast Chataqua. The Methodists, like Thomas Ince, were premature in realizing their aspirations on the high palisades next to the ocean, but many artists and writers began to migrate to the area anyway, to live in the woodsy little houses away from the city.

Movie stars, who sometimes built cabins out of discarded movie sets, were also attracted to the area about the same time, along with a group called the Uplifters, a collection of well-off businessmen and writers. Will Rogers moved to Pacific Palisades in the 1920s, and Thomas Mann lived in the area for 13 years before the rise of McCarthyism drove the Nobel prizewinner to move to Switzerland.

The Man Who Never Met a Man He Didn't Like

Will Rogers, the national humorist, was "an Oklahoma cowboy, a laconic lasso artist with a homespun philosophy and yen for real estate," who moved to Santa Monica in the 1920s and became probably the town's best-loved resident.

First attracted to Southern California to be in the movies ("pleasant outdoor work"), Rogers soon moved up the coast to Pacific Palisades and bought 300 acres in the Santa Monica Mountains, installing a ranch with polo field and "the house that jokes built." While dabbling in real estate, Rogers acquired more than two miles of valuable beachfront near the mouth of Santa Monica Canyon, which was eventually condemned by the State to make Will Rogers State Beach.

Richard Neutra at the Beach

The Holiday House Motel at 27400 Pacific Coast Highway was designed by Los Angeles's most influential architect, Richard Neutra. Neutra's clean white houses speak of a cerebral world of high design in which architecture refuses to submit to anything, least of all the natural environment.

The building expresses Neutra's favorite characteristics, which have become almost the embodiment of Modern Architecture in California: flat roof crispness, precise detailing, and an abundance of glass and severe edges. All this is rather humorlessly presented, even though Neutra's stringency always achieves a graceful elegance.

Born in Vienna in 1892, Neutra moved to California in the mid-1920s when a travel poster reading "California Calls You," called him. His International Style buildings created a reference point for a generation of California architects whose clear, sparse buildings dot the LA landscape. In addition to designing buildings, Neutra also wrote books about spatial relationships and—to prove that he was capable of a good joke—designed the world's first drive-in church in 1967 in Garden Grove.

Environment

Malibu Lagoon

Just north of the Malibu Pier, PCH crosses Malibu Creek, a stream that flows from the mountains, through a floodplain and a lagoon, and out to a small promontory called Malibu Point. Until recently, the Malibu Lagoon was a barely-noticed fresh water system, isolated from tidal action by a sand-closed mouth, and lacking much in the way of marsh of mudflats. Some birds stopped here, but not nearly the number that usually enjoy healthy coastal wetlands.

After years of planning, hearings, and studies, the State of California undertook an ambitious restoration project at the lagoon. The $1 million project restored 23 acres of land around the existing lagoon, now part of the Malibu Wildlife Preserve. The restoration required extensive engineering, reshoaling, and opening the mouth of the lagoon to the sea, as well as development of new public trails and interpretative signs. Not long after April 1983 opening ceremonies, environmentalists were rewarded by numerous new sightings of green and blue herons, snowy egrets, mallard ducks, and all types of shorebirds. The project has now become a national model for restoration of healthy wetland systems in highly developed urban areas.

Point Dume

Point Dume marks the upcoast limit of Santa Monica Bay. The point is a 215 foot high mass of erosion-resistant volcanic rock that may have once been an offshore island, connected to land by a sand bridge, or tombolo ages ago. The steep, nearly verticle cliffs shelter Dume Cove, an attractive rocky beach situated in the lee of Point Dume. From Santa Monica to Point Dume the coastline rises inland as much as 3,000 feet above sea level within three miles of the coast. These are the western rims of the Santa Monica Mountains, and are responsible for the predominantly rocky and rugged shoreline. In the Point Dume area, traces of two marine terraces are visible. The first, near shore, is about 150 feet high, and the second follows the path of PCH, rising about 250 feet above sea level.

Surfriders R.I.P.

Soon after work was completed on the restoration of the Malibu Lagoon, surfers began to notice change in the once perfect parabolic shape of Malibu's waves. Two canals that were carved through the reefs offshore not only enlarged the tidal outlet at the lagoon, but by changing the consistency of the ocean floor, have forever changed the wave patterns. Surfers agree that the new waves are dangerous, the once-ideal patterns at Surfriders Beach are broken and, according to Lance Carson (star of *The Endless Summer*), the beach has been wrecked. The Parks and Recreation Department, engineers of the restoration project that was aggressively supported by local environmentalists, note that you can't please everyone.

The J. Paul Getty Museum

The Getty stands above the Pacific Coast Highway as one of those odd monuments, a palpable contract between the very rich and the people who distrust them least.

Joan Didion

The only thing the very rich like to do more than build castles is to build museums. It is, perhaps, a kind of immortality they are after. Consider the example of J. Paul Getty, who constructed his opulent museum above the Pacific in 1974, when his fantastic art collection overflowed the confines of his elegant Malibu villa.

To make his mark in the museum world, Getty chose to have constructed what is surely California's most heroic house of art—a replica of Herculaneum's seaside villa of the Papyri, buried by Vesuvius' volcanic mud in AD 79 and partially uncovered in 1709. Getty disovered that one could bring the glories that were Rome to the apparent grandeur that is Malibu for little more than $7 million.

As a museum for antiquities set in Malibu, the mythical home of California's movie stars, it's hard to imagine a more appropriate structure: with illusory windows, *trompe l'oeil* columns and garlands, and murals that imitate first-century imitations of marble, the Getty is one of the world's great tributes to the virtue of impersonation. As Charles Jenks puts it: "A very amusing and colorful recreation whose wit is perhaps not intended."

What is real, however, probably matters significantly less than what is magnificent, and the Getty delivers magnificence in full measure from its opulent architecture to its great antiquities, with the classical sculpture being the most impressive of the lot. The Getty Bronze, a statue of a victorious athlete by Lysippos (c. 310 BC), is perhaps the finest classical antiquity in the United States.

Art and Architecture

Visiting the Getty
17985 PCH
459-8402

Due to the Getty Museum's limited parking facilities, visitors with automobiles must have an advance reservation for parking (one week prior). Alternatively, visitors may be admitted without reservations, but only if they are dropped off or arrive by taxi or RTD bus #434 (Driver dispenses museum passes). Because of an agreement with local homeowners, you must have an RTD pass to be admitted without a parking reservation, but admission is free. Hours: Tuesday–Saturday, 10 a.m. to 5 p.m.

For a complete listing and description of LA's museums, galleries and visual art resources, see:

INSIDE LA ART
Deborah Ashin
Chronicle Books
San Francisco. 1980.

The following reading will enhance your appreciation of LA County's impressive architecture and archetypal urban form.

LOS ANGELES, THE ARCHITECTURE OF FOUR ECOLOGIES
Reynor Banham
Penguin Books
New York. 1982.

A GUIDE TO ARCHITECTURE IN SOUTHERN CALIFORNIA
David Gebhard and Robert Winter
Peregrine Smith
Santa Barbara. 1976.

DAYDREAM HOUSES OF LOS ANGELES
Charles Jencks
Rizzoli Publications
New York. 1978.

THE IMAGE OF THE CITY
Kevin Lynch
MIT Press
Cambridge. 1982.

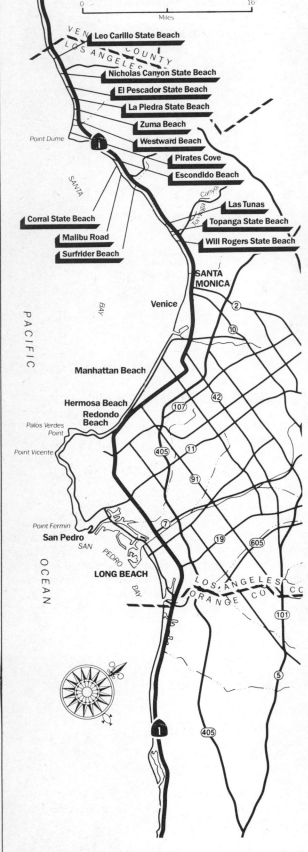

The Kingdom of Malibu

The problem at Malibu has always been those invaders of the kingdom. So it was in the beginning when Frederick Hastings Rindge and May Knight Rindge from Massachusetts purchased the Rancho Topanga, Malibu y Sequit in 1887. The Rindges were wealthy enough to establish a feudal duchy along the 20 miles of untouched Malibu shoreline. Although trespassers were always a problem, the Rindges were able to maintain their isolated paradise by the sea for almost 20 years.

Then unexpectedly in 1905, Frederick Rindge died. Shortly afterward the State initiated efforts to forge a highway through the rancho that would allow passage north from Santa Monica up the coast. But May Rindge refused, feeling bound to maintain the land as she and her husband had known it.

Passage Through the Kingdom

As the State pressed its condemnation suit through the courts, May Rindge patrolled her property boundaries on horseback, straining to maintain intact the last old rancho in Los Angeles County. May Rindge's resistance quickly turned to an obsession. Her inability to separate the past from the present rivaled that of Dickens's Miss Havisham. To prevent incursion by the Southern Pacific, Rindge constructed her own railroad (making her the only female railroad president in history). For 15 years the expensive litigation continued— four times the case went to California's highest court,

twice to the U.S. Supreme Court—while the Rindge fortune was being drained.

In 1923 the State's right of eminent domain through the Rindge property was affirmed, but armed guards still prohibited all entry for two more years until the amount of compensation was determined for the right-of-way. For passage through the kingdom, May Rindge asked $9,180,000. The courts granted $107,289.

Finally surveyors gained access to the land. Soon bulldozers and roadbuilders followed. By 1928 a paved highway was completed through the 20 miles of untouched shorefront. The public was at last able to see the unmatched Malibu coast, even if the newly built high fences and patrolling armed guards paralleled the public right-of-way.

Movie Stars

May Rindge had spent so much money on lawyers' fees that even before the coast highway was opened for use, she was forced to lease out beachfront lots. The extreme seclusion of the area appealed to movie stars, who became the first lessees of the tiny 40-foot beachfront lots. In 1927 John Gilbert, Ronald Coleman, and Corrine Griffith led an exodus to what soon came to be called Malibu Colony. The Colony's strict gatekeep inaugurated another era of prohibited entry to the kingdom, different only in kind from May Rindge's.

The Depression further decimated Rindge's fortune, and in 1936 she declared bankruptcy, which forced a reorganization of her holdings into several categories. In 1940 the entire ranch was put up for public sale.

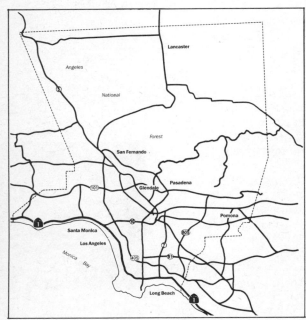

Environment | ## Roadside Attractions | ## Resources

Plastic Trash

Plastic litter on the beach is a nuisance and a detraction for beach visitors, but for fish, seals and birds that live in or depend on the ocean, it can be a death sentence. Plastic pollution is killing millions of members of the ocean environment as surely as if they were being intentionally exterminated.

The problem is so great that one to two million sea birds such as albatrosses, puffins, gulls, terns, murres, and petrels die each year from eating bits of plastic litter or becoming entangled in plastic nets. Another 100,000 or more whales, dolphins, seals, and manatees meet the same fate.

Plastic and More Plastic

The problem has become epidemic due to the world-wide rise in the production of plastic products, particularly monofilament fishing nets. The National Academy of Science estimates that commerical fishing fleets dump more than 52 million pounds of plastic packaging into the sea and lose more than 298 million pounds of plastic fishing gear each year.

Monofilament fishing nets, which are cheaper to produce than traditional nets, do not biodegrade

and are difficult for marine inhabitants to detect acoustically, so sea mammals often become entangled and drown. Seabirds become ensnared in the plastic nets when they dive for fish. Young seals are increasingly sighted with netting around their necks that strangle them as they grow. Many more marine inhabitants are being killed by eating plastic. Pieces of styrofoam, plastic wrappers, and bottle caps have been found in the stomachs of over 50 species of sea birds, as well as numerous fish, turtles, and mammals. Plastic in their stomachs remains there displacing real food and

causing death by starvation.

The evidence is extremely strong in favor of needing new, more bio-degradable marine products and educating people to be more careful with litter. Plastic can kill.

Malibu

Malibu is the only place in the world you can lie on the sand and look at the stars—or vice versa.

Joan Rivers

Once described in *People Magazine* as the G-spot of North America, Malibu is actually less a physical location than a state of mind, a condition of desire stimulated by the presence of celebrities, climaxed by the free spending of vast amounts of money.

Although Malibu occupies 27 miles of Los Angeles County shoreline, it does so in certain figmentary ways: there are no laundromats here, no carwashes, no undertakers, and barely a decent restaurant. There are certainly no poor people, and few blacks, Hispanics, or Asians. Housing is available, but again only in figmentary fashion—at prices beyond irrational belief. Malibu's best-known residents are America's most mythic: movie stars who tred lightly the bounds between reality and illusion, harbormasters at the sea of make-believe.

Many Malibuvians live in mythical Malibu Colony or along the storied Malibu wall, a string of connecting bungalows along PCH that make the beach (and access to it) vanish. Many are famous: Herb Alpert, Julie Andrews and Blake Edwards, Anne Bancroft and Mel Brooks, Christie Brinkley and Billy Joel, Lloyd Bridges, Bryan Brown and Rachel Ward, Genevieve Bujold, Johnny Carson, Cheech, Dick Clark, Bruce Dern, Bob Dylan, Sam Elliot and Katharine Ross, Farrah Fawcett and Ryan O'Neal, Mick Fleetwood, Steve Lawrence and Eydie Gorme, Lou Gossett, Lorne Greene, Larry Hagman, Goldie Hawn, Jascha Heifetz, Dustin Hoffman, John Houseman, Tim Hutton, Bruce Jenner and Linda Thompson, Jennifer Jones and Norton Simon, Stacy Keach, Billy Jean King, Jack Klugman, Kris Kristofferson, Michael Landon, Jack Lemmon, Rich Little, Ali MacGraw, Shirley MacLaine, the Maharaji Ji, Lee Majors, Dick Martin, Walter Matthau, Burgess Meredith, Joni Mitchell, Olivia Newton-John, Carroll O'Connor, Tatum O'Neal, John Peters, Robert Redford, Don Rickles, Londa Ronstadt, Martin Sheen, Dinah Shore, Steven Spielberg, Rod Steiger, Barbra Streisand, Flip Wilson, Shelley Winters, and Pia Zadora.

Many of the other people at Malibu are visitors, adventurers from the outside searching for the place that is not there. Most of them drive up and down PCH or go to the beach.

Celebrities, Automobiles

To many people, Malibu Beach images the attainment of fame and fancy automobiles. The following books comprehensively treat these two enduring California passions.

CALIFORNIA PEOPLE
Carol Dunlap
Peregrine Smith
Salt Lake City. 1984.

One of the most fascinating contemporary books about California from any perspective, California People is a compendium of over 500 biographies of virtually every noteworthy California celebrity from Upton Sinclair to Richard Nixon, from Clara Bow to Huey Newton. Informative and entertaining.

AUTOMOBILE AND CULTURE
Gerald Silk
Harry N. Abrams, Inc.
New York. 1984.

Guides

THE BEST OF LA
By the Staff of the LA Weekly
Edited by Mary Beth Crain
Chronicle Books
San Francisco. 1984.

More than 500 eclectic selections of LA's "best"—Included: Best restaurants, sights, services as well as the best tuna sandwich and the best sexuality seminar.

LA ACCESS
Richard Sam Wurman
Access Press
Los Angeles. 1982.

Colorful and informative.

WPA GUIDE TO CALIFORNIA
New Introduction by
Gwendolyn Wright
Pantheon Books
New York. 1984.

Originally compiled in 1939, the WPA Guide to California is the best guidebook ever done on the nation's most populous state, and is as invaluable today as when first written by a collection of out of work writers including Kenneth Rexroth and Tillie Olson.

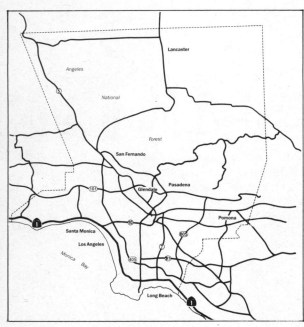

A Road for the Ages

Construction on the coast road continued at a pace coinciding with the automobile's rise in popularity, at least as far north as Rancho Malibu, where May Rindge defied efforts by the State to build a highway through her property. Funds for the construction of a paved coast road from San Juan Capistrano to Oxnard had been authorized in 1919, but although construction was underway in 1921, continual litigation at Rancho Malibu dimmed the prospects of a "travelable highway in

sight of the ocean from San Diego to Santa Barbara" for years.

The problems at Malibu were not only legal—the only available terrain was flat against the face of the cliffs that stood next to the ocean. Only at Point Dume was the close approach to the ocean edge avoided.

To make a road where no road would go, 2.5 million cubic yards of mountainside had to be moved before a 20 foot wide cement pavement could be laid aside the ocean. More than 40,000 cubic yards of heavy rip rap had to be dumped into the sea to forestall erosion.

Finally on June 29, 1929, the Coast Highway from Santa Monica to Oxnard was finished. The ceremonies that marked the event included speeches by the Governor and poses by Miss Canada and Miss Mexico, symbolic representatives of the two countries hoped to eventually be linked by the highway. A low-flying blimp led a long and colorful caravan of automobiles. The rhetoric was bombastic. Claimed one speechmaker: "This road will belong to the ages and will stand as a monument to the peace of the Golden Age, as the Roman roads stand today as a monument to the soldiers of the Caesars."

Surfer Against Surfer

Vals Must Die!
Graffito scrawled on life guard tower, Malibu Beach

The problem is one of supply and demand—too many surfers, too few waves. Of the State's approximately one million active surfers, most live in Southern California, where, according to *Surfer* Magazine, there are about 100 good surfing spots. The resulting competition for waves often resembles a Hobbesian world of surfer against surfer, where the most aggressive rule over a pecking order based on superior skills and territorial dominance.

Fights in the water are not uncommon. On a crowded day dozens of altercations may occur on any good surfing beach as surfers, kooks, and wannabes complete with infinite amounts of passion for a finite number of waves.

Prime surfing spots are controlled by locals who attempt to bar "invaders" by intimidation and violence. At Malibu the turf dispute is between locals and inland residents, particularly those from the San Fernando Valley, "Vals." *LA go Home* is a frequent spray can expressed sentiment on prominent walls, rocks, and fences.

Uncool Behavior

There is probably more to the conflict than supply and demand. The competition reflects the hardening edge of a culture. For about a ten-year span beginning in the late 1960s, localism was hardly apparent. "To be possessive, competitive, or worse, imperialistic about waves was not socially acceptable," says Jim Kompton, editor of *Surfer* Magazine. But today a band called the Surf Punks has an album, *My Beach,* that has sold more than 50,000 copies, mainly in Southern California. The song titles include "Punch Out at Malibu," and "Beer Can Beach," and "Somebody Ripped My Stick," which puts it simply: "I'll beat him, I'll pound his head. And if I ever find him, he's gonna be dead."

For years surfing garnered unfair criticism as an activity of escape from the "real" world, a meaningless quest on a glass board for a sunshine paradise. It may be more than a measure of paradox that surfing now imitates some of the worst of the push-and-shove world it was once accused of attempting to avoid.

Environment	Roadside Attractions	Resources

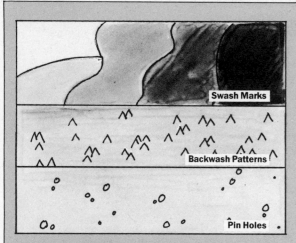

Reading the Beach

The next time you bore of people watching, and have forgotten to bring a good book to the beach, you might try amazing your friends by identifying swash marks, backwash patterns, and pin holes—the key to reading the beach. These subtle patterns tell something about the nature of the sand, the shape of the beach, and the action of the surf.

Swash marks are thin lines of sand left by the upward reach of incoming waves. The water, called a swash, spreads out into a thin film, traveling up the beach face and pushing sand particles along until the swash expends its energy, leaving the definitive marks.

Backwash marks are shallow, triangular gullies cut by the force of backrushing water, usually found on beaches that have an intermediate slope composed of moderately coarse sand. These marks can criss-cross into six-inch long diamond-shaped patterns of great diversity.

Pinholes are created when water sinks into especially dry sand and displaces the air between the grains. The displaced air rises to the surface in a series of bubbles which create the small pinholes.

Beaches

A beach is more than just the place where sand meets water. It is part of a complex ecosystem that consists of at least seven distinct life zones.

BAR. An offshore ridge submerged permanently or at least at high tide.

TROUGH. A natural channel running between the bar and beach front.

FORESHORE (FOREBEACH). The part of the shore lying between the crest of the most seaward berm and the ordinary low-water mark, usually traversed by the uprush and backrush of the waves as the tides rise and fall.

BACKSHORE (BACKBEACH). The part of the beach that is usually dry, lying between the foreshore and duneline and acted upon by waves only during storms and exceptionally high tides.

BERM. A wave-deposited ridge of sand on the backshore, marking the upper limit of ordinary high tides and wave wash.

BEACH RIDGE. A more or less continuous mound of beach material behind the berm, heaped up by wave action during extreme highwater levels; the ridge becomes a dune if it is largely wind-built and vegetated.

DUNES. More or less continuous mounds of loose, wind-blown material, usually sand, behind a berm. These areas are often vegetated with plants such as evening primrose, hottentot fig or salt bush that stabilize the dune formations. The secondary, or rear, dunes are usually more stabilized, linking the ecological chain of inland vegetation and animal life to the marine system.

Malibu Beaches

The celebrities may give Malibu its glitter, but it is the beaches that furnish the gold. Along its 27 mile length, Malibu has some of the best swimming and surfing beaches in California.

Will Rogers State Beach: Long and wide beach with lots of room and excellent even surf.

Topanga State Beach: A fine sandy beach is Topanga's most outstanding virtue; scheduled improvements should make the area even better.

Las Tunas: Similar to Topanga; immediately north are a series of stairways and walkways that lead to good, even beaches between Las Tunas and Malibu Pier, including the famed Zonker Harris Accessway (next to the Nantucket Light and Carlos Pepés), named for Gary Trudeau's quintessential laid-back Californian.

Surfrider: Stretching for almost a mile, Surfrider has traditionally been one of the best surfing spots in California (where Mickey Dora rode to fame and legend) although construction of the new Malibu lagoon State Park appears to have seriously affected the quality of waves for surfing.

Gidget Grows Up

Of all the cinematic depictions of California beach life, none so well expressed such a clean-cut, virginal, thoroughly middle-class image of American youth as *Gidget,* a 1959 movie starring Sandra Dee and James Darren. As unlikely as it may seem, the film was based on a real-life character, who is today a 44-year-old resident of Pacific Palisades, a few miles beyond the Malibu beaches where she spent a great deal of time in the mid 1950s outsurfing the immaculate young boys who rode the big waves.

All it took was an idle comment by Kathy Zuckerman about the "surf bums" at Malibu for her father, a Yugoslavian-born playwright and screenwriter, to knock out a story in six weeks about a 15-year-old girl at Malibu who learns how to surf and becomes accepted into the boys-only teenage surfing world. A *gidget,* it seems, was "a small girl—sort of a midget, a girl midget, a gidget."

Soon the book became a movie, and soon the movie spawned other movies: *Gidget Goes Hawaiian, Gidget Goes to Rome, Gidget Grows Up,* and *Gidget Gets Married.* There was also a short-lived television series starring Sally Field. The name Gidget, connected to any location or activity, evoked one of the times' strongest images of cute, girlish cheerfulness: Doris Day in adolescence.

All of this was a bit much for Kathy Zuckerman, who found the image of Gidget the perennial child increasingly embarrassing and irrelevant as she grew up, began a career, married, and had children. Today, however, as a middle-aged travel agent, Zuckerman recalls her association with Gidget fondly, sometimes referring to herself by the famous name to her clients, all in good clean fun of course.

Malibu Road: Exit PCH at Webb Way past Malibu Colony Coffee Shop to Malibu Road—4 stairways to excellent beach area near heart of one of Malibu's most private beach areas.

Corral State Beach: Narrow beach, excellent surfing.

Escondido Beach: Stairways from mouth of Escondido Creek and nearby restaurant lead to small, beautiful portions of beach, hampered by adjoining estates.

Paradise Cove: A fee access beach with a 400 foot

fishing pier, superb beach, and a romantic restaurant; where James Garner parked his trailer in Rockford Files; surfing not allowed.

Pirates Cove: One of the few clothing optional beaches in Southern California, access is gained from nearby Westward Beach.

Westward Beach: Excellent swimming beneath sandstone cliffs of the Point Dune headlands, often strong surf and good body surfing, tidepools.

Zuma Beach: One of Malibu's most heralded beaches, miles of uncrowded beach break; north are stairways off Broad Beach Road.

El Matador, La Piedra, El Pescador, and Nicholas Canyon: 4 superb beaches in highly scenic setting; El Matador is the prettiest and most interesting; minimum facilities.

Leo Carillo State Beach: Part of a 1600 acre park that concludes Malibu; the beach is more than a mile long, one part of which has sea caves and a tunnel carved by erosion; three campgrounds.

WAVES AND BEACHES
Willard Bascom
Anchor Books, Doubleday
New York. 1980.

VENTURA

VENTURA COUNTY is seldom granted sufficient recognition for its interest and charms, even though it occupies 43 miles of highly scenic shoreline and has a fascinating early history. Although its adjacency to one of the country's largest metropolitan areas has significantly influenced Ventura County, its character remains largely its own: an easy-going place that quietly admits to possessing one of the most beautiful coastlines in the state, two unique coastal urban areas, and proprietorship of the unmatched Channel Islands.

California Route 1, Pacific Coast Highway, begins in the south on a narrow ledge between the Santa Monica Mountains and the deep blue sea. Racing northward past Point Mugu, PCH soon levels out upon the Oxnard Plain, a huge former delta area of the Santa Clara River, which has left a swath of fertile farmland through the center of the county.

The Oxnard Plain embraces the cities of Oxnard and Ventura, two of California's pleasantest and least pretentious urban areas. Past Oxnard, PCH joins U.S. 101 for a rare appearance as a Southern California freeway. North of the city of Ventura, PCH disappears just before the county line, as if to register its dissent from continued regard as a wide lane freeway.

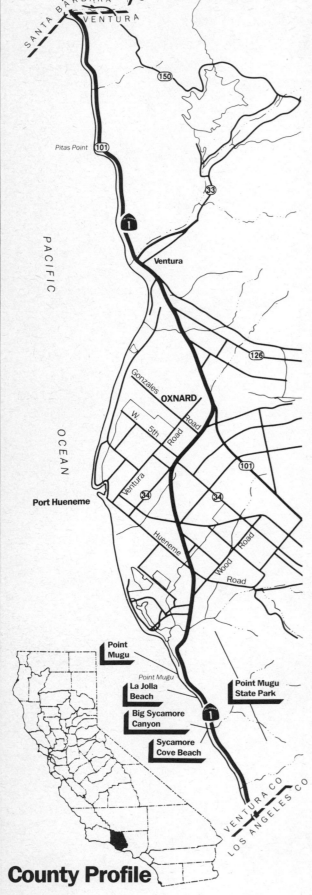

The Archenemy of the Unwary Traveler

The irregular, rocky, sharply sloping coastline that begins at the southern boundary of Ventura County has always played hell with road travel. For decades the ocean adjacent to this rugged stretch of coast was judged to be "an archenemy" that lay in wait for the unwary traveler.

In 1921 construction began on a highway along the most formidable section of Ventura's coastline.

Although the road north had been completed in 1913, the crew had not attempted to complete the section over Ventura's most difficult terrain. One segment, around the main edge of Point Mugu, was called at the time "probably the most dangerous and difficult single piece of construction work in the California highway system."

When construction began on the Ventura coast road many immediately compared the challenge to that posed by the road from Carmel to San Simeon through Big Sur, where crews had a few months earlier dared the difficult terrain of Monterey County.

The Ventura road, however, required even deeper excavations, and the blasting out of greater quantities of earth and rock. One section, south of Big Sycamore Canyon, required crews to blast through an uninterrupted mile of solid rock cliff and to move 334,086 pounds of earth and rock. A giant railroad steamshovel chewed up mountains of fallen debris and dumped them into the ocean.

Unreal Places

California has always had a special relationship with the figmentary, appealing to dreamers and searchers for paradise like few places in the world. Part of this is due to the state's magnificent scenery, which often seems to express the character of imaginary worlds, unreal and serene.

California, in fact, has been historically regarded as a kind of Atlantis by many. Its potential as an environment for living has been enhanced for centuries by the imagination of explorers and story tellers. Coronado's quest for the Seven Cities of Gold included stories of a place called Quivira—sometimes described as one of the Seven Cities, sometimes a separate Kingdom—that frequently appeared on maps along the California coast.

The Promised Land

The quest for paradise has often led to Southern California. Ventura County has attracted perhaps the most imaginative of California's seekers after the promised land. In the 1920s Albert Powell Warrington relocated his Krotona, "the place of promise," from Hollywood to Ventura's Ojai Valley. The Ojai Valley was also the home of Edgar Holloway, "the man from Lemuria," who claimed that he arrived in Ventura County from the sky as a "great flying fish."

Much of Ventura's original psychic appeal stemmed from a magazine article by a Dr. Hrdlicka, who predicted the rise of a "new sixth subrace" in the Ojai Valley based on a series of psychological tests given to California students that reportedly revealed a large number of child prodigies. Suddenly the area became regarded as the new "Atlantis of the Western Sea," attracting thousands of Theosophists from all over the world, including the "world teacher" Krishnamurti, who was believed to be the messiah of the select sub-race.

Atlantis has always been an extremely elusive place, usually appearing just ephemerally enough to stir a desire of how people might live better. From this desire comes a great deal that is not so impractical. From the unfettered imagination of Thomas More to Frank Lloyd Wright to Paolo Soleri, the idea of designing new communities and creating an improved society has been vitalized by the presence of unreal places. "What is now proved," said William Blake, "was only once imagined."

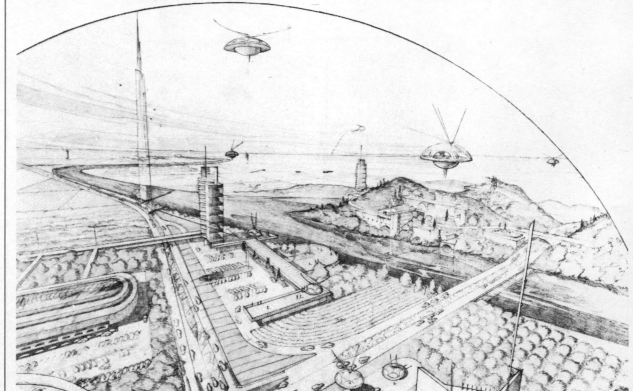

County Profile

Geographic

Land Area (acres)	1,184,640
Land Area (sq. miles)	1,851.0
Water Area (acres)	8,040
Water Area (sq. miles)	12.6
Acres in Public Ownership	645,585.74
Percent in Public Ownership	54.50
Miles of Public Roads	2,573
County Seat	Ventura

Demographic

Population	565,600
State Rank by Population	12
Projected 1990 Population	739,600
Unemployment Rate (state avg. = 9.9)	9.0
Per Capita Personal Income	$10,864
State Rank by Income	16
Total Assessed Property Value	$17,409,392,232

Environment

Ventura Riches

Ventura County's environment is surprisingly rich, encompassing a self-contained mountainous watershed, intermont basin, broad coastal plain, advantageously situated stream and groundwater systems, mild Mediterranean climate, and abundance of deep and fertile lowland alluvial soils. In welcome contrast to the Los Angeles Basin, Ventura offers fresh air cooled by prevailing ocean breezes and vast vistas across agricultural plains.

This geologically diverse county is bounded by the Santa Monica Mountains on the south, and, on the north, by the Santa Ynez segment of the Transverse Ranges. In between the mountains lies the Oxnard Plain, one of the country's most fertile agricultural areas, and offshore from the low coastal bluffs are the crown jewels of California islands: the Channel Islands.

California Condor

The giant black profile of the California condor once loomed over Western North America, uplifted by thermal air currents from British Columbia to Baja California. Today fewer than 30 condors remain, and that number shrinks each year. Experts predict that soon the only remaining specimens will be in zoos and captive breeding programs.

The California condor is North America's largest land bird, a vulture twice the size of the common turkey-vulture. Condors weigh about 20 pounds and their wings stretch to nine-foot spans. The bird's featherless head is gray until maturity (six years) by which time it has developed the characteristically gruesome mixture of wrinkled red and orange. Both sexes have identical plumage and broad wings ending in primary feathers than spread out like fingers at the end of a hand.

Condors take as long as seven years to reach breeding age, and then the female lays no more than a single egg once every two years. The parents spend almost two years raising their offspring, which even at ten months is still learning to fly.

Roadside Attractions

County Line

Southern Ventura County begins at one of the most beautiful spots on the California coast. Suddenly the Santa Monica Mountains rise up to present a stunning panorama of rock aside a roaring sea. From the county line to Point Mugu, the rolling ocean and implacable mountains lend exaltation to the Pacific Coast Highway journey.

Neptune's Net announces the down-to-earth pleasures of Ventura County, while it interrupts only briefly the tableau of dramatic natural elements. Neptune's is a festive eating spot that offers everything desirable in an oceanfront roadside stand. You may select from a variety of live shellfish and have them cooked in front of you. All manner of locally caught shellfish is available, as is fresh corn, according to season, and an outdoor deck provides the perfect spot for enjoying wonderfully fresh and inexpensive seafood.

South of Point Mugu are a series of superb beaches with often dramatic waves and an unspoiled character. There are facilities at Sycamore Cove Beach (showers, cooking grills, picnic area), and La Jolla Beach (campsites, water, picnic tables). La Jolla is the trailhead for the 13,000-acre Point Mugu State Park.

Resources

AREA CODE: 805

Rules of the Road

PCH in Ventura County offers a variety of driving experiences. In the southern portion of the county, it is a fast-traveled two lane roadway that hangs between the Santa Monica Mountains and the ocean. The magnificent views are best appreciated by using pull outs. North of Oxnard, PCH merges with the Ventura Freeway, which sometimes becomes an inpenetrable mass of automobiles during rush hours. Check your radio for traffic reports. North of the city of Ventura, look for PCH's brief departures from Freeway 101 along the North Rincon Parkway.

Public Transportation

487-4222 South Coast Area Transit (Oxnard)
643-3158 South Coast Area Transit (Ventura)
648-3850 Amtrak

Climate

Ventura County hosts mild, Mediterranean weather. Average low temperature in January is about 42°. Highs that month average 64°. A mild summer day is likely to be around 74° tops, 56° low. The average annual rainfall is 14.22 inches.

Condor Protection

California Condor Range

To find out the most recent status of the California condors, and to discover how you may help in their recovery, contact:

CONDOR CAMPAIGN
Friends of the Earth
124 Spear Street
San Francisco, 94105

DIRECTOR, CALIFORNIA
DEPARTMENT OF FISH
AND GAME
Sacramento, 95814

NATIONAL AUDUBON
SOCIETY
950 Third Avenue
New York, 10022

SECRETARY OF THE
INTERIOR
Washington, D.C. 20240

Blasting a New Road

In order to set the earthshaking explosions to make the new road, trails were built over the edge of the high cliffs and ropes and ladders hung over the side. Men in safety slings were lowered over the edge to dig concrete holes, which were filled with black powder—as many as 3,200 cans holding 25 pounds of black powder each were used to make a single explosive.

The blasts shook the mountains with force and filled the sky with dust. Such thunderousness had never been heard along this unpopulated portion of coast, though for millennia the sea had stormed and earthquakes had cracked the ground.

Danger and Daring

Each blast was an extremely uncertain endeavor. Once, when a powder foreman miscalculated the impact of a blast, the top of a 150-foot cliff broke loose and carried away the ground on which he and two helpers stood. The three men slid 200 feet to the ocean amid an avalanche of rock and earth. All three survived.

Danger and daring came with the territory. Climbing perpendicular cliffs and dangling from ropes over the deep blue sea was just part of a day's work for men who pushed themselves to untried levels of roadbuilding courage and heroics.

Point Mugu

Point Mugu is a remnant of igneous dyke that juts out into the ocean. Before the road cuts and excavations pushed a four-lane road 200 feet through its center, Point Mugu stood as the proudest promontory on the south coast, resting in the deep ocean with raging surf on three sides. The still-visible original road veered seaward of the point, leaving it with dignity intact. In the late 1930s and for two years to the day, crews blasted, dug, and shoveled out enough earth and debris to build a 150-foot thick hard rock ledge to carry a two-lane road.

The Military Presence

Much of coastal Ventura County's character is determined by the historic and continued presence of the military, particularly at Port Hueneme and Point Mugu.

Port Hueneme first achieved military importance in the 1930s when its harbor was dredged to allow entry of large naval ships. Today the Port is home to the Pacific Coast's most important Naval Construction Battalion ("Seabee") base, which provides thousands of military and civilian jobs in its operations as a shipping point for materials going to Pacific outposts.

The second major military presence is at the Point Mugu Naval Air Missile Test Center, which was created after World War II to test modern weapons. The missiles are fired regularly in a southwestwardly direction across the Pacific ocean. Observation stations are maintained in the Santa Monica Mountains and on the Channel Islands.

The most obvious impact of the military on Ventura coastal uses in visual presence—trucks on the roads and fences and locked gates surrounding miles of coastal property. Other impacts are less noticeable, but just as critical, including effects on the area's demographics such as income level and racial mix, housing and job markets, and the general state of the local economy.

Both Oxnard and Port Hueneme have been influenced by the military for decades. Service personnel have traditionally found housing in Oxnard, making this Ventura County's most racially diverse population, with a 1979 black population of about six percent. In Port Hueneme, the population for years was mainly either military or military-related. Today that trend is giving way as new residents are attracted by expensive new developments around the yacht basin. As the existing low/middle-income population is squeezed out by more affluent housing consumers, however, local planners contemplate a potential affordable housing shortage for military personnel, much like the one at Fort Ord near Monterey to the north.

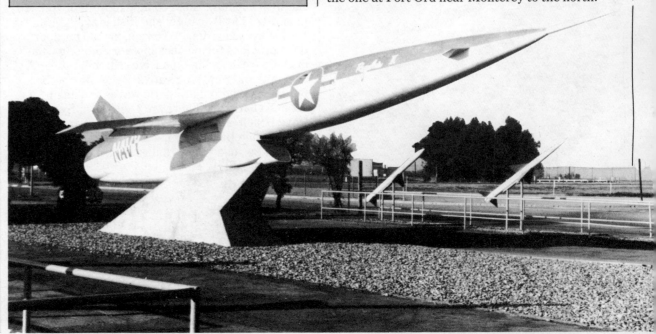

Environment

Roadside Attractions

Resources

Mugu Lagoon

Although only half of its original size of 3,000 acres, Mugu Lagoon remains an impressive example of the marshland ecosystems that once lined Southern California's coastline. The lagoon is fed mostly by Calleguas Creek at the northwest and is separated from the ocean by a barrier beach consisting of two distinct sand spits. The ocean's salt water enters with the tides at an opening just upcoast from Point Mugu to create the salt-fresh water mix that is the source of life for a wetland. Below the water, a rich substrata of ancient beach sands underlies eons of silt and clay deposits delivered by Calleguas Creek and prevented from escape to the open sea by the sand spits.

Within Mugu Lagoon are freshwater ponds, salt marshes, mudflats, deep water channels and sand dunes. This is one of California's richest natural habitats, with diverse marine and bird life. Among the more than 10,000 birds visiting the lagoon annually are the endangered California least tern, the peregrine falcon, California brown pelican, and lightfooted clapper rail. Harbor seals and California sea lions come here each year to breed.

All of Mugu Lagoon lies within the Navy's

Point Mugu

Point Mugu is one of the most striking landmarks on the Pacific Coast Highway. A noble rock that held its own for centuries against the assault of the Pacific, it was blindsided twice by overly eager highway construction crews bent on "conquering nature." Though it bears the scars of those road-building attacks, Point Mugu still stands with much of its dignity intact. It's worth stopping at, if for no other reason that to congratulate the old fellow on his proud endurance.

Point Mugu State Park

P.O. Box 2678
Oxnard 93034
(213) 457-5538

Point Mugu State Park begins west of PCH 3.5 miles south of Point Mugu and covers almost 15,000 acres along the road. The park area ends where Mugu Peaks mark the western end of the Santa Monica Mountains, rising 1,226 feet in less than .5 mile. The area is accessible by foot, horseback, or more than 70 miles of trails. Look for deer, coyote, bobcat in the chapparal and sage country. The park's beaches (Sycamore, LaJolla, and Point Mugu) offer excellent body surfing, sand dunes, and sun. There are two campgrounds (155 sites), reservations recommended. Maps available from headquarters.

Mugu Lagoon Wildlife Sanctuary

Point Mugu Testing Center Public Affairs Office
982-8094

Contact PMTC Public Affairs Office for information on restricted tours of the sanctuary, all of which is within the missile testing boundaries. Group interpretive tours are given only on weekends, by reservation only. Reservations must be made in advance, and there must be at least 15 people in the group. Oddly for an environmental interpretive program, no children are allowed.

Pacific Missile Test Center. As such, access is limited to weekend group interpretive tours which must be arranged at least a month in advance through the Center's Public Affairs Office. However, the southern end of the lagoon may be viewed (but not visited) from an overlook platform west of PCH about one half mile north of Point Mugu rock. An interpretive display depicts shellfish, birds, fish and plant life of the lagoon. On a clear day Anacapa Island and the cliffs at the east end of Santa Cruz Island can also be seen from the lagoon overlook.

Roadside Art: The Pacific Missile Testing Center

Like the famous Cadillac Ranch, a string of tail-finned Cadillacs buried nose down along a west Texas roadside, the Pacific Missile Testing Center exhibit at Wood Road commands the attention of passing motorists. This tightly fenced but public exhibit demonstrates that the U.S. Navy has not missed the pop art significance of its weapons system. Models of missiles point bravely toward the sky in mock seriousness, sparing little in authentic detail.

Parking is limited to 30 minutes, although you will surely want to stay longer.

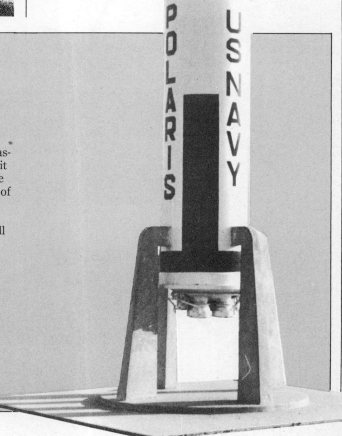

Ventura County, 1861

For the first half century of its existence, Ventura County relied on ships and stagecoaches to meet its transportation needs. Travel by steamer was considered less risky than a stagecoach ride, but expensive tickets limited the number of sea travelers. For most excursionists, the stagecoach was the usual conveyance of the day, and the coast road was the main route.

Stagecoach travel began in Ventura County even before it was a county. In 1861, ten years before the southern segment of Santa Barbara County was reformed as San Buenaventura County, a dirt road was laid out along the route of El Camino Real. The road was built by James Thompson and his crew and paid for by the county of Santa Barbara in anticipation of the Overland Stage Company's new route between San Francisco and Los Angeles, which was to run from Santa Barbara to Malibu along the Ventura coast.

El Camino Real was no pleasure for stage travel—although it had served the Spanish *padres* well as a footpath and oxcart trail, it required substantial improvement to be suitable for stagecoach travel. Near Rincon Point and Punta Gorda, the

terrain was so formidable that no stage road could be built—coaches had to take to the beach and negotiate the surf as best they could. Said the *Santa Barbara Press:* "The down stage from Santa Barbara upset at Punta Gorda on Sunday night, throwing passengers, baggage, mail, etc. into the surf. Everything was thoroughly drenched, the way bill lost and one man was thrown clear over the driver's head into the breakers, but luckily no one was injured."

The Town that Oxnard Killed

In 1876 Hueneme was the liveliest port on the Southern California coast, shipping more grain than any port south of San Francisco. Coastal steamers called for freight and passengers, entrepreneurs did a land-office business, and the wharf grew by increments. The wharf's ultimate 1,500 foot span into the sea proudly symbolized the port's success.

Prosperity at the wharf meant prosperity in town: hotels, stores, saloons, a telegraph, a post office, and steamship offices sprung up. A 7,000-foot dancehall with a shiny polished floor kept Huenemenites stepping to the rhythm of an upbeat future.

In the late 1890s the Southern Pacific Railroad came to Ventura, but it did not come to Hueneme. Instead, Oxnard became the area's new focus for growth, flourishing at the expense of Hueneme—a Chumash word for "resting place."

For years Hueneme was angered by the railroad's snub of its varied charms. Animosity toward Oxnard grew stronger, and many in the port town thought of their community only as "the town that Oxnard killed." But modern times and urban sprawl have now melded the two places into a single growth area.

California Farmworkers

Through various periods since 1870, agricultural workers in California have suffered job repression, prejudice, and social and economic barriers as drastic as any element of the American labor force.

Even until the Progressive Era of the 1930s, the certainty of violence against those struggling to improve unbearable conditions was often enough to stifle change. It took the "Great Upheaval" year of 1933, when the farm labor ranks swelled with Depression-era white unemployed men, for workers to organize against exploitive conditions. By the end of the bloody 30s, the plight of the California farmworker had received national notice, some union organizing and strikes had been called successes, and the farmworker had taken the first step on the long road to improved economic status.

A New Era: The United Farmworkers

In 1962 a young migrant worker from Yuma, Arizona, announced a strike of grape growers and support of a nationwide boycott, forming the base of what was to become the United Farm Workers

Union (UFW). The place was the Sierra Vista labor camp near Delano, California. The worker's name was Cesar Chavez.

Since then, Chavez has led organized farmworkers through the pages of what has been called "the greatest chapter in the history of California labor." By 1977, the UFW had some 70,000 members, several contracts, many successful actions behind them, and the eyes, ears, and purses of the state legislature and the Governor, Jerry Brown. The charismatic Chavez was by far the most well-known and respected Chicano in the country, and

the farmworkers finally had a national forum for their long-term grievances.

During the decade of the 70s, California passed legislation to protect workers from pesticides and unsafe farm machinery, to control child labor, and end the harsh exploitive *bracero* program, which relied on undocumented Mexican laborers. Wages rose for union members from below minimum levels to about $6 an hour, often higher on piece rates.

Today the UFW's ranks have shrunk in numbers, and the anticipated leap to an influential national membership has not yet been realized.

Environment	Roadside Attractions	Resources

Chemical Change

American farmers provide an astounding amount of food products: 15% of the world's wheat, 21% of the oats, and 46% of the maize, all on only 11% of the world's croplands. But decades of such production have taken a toll that is only recently begun to be measured. It affects the worker in the field, the animal life in agricultural areas, and—ultimately—all life on this planet.

According to the authors of *Gaia,* synthetic fertilizers are applied to American soils at an average rate of 125 kilograms per hectare per year. These fertilizers, and the pesticides used in conjunction

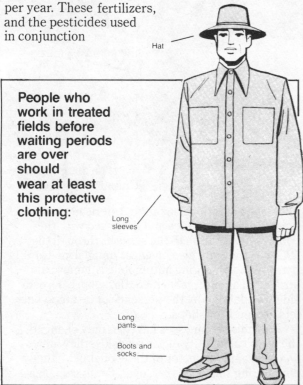

People who work in treated fields before waiting periods are over should wear at least this protective clothing:

Hat

Long sleeves

Long pants

Boots and socks

with them, are responsible for over half of all our nation's water pollution. Direct effects of such chemicals on farmworkers, their families, and nearby communities are still under study. It often takes years to prove causal relationships (and there are a multitude of individual chemicals to test), but few doubt that there *are* relationships between agricultural chemicals and the closed and fragile eco-system that comprises our world.

DDT: Lessons Learned or Just Lessons?

Prior to 1972, DDT was one of the most commonly used pesticides on the California coast. It is now one of the best documented examples of how a pesticide enters the food chain to deadly effect. The presence of DDT was traced with scientific certainty from field to fish and birds. It showed up in increasingly concentrated rates as it climbed from streams polluted by agricultural run-off to small fish that absorbed the pesticide through their gills. From the small fish, it moved to larger fish in the dietary chain, and ultimately to the birds that ate the large fish. The final link was to the eater of large fish and some birds—people.

The evidence of DDT pollution was shocking—deformed and dead birds, entire nesting colonies with generations aborted by eggs that had thinned and fragile shells, and dead water systems adjacent to agricultural fields worked by humans, producing foods for human consumption. So horrible was the evidence, in fact, that DDT use was prohibited in the United States by 1972. This might bring comfort was it not that this country still allows *production* and *export* of over 18 million kg of DDT a year, most of which goes to Third World countries, having little knowledge of the chemical's dangers nor the ability to regulate its use. One result is that farmworkers in Central America are estimated to have 11 times as much DDT in their bodies as an average person in this country.

Port Hueneme

PCH leaves the shoreline at Mugu Lagoon, part of the Point Mugu Pacific Missile Range. Channel Islands Boulevard leads to Port Hueneme and the ocean beaches to the north. At Oxnard's Channel Island Harbor the amenities include a re-created New England fishing village that, despite its ill-considered motif, has several satisfactory restaurants tucked away within the fakery.

There are good beaches nearby—Ormond, Silver Strand, Hollywood, Oxnard Shores, and

Mandalay—that have always rewarded visitors with fine surf and sand and not many crowds. Because most development was concentrated around the town of Oxnard, for years the beach area was almost desolate. (In 1921 these beaches passed for Araby when *The Sheik* with Rudolph Valentino was filmed here.) Recently, however, new investment has deserted Oxnard proper, or at least its downtown, for the harbor. The result has not been the most successful mix of residential, maritime, and recreational uses.

Ventura County Agriculture

Ventura County leads the state and the nation in growing cabbage, green lima beans, lemons, Romaine lettuce, and spinach. The county is second in place in bell peppers, celery, and avocados. Total value of annual county farm products is about $500,000,000. Crops include:

  7 different livestock commodities
  6 kinds of fruit and nut crops
12 major vegetables
14 minor vegetables
  7 field crops
  & cut flowers, nursery stock, and apiary products of beeswax and honey.

Ventura County Farm Trails
P.O. Box 1072
Ventura 93002

Provides a brochure with maps and lists of many small farms that offer produce directly to the public. Pick your own peaches, pomegranates, or persimmons.

Farm Facts

In 1980, the average California farm was 538 acres in size, valued at $503,500. The national average was 450 acres, valued at $251,000.

Two-thirds of California farms are 100 acres or less in size, but 10% of these farms produce ¾ of the total farm revenues.

California has more than 5,200 farms of 1,000 acres or more.

Eight of the ten top agricultural counties in the United States are located in California.

California Farmworkers

Few books render the inspiring story of an American people like these three volumes. McWilliams and Steinbeck, writing more than 45 years ago, provide shockingly realistic detail in novel format. Daniel summarizes facts, figures, politics, and movements with the eye of a scholar and the heart of a passionate defender of individual freedom and dignity.

FACTORIES IN THE FIELD
Carey McWilliams
Little Brown
Boston. 1939.

THE GRAPES OF WRATH
John Steinbeck
Viking Press
New York. 1939.

BITTER HARVEST: A
HISTORY OF CALIFORNIA
FARMWORKERS, 1870-1941
Cletus E. Daniel
University of California Press
Berkeley. 1981.

The First Oil Well in California?

California's first oil well was not drilled in Ventura County, although for years Ventura was credited as the original location.

California's first well was actually drilled in Petrolia, a few miles south of Eureka near the Lost Coast in Northern California. The year was 1861, about the same time that George S. Gilbert, an entrepreneur from San Francisco, moved to San Buenaventura and attempted to refine the black sticky stuff into lamp oil and wheel lubricant.

Gilbert didn't have much success, despite the pools of oil that seeped up out of the ground and blackened the beaches. The abundance of natural oil deposits in Ventura had always been evident. The Native Americans who first lived in the area used the thickest part of the goo—asphaltum—to line their baskets and waterproof their canoes.

Struggling to the Surface

In 1864 Thomas A. Scott, vice president of the Pennsylvania Railroad, dispatched Benjamin Silliman to California to investigate the possibilities for locating oil. It had been Scott and Silliman who sank the world's first

commercial oil well in Titusville, Pennsylvania in 1859.

Silliman, a Yale professor of geology, went straight to George Gilbert, the unlucky oil refiner in Ventura, to ask his opinion of the prospects of oil discovery in California. After listening to Gilbert's unqualified optimism and witnessing the oil seeping out of the ground, Silliman wired back to Scott, "California will be found to have more oil in its soil than all the whales in the Pacific Ocean. [In Ventura] the oil is struggling to the surface at every available point and is running down the river for miles."

Scott quickly sent Thomas A. Bard to California to buy up all the land in sight. Optimism ran high—until the first wells were drilled. Extracting the oil proved far more difficult than had been expected. California's geology—its folded and tilted strata—was a far cry from Pennsylvania's. And the oil was much heavier; its denser content of asphalt made it gummier. It wasn't much good for lubricant, and the kerosene burned poorly and smelled worse. In 1897 Scott refused to finance any further exploration.

Although deeper drilling eventually yielded larger quantities and higher-quality grades, profits were slow. Thomas Bard, however, who was nobody's fool, subdivided much of the land for ranches and made a quick fortune. And since he retained the oil rights to the land, he made millions when oil eventually proved profitable. Oil baron Bard became the first president of Union Oil Company.

Franchises at the Roadside

First there were the Howard Johnson's. Then Holiday Inns arrived as night follows day. Then came AAMCO Transmissions, McDonalds, H & R Block, Kentucky Fried Chicken, Dunkin' Donuts, Burger King, Taco Bell, Pizza Hut, Ramada Inn, and Midas Muffler, until enough franchises cluttered the roadside landscape that little else could be seen. And the motorists who stopped, more often in urgency than in tribute, felt that if it was not good, at least it was convenient.

The transformation of the American roadside began in the late 1940s and advanced with the country's migration to the suburbs through the 1950s as the franchise business found its natural home along emerging automobile commercial strips. All at once, it seemed, the suburban roadside was defined by the presence of fast food outlets and muffler shops.

Franchise businesses have not only changed the physical identity of the roadside, they have changed a major sector of the economy, virtually eliminating the small, personal, family-run business. Although most franchises do not make a great deal of money (most cannot expect to make more than $25,000 per year), their allure to the small investor-operator is tremendous, even though they afford little of the individual autonomy that has traditionally made small businesses attractive. (Working within a "straightjacket of corporate regulations," franchise owners have practically no say in individualizing their shops.)

The largest segment of roadside franchises is, of course, devoted to fast food. More than five million people work in fast food franchise jobs, but most of these are dead-end jobs that pay little above the minimum wage with few benefits. All fast food franchise stores are non-union. With an average term of employment of approximately four months, most employees find the work unrewarding, too low paying, and too depersonalized to continue for long.

Main Street America

Franchise strips have become the new Main Streets of America, substituting a homogenized landscape for one of variety and local character. At first designed with flashy colors and bright signs, most franchise operations have been toned down in recent years by local zoning requirements. In place of gaudy, eyecatching stores, are ones with earth tone facades and more discreet signs. Less conspicious, they are no less sterile or depersonalized.

For all of their association with the automobile and suburbs, franchise businesses also bear a great affinity with television, not only benefitting from national TV advertising ("you deserve a break today"), but in many ways imitating the experience of television watching itself. Bright and banal, almost instantaneously available, roadside franchises provide an unvarying pre-selected program of services and good, usually conveyed with smiling rigidity. The choice is only among channels all the same.

Environment

Strawberries, A Suburban Survivor

Urban growth adjacent to the Oxnard Plain is slowly encroaching on once-productive agricultural fields, pushing many sensitive crops even further back behind buffer zones that separate farms from factories and houses. Strawberries, however, are one crop that is often cultivated along the immediate suburban edge. The strawberry's per-acre production value is unusually high, making them more competitive against alternative land use. Look for the lush red fruits around harvesting time in early summer (strawberries are harvested by hand). The rest of the year, however, strawberry fields are often covered with polyethylene tarps to entrap fumigated soil and provide a temporary greenhouse to nurture young plants.

Every spring Oxnard hosts the California Strawberry Festival held at Channel Island Harbor. Appreciation of the sweet fruit is celebrated through theater, music, arts, crafts, and gourmet strawberry concoctions of all sorts.

Lemons and Limas

The Oxnard Plain produces almost half of the entire national lemon crop and has long been one of the world's chief large-lima bean producers. Both of these crops require a frost-free environment, but can tolerate the relatively cooler temperatures of coastal Ventura County. Ventura also ranks high in production of Valencia oranges, strawberries, avocados, celery, tomatoes, lettuce, green beans, and cabbage.

Roadside Attractions

Oxnard

Oxnard begins with a sudden departure from the wide agricultural fields to the south. The Coast Highway is transformed into Oxnard Boulevard and the roadside suddenly becomes a montage of signs for the All-American Car Wash, Kozy Kitchen, Pep Boys, and other declarative indicators of life along the commercial strip.

As Oxnard Blvd continues north, the median strip becomes landscaped and intersections feature tiled pedestrian crossings, but the lifelessness

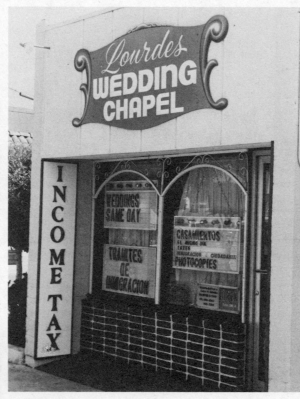

of Oxnard's central city belies the decoration—numerous out-of-business storefronts dot the roadside crying out for more substantial solutions. The Teatro Theater, a small authentic gem, shines through the dimness.

North of Oxnard's drowsy central city, signs of economic vitality reappear. As the street widens, commercial lots increase in size, and the character of roadside business changes. Corporate trademarks and large stores become everywhere evident, and in one short distance starting from the central city and going north, Oxnard Blvd displays a half-century in the evolution of the American commercial strip: from storefront to blockfront, from small entrepreneur to regional or national corporation, and from identifying signs observable by a passing motorist to flamboyant, rotating, illuminated displays visible blocks away.

Nor could Oxnard Blvd be without a shopping center on its evolutionary march northward. At Gonzales Road, the Carriage Square Center features a multiplex movie theater with five screens. Past the Levitz Furniture Store, Carl's Junior, and Handyman, just before Oxnard Blvd turns into a freeway, is the Esplanade.

The Esplanade

A good center in which to spend the day if you wake feeling low in Oxnard, California, is the Esplanade, major tenants the May Company and Sears.
Joan Didion

The Esplanade, a double-anchor regional mall, has (in addition to the May Company and Sears) 10 shoe stores, 15 women's apparel shops, 7 men's apparel shops, 5 jewelry stores, 7 restaurants, and one of each of the following: childrens' clothing shop, hair stylist, bookstore, optometrist, pet store, cable TV store, fabric store, cookie store, caramel corn store, candy store, and general nutrition store.

Resources

Oxnard Area Beaches

Between Mugu Lagoon and the Santa Clara River are a series of excellent beaches that stand out for their excellent facilities and pleasurable surf. Usually uncrowded, these south county beaches offer a variety of recreational opportunities.

Ormond Beach: access is from Perkins Road to this varied beachfront area with small dunes and wetlands.

Port Hueneme Beach Park: adjacent to the fishing pier are a wide beach, picnic tables, snack bar, playground and bike path.

Silver Strand Beach: take San Nicholas Avenue to this large, sandy beach with plenty of parking and volleyball facilities.

Channel Islands Harbor: In addition to Harbor facilities (boat ramps, berths, hoists), Channel Islands Harbor Park offers a well maintained grassy area and superb beach (showers, picnic area, restrooms).

Hollywood Beach: take Ocean Drive to Beach; outdoor showers and volleyball.

Peninsula Park: Next to Channel Islands Harbor, Peninsula Park has a childrens' playground, two tennis courts, cooking grills, and a grassy area for picnics.

Oxnard Shores: although access to this beachfront next to a subdivision is limited, entry can be obtained at the end of Seabreeze Way; picnic tables and a small park.

Mandalay County Park: a large County-owned beach area without facilities, but excellent beach and dunes; fine surfing.

McGrath State Beach: the largest beach area in the vicinity (2 miles) McGrath has campsites, picnic facilities, and a fascinating nature trail that leads through a wilderness area.

ROADSIDE EMPIRES: HOW THE CHAINS FRANCHISED AMERICA
Stan Luxenberg
Viking Penguin Inc., New York. 1985.

Roadside Empires is a fascinating examination of the franchise business, which has utterly transformed the American landscape, diet, and economy since the Second World War. Everybody is here from Howard Johnson to Ray Kroc and Colonel Sanders, and every glittering franchise operation is discussed from motel chains and muffler shops to hair salons and tanning parlors.

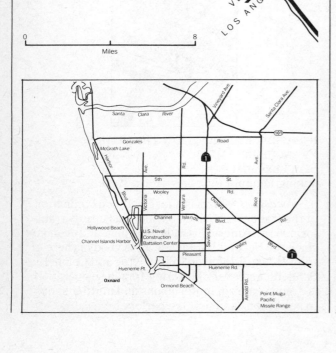

Twentieth Century

With the demise of the stagecoach about the turn of the century, the coast road along Rincon entered a period of disuse. But not for long. Within a few years the automobile made its first appearance on the Southern California scene. As the importance of the automobile to tourism became readily apparent, the construction of a coast road through Ventura County to link Santa Barbara to Los Angeles became inevitable.

In early 1911 a meeting was called at the Potter

Hotel in Santa Barbara by Milo "Mile-a Minute" Potter, owner of Santa Barbara's most expensive and elaborate tourist attraction. The topic: How to build the coast road through Ventura County that Ventura County would not build for itself.

The upshot of the meeting was a decision to raise private funds for a new highway through neighboring Ventura County so that visitors from Los Angeles could drive to Santa Barbara. Santa Barbara residents judged the need for the new highway to be so urgent that Ventura County's near-unanimous sentiment against the project was

ignored, as was the fact that a State highway bond issue to finance the new road with public funds was imminent.

Nothing meant more than the plight of visitors from Los Angeles who were so anxious to enjoy Santa Barbara's new seaside tourist attractions what they were stranding themselves in the breakers as they attempted to negotiate the old stage road up the coast.

The Biggest Little City on the Coast

Oxnard began not as a town but as a sugar factory, and for years it resisted any other identity. The town was wrought from a few small houses, a store, and a saloon adjacent to Henry J. Oxnard's $2 million sugar-beet processing plant.

Despite the early railroad connection to the outside world and the completion of a decent road to Los Angeles in 1925, the town's economic dexterity was hindered by the presence of a single dominant industry. Located near an expanding Southern California economy, Oxnard maintained an inward focus until the tentacles of Los Angeles urban sprawl eventually transformed the "biggest little city on the coast" into an annex of the third-largest city in America.

Pedestrian Malls: Oxnard's Plaza Park

Vehicle-free pedestrian malls were not invented in the 1960s: both Greek agoras and Roman forums isolated themselves from the push-and-shove of ancient street traffic to preserve their special public functions. In California, though, the conversion of city streets to pedestrian malls is a relatively new phenomenon.

Pedestrian malls have become the easiest way for a municipality to achieve the appearance of "doing something" to improve run-down areas. Less costly and controversial than addressing the social and economic causes of urban decline, malls have sprung up everywhere. Even the cynic must acknowledge that some malls have helped local businesses, and some have made a positive contribution to the store of urban open spaces.

Social Value

Ideally, a pedestrian mall brings people together for a variety of purposes and activities. A consummate mall conveys a sense of personal freedom as well as a sense of public involvement

that informs our understanding of ourselves as social beings who belong to a diverse group. In addition to such social values, a pedestrian mall enables residents and visitors to enjoy an urban area, to experience an emotional and intimate civic relationship, and to identify with the mood and movements of a city.

Unfortunately, many cities have jumped on the mall bandwagon without considering the social characteristics and requirements of surrounding areas. Thus, Oxnard's Park Plaza mall barely survives in a state of stupor and social irrelevance. It is ignored as an urban amenity and activity center, chiefly because it was conceived in a social vacuum. Its designers hoped it would "revitalize" a declining area, a burdensome expectation for a few acres of greenery.

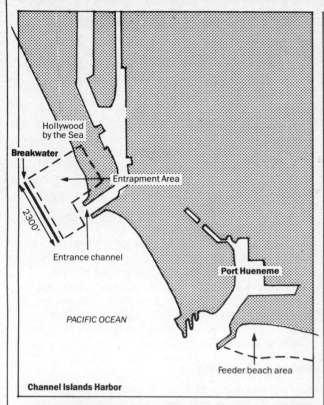

Channel Islands Harbor

Labels on map: Hollywood by the Sea; Breakwater; Entrapment Area; 2300'; Entrance channel; Port Hueneme; PACIFIC OCEAN; Feeder beach area

Sand Entrapment at Channel Islands Harbor

The small craft harbor at Oxnard sits right in the middle of what was once a major sand dune field. The sands were hauled away, the harbor dug from solid ground, its sides concreted over, and an entrance channel opened to the sea to develop what now looks like a natural waterway, port for more than 1,800 small craft.

Opening the mouth of the harbor was simple compared to keeping it open. Huge amounts of sand

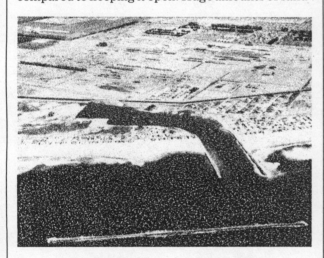

travel on the littoral drift (the "conveyor-belt" current that runs parallel to the shore). But left alone, the sand would soon shoal the harbor's entrance. To solve the problem, engineers created a sand entrapment area just north of the harbor mouth.

A sand entrapment area is a protected spot formed by breakwaters and jetties, which cause sand to settle out before reaching an undesired destination. At Channel Islands Harbor, the sand drops out in the zone formed by a 2,300' long detached breakwater and a jetty at the north end of the harbor entrance. The trapped sand is removed by a series of submerged pipelines and by periodic dredging. It is replaced on shore at a feeder beach south of Port Hueneme.

Erle Stanley Gardner at Oxnard

Oxnard's most famous literary resident is Erle Stanley Gardner, one of the best-selling novelists of all time. The creator of Perry Mason and a self-described "one-man fiction factory," Gardner moved to California in 1911 to practice law. His legal career had begun with a crash in Indiana when he was thrown out of school at Valparaiso University for engaging in a bottle-throwing melee with a professor.

In the small, wide-open town of Oxnard, Gardner met with little professional success, though he developed a reputation for challenging authority, using unorthordox tactics and representing the poor. "I have built up a law practice in which I am dealing with large numbers of clients of all classes—except the upper and middle class," he said.

Eventually Gardner's eye for unusual precedents led him to writing stories, which in lawyerly fashion he dictated to his secretary. Beginning with westerns, he soon advanced to pulp detective stories that drew on his legal knowledge. In 1933 Gardner spent three and a half days dictating to produce the first of his Perry Mason stories, *The Case of the Velvet Claws.* The book's jacket carried the copy line "Perry Mason—

Criminal Lawyer. Remember that name. You'll meet him again. He is going to be famous."

Perry Mason, Della Street, and Paul Drake

The new medium of paperbook books helped Gardner attract galaxies of readers. The smooth and brilliant Perry Mason, his beautiful, loyal secretary Della Street, and the always-there-at-the-last-second Paul Drake became national figures.

Although Gardner always saw himself as an "advocate for the downtrodden," there is little criticism of the system in his book. Justice always triumphs in an even-handed world that never punishes the wrong party. For Perry Mason's clients the system works as well as Gardner's genre formula did for him: "Ordinary readers see me as somebody they can identify with," he said. "I'm for the underdog. The average man is always in a state of supreme suspense because life is all complication with no conclusion. In my books he sees people get out of trouble."

The U.S. Army Corps of Engineers

South Pacific Division
630 Sansome Street
San Francisco 94111.
(415) 556-5630.

San Francisco District
211 Main Street
San Francisco 94105.
(415) 974-0356.

Los Angeles District
300 N. Los Angeles Street
Los Angeles 90012.
(213) 688-5320.

Sacramento District
650 Capitol Mall
Sacramento 95814.
(916) 440-2183.

The U.S. Army Corps of Engineers is a federal agency with broad powers and programs along the nation's coast and waterways. Breakwaters, jettys, shore engineering programs, erosion control projects, dredging, bay and harbor development, and many other types of California coastal projects are designed, approved, and/or maintained by the Corps. The agency's library and public relations officers offer excellent referrals and information on most technical subjects.

The Corps also conducts a wide-spread general public information and education campaign. Among the most outstanding recent contributions is the 1980 *California Coastline Explore Series* of 13 booklets, which tour the California Coast from Mexico to Oregon. The series has recently been re-issued and is available from the District offices.

CALIFORNIA COASTLINE EXPLORE SERIES:

1. Border to Klamath River
2. Klamath River to Punta Gorda
3. Punta Gorda to Arena Cove
4. Arena Cove to Golden Gate
5. San Francisco Bay
6. Sacramento–San Joaquin Delta
7. Golden Gate to Davenport
8. Davenport to Cape San Martin
9. Cape San Martin to Point Conception
10. Point Conception to Point Mugu
11. Point Mugu to Point Fermin
12. Point Fermin to Newport Beach
103. Newport Beach to The Mexican Border

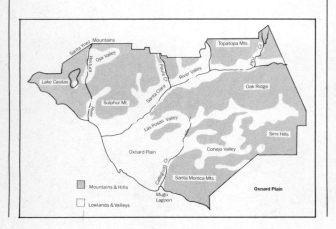

The Coast Highway

To finance the new highway up the coast, more than $50,000 was raised by private subscription, including a $5,000 donation from the San Francisco Chamber of Commerce. Not much money was raised in Ventura, where people foresaw slight economic opportunity from a highway that they thought would carry travelers straight through the county without stopping.

In order to maintain the State's interest in financing the coast highway, the funds raised by private subscription were earmarked for construction of causeways around the points where the old Camino Real road ran down on the beach, the spots frequently cut off by high tides and storms.

Because the railroad tracks lay at the foot of the bluffs, the Rincon causeway had to traverse the sea on a pile of bridges. From Rincon Point to Punta Gorda Beach three causeways were built over piles sunk in the sand. Many doubted that such a road could hold up against the assault of the sea. High waves from winter storms crashed so forcibly against the low-slung structures that they resembled matchsticks in a raging sea.

The Rincon road was completed and opened to

the public early in the summer of 1913, although the final connections were not completed until the middle of the next decade. The City of Ventura celebrated, and Santa Barbara—now linked to points south—rejoiced.

The fever of the Good Roads Movement gripped Ventura; suspicion and caution were banished. The Fourth of July celebrations on the main street featured a parade that marched across the new bridge. The festivities seemed to proclaim the community's faith in the four-square virtues of patriotism and road building.

San Buenaventura Becomes Ventura

Ventura began as a white settlement in the 1860s and 70s, originally taking the name of the nearby mission, San Buenaventura. For decades the town suffered severe isolation because of the high tides along Rincon Point that seriously hindered land travel to expanding commercial markets in Santa Barbara.

Eventually the railroad came to Ventura—its name shortened from San Buenaventura to fit on Southern Pacific's timetable—connecting the town to S.P.'s main line at Saugus, where the train from Los Angeles to San Francisco passed. The arrival of the railroad launched a land boom, which prompted construction of fine hotels like the Rose and Hotel DeLeon. But it also put the stage and steamship out of business, delaying actual prosperity until the 1920s when oil was discovered.

The Nation's Innkeeper

Ventura's most visible landmark is the highrise Holiday Inn that looms over the city with a revolving roof-top restaurant. Indeed, in three decades the Holiday Inn has influenced the appearance of practically all of roadside America.

The first Holiday Inn was established in 1952 on the outskirts of Memphis, Tennessee, by Kemmons Wilson, a devout Baptist real estate developer. Wilson had the simple idea of providing motoring Americans with a clean, reliable, inexpensive place to stay. He named his motel after a Bing Crosby–Fred Astaire movie, *Holiday Inn*.

Shortly after his first motel proved highly popular, Wilson built two others in the Memphis area. Soon he was franchising his concept to eager buyers across the country. Wilson seemed to have come up with an idea with just the right combination of middle-class respectability, family wholesomeness, and antiseptic cleanliness to defeat the unsavory image of motels as sleazy stops for salesmen and clandestine lovers.

So Long, Mom and Pop

In the process, Holiday Inn has put mom-and-pop operations out of business and launched a fast-growth industry. In 1971 a new Holiday Inn was being completed somewhere in the world every 2.5 days. By the end of the 1970s, the inns were grossing more than $7 million a day in room rentals, in addition to gigantic profits from the Holiday Inn restaurant chain, the country's second-largest (McDonalds is #1).

For years Holiday Inn built its reputation by appealing to the budget-minded family, offering predictable accommodations that provided security for the disoriented traveler. But recent years have brought significant changes to the company whose Southern Baptist directors until 1960 for-

bade liquor sales in all of the inns.

Holidomes—as inns with complete recreational facilities (swimming pools, saunas, exercise rooms, miniature golf, and table tennis) are called—are now leading the corporation's growth, as are hotel high-rises, many near airports. In 1977 Holiday Inn, displaying a surprising disregard for its conservative moral heritage, voted to go into the gambling business at Atlantic City. Despite detractors' frequent ridicule of the chain's conservative style, the inns' popularity has continued to grow.

Environment	Roadside Attractions	Resources

The Oxnard Plain

The Oxnard Plain is one of California's most fertile coastal lowlands and the economic center of Ventura County. The plain is bounded by segments of the Transverse Ranges, including Sulphur Mountain to the north, South Mountain to the northeast, and the Santa Monica Mountains to the southeast.

For more than 10,000 years, the Santa Clara River has brought rich deposits of alluvium to the plain from the surrounding mountains. The resulting five foot deep loamy sands and several hun-

dred feet of silty clay loams make the Oxnard Plain among the world's most fertile agricultural land. The soil here is especially suited to machine cultivation because of its organic content, great depth, lack of profile, effective moisture retention, and loamy texture.

The mountains surrounding the plain also protect it from harsh weather conditions. The weather is a modification of a typical dry-summer subtropical climate with few extremes of heat and cold, permitting a year-round growing season.

Ventura

California 1 joins the Ventura Freeway (US 101) at Wagon Wheel Road, home of the Wagon Wheel Restaurant, Wagon Wheel Motel, and the Wagon Wheel Bowling Alley. Very soon is the exit for Montalvo, named by the Southern Pacific Railroad for the Spanish author who coined the word California in his 16th-century romance *Las Sergas de Esplandiàn*. From the freeway quick glimpses of a truck stop and miniature golf course float by, roadside ephemera at 55 mph.

The high-rise Holiday Inn on California Street marks the heart of the town of Ventura's waterfront area. There are the promenade and the pier.

Old People, Lovers, and Others

Ventura's promenade, which runs from San Buenaventura Park to E. Figueroa Street, is an extremely well-designed public open space that gives form to the entire waterfront area. This landscaped concrete walkway accommodates the young, the old, the rich, the poor, and also sets a border between public and private areas, preventing the encroachment of either.

Stroll past Surfer's Point and watch experts on the glass boards, or observe the back-and-forth of volleyball players on the beach. There is a wealth of things to do around the promenade, from people watching to dining at the popular Pier Fish House, although nothing may surpass the simple pleasure of sitting on a bench on the promenade facing the sun and watching the ocean.

When the sea is in the proper mood, the sky has just the right shade of light, and the sea breeze is just sensuous enough to caress in a certain unexpected, loving way—then, sitting on a park bench in front of the ocean in Ventura, California, may be the very best that any day can offer.

City of Ventura Waterfront

The City of Ventura has taken good advantage of its waterfront area, preserving and developing a remarkable diversity of interest on the city's shoreline. Practically every type of beach goer is well accommodated along the 7.5 miles of shorefront between the Santa Clara to the Ventura Rivers.

Santa Clara Estuary Nature Preserve: a superb spot to view marshland wildlife habitat, especially birds. Located at the mouth of the Santa Clara River.
Peninsula Beach: offers good surfing and a protected swimming area along the southern peninsula of Ventura Harbor.
Ventura Harbor: there are two marinas in this inland harbor and a wealth of facilities for boat owners and fisherman. Channel Islands National Park Headquarters.
Marina Park: Picnic facilities, playground, bikepath, and sand dunes.
San Buenaventura State Beach: offers the area's best swimming along a handsome wide beach in addition to complete facilities, including showers, dressing rooms, picnic areas, bike path, volleyball, beach equipment rental, and snack bar.

Ventura Pier: originally constructed in 1872, the 1700 foot long pier is one of the longest on the west coast. Restaurant.
Promenade Park: A well-designed promenade that offers Ventura's best spot for a stroll, whether to watch the rolling blue ocean, volleyball players on the sand, or the varieties of human behavior at a California beach.
Surfers Point Park: has not much to recommend it but excellent surfing, which for many is enough.
Ventura County Fairgrounds Beach: A small rocky beach south of Ventura River.

Ventura Historical Sites

OLIVAS ADOBE
654-7837

ORTEGA ADOBE
654-7837

SAN BUENAVENTURA CITY HALL
654-7800

SAN BUENAVENTURA MISSION
643-4318

PACIFIC

OCEAN

SANTA BARBARA CO
VENTURA CO

150

Pitas Point

101

33

①

Ventura

★ CHANNEL
ISLANDS
NATIONAL
PARK VISITOR
CENTER

126

Gonzales Road

OXNARD

W. 5th Road

Port Hueneme

Ventura

101

34

34

Hueneme Road

Wood Road

Road

Point Mugu

①

0 ————— 8
Miles

VENTURA CO
LOS ANGELES CO

Island History

Although they are remarkable principally for the absence of most marks of civilization, the Channel Islands have been inhabited since prehistoric times. The Chumash Indians built habitations on the islands and traded the game and fish they caught to mainlanders.

For hundreds of years the Chumash existed on the islands, in easy concord with their environment, until they were eventually removed by Europeans to coastal missions on the mainland. The first European to visit the Channel Islands was Juan Rodriguez Cabrillo in October, 1542. Cabrillo is believed to be buried on San Miguel Island, although his grave has never been located.

The arrival of white adventurers, whalers and fur hunters in the mid-1800s inaugurated a new era on the quiet islands. Death filled the air as whales were killed in droves and thousands of sea mammals were hunted for their pelts nearly to extinction.

Near the turn of the 20th century, several attempts at farming were undertaken. Forage crops were tried, generally without success. More successful were cattle ranching and sheep herding. In 1880 Justinian Care established a colony of French and Italian immigrants on Santa Cruz Island who produced, in addition to sheep and cattle, walnuts, olives, honey, almonds, and some of the highest regarded wine grown in early California.

In 1938, President Franklin Roosevelt declared Santa Barbara and Anacapa Islands to be a national monument. Ranching and farming activities were stopped, and few residents remained. One exception was "Frenchy" Le Dreau, a hermit who lived in a seaside shack at Anacapa Island and greeted visitors from 1928 to 1956.

At various times Anacapa, Santa Barbara, and San Miguel Islands have been sites of military installations. From the 1930s to 1963, San Miguel Island was used as a bombing range and missile target area, a practice that stopped when the Navy transferred management of the island's natural and cultural resources to the National Park Service.

Santa Cruz Island and the Nature Conservancy

The largest and most topographically diverse of the Channel Islands, Santa Cruz Island rises wild and rugged out of the Pacific Ocean like a miniature continent. Its 96 square miles include major earthquake faults, Indian middens, freshwater streams, creeks, springs, and pristine coastal beaches and dunes.

The majority of Santa Cruz Island has been owned since 1937 by the Stanton family under the name of the Santa Cruz Island Company, which runs a "functional 19th century cattle ranch" on the property. Yet despite its private ownership, Santa Cruz Island faces a secure future, protected from the possibility of harmful development.

In 1978 Dr. Carey Stanton entered into a partnership agreement with the Nature Conservancy to preserve the natural resources of Santa Cruz Island in perpetuity. The Conservancy, a national non-profit membership organization that protects and manages ecologically significant natural areas, raised $2.5 million to purchase the Santa Cruz Island Company property, part of which was bought out

right and part of which will be transferred to the Conservancy in 2008. In the meantime, a conservation easement over the property ensures the preservation of its unique natural resources.

The Conservancy's acquisition of Santa Cruz Island was initiated by a major corporate gift. Foundations and individuals also provided donations that made the project possible and helped establish a management program that allows careful stewardship of the island and directed scientific research. A Public Use Plan outlines allowable uses of the island that do not threaten its resources and emphasizes the island's biological and historical importance.

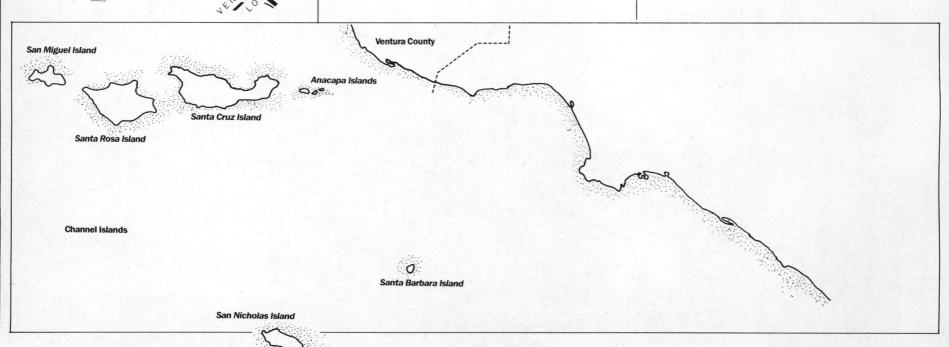

San Miguel Island

Ventura County

Anacapa Islands

Santa Cruz Island

Santa Rosa Island

Channel Islands

Santa Barbara Island

San Nicholas Island

Environment	Roadside Attractions	Resources

Life on the Islands

The five islands within Channel Islands National Park mark the western tip of the Santa Monica Mountains segment of the Transverse Range, having been uplifted by folding and faulting approximately 3 million years ago. At that time, the islands were connected to the mainland by the ancient Cabrillo Peninsula, which eventually subsided, leaving the peaks adrift at sea.

Most of the islands consist of open wind-swept land areas with short and scrubby vegetation that

causes a brown and somewhat desolate appearance. One noteable exception to the uncolorful landscape is the rare giant coreopsis, or tree sunflower, that reaches heights of ten feet in some of Anacapa Island's protected canyons. In the spring this unusual looking plant sprouts huge yellow flowers, which cause the island to appear in the distance like a giant green and yellow table.

Although San Miguel Island is the westernmost of the Channel Island chain and thus the most exposed to harsh weather conditions, it hosts several rare plants, including live-forever, wild buckwheat, and rose mallow.

All of the islands are surrounded by rocky cliffs, usually quite steep. There are few sandy beaches, but several rocky coves that attract divers from all over the world. The cliffs themselves are home for several major sea bird colonies, including anklets, cormorants, gulls, guillemots, snowy plovers, and brown pelicans.

Along the edges of most of the islands are enormous colonies of California Sea Lions, harbor seals, Northern fur seals, and elephant seals. In the turbulent waters around the islands, giant kelp forests provide shelter for frolicking dolphins and porpoises. Whales and sharks swim in deeper waters near the islands with a variety of game fish including rockfish, perch, sanddabs, and sheepshead.

Channel Islands Visitor Center

Within Ventura Harbor is the headquarters for the Channel Islands National Park, a modern $2 million visitors' center that is its own attraction. In the open-air entry an interesting photo exhibit portrays the islands' highlights and most appealing features. Inside, the center features a living tidepool, a garden of island plants, three-dimensional models of the islands, and a series of engaging dioramas. There is also a bookstore, and movies

about the islands are screened regularly.

The stairway above the Visitors' Center leads to an observation deck that has its own unique display—an interpretive marine exhibit that illustrates life at various levels of the sea. From the observation deck you can view the islands beyond the coastline to the north and south. Should you require encouragement to visit the Channel Islands, the Visitor Center will supply it.

Channel Islands National Park

Visitor Center
1901 Spinnaker Drive,
Ventura 93001.
644-8464.

In 1980, Channel Islands National Monument was redesignated a national park. The National Park Service administers three of the five islands: Anacapa, Santa Barbara, and San Miguel. Santa Cruz and Santa Rosa Islands are privately owned, although most of Santa Cruz Island is in the process of being turned over to the non-profit Nature Conservancy. The Channel Islands Visitor Center is open daily 8:30–5:30 p.m. Free.

Visiting the Islands

Commercial Boat Service is available from many Southern California ports, although sometimes on an irregular basis. Contact Park Headquarters in Ventura for up-to-date transportation information.

ISLAND PACKERS CRUISES
1867 Spinnaker Drive,
Ventura 93001.
642-1393.

Extensive programs to the islands, including 1 and 2 day powerboat and schooner sailing day trips. Advance reservations advised.

CHANNEL ISLANDS LANDING
3821 Victoria Avenue,
Oxnard 93030.
985-6059.

Sailboat rental by the hour. Open daily.

CAPTAIN JACK'S
Channel Island Sportfishing Center
4151 South Victoria Avenue,
Oxnard 93030.
985-8511.

Day trips for excursions, deep-sea fishing, whale watching. Open 24 hours a day.

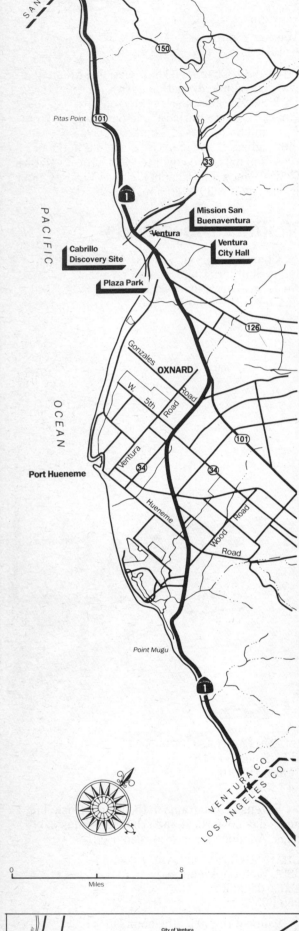

When Cabrillo Discovered California

Although California 1's route through Ventura County is no longer called Cabrillo Highway, the first European discoverer of California probably set foot on Ventura's shore on October 10, 1542, while looking for an island paradise populated by black Amazon women. (Designation of State Highway 1 as Cabrillo Highway was removed on July 7, 1959 south of Santa Barbara because of confusion with Santa Barbara's Cabrillo Boulevard. Between Santa Barbara and San Francisco, California 1 is still designated Cabrillo Highway, although rarely referred to as such.)

Juan Rodriguez Cabrillo was a Portuguese-born sailor who sought the Northwest Passage to the Atlantic and found instead the "land of the Califanos," first at San Diego in September 1542, and then at the Channel Islands and Ventura a month later.

When Cabrillo came ashore at Ventura he found not Amazons but Chumash Indians who lived in a large village that soon came to be called El Pueblo de las Canoas (the town of the canoes) after the well built boats caulked with Ventura asphalt that crowded the shoreline.

A great deal of uncertainty surrounds the actual location of the spot where Cabrillo discovered El Pueblo de las Canoas, although most historians place the location near Figueroa and Palm streets. Others, however, place the spot at Mugu Lagoon or even Rincon Point.

While investigating nearby San Miguel Island, Cabrillo fell and broke his arm. Undeterred, he continued his voyage north to Monterey and Fort Ross, where he soon returned due to heavy seas. Shortly after his arrival at San Miguel Island, Cabrillo died, probably from an infection to his arm.

The Spanish Influence

Cabrillo first sailed to California on behalf of the Spanish flag in 1542. From that year forward, land use patterns in the state were established according to a highly sophisticated Spanish settlement strategy. By the 1770s, the strategy was well-developed and ingrained on the California landscape.

The reasoning behind Spanish land use planning was based on international competition, as was the case in all development in the new world. The Spanish realized the importance of protecting their stronghold, and the best way to do this was by a three part program: presidio—mission—pueblo.

The presidios were established first. These were the military encampments, whose goals were to defend the coastline, subdue hostile natives, and begin to develop friendly relations with non-hostile natives. But perhaps the most important task of the presidios was to set up a protective envelope of land control so the next phase of development could peacefully occur—the missions.

Missions were at the heart of Spanish expansion. Guided by economic as well as spiritual imperatives, the missionaries were sent to save the heathen soul and to convert Native Americans into the embrace of European ideals of civilization, culture, and commerce. This could only be done under the military protection of the presidios, and so it was that the Spanish missions stretched along the first road in California's coastal zone—the Royal Road, or El Camino Real.

The last step in the planned Spanish land use development was the pueblo, or civilian community established to provide a legitimate long-term Spanish presence, and to offer examples of behavior to the mission natives. A good plan, but in fact, only three pueblos were actually founded before Spanish influence gave way to Mexican dominance, and eventually to American occupation.

Despite its ultimate failure in dominating the California coastal landscape, the Spanish presidio, mission, pueblo system did establish a stronghold for many of today's coastal towns, all linked by El Camino Real, which in many places coincides with Highway 1's present route.

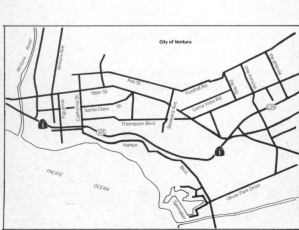

Environment

Roadside Attractions

Resources

Ventura's Pride

A burst of flame on every side,
  Poinsettia;
Our California winter's pride,
  Poinsettia;
In your rare beauty you arise
Beneath the blue Ventura skies,
Of all the flowers the greatest prize,
  Poinsettia.

When summer's gone and with it all,
  Poinsettia,
Queen Flora's offspring, great and small,
  Poinsettia,
'Tis then you wondrous, brightest thing,
Flash like flamingoes high awing,
In dazzling red, and pleasure bring,
  Poinsettia.

In raiment of a Balkan bride,
  Poinsettia,
You match the sunset o'er the tide,
  Poinsettia;
Your throne is here and you preside
Queen by Pacific water's side;
Small wonder you're Ventura's pride,
  Poinsettia.

Poinsettia, E. M. Sheridan, 1925.

Ventura calls itself "The Poinsettia City." Since 1925 residents have celebrated a festive annual Poinsettia Festival to honor the scarlet flowers that grow in such profusion in the favorable Ventura climate.

The large red poinsettia with its flower-like bracts (they are not the flower) is actually a tropical American species of Euphorbia. The plant is commonly associated with Christmas and usually seen in pots elsewhere, but in Ventura it abounds in its natural form as a shrub, reaching stunning heights of ten or even twenty feet.

Downtown

Ventura's main street boasts some of the oldest attractions of any rehabilitated California "old town" area—about 3,500 years old, in fact. In 1973, when bulldozing for a better Ventura, construction crews and archeologists came upon a fire hearth dating to 1600 BC, a 2,300-year-old earth oven, and the remains of the original San Buenaventura mission. All these uncovered artifacts are on display at the Albinger Archaeological Museum at the site, along with such intriguing esoterica as Chinese opium pipes, early American glassware, and age-old ceramics.

Plaza Park

Ventura's main district also contains the reconstructed Mission San Buenaventura, founded by Father Junípero Serra and the ninth of 21 Spanish missions in California. See too the nearby Ventura County Historical Museum. Figueroa Plaza deserves little comment, but nearby Plaza Park is a quiet pleasant open space, with a 100-year-old Morton bay fig tree. Facing Plaza Park is the Mitchell Block, on Thompson Blvd, which is the only intact residential block left in downtown Ventura (built between 1885 and 1826). Pierano's Store, the city's oldest brick structure (1874), is worth visiting for its historical interest or for its array of picnic food.

Should you desire to shop in a restored livery stable, the Old Town Livery (1870) awaits you. Downtown's most dazzling attraction, however, is City Hall. Designed by Albert C. Martin and dedicated in 1913 as the County Courthouse, this elaborately handsome Beaux Arts building with an Italian marble staircase and stained-glass domes speaks from an era when public architecture declared itself in heraldic terms.

History

Ventura County Historical Society Museum
100 East Main Street,
Ventura 93001.
653-0323.

Open 10 a.m. to 5 p.m. Tuesday–Saturday. Free.

Albinger Archaeological Museum
113 East Main Street,
Ventura 93001.
648-5823.

Open 10 a.m. to 5 p.m. Tuesday–Saturday. Free.

Carnegie Cultural Arts Center and Historical Society Museum
424 South C Street,
Oxnard 93030.
486-4311.

Photos, historical displays (downstairs, 1–4:40 p.m.) and cultural and archaeological exhibits (upstairs, 10 a.m.–5 p.m.). Tuesday–Saturday. Free.

Visitor Assistance

Oxnard Chamber of Commerce
228 S. "A" Street,
Oxnard 93030.
487-6305.

Oxnard Convention Bureau
325 Esplanade Drive,
Oxnard 93030.
485-8833.

Greater Ventura Visitor Bureau
185 South Seaward Avenue
Ventura 93003.
648-2075.

Channel Island
Chamber of Commerce
116 West Channel Islands Blvd.,
Oxnard 93030.
985-2244.

SANTA BARBARA

SANTA BARBARA COUNTY is divided into two distinctly different geographic halves, separated by Point Conception on the coast and Gaviota Pass a few miles inland. The southeastern half of Santa Barbara is polished and beautiful, the western half is rough and wild. Traveling from one end of the county to the other is nothing if not a study in contrasts.

A major aspect of the county's identity is defined by the City of Santa Barbara, California's most well-groomed coastal city. Offshore, oil derricks stand forelornly against an uneven horizon, industrial giants from an unpretty world.

Highway 1 begins just beyond Gaviota Pass and rambles quietly through the Lompoc Valley heading generally north. Just before Lompoc, the rough uneven landscape gives way to fields of flowers and miraculous contrasts of colors, as Highway 1 courses through the heart of the world's major flower seed growing area. Just past Lompoc is Vandenberg Air Force Base, the future home of the space shuttle. Highway 1's northward route ends at the town of Guadalupe, just south of the Santa Maria River, the County line.

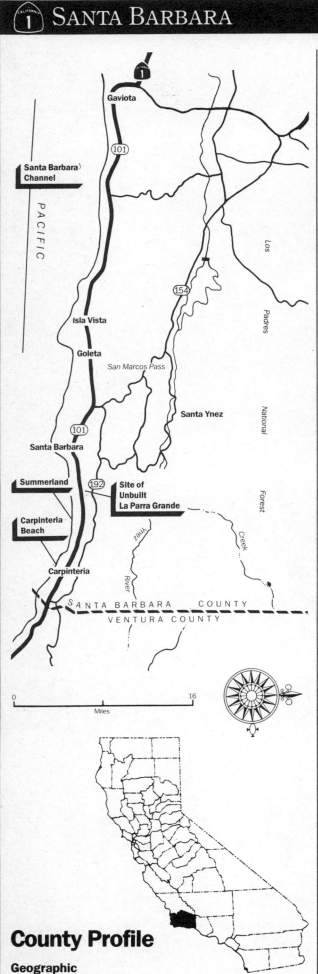

A Mecca for the Moribund

The first travelers to Santa Barbara were attracted by publications that rhapsodized over the area's healthful environment. From about 1870, Santa Barbara was aggressively promoted as the "Sanatorium of the Pacific," where visitors could luxuriate near the "quiet restfulness of the wave-caressed sand," or enjoy ocean breezes "laden with the vital elements that inspire one to exertion."

Southern California for Invalids

The principal advocate of Santa Barbara's healthy charms was Charles Nordhoff, an easterner whose *California for Settlers and Travelers* became a best-seller from the day it was first serialized in *Harper's Magazine* in 1873. The book was immeasurably influential in the early development of Santa Barbara. After reading Nordhoff's chapter "Southern California for Invalids," the sickly, feeble, and frail came from all over the world to be cured by the wholesome therapeutic climate.

In his enthusiasm for the region, Nordhoff claimed that Santa Barbara had the most beneficial climate of any city on the coast, although he admonished consumptives to avoid the cold and foggy beach. Near-magical powers were attributed to the town's environment, as Nordhoff and others indulged in unshy hyperbole.

One proponent of Santa Barbara's healthful environment, Dr. Samuel Brinkerhoff, even went so far as to claim wonder-working powers for the petroleum fumes that reeked from cracks in the ocean floor. According to Brinkerhoff, the fumes cured respiratory ailments.

By 1872, Santa Barbara had become "a crowded sanatorium," with throngs of people arriving on every steamer. The possibilities for healthy profits were impossible to overlook.

La Parra Grande

Among coastal California's unbuilt glories and magnificent might-have-beens is La Parra Grande at Montecito, designed in 1914 by architect Louis Christian Mullgardt, whose fantastic Court of the Ages graced the 1915 Panama-Pacific Exhibition in San Francisco.

La Parra Grande was to have featured a grandiose center hotel and court, adapting Spanish street architecture to California by means of cottages and hundreds of gardens. La Parra Grande surely would have been the crown jewel among Santa Barbara's collection of elite, luxury hotels and a coastal art piece *non plus ultra*.

County Profile

Geographic

Land Area (acres)	1,752,320
Land Area (sq. miles)	2,738.0
Water Area (acres)	4,260
Water Area (sq. miles)	6.7
Acres in Public Ownership	870,802.17
Percent in Public Ownership	49.66
Miles of Public Roads	2,288
County Seat	Santa Barbara

Demographic

Population	313,500
State Rank by Population	16
Projected 1990 Population	329,400
Unemployment Rate (state avg. = 9.9)	7.4
Per Capita Personal Income	$12,218
State Rank by Income	10
Total Assessed Property Value	$9,954,962,733

Utopia by the Sea

When H. L. Williams came to Santa Barbara County in 1888, it was to form a new utopian community based on the precepts of Spiritualism. Williams held camp meetings, and people came from all over the country to feast and dance, important rituals to the utopians. Williams sold them 25' × 60' lots for $25, and many built houses.

For seven years the community developed unobtrusively. Williams set aside land for a school, a temple, and four parks. The utopians named their community Summerland for its even, pleasant climate.

Then in 1895 the outside world impudently intruded when a giant pool of highly profitable oil was discovered. Suddenly Summerland was covered with long wharves and derricks; the stench of oil filled the air. The Southern Pacific Railroad advertised: "See the oil wells in the sea."

The utopians who had purchased their small lots for $25 were suddenly rich—although many of them sat contemplating the sudden arrival of the dark industrial world and wondered what had become of paradise.

The Santa Barbara Channel

The Santa Barbara Channel extends offshore for 70 miles between Oxnard and Point Conception, bounded on the seaward side by the northern shores of the islands of San Miguel, Santa Rosa, Santa Cruz, and Anacapa. This is one of the most productive and diverse marine ecosystems in the world, a product—like much of the rest of Santa Barbara's environment—of the unusual east-west alignment of the continental mass.

Within Santa Barbara's Channel, northern

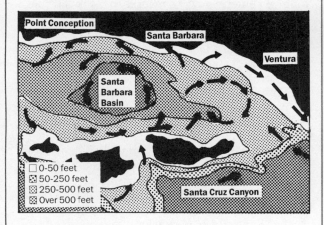

Point Conception
Santa Barbara
Ventura
Santa Barbara Basin
Santa Cruz Canyon
☐ 0-50 feet
▦ 50-250 feet
▨ 250-500 feet
▥ Over 500 feet

currents sweep their cold, nutrient-rich waters southward toward a swirling marriage with warm-temperature waters moving up to the northwest from Southern California.

Here the abrupt coastal geological reorientation of the state at Point Conception creates an offshore eddy or gyre that works like a giant mixer, blending waters from two very different Pacific provinces. The resulting concoction is a third world of the ocean—a unique water climate that combines characteristics of both north and south.

Circular Motion: Gyres and Waterspouts

A gyre, also called an eddy, is a circular current of water caused by a sudden interference of a current by a point of land such as Point Conception or the Channel Islands. A gyre's speed, size, and power depend upon the land's configuration and the speed and direction of the current's movement. In the Santa Barbara Channel strong currents from both the north and south meet in a varied geological cradle of islands, shore, and ocean floor to create many complex gyres.

Gyres are constant, natural phenomena in the Santa Barbara Channel. Rarer are waterspouts, fascinating to behold, but awesome and extremely dangerous. Since antiquity writers have recorded the antics of waterspouts, calling them variously sea dragons, great serpents, or magical spirits.

On New Year's Eve of 1878 such a spirit reared its head in the Santa Barbara Channel. Within minutes, the spout had skimmed across the water's surface and come ashore, smashing anchored ships near Stearn's Wharf and cutting a swath of destruction across the lower West Side north to Canon Perdido Street. Houses were demolished, people injured, and at least one person died.

Waterspouts obey few natural laws. They vary in size and behavior, color and intensity, location (from the cold arctic waters to balmy tropics, from sea to bays, river, even lakes), and character (appearing within storm systems or as blazing whirls on the clearest, most blue-skied of days). Sometimes a spout seems to emerge from the ocean; other times to touch down from the heavens. It may radiate no sound or arrive with the roar of a locomotive.

A true waterspout always dissipates quickly on land. But, like the one in Santa Barbara, it can wreak havoc first and deposit rains of worms, fish, frogs, and driftwood miles inland.

County Line

California l's northward route through Santa Barbara begins above Gaviota Pass, about 50 miles northwest of the Ventura County line. But much of Santa Barbara County's identity is defined by the presence of the City of Santa Barbara, the county seat, major metropolitan area, and one of the most popular tourist destinations in the state.

Santa Barbara

Even tempered and well manicured, Santa Barbara has always prided itself on its good looks and appeal to California's moneyed class. Its careful appearance has come to illustrate a particular type of the California good life that is neither extravagant, flamboyant nor shrill, that assumes the satisfaction of well-earned reward.

Although Santa Barbara is the home of many who are stupendously wealthy, and has cultivated its image of a playground for the rich since its earliest days, there's another Santa Barbara, described in the city's 1936 *WPA Guide,* as "not merely a show city; not just a resort of suave leisure and play:"

There are thousands of storekeepers, clerks, stenographers, laborers, taxi drivers, salesmen, agents, and professional men and women, and these make up the average Santa Barbaran, a very regular, ordinary American citizen. He has an automobile in his stucco garage, a radio in this red-tiled bungalow, an orange or an avocado tree behind his kitchen, a strip of yellow poppies or rosebushes, giant poinsettas or a pepper tree in the back corner of the lot, and tries to have at least one window that catches a glimpse of the blue ocean or the majestic purple of the mountains.

AREA CODE: 805

Public Transportation

965-5184 MTD Bus & Transit Center
965-5184 Mini Bus
963-3844 Dial-A-Ride
252-0001 Amtrak (1-800)
963-1351 Greyhound
963-3717 Open Air Bikes

Rules of the Road

For most of its route from the southern county line, the coast highway (U.S. 101) races astride the ocean as a freeway. In the heart of Santa Barbara, however, the highway loses its freeway status, and serious traffic congestion is often the result. North of the Gaviota Pass, Highway 1 resumes after an approximate 50 mile hiatus. Be sure to watch for the exit sign.

133° in the Shade

On June 17, 1859, Santa Barbara and the Goleta Valley were seared by a freak simoon, a hot dry wind, blowing from the northwest. Temperatures reached 133 degrees by mid afternoon and stayed there for more than two hours. Birds died on the wing, livestock dropped at their watering troughs, fruit fried on trees, and residents sought the insulation of the thick-walled adobe buildings in town. According to the U.S. Coastal Survey, the heat wave set an unofficial high for the U.S., broken in 1934 by a 134° reading in Death Valley.

Climate

Santa Barbara's climate is what gives it its reputation as a true Garden of Eden. The weather is mild and balmy, and in the City of Santa Barbara itself, because of the unusual east-west alignment of the coast, one may sit on a beach in sunshine for the entire day. Average winter temperatures for the county are lows of 47°and highs of 66°. In the summer, the average ranges from 56° to 72°.

The Approach of Civility

As Santa Barbara matured, the invalids' sanctuary became the pleasure seekers' resort. The town assumed the character of a city, and its appeal to tourists increased. Gas lights were installed on State Street in 1872, adding charm and symbolizing a shining future for the town. That same year the Lobero Theater was completed. With a suspended balcony and a curtain that had once adorned the proscenium of a San Francisco opera house, the Lobero was the largest adobe

structure in California and an emblem of cultural sophistication for 50 years.

By the mid 1870s, Santa Barbara boasted several bathhouses that catered to a new breed of beachgoers who sought pleasure instead of cures. Proprietors charged 15 cents for bathing, towels, and bathing suits.

Indecent Exposure

A faint aura of impropriety and sexual misconduct seemed to emanate from the bathhouses, though they allowed little real opportunity for improper conduct, sexual or otherwise. Charges of "indecent exposure" by local bluenoses prompted owners to enforce a dress code that required frolickers to be covered from "the shoulder to the knees." Bathers swam in the calm surf and wondered what all the commotion was about.

The quest for pleasure in Santa Barbara also inspired racetracks to be developed near the waterfront. At Ocean Beach Park, or Bradley's, near the present-day bird refuge, daily races attracted good crowds despite the soggy marsh that made for poor footing for the horses. Later, the old *estrero*—a one-time garbage dump—was

converted into a fine fairground with an agricultural pavilion and a grandstand from which visitors could watch horse races, circuses, and balloon ascensions.

With more tourists came improvements in transportation. In 1876 a mule-drawn streetcar was put into service from the bathhouses along West Beach into town, where new hotels were rising to meet the transient influx. Following Charles Nordhoff's advice, new hotels were not built near the beach for the sake of the consumptives. The finest hotel of the century, the Arlington, was located here.

The Santa Barbara Oil Spill

On January 28, 1969, a tragic oil spill focused the eyes and minds of the world on the Santa Barbara Channel. The Santa Barbara oil spill tragically high-lighted the potential dangers of spills and the inadequcy of clean-up technology in the 1960s.

On Tuesday, the 28th, the Union Oil Company began sinking a fourth well on its newly constructed platform in the Santa Barbara Channel. At 10:45 AM, gas broke out from a hole and started spewing up through the drill pipe. Workers followed emergency procedures to block the hole, but the pressure of the blockage caused fracture lines on the ocean floor to break apart. The well was out of control, and oil and gas bubbled up to the water's surface from at least four spots around the platform.

The oil flowed uncontrolled for 10 days, releasing close to 2,000 barrels of oil a day into the Santa Barbara Channel and producing a slick that covered 803 square miles. The total spill was estimated at 3.25 million gallons, which contaminated miles of beautiful beaches and marshes. At least 3,600 birds died, and a valuable fishery and recreation area was despoiled. The long-term effects of the spill are still not fully understood.

The Santa Barbara spill served as a rallying point for advocates of closer review and regulation of offshore drilling. Offshore activities became an important issue in the 1972 California election, when voters approved a development moratorium along the coast, a prelude to the establishment of the California Coastal Commission. The spill also helped shock Congress into passing the National Environmental Policy Act, cornerstone of federal environmental legislation. Outraged Santa Barbara citizens organized GOO (Get Oil Out) to undertake a massive educational and lobbying campaign, and the oil companies and responsible public agencies pushed forward to develop elaborate and effective safety controls and spill clean-up technology.

Oil on the Ocean

Except for major accidental spills, these are the sources for most of the oil occurring on the ocean's surface:

29.4% Auto crankcase oil
28.4% Tankers
17.3% Other vessels
15.3% Industrial waste oil
 6.1% Refinery, petrochemical plants disposal
 2.1% Offshore production
 1.4% Tank barges

Oil In the Environment

Oil is a noxious presence in a marine environment. Even when it occurs naturally, seeping up through underwater crevices, it can coat the ocean's floor, destroying bottom life and coming ashore in "tar blobs" that blacken the bottoms of the feet of birds and humans, suffocating tidal grasses and seaweeds in the process. And when quantities of oil are deposited in the ocean as a result of human misadventure, the effect can be disastrous.

Impacts to Birds and Marine Life

Seabirds rely on their feathers for warmth and insulation from icy ocean waters, as well as for buoyancy. When a bird's feathers pick up oil—whether from accumulated small "normal" industrial discharges or a major spill—the bird is in grave danger. Its metabolism triples in order to maintain normal body temperature, feeding usually ceases, and stored fat is quickly dissolved for warmth. Death from starvation often follows.

If the bird does not starve, it may become waterlogged and—although one of the most buoyant creatures on earth—it may sink and drown. Yet other birds suffocate from oil clogged in the mouth and nostrils. Birds who survive oil contamination may experience severe dehydration and persistent infirmity, as oil swallowed during preening interferes with the creature's digestive ability to turn seawater into freshwater.

Marine mammals, especially the sea otter and fur seal, are also vulnerable to oil. Otters and fur seals, for example, rely on air pockets trapped in their thick underfur for both warmth and buoyancy. When oil penetrates the outer hairs, they—like seabirds—may lose buoyancy and warmth. Oil in the food chain of seals, sea lions, and whales also leads to both immediate and chronic ailments.

Animals at the lower levels of the marine food chain also suffer the toxic effects of oil. For instance, the Northern Gulf spill in Maine killed 33,000 pounds of lobsters and almost 3 million pounds of clams, and for a decade, hydrocarbons persisted in local sediments and clams.

Concentrations of oil of only 10 parts per million (ppm) can kill shellfish; 1 ppm reduces oysters' growth rates and is deadly to fish eggs and larvae. (Simon visualizes 1 ppm as a martini with an ounce of vermouth to 32,000 quarts of gin.) In mature fish like the anadromous striped bass and salmon, oil destroys chemical sensory processes and interferes with a homing mechanism critical for survival of the species.

When oil sinks to the ocean floor, it spreads out like an asphalt desert, killing all life and remaining toxic for as long as 10 years, aiding erosion and the spread of pollution during that time. Onshore and in tidal flats, eelgrass and marine algae are stunted by low oil concentrations and seldom survive high ones.

The Waterfront

Santa Barbara's quest for the City Beautiful has resulted in a superb waterfront area, one of the most elegant on the Pacific coast. Along Cabrillo Boulevard many stately elements combine to form an ordered shorefront environment that achieves an almost majestic quality. The uniform Corinthian palms and manicured green lawns evoke a world of grand and courtly Mediterranean palace grounds.

But Santa Barbara remains in California, and the principal appeal of the waterfront area—its vitality—remains totally Californian. Bright sunshine and smiling faces bicycling, roller-skating, jogging, strolling, and swimming. The waterfront is Santa Barbara's most democratized area, where an array of attractions and activities are available for everybody.

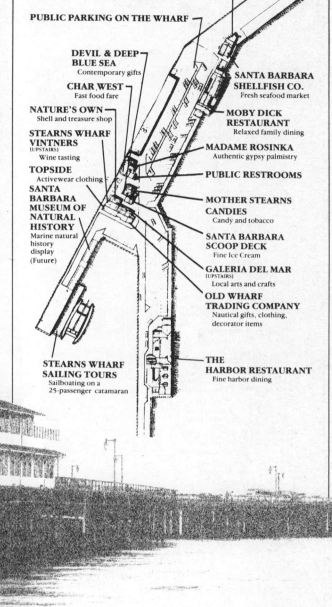

J.P.'s BAIT AND TACKLE
Bait and tackle

PUBLIC PARKING ON THE WHARF

DEVIL & DEEP BLUE SEA
Contemporary gifts

CHAR WEST
Fast food fare

NATURE'S OWN
Shell and treasure shop

STEARNS WHARF VINTNERS
(UPSTAIRS)
Wine tasting

TOPSIDE
Activewear clothing

SANTA BARBARA MUSEUM OF NATURAL HISTORY
Marine natural history display (Future)

STEARNS WHARF SAILING TOURS
Sailboating on a 25-passenger catamaran

SANTA BARBARA SHELLFISH CO.
Fresh seafood market

MOBY DICK RESTAURANT
Relaxed family dining

MADAME ROSINKA
Authentic gypsy palmistry

PUBLIC RESTROOMS

MOTHER STEARNS CANDIES
Candy and tobacco

SANTA BARBARA SCOOP DECK
Fine Ice Cream

GALERIA DEL MAR
(UPSTAIRS)
Local arts and crafts

OLD WHARF TRADING COMPANY
Nautical gifts, clothing, decorator items

THE HARBOR RESTAURANT
Fine harbor dining

Stearns Wharf

Stearns Wharf is a focal point of activity that defines the center of the waterfront area. Although a number of shops and restaurants are located on the wharf, the city has sought to prevent the overcommercializing of one of Santa Barbara's most enduring resources.

You might enjoy taking a tour on a 25-foot catamaran from Stearns Wharf Tours or simply listening to a free Wednesday afternoon concert. Marine living lab sessions are held on Fridays. Any day is superb for strolling the pier to view the beautiful Santa Barbara Channel and to observe how fine the city appears. Should you desire to fish, rental equipment and bait are available.

On the arm of the pier is the Nature Conservancy, a nonprofit organization that protects and preserves resource lands. Their informative exhibits include a display on their preserve at Santa Cruz Island. At the other end of the wharf the Santa Barbara Shellfish Company, a first-rate fresh fish stand, will cook your selection to order for a wonderful picnic on the pier.

From Ruin to Restoration

John Stearn's wharf has figured prominently in the life of Santa Barbara since the first health seekers came to town in the early 1870s. Six years after the pier was built, a rampaging storm dashed it to ruin. Almost as soon as the pier was repaired, it was damaged again by Santa Barbara's famous waterspout.

In 1941 moviestar Ronald Coleman opened a restaurant on the wharf. James Cagney assumed its ownership after World War II. For decades Stearns Wharf existed in relative tranquility. But in 1973 a fire swept the wharf and burned it to bits. It sat in hulking ruin until the end of 1981, when a new Stearns Wharf rose from the ashes, rebuilt with the aid of public funds that included oil industry compensation for the 1969 spill.

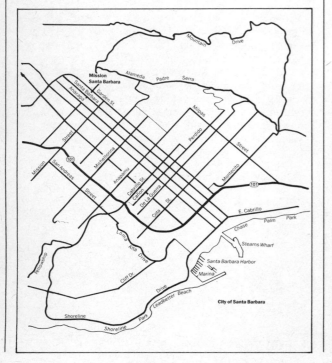

City of Santa Barbara

The Arlington

The Arlington Hotel was built for $160,000 by the hard-driving Colonel Hollister, who formed a syndicate to accommodate wealthy pleasure seekers desirous of well-being amid an atmosphere of coastal luxury. Each room had a bathtub with silver fixtures and a private fireplace that burned almond wood.

The Arlington was one of the grand coastal resort hotels of 19th-century California, along with the Del Coronado in San Diego and the Del Monte in

Monterey. It expressed opulence and exotic refinement while pandering to the richest of the rich.

A Wheeled Future

The end of the 19th century brought foreshadowings of a future Santa Barbara could little imagine. In 1896 the horse-drawn streetcars were replaced by up-to-the-minute electric trolleys. A parade up State Street to celebrate the event included a tram pulling a flatcar with an old gray mule on top—a horse-car veteran saddled with a sign "My Last Trip—1876–1896."

By 1899 the first Oldsmobile "automobile wagon" made its way up State Street, marking the advent of a wheeled future. The first order of business for the new century, however, was to make ready for the arrival of the railroad.

Tourism and Santa Barbara

Santa Barbara's beauty, scale, land use, and architecture reflect long-standing local values of what constitutes "good" development. Santa Barbara is a town originally built by, and then for, tourists. People came here for the beauty and health of the place, then fought to preserve those attributes. The early wealthy bought waterfront land to prevent "undesirable" commerce, and they enacted some of the state's earliest and strongest land-use controls.

Tourism is good business in Santa Barbara, and business has never been better. In 1963 visitors spent an estimated $39 million; 21 years later visitor expenditures topped $490 million. Hotel transient occupancy taxes raised an additional $3,375,901 for the city in 1984, more for the county. Tourist-related jobs account for one of the largest employment categories in the city.

Most of the money collected from the hotel tax is plowed back into promoting tourism and supporting major annual tourist events such as the Fiesta. Thousands are spent on professional advertising campaigns to convince residents of nearby cities that Santa Barbara is the place for short or extended vacations. Advertisements proclaim the historic interest, the healthy air, the resort amenities, and—most of all—the beauty of Santa Barbara, a beauty that is good for business.

The Flying A Studios

Once Santa Barbara had a far different hold on California's dream life than it does today. For a short period before the 1920s Santa Barbara reigned as the capital of the film industry. More than a dozen local film studios pumped out thousands of major productions for worldwide distribution. Local mansions doubled as make-believe villas, chateaux, and castles. A decade of shoot-em-ups were filmed amid the dust and chaparral at San Marcos Pass.

In 1910 the American Film Company came to Santa Barbara and three years later built the Flying A Movie Studios with a western set and other elaborate backlot fakery. In one studio the first animated cartoon was developed. Cinematic luminaries like Fatty Arbuckle, Wallace Reid, and D. W. Griffith lent glamour to the Santa Barbara environs in their off-studio

hours. Then in 1921, the entire enterprise ended as abrubtly as it had begun—Santa Barbara forsaken for Tinsel Town.

Environment

The Town of the Trees

Santa Barbara loves its trees. The city's climate encourages more than 1,000 species to thrive here, and over 100 city streets have been named after trees. Historic specimens (many sporting individual colorful titles), trees cherished for their food and resource values, and an astounding array of cultivated trees line the city's 300 miles of streets. Two of the most unusual historic trees are the Moreton Bay Fig Tree and the Eastside Bottle Tree.

The Moreton Bay Fig Tree

Toward the waterfront, just off the highway at Chapala and Montecito streets, stands a gargantuan Moreton bay fig tree, among the largest of its kind in the world. This tree arrived as a seedling from its native Australia, brought by a sailor who claimed it was a rubber plant. Planted by a local family in 1877, the tree today has a trunk circumference that extends 31 feet, and its regularly pruned branches would cover half a football field. It is said that more than 10,000 people could stand it the tree's shade at noontime.

Eastside Bottle Tree

The bottle tree that stands at the corner of Carpinteria and Canada streets is over a century old, and is among the largest of its kind in the state. Its 5-foot-thick trunk, sporting the shape of an old-fashioned milk bottle, is home to swarms of bees who find shelter in its hollow (a blatant violation of a city ordinance against beekeeping in this pollen-rich urban area). Native Indian tribes used to tint the odd-shaped seed pods of bottle trees with natural dyes and string them in charm necklaces, a practice continued today by local artisans.

Burton's Mound

More than 10,000 years ago, native Americans populated an obscure Santa Barbara hill that rose 30 feet above sea level, covering an area about 600 feet long and 500 feet across. When Father Juan Crespi of Portola's expedition came upon the place in 1769, he found the thriving native village of Yanonolit. By the early 1880s the Chumash Indian village of Syujtun had surrounded the central hill, which was sanctified as a burial ground.

After the Europeans arrived, the natives soon dispersed. The mound eventually fell into the hands of Lewis T. Burton, a Yankee fur trader who owned it until 1879. Burton's Mound was finally graded in 1901 by a new owner, Milo M. Potter, who constructed his massive Potter Hotel atop it. Potter also sealed the natural sulfur springs that had been valued for centuries for their medicinal powers.

Today this part of Santa Barbara is called West Beach. Burton's Mound is just a spot on the map in the heart of the city's tourist corridor. An apartment complex sits atop the central hill, guarding untold archeological and spiritual secrets until a change in land use or an enlightened public policy reveals them.

Roadside Attractions

The Breakwater, West and East Beaches

Although Santa Barbara's breakwater has caused erosion that has seriously interrupted the offshore flow of sand, it is still a splendid place for a walk. Best enjoyed when the sea spray cascades over its edge, the breakwater is an excellent spot to watch the commercial fishing fleet unload its catch at the end of the day, a real-life attraction that reminds you why people took to the oceans in the first place.

West Beach

Nearby Ledbetter Beach, formed when a groin was added to halt erosion, and Los Banos Pool at West Beach provide excellent spots to take to the water. The Los Banos Pool, built in 1901, is one of the many fascinating architectural treasures in Santa Barbara.

Also at West Beach is tiny Ambassador Park, all that remains to the public of the site where the Potter Hotel once stood; the rest of the parcel passed into private hands when the City failed to acquire it for public use. At Sea Landing you can catch a cruise for whale watching, sport fishing, or cocktails and dinner. What could be more sublime than cocktails for two while cruising the powder blue Pacific?

East Beach

Along the East Beach area you'll find the bird refuge and the Cabrillo Arts Center. Across the street from the Arts Center is the Sheraton Santa Barbara Hotel, the informal headquarters of the White House press corps during the Reagan administration.

Palm Park, the heart of the East Beach area, is the most pleasureful open space in Santa Barbara. Filled with activity beneath soaring palm trees, Palm Park exudes gladness. A crafts fair takes place every Sunday and the Cabrillo Bikeway adds wheeled liveliness to the park. On a summer day hundreds of people find countless ways to enjoy themselves in this beautiful green area along the beach.

Resources

The City's Street Trees

Several hundred species of trees border Santa Barbara's streets, adding immensely to the beauty and health of the area. Among the most stunning are these:

FLOSS-SILK. Large pink-to-maroon flowers bloom September to December, followed by oval 3–4″–long fruits that burst into heads of fluffy silk cotton.

STONE PINE. Flat-topped, spreading tree to 60 feet in height, valued for compatibility in masking utility poles and wires.

RED-FLOWERING GUM. Stunning clusters of red flowers make it the most colorful tree in the city during summer.

PINK FLAME. Rose-pink flowers and large pods covered with rusty wool adorn these maplelike trees.

CHINESE LANTEN. Spreading tree with unique terminal sprays of small yellow flowers and pink-to-red papery capsules.

CAJEPUT. Look for the oval-crowned tree with peeling, spongy white bark.

Knowing the Trees

Check Kolsbun and Burgess's *Discovering Santa Barbara* for botanical details, and visit the Botanical Gardens, Courthouse Grounds, Franceschi Park, Orpet Park, and Alameda Park to view labeled specimens. Two fine books on the city's trees are available in local bookstores: *Santa Barbara's Street and Park Trees* (Will Beittel) and *Trees of Santa Barbara* (Muller, Broder, and Beittel).

Historic and Unique Trees to Visit

Moreton Bay Fig Tree	Chapala & Montecito
Showdown Sycamore	309 N. Ontare
Hangman's Tree	Castillo & Islay
Sailor's Sycamore	Milpas & Quinientos
Cota Sycamores	Los Olivos at Old Mission
Juniper Serra Olives	Garden & Los Olivos
Franceschi Flame Tree	State & Gutierrez
Hayward Hymenosporum	Dibblee & Castillo
Mystery Oak	Junipero & Castillo
Eastside Bottle Tree	Canada & Carpinteria
Witness Tree	5555 Hollister
Old Kellogg Sycamore	San Jose Creek
Old Pepper Tree	City Hall
Laurel of San Marcos	1066 Old San Marcos
Arlington Silk Oak	1309 State
Santa Barbara's Tree of Light	Carrillo & Chapala
Santa Barbara's Orchid Tree	Garden & Carrillo

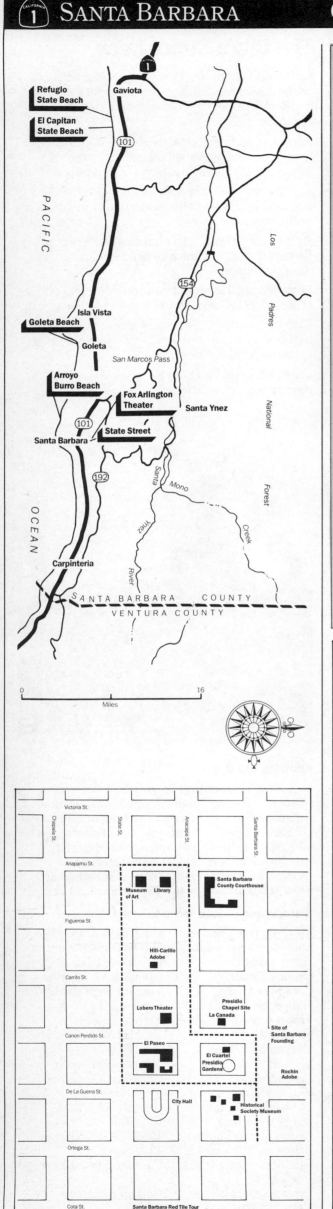

Streets of Santa Barbara

Santa Barbara never realized how chaotic order could be until 1851, when it commissioned Salisbury Haley to lay out a street-grid system that would rectify the meandering paths that wandered through the adobes.

Haley was evidently his own man and followed his own drummer—or in this case, compass. He chose to orient Santa Barbara's streets so that they ran on a diagonal to the coastline and to the four points of the compass. Confusing enough, even if the measurements had been accurate, which they weren't. Perhaps because Haley used humidity-sensitive leather straps to mend breaks in his measuring chain, dimensions were off by as much as 45 feet. When Haley finished his survey, some of the adobes were found to be standing smack in the middle of the new streets.

Why Santa Barbara Looks Like Santa Barbara

By the 1920s, Santa Barbara's upper class had taken stewardship of most of the beach and waterfront area. With refined sensibility, they sought to banish unsightly and unharmonious land uses from the prospering city and establish an environment that was pleasant to live in and good for business.

Santa Barbara's native Spanish architecture—with simple hierarchal lines that harken to an era of land-grant wealth—was extremely compatible with Santa Barbara's new prosperity. California Spanish architecture also gave distinction to the town that was modeling itself into a playground for the discriminating Southern Californian. When the Plans and Planting Committee was formed to beautify the city and influence land-use decisions, the preservation of Santa Barbara's Spanish architecture became the group's primary focus.

The Plans and Planting Committee

The Plans and Planting Committee is singly responsible for the present-day appearance of Santa Barbara. The town's architecture, landscaping, and some of its land-use patterns all derive from the goals and accomplishments of a group of well-heeled, hardworking Santa Barbarans who enacted significant urban design controls before almost any city in America.

On June 29, 1925, an earthquake significantly damaged Santa Barbara, leveling entire areas and dismantling buildings. The earthquake created an opportunity to plan for a new Santa Barbara, and the Plans and Planting Committee, which had been working for years for the beautification of the city, quickly came to the fore with plans for a "California Spanish" Santa Barbara. Ideally, every structure would have plaster walls, tile roofs, enclosed patios, and cascades of wrought iron.

Shortly after the earthquake an architectural Board

Downtown Santa Barbara: Interest & Vitality

In the late 1950s and 1960s many American cities were targeted for urban renewal. The too-frequent consequence was serious urban disruption, as entire districts were razed and people left homeless. The urban renewal campaign was a debacle of tragic proportions, leaving vast stretches of rubble that suggested postwar ruin.

But Santa Barbara chose a different type of downtown renewal, one that eschewed the clearance of whole blocks and focused on restoration that would maintain the downtown area's small scale and high density. Rather than obliterating its downtown, as many cities were doing, Santa Barbara reclaimed its downtown, polished it up, and made it shine as one of the most appealing urban centers in the state.

The city's architectural heritage was preserved and revived without phoniness or cuteness, underscoring Santa Barbara's distinctive image. An infusion of small stores, cafes, and restaurants brought new vitality to the central city.

Santa Barbara has always taken great civic pride in responsible planning and its striking architectural identity. Since 1915 the town has pioneered design standards and an indigenous Southern California aesthetic that has come to represent one of the country's purest examples of regional architecture. Always mindful of its most appealing assets, Santa Barbara has been able to safeguard much of what makes a downtown a satisfying place to be.

of Review was established. Although it lasted only eight months, its efforts were significant, both in underscoring local concern for a harmonious environment from which developed a regional architecture style and in setting a national precedent for design review.

Mediterranean-Style Gas Stations and Replicas of Bull Rings

But it was the dedication and hard work of the Plans and Planting Committee, more than any municipal board, that determined architectural standards in Santa Barbara. Even when builders would propose to erect a seemingly insignificant new structure, they could expect a visit from Pearl Chase, the group's steadfast representative, to advocate a Spanish-style façade. Chase even persuaded the oil companies to build Mediterranean-style gas stations, and convinced Southern Pacific to convert a roundhouse into a replica of a Spanish bull ring.

The end of World War II set off a building boom that threatened, in the minds of Santa Barbarans, to transform the town into a hodgepodge of ticky tacky. In 1947, a new architectural Board of Review was created to establish guidelines for color, design, and compatibility for new structures. Although it proved not always equal to the task, the board attempted to safeguard the city's unique character against an onrush of new development.

Design standards have been written into zoning requirements in specific sections of Santa Barbara, although certain areas remain unprotected, as Santa Barbara struggles to maintain, in the words of its general plan, "her historic role as home for those who seek refuge from the commonplace."

Street Ornamentals

Santa Barbara distinguishes itself from much of the natural Southern California landscape by its lush verdancy, which has been carefully cultivated to present the appearance of a well-maintained garden.

Here the climate and soil accommodate a botanical profusion that thrives with little moisture and even less care. Three good examples are the shrub oleander, the vine bougainvillea, and aloe, a succulent.

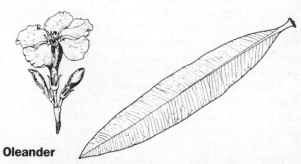

Oleander

A spectacularly beautiful evergreen shrub or small tree, the oleander beckons one to sniff its rose-colored, deep cream, velvety crimson or vanilla-scented white double blooms. Oleanders are a favorite street or avenue ornamental, and you will see many of them in Santa Barbara. This shrub thrives on sandy soil and produces an incredible profusion of blooms with minimal care and water. However, like the coral snake, the oleander hides a deadly poison beneath its beauty. Don't eat, and think twice about even touching.

Bougainvillea

Among the most colorful and long-flowering of the semitropical vines, bougainvillea comes in dozens of species and varieties. In Santa Barbara they are especially favored along highway walls and dividers, providing yet another splash of color to the manicured design and landscaped palette.

Aloe

Aloe is a perennial succulent with large leaves and tubular red or yellow flowers. Aloe loves the sun, requires very little water, and flowers abundantly for years in sandy soil. Appreciated by the Chumash and Spanish for its medicinal power to heal burns, and by today's landscape architects for its hearty beauty, aloe adorns street edges and yards throughout Santa Barbara.

State Street

Central street districts have been refurbished and revitalized in almost every California city that is old enough to possess a past. Once the center of downtowns, these two-to-five-story rehabilitated districts hold a special charm for young urban professionals and college students. The districts are experiencing an unprecedented vogue in a state that never used to have time to look back.

Santa Barbara's State Street achieves the best of what such rehabilitated areas strive for. It preserves the area's history, heritages, and intimate scale, while creating a pleasing spot for pedestrians, one that induces people to get out of their cars and stroll.

A stroll along State Street is a gladdening experience: three movie theaters provide silver-screen romance, the Santa Barbara Art Museum offers an entire day's fascination, and several good bookstores and many good cafes and restaurants provide entertainment for the solitary stroller. There is always something to do or see on State Street; its pleasant ambience prepares you for pleasant surprises.

State Street's delightful mood owes a lot to its meandering tiled sidewalks, abundance of greenery, fountains, benches, and street lanterns. But the pedestrian area also benefits from its proximity to a street with considerable automobile traffic. The traffic imparts a sense of constant activity and prevents the street from becoming deserted and scary at night or too still and settled during the day. A city street is, after all, a city street.

Movie Magic on State Street

State Street's most exquisite attraction is the Fox Arlington, a movie theater and performing arts center as magical and exotic as any in California.

Designed in 1929 by Edwards and Plunkett, the Fox Arlington was conceived to rival the opulence of the Arlington Hotel, which had earlier occupied the site. The new theater was arrayed with furnishings fit for a palace: thirteenth-century Tunisian tiles, antique chandeliers, and European carpets summon a world of Moorish castles and enchanted nights, a fantasy equal to many on the screen.

The Fox was designed to recreate the illusion of a nighttime square in a Spanish village. The auditorium has beautifully detailed Spanish street facades on both sides and shining stars above, and the lobby is a recreation of a room at the Castillo de los Condes de Perelado.

Restored in 1976 to its original magnificence, the Fox Arlington shows first-run single features. The theater is also booked for live performances.

Historic Districts and Landmarks

Santa Barbara began to officially designate historic sites in 1960, when the Historic Structures ordinance was adopted. El Pueblo Viejo Landmark District was then established, encompassing 16 blocks around the old Presidio site. Over the years buildings have been added to the historic list, and new districts designated. *A Visit to Santa Barbara's Historical Architectural Highlights* briefly describes and maps most of the designated city landmarks, as well as several other significant buildings. The pamphlet is available from the City, the Historical Society, or Chamber of Commerce.

Santa Barbara Historical Society Museum
136 E. De la Guerra Street,
966-1601.

Here you will find detailed information on the four early eras of the county's history: Native American, Spanish, Mexican, and American. There are period costumes, a model of Richard Henry Dana's ship *Pilgrim,* and much more.

Santa Barbara Museum of Natural History
2559 Puesta Del Sol Road,
682-4711.

Founded in 1916, the original collection of bird eggs has expanded to include exhibits of flowers, native wildlife, insects, minerals, and marine life. Located in the historic Mission Canyon District, the museum has a planetarium, research library, and exhibits and special programs on the Santa Barbara Channel, the Channel Islands, and the Chumash Indians. The museum shop is filled with books and gifts celebrating the natural world of the Santa Barbara coast. Open seven days a week.

Two Tours

Add to your appreciation of Santa Barbara by taking one or both of two self-guided tours, one by foot, the other by car or bike. Tour maps and details on the highlights are available from the city.

The Red Tile Tour

Park your car at one of ten city-owned downtown parking lots (free for the first 90 minutes) and follow the red tiles around a 12-block walk through old Santa Barbara. Among the highlights: the Spanish-Moorish Courthouse (a good place to start your walk), the Santa Barbara Museum of Art, several adobes—including the Casa de la Guerra, made famous in *Two Years Before the Mast*—the Santa Barbara Historical Society, and the Lobero Theater.

Scenic Drive

Follow the road signs for a 15-point scenic tour that hits all the main spots, including the Bird Refuge and Zoo, Stearns Wharf, Mission Santa Barbara, and the city's waterfront.

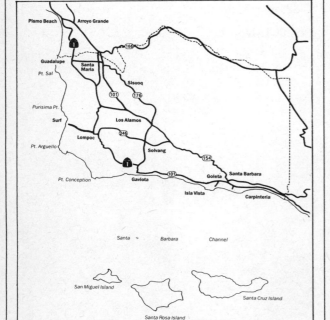

Geranium-Bordered Paths

The Southern Pacific Railroad arrived in 1901, carrying new crowds of tourists anxious to spend money. Entrepeneurs in Santa Barbara, eager to capitalize on its image as the poshest resort town on the coast, set to planning another luxury hotel, more elegant than even the Arlington. The Burton Mound, a major Chumash burial ground and archaeological site, was quickly chosen as the spot for a seafront hotel as splashy as any along the California coast.

The admonitions of Charles Nordhoff to avoid the cold, foggy waterfront no longer held sway. Instead, the practical realities of big profits predominated. From Los Angeles came Milo "Mile-a-Minute" Potter to give Santa Barbara its most luxurious resort hotel.

The glamorous Potter Hotel opened on June 19, 1903 with a celebration heralded as one of the greatest social events on the Pacific Coast. The Potter went to elaborate lengths to appeal to California's wealthiest travelers. Furnishings bespoke a sense of luxury and refinement that was intended to lure California's ruling class to the sea from behind the thick walls of their palatial man-

sions. Andrew Carnegie was one of the first to stay at the hotel, and John D. Rockefeller, Jay Gould, Charles Schwab, and various Swifts, Armours, and Vanderbilts all spent time there.

Little was spared in the creation of the prestigious Potter. A 300-seat dining room featured individually designed pieces of china from Limoges, France. Geranium-bordered paths led to a 36-acre park with a stable of show horses and a children's zoo. In addition to its own hothouse, the hotel had its own fire department, butcher shop, and bakery.

When it opened, most of the Potter's well-fixed guests arrived by train, some in their own private railroad cars. However by 1915, a great many guests arrived by the newly fashionable automobile, and the hotel's garage soon filled with Cadillacs and Stanley Steamers.

With the automobile came a different type of traveler. No longer did guests travel to Santa Barbara for an entire season. The automobile permitted tourists to visit a variety of destinations for shorter stays. The seasonal guests became a seldom-seen rarity, the seasonal hotel a relic awaiting extinction. In 1919 Potter sold his hotelery, which was rapidly fading into unfashionability. Most of the hotel went up in flames in 1921.

The Empire Strikes Out

Almost all the land that runs from Highway 1 to the sea near Point Conception and from Gaviota Beach to Vandenberg AFB belongs to one of three giant ranches that have dominated this section of Santa Barbara County since Spanish times. The 20th century has been forestalled in much of this area, as these empires have been preserved for the privileged use of a small group of land barons, their hired help, and the foxes, gophers, roadrunners, puma, and cattle.

Ranches San Julian, El Cojo-Jalama, and Hollister

The land adjacent to Highway 1 as it winds toward Lompoc is still controlled by the blood heirs of its original Spanish grantee, José de la Guerray Noriega. Rancho San Julian is now considerably smaller than its former half-million acres, but the land is used primarily as it always has been for sheep and cattle grazing, although the grazing land is leased out. Until not too long ago cattle drives still took place on Highway 1, with CHP patrol cars leading the way as outriders.

The nearby El Cojo-Jalama still operates as a working ranch. The 24,000-acre ranch, which surrounds Point Conception and its lighthouse, was originally bought up from land grants in the 1850s by the Bixby family, New Englanders who migrated west and purchased much of the coast, including half of the Irvine Ranch and all the oil fields in Long Beach, for as little as 3 cents an acre from Californios whom they dismissed as "ignorant, lazy, and semi-barbarians." Today the Bixby property is run from the Bixby Corporation's offices in a Los Angeles high-rise.

Adjacent to the Bixby Ranch is the Hollister Ranch, which occupies more than 8 miles of coastline that few Californians have seen—lest it be fleetingly from the window of the Amtrak Coast Starlight as it runs through the property. In 1965 the family that had owned the Hollister Ranch for 100 years sold it to meet taxes. Much of the property was divided up into 100-acre parcels. For more than a decade the state legislature and the California Coastal Commission have unsuccessfully tried to establish public access to the shoreline through Hollister Ranch.

These big anachronistic ranches thus continue to exist in their odd way—preserving much of the land, but preventing the public from seeing it or using it. Inevitably the times—or taxes—catch up with such massive holdings, however, as they did with Hollister Ranch. More imminent yet is the prospect of another type of doom: a giant liquid natural gas (LNG) facility proposed for Point Conception.

Tent City

Despite its well-earned reputation as a seaside retreat that catered mainly to the moneyed and influential, early Santa Barbara also went out of its way to provide simple, low-cost seaside accommodations for the less well-heeled. Until the mid 1920s, Santa Barbara's beach area sported a motley of canvas sleeping tents that were available to tourists for a fraction of the tariff at the Arlington or Potter.

In 1908, the Santa Barbara Chamber of Commerce proposed the establishment of "moderately cheap accommodations for light housekeeping" to increase the number of summer visitors. Shortly afterwards a brand-new tent city sprung up along East Boulevard, where flowers and a row of palm trees decorated its presence. Another tent city was inaugurated at West Beach until local complaints protested their "shantytown" character, ending an enterprise that allowed inexpensive enjoyment of the seashore with minimum environmental impact and a great deal of striped-canvas color.

Environment

The Santa Ynez Mountains

Much of the roadside landscape in Santa Barbara is defined by the 5,000-foot high Santa Ynez Mountains, the region's most dramatic backdrop. No more than 16 miles wide in places, the Santa Ynez are the narrowest and most western segment of the 300-mile-long Transverse Ranges.

The Transverse Ranges

The Santa Ynez Mountains are the only coastal mountains that run east-west, reflecting the ancient geological forces that formed Point Conception and turned the edge of the continent from its prevalent north-south orientation. The Transverse Ranges divide the Peninsular Ranges to the south from the California Coast Ranges, which run from here north to Oregon. Besides the Santa Ynez, the Transverse Ranges include the Santa Monicas to the south, and to the east, the San Gabriels, San Bernadinos, and Eagle Mountains, which frame California's Mojave Desert.

Many Faults and Many Rocks

The Santa Ynez are defined on the north by the Santa Ynez River and the Santa Ynez fault zone. This range, like the other mountains in the Transverse Ranges, is extensively faulted and geologically very unstable. The origin of the unusual faulting and geological folding has long been debated by geologists, but recent offshore explorations suggest that the unusual land mass is the extension of a dominant massive sea-floor configuration that runs predominantly east-west for hundreds of miles offshore.

The Transverse Ranges feature a wider age sampling of rocks than does any other natural province in California. Rocks date from Precambrian gneisses, 1.7 billion years old, to modern alluvium,

and show all manners and types of structures. In the Santa Ynez, the basement rock formations are typical Franciscan and serpentine, displaying superb successions of sedimentary rocks with folds aggregating tens of thousands of feet in thickness, many of these visible from the highway.

These geological characteristics make for the rich deposits of oil that bubble up and seep out of the Santa Barbara landscape.

Roadside Attractions

When Zorro Lived in Santa Barbara

In California the image of the outlaw as hero has always been appealing. Consider the case of Salomón Pico, an early resident of the Santa Barbara area and member of one of early California's richest families. Pico chose to spend his off hours outfitted in black cape, mask, and shining sword, ambushing gringos along the roadside.

Romantic and dashing, Pico became the subject for

a popular series of novels—the tales of Zorro—the first of which was written by Johnston McCulley in 1919. The trademark of the fictional Zorro—three slashes with a silver sword that formed his insignia "Z"—was far more eloquent than Pico's habit of cutting off the ears of his victims and stringing them on a braid that he saved for an admiring paramour.

Although Pico never failed to relieve his gringo victims of their bulging gold purses, his true motive for banditry is said to have been revenge for a beating and robbery he had suffered at the hands of a group of Americans.

Events

Old Spanish Days Fiesta

When the new Lobero Theater was dedicated in August 1924, it was heralded by a week-long Spanish fiesta including an equestrian parade on State Street and much music and theater. The festival was such a success that it was repeated the next year, and in 1926 declared an annual event. Today it is one of Santa Barbara's most famous attractions. During festival week there are free nightly shows in the Sunken Garden of the Courthouse, flamenco shows at the Lobero, a historical parade one day, an equestrian promenade another, and on yet another day, a children's parade. A rodeo and Spanish marketplace add to the excitement.

Summer Solstice Celebration

Santa Barbara pays homage to its shining sun during an annual summer solstice celebration. The all-day celebration begins with a noontime parade on the Saturday closest to the first day of summer. At sunset local stages explode with music, dance, and theater.

Resources

Santa Barbara History

SANTA BARBARA BY THE SEA
Rochelle Bookspan, Editor
McNally & Loftin
Santa Barbara.
1982.

This intelligent collection of essays on the history of Santa Barbara's waterfront not only documents the past but also enables readers to understand why Santa Barbara now is as it is and how its future is being determined by today's decisions. Other editions in this UC Santa Barbara Public Historical Studies Series include *Old Town Santa Barbara, Environmental Hazards and Community Response: The Santa Barbara Experience,* and *A History of Environmental Review in Santa Barbara County, California.*

SANTA BARBARA: PAST AND PRESENT
Walker A. Tomkins
Telcolote Books
Santa Barbara 93101.
1975.

Walker Tomkins is Santa Barbara's most prolific historian. Author of 46 books, including such local histories and *Santa Barbara's Royal Rancho, Stearns Wharf,* and *Santa Barbara County: California's Wonderful Corner,* Tomkins is also well known for his radio and newspaper work. This book capsulizes all his experience and knowledge into an entertaining and concise description of changes in Santa Barbara from 1542 to the present. Many historical photos.

DISCOVERING SANTA BARBARA WITHOUT A CAR—A GUIDE FOR PEOPLE USING BICYCLES, BUSES, THE TRAIN, HORSES, OR WALKING
Ken Kolsbun and Bob Burgess
Friends for Bikecology
Santa Barbara.
1974.

The authors of this superb guide hope their readers will sever the "automania umbilical cord" and discover the individual freedom of movement and positive effect on the environment and community that nonmotorized transportation allows. The booklet makes a convincing case, but it will be useful even if you aren't quite ready to abandon your car.

Polo

Santa Barbara County's thick layers of tough, well-drained turf inspired Max Fleischman in 1921 to indulge his love for polo here; he was soon joined by friends David Niven, Will Rogers, and others. The Santa Barbara Polo Grounds quickly earned a national reputation, one that continues today. This is the only place along the road where you may observe free practice matches during the week and trophy matches every weekend during the season (April–December). The grounds are located south of Santa Barbara on Highway 101 at the Nidever River. Phone: 684-5819.

Beach Arts & Crafts Show

Every Sunday afternoon of the year more than 400 local artists stretch out for blocks along the Cabrillo Walkway for a nonjuried show of their work. Items for sale.

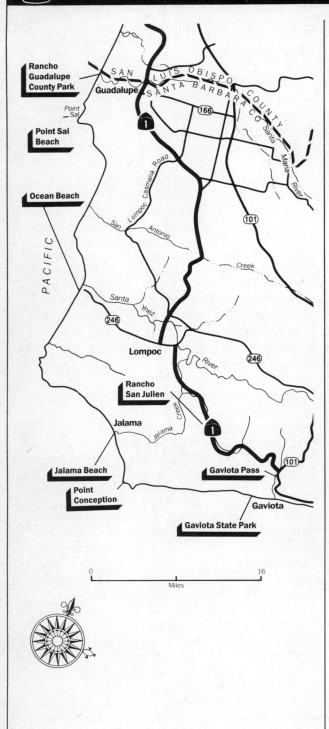

A Struggle Against Distance

Beyond Gaviota Pass, Highway 1 resumes a straight-line journey through the Lompoc Valley. This section of California has historically been forced to struggle against the distances and isolation imposed by mountain barriers on three sides and a wild coastline with shifting dunes on the fourth.

Because of its remoteness, the Lompoc Valley was extremely slow to develop. Passenger service became available after 1861, on the San Francisco–to–Los Angeles stage, but shipments to and from

markets remained burdensome and expensive. Two full days of travel were needed to reach Gaviota, where a reliable port waited on the Santa Barbara Channel, or to arrive at Point Sal, 21 miles north of the valley.

The Lompoc Colony

Had it not been for the desire to avoid temptation, Lompoc might never have been founded. In 1874 W. W. Broughton, president of Santa Cruz's Temperance Society, brought a group of teetotaling colonists to the Lompoc Valley to set up a perfected world where the evils of strong drink could not seek them out.

The Lompoc Colony was established in 1874 to convert the wilderness into the promised land. The rich valley floor was subdivided, roads and bridges built, and wharves constructed. The most important road prefigured the route of Highway 1 through Santa Barbara County. In complete and enduring moral turpitude the temperance colonists settled in their new town. To their credit, the practical-minded utopian founders immediately established a school, picnic area, cemetery, and municipal water system, as well as underwriting the establishment of a newspaper. To give the town the appearance of permanence and stability, inhabitants were encouraged to plant thick foliage trees in their front yards.

Despite the isolation of the valley and the poor transporation to markets, the colonists prospered. When a domestic variety of mustard seed was introduced into the valley's alluvial soil in the 1880s, it took hold so assertively that Lompoc soon replaced Salinas as the world's mustard capital. The temperance colony then launched a publicity campaign to attract other settlers. Thousands of acres were auctioned, and the wilderness was pushed into the background.

Banning Billboards

The first thing is to get rid of the billboards. They are a desecration to the landscape. And that is the reason to get rid of them.

—William H. Whyte

Even before California's Scenic Roads Program, which banned billboards along major segments of Highway 1, Santa Barbara had seen fit to prohibit roadside advertising in selected portions of the county. In recent years, communities all over the nation have taken steps to limit the presence of the big wide structures that inveigh on our attention for brief seconds but often transform the character of the roadside landscape. Key court decisions have generally upheld the right to regulate billboards, despite objections that such regulation interferes with private property rights and even freedom of expression.

The justification for banning billboards is based on the need for scenic preservation. A billboard is an unsightly thing against a scenic backdrop. Not only do billboards often interrupt visual corridors, blocking out mountains, trees and valleys, but they do so in a way that is a too harsh reminder of the non-pastoral world of buy and sell.

Highway 1's route through the Lompoc Valley makes an extremely strong case against roadside billboards. In this wild, unspoiled stretch of countryside the dignity of the land is able to assert itself without compromise. Billboards here would be a ruthless imposition of ticky tacky in an area of high scenic values.

The case against billboards, however, is not unanimous. Supporters of billboard advertising point to the need of out of the way tourist attractions—particularly small motels, cafes and shops—to attract business if they are to survive and compete with nationally-advertised chain operations. Landscape architect J.B. Jackson argues that billboards have a valid place on the rural periphery of cities to acknowledge the presence of the motorist and enliven the landscape.

Others point to the pop-art quality of billboards to justify their roadside presence. Although pop art may seem more appropriate in an urban locale, there was a time when the roadside sign achieved universal popularity as part of the American countryside, scenic or not:

MY JOB IS

KEEPING FACES CLEAN

AND NOBODY KNOWS

DE STUBBLE

I'VE SEEN

BURMA SHAVE

Environment	Roadside Attractions	Resources

California's Elbow: Pt. Conception and Gaviota Pass

Point Conception is California's most significant promontory. Here the coastline dramatically turns from the predominant north-south direction to an east-west orientation. The abrupt shift affects both inland and coastal characteristics.

The difference is especially apparent in the unusual and spectacular geological patterns around Gaviota Pass, where Highway 1 follows the contours of Pt. Conception by turning north inland at Gaviota State Park, and then continuing in a generally northern direction.

Before the turn, the highway sits astride one of the many white shale (Monterey) terraces that distinguish this section of the Santa Barbara coast. Geologists count as many as 22 levels of marine terraces, or land benches, ranging in elevation from 6 to more than 300 feet above the sea. Steep cliffs fronting the ocean along the beach provide a visually fascinating geological composition of layers of shales, diatomites, and sandstone, all uplifted and folded together during ancient seismic activity. The sand on northern Santa Barbara beaches come mostly from these formations.

North to the Pass

Upon first turning north, the road dips toward Gaviota Creek—the cuts alongside are light-colored Monterey shale. But just beyond, brown shales appear, and soon brownish Vaqueros sandstone, a remnant of a formation that extends to depths of hundreds of feet all the way to Santa Barbara.

At Gaviota Gorge, the highway disappears in a tunnel through a massive resistant sandstone unit, the Gaviota Formation, and exits on the other side toward a canyon of shale beds and thinner sandstones. The south branch of the Santa Ynez fault crosses the road about a half mile beyond the tunnel; the confused piles of rock here are remains of an ancient earthquake-induced landslide.

The Mesa Fault

The 1925 earthquake was centered on the Mesa Fault, which extends from the channel along the mesa bluffs to the foothills of the Santa Ynez around Tucker's Grove County Park. At 6:42 AM on June 29, the Mesa Fault slipped, causing a violent shock that rippled until it reached the South Santa Ynez Fault and set off major quaking for the next 19 seconds.

North of Gaviota Pass

When California 1 resumes north of Gaviota Pass, everything is different. Now 15 miles inland, the Coast Highway courses through a serene valley topography, and the landscape assumes almost a wilderness character. The coastline, on the other side of the hill, reverts to its general north-south orientation at Point Conception. Some people call this spot the divider between Southern and Northern California.

Highway 1 winds down out of the Santa Ynez

foothills through a countryside that once was part of the 48,000-acre Rancho San Julian, and the land assumes a harshness not evident nearer the coast. But a majesty accompanies the harshness, and the terrain's nobility surpasses mere prettiness. Ruggedly beautiful, the landscape is its own master, resisting its place on postcards for the sake of its own desolate integrity.

Within only a few miles of the freeway, the land's desolation envelops the Highway 1 traveler, so much so that by the time the cutoff for Jalama Beach appears, it seems improbable that the ocean still exists. If you decide to take this 10-mile ride over the coastal hills in search of the sea, such doubts may haunt you until you actually arrive at Jalama Beach County Park.

Jalama Beach is one of the rarest of beaches in Southern California: sparsely attended and spectacularly beautiful. The wide beach and rising cliffs are set against a backdrop of magnificent rolling foothills completely unmarred by development. Jalama is the place to go in Santa Barbara County to contemplate the sea or contemplate the soul. It also has excellent surfing, campsites, and a snackbar.

North County Beaches

The Santa Barbara coastline north of Pt. Conception displays a vastly different character than in the rest of the county. The beaches here are near-wilderness in character, with magnificent sand dunes and only slight traces of human presence.

All of the Santa Barbara beaches north of Pt. Conception are accessible from Highway 1, although each requires a 10 to 15 mile sidetrip over usually less than ideal roads. The difficulty in reaching them, however, is part of their appeal.

Jalama Beach County Park: The first public beach north of Point Conception, Jalama Beach is a relatively undiscovered gem. With beautifully eroded cliffs and a sweeping beach, this 28 acre beach showcases the shore of the Pacific on its own terms. Facilities include: 120 campsites, a snackbar, and store. A small wetland attracts numerous species of birds and waterfowl. Jalama is also legendary for excellent surfing.

Ocean Beach County Park: This 28 acre county park is located in a gap of Vandenberg Air Force Base's grasp of Santa Barbara's north coast. Accessible from Lompoc via State Highway 246,

Ocean Beach may not be the most scenic of Santa Barbara's beaches, but it's the only one publically accessible for 25 miles north or south, and the birds and shore life are exceptional. Ocean Beach is also the location of the mysterious town of Surf.

Point Sal State Park: Point Sal has the most pristine publically accessible coastal environment in Santa Barbara County, with an abundance of shore and marine life and spectacular dunes, a harbor seal haul out area and a sea bird rookery. Nine miles west of Highway 1, Point Sal offers some of the most dramatic scenery on the coast.

Rancho Guadalupe County Park: The northernmost beach area in Santa Barbara County, Rancho Guadalupe is also the location of the highest sand dune on the west coast—Mussel Rock. Accessible from the town of Guadalupe; 26 acre dune habitat with abundant birds, wetland.

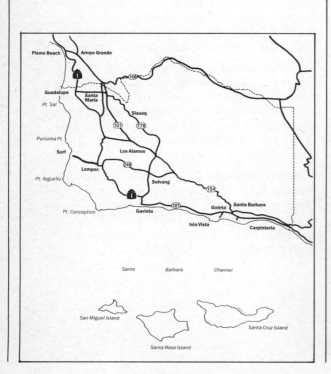

Driving Out Demons

The ability of the colonists to extract a livelihood from such an isolated region indicates how hard they worked. And at nothing did the group work harder than the cause of temperance itself. Maintaining a prohibition against drinking alcohol may have been the most difficult of tasks in a region where the Devil appears to have had a lot of hard-drinking friends.

Perhaps as the imbiber may take unique satisfaction in tippling where drinking is forbidden, so

the temperance advocate may take a measure of joy in smashing a glass of alcohol. So it was in quiet Lompoc on March 15, 1875 when "a goodly number of the fair sex entered the 'drugstore' and set about destroying the liquor stock, knocking in the heads of barrels containing anything and everything that would intoxicate, from bay rum to Schedam Schnapps."

Maintaining complete prohibition in Lompoc was an enduring struggle. Bootleggers passing through seemed to take extra pleasure in selling their wares to the sanctimonious Lompocians. But the prohibitionists remained feisty: in 1881 they threw a bomb into Walker's Saloon, obliterating the building. A few years later they tied a rope to Drum & Davis's occupied saloon, pulled the building from its foundations, and dragged it halfway down the block, spilling every drop of booze in the place and shattering every glass.

But intemperance eventually held sway. After Lompoc was incorporated in 1888, a California court nullified the ban on the manufacture and sale of alcohol enforced by deed restriction, which was the only power the colonists had. Shortly afterward the town voted to license a saloon.

The World's Flower Seed Capital

It is without exaggeration that Lompoc claims to be the world's flower seed capitol—Lompoc accounts for half the U.S. flower seed acreage and produces 90% of the nation's crop. Local growers specialize in an ever changing rotation of high value varieties of marigolds, zinnas, alyssum, lobelia, stock, and sweet peas. Historically, the growing of flower seeds has been the most stable element of Lompoc's economy.

Seed growing began in the Lompoc Valley in the 1890s with the production of vegetable seeds, but did not really gain a foothold until 1909 when the W. Atlee Burpee Company purchased 160 acres near the center of the valley. Burpee's interest enticed other growers to the area, and by 1940, 90% of the world's flower seeds were being produced in the Lompoc and Santa Maria Valleys.

Two factors aided the Lompoc's rise as the flower seed capitol. First, urban encroachment in other flower seed growing areas (particularly in Santa Clara and Ventura) led to an increased concentration of growers in Lompoc, which has remained relatively free of the same threat. Second, the area's climate is extremely varied, offering several microclimates that allow for many varieties of seeds and greater capabilities of production. Cool weather annuals (sweet peas, larkspur, nasturtiums, pansies, and poppies) thrive near the coast; warm weather varieties (marigolds, cosmos, snapdragons, petunias) thrive a few miles inland.

For 4 decades flower seed acreage has remained relatively stable in the Lompoc area, creating a solid ground against the boom and bust cycles of the area's other main economic influence, Vandenburg Air Force Base.

No matter how economically constant, however, flower seed fields provide an ever changing visual variety. Different seeds are grown in different years due to market demands, and varieties must be continually rotated. Even within fields there is a stunning range of variation, all of which contributes to one of the most unarguably beautiful uses of the land this side of paradise.

The Keeper of Deer

Felis concolor, cougar, puma, panther, painter, leon, the cat of God, mountain lion—these once-common predators are today among the world's rarest mammals. They are also among the most beautiful and mysterious, subject of centuries of myths, fears, and reverence.

A mountain lion is long, slung close to the ground, and reaches body lengths of up to eight feet. A female can weigh 135 pounds, a male 225. The long, sleek body is set on short muscular legs capped by great padded paws. Mountain lions are golden in color, with a black tip at the end of the longest feline's tail in the world. The studious face of this intelligent and elegant animal is marked by stunningly beautiful large eyes that glow a translucent green-gold.

Native Americans called the mountain lion the keeper of deer in honor of the animal's critical ecological role as predator of the sick, weak, old, and very young among herds of deer and elk that once roamed the range. The presence of mountain lions also kept the herds moving, spreading their grazing throughout a region that once stretched from British Columbia to South America. The cat is among the world's most adaptable of animals, at home in mountains and deserts, forests and swamps, on the prairie and on coastal plains.

The Supreme Predator

The one force that the lions could not adapt to, however, was the human presence. The cat was always a target for hunters, but in 1948 a program to systematically eliminate mountain lions was implemented by the California Department of Fish and Game and the Department of the Interior's Fish and Wildlife Service.

Using the undocumented premise that mountain lions posed a threat to livestock and people,

the State employed 5 lion hunters and 40 trappers to work in "predator control." A bounty of $630 for each dead lion was paid. By 1963, when the program was finally acknowledged a mistake, more than 12,400 bounties had been collected. Today fewer than 3,000 mountain lions remain in the state, driven into tiny corners of wilderness as people, roads, dogs (of which the lions are terrified), and offroad vehicles invade their shrinking territories. The State now considers mountain lions as "specially protected mammals," and a moratorium on sport hunting has been extended through 1986. Still, the future of these mythically majestic creatures is precarious at best.

Lompoc

Lompoc (pronounced 'Lom-poke') is an unusual town that owes its contemporary existence to two antithetical industries: flowers and the military. The flowers are grown in nearby fields for their seeds, and the military presence is located at nearby Vandenberg Air Force Base. Lompoc owes its economic sustenance to their coexistence.

As you descend into the Lompoc Valley, you may smell the fragrance of the flowers before they come into view. In the early summer, when the flower fields are exploding in flashes of pink and blue and purple and yellow and red, Lompoc dazzles. Few roadside sights are as stunning as the

endless rows of multicolored flowers. The brilliant color combinations sometimes outshine neon lights in their vibrancy.

Lompoc, which produces more than half of the world's flower seeds, has but a slight tourist industry. For the most part, Lompocians are used to transacting business with other Lompocians. As a result, the town's attractions are nothing if not unaffected, and few places on Highway 1 are more unaffected and sincere than the Hi! Let's Eat Restaurant, which serves excellent food in a warm, personal, and good-natured manner. Their breakfasts are top-notch.

Lompoc also has a fine municipal swimming pool and a wonderful drive-in movie theater, the Valley, north of town. At the Lompoc airport you can arrange for a private plane flight over the dazzling flower fields or examine the airworthiness of an ultralight. Surf, west of the town, is not a town at all (despite its perfectly appropriate name), but the location of Ocean Beach County Park and an entry gate for Vandenberg Air Force Base.

Lompoc Community Profile

	1983
Population in City Limits	28,277
Adjacent Areas (Vandenberg)	48,200
Occupied Dwellings (City)	10,441
Total Taxable Retail Sales (City)	118,003,000
School enrollment, K-12	8,550

Employment

Agriculture, Forestry, and Fisheries	263
Construction	355
Manufacturing	2,754
Transportation, Communication, Utilities	861
Mining	620
Retail and Wholesale Trade	2,634
Finance, Real Estate and Insurance	553
Services	3,139
Government	1,700

Housing

Apartment Rentals (1-2 BR)	$350 – 750/mo.
House Rental	$475 up
House Purchase	$65,000 up
Condominiums	$62,000 up

Motels: 8 Operations, 371 total rooms
Mobile Homes: 6 Parks, 668 spaces

Lompoc Flower Festival

P.O. Box 505
Lompoc, CA 93438.
736-3110.

During the last full weekend in June every year, Lompoc celebrates its distinction as the flower seed capital of the world with a colorful salute to the "Valley of Flowers." Highlight of the festival is the parade, with floats elaborately adorned with valley grown blossoms. Additional festivities include flower shows, exhibits, art and craft booths, a carnival, tours of flower fields, and concerts.

The Approach of the Railroad

Throughout the 1880s Lompoc Valley continued a quiet economic and population expansion while the isolation enforced by poor access persisted. The remoteness that had been the valley's initial attraction for the Lompoc colonists also thwarted progress.

By the turn of the 20th century, Lompoc had become a proven "agricultural frontier." Local boosters distributed pamphlets singing the area's praises. What the boosters described with hyperbole, corporate investment quietly gained control over. The Southern Pacific Railroad, called the Octopus for the tenacious reach of its influence, put in a railroad and then helped take over the land.

By 1894, Chinese labor crews had completed tracks into San Luis Obispo to the north over Cuesta Ridge. But construction over the Cuesta had proved so expensive that Southern Pacific looked for a more level route as it proceeded south, seeking to avoid any more crossings of the Coast Range.

So the railroad came down the flatter terrain near the coast, generally ignoring the problems of running a train route through an active dune field. And a decent shipping connection to the outside world finally appeared in northwest Santa Barbara County in 1901. The region was one of the last agricultural districts in the state to obtain railroad services.

Lompoc was 9 miles east of the main line, but a spur line ran into town. The depot placed at the juncture was called Surf after the only thing evident at the site. This inauspicious depot location became the site for another subdivision attempt by the Lompoc Valley Company. But few settlers chose to buy property at the windswept, desolate area.

Gin Chow, Weather Prophet

Just north of Lompoc is the former home of Gin Chow. Gin Chow was a weather prophet who became famous throughout Southern California for his amazing predictions. The diminutive Chow foretold the earthquakes that struck Yokahama in 1923 and Santa Barbara in 1925. He foretold rains, floods, and heatwaves, all of which came to pass with uncanny punctuality.

With the publication of his *First Annual Almanack* in 1932, Chow became a California celebrity, appearing in newsreels and as a featured speaker at Southern California business clubs. Chow maintained that his success at weather prediction resulted from his understanding of the "key" to weather cycles based on the Chinese lunar calendar.

Chow moved to Lompoc in 1911 and bought land just prior to the enactment of a law that prohibited the purchase of real property in the U.S. by persons of Chinese ancestry. A sharp, down-to-earth man, Chow was the originator of a lawsuit against the City of Santa Barbara over Santa Ynez Valley water rights.

In the summer of 1933 Chow was run over by a truck and killed, in line with his earlier prediction.

Missiles and Mountain Lions: Vandenberg Air Force Base

Vandenberg AFB presents an unparalleled mingling of past and present, technology and wilderness. It serves as a satellite-launching site for the NASA Western Test Range and as a base for the Strategic Air Command, the center for missile-combat crew training and testing of ICBM missiles. On the base's 153 square miles there are 12,000 military personnel, 421 Native American petroglyphic and pictographic sites, and some of the coast's most diverse, fragile, and beautiful natural resources.

Vandenberg missile sites require extensive personnel, sophisticated electronic equipment, exotic fuels, and mammoth power resources. These are sited on some 20,000 acres, with the other 68,000 acres remaining wild, undeveloped, and inaccessible to the public. The military preserves this open space as a buffer zone that minimizes public hazards from toxicity, noise and falling debris from malfunctioning missiles. This zone also serves the local environment by just leaving it alone.

Vandenberg's open areas shelter elusive mountain lions, cocky coyotes, herds of some of the state's healthiest deer, and a wild pig population of about 300. There are rattlers and their only natural enemy besides man, the king snake. Hawks, owls, buzzards, rare black rails, and California valley quail take wing here. And the rocky 35-mile coastline holds some of the state's richest tidepools.

The Air Force takes pride in its concern for the resources surrounding the military operations here. In 1973 the base established an Environmental Protection Programs Office to sponsor management studies, develop and enforce an elaborate recycling program, maintain a natural resource library, and work with public agencies, universities and individuals to responsibly explore, protect, and manage the historical and natural resources of this singularly majestic, if generally inaccessible, part of California's coast.

Environment

Roadside Attractions

Resources

Overdraft and Salt Water Intrusion

Most of the water used to irrigate crops in northern Santa Barbara County comes from aquifers, nature's underground reservoirs that store up groundwater.

For decades farmers pumped water from local aquifers with little thought of the consequences. Since the 1950s, however, it has become evident that in portions of northern Santa Barbara County, more water is being pumped out than is being restored from runoff and seepage. The resulting "overdraft" of groundwater supplies holds serious implications for the future of agriculture in the area, as well as any type of new development.

Even before overdraft leads to dried-up groundwater supply, it may lead to an equally serious consequence—salt water intrusion, which would render the area's farmland useless.

Because the Santa Maria Valley's water-bearing alluvial layers tilt toward the ocean, the outflow of groundwater serves as a hydraulic barrier to the landward flow of seawater beneath the surface. Continued overdraft could reduce the water table to levels insufficient to block out salt water intrusion into the aquifers. Once this happened, water pumped up would be brackish and unsuitable to life.

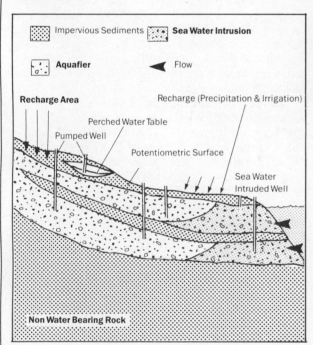

Deposits of Diatomite

Lompoc's diatomite deposits are among the world's largest and purest, making diatomite mining and processing an important industry in this part of California. Diatomite is a sedimentary organic composition made up of the skeletons of diatoms, small ocean-dwelling single-celled plants. These skeletons are pure silica and are thus chemically inert. Processed diatomite is about 10% solid matter and 90% air, and is adaptable to over 300 commercial uses, among them as a filtering medium for a multitude of fluids from oil to syrup, as a filler in paints, and as an insulator.

La Purisima Mission

La Purisima Mission, north of Lompoc, is one of coastal California's most fascinating undiscovered attractions. Because its quiet rural setting effectively isolates it from the 20th century, La Purissima evokes the strongest sense of mission life of the state's 21 missions. Careful and detailed reconstruction by the Civilian Conservation Corps (CCC) from 1934 to 1941 left La Purissima as authentically beautiful and appealing as any of the other missions.

The La Purisima Mission was abandoned sometime during the mid 1850s, after most of the Chumash Indians who worked there had died of disease or grown disillusioned and left. The Mission then deteriorated. After seeing use as a blacksmith's shop, a stable, and a saloon, the structure eventually burned. For the first three decades of the this century, winter rains turned the exposed adobe to goo.

In 1934 the Work Projects Administration (WPA) undertook the Mission's restoration, one of the largest authentic historical restoration projects in the country. Crews of the CCC were assigned the painstaking task of restoring the adobe mission that had been reduced to a few relics and rubble.

After excavation of the site, new walls were matched to old ones, following the original method of construction. More than 100,000 adobe bricks, identical in composition to the originals, were cut and sun-dried for the new 4-foot-thick walls. The roofs required over 32,000 handmade tiles.

Close attention was paid to every aspect of construction. Hardware was forged, wood trim was carved by hand, furniture was built from scratch, and structural improvements were incorporated into the original primitive construction methods.

As many as 200 members of the CCC worked on the project. Artist Henry Helmle supervised the decoration under the WPA Art Project of California. On December 7, 1941, the day the U.S. entered World War II, the beautifully restored La Purisima Mission was opened to the public.

La Purisima Mission State Historic Park

RFD Box 102–Purisima Road
Lompoc 93436.
733-3713.

La Purisima Mission is administered and operated by the California Department of Parks and Recreation and is open to the public seven days a week. A small fee is charged for entry.

The park closes at 6 PM during the summer months, 5 PM from October through April. There are no camping facilities connected with the park, but there are several commercial facilities nearby. Park attendants are usually available to answer questions, and a self-guided tour pamphlet is available free to explain the numerous fascinating elements of La Purisima Mission. Write for further information and a schedule of special events.

Guide to California State Parks

P.O. Box 2390
Sacramento 95811.

A folder listing all state parks and their facilities, including La Purisima State Historic Park, is available from the Department of Parks and Recreation for $2. In addition, they will also send (free) an order form for all State Parks publications.

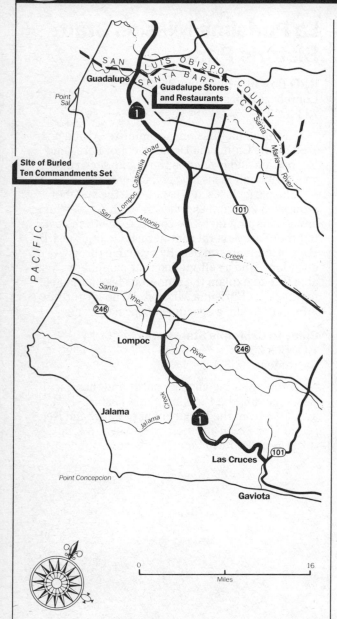

Losing the Heartbeat of the Land

The rail lines brought prosperity and the attentions of larger agricultural companies, which introduced intensive agricultural methods and irrigation. The arrival of the railroad also brought outside speculators, who soon forced out those marginal family farmers unable to adapt to more competitive markets. Most of those who stayed became contract growers, still working the land,

Guadalupe In a Field of Gold

Guadalupe, founded two years before Lompoc, was never subject to the same prohibition on alcohol as its neighbors down the road. In 1883 it was described as "a wide-awake little village" of about a hundred dwellings, six stores, including a fruit store, two hotels, two stables, a post office, an express office, a blacksmith shop and five saloons.

Most of Guadalupe's early residents were dairy farmers of Italian Swiss and Portuguese descent. A "bright gem set in the midst of a vast field of purest gold," Guadalupe was fortunate enough to attract a stage route and later the Southern Pacific Railroad, which sustained it economically—until the advent of modern times paid off less handsomely.

but more distant from its heartbeat.

Soon a new highway was built to further facilitate the production and shipping from the corporate farms. State Highway 56—later changed to Route 1—dealt the railroad a severe blow as it aided the growth of Lompoc and Guadalupe. Each passing year provided more evidence of what everybody already knew: The valleys had become gardens for outside investors.

By 1920 the number of farms peaked, then began to decline as each year brought more consolidations. The rows of windbreaks planted by farmers were uprooted, leaving a bare landscape, because they drank up too much water and shaded valuable crop land. Farmhouses and barns disappeared as the family farm became a relic of a departed era. Eventually, even the mustard fields vanished as prices shifted on what was now a national market.

The Lost City

Far beneath the deep-piled sand near Guadalupe lies an ancient city with 110 foot walls and an avenue of 20 foot sphinxes and 35 foot pharoahs. Chariots once raced down the main avenue of this lost city now covered by rolling sand dunes. Biblical ceremonies were silently carried out behind its towering gates.

Egyptian civilization once had its day on the California coast. But its architect was Cecil B. DeMille, not Ramses II. The time was 1923, and the occasion was the filming of DeMille's original silent film classic, *The Ten Commandments*. The film was an extravaganza of its day, costing $1.4 million and employing more than 1500 performers.

In 1984 two men working their way up the dune covered section of coastline near Point Sal unearthed parts of the movie's monumental set, which had been covered over with sand and abandoned when the film was completed. The discovery of a six foot wide horse's head, sculpted in the style of ancient Egypt, has led to the strong possibility that one of Hollywood's most monumental creations lies relatively intact beneath the rolling dunes. Plans are currently underway to excavate the huge creation, to salvage what may be one of the most exotic artifacts of Hollywood history. Filmmaker Peter Brosman, who with his friend Bruce Cardozo, discovered the artifact after noting a reference to the site in DeMille's autobiography, formed an organization to uncover the ancient Hollywood treasure, called Lost City Productions.

DeMille's set was used as a backdrop for chariot races and scenes depicting the worship of the golden calf and the destruction of the Ten Commandments. Designed by Paul Iribe of France, the 750 foot long set with 109 foot high walls was constructed in one month by a crew of more than 1,000 who worked night and day. Some of the 21 plaster and clay sphinxes that lined the avenue weighed as much as 11,000 pounds.

If the set can be saved from the sands of time relatively intact, it will most certainly be put on public display. Already the Smithsonian Institute has expressed interest, and several museums in the Los Angeles area would like to purchase some of its statues.

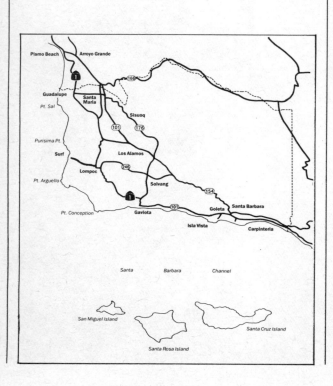

Bald Eagle

Aloft in the Santa Barbara sky soars an occasional majestic silhouette—a bald eagle, unmistakable in size, shape, and color.

Field Identification

An adult bald eagle's large, shining chocolate-brown body is sandwiched between a heavy, brilliant white head and matching snow-white tail. The tail is thick and short, the bill large and yellow. A mature bird weighs about 14 pounds and its

wings span a distance exceeding 8 feet. The only thing less than impressive about this bird is its voice—a surprisingly thin, squeaky chitter.

Young birds are harder to identify since they do not obtain the distinctive bald eagle coloring until they have molted for three to five years. Prior to maturity, a bald eagle is almost all brown, including the tail, head, and beak. In both youth and old age, the sexes are similar in appearance.

Endangered Species

Bald eagles once bred throughout North America, with large populations in Southern California and on the Channel Islands. But recently the bird's range has been drastically reduced, and the bald eagle is now on both state and federal lists of endangered species. Today fewer than 900 bald eagles nest in California, almost 70% of these within protected U.S. Forest Service lands like Los Padres National Forest.

Bad Eating Habits

The downfall of this majestic buteo was occasioned by its eating habits. Sometimes the bird will catch small live prey, but mostly the bald eagle is a beachcomber, dining on wounded or dead waterbirds and fish, two of the links in the global food chain that have the highest concentrations of pesticides and other toxic pollutants.

Recent studies indicate that the bald eagle population in Santa Barbara and the rest of California is holding fairly steady after an alarming decline over the past two decades. Improved pesticide management and increasing protection in wilderness areas encourage modest optimism for the continued stability of the species and, with luck, someday even an increase.

In the meantime, the rare sight of a bald eagle soaring on coastal updrafts or perched in a Santa Barbara seascape is a Highway 1 car-stopper.

Guadalupe

As Highway 1 climbs over the Purissima hills headed north, stunning southern views of the Lompoc Valley present themselves. If the flowers are in bloom this vista may do for a portrait of paradise.

Past the occasional oil derrick and storage tank, Highway 1 and State 135 enter a brief joint venture as a four-lane divided freeway. At the Orcutt–Santa Maria cutoff Highway 1 returns to its single-lane self through pretty rolling hills, sometimes spotted by crops, sometimes by oaks. Just before Guadalupe, Point Sal Road leads to a huge and magnificent wilderness beach, secluded and sublime.

The entrance to Guadalupe is marked by the Guadalupe cemetery, a heraldic and striking roadside presence that seems to be celebrating the arrival of the dead rather than mourning their departure.

The marble monuments marking the oldest graves in the Guadalupe cemetery seem from another world. Actually, they are modeled after monuments in the canton of Ticino, the Lake Maggiore region that was home to many of the valley's Italian-Swiss dairymen. Ticino, an impoverished area, lost half its population to immigration between 1850 and 1900. The Guadalupe

Cemetery contains the remains of those who found their way to northern Santa Barbara County.

Should you pass through Guadalupe during the day, you may mistake it for a quiet sleepy place where nothing much goes on. Do not be misled, however, just because most of Guadalupe's residents vanish during the day. Once the workday is over, Guadalupe transforms itself into a hard-drinking, racket-raising township, hell-bent on having a good time.

Guadalupe is also the place to have the best-tasting Mexican food on the coast. The Guadalupe Restaurant is excellent, but so are a half a dozen or more places stretched out along Guadalupe's main street, Highway 1.

An unusual spot by any standards, Guadalupe marks the end of Santa Barbara County. Enduring most mysteriously, Guadalupe stretches out by the railroad tracks that once meant a great deal to its economy, but now just seem
to be
going
somewhere
else.

The Amtrak Coast Starlight

Among the most rewarding traveling pleasures along the coast is the Amtrak Coast Starlight, a passenger train that runs daily between Los Angeles and San Francisco. The Coast Starlight is the only way to see much of the Santa Barbara Coast, especially the area within Vandenberg Air Force Base.

The Coast Starlight enters Santa Barbara County 30 minutes outside of the Ventura station, crossing Rincon Point along a route that parallels

the Highway 1. From the county line, the tracks follow the elbow-coastline to Point Conception, Point Arguello and Purisima Point. The upper deck observation cars are particularly enjoyable for this segment of the trip. The train passes through Guadalupe and crosses the Santa Maria River into San Luis Obispo County a short two hours from departure at the Santa Barbara station. Call the Amtrak office nearest you for current schedules and reservations.

Visitor Assistance

SANTA BARBARA CONFERENCE & VISITORS' BUREAU
1330 State Street
Suite 200, P.O. Box 299
Santa Barbara 93102
965-3021

SAN LUIS OBISPO

HIGHWAY 1'S JOURNEY through San Luis Obispo County provides some of the most varied pleasures on the coast. Stretching from the Santa Maria River to the edge of Big Sur, San Luis Obispo distinguishes itself from other coastal counties by its amazing diversity of environments and numerous unusual attractions.

Beginning at the edge of the Nipomo Dunes, among the country's largest and most spectacular dune systems, Highway 1 quickly winds its way to the ocean and Pismo Beach, one of the few places on the coast where vehicles are permitted on the sand. Beyond Pismo, Highway 1 departs briefly from the coast and detours around Diablo Canyon to take in the interesting city of San Luis Obispo.

Highway 1 regains the coast at Morro Bay, which is marked by the mysterious presence of 22 million year old Morro Rock and decorated by the nearby presence of Montana de Oro State Park. In a trace, the landscape seems to have assumed a Northern California mode, with noticeable differences in the coast south of here.

Before long the northbound traveler approaches the Hearst Castle, the most elaborate American dream house ever built, but only one of a collection of magnificent oddities in one of coastal California's most pleasurably diverse counties.

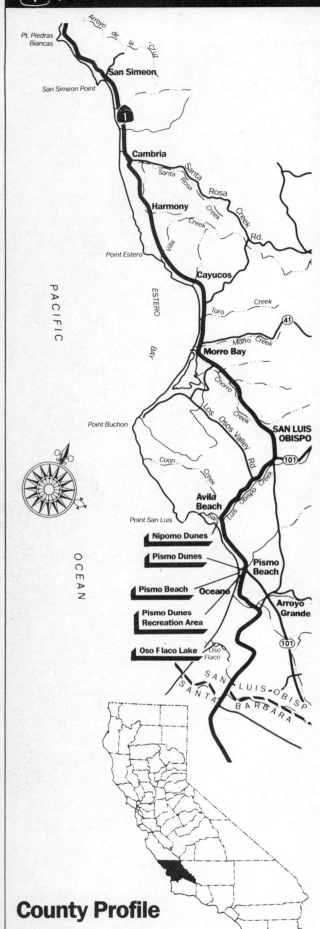

Wheeled Travel Along the Coast

It was a long time until the trails made by the light-footed Chumash evolved into a coastal wagon road. In 1850, the same year the county was formed, wheeled travel along San Luis Obispo's coast was inaugurated when Captain Dana used a *carreta* over the coastal horse trail to haul pine logs down the shoreline. Before Dana, transport had relied on pack mules to negotiate the arduous hills, gullies, and washes that slowed passage and hindered settlement.

South of Pismo, coast travel was less difficult, with a hard-packed beach providing the smoothest of possible surfaces. A 19th century description by *San Luis Tribune* editor Myron Angel testifies to the beach's early appeal for vehicular use: "For twenty miles the broad beach extends as level as the sea and as smooth as a floor washed by the ever coming and receding waves, the sand hardened by the beating of the water so the tracks of horses and wagons scarcely leave an imprint."

At first not many wagons rolled over Pismo's hard beaches, regardless of the smooth ride. Connections to the south coast were poor and, though passage along the beach may have been easy, getting to the beach was torturous. The coast's economic lifeline ran east and west from Port Harford (later Port San Luis) to the township of San Luis Obispo, not north and south to include Pismo Beach. In the minds of most county residents there was little occasion to journey to the sparsely populated south coast. Until late in the century, Pismo Beach remained a largely unpopulated dune fields.

But eventually the tourists came. And what they wanted to do most was drive their carriages and wagons along the edge of the sea. Hundreds of vehicles paraded along the hard sand while white-foamed breakers rushed at their painted wooden wheels.

Once the beaches' recreational appeal became evident, it didn't take long for adjoining land development to follow. In 1887 P. C. Dolliver announced that an eastern syndicate, known as the "managers and manipulators" of magnificent Long Beach, was interested in "El Pismo Beach." The syndicate, he promised, would transform Pismo into the Pacific's grandest beach resort. Once the railroad arrived land values would skyrocket, but right now he had lots to sell at bargain prices. Would anyone like to buy one cheap?

The Roar of the Machine at Pismo Beach

Southern San Luis Obispo's beaches are frequently covered with two-, three-, and four-wheeled vehicles that scramble across the tightly packed sands, leaping over the dunes in ungainly flight and emitting a steady-pitched drone like a swarm of locusts out of a Biblical nightmare.

These are off-highway vehicles (OHVs), also called off-road vehicles (ORVs), or all-terrain carriers (ATCs) and Pismo's beaches are one of the few places on the California coast where they may legally cavort along the ocean's edge and atop a major dune system.

Off-road vehicular recreation is a popular, thrilling sport that each year draws more than 2 million visitors to Pismo. The drivers contribute truckloads of dollars to the local economy in the form of equipment rentals, services, and visitor accommodations. But it can be a dangerous sport (there are over 200 accidents at Pismo each year, approximately 10 of which are fatal), and if not managed well, it can cause environmental damage and conflicts with other beach and dune uses.

A Day on the Dunes

Because of the inherent conflicts between vehicle use on the beach and other forms of recreation, nonenthusiasts display an abundance of perhaps unjustified antipathy toward the sport. ORV aficionados race to point out, however, that they are entitled to some area along the state's 1,100-mile coast to enjoy their sport, which requires dunes and beaches as certainly as the diver needs a clear water cove, or the pier fisher a pier. The State is obligated to provide areas, protection, and services for their sport just as it does for other forms of recreation, they argue.

Accommodating such disparate recreational activities is a complicated matter that requires attentive resource monitoring to ensure protection of the magnificent Pismo Dunes and the safety of all its visitors. Carefully managed—which means strict boundaries between vehicle use areas and non-vehicle use areas, along with some protected portion of the beach itself—there's plenty of room for everybody.

County Profile

Geographic

Land Area (acres)	2,122,240
Land Area (sq. miles)	3,316.0
Water Area (acres)	6,560
Water Area (sq. miles)	10.2
Acres in Public Ownership	352,554.53
Percent in Public Ownership	16.61
Miles of Public Roads	2,518
County Seat	San Luis Obispo

Demographic

Population	170,200
State Rank by Population	24
Projected 1990 Population	199,400
Unemployment Rate (state avg. = 9.9)	6.5
Per Capita Personal Income	$9,387
State Rank by Income	35
Total Assessed Property Value	$5,909,880,462

Environment

A Seaside Desert: The Nipomo Dunes

One word describes southern San Luis Obispo terrain: sand. The Nipomo Sand Dunes, which run for 18 miles from Point Sal in Santa Barbara to the northern end of Pismo State Beach, comprise one of the largest relatively undisturbed dune complexes in the country. The Nipomo are part of the Santa Maria Dunes, which include the Oceano Dunes, highest and whitest sand dunes of California, and the 450-foot tall Mussel Rock sand dune, highest single dune on the West Coast.

The Santa Maria fields were developed over thousands of years, the result of Ice Age evolution, deposits by the Santa Maria River, and constant rearranging by coastal winds and tides. They include a chain of freshwater lakes trapped in the interior of the impermeable dune system. Few of the lakes contain fish, but they do provide sanctuary for waterfowl and dune mammals.

Sand Dune Vegetation: The Pioneers

Plants that grow on shifting sands have to be a hardy lot. Such species have developed special adaptive characteristics that make them easy to recognize, earning them the title of "pioneer plants." Sometimes also called "invaders," these plants put most of their energy into their reproductive process, flowering quickly and over a long period of time, dispersing a multitude of unusually small, light seeds to enhance their opportunity for reproduction in an unfriendly environment.

The pioneers all have markedly extensive root systems, and many have long runners that weave over the surface of the sand as they spread out. The plants are low, often of a clinging variety, and many are succulents, which retain moisture inside their leaves despite the wind's attempt to evaporate every available dew drop. None of the pioneers require large amounts of nutrients, and all add colorful relief to the sandy landscape. Three of the most typical pioneer plants on the Nipomo fields are the ice plant (or sea fig), European beach grass, and beach strawberry.

European Beach Grass

European beach grass was introduced to California in the late 1800s and is now one of the most widely used dune-stabilization grasses in the world. Its stems, or rhizomes, grow up and down but also out, sending horizontal and vertical shoots in all directions to trap and stabilize shifting sands. Its scientific name, *Ammophila arenaria*, derives from the Greek *ammos* ('sand') and *philos* ('loving'), a suitable title for a dune pioneer.

Roadside Attractions

County Line

Across the Santa Maria River, Highway 1's journey through San Luis Obispo County begins with slight heraldry, the landscape marked by quiet signs of agricultural production and farmworkers' housing. Lettuce is the principal roadside crop, although you may also see artichokes, corn, and flowers, as well as some oriental specialties such as snow peas and bok choy. From March through October strawberries are sold at several roadside stands: Tioga, Fresno, "105", Tuff, or—sweetest of the sweet—sequoia berries.

Oceano Dunes

Approximately 2.5 miles north of the county line is the cutoff to Oso Flaco Lake, the largest of the lakes that lie within the Oceano Sand Dunes (75 acres of water and 80 acres of marsh). This is the southernmost (non-vehicular) access to the most superlative coastal dune system in California, with amazing mountains of high white sand and an accompanying wilderness magic that makes plausible the chance of encountering Lawrence of Arabia or mounted riders of the French Foreign Legion.

The access point at Oso Flaco is a good place to enter if you have come to experience the dunes without a vehicle, since most of the nearby area has been designated as a preserve, which means that off-road vehicles (ORVs) are prohibited (although vehicle use of the beach is not, so watch out).

North of the Oso Flaco cutoff begins a stand of eucalyptus trees that accompany Highway 1's inland side for miles while the road takes a number of abrupt 90-degree turns. On the shore side of Highway 1 the Santa Maria refinery of the Union

Oil Company sits in stinking splendor astride the sand dunes. If you are traveling north, you may take a certain amount of olfactory relief in noting that this is the last such shorefront facility you will encounter along Highway 1.

Past Mesa View Road is a stunning view of the Oceano Dunes, the ocean, and the pleasing motley of roadside agriculture. As the road descends from the Nipoma Mesa to the valley floor, keep an eye out for the "Hayashi Produce" sign, a stand owned by grower Robert Hayashi that dispenses excellent produce year round.

Resources

AREA CODE 805

For 24 hour road conditions: 544-4256

Rules of the Road

Highway 1 through San Luis Obispo County is variously a country road, a freeway, a city street, and a narrow cliffside highway with sudden curves and tight switchbacks. Each of these types of roadway requires individualized attention, so be alert and adaptable to changes in road characteristics.

In San Luis Obispo city, northward Highway 1 separates from U.S. 101—look for the sign for Morro Bay and Hearst Castle. Sudden fog is often part of the road's environment near Morro Bay, so be prepared for reduced visibility. Increased traffic is a tourist season phenomenon anywhere near the Hearst Castle at San Simeon, California's second-most popular tourist attraction.

North of Piedras Blancas, Highway 1 narrows, often creating a clog of traffic as slow-moving RV's make passing difficult. As Highway 1 climbs the Santa Lucia Mountains, the road becomes more serpentine, the vistas more spectacular. It's always preferable to use turn outs in such conditions. The best way to savor the stunning views is to pull off the roadway.

Public Transportation

All of Highway 1's route through San Luis Obispo County may be traveled by public transportation. The south county is served by South County Area Transit (SCAT) and Greyhound Bus. The Coast Starlight (AMTRAK) also stops in the City of San Luis Obispo.

The north county is served by San Luis Obispo County Transit (SLOCAT) and Coastlines Bus Service, which travels Highway 1 all the way to Monterey. Check these numbers for schedules and routes.

541-0505	Amtrak Passenger Service
772-2744	City of Morro Bay Dial-a-Ride
772-1214	Clam Water Taxi Service, Morro Bay
649-4700	Coastlines Bus Service (area code 408)
489-1155	Five Cities Taxi
773-5851	Greyhound Bus, Pismo Beach
543-2121	Greyhound Bus, San Luis Obispo
541-BUSS	North Coastal Transit
541-2544	Runabout, San Luis Obispo for the disabled
541-1000	San Luis Obispo City Buses
549-5252	San Luis Obispo County Area Transit, SLOCAT
773-5400	South County Area Transit, SCAT

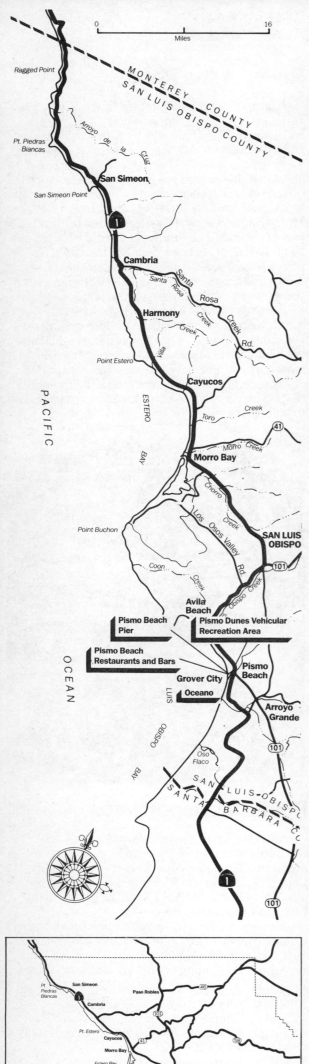

The Dunites

For more than half a century mystical pursuit thrived amid the shifting sands of the Oceano Dunes. Individual mystics, poets, artists, musicians, and drifters began to come to the Oceano Dunes in the early 20th century to live on the sand, unencumbered by social convention and constraint. They chose the dunes at Oceano because they were located at the "intangible center of gravity" between the state's two great cities where the vibrations were the strongest. The followed astrology, nature spirits, and Hindu sacred writings. They practiced social nudism and called themselves "Dunites."

Most of the Dunites lived in driftwood shacks that were built amid vegetated dunes from Oso Flaco Lake to Oceano. Their shacks, ornamented with mystical symbols and occult trappings, were often constructed by the light of the full moon to obtain the most auspicious spiritual alignments. Though they lived almost entirely to themselves, they frequently bartered with the outside world, trading clams for fresh vegetables and potatoes.

Almost all the resident Dunites held strong beliefs in astrology, and many were followers and believers in the myth of Lemuria, which tells of an ancient continent that sank beneath the Pacific. Descendents of

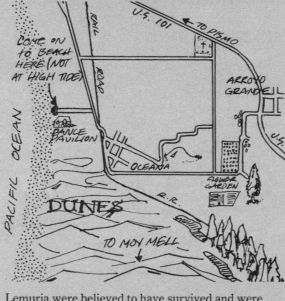

Lemuria were believed to have survived and were hiding out in California until the reemergence of their land. Traces of them had been reported at Mount Shasta and on the Channel Islands. Visionaries, prophets, yogis, and seers all confirmed the imminent reemergence of Lemuria from the Pacific and the rise of the Lemurian people.

In 1931 Gavin Arthur established Moy Mell ('Pasture of Honey'), a utopian commune that lasted for eight years. Arthur, the renegade grandson of Chester A. Arthur, the 21st president of the United States, had a vision of an economic and social union that would diffuse from Dunite society. The principle—epitomized by the group's motto "Individualism within a community"—relied on a society of artists who worked for the communal good while maintaining individual integrity.

Moy Mell was a gathering place for artists, astrologists, and intellectuals—a refuge from the harsh reality of Depression-era California. To spread the influence of new ideas, as well as help support itself, Moy Mell published an impressive magazine, *Dune Forum*, a highbrow journal of artistic, political, and social ruminations. Although the journal lasted only six issues, it published a number of serious articles, including one on modern music by John Cage.

Dunites survived in one form or another amid the Oceano sands until 1974, when Bert "Bourke" Schievink, the last dune resident, died near his driftwood-and-grass shack. Others still live in the general area, safely out of the path of roaring vehicles flying over the dunes. Elwood Decker, an 80-year-old Arroyo Grande resident, who left the dune in 1946 to move to Hollywood and a film career, has no regrets about leaving or the loss of utopia. "I had a wonderful time," he said, "I took the dunes with me."

Home Sweet Mobile Home

Sometime during the 1920s, Americans' interest in mobility rose to a high enough pitch that travel trailers began to roll off automobile assembly lines. The first trailers looked odd and attracted a new breed of highway vagabonds who were generally regarded as even odder.

Eventually the travel trailer became the mobile home, although "relocatable home" might be more accurate since much of its mobility was lost due to its size and the high costs of moving one. During their highpoint in the mid 1970s, new mobile homes accounted for one-fourth of all homes built annually. In 1973, *Forbes* magazine ranked three manufacturers of mobile homes among the most profitable American corporations of the decade.

A Meaningful Life

Entirely prefabricated, mobile homes are much cheaper to build that conventional housing and thus represent the least expensive way for many Americans to fulfill their vision of the American dream.

But there are some problems. For one, mobile homes are small, averaging less than 750 feet of floor space, half the square footage of a conven-

tional house. Their scale restricts their suitability to limited segments of the population, such as retired couples and couples without children. Double wides—two joined single units—double not only the size but also the price.

Of further consequence are the financing arrangements that make mobile homes difficult for low- and moderate-income buyers to purchase. Because banks do not consider mobile homes real property, long-term mortgages are not available, and most buyers must finance their mobile homes as they would an automobile, under a short-term conditional sales agreement. The interest rates and short amortization period make mobile home installment payments as high as house payments.

Mobile homes are also often subject to unfair judgments and undeserved social stigma, a great deal of which is reflected in public laws. Local zoning ordinances severely restrict the siting of mobile homes, when they allow them at all. More than 60% of the nation's zoning ordinances ban mobile homes altogether, unfairly limiting a potentially plentiful source of low-cost housing in an economy that thirsts for any source of new housing.

Environment

Roadside Attractions

Resources

Pismo's Clams

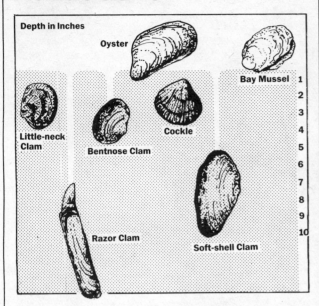

Cold, rough water like that off San Luis Obispo's Pismo coast is extremely high in oxygen and nutrients. This harsh marine environment is perfect for the Pismo clam, one of the toughest and largest of the bivalves. In fact, the oxygen-dependent Pismo clam would suffocate in the quiet water of the mudflats and estuaries where most other clams live.

The Pismo grows to shell diameters of over 7 inches and may live for 35 years. The shell is thick and grayish-white, marked with darker annual growth bands. The clam is easy to locate since it settles down just under the sand at a depth about equal to its shell length. Usually positioned with its hinge portion facing the sea, it seldom resides under more than 10 feet of water, even at highest tides.

Pismo clams once dotted the tidal zone like pebbles and were the mainstay of the diet of coastal Indians. In 1914 the individual bag limits were 200 Pismo clams per person. Clam colonies soon diminished, however, and commercial harvesting was outlawed in 1947. The private individual sport of gathering Pismo clams is still legal and popular, subject to certain Fish and Game regulations. Resource managers today are less concerned about human impacts on the Pismo clam than about those of the clam's major predator—the sea otter. There is serious concern that the depleted clam populations may not be able to withstand the onslaught of an expanding sea otter population, which does not abide by size and bag limits.

Pismo's Beach

The beach at Pismo is comprised of a fine sand that has been packed to a remarkably hard surface by the relentless pounding of the surf. The word *Pismo* comes from a Chumash term meaning 'lumps of natural asphalt'—which still are to be seen along the beach's shore. Used in the 1900s for caulking and sealing, the asphalt contributes to the tough surface of the beach, a surface enjoyed by the beach's many off-road-vehicle users.

Oceano

Next come trailer parks with a series of affinitive appellations: Rancho del Arroyo, Casa del Rey, Duna Vista, Cienaga Seabreeze, and United States Vacation Resorts. Here you can park your aerodynamic Airstreams or settle down within a community that always knows where its mobility lies.

Oceano is a special place with veiled charms that mysteriously surprise: there is a card room, a couple of Chinese restaurants, and the great American Melodrama and Vaudeville Theatre, a distinctive evening's entertainment on any part of the coast. When Oceano's airstrip hosts the annual National Rotorcraft Society Airshow, more than 100 gyrocopters come from all over the state to flutter above the dunes.

Of architectural and historical interest are the 1896 Southern Pacific Railroad Depot and the Coffee Rice Home, a Victorian built in 1885 as a vacation duplicate of Rice's San Francisco mansion to ease the family's transition from city to countryside. At the cutoff for the airstrip is the Oceano Railroad Company, two Southern Pacific dining cars that have been converted to a restaurant open on weekends.

Pismo Beach

There's no place like Pismo, and though some may find the place unappealingly rowdy, unkempt, and out of date, others are attracted to it for just those characteristics. Pismo Beach wastes no time trying to be other than itself; what it lacks in precious, chichi appeal, it more than makes up for in personable, gritty charm.

Named for the Chumash Indian word for *tar,* Pismo had almost every recreational attraction that a seaside resort town could want: a 900-foot pier for excellent fishing and crabbing, a fine beach for good swimming and surfing, and a bowling alley, a roller rink, an art deco movie theater, two arcades, a dance hall, and several night spots where you can trip the light fantastic to your favorite style of country and western music.

And should you desire to dine or recline, the Clam Digger Motel has moderately priced oceanfront cabins with soft beds, and Brad's Restaurant serves sturdy all-American food. The Burger Factory Drive-In offers a distinct flash from the past with carhops on roller skates.

Campgrounds

Here are the major campgrounds along Highway 1, south to north. Make reservations early during the summer.

PISMO BEACH AND DUNES VEHICULAR RECREATION AREA *(State)*. 1.5 miles south of Pismo Beach at Highway 1. 145 primitive sites, 42 electric & water sites, restrooms, showers, motor and sail boating, fishing, dump station. 489-2684.

SAN LUIS OBISPO CAMPGROUND *(County)*. Off Highway 1 at 1330 Dewey Road. Playground, basketball, camping. 549-5930.

LESAGE RIVIERA *(Private)*. Half mile south of Pismo Beach, 60 spaces, 9 holes of golf, restaurant. 489-5506.

HOLIDAY RECREATIONAL VEHICLE PARK *(Private)*. 100 South Dolliver Street, Pismo Beach. 195 full hookups, laundromat, heated pool, hot showers. 773-1121.

PISMO DUNES TRAVEL TRAILER PARK *(Private)*. 200 South Dolliver, Pismo Beach. 391 spaces, laundromat, showers, tables, pets. 773-4807.

EL CHORRO REGIONAL PARK *(County)*. Highway 1 north of San Luis Obispo. Baseball, playground, primitive camping. 549-5219.

MONTANA DE ORO STATE PARK *(State)*. Off Los Osos Valley Road. 46 primitive sites. 772-2560.

MORRO BAY STATE PARK *(State)*. Quarter mile east of Morro Bay, Highway 1. 115 developed sites, showers, boating, golfing, Museum of Natural History. 772-2560.

BAY VIEW TRAILER PARK *(Private)*. 714 Embarcadero, Morro Bay. 22 developed sites, cable TV. 772-3300.

MORRO DUNES *(Private)*. 1700 Embarcadero, Morro Bay. 70 complete hookups, 80 others, tent sites, laundry, showers. 772-2722.

ATASCADERO STATE BEACH *(State)*. North of Morro Bay on Yerba Buena Avenue off Highway 1. 104 developed sites. 772-2560.

SAN SIMEON STATE BEACH *(State)*. 5 miles south of San Simeon on Highway 1. 134 developed sites. 927-4509.

Pismo Beach

Driving

Pismo Beach is the last oceanfront community in the state where visitors can still drive autos on the beach. There are ramps all along the 23-mile stretch of beach, a multitude of rental shops for vehicles, equipment, and supplies, and lots of rolling and sturdy flat surface to drive along. Vehicle-use areas are expansive and clearly marked.

Riding

If you prefer to see the beach on horseback, stop at the Livery Stables in Oceano (489-8100) or north of Pismo Beach on Avila Road.

Clamming

Pismo clams burrow into the sand only a few inches, so a clamming fork with 8- to 10-inch tines is adequate. It's not a difficult hunt. Just walk along and into the surf as far as you wish, probing the sand every two inches or so, about six inches down, until you strike something hard. If it's a clam, dig it up and measure it. It must be 4.5 inches long and your daily limit is 10 a day. License required.

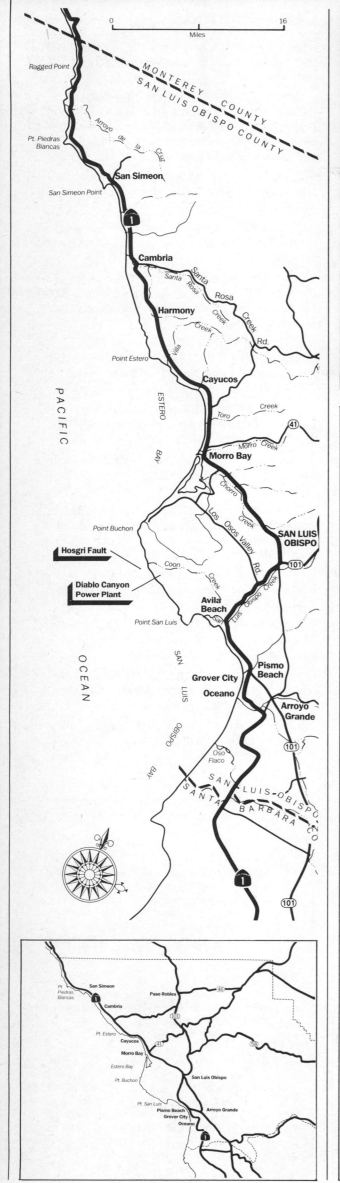

Diablo Canyon

In the fall of 1966, the Pacific Gas and Electric Company (PG&E) announced plans to build a nuclear power plant 12 miles southwest of the city of San Luis Obispo at Diablo Canyon. The plant, consisting of two large electricity-generating units plus support structures, towers, and transmission lines, was budgeted at $350 million, and was expected to be "on line" by 1973. However, because of serious questions raised concerning seismic safety, the project was delayed for almost two decades beyond its start, with costs rising to more than $5 billion.

When PG&E first proposed its mammoth plant, few voices were heard to dissent. The Sierra Club, in an action they would have difficulty living down for years, endorsed construction at Diablo Canyon in preference to the originally proposed site at Nipomo Dunes. Meanwhile PG&E initiated licensing procedures with the Public Utilities Commission, the Atomic Energy Commission, and its successor, the Nuclear Regulatory Commission.

At first only a few individuals contested the project as it moved through the permit process. Because most people believed the nuclear power plant would lower their taxes, the project enjoyed strong public support. But eventually voices began to be heard raising questions about permanent impacts to the environment and seismic safety.

The Pristine Character of the Land

Diablo Canyon was once among the loveliest spots on the California coast, nourishing some of the largest oak trees in the world, as well as ferns, brush, and coastal mesa vegetation. The waters of the rocky coves at the foot of the crescent-shaped headlands were nurseries to thousands and thousands of abalone that clung to the rocks like barnacles on a whale. Giant beds of bull kelp floated offshore, sheltering sea otters, abalone, and other marine life from the powerful San Luis Obispo breakers.

To convert Diablo Canyon to a nuclear power plant site, the oaks in the Canyon were razed and roads were cut that slashed the open mesas with deep scars. Marine life was seriously depleted: in 1974 thousands of abalone died and forests of kelp withered after the plant's cooling system dumped millions of gallons of thermoheated water into the ocean.

During initial construction, efforts to mitigate major environmental impacts sometimes became absurdly comical. At one point, the bulldozed hillsides and eroded road cuts were painted green to "cover" the canyon's huge scars.

While Diablo Canyon moved through the lengthy permit process, challenges increased, but conditional approvals were obtained despite some commissioners' misgivings. Said one: "PG&E [has] demonstrated planning which is cold in concept and ruthless in practice as far as nature is concerned."

Seismic Safety

First to press the issue of seismic safety was the Scenic Shoreline Preservation League, which raised the issue of the Hosgri fault as a potential danger to the plant. In 1971 a 6.5 earthquake in the San Fernando Valley created substantially more ground shaking near Diablo than had previously been thought possible.

Not until 1973, however, did PG&E admit the existence of the Hosgri fault. Once again the sceptre of earthquake damage rose up to haunt PG&E, who seemed to have a penchant for building or planning nuclear power plants near earthquake faults. PG&E's first nuclear plant at Vallecitos (since shut down), near Livermore, was constructed 200 yards from the Verona fault. Its Humboldt plant (shut down in 1976) was located next to a series of faults that in 1980 shook to a Richter magnitude of 7.0, toppling an overpass a few miles from the plant. PG&E also planned nuclear plants at Bodega Bay and Point Arena, each within fidgeting distance of the San Andreas fault.

As the danger of a nuclear energy plant so near a major fault line grew more evident, attitudes began to

change against the plant. San Luis Obispo residents grew more concerned and local newspapers editorialized against the project. Groups like Mothers for Peace and Abalone Alliance organized demonstrations.

By 1978 thousands of people were demonstrating against the project, and hundreds were arrested. A year later the near melt down at Three Mile Island prompted even greater demonstrations. A rally in June, 1979 drew 40,000 people to voice their objections to the Diablo Canyon Plant. Governor Jerry Brown addressed the crowd. Despite protests, certification proceeded, with PG&E's rising investment in the project creating its own momentum. In late 1984, PG&E's Diablo Power Plant went "on line."

The Hosgri Fault

One of the greatest dangers to public safety from a nuclear facility in California is, of course, from earthquakes. At Diablo Canyon an earthquake fault lies less than 2.5 miles offshore. So close is the active fault to the nuclear plant, that critics have charged that putting Diablo Canyon on-line is the equivalent of taking an atom bomb for a ride on a roller coaster.

The Hosgri fault was discovered in 1969, after construction of the nuclear plant was underway, by two Shell Oil Company geologists, Hoskins and Griffith, who mapped over 90 miles of the system. In 1971, a U.S. Geological Survey team confirmed the presence of the fault, naming it after the two men who discovered it. But information about the fault was not made public for several years, although earlier reports placed the nearest fault 45 miles away.

The Hosgri system is a series of broken segments rather than one main fault. Geologists think it may have been the source of a 1927 quake in Lompoc (7.3 on the Richter Scale) and that the system may extend for over 400 miles, interlacing with the San Simeon, Big Sur, and San Gregorio faults. In June 1984 a 4.3 quake was centered in the Hosgri Fault about 20 miles southwest of San Luis Obispo, and new evidence suggests that some of the system's segments may run much closer to the nuclear site than even 2.5 miles—indeed, the system of faults may run directly under the plant.

Diablo Canyon

Seven miles south of San Luis Obispo is the cutoff for the Energy Information Center, which offers a free program of films and information put together by Pacific Gas and Electric (PG&E) as a public relations gesture to improve the image of nuclear energy facilities.

Nuclear energy is extremely controversial in California, and no facility has been more controversial than the Diablo Canyon Power Plant. Located near an active earthquake fault, the plant has thus far cost PG&E $5.2 billion.

This is a listing of major groups concerned with nuclear energy issues in California. Some of these organizations are described in detail in other resource columns. Check the index.

ABALONE ALLIANCE
2940 Sixteenth Street
Room 310
San Francisco, 94103
(415) 861-0592

ABALONE ALLIANCE
Diablo Project Office
452 Higuera Street
San Luis Obispo, 93410
(415) 543-6614

ALLIANCE FOR SURVIVAL
1473 Echo Park Avenue
Los Angeles, 90026
(213) 617-2118

AMERICAN FRIENDS
SERVICE COMMITTEE
2160 Lake Street
San Francisco, 94121
(415) 752-7766

FRIENDS OF THE EARTH
124 Spear Street
San Francisco, 94105
(415) 495-4770

GREENPEACE
Building E
Fort Mason
San Francisco, 94123
(415) 474-6767

SIERRA CLUB
530 Bush Street
San Francisco, 94108
(415) 981-8634

NATURAL RESOURCES
DEFENSE COUNCIL
25 Kearny Street
San Francisco, 94108
(415) 421-6761

NUCLEAR WEAPONS
FREEZE CAMPAIGN
5480 College Avenue
Oakland, 94618
(415) 652-5231

UNIVERSITY OF
CALIFORNIA NUCLEAR
WEAPONS LABS
CONVERSION PROJECT
944 Market Street
Room 508
San Francisco, 94102
(415) 982-5578

NUCLEAR CALIFORNIA, AN INVESTIGATIVE REPORT
Edited by David E. Kaplin
Greenpeace and the Center for Investigative Reporting, 1982.

This is an excellent report on the state of nuclear technology in California in the 1980s compiled by experts in their field. Chapters cover topics such as California nuclear nightmares, science and industry in the nuclear state, cleaning up the nuclear state—and a nuclear atlas of California.

Low Level Radiation and Radioactive Wastes

As a matter of course, nuclear power plants release small amounts of radiation into the air and water, which is often dismissed as being of too low a level to be significant. Studies of "low level" radiation, however, have consistently shown that any radiation will increase the chances of cancer and birth defects.

But the dangers associated with nuclear energy are not limited to the reactor site. Nuclear power plants create huge stockpiles of lethal radioactive waste (Diablo Canyon is capable of producing 37 tons of nuclear waste materials annually) that must be isolated from any human contact for hundreds of thousands of years.

The Diablo Canyon Power Plant produces nuclear waste that contains such toxic and long-enduring elements as plutonium, strontium, and cesium. At present there is no safe and comprehensive solution for the disposal of nuclear waste.

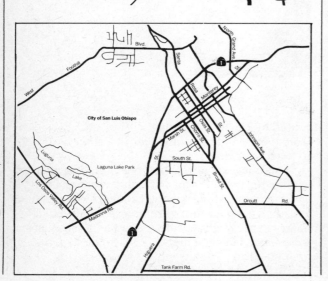

The San Luis Obispo Stage

San Luis Obispo was always an important way stop for travelers on the El Camino Real, but because the railroad did not arrive until late in the 1800s, modernity approached slowly.

Until 1894 the stagecoach remained the principle means of travel for coast journeyers in San Luis Obispo. Connections could be made for Santa Barbara and Los Angeles on the down stage, or—on the up stage—to the bay city beside the Golden Gate. In 1861 a triweekly stage passed through San Luis Obispo between San Francisco and Los Angeles. A year later daily service began, and four-horse relays made the entire run in 3.5 days.

Like the sailing ship, the stagecoach was accompanied by its own romantic allure. Children and barking dogs greeted the arriving stages with excitement and anticipation, running alongside from the outskirts of town to the depot. Terms of the stagedriver's craft—*off leaders, near diving horses,* and *wheelers*—were spoken with informed pride by young and old, who warmed as they shared in the lore of the stagecoach.

Knights of the Ribbons

As the stage arrived, spectators would call out enthusiastic greetings to the drivers, who were referred to by such affectionate appellations as *Jehu, Whit, Whipster, Charlie,* and, most poetically, *Knight of the Ribbons.*

Men like John Waugh and Jim Meyers drove one-ton concord stages through the mire and muck of the lowlands and over the unpredictable heights of the Cuesta Ridge—all for the handsome pay of $125 a month plus keep. The spirited teams were pushed to make an average of 10 miles an hour and trained not to stop on flat ground. When the stages made meal stops, teams of alacritous

horses tore around in wide circles, never stopping, while passengers ate.

Travelers were charged nine cents a mile to be carried over always rough roads. Some stage roads were not completely insufferable, but most that were not, were not in San Luis Obispo County.

Because It Is There

San Luis Obispo Mountain looms on the horizon just south of the City of San Luis Obispo, the first in the county's chain of volcanic peaks. The mountain is easily recognized by the mammoth "M" carved into its side and the curving scar of a widely bladed road ascending its peak.

Shortly after Alex Madonna (developer of the Madonna Inn) monogrammed the mountain and cut the road up it, local citizens decided it was time to protect this and the other peaks from development.

Save the Peaks

Once committed, the group organized to raise money to buy the mountaintops, intending to develop trails and a park system what would reach from San Luis Mountain to Morro Rock, the last of the nine-mountain volcanic chain. Calling themselves the "Save the Peaks Committee," they had some success in raising money and public support and in getting the county to change its ordinances to require public notice of roads like the one on Madonna Mountain.

Most of the property owners on the mountains, however, soon proclaimed their stewardship of the

land to be adequate: they weren't intending to develop the land, but neither did they intend to sell it for public use. The Save the Peaks Committee recruited the help of the State Parks Foundation, hoping that should the owners ever change their minds, they would offer their land first to the state parks system.

Solidifying Private Stewardship

Private stewardship of important natural areas entails uncertainty—people and situations change. One owner may carefully protect a parcel during his or her lifetime, but heirs may act differently, depending on inclination and finances. In such a case, a private nonprofit land trust may be the solution.

A land trust can negotiate with the living steward for a gift of a conservation or recreational easement on the property. Easements achieve a public purpose, protect the private interest, and provide tax benefits to the donor as well. A new land trust has been established in San Luis Obispo County to focus on agricultural protection, but many local conservationists hope it will eventually become an important agent in efforts to protect the undeveloped mountaintops.

Stage Robbers

And there were stage robbers: masked men with double-barreled shotguns who accosted stages with derring-do and a strict order to "throw down the box!" Most of the road agents were less vicious than legends often hold, frequently forced to outlawry by economic injustice and unfair treatment by the railroads.

A sense of Robin Hood redistribution often accompanied the holdups. In fact, Wells Fargo and Southern Pacific provoked so much resentment along the coast that people often sided more with the outlaws than the stage owners. One holdup man—Black Bart—even became a popular hero as he evaded Wells Fargo detectives and law enforcement agents. Black Bart never stole from women and he never killed, but he led Wells Fargo on a merry chase for almost a decade. His robberies were ceremonialized with poetry, which he would bestow on his victims at his departure.

I've labored long and hard for bread,
For honor and for riches,
But on my corns too long you've tread,
You fine-haired sons of bitches.

Rosebuds & Rosettes at the Roadside

Once described as resembling a wedding cake designed by someone who had just grasped the technique of making rosebuds and rosettes, the Madonna Inn stands adjacent to Highway 1 as one of California's most elaborate pop art icons. Hearst Castle is still 45 miles to the north, but getting closer.

The Madonna Inn possesses the only men's urinal in recent memory to have been singled out in the travel pages of *The New York Times*. The men's room is famous for its solid rock urinal flushed by a waterfall set off by an electric eye. But it is no more elaborate than any other aspect of the 110-room unpityingly pink motel. Gilt cherubs, red flocked wallpaper, and floor-to-ceiling plastic plants elevate kitsch to new heights of thick-skinned taste.

The mood and design of Disney inhabit the Madonna Inn. An inscription in the dining room reads "Eat and be happy." This is where Snow White and the 7 Dwarfs would choose to stop on their travels from Los Angeles to San Francisco. To be sure, the Madonna's relentless whimsey leads to unexpected delights. The renowned architect Charles Moore called the Madonna "one of the most surprising and surprisingly full experiences to be found along an American Highway."

All the rooms are different—not just from other motel rooms but from each other. With names like Time of Your Life, Old Fashioned Honeymoon, and Cloud Nine, the rooms each have a distinctive appeal— enough to account for 37% of all room rentals in San Luis Obispo.

Among the 110 fantasies at the Madonna are four rock rooms with real rock floors and showers, and the traveler's suite, which portrays a turn-of-the-century bordello. So enchanting is the Madonna that many guests check in for a week and stay in a different room every night. The first person to sleep in all 110 rooms took 7 years to achieve the feat, finishing in 1977.

Under the Volcano

The terrain along Highway 1 between San Luis Obispo and Morro Bay is distinguished by a series of nine volcanic peaks that abruptly emerge from the rolling landscape. These peaks are volcanic "plugs," remnants of oceanic volcanic activity that occurred over 20 million years ago, when these mountains were great masses of molten rock that boiled and bubbled up from the earth's center inside the necks of ancient volcanos. But the liquid rock never spilled over the outer rim of the volcano, instead remaining inside about 1,000 feet from the older Franciscan Formation volcanic edge. When the fire and smoke finally subsided, time began to work on the terrain, eventually wearing away the softer rocks and earth of the outer volcanic layers until only the solid cores remained.

The first of the volcanic peaks is San Luis Mountain; Morro Rock is the last in the series, standing 576 feet high in its watery bed at the mouth of Morro Bay. Other peaks include Islay Peak in Montana de Oro State Park, Bishop Peak, Hollister Peak, and Black Mountain, the last in the series before Morro Rock. A 1.5-mile hike up Black Mountain's face rewards the traveler with a spectacular view of the entire Morro Bay Estuary, the sandspit, ocean, and the hills of Montana de Oro State Park.

San Luis Obispo

The Madonna Inn, in one great garish cartoon gesture, marks the northern boundary of Southern California, as the town of San Luis Obispo marks the southern limits of Northern California. In Southern California experiences are meant to be entertaining; in Northern California they must be interesting. San Luis Obispo is an interesting town.

The Avila Beach off ramp leads to Port San Luis, which has a fascinating pier, a fine beach, and two mineral spring resorts. Sycamore Mineral Springs offers hot mineral springs in private hot tubs under the stars.

Going north, Highway 1 splits from 101 at the Santa Rosa Avenue exit, but if you delay your exit for one freeway stop—taking the Monterey exit instead—you will have an opportunity to view the world's first motel. In 1924 Arthur Heineman built the Motel Inn, coining the word *motel*. Heineman envisioned a national chain for his new invention, which, in advance of its time, never materialized.

San Luis Obispo's most interesting attraction is Mission Plaza, located in the center of town. Take Monterey Street off Highway 1 past the Fremont Theatre, a magnificent Streamlined Moderne movie house, and Muzio Deli, a big-city quality deli with antique charm. At the foot of Monterey Street, Mission Plaza begins.

Environment

For expert advice and information on the San Luis Obispo natural environment, consult any of these groups.

Natural History Association of San Luis Obispo Coast, Inc.
Morro Bay State Park Museum
Morro Bay 93442

A nonprofit affiliate of the California State Parks System, the Association provides special programs on natural history, publishes and distributes a monthly newsletter, and maintains a natural history museum particularly well-versed in coastal and bay resources.

San Luis Obispo County Land Conservancy
P.O. Box 12206, San Luis Obispo 93401.
544-9096.

The primary purpose of this new land trust is to protect the county's agricultural lands, but the Trust is also pledged to seek innovative solutions to local environmental, scenic, ecological, recreational, and historical challenges.

California State Parks Foundation
1212 Broadway, Suite 438, Oakland, 94612.
(415) 834-4411.

The California State Parks Foundation was formed in 1969 to receive bequests and gifts of cash, securities, real estate, and other property for the benefit of the California State Parks System. Since then, the Foundation has raised over $50 million for acquisition and development of parks and has organized volunteer and cooperative associations throughout the state to interpret, improve, and protect public lands.

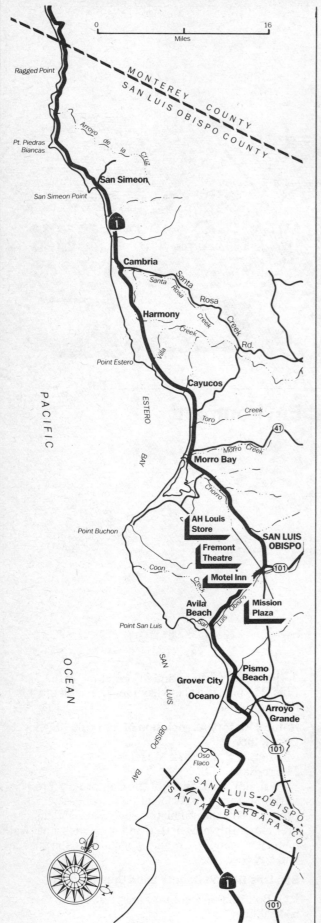

Elegance and Good Taste

Most early travelers to San Luis Obispo were utterly relieved to step off the stage and hobble to feather beds at the Andrews Hotel, which burned to the ground in 1886 and was reconstructed as the Ramona. In the years that followed the Ramona became the central attraction for the traveler seeking elegance and good taste in San Luis Obispo. With a grand ballroom, 300 guest rooms, and brick construction, the Ramona was visited by presidents and widely advertised as *the* spot for the traveling elite.

Guests at the Ramona enjoyed elegant dinners, billiards, croquet, and lawn tennis as well as band concerts and dances. For $2 and $3 a night guests stayed in rooms or suites with individual fireplaces, a dumbwaiter, and a magical electronic innovation—buzzers that summoned uniformed bellboys in pillbox hats. The outside veranda was often used as a stage, while guests wrapped in blankets watched from carriages and wagons in an early incarnation of the California drive-in movie.

Finally on May 5, 1894, the Southern Pacific reached San Luis Obispo, setting off a celebration unmatched in the city's history. The entire county joined in the festivities that signified the end of one era and the beginning of another. San Luis Obispo was on the map.

Ah Louis

The name Ah Louis over this San Luis Obispo storefront preserves the memory of one of the area's most influential settlers. In the 1870s, Ah Louis brought thousands of Chinese laborers into San Luis Obispo County to build stage roads and railroads and to work the quicksilver mines. He became a patriarchal figure to the new immigrants, pioneered the county's flower seed industry, and served as honorary mayor of Chinatown, which he founded. The store, state historical landmark #802, still operates, although at a somewhat slower pace than when it served as a bank, post office, counting house, and emporium for San Luis Obispo's lively Chinese community.

Progress of a Public Plaza

Aristotle, in *The Politics,* described the ideal public square: "Nothing here may be bought or sold, and no member of the lower order may be admitted unless summoned by the authorities. . . the market proper, where buying and selling are done, must be in a quite separate place, conveniently situated both for goods sent up from the harbor and for people coming in from the country." As it happened, the citizens of Athens ignored Aristotle's recommendations for a public square removed from other functions of urban life, and fortunately, so too did the citizens of San Luis Obispo when they relied on a mixture of commercial, cultural, and woodland features for Mission Plaza.

It all started with the crash of an egg truck in 1953. A runaway egg truck whose brakes had failed on the Cuesta Grade came roaring through town and plowed the Mission Garage broadside. A year later the city ordered the damaged building demolished. Once the building was gone, San Luis Obispo Creek became visible for the first time in a century.

Soon afterward, the "Citizens for Mission Gardens Plaza" commissioned some Cal Poly students to draw up plans for a central open space

that would rely on San Luis Obispo Creek to unite the town's historical buildings and its commercial center. Other citizens meanwhile garnered city council support for a parking lot to be constructed over the creek.

Revitalizing the Urban Core

For years the debate continued about how best to revitalize San Luis Obispo's declining urban core, which was rapidly losing business to outlying shopping areas. Proponents of the proposed parking lot assumed that waning use was related to inconvenience—and that improved parking would bring shoppers back downtown. But proponents of the plaza defined the problem as one of public disinterest, which could be remedied only by enhancing the inner city's attributes.

In April 1961 the City Council, on the recommendation of the planning commission, approved the city's first comprehensive general plan. The mission area was designated public open space, and one of the plan's major objectives was "to protect and preserve natural amenities—scenic hills, creeks, view areas, and other open space—by indicating areas that are to be withheld from private development."

Over the next ten years, the plan for Mission Plaza was nurtured and developed by local citizens who participated in virtually every phase of the project, including approval of the final design by architect Richard Taylor of Santa Barbara. In 1969, Montgomery Street was closed, and in 1970, landscaping began. Soon new shops and restaurants were springing up, followed by other forms of new life in San Luis Obispo's revitalized downtown.

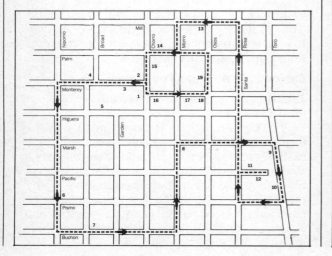

Environment

Varied Climates

Highway 1 makes a sudden departure from the coast north of Pismo Beach, and the difference in temperature and climatic conditions is often dramatic. In the summer months it is not uncommon for inland areas near San Luis Obispo city to be more than 15 degrees warmer than the coast. In the winter, conditions often reverse themselves, and the coast becomes the comparative warm spot. Coastal fog and overcast skies, frequent visitors near the shoreline, are of course much more of a rarity in the inland areas.

It has been said of San Luis Obispo County's climate that, like Gaul, it is divided into 3 parts: south county, north county, and coastal. The south county, which takes in San Luis Obispo city and the non-coastal areas south to the county line, is reliably sunny (265 days in the growing season), with only moderate amounts of moisture (21.92 inches annual average), concentrated in the winter months.

The north county, north and east of San Luis Obispo county, is drier and hotter in the summer and colder in the winter. Seasons are more marked.

San Luis Obispo's coastal area is the most even in temperature, with an average variance of less than ten degrees between winter and summer months. With the exception of Avila Beach, a usually sunny "pocket" nestled behind Point San Luis, the coast also has far fewer days of sunshine than other areas. Coastal fog, however, is an often unpredictable phenomenon, departing or arriving without warning, or burning off suddenly in the afternoon.

Each climate, of course, has its advocates. To some, a hot and dry climate is most preferable, while others find no substitute for the invigoration of a cooler shoreline climate.

Roadside Attractions

Mission Plaza

The two square blocks of Mission Plaza decorate San Luis Obispo Creek with a tasteful accompaniment of walkways, bridges, benches, wooden flower boxes, and colorful tiles. Designed by Santa Barbara architect Richard B. Taylor with a great deal of community input, Mission Plaza is one of the best-executed pedestrian areas in any of California's central cities.

The Creek

The plaza is enjoyable because it uses the creek as the vital center of a coherent whole. Rather than singularly orienting the visitor to the several commercial enterprises along the creek, the creek itself draws the focus, providing natural sights, sounds, and smells in an environment that is both woodsy and pleasingly urban.

Besides the several shops and eating places that dot the creek, visitors can tour an art center, the Murray Adobe, the San Luis Obispo County Historical Museum (located in a Carnegie Library Building), and the Mission San Luis Obispo. You can wander through two centuries of history on your journey through Mission Plaza, then enjoy a

meditative moment on the sloping lawns, where aromas of jasmine and eucalyptus pervade. Or walk along the creek, savoring the cool shade and musical sound of water running over stones.

Should you desire a repast, Sebastian's has very good food for both inside and outside dining, and on Sunday a fine champagne brunch is served. Down the street the Cigar Factory deserves attention, and the Bakery Cafe is also worthy of recommendation.

Resources

Walking San Luis Obispo's History

Park your vehicle and enjoy a two-hour walking tour through San Luis Obispo's charming history. Begin at Mission San Luis Obispo at Mission Plaza and simply follow the green lines painted on the city streets.

1. MISSION PLAZA, historic and social center of the city.

2. MISSION SAN LUIS OBISPO DE TOLOSA, the fifth of 21 missions in the state, founded by Father Junípero Serra in 1772. Open daily.

3. JUDGE WALTER MURRAY ADOBE, 1846 home of writer and journalist Walter Murray.

4. SAN LUIS OBISPO COUNTY HISTORICAL MUSEUM, originally the Carnegie Library, built in 1905; the museum located here in 1956. Open daily except Monday.

5. CIGAR FACTORY, an 1897 Victorian cigar factory, now a restaurant backing on San Luis Creek.

5A. CREAMERY, a full-service creamery operated here from 1906 until 1974, now a mall of shops and restaurants.

6. ST. STEPHEN'S EPISCOPAL CHURCH, one of the first Episcopal churches in the state (1867). The original pipe organ was donated by Phoebe Apperson Hearst.

7. MYRON ANGEL HOME, home of the original historian of San Luis Obispo County and founder of Cal Poly State University.

8. PRESBYTERIAN CHURCH, 1905 church built entirely of granite rock from Bishop's Peak, the second peak in San Luis Obispo's majestic row of mountains.

9. SAN LUIS CREEK, meanders underground through the city, becoming visible at Mission Plaza.

10. DALLIDET ADOBE, 1853 home built by Pierre Hyppolite Dallidet, a French vintner.

11. KUNDERT MEDICAL BUILDING, designed by Frank Lloyd Wright (1956).

12. RAMONA DEPOT, official depot built by the SP Railroad Company in 1889 and all that remains of the elegant Ramona Hotel, which burned down in 1905.

13. FREMONT MARKER, a granite column marking the spot of an overnight encampment by General John Fremont.

14. AH LOUIS STORE, store built by the leader of the town's Chinese settlement in 1874 and made entirely of bricks from his brickyard. The store served the more than 2,000 Chinese laborers who built the railroad tunnels.

15. SAUER ADOBES, circa 1860, includes examples of technique of covering adobe walls with clapboard to protect them from rain.

16. SINSHEIMER BROTHERS STORE, 1874 boasting the only iron-front facade on a building anywhere in the county. The front was cast in San Francisco and transported by boat.

17. SITE OF CASA GRANDE, adobe built by William G. Dana in 1851.

18. BULL & BEAR PIT, site of the deadly spectator sport of the early settlers.

19. ANDREWS BANK BUILDING, built in 1893 by J. P. Andrews, who also donated the land across the street for the County Courthouse.

Four Days from Bakersfield

At first they came by horse and wagon to stay at Schneider's campground, where Mathias Schneider set up a camping resort amid a eucalyptus grove south of Morro Bay. In those days there were Fourth of July fireworks off the top of Morro Rock and dances under the stars. Midnight clambakes were held on the sandspit beneath the shadows of the moon as young couples put aside the drudgeries of valley farmlife—with 100° heat and 16-hour workdays—for the pleasure and refreshment of Morro's sea-cool breezes.

By the turn of the century, each summer brought hundreds of campers to the "point" just north of the isolated little village of Morro, which eventually added "Bay" to its name at the request of the postal service to avoid confusion with Mono, California. When Schneider's campground built a dance hall, local people were drawn as well, traveling over poor roads that created excuses to dance all night rather than return through hazardous darkness.

It took four arduous and exhausting days to reach Schneider's from Bakersfield, but they came in droves. By the early 1920s, the road to San Luis Obispo had been paved, making travel much faster and tourists more numerous. A celebration in Morro Bay accompanied the opening of the newly paved road, and the Chamber of Commerce was effusive:

The call of the sea over splendid highways in picturesque scenes and ever balmy weather leaves only one other factor to make for complete happiness in this wonderful playground of the west—the automobile. And this factor is one almost universally possessed in this land of Cornucopia. Everybody motors and everybody enjoys it to the uttermost.

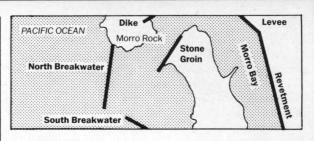

Morro Bay

Morro Bay is the only landlocked anchorage along the San Luis Obispo–Santa Barbara coastline. Its waters protect a major fishing fleet and provide fertile grounds for one of the largest West Coast oyster cultivation operations. The bay's 500 acres of marshlands and adjacent mudflats also encompass the most important coastal estuary south of Elkhorn Slough in Monterey County.

An amazing 80% of the central coast's marine life originates in the Morro Bay estuary. The area ranks in the nation's top ten for the number of bird species sighted in a single day.

Morro Bay is separated from the ocean by a 4.5-mile-long sandspit that varies in width from 1,000 to 2,000 feet and contains 80-foot-high sand dunes. The entrance to the bay was originally between Morro Rock and the mainland, but that was filled by a revetment, or stone dike, when the Corps of Engineers built a paved road in 1933 to connect the rock and the mainland. The only remaining entrance lies between two highly engineered breakwaters designed to calm the waters in the entrance channel. The north breakwater, composed of locally quarried rock, extends 1,885 feet south from Morro Rock. The south breakwater, 1,832 feet long, was built in 1946 to define the mouth of the bay's entrance channel. Additional revetments, levees, dikes, and groins have been constructed on the bay's interior.

Blue-Sky Salesmen

In 1919 Morro's mysterious rock captivated the attention of E. G. Lewis, a developer who had established University City, Missouri, and the Atascadero Colony, inland from Morro Bay. When he viewed Morro Bay, Lewis imagined it as a mecca for American easterners and midwesterners. He would sell them their portion.

After purchasing 463 acres of land on the ocean side of Highway 1, Lewis set out to sell off small lots of what he named Atascadero Beach. Pictures of the imposing rock in the bay graced his promotional brochures—*The Illustrated Review* and *California, the Beautiful*—and land buyers from the east and midwest with stars in their eyes rushed to buy a portion of paradise.

To focus eager land buyer's dreams, Lewis built an oceanfront resort on Atascadero Beach. Named the Cloisters Inn, the Mission Revival structure with open views of Morro Rock was the headquarters for Lewis's lot auctions. Buyers crowded the Cloisters and ignored the warnings of pamphlets that spoke of "those who have had some experience with superficial or dishonest 'boomers' and have become suspicious [of] land sharks, fakers, and lying blue-sky salesmen."

Lewis put in streets, curbs, and gutters, even added decorative iron lamps, but ignored services such as water and sewage. In nine years only one structure was ever built. Eventually the California Land Commission seized the property for unpaid taxes.

Other Morro Bay subdivisions had less catastrophic consequences than Lewis's Atascadero Beach. During the early 1920s a group of local investors formed a syndicate and launched Morro Heights. Their success in selling $300 lots attracted other developers, many from Los Angeles, where the fine arts of subdivision, speculation, and hard sell had reached connoisseur standards.

Environment | Roadside Attractions | Resources

Circling, Circling

Overhead at Morro Bay flashes the occasional glimmer of predatory hooked bill and strong curved talons. A state ecological reserve at the rock protects one of the few remaining California habitats of the endangered peregrine falcon.

The peregrine falcon is among the swiftest of all birds, surpassed in speed only by the prairie falcon. A peregrine can reach a speed of over 200 miles an hour as it dives from the heavens to feed on the terns, coots, wild ducks, and other marsh birds around Morro Bay. Falcons, sometimes called streamlined hawks, are identifiable in the field by pointed wings which average 3 feet in length, and tails that narrow at the tip. The peregrine's body is similar to that of a common crow in size. The male is slate gray above, pale below, with white unstreaked throat and fine barring on its buffy breast. The call of the bird, which is silent in flight, is a long series of slurred notes.

Peregrine falcons nest on rocky ledges like Morro Rock, laying two to four spotted eggs in nests composed of merely a few sticks. Until recently the theft of eggs and young birds by would-be falconers and extensive damage to the

falcon food chain by pesticides seriously depleted falcon populations in California. Today their few remaining habitats are fiercely protected and studied by environmentalists and public agencies in yet another of the widening gyres of relationship between falcon and falconer, humans and their world.

Morro Bay

Despite an active tourist economy, Morro Bay maintains an authentic maritime character on its Embarcadero. Commercial fishing is still a vital presence, and a number of charters are available for sport fishing. From the marina you can take a $3-ride on a "clam taxi" that drops you at the sandspit, where you may clam, swim, or explore the dunes. Boats are also available for personal use by the hour.

Along the Embarcadero are several fine places

to dine and watch shorebirds and boats in the harbor. Zeke's has very good seafood and is a local favorite. Rose's restaurant has good food, a good view, and a waterfront deck where you may stroll on the edge of the bay and watch the fog silently slink in over the watertop.

One of Morro Bay's most interesting overnight accommodations is also located on the Embarcadero—Gray's Inn, which has moderate rates for one-bedroom cabanas with individual decks on the edge of the bay. The Embarcadero has plenty of souvenir shops, salt water taffy, and an aquarium–gift shop where 70¢ buys you a ticket to see captive seals that beckon with their flippers for food and, presumably, their freedom.

Morro Rock

But nothing along this part of the coast stands out like Morro Rock, whose presence looms over everything in the town and imbues the place with a mystical significance. You can get to the Rock easily—drive out on the causeway built in the 1930s from rock quarried off the inland side. Morro Rock is now a state ecological preserve, protected from atrocities like those that left a 500-foot gash

in its 22-million-year-old face. Morro Rock is also a wildlife preserve, a protected nesting area for the endangered peregrine falcons that roost atop the 576-foot volcanic plug.

At the north end of Morro Bay is Atascadero Beach, which has good sport fishing and perfect appeal for long strolls. Above the beach is the Point Motel, a pink-walled blufftop motel that has topmost seaside charm and low prices. The rooms with great views are booked years into the future, but other attractive rooms are more readily available, and cancellations are always a possibility.

Montana de Oro State Park

Lower State Park Road
Morro Bay, 93442.
528-0513.

"Mountain of Gold," State Park embraces 6,900 miles of coastal meadow, mountain, and cliffs just north of Diablo Canyon. There are several beaches and pocket coves, including Spooner's Cove, whose history includes protection for contraband hides during the Mission days and bootleg liquor during Prohibition. Valencia Peak (1,345 ft.), two streams, and miles of hiking trails, equestrian trails and camps, and primitive camping areas cover the park, culminating in 1.5 miles of coastline. Fees for camping.

Montana de Oro State Park, the Pismo Dunes, and San Luis Obispo's volcanic peaks long to be walked upon. The trails in the county are extensive and rewarding.

SAN LUIS OBISPO COUNTY TRAIL GUIDE
Santa Lucia Chapter, Sierra Club. 1984.

Lucid maps and trail descriptions of 25 of the county's most popular hiking trails, many accessible from Highway 1. Also includes a summary of the county's natural history and charming black-and-white line drawings of trails and sites.

NATURE WALKS ON THE SAN LUIS COAST
Harold Wieman
Padre Productions, San Luis Obispo. 1980.

Published in cooperation with the Natural History Association of the San Luis Obispo Coast, this book provides general information on coastal ecology, especially of the Morro Bay Estuary, and a vibrant and informative dialogue on trails and sites.

Hikers shouldn't forget *California Coastal Trails,* Volume 1, by John McKinney (see Index).·

After the Steamers

In the early 20th century residents up the coast from Morro Bay found themselves more isolated than they had been a few years before, when shipping thrived and steamers could be boarded for connections near and far. The evolution of transportation had left residents of Cayucos, Cambria, and San Simeon in the lurch: the railroad had supplanted the cargo ship, but the railroad did not reach the coast.

Travelers to San Luis Obispo could spend 10 to 12 hours in bad weather on a bad road before the automobile came. Wagon travel did not sit well with north county residents who recalled days of nobler forms of transportation, when tall ships and steamers docked at Cayucos and San Simeon.

In Cambria, Orle Mayfield brought the modern age to the north coast when he replaced the horse-drawn stage with two smart Packards in 1910. Though the coast road was rutted, rock-strewn, and rough enough to break an axle, Mayfield's stylish auto-stages negotiated the route with comparative ease. His Packards became immediately popular as coast residents wheeled into the future on hard rubber tires.

Everything Changed

By the time an oiled and improved road was completed through Cayucos into Cambria in 1924, the automobile had changed everything: commerce now looked to the road, and opportunity seemed to have as asphalt face, as the pace of life assumed a four-wheeled hum it had never known before.

In 1927 the Cambria Development Company followed the newly surfaced road up the coast and built a mountain lodge in the pines above Cambria. The lodge was the lure for an adjacent subdivision that sold small lots for vacation dream homes through an extensive nationwide advertising campaign. Many lots were sold sight unseen to a trusting group of radio listeners and magazine readers who rarely got around to building on the lots. A few miles up the road, however, construction went on apace where the idea of the California dream home assumed its most heraldic and gaudiest dimension.

Two Californias

Northern and Southern Californians are never so strongly in agreement as they are in the opinion that the state is sharply divided into two distinct social, political, and economic halves. The line of demarcation between the two cultures is often placed in or near San Luis Obispo County, which contains enough of each realm's characteristics to function as the zone of transition between the Land of the Redwoods and the Sunny Southland.

The perception of California as two discrete regions predates statehood. In the 18th century, Franciscan Fathers found the California region too large and difficult to govern and recommended that it be severed just north of Santa Barbara. In 1941 an effort to establish the new northern California state of Jefferson advanced far enough that residents formed a provisional government. Armed with deer rifles, they stopped cars on the Klamath River highway and pressed copies of Jefferson's Declaration of Independence on passing motorists.

Each of the state's halves has considerable economic presence and power. As Dileo and Smith observe in *Two Californias*, Northern California possesses "valuable farmland, timber, water, a growing high-technology industry, one of the world's leading ports, the state's banking and commercial center, respected institutions of higher learning, a thriving tourist industry, the State Capitol, and one of America's largest metropolitan areas surrounding San Francisco Bay." Southern California possesses "America's second largest city, an economy bigger than many countries, agriculture, high-tech industries, the movie business, and most important of all, well more than half the state's population in a sprawling megalopolis."

So deep is the disparity of cultures and cultural values that Northern California visitors to Southern California often feel they have arrived on another planet, as do Southern Californians visiting the North. Not only are the natural environments extremely different, with the drier Southern California climate creating a less verdant landscape with wider vistas, but the aesthetic styles are also quite dissimilar. Southern California has more interesting contemporary architecture, Northern California has more interesting older architecture.

Where does the boundary between these two unlike states within a state occur? Some say it is at the exact point that the newspapers in driveways change from the *San Francisco Chronicle* to the *Los Angeles Times*.

Environment

Pier Fish

A variety of surfperch, rockfish, and other pier fish abound off San Luis Obispo's several municipal piers, including the ones at Cayucos, San Simeon, and Pismo Beach.

Surfperch

The term *surfperch* generally includes those species of saltwater perch that frequent the sandy surf zones. (Seaperch are found in deep water or along rocky shores.) Surfperch have compressed, deep bodies that are elliptical in outline, marked with one long dorsal fin. Among the most common of surfperch are the walleye, silver, redtail, and barred. Surfperch will usually bite a hook baited with mussels, bits of fish, marine worms, or shrimp. The fish follow the tide in to feed in very shallow water during high tides. Look for them when the water is clear.

Rockfish

Within the California coastal range are 52 species of fish referred to as rockfish. Rockfish come in a variety of sizes and shapes, but they bear absolutely no resemblance to rock cod, the name commonly applied to them. Though fish commissioners on the West Coat have aggressively campaigned for years to clear up the confusion caused by anglers' misnaming the fish, success has been limited. The spiny-rayed catch you take in San Luis Obispo may be one of the several different colors and sizes of rockfish that frequent the surf here, but some local fisherman will probably identify it for you as rock cod, red snapper, sea bass, black snapper, big red rock cod, or sugar bass. Correctly labeled or not, it will taste just as good when you get it home.

The Ecology of a Piling

The piers at San Simeon and Cayuos are supported by pilings which themselves contain whole universes of life. As many as 100,000 microscopic organisms have been found to occupy a single square of a piling's surface. These living things organize themselves among their neighbors in socially-cooperative patterns adapted to their own survival and that of the community. Life on a piling can be viewed generally in layers according to the tidal zones. The lower part which is always underwater is likely to yield starfish, the mid-tidal zone is marked by the California sea mussel and barnacles such as the common acorn barnacle will dominate the high tide zone and splash zone above the tide line.

Roadside Attractions

Cayucos

Approximately 7 miles north of Morro Bay is the town of Cayucos. Take the Highway 1 business route, which is just the old Highway 1 before Caltrans built a bypass freeway during the glory days of concrete expansionism.

Cayucos is a wonderful place. It has everything of expectation and surprise against a background of an always available sea. Cayucos' handsome 940-foot pier defines much of the waterfront activity. Lit at night, the pier is a superb location to fish

for red snapper, rock cod, and perch.

Should you desire to go more than 940 feet into the ocean, party boats are available for charter, and scuba gear may be rented.

Cayucos' main street has several good places to eat and drink—start with a cocktail at the old Cayucos Tavern and you may not make it any further. Only steps away, however, is the Way Station and the Back Door Cafe, which serve fine food in a friendly atmosphere. Doc's Dance Hall keeps Cayucos stepping.

North of town Gull Cottage offers an unusual collection of dolls, pillows, toys, ornaments, and clocks. A bright-yellow Victorian cottage covered with an eclectic arrangement of bizarre and decorative doodads, Gull Cottage may appeal to your surrealistic impulses.

Harmony

Harmony, population 18, is about as small as a place can be and still be called a town. But Harmony survives on its romantic allure. Once an active dairy town that made good tasting butter and cheddar cheese, Harmony has been transformed by modern roadside economics into a charming spot with a gallery, wine shop, pottery, antiques store, and a first-class restaurant, the Harmony Valley Inn, which uses carefully chosen ingredients in its rare-flavored dishes.

Cambria

At Cambria, the roadside landscape becomes Alpine in character, with thick pines and steep hills. Cambria has grown so much and so quickly since the 1950s that the correct pronunciation of its name has been lost in the deluge of new arrivals. Three current versions have their own constituencies, so no matter how you say it, you're certain to antagonize somebody. You can reach the beach off Ardath Drive.

If you pull off the road at Cambria, you'll find rewarding, fine-tasting breakfasts, lunches, and dinners at the Ridge Street Cafe. The Hampton's Motel offers charming and inexpensive family-style cottages.

Resources

Visitor Assistance

CAMBRIA CHAMBER OF COMMERCE
767 Main Street 93428.
927-3624.

CAYUCOS CHAMBER OF COMMERCE
200 South Ocean Avenue 93430.
995-1200.

GROVER CITY CHAMBER OF COMMERCE
883 Grand Avenue 93433.
489-9091.

LOS OSOS CHAMBER OF COMMERCE
2238 Bayview Heights 93402.
528-4884.

MORROW BAY CHAMBER OF COMMERCE
385 Morro Bay Boulevard 93442.
772-4467.

PISMO BEACH CHAMBER OF COMMERCE
581 Dolliver Street 93449.
773-4382.

SAN LUIS OBISPO CHAMBER OF COMMERCE
1039 Chorro Street 93401.
543-1323.

SAN SIMEON CHAMBER OF COMMERCE
Highway 1 93452.
927-3500.

Nitwit Ridge

Cambria is also the home of Nitwit Ridge, one of the most peculiar structures in a county of peculiar structures. Lying somewhere near the edge of the realm of improbability, Nitwit Ridge is the product of the overactive imagination of Art Beale. Captain Nitwit's structure demonstrates what may result when creative inspiration, whimsy, and an advanced appreciation of the absurd meet an abundance of abalone shells, knickknacks, and found objects.

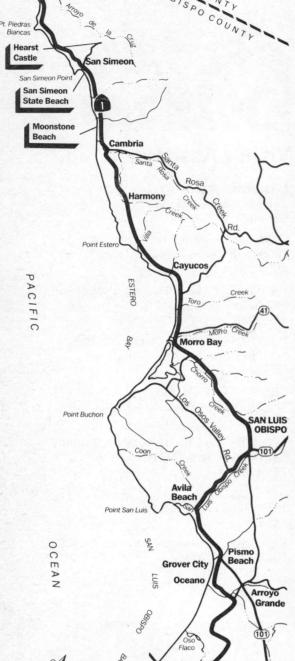

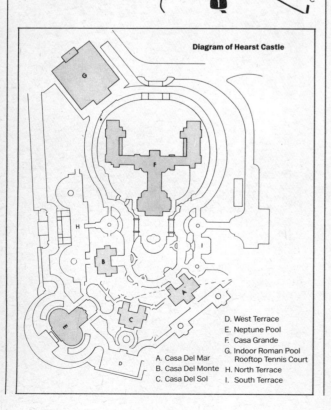

Diagram of Hearst Castle

A. Casa Del Mar
B. Casa Del Monte
C. Casa Del Sol
D. West Terrace
E. Neptune Pool
F. Casa Grande
G. Indoor Roman Pool
    Rooftop Tennis Court
H. North Terrace
I. South Terrace

Sailing to Byzantium

In 1919 construction began on La Cuesta Encantada, the castle of William Randolph Hearst, which would become the single most ornate monument to the grandiosity of the individual ego, the magnificence of artifice, and the flagrancy of California fantasy. Upon a hill, Byzantium was built.

Camp Hill

The hill had been the location for camping retreats initiated by Hearst's father, an illiterate, multimillionaire who drank heavily, drooled tobacco juice, cursed continuously—and became a United States Senator in 1886. George Hearst, rich from mining, owned almost the entire coastal area near San Simeon. It became his habit to retreat to the ridgetop—called "Camp Hill" by the family—with parties of friends. William Randolph accompanied the parties and came to view the hilltop as akin to the seat of paradise.

What Maturity Brought

William Randolph Hearst matured into a man for whom flamboyance paid off handsomely. Taking over his father's failing *San Francisco Examiner,* he developed a fantastically successful newspaper chain that mixed splashy tabloid graphics with lurid reporting. With maturity Hearst indulged an iconoclastic style. He kept a mistress, Tessie Powers, without apology, and favored bright-colored clothing, vivid cravats, and walking sticks, one of which whistled.

Unimpressed with William's flamboyance and cavalier regard for the importance of money, George Hearst willed every cent of his $18-million estate to his wife Phoebe Hearst. When his father died in 1891, the 27-year-old William was thus spared the challenge of seeing how fast he could spend his inheritance.

Expansion of an Empire

For more than 25 years, San Simeon remained Hearst's satori. Throughout the early years of his career as a publishing baron, congressman from New York, kingmaker, and frustrated presidential aspirant, San Simeon remained pleasurably present in his mind, and he frequently returned to Camp Hill for elegantly outfitted camping parties, "roughing it deluxe."

In 1919 Hearst's mother died. Phoebe Hearst's passing left the entirety of the Hearst estate to William Randolph, which hastened the expansion and elaboration of his empire. Now 56, Hearst undertook the construction of a world from what he imagined to be the artifice of eternity, in

. . . such a form as Grecian goldsmiths make
Of hammered gold and gold enamelling
To keep a drowsy Emperor awake;
Or set upon a golden bough to sing

To lords and ladies of Byzantium
Of what is past, or passing, or to come.

W. B. Yeats, "Sailing to Byzantium"

Living in Windsor Castle

The idea for a castle upon the hill near his birthplace may have been in Hearst's mind since childhood. W. A. Swanberg writes in *Citizen Hearst* that "he once had told his mother he would like to live in Windsor Castle and had asked her to buy the Louvre." Yet at age 56 Hearst had other reasons as well. One was the frustration he had experienced in his aspirations to be president—perhaps the only prize he had ever been refused. A castle—a hilltop shrine to the self—offered kingly compensation. A second motive concerned his relationship to Marion Davies.

The Virginal Young Heroine

Marion Davies was a Ziegfeld showgirl, 34 years younger that Hearst, for whom he established a movie production company that spent more than $7 million to advance her career through a series of idealized virginal roles. As Hearst's mistress during the San Simeon days, it was she rather than Millicent, Hearst's wife, who was the queen of the castle.

One cannot overestimate Hearst's affection for Davies: certainly far more than a sexual plaything, she was the object of his devotion and adoration until his death. Yet so possessive was he that he hired detectives to keep her under constant surveillance.

Hearst not only oversaw Davies's career, he showered her with jewels and built her castles—first San Simeon and then, when she grew tired of the big castle's isolation, he built her another on the beach at Santa Monica, a compound of five connecting colonial mansions. As Hearst's feelings for Davies deepened, San Simeon became more exotic yet, and it is not hard to relate the castle's sensual, often erotic art and architecture to the worshipful desire of an older man for a much younger, sexually attractive moviestar.

Touring the Castle

Access to the castle is by guided tour only and reservations are required. Visitors must make their reservations, obtain their tickets, and arrive at the visitor center's staging area to catch the shuttle bus that ascends to the castle. Visitors must leave with the tour they came with and return to the staging area even if they have tickets for another tour shortly thereafter.

All tours require lots of walking and stair climbing, so dress comfortably. Special tours are provided for the disabled (phone 927-4621). To make a tour reservation contact the nearest Ticketron outlet:

1-800-952-5580	Anywhere in California for forms & information, toll-free
(213) 642-3888	Los Angeles
(619) 565-9949	San Diego
(415) 393-6914	San Francisco
(916) 445-8828	Sacramento

The Tours

Four tours are offered, beginning at 8:20 am daily and continuing until around 3 pm. Each tour lasts just under two hours.

Landscaping Xanadu

The creativity, personal attention, and money that William Randolph Hearst devoted to the landscaping outside his castle nearly matches the efforts devoted to the architecture itself.

A Firm Fountain

Hearst Castle sits atop Camp Hill, originally the Hearst family campground. The hill had expansive views of the ocean, grazing lands, and—to the north—the rise of the imposing Santa Lucia Mountains. At the top of the hill was a majestic stand of native oaks, remembered fondly by Hearst for their shade during family outings. Other than the oaks and views, however, there was little else, just a thin cover of dusty dirt, scrubby sage, and lots of solid rock.

Turning this barren acreage into a garden fit for a castle was a monumental feat that required imagination, skill, hard work, and hectares of money. First, to get water to the site, pipes were run from a system of natural springs 5 miles away. Next, tons of rich topsoil were hauled from the fertile bottom lands of the ranch to the mountaintop.

Planning the Gardens and Grounds

Like the buildings, the gardens were designed and redesigned as construction proceeded and according to the latest desires of three eager minds: Hearst, Julia Morgan, and Nigel Keep, an Englishman who was in charge of the grounds for the first 22 years of the castle's existence. This piecemeal design process discouraged any grand scheme for an enormous formal garden, much to Hearst's intent.

Trees were planted at slight angles to prevent them from looking too unnatural, and the castle and its buildings were surrounded by a complex series of gardens, paths, walkways, and terraces that were planned to give the impression of an unplanned garden that, even in the beginning, seemed aged.

San Simeon

Just past Cambria is Moonstone Drive, which races past Moonstone Beach and actual moonstones (a translucent agate). Further north is the Sea Chest, which boasts a superb oyster bar.

Past the garish commercial strip at San Simeon, a pleasanter town of San Simeon awaits at the turnoff for William Randolph Hearst State Beach, where there is a fine pier and the Sebastian store, built in 1873. Several of the adjacent buildings were constructed to house Hearst Castle employees and to warehouse Hearst's superabundance of art treasures.

Hearst Castle

You never know what is enough unless you know what is more than enough.

William Blake

Welcome to the center of the realm of improbability, where once diamonds fell like rain. Conspicuous consumption has never known such a tribute, and freely reigned sensuality has never had such a shrine.

Leave your car in the parking lot and board the shuttle to the top of the hill. You'll ascend 5 miles through the center of what was once one man's kingdom: 250,000 acres that included 50 miles of coastline from Big Sur to Cambria.

On approaching the hilltop, take note of the magnificent pergola with vine-covered columns and carved birds and beasts and espaliered fruit trees. Here Hearst and his entourage would stroll to witness spectacular coastal sunsets.

The Enchanted Hill

Once you arrive at La Cuesta Encantada, the ordinary world evaporates and wafts away on perfumed winds that issue from the castle's terraces, plazas, and gardens. Beneath the imposing presence of La Casa Grande, a too-abundant assemblage of glazed Italian pottery, antique stone oil jugs, fountains, and sensuous statuary decorate the ground and enforce the presence of unreality.

Ancient sculptures, such as granite figures of the goddess Sekhmet from Egypt's 18th and 19th dynasties, are mixed with 19th- and 20th-century art, some of which—like Paul Manuat's *La Source,* a Moderne sculpture group of the 1930s—are as rapturously expressive as the ancient art. If there is a single dominant theme to the grounds, it is certainly the sensual enrapturement of love.

TOUR 1 *(Capacity 53 persons):* covers the gardens, the two pools, one of the three guest houses, and the lower level of the castle (refectory, assembly hall, and movie theater). About 150 stair steps.

TOUR 2 *(capacity 12 persons):* traverses the upper levels of the castle, including intimate views of Hearst's private Gothic Suite and the Celestial Suite, the libraries, a two-level guest room, kitchen, and pools. About 300 steps.

TOUR 3 *(capacity 14 persons):* focuses on the castle's guest wing, its 36 bedrooms, sitting rooms, and bathrooms—all elaborately furnished—and works of art, the pools, gardens, and a guest house. About 300 steps.

TOUR 4 *(capacity 15 persons):* ranges over different aspects of the castle, emphasizing the gardens, and provides a behind-the-scenes look at a hidden terrace, the wine cellar, the lower level of a guest house, the pools, and the filter and dressing rooms of the indoor pool. About 300 steps.

Architectural Exoticism

No private home has ever had such art as at San Simeon: Hearst stockpiled medieval and Renaissance treasures that would be at home only in a castle or a museum, and in such quantity—spending perhaps $1 million a year—that no ordinary castle could accommodate them. Hearst's collection of antique paintings, tapestries, silver, statues, and furniture was most likely the largest collection ever held by a private individual.

To create a house worthy of the magnificent art, Julia Morgan was hired to design Hearst's castle; with her Beaux Arts background and experience in public architecture, she was eminently suited to construct an ornate building of museum proportions. That she designed a group of buildings which complement the art they contain is an enduring credit to her craft.

First to be built was a road from the coast up to the top of the hill; then the guest houses: La Casa del Mar, La Casa del Monte, and Casa de Sol, each named for its views. Their Spanish Renaissance red-tiled roofs and white walls were more subdued and far less elaborate than what was to follow.

Planning for the castle was extremely sponta-

neous, with much of the design created or refined after construction was underway. Before the last guest house was finished, construction was begun on La Casa Grande, the castle itself, which would combine glass, walls, and ceilings from European palaces with newly built concrete structures that describe and exclaim a level of architectural exoticism previously unseen save for the excesses of Pashadom.

Julia Morgan, Architect

The first woman graduate of the Ecole des Beaux Arts in Paris (class of 1902) and the first woman architect licensed in California, Julia Morgan was decidedly different in personal style from the exotic and flamboyant Hearst Castle that she designed.

An extremely restrained woman who favored Queen Mary hats and old-fashioned clothing, Morgan oversaw the construction of YWCAs, chapels, and institutional buildings in every style from Italian Renaissance to Mission Revival. Morgan's first major work was the rebuilding of the interior of San Francisco's Fairmont Hotel after the 1906 earthquake and fire. She also designed over 600 residences, frequently shingled and often displaying Tudor arches and half-timbered exteriors. Morgan's architectural style shares certain resemblances with the work of Bernard Maybeck, for whom she worked prior to 1905 and with whom she later built the Hearst Gymnasium for Women at the University of California, Berkeley.

Designing Hearst Castle may have been an architect's dream—with an unlimited budget and a treasure trove of decorative materials. But it was also an architect's nightmare, offering little autonomy and much pressure to accommodate Hearst's every extravagant whim. Morgan held up, however, to her credit or not, and became a very wealthy woman in the process of completing the most unusual long-term design project any American architect ever had.

The Stars at San Simeon

As if to foster a mythos of make-believe at his castle, William Randolph Hearst filled its ballrooms, gardens, and guest houses with constant rounds of Hollywood moviestars. The stars, for their part, journeyed to San Simeon as if it were a shrine at the temple of tinsel and glamour.

Greta Garbo, Charles Chaplin, Cary Grant, Clark Gable, Buster Keaton, Hedda Hopper, Douglas Fairbanks, Joan Crawford, Howard Hughes, Gary Cooper—make up only part of the list of frequent Hollywood visitors that included almost every major and minor Hollywood light of the 1920s, 30s, and 40s.

Visits to San Simeon were conducted with a sense of ceremony and importance comparable to a trip to the Vatican. After receiving a formal invitation from Hearst, guests were chauffeured up the coast from Hollywood in a procession of limousines or railroad cars with catered food and accompanying musicians. Arriving at San Simeon, they were met by floodlights that rivaled a Hollywood opening.

Environment

Roadside Attractions

Resources

Trees and Flowers

In addition to the gardens directly around the castle, Hearst wanted the nearby visible ridgetops converted from rangeland to forest. During the first several years of development, some 4,000 to 5,000 native and exotic trees were planted on the hills.

The main drive to La Casa Grande was lined with 1,500 oleanders, 151 citrus, 61 pomegranates, 28 persimmons, and 18 quinces. Many of the large trees visible today were already half-grown when they arrived at San Simeon. Most weighed more than several tons. The beloved native oaks were either built around or uprooted and replanted, despite their weighing hundreds of tons each.

Hearst himself selected many of the individual trees. The cypress around the outdoor pool, for example, were saved from a woodsman's axe in Paso Robles. Hearst simply ordered all thirty of the tall trees to be dug up, encased in wooden boxes, and brought to San Simeon, where they were watered and fertilized for over two years before being transplanted.

Today's Gardens

During Hearst's lifetime, five greenhouses operated on the grounds, nurturing 650,000 to 700,000 annuals each year. Once the castle passed under control of the State, the greenhouses were abandoned, but the job of keeping the grounds in bloom is still staggering.

Every year between April and October the grounds staff plants some 25,000 annuals, to ensure that there are always plenty of blossoms. At the beginning of each season the soil is conditioned with about 25 tons of nutrients. Tree trimming is a constant chore, and each year as many as 50 new trees are planted. In the summer of 1984, for example, the eight-member full-time ground staff and their seasonal assistants planted some 30 citrus trees.

The annual budget for the gardens is around $75,000, which includes funds to replace plants lost to the havoc of the weather. Temperatures here can soar to 100° during the day and dip to a moderate 60° or less in the evenings—conditions that some exotic species cannot endure.

Neptune's Pool

At Neptune's Pool, the exaltation of the senses gains deeper dimension. Between a marble monument to Venus rising from the sea (*Naissance de Venus*, executed by Parisian sculptor Charles Cassou) and the magnificent facade of an ancient Greco-Roman temple, lies the 104-foot shimmering pool, which requires 345,000 gallons of water to fill. The basin is lined with white Vermont marble and covered with a grid-and-key design made from verde antique, a jadelike mineral.

The ancient Greco-Roman temple is the thematic center of the outdoor pool: the glory of Greece and the grandeur of Rome are evoked in an orgy of white marble amid symbols of ripening sexuality. Where else could the Three Graces (Brilliance, Joy, and Bloom) find harmony with four white marble Ledas and the Swan, a statuary birth of Venus, marble mermaids, sea nymphs riding on dolphins—all superintended by a 16th-century sculpted Italian Neptune with a broken trident?

La Casa Grande

But nothing dazzles like the castle itself. Principally defined by two Spanish Renaissance towers that house 36 bronze carillon bells, the "castle" looks more like a cathedral or a Hollywood facsimile created for an epic film.

The main structure contains approximately 100 rooms and 40,000 square feet of living space. The largest room is the Great Assembly Hall, where Hearst hosted his guests at 7:30 each evening before adjourning to the refectory for dinner. The huge chamber measures 100 × 42 feet with two-story walls ascending to an antique carved wooden ceiling.

Most of the room contains pieces from either the French or Italian Renaissance, although art deco furniture and art pieces are mixed throughout.

Around the room are a group of wooden citair statues from an ancient Italian monastery, a French Renaissance stone mantel once owned by architect Stanford White, numerous antique tables, benches, vases, and chests, and a series of 7th-century Flemish tapestries—once the property of the Spanish Royal Family—one of which portrays Neptune and Venus.

No less grand than the Assembly Hall is the Refectory, where art of the Middle Ages prevails and where Hearst held court around a kingly dinner table with bottles of ketchup, relish, and pickles in the center to undercut the room's formality.

This room too has a magnificent hand-carved ceiling—more than 400 years old, originally created for an Italian Monastery. Sienese banners hang from poles high on the walls, silver pieces—candlesticks, cisterns, and serving dishes—stand opulently on every level surface, and a gigantic French Gothic mantel covers an end wall as it would in a palace.

Castle Books

THE ENCHANTED HILL: THE STORY OF HEARST CASTLE AT SAN SIMEON
Carleton M. Winslow, Nickola L. Frye, and Taylor Coffman
Rosebud Books, Los Angeles. 1983 *(3rd edition)*.
A souvenir book, offering a brief but well-written text and impressive color photographs.

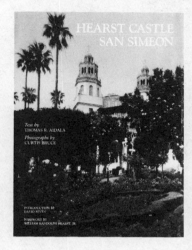

HEARST CASTLE: SAN SIMEON
Thomas R. Aidala
Curtis Bruce, photographs, Hudson Hills Press. New York. 1981.
This is the most lucid and comprehensive presentation of the story of the castle. Lively anecdotes recount how Hearst and Morgan built this architectural monument, and the text details the lives of both—from Hearst's relationship to his family, to Morgan's struggle to become one of the world's most recognized architects—at a time when women were unheard of in the profession. Fully illustrated, showing grounds, gardens, rooms, and works of art.

HANDBOOK OF THE PAINTINGS IN THE HEARST SAN SIMEON STATE HISTORICAL MONUMENT
Burton B. Fredericksen
Delphinian Publications, California Department of Parks & Recreation. 1976.
A complete survey of all the major paintings in the castle, many of which are of museum quality. This little handbook is a help for the visitor and also a hint of Hearst's personal taste.

THE ART OF SAN SIMEON: INTRODUCTION TO THE COLLECTION
Carol J. Everingham
Haagen Printing, Santa Barbara. 1981.
An art book that makes no attempt to catalogue and describe the collection but rather to evoke through verse, historical quotations, and representative pieces the warmth and quality of Hearst's acquisitions within each medium, including pottery, earthenware, tiles, ceramics, brass, bronze, iron, rugs, and tapestries.

MONTEREY

IN MONTEREY County, Highway 1 achieves a road-going glory beyond compare. Threading along the edge of the continent through Big Sur, the Coast Highway hangs mystically above the sea, serene and sublime. Big Sur is like no place on earth. "Its majesty is almost painful to behold," said Henry Miller. "That same prehistoric look. The look of always. Nature smiling at herself in the mirror of eternity." Yet it is Big Sur's attractive majesty that perhaps threatens to bring about its own demise by drawing so many visitors and mansion builders that its face is made ordinary, its wildness tamed.

Upon descending to Point Lobos and the Monterey Peninsula, the Highway 1 traveler is greeted by the storybook appeal of Carmel, California's quaintest city. In Monterey, the newly opened Monterey Bay Aquarium at Cannery Row provides the most dazzling maritime interpretive exhibits to be found on the coast.

North of Monterey, the presence of the sea once again asserts itself as Highway 1, disguised temporarily as a multi-lane freeway, speeds along white sand beaches to the appealing town of Moss Landing and nearby Elkhorn Slough, whose warm colored marsh grasses harbor a multitude of natural life.

Monterey County contains some of California's most stunning coastal wilderness and unspoiled habitats, as well as being a focal point for extremely intense development pressures. A magnificently beautiful county, it is also a tremendously threatened one, whose value as a scenic treasure cannot be overestimated or too agressively preserved.

Pebble Beach
Del Rey Oaks
Carmel
Point Lobos
Carmel Highlands
Wildcat Creek
Granite Creek
Little Sur River
Point Sur
Los Padres National Forest
Big Sur River
Big Sur
Sur River
Santa Lucia Range
Andersen Creek
OCEAN
Big Creek
PACIFIC
Lopez Point **Lucia**
Nacimiento Fergusson Road
Jade Cove
Cape San Martin *Willow* **Gorda**
Salmon Creek
SAN LUIS OBISPO CO / *MONTEREY CO*

County Profile

Geographic

Land Area (acres)	2,127,360
Land Area (sq. miles)	3,324.0
Water Area (acres)	70
Water Area (sq.miles)	.1
Acres in Public Ownership	634,536.70
Percent in Public Ownership	29.83
Miles of Public Roads	2,324
County Seat	Salinas

Demographic

Population	309,600
State Rank by Population	18
Projected 1990 Population	313,800
Unemployment Rate (state avg = 9.9)	11.5
Per Capita Personal Income	$11,981
State Rank by Income	11
Total Assessed Property Value	$8,535,291,596

The Unknown Coastal Wilderness

Despite its spectacular presence, Big Sur was an unknown coastal wilderness until late in the 19th century. Formidible in its beauty, it remained untouched far longer than the less-wild adjacent lands.

The area's once-extensive native American population, the Esselens, eventually moved on to less difficult terrain. The only native Americans to be seen in Big Sur by the middle of the 1800s were sojourners from the Salinas who might show for a season to hunt or fish.

Even the Spanish explorers, saw the region no more distinctly than *el país grande del sur*—"the big country to the south." Simply naming the area seemed enough for the Spanish, who were used to seeking glory and grandeur where the topography was less imposing.

One of the first white settlers to arrive to this magnificent unpopulated land was George Davis, who left Monterey after an argument with his wife and built a small cabin along the Río Grande del Sur in 1853. It took Davis eight years to cool off and return to his wife in Monterey, after having sold his 160 acres and cabin to Manuel Innocenti for $50.

The uninhabited land had little need for roads. Trails furnished suitable access for the occasional hunters who arrive on horseback seeking wild grizzly or deer. By the 1860s a semblance of a wagon road ran from Monterey to Wildcat Creek south of the present-day Highlands Inn. There the road changed into a trail that ran along the coast to Granite Creek before scaling the mountains to the Big Sur River.

Eventually more settlers were attracted by the government's pre-emption policy, which enabled homesteaders to gain title to 160-acre parcels of unappropriated public lands for $1.25 an acre by merely filing a declaration of intent and settling on the land. The promise of dirt-cheap land brought the first families to Big Sur.

Because of the paucity of roads, many of the homesteaders, like William Post and Anselma Post, had to pack in household equipment—stoves, beds, and furniture—using teams of mules that plodded over the uncertain trails beyond the wagon road at Wildcat Creek. And even at that, the trails frequently disappeared into the wild brush or forest, leaving the new settlers to find their own way through the untrammeled countryside.

Many of those who came gave their name to the land. Michael Pfeiffer and Barbara Pfeiffer arrived from San Francisco on the sidewheeler *Nevada* with their four small children and their cattle and horses. They then climbed the mountains on foot to the redwoods and shoreline south of the Big Sur River. Laura Partington and John Partington came with a pack train of 15 mules carrying household goods and furniture over the rugged trails from Monterey. But one of the mules lost its footing on a steep cliff and plunged into the depths, pulling three other mules packed with supplies into the abyss.

Big Sur Nation

Few places in the world rival the superlative scenic splendor of Big Sur, and among them even fewer remain without government controls to preserve their beauty. Many nations, including the U.S., have seen fit to protect their most important scenic treasures for reasons of both national pride and obligation to future generations. Yet, unlike Yosemite, the Grand Canyon, or the Everglades, Big Sur is not a federally protected area.

The conspicuousness of this omission was not missed by Ansel Adams, who helped set up the Big Sur Foundation to work for the establishment of a Big Sur National Park. The legislative procedure seemed simple: since Big Sur abuts the Los Padres National Forest, have Congress expand the Los Padres' boundaries to include Big Sur's undeveloped scenic lands. In one legislative act, Big Sur could be protected forever.

Unfortunately, things proved more complex. National pride is one thing, local pride sometimes another. To many of the few hundred permanent Big Sur residents, who treat their relationship to the coast as an independent stewardship, the proposed federal designation smacked of intervention by insensitive outsiders. Some feared a decline in property values, others an increase in tourism. Together they were able to put the kibosh on the move to extend federal jurisdiction and protection to the area.

Leon Panetta, Big Sur's congressman, attempted a compromise settlement that would have granted local residents a voice in the management of Big Sur once it was under U.S. Forest Service jurisdiction. But his proposal still met opposition from local residents whose suspicions of federal bureaucracies run deep. In 1980, Panetta's legislation was opposed by conservatives in the Senate. When the bill was reintroduced by Alan Cranston, it was stalled through two legislative sessions.

Present prospects offer no real promise of federal protection for Big Sur. The area's fate is now in the hands of the California Coastal Commission and the County of Monterey, which together have forestalled many proposals for large-scale development as they have gone about the complicated process of developing a local coastal program for the highly sensitive land.

In September of 1984 the LCP was finally approved by the Coastal Commission. The plan allows construction of 300 more hotel rooms in small scattered sites, each holding 30–60 units. About 900 new homes may also be built, but they must be sited out of view sheds (the areas visible from Highway 1). As soon as the county amends its zoning ordinance to reflect the new plan, development permits will once again be issued in Big Sur.

Environment

Big Sur

Big elbows of Rock rising everywhere, sea caves within them, seas plollocking all around inside them crashing out foams, the boom and pound on the sand dipping quick (no Malibu Beach here). . .you look into the sky, bend way back, my god you're standing directly under that aerial bridge with its thin white line running from rock to rock and witless cars racing across it like dreams! From rock to rock! All the way down the raging coast! So that when later I heard people say, "Oh, Big Sur must be beautiful!" I gulp to wonder why it has the reputation of being beautiful above and beyond its fearfulness, its Blakean rough-rock creation throes, those vistas when you drive the coast highway on a sunny day opening up the eye for miles of horrible washing, sawing.
Jack Kerouac, *Big Sur*

Enter the gates of an unpredictible paradise. No bucolic angels plucking harps on fluffy clouds here. Rather—power, collision, soaring freedom, and the California coastline that is nothing if not adamant about its presence.

Big Sur is 80 miles of a battling ocean and shore, where only the courageous and strong survive. Inland rise the jealous sentinel of the Santa Lucia Mountains, whose rocky toes test the icy waters of the Pacific and whose shoulders extend almost straight up for hundreds and then thousands of feet. The mountains are slashed by canyons and gorges, sparkling streams and waterfalls. Under the surface ancient volcanic interiors bubble up hot springs that contain sulpher, iron, soda, and magnesia and that reach temperatures of 160°. The world's largest trees, the coastal redwoods, blanket the sloping mountainside, habitat for hawks, falcons, bear, and the powerful tusked wild boar.

Offshore crash breakers of brilliant blue and sparkling turquoise in an ocean that appears to change color according to its daily mood or the phases of the moon. Beds of the largest kelp known to the sea create underwater forests hundreds of feet high. Otters, sea lions, whales, and sharks move in mysterious patterns offshore. The beaches yield jade; the mountains gold, silver, lime and granite.

Within the natural universe, Big Sur stands alone.

Roadside Attractions

County Line

Monterey County: see it invent itself upon the ascent of the Santa Lucia Mountains; beauty shaped from forest and rocks and tide and elevation. Big Sur comes from nowhere and nowhere seems as blessed.

This is the ethereal kingdom, where spirit and beauty commingle in lurid movements of earthly paradise pantomime. Drench the senses.

Past the county line to Salmon Creek, a waterfall announces Eden where the redwood trees begin. You may wish to adventure up the creek to the falls and immerse yourself in this seductive portion of Big Sur's lush verdure. Perhaps to shed your clothes and shower beneath the chilling cascade of mountain water racing to the sea. No pagan baptism was ever more sensuous or more appropriate to place.

From Big Sur's southern entrance, Highway 1 conducts itself through the Los Padres National Forest, where several public picnic areas on the west side of the highway provide magnificent vistas and wonderful stopping places. East of the Highway a number of trails allow rewarding access to the Los Padres Wilderness.

At Gorda a grocery store and gas station offer roadside accompaniments along with a restaurant, Sorta Gorda, which is as good as its name. From 1979 to 1983, the town of Gorda was owned by KIDCO, a corporation made up and run by local kids.

On the small rise behind the gas station a short trail leads to the Big Sur Jade Company. Proprietor Ken Comello collects, cuts, and polishes nephrite jade that he finds underwater and on the beach at nearby Jade Cove. Here you can buy any size piece of jade practically cheaper than anywhere else. Should you desire to find your own stones at Jade Cove, Comello will polish them or show you how to do it yourself.

Resources

AREA CODE: 408

Public Transportation

899-2555 Monterey-Salinas Transit
649-4700 Coastlines Bus Service
372-4492 Monterey Peninsula Transit

Rules of the Road

Highway 1 in Big Sur offers a driving challenge unmatched on the California coast. On busy weekends, the challenge may be to restrain oneself from hasty action after being stuck for miles

behind slow-moving traffic on the narrow two-lane road. But more often, the road winds ahead in sinuous splendor, vying with spectacular views and an occasional glimpse of wildlife or waterfall for the driver's attention. It's usually best to use one of the roadside turnouts to indulge in that glimpse straight down to the pounding sea. The Big Sur emergency road service phone number is 667-2518.

Climate

Monterey coastal weather is mild and temperate, although fog and strong winds are often part of a Big Sur day. The seasons are marked by variation in rainfall more than temperature, with January and February usually the wettest months. An average winter day is about 57°. In summer, average temperature is 67°, slightly cooler at Big Sur heights and in its forested canyons. Summer fogs can be heavy throughout Monterey, but they usually burn off during mid-day.

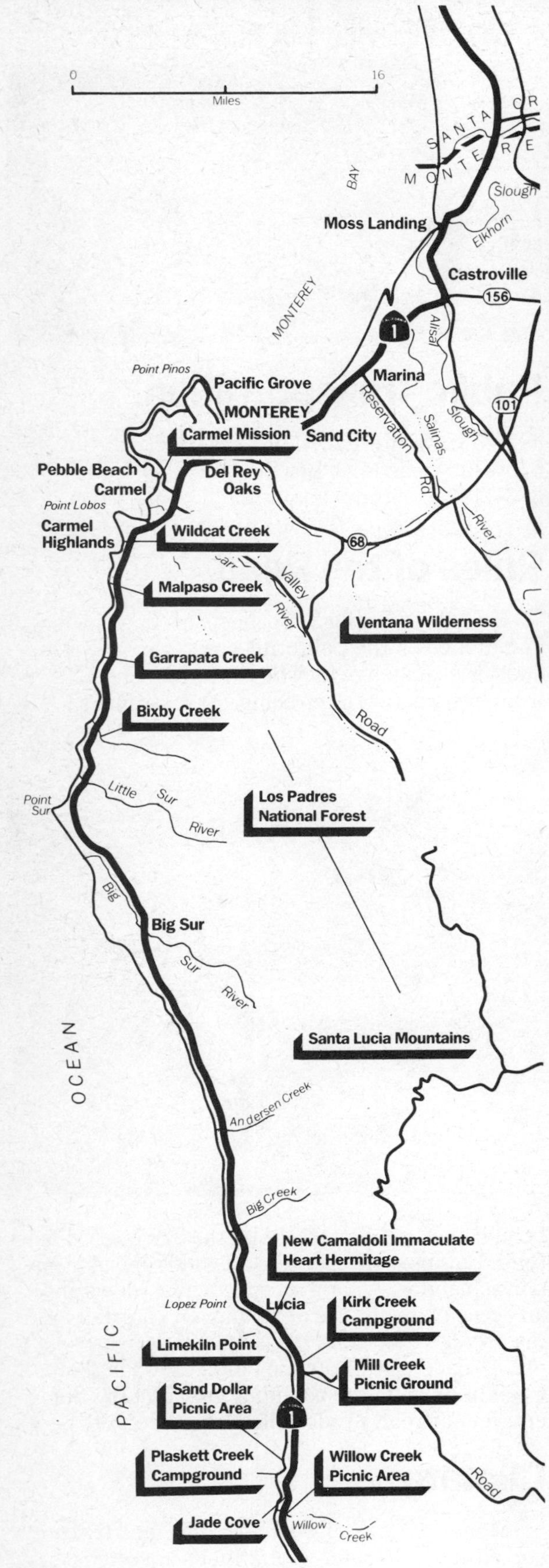

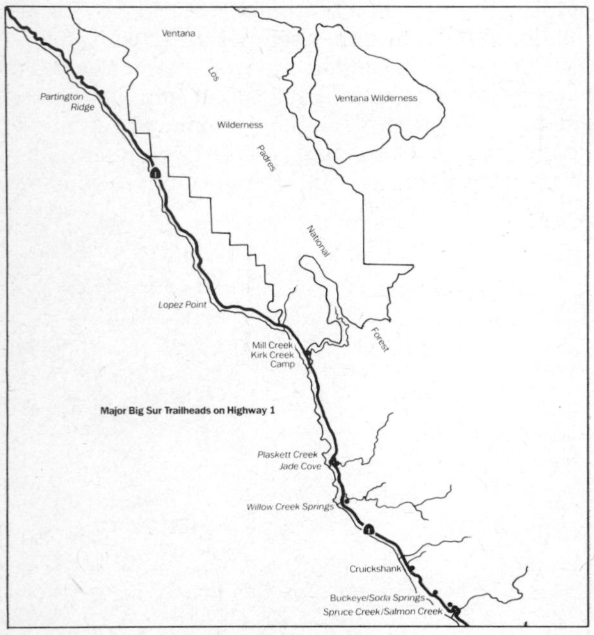

Map labels (left column)

Miles 0 — 16

SANTA CRUZ
MONTEREY
BAY
Slough
Moss Landing
Castroville
156
Elkhorn Slough
Point Pinos
Pacific Grove
Marina
MONTEREY
Carmel Mission
Sand City
Pebble Beach
Carmel
Del Rey Oaks
Point Lobos
Carmel Highlands
Wildcat Creek
Malpaso Creek
Ventana Wilderness
Garrapata Creek
Bixby Creek
Los Padres National Forest
Point Sur
Little Sur River
Big Sur
Sur River
Santa Lucia Mountains
Andersen Creek
Big Creek
New Camaldoli Immaculate Heart Hermitage
Lopez Point
Lucia
Kirk Creek Campground
Limekiln Point
Mill Creek Picnic Ground
Sand Dollar Picnic Area
Plaskett Creek Campground
Willow Creek Picnic Area
Jade Cove
Willow Creek

101
Alisal Slough
Salinas River
68
Carmel Valley Road
Reservation Rd

OCEAN
PACIFIC

Inset map

Ventana
Partington Ridge
Ventana Wilderness
Los Padres Wilderness
Lopez Point
Mill Creek Kirk Creek Camp
National Forest
Major Big Sur Trailheads on Highway 1
Plaskett Creek Jade Cove
Willow Creek Springs
Cruickshank
Buckeye/Soda Springs
Spruce Creek/Salmon Creek

Building a Wagon Road

Eventually the early Big Sur settlers complained that travel was too harrowing and too slow. They petitioned the County to build a wagon road that would allow supplies to be brought into the area and mitigate the crushing isolation. But the county government showed little concern: "Show us the road is feasible first." So the few residents of Big Sur decided to build the road themselves—across Malpaso Creek ("Bad Crossing") and all the way south to Garrapata.

A small crew of farmers and settlers with picks and shovels began to forge a road out of the hard granite. With the same pioneer determination they had brought to settling the land, they tirelessly carved the new passageway, constructing wooden plank bridges across creeks and ravines. Twenty-three bridges were required to cross the creeks from Carmel Mission to the new road's endpoint 18 miles south. These settlers sacrificed the tending of their own homesteads, neglecting their chores, for the community's need of a new road.

The new road was also intended to satisfy the economic needs of the isolated area—a consequence not lost on Charles Bixby, an ambitious rancher who had a homestead at Mill Creek, now Bixby Creek. Bixby assumed the supervision of the road crew, paying extra men $1.25 a day and providing them with food and lodging at his ranch. Under Bixby's hard-driving supervision, the road was soon completed and the County committed to its financial assistance. Conveniently, the road terminated at Charlie Bixby's front door, connecting his ranch to the outside world and the expanding economic markets at Monterey. But Big Sur had a road—at least part of the way into the wilderness.

The Dilemma of the Automobile at Big Sur

Big Sur is a formidably strong granite wilderness with an unforgiving terrain and a heroic seacoast. But it is as fragile and susceptible to harm as the most delicate patch of countryside. Among the most indelicate of impacts to the area are those caused by the automobile.

During the peak summer months an average of 112,000 automobiles pass through Big Sur on any given day; more than 3 million travelers a year. Traffic at times achieves urban rush-hour proportions and, with an increasing rural population and an expanding statewide tourist industry, all forecasts predict more traffic. Sustained high traffic on Highway 1 has four major effects on Big Sur's environment:

Traffic threatens the region's character

Highway 1's two uninterrupted strings of loud, smoking automobiles are hostile to Big Sur's wilderness topography and serene rural atmosphere. The throngs of cars reduce Big Sur's sublimity to a harsh ordinariness.

Traffic causes pollution

Heavy traffic changes the air from pristine to noxious, and noise pollution rises in direct proportion to traffic levels. As a result, visitors often hear the racket of the highway above the subdued roar of the sea; pollution also seriously affects wildlife.

Traffic makes the journey nerve-racking

Travelers can easily become so immersed in traffic and so agitated by frustrations that their visit may be no more visually or emotionally exceptional than the sight of the rear bumper of an RV camper pasted with stickers from Niagara Falls to Disneyland.

Traffic changes the local economy

Local retail enterprises—from gas stations to motels—must adapt to the design economics and cost efficiencies of the commercial strip, forgoing their out-of-the-way rustic character to appeal to the passing motorist in a hurry.

What can be done? Can traffic be reduced on a public highway in an equitable fashion to protect the surrounding environment?

The Santa Lucia Mountains

Big Sur *is* the Santa Lucia Mountains. Nowhere else are land and sea so equally matched in eternal conflict. The cliffs here bear the scars of battles fought for over 200 million years, rocks' struggle to be free from the watery face of the planet.

The Santa Lucia were once a solid mass of sedimentary rock on the ocean floor. Then, about 10 million years ago, the sediment was covered by successive layers of lava flows, arriving from inland volcanos. Eventually, the volcanic rock rose above the ocean's depth at a spot several miles east of Big Sur's present location.

Later, but still long before human arrival, violent earthquakes thrust the volcanic rocks up, breaking them apart and pushing them west. Since then, the southwestern exposure of the mountains' face to the relentless erosion of wind, waves, and inland water flows have molded the gracefully powerful contours of Big Sur. Daily the battle is waged. Sometimes the cliffs encroach upon the ocean through land- or mudslides. Other times the powerful surf breaks away another segment of the mountainside, returning it to its ancient residence at the bottom of the sea.

Minerals in the Mountains

The Santa Lucia contain minerals to satisfy the most ardent geologist: copper, iron, lead, gold, antimony, chromium, soft-grade coal, lime, and silver in the form of argentiferous galena (a mixture of lead and silver). There are jasper and iron pyrite, rhodenite, agate, and garnet along the shores. And, of course, there is jade.

Nephrite jade, one of the two true types of jade, is found in concentrated areas around Plaskett and Willow Creeks. A piece of jade lying on the beach has a waxlike luster—it feels like a piece of soap. But when the stone is polished, its color usually reveals patterns of green that reflect the chromium content. Sometimes the color varies to yellow, white, pink, or black.

At Big Sur, you may see *botroydal* or "bubble" jade, jade shaped like a cluster of grapes. Other pieces are heart-shaped, or another find might be translucent or *chatoyant*, having inner movement like a cat's eye.

Jade is too hard for a knife to scratch it (a good test to identify a stone) but not hard enough for industrial use. The lucky scavenger is likely to receive only about $100 for a 10-pound piece. Jade's value is in its beauty, and in that it is unsurpassed.

Jade Cove

Just north of Gorda is Jade Cove, where fine pieces of jade may be found on the beach and off the rocky shore. In 1971, a 9,000-pound piece of nephrite jade was excavated from the cove. The Guinness *Book of World Records* lists the 8.5' × 5' rock, which had a value of $180,000, as the largest piece of jade ever found.

Willow Creek, Plaskett Creek, and Sand Dollar Picnic Area each provide access to the beach. Plaskett Creek has RV camping, and Sand Dollar has a popular hang-gliding area. All three spots offer offshore vistas of Gorda Rock, named for its feminine contours.

Pacific Valley

Offshore sea stacks are prominent as Highway 1 levels out across the coastal mesa. Several informal access trails lead to the rocky beaches below. Past Pacific Valley (store, gas) is Mill Creek, Mill Creek Picnic Ground, and Kirk Creek Campground with 33 campsites and a sandy beach. Close by is the trailhead for Vicente Trail.

Just north is Limekiln Point, where a fine private campground is located in the redwoods and on the beach. You can take an easy half-mile walk to see the remains of limekilns that the Rockland Cement Company used in the late 1800s to fire lime into bricks that were shipped from the cove aboard schooners. Jasper and iron pyrite can be found on the trail, and just off the path is another waterfall. (There is no shortage of waterfalls in Arcadia.)

The entrance to the New Camaldoli Immaculate Heart Hermitage stands on the east side of Highway 1 just north of Limekiln Creek. Beyond the mosaic sign, a road leads up the hill to the hermitage, which is the only American branch of an 11th-century Benedictine order. In the spiritual and aesthetic splendor of Big Sur's hills, Camaldolese monks live lives of quiet prayer and devotion to their god.

The hermitage is open to the public for twice daily masses, and there is a gift shop. Should you desire a place to meditate, you may rent a small ascetic room where your meals will be brought to you. Because monks are monks, however, rooms are available only to men. The fruitcake, sold in the giftshop, made in the traditional unhurried manner, is available to everybody.

Los Padres National Forest and the Ventana Wilderness

Highway 1 from the San Luis Obispo county line up as far as Lucia is bounded by the coastal edge of the Los Padres National Forest, a 2-million-acre forest extending from the shores of Big Sur over five California counties. The forest has close to 2,000 miles of recreational trails and some of the wildest, most splendorous and challenging camping opportunities in North America.

Above Lucia, the forest boundary moves inland, but there is easy access from the many trailheads on the Highway (see map). The National Forest includes the Ventana Wilderness, a 150,000-acre natural wilderness area with its own trails and campsites linking to the rest of the forest system. A hiking permit is required if you plan to stay overnight. Permits and advice on road, trail, and camping conditions can be obtained from any of the following U.S. Forest Service offices or information stations.

U.S. Forest Service District Office
406 South Mildred Street, King City 93930.
385-5434

Arroyo Seco Guard Station
Arroyo Seco Road.
674-5726

Big Sur Guard Station
Big Sur.
667-2423

Bottchers Gap
Palo Colorado Canyon Road.
(off Highway 1)

Chew's Ridge Lookout
Tassajara Road *(summer only)*.

The Indians Guard Station
The Indians Road *(summer only)*.

Nacimiento Guard Station
Nacimiento-Fergusson Road *(summer only)*.

Pacific Valley Guard Station
Highway 1.
(806) 927-4211

4th Edition

TRAIL GUIDE
to
LOS PADRES
NATIONAL
FOREST

TRAIL GUIDE TO LOS PADRES NATIONAL FOREST, Monterey Division,
Ventana Chapter, Sierra Club
Angel Press,
Carmel. 1983.

This small, easy-to-lug-around trail guide was first published in 1969 and has been revised three times since. The information is practical and succinct: location of water sources, summary of vegetation, links to all other trails, distance points, and general descriptive information. A detailed comprehensive map fits into the back pocket.

CALIFORNIA COASTAL TRAILS
John McKinney

Don't forget *California Coastal Trails,* volume 1, which ends with the southern part of Big Sur. (See *Index*).

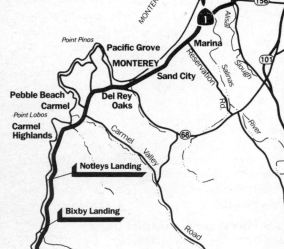

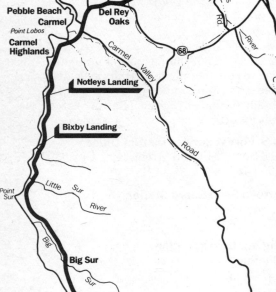

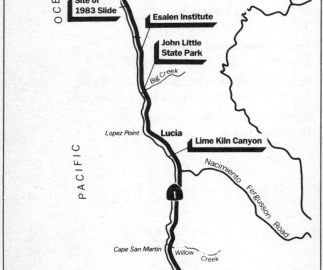

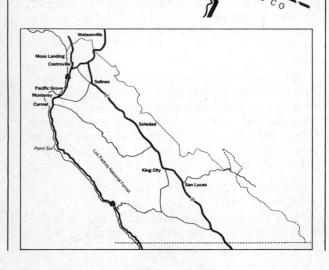

Early Landings

For years Big Sur depended on the sea for its main means of transportation. Several landings were built for loading products bound to market. For example, Charlie Bixby's landing at Mill Creek was the loading point for wood products. First-growth redwoods were cut into railroad ties, shakes, and shingles, and shorn into tanbark that was loaded on ships for San Francisco and Monterey. A small settlement grew up around Bixby Landing until the availability of easily cut trees diminished, and residents were forced to find work elsewhere.

Other landings sprung up to accommodate the briefly prosperous lumber and tanbark trade. At Notley's Landing a thriving logging operation and a small village persisted until the end of the century. At the mouth of the Big Sur River another loading facility transferred tanbark from wooden sleds to waiting ships by way of cables anchored offshore. And at Partington Landing goods were transported through a 1,000-foot tunnel (which remains today) to ships waiting in the cove.

Lime Kilns

Other natural resources brought short-term economic livelihood to Big Sur. Rich deposits of lime were mined at Limekiln Canyon in the 1880s and at Bixby Canyon in the 1900s. From giant kilns limestone bricks were turned out and loaded on waiting schooners at Rockland Landing.

In 1904 Charlie Bixby sold his holdings to the Monterey Lime Company, which produced up to 75,000 pounds of limestone a year. The lime was transported in kegs from Long Ridge to warehouses at Bixby Point by a system of chutes, pulleys, and cables. The company had to cease production in 1910, when it could no longer rely on Charlie Bixby's cutover canyon as a cheap source of wood to keep the kiln fired.

Closing the Highway

To many the most obvious solution to Big Sur's traffic problem is to restrict entry to the area. One proposal, which required imposition of a toll, even got as far as the Board of Supervisors, although such an action would require state legislation.

In 1982, Harold Gilliam suggested that the solution to Big Sur's automobile problem was to close Highway 1 near Big Sur, at least to through traffic: "Put a barrier on the coast road somewhere near Monterey–San Luis Obispo county line, possibly a gate to be used for emergency use only. The entire Big Sur coast would still be accessible from one end or the other, but the elimination of through travel would reduce traffic by several orders of magnitude."

In 1983 natural events unexpectedly provided the opportunity to test and evaluate Gilliam's proposal. Severe storms and slides closed Highway 1 in Big Sur to through traffic, making it the state's longest cul-de-sac. Highway 1 remained closed for more than a year, longer than any major state thoroughfare in California history.

Without the through traffic, daily automobile traffic fell to a fraction of what it had been. Big Sur gained a quietness it had not known in decades. Coons, bobcats, and fox returned, replacing the motorists who now made their way between Los Angeles and San Francisco on Highway 101.

Some Big Sur locals greatly appreciated the change. Said Walter Trotter, who manages a ranch in Big Sur, "Hell, a lot of my friends around here enjoy not having the tourists around. It's like how it used to be. It was a lot better here before the road was open."

Trotter did not speak for all Big Sur residents, however. When closure of the road forced numerous layoffs and cutbacks, a great many discovered a harsh reality: that regardless of how well the beauty and spirituality of Big Sur nourished their souls, it was tourism that supported their livelihoods. After a few months' reprieve from the press of tourism, those Big Sur residents who were not financially independent grew eager to see the road reopened.

For some this may amount to a devil's bargain, but it does provide for mobility in the quotidian world. Tourism is the only economy Big Sur has, without it most working people would be forced out of the area.

Lucia

Lucia is a bit of a place perched on a cliff at Lopez Point. You may obtain gas and supplies or rent a cottage with a view. A small restaurant offers good food, but best of all is the backside deck that sits like an aerie above the Pacific. A glass of wine may never again taste so sublime.

The next four miles of shoreline, once the Big Creek Ranch, now preserved by the Nature Conservancy and the University of California, which uses the site for an outdoor biological laboratory. Adjacent is John Little State Reserve, which is unmarked but available for public use—check at Julia Pfeiffer Burns State Park.

Esalen Institute

Big Sur 93920.
667-2335

To subscribe to the catalog of classes, published tri-annually, send $6 to the Institute (or $2 for the current issue). All workshops are by prepaid reservation. (The form is in the catalog, or you may charge to a major credit card by phone.) Unfilled beds are rented on a daily basis, and the hot tubs are available to non-participants after midnight on weekdays. Workshops may last a weekend, five days, or two, three, or four weeks. Prices are $50 to $400, room and board included. Esalen will arrange your transportation from the Monterey airport or the bus station and hopes you will leave a better person.

THE UPSTART SPRING: ESALEN AND THE AMERICAN AWAKING
Walter Truett Anderson
Addison Wesley. 1984.

The story of the birthplace of America's human potential movement, told in sympathetic and thorough narrative that describes the people, places, and philosophies.

Slide!

In Big Sur, where brave attempts at civilization—roads, houses, stores—are perched on the edge of mountains, above the pounding surf, *slide* is as formidable a force of nature as *flood* on the banks of the Mississippi or *blizzard* in the Northern Rockies.

Slides are of four general types: rockfall (rock mass falling), debris (broken-rock slides), slump (mass movement by rotational slip), and earthflow (soil and water movement downslope like a viscous fluid). In Big Sur, it is the last, earthflow or mudslide, that is most common and most dangerous.

Mudslides occur when a unified area of topsoil becomes saturated with moisture and breaks away from its subsurface bedrock anchor. The surface earth becomes a river of mud and if located on a slope, the river flows. How quickly a patch of topsoil becomes saturated depends on the type and abundance of plants, trees, and grasses that provide drainage and channel runoffs. When ground cover is sparse or damaged, usually by fire, heavy rains can cause flash-flood conditions on the earth's surface. When this happens on the slopes of the Santa Lucia, the earth moves.

The 1983 Slide

Between the entrance to Julia Pfeiffer Burns State Park and Partington Ridge is the site of the infamous 1983 slide that closed Highway 1 in Big Sur for more than a year. The slide originated 1,324 feet above sea level (1,030 feet above the roadbed). More than 150 men and women worked 7 days a week, using 30 bulldozers and 3 loaders, consuming 1.3 million gallons of diesel fuel and 7,700 pounds of quadrex (explosives) to move 3 million cubic yards of material. Cost: $7.4 million.

Esalen

There's no doubt about it. We're going to explore the mind. We come into it as adventurers, sometimes as drunken sailors, and some aspects of this thing get very crazy and demonic. The power of the group process is almost limitless . . . I'm aware that we're assuming responsibility for human lives, and it can be very, very dangerous . . . I'm aware that Madness Gulch is just around the corner.
Michael Murphy, Esalen's founder

From the first, the hot springs on the bluffs were the attraction. In the 1870s Tom Slate was enticed by the warm waters that were believed to have special curative powers. When a local Indian doctor told him of magical healing hot springs that could cure his crippling arthritis, Slate went. A few years later Slate opened his springs to the public; as a tourist attraction, the springs were a natural.

After Slate died others continued to operate the hot springs as a resort. The property eventually fell into the hands of the Murphy family; Michael Murphy, who had dropped out of Stanford to study Indian philosophy, wound up running the place in 1961.

Murphy soon became interested in establishing an environment in which fellow seekers could come to "explore mind" and take part in group process. Murphy started with exercises based on Fritz Perls' gestalt therapy, and soon other innovative therapists and thinkers were drawn to the place: Abraham Maslow, theorist of self-actualization; Ida Rolf, originator of a method of deep muscular bodywork; George Leonard and his transcendent aikido. Alan Watts was a frequent lecturer, as were other luminaries of the era.

While Esalen was inaugurating encounter therapy, the rest of the country looked on and tittered. A movie was made, *Bob and Carol and Ted and Alice,* loosely based on Esalen, which equated encounter groups with wife-swapping. But Esalen remained

above and apart. In the vernacular of the times, it knew it was where it's at.

But something happened on the road to the new age. Esalen became an institution, for one, and those who came to weekend seminars were now older and vastly richer, pilgrims from comfortable homes who arrived to study zero balancing and take a massage intensive. The cynical might say that Esalen today looks more like a country club than any enclave of radical thought. But what country club challenges its members with courses on the Existential Model, or Applied Vulnerability, or a workshop on New Approaches to Birth, Sex, and Death?

The hot springs are still there of course, and open to the unrepentant for a nominal cost after midnight on non weekends. Esalen also offers lodging with meals—the prices aren't cheap, but neither are many places that lack Esalen's particular brand of idyllic, explorative charm.

Early Resorts

The Pfeiffer resort was a rustic and homey retreat located on the present site of the Big Sur Lodge in Pfeiffer–Big Sur State Park. Guests arrived by stagecoach from Monterey three times a week to sleep in fancy brass beds and dine on the rose-covered porch. The stage trip took a harrowing 10 hours, but upon arrival, guests fell easily into the serene mood of the place.

Within a few years the hotel Idlewild started up business on the banks of the Little Sur River.

The Big Sur Land Trust, David Packard, & 3,040 Acres of Pristine Land

The story of how 3,040 acres at Gamboa Point, known as Potter Ranch, were forever removed from the threat of private development is a superb example of effective private conservation efforts. In 1979 the Big Sur Land Trust obtained Potter Ranch for $1.12 million, held it just long enough to load the title with protective conservation ease-

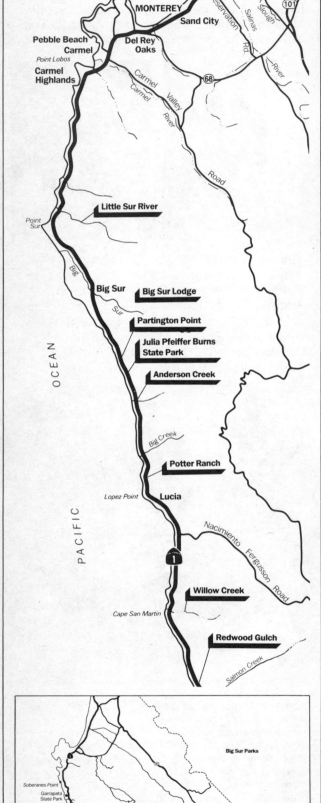

Fishing was the main attraction, with a full limit of trout guaranteed. Accommodations at the hotel cost $1.50 a day, or visitors could stay in platform tents for $2 a week.

As word spread of the magnificent land south of Monterey, larger numbers of tourists came to the area, and new resorts eagerly awaited them.

As Big Sur's economy grew more dependent on tourism, more residents were convinced that Big Sur needed a decent road to protect and enhance its major industry, and by now practically its only industry. If tourists were willing to travel for long hours over a horrible road to reach the beautiful kingdom, then greater convenience would surely mean more visitors—why not a new road?

How the Resort Business Began in Big Sur

The resort business in Big Sur was initiated by a strong-willed woman who entered the Pfeiffer family in 1902 by marrying the good-natured if somewhat weak-willed John Pfeiffer.

Florence Sweetnam Brown, an energetic widow with two children, did not lack for intelligence, drive, or common sense. After marrying John Pfeiffer, she applied each of these skills to manage the Pfeiffer ranch and restore it to financial solvency.

Life at the Pfeiffer Ranch was relaxed, informal, and sociable. John Pfeiffer maintained an always convivial atmosphere, and if he cared more about a good conversation than he did about debts and the mounting costs of the numerous unexpected guests who dropped in for visits of various lengths, Florence always kept things on an even keel.

No one knows what frustrations Florence Pfeiffer might have felt as she faced rising stacks of dirty dishes and dirty laundry while she worried about mounting debts. But it was the accumulation of such drudgery that snapped Florence into action.

One day from the kitchen she watched a freeloading boarder pick up a heavy picket and whip a mule. She rushed into the yard, angrily confronted the boarder, and informed him that enough was enough. In the future he and his friends would pay $3 a day for bed and board, or they would be asked to leave. Thus did the resort business begin in Big Sur.

ments, and then transferred the title to a private party. The Trust accomplished all this after several years of hard work, some luck, and no financial investment of its own.

Potter Ranch, rich in mineral, timber, wildlife, and Big Sur beauty, was transferred by foreclosure to a New York development corporation in the 1970s. Having no use for the property, the corporation immediately put it on the market.

Over a two-year period, several developers demonstrated a strong interest, including a group of Oklahoma businessmen, some Southern California recreational vehicle park developers, and the government of Kuwait. During the same time, the Big Sur Land Trust and other conservation groups explored all avenues for protecting the site, either through public purchase or private conservation. Nothing materialized.

Just as the Oklahomans were ready to make a purchase offer, industrialist David Packard expressed interest in the ranch. Directors of the Big Sur Land Trust moved quickly to contact Packard and convince him to buy the property with their help. Together, Packard and the Trust agreed on a package that allowed the Packard family's private use of the property but that also protected the resources and open space in perpetuity. Only four structures would be built, and those on a concentrated, carefully selected 300-acre area. The remainder of the ranch was blanketed with mining, timber, and other conservation easements. The University of California was granted access for scientific research. The Big Sur Land Trust performed the negotiating and title and transfer work, and Packard acquired a portion of Big Sur whose unmatched beauty was forever protected by conservation easements.

Environment	Roadside Attractions	Resources

Sequoia Sempervirens: The Coast Redwood

North of Salmon Creek, Highway 1 arrives at Redwood Gulch, the southernmost point of growth of the *Sequoia sempervirens,* the coast redwood. For the next 450 miles north along the California coast grow these most majestic of trees—in a long, narrow belt, seldom more than 20 miles wide, that marks the fog line and rainfall of the coastal ridges.

Over all the earth no other forest growth compares to that of the redwood. It is the tallest tree in the world, of a titan race whose members average 200 feet, and sometimes exceed 360 feet. Their density reaches 2.5 million board feet an acre in coastal stands; a single tree can yield over 490,000 board feet of lumber—enough to build 20 houses.

The coastal redwood's sibling, *Sequoia gigantea* of the Sierra Nevada, grows wider at the base and lives longer, but the graceful, tall coastal redwood will live for about 1,500 years; the oldest surviving redwoods are over 2,200 years old.

Many of the redwoods in Southern Big Sur are of first or second growth, but most are smaller than the redwoods further north because the rainfall at Big Sur (about 40 inches a year) is insufficient to nurture the giants. In Big Sur, however, redwoods grow to the sea's very edge, while up north they generally stand at least a mile inland.

As Highway 1 winds past the Santa Lucia's northfacing slopes, it passes more than 30 canyons plummeting to the ocean, canyons usually distinguished by groves of the coast redwood. At Willow Creek, site of the largest of these groves, a 2.5-mile dirt road to the campground followed by a 3-mile hike takes you into a lovely redwood-lined canyon.

Julia Pfeiffer Burns State Park

Next is Julia Pfeiffer Burns State Park, which marks the entry to some of Big Sur's most stunning natural attractions. Several trails strike for the depths of the 1,800-acre park. Take the paved foot path to McVay waterfall, which dives eloquently 50 feet into the dark blue ocean near Saddle Rock or take another trail to the picnic area at McVay Creek.

A little less than two miles north is Partington Cove, where an easy trail (unsigned) on the west side of Highway 1 leads across Partington Creek on a wooden footbridge to a 200-foot tunnel cut through the cliff. On the other side of the cliff is the cove, a serenely still inlet of deep-blue water and gray rock where you may view the remains of a cargo hoist—a relic of Big Sur's shipping days—or gaze on a pool of paradise.

Anderson Creek

Anderson Creek marks the location of Big Sur's largest prisoner work camp during the construction of Highway 1 and, perhaps appropriately, is also the site where "literary gangster" Henry Miller lived on his arrival to Big Sur in 1944. With little basis, a series of articles in William Randolph Hearst's *San Francisco Examiner* charged that Miller was the guru of a cult of sex anarchists at Anderson Creek, which of course drew would-be "sex anarchists" from near and far. Miller, then 56 years old and suffering from writer's block, found the *Examiner's* exposé entertaining, at least until the arrival of intruders forced him to move to more secluded living arrangements in Partington Ridge.

Big Sur's Parks and Beaches

Refer to the *Coastal Access Guide* (see index), or call the numbers below to plan your time in Big Sur's expansive parks, campgrounds, trails, beaches, and wilderness areas.

385-5434	Los Padres National Forest
385-5434	Ventana Wilderness
667-2315	Julia Pfeiffer Burns State Beach
667-2423	Big Sur Ranger Station
667-2315	Pfeiffer Big Sur State Park
385-5434	Pfeiffer Beach (a unit of Los Padres)
667-2315	Andrew Molera State Park
667-2315	Soberanes Point
667-2315	Garrapata State Beach
649-2840	State Parks, Central Coast Region
822-CAMP	All County Parks (800)

All Those Pfeiffers

Two state parks, a federal beach, a waterfall, a point, and a ridge carry the Pfeiffer name, indicative of the influence of this early settling family. These are the parks.

Julie Pfeiffer Burns State Park

Here are 3,543 acres of hiking tails, redwood groves, environmental campsites, and access to Partington Cove, the park's northern boundary. There are kelp beds, sea otters, and whales, but the main attraction is the waterfall. Take the turnoff to the right marked on Highway 1. From the parking area walk along he signed trail to the ocean for a view of Anderson Canyon Creek tumbling 80 feet down sheer granite into the ocean while the silhouette of Saddle Rock overlooks the majestic scene. The trail is wheelchair accessible. Longer hikes extend back up the slopes of the Santa Lucia among the redwoods.

Pfeiffer Big Sur State Park

North of Julia Pfeiffer Burns State Park, past Ventana campground, lies one of Big Sur's most popular parks. Here, where the Big Sur River runs to the ocean, are 810 acres of river flats, canyons, ridges, and backcountry. Trails link to Los Padres National Forest from Highway 1 at the USFS Ranger Station about a mile south of the entrance. The commercial lodge, two groceries, and a laundry are open during the tourist season, and rangers conduct daily nature walks, hold campfire meetings, and give slide shows and lectures. Reservations advised for camping, and there is a seven-day limit from June to September.

Big Sur Land Trust

Box 1645, Carmel 93921.
625-5523

One of the oldest and most successful land trusts on the coast, the Land Trust was organized in 1978 and has since completed projects that preserve almost 5,000 acres in Big Sur and Monterey County. The estimated contributed value of conservation easements, deed restrictions, land-free title and estate-planned gifts exceeds $4 million. The Trust also conducts public information campaigns and has organized volunteer programs to restore burned or flooded mountain slopes, clear clogged streams, and assist local property owners in responsible resource management of their lands. Contact the Trust for a copy of their poster (for a tax-deductible contribution) and more information.

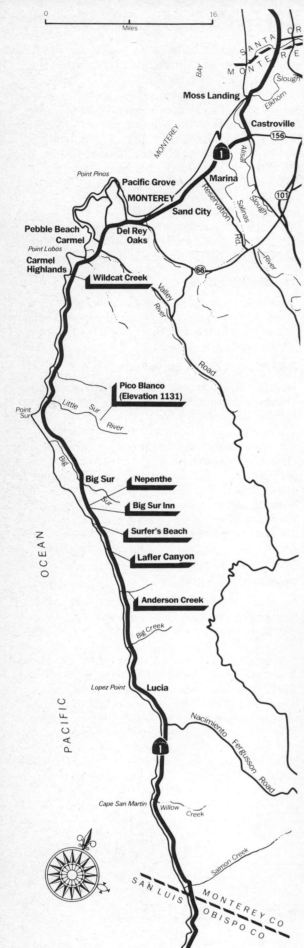

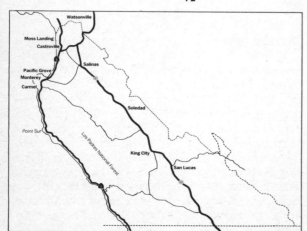

A Road on the Edge of the Continent

The first proposal for a road along the edge of the Pacific through Big Sur came from Dr. John Roberts, a physician and 20-year member of the Monterey Board of Supervisors. In 1897 Roberts traveled on foot from Monterey to San Luis Obispo, mapping the contours of the land for a new road as he walked.

After years of frustration, Roberts enlisted the assistance of a state senator from San Luis Obispo, James Rigdon. Rigdon secured the ardent doctor from Monterey an appearance before the legislature in 1915. So compelling was Roberts' presentation—which included the first color slides ever taken of Big Sur—that initial funds for the project were appropriated, but only after the original designation of the road was changed from the "Scenic Carmel–San Simeon Highway" to one "necessary for defense." In 1919 California voters approved the first $1.5 million to begin construction.

Approval of the road did not gladden the hearts of all Big Sur residents, however. Some suspected the road was actually being built to enable easier access to the Hearst Castle; they referred to the road as William Randolph Hearst's private driveway.

Planning the Road

At the time voters approved the funds, there was only a narrow, winding, steep 35-mile road from Carmel south to Anderson Creek. The road wound around the banks of the coastal streams and rivers, crossing over wherever the water was not impassable. The distance from Anderson Creek to San Simeon could only be traveled on horseback or on foot.

The planning and surveying of the new highway took three years, starting with surveys made in 1919. These were not the usual survey parties, however; engineers had to be lowered over cliff edges by rope to obtain the necessary topographic readings.

The informality of the planning is illustrated by an often-told story. The famed photographer Edward Weston and planners from the Department of Highways were discussing a bridge for Wildcat Creek. At one point, Weston took out an envelope and hastily sketched his idea for the bridge's design. A few days later the envelope appeared in Sacramento on the desk of a highway engineer, who used Weston's design much as he had sketched it.

The Battle of Pico Blanco

The Little Sur River cuts open a broad canyon as it flows under Highway 1 to the ocean. Views up the vast canyon—habitat for steelhead trout, mountain lions, hawks, falcons, and the coast redwood—culminate in the majestic silhouette of Pico Blanco, the second highest summit of the Santa Lucias and the focus of one of Big Sur's biggest land-use battles.

A Mountain of Limestone

Pico Blanco's distinctive white top is not snow, but limestone. The entire mountain, in fact, is mostly limestone, of a rare high chemical grade, and on Pico Blanco, it is unusually close to the surface. Its mineral content make the summit a beautiful part of Big Sur. It also makes the peak a highly valuable piece of property.

The Granite Rock Company owns 1,000 acres here and has mineral claims on another 1,800 acres within the Los Padres National Forest. In 1980 the company obtained permission from the U.S. Forest Service to open a quarry in the national forest and conduct what it termed "exploratory operations" that would remove up to 32,000 tons of limestone a year. Because this quarry was to be on federal property, the company claimed it was not subject to permit requirements of the California Coastal Commission; once federal permission was granted, the company argued, mining could begin.

Public reaction was swift. Opposition was headed by the Big Sur Foundation, joined by the Sierra Club, the Audubon Society, the California Native Plant Society, the Big Sur Land Trust, and others who agreed with Ansel Adams that "the Granite Rock people apparently have no understanding or appreciation of what the natural scene means to us and to future generations. The damage they would do would far outweigh any profit they can expect from mining."

The effects of even the "exploratory operations" were clear, and the impacts of any full-scale operation were obvious. In the worst case, an ugly scar would be slashed across the mountain's face to remain there for years. But even if mining were limited to less visible areas, effects of blasting would close trails and campgrounds, and the loading and crushing of the rock would be, as the environmental reporter for the *Chronicle* stated: "an infernal commotion of noise and dust in the midst of a prime scenic area, including the Ventana Wilderness on the east and the Molera State Park to the south."

The Coastal Commission has insisted that Granite Rock must meet the terms of the California Coastal Act. Granite Rock has declined to apply for any state permit. Whether the state agency has jurisdiction over this federal property is still being decided in the courts, and the issue of mining at Pico Blanco remains unresolved.

Environment

Passionate and Poisonous Petals

Monterey's fields and coastal bluffs come alive in spring and summer with a brilliant mixture of central coastal wildflowers. Comparatively few stems sport red blossoms, but those that do are stunning.

Indian Paintbrush

Perhaps the best-known wildflower in this country, the woody paintbrush appears in several varieties along Monterey's coastal headlands. Fond of sandy or rocky terrain, the woody paintbrush flashes into a scarlet blossom at the end of a bushy base. Most of the flower's color is within the bracts subtending the blossom. Splashes of white or yellow often add to the palette. The paintbrush is related to the monkey flower and the foxglove, and tea made from this passionate flower is said to add new spice to love.

Red Elderberry

The flats and coastal bluffs of Monterey are likely to provide the unusual sight of red-berried species of elderberry. Similar to its common blueberried relative, elderberry shrubs stand 6 to 18 feet high, dripping with glossy seven-clustered leaflets and heavy with bright scarlet fruit.

Red Maids

When the sun shines in Monterey County from February through April, inland hillsides may produce a brilliant patch of unusual and lovely shaded rose-red-purple red maids. A delicate beauty, this low-crawling wildflower embraces the sun for only a few hours before wilting, its expectations of existence fulfilled. During these short hours, however, the red maids provide a solid carpet of passion to complement an equally-emotional surrounding.

Poison Oak

If you have not already encountered poison oak along Highway 1, you most certainly will in Big Sur. This irritating leafy plant abounds in the underbrush of the canyons, forests, and shores of the entire California coast. Even if you don't care a bit about botany, this is one plant you'll want to be able to identify.

The most distinctive characteristic of poison oak is its three-lobed compound leaf. The leaves are similar to the California blackberry leaf, but they lack thorns. Many people identify poison oak by the glossy red or red-orange sheen of its leaves, but at other stages in the life of this long-lived plant its leaves are a dark, shiny olive color, or a glistening kelly green. And not only the leaves but also the oils of the stems, roots, and berries can produce a skin irritation on contact. In winter the slender woody stems are a light brown and retain some small buds, but they are difficult to identify among other brush. Since even breathing smoke from burning poison oak can cause a severe internal reaction, campfires are best compiled from known woods only.

Native Americans are said to have eaten small pieces of poison oakleaf each spring to provide immunization the rest of the year, but medical science disputes this as effective. The best protection is caution. If you do come in contact with poison oak, remove clothing, wash with soap immediately—and hope your reaction is not too severe.

Roadside Attractions

Coast Gallery

Past the cluster of mailboxes at Partington Ridge is the Coast Gallery, an interesting structure based on two large round redwood tanks. The gallery sells a mixture of artsy-craftsy schlock and interesting art pieces. Original prints of Henry Miller's festive watercolors are available.

The Coast Gallery is situated on Lafler Canyon where Harry Lafler, a former editor, once lived in a house he carved out of the trunk of a redwood tree.

Between the Coast Gallery and the Big Sur Inn

is a narrow unsigned trail that winds down the cliff to a fine beach, sometimes called Surfer's Beach. The trail, maintained by the Big Sur Land Trust, is not easy to locate, but if you find it, your effort will be rewarded.

Deetjen's Big Sur Inn is a distinctive Highway 1 attraction that has participated in the lore of Big Sur since the 1940s when Robinson Jeffers used to trek down from Carmel. During the 1970s its practice of haughty hipness was notorious for refusing rooms to the unhip hoi polloi.

The Big Sur Inn is a special place with 17 uniquely decorated rooms and cabins that are nothing if not out of the ordinary. There are books in every room and each room represents a different facet of founder Helmuth Deetjen's intellectual creativity, and all the rooms loosely relate to an encompassing spiritual ideal. Deetjen's Big Sur Inn evokes Bohemian Big Sur life more ably than any accommodation in the area. Its dinners are superb and moderately priced.

Nepenthe

Named after a mythical Egyptian drug, Nepenthe is Big Sur's best-attended gathering place, attracting local people as well as tourists with its engaging vitality and garrulous nature. If there were a town hall to Big Sur, this would be it. You can spend quiet moments on the patio with the sea before you and the mountains behind, or you can converse with good-natured residents and visitors at the inside bar. Nepenthe does far better as an eating and drinking place than it did as a honeymoon home for Orson Welles and Rita Hayworth. Despite Welles' romantic expectations of the place, Hayworth thought little of the isolated pied-à-terre above the sea, and if she stayed there at all, she could not wait to return to the bright lights of Hollywood.

Beyond Nepenthe is the cutoff for Ventana Inn and Restaurant. Should you desire the height of luxury accommodations you may rent a suite with hot tub and fireplace for $525 a night, which includes continental breakfast. Children are "not encouraged."

Resources

Roadside Stops

Big Sur's remote location makes some advance planning helpful. Major services available along the road from south to north are listed below (excluding public campgrounds and parks, listed elsewhere). The mailing address for any of these businesses is simply the name of the business, Big Sur, California 93920.

927-4502 RAGGED POINT. Motel, Take-Out Food, Gas (805).
927-3918 GORDA. Grocery, Restaurant, Gas (805).

927-8655 PACIFIC VALLEY CENTER. Grocery, Restaurant, Gas (805).
667-2335 LUCIA LODGE. Inn, Restaurant, Provisions, Gas.
667-2301 COAST GALLERY. Art and Gift Shop.
667-2377 DEETJEN'S BIG SUR INN. Inn, Restaurant.
667-2347 THE PHOENIX SHOP. Jewelry and Crafts.
667-2660 NEPENTHE. Restaurant.
667-2331 VENTANA. Inn, Restaurant.
667-9997 LOMA VISTA. Gardens.
667-2197 BIG SUR BAZAAR. Local crafts.
667-2171 BIG SUR LODGE. Inn, Restaurant, Grocery Stores, Gift Shop, Laundromat.
667-2422 FERNWOOD. Lodging, Restaurant, Gift and Wine Shop, Grocery, and Gas.
667-2623 GLEN OAKS RESTAURANT.
667-2101 PENNY'S HAIR CARE. By Appointment.
667-2105 GLEN OAKS MOTEL.
667-2209 MONIQUE ORIGINAL DESIGNS. Handcrafted women's clothing.
667-2242 RIPPLEWOOD RESORT. Cabins, Cafe, Grocery, Camping Equipment, Gas.
667-2414 RIVERSIDE CAMPGROUNDS AND CABINS. Playground and Laundry.
667-2322 BIG SUR CAMPGROUNDS AND CABINS. Store, Laundry, Playground.
667-2237 RIVER INN. Motel, Pool, Restaurant, Bar, Live Entertainment, Gift Shop, Grocery Store, Health Center, Gas.
667-2666 BIG SUR TRAIL RIDES. Reservations only.
624-2933 ROCKY POINT. Restaurant.

Public Phones. River Inn, Big Sur Campground, Riverside Campground, Ripplewood, Fernwood, Big Sur State Park, Ventana, Nepenthe, Big Sur Inn, Julia Pfeiffer Burns Park, Esalen, Pacific Valley Center, Gorda.

Gas Stations. Most close in early evening, so plan ahead. River Inn, Ripplewood (Chevron); Fernwood (Union 76); Loma Vista (Chevron); Lucia Lodge (Arco); Pacific Valley (Mobil); Gorda (Mobil); Ragged Point (Union 76).

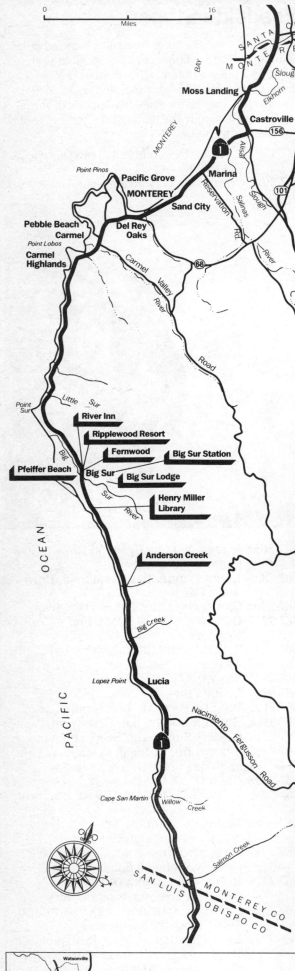

Construction Begins

Construction of the Carmel San Simeon Highway began in 1921 from the Highway's southern end with the grading of six miles of more or less even terrain between Piedra Blanca Light-station north of San Simeon to Salmon Creek.

During most of the effort, two crews worked from the ends of the road toward each other much after the fashion of the crews laying the Transcontinental Railroad. In September 1922 the George Pollock Company of Sacramento began grading along the 13 miles of oceanfront between Anderson Creek and the Big Sur River.

But nothing seemed to go right. From the first, the difficulty of access had made this no ordinary job. Because of the impassable mud that followed winter rains, a boat service was inaugurated to bring in workers, equipment, and provisions. In the summer so much dust was created from digging through the fine volcanic formations that construction had to be periodically halted until the dust clouds subsided enough for workers to see.

And there were accidents. One worker was hurled down a cliffside by a landslide. When he landed at the bottom, he was surprised to find

himself uninjured. Thus fortunate and relieved, he doffed his cap and walked straight off the job, leaving his uncollected pay to a previous life. Another worker had no luck in a similar spill that crushed his legs so badly that they had to be amputated. It took 10 men all night to carry him over slides and narrow, steep trails through a rainstorm to reach help. Pollock's run of misfortune continued when his contract was cancelled by the State after three years of work. Pollock simply ignored the state's action and continued working. When he finished the contracted section, he sued the state and won.

Out of Sight, Out of Mind: Viewshed Protection at Big Sur

Among the many precious resources in Big Sur, none is rarer or more compelling than the magnificent views from Highway 1. Because few places in the world offer more dramatic scenery, the protection of Big Sur's views is seen as a local, county, and state priority.

The established method of preserving valuable

roadside scenery is by viewshed protection. In Big Sur the viewshed is measured from Highway 1 and encompasses everything that can be seen on the land from that point. Consequently, the viewshed from a heavily forested section of Highway 1 is much smaller than a section where the views from the road are unobstructed.

The basic idea of viewshed protection is that a house or motel smacked down in the middle of a natural landscape is an unwarranted intrusion that unfairly destroys the land's unspoiled qualities. By prohibiting development within a sensitive viewshed, the beauty of the land is preserved for everyone to enjoy. Unfortunately, those who own land within a viewshed where development has been prohibited are suddenly left with significantly reduced property values.

One method to compensate these landowners is through Transfer of Development Credits (TDCs), a device that awards a certain amount of transferable value to landowners with unbuildable land within a sensitive viewshed. The credits allow for extra development outside a viewshed and may be traded or sold. The objective of a TDC program is to protect sensitive lands—a goal from which everybody benefits—without placing an unfair burden on anybody.

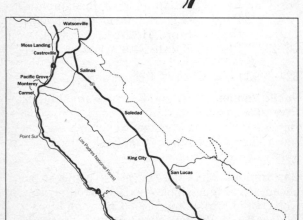

Environment

Roadside Attractions

Resources

Big Sur Birds

The powerful updrafts created by the steep rise of the Santa Lucia cliffs above the ocean at Big Sur encourage the antics of several soaring birds, especially the impressive red-tailed hawk.

Red-tailed hawks belong to a group of large hawks called *buteos,* birds whose broad wings and tails enable them to ride the updrafts cause by the sea winds deflecting off the coastal cliffs. This assist from nature is critical for these heavy-bodied birds, who spend many hours cruising the continent's edge looking for ground squirrels, lizards, and rodents.

The traveler may also spy the red-tailed hawk perched for hours on a pole or wire next to the highway, waiting for prey to appear. With a wingspan of up to 54 inches, the red-tailed hawk cuts a noble figure in flight, its heavy, sharp hooked bill and strong, curved talons flashing. The uniformly colored tail—reddish above, light pink below—and the dark band are the surest field marks of this variably plumed bird. The call of the red-tail is a high screaming noise.

While the hawks soar the skies in Big Sur, sandpipers scurry along the beaches. There are

over 90 species of shorebirds, 35 of which are found in California. All sandpipers are wading birds, but species vary in size and in length of bill, neck, and legs. Their plumage usually matches their background, changing with seasons.

Around the Big Sur beaches and shore you are most likely to see the sanderling, the dunlin with its turned-down bill, the western, and the tiny least sandpiper. You may also see an occasional spotted sandpiper, one of the few loners of these generally gregarious birds.

The sanderling is most commonly recognized by casual beach visitors. The only sandpiper that regularly feeds in the immediate backwash of the big waves, it is also the whitest sandpiper. Watch for a mass of sanderlings flocking in behind the ebbing water on fleet feet, probing frantically for a few seconds while the breakers retreat, then scrambling en masse up the beach to escape an incoming breaker.

Sandpipers dig for the tiny sand crabs that survive under the surface of the beach, dependent on the surf for food and oxygen. Because of the diversity among the species of sandpipers, many people simply group the smaller ones, including sanderlings, into a single classification: "peeps."

Pfeiffer Beach

The entrance to Pfeiffer Beach is just north of the Pfeiffer Canyon Bridge at Sagmore Canyon Road. The turnoff is unsigned because some local residents prefer anonymous beaches and are given to the impulse of stealing signs. But anonymous or not, Pfeiffer is a fine beach, beautiful with near-shore granite sea stacks, and romantic enough to be used as the backdrop for Elizabeth Taylor and Richard Burton's love scenes in *The Sandpiper.*

At Big Sur Station is the post office and the National Forest Headquarters, where permits into the Ventana Wilderness can be obtained. Big Sur Lodge, nearby, has supplies of all kinds, cabins, and a campground. Fernwood, not far south, offers the same facilities.

Just past Higuera Creek in Glen Oak's restaurant. Its excellent Italian-French style food has received high marks from *Gourmet* and *New West (California)* magazines.

A little down the road is Ripplewood Resort (cabins, groceries, cafe) which a lot of people think of as the center of the town of Big Sur, but there is no town of Big Sur, and if there's a center it's likely not here. Nearby is the Big Sur Library,

housed in a trailer, which provides the saving grace of the written word to inarticulate Big Sur beauty.

Before regaining the pleasure of an unbuilt roadside, Highway 1 passes the River Inn, which has supplies, a bar, and a fire engine out front. Within a short distance, the panorama widens as the dense pines and redwoods adjacent to the Big Sur River thin out, opening up the countryside.

Henry Miller Memorial Library

Henry Miller, who lived in Big Sur for 18 years, was an splendorously irreverent wiseacre of a prose stylist—whom Norman Mailer has called the greatest American writer of the century. His novels and other works shattered sexual taboos and challenged the vapidness and phony propriety of American literature. Yet because Miller chose to speak directly and undecorously of his experiences, many of his works were banned in the United States until the early 60s, although they had been published in France in the 1930s.

In 1944 Miller came to Big Sur at the invitation of Jean Varda. ("I have found the perfect place," he wrote to his friend Emil White.) Although most of Miller's major works were written prior to Big Sur and set in urban locales, Miller has become identified with Big Sur from a book he wrote in 1959, *Big Sur and the Oranges of Hieronymus Bosch:* "Out yonder they may curse, revile and torture one another, defile all the human instincts, make a shambles of creation," Miller wrote, "But here, no, here it is unthinkable, here there is abiding peace . . . and sea and sky unending."

By the 1960s, Miller's disregard for social conventions and contempt for the banality of middle-class American life had made him a hero to a dissatisfied younger generation. By inexplicable association, Miller and Big Sur came to represent a purity of being that Miller had never claimed for himself as an author whose works deal chiefly with the carnality of the soul. In 1962 Miller moved to Pacific Palisades, where he died in 1980.

The Henry Miller Memorial Library is a loving and intimate shrine to a great writer. Run by Emil White, Miller's closest friend, the library is a treasure trove of Miller memorabilia—books, criticism, drawings, paintings, treatises, and letters. The museum is located in White's home, and although he is a sick man, he is usually present and eager to show visitors around.

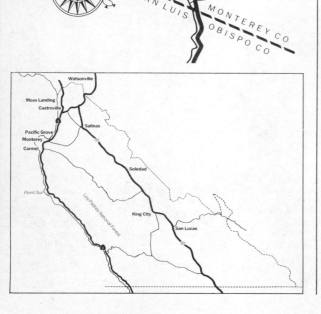

Breaking Rocks

For years the Carmel San Simeon Highway stayed in an unfinished state. After the original contracts were completed, no further work except maintenance was done on the highway until 1927. Governor William Friend Richardson who served between 1923 and 1927, had little enthusiasm for a project he considered fanciful and ill-conceived. When a new governor, Clement C. Young, was elected in 1927, construction resumed, this time with prison-gang labor.

The prevailing method of construction—pick and shovel station-gang labor, often augmented by a steam power shovel—seemed well-suited to the prison inmates, who were enthusiastic about the opportunity to break rocks outside the prison walls. The Department of Corrections claimed that road camps "prepared prisoners for return to free society—both physically and psychologically."

Prisoners from San Quentin and Folsom were transported to Big Sur, and work camps were established at Little Sur River, Anderson Creek, and Salem Creek. For a 14-hour day of hard labor prisoners were paid up to $2.50 a day. These earnings, however, were subject to a number of deductions, including a levy for any reward money paid for the capture of escaped road camp prisoners. Since the reward was $200 for each returned escapee, only a few prisoners risked the disfavor of their inmates by trying to escape. Among many heroic deeds attributed to the prison gangs is one that occurred on a winter night when slides had blocked the road. The wife of a workman went into labor with complications. When told of the emergency, a hastily assembled contingent of convicts blasted a new trail in the dark of night and carried her over the mountain to medical help.

The convict road crews worked industriously to complete section after section of the new highway. Accompanied at times by wage-exploited Chinese laborers, the prisoners worked for nine years to carve, grade, and pave the byway that would open up Eden to the world.

California's First Scenic Highway

When the California Department of Highways (now Cal Trans) began pondering the reconstruction of Highway 1 through Big Sur to freeway standards in the early 60s, a movement was born. Suddenly the vision of four or a eight lane highway through one of the world's most scenic corridors grounded the resistance of conservationists and lovers of coastal beauty. A group was formed, and with the help of state senator Fred Farr, the state legislature was persuaded to undertake a scenic roads study.

Public Progress

For years a significant mark of public progress had been the unquestioned allocation of funds to lay increasing amounts of concrete upon the untrammeled landscape. But now the legislature was being asked to leave certain highly scenic roadways alone. For the first time legislators were forced to consider the pleasure of driving on a beautiful road, regardless of its inefficiency or its lack of straight-line engineering excellence.

So strong was the scenic identity of the Carmel-San Simeon Highway that it became the perfect emblem for conveying the public value of preserving certain roadways. Soon California launched the nation's first scenic roads program. Highway 1 through Big Sur was designated the first of the state's scenic roads.

California's lead sparked nationwide interest in preserving scenic roadways, which brought about the Highway Beautification Act, a federal program to protect and enhance the appearance of the American roadside. Although several aspects of the program have been compromised in succeeding years, its ability to protect many of the nation's "blue highways" from reconstruction to freeways has been significant. There are places for freeways, but as Highway 1 in Big Sur makes dramatically clear, there are places where no freeway should ever go.

Environment	Roadside Attractions	Resources

Big Sur Boar

If you hike into the forests of the Santa Lucia you are very likely to see signs of, or even encounter, a truly unfriendly mammal that still roams these backlands. Wild pigs were introduced to Big Sur in the 1920s by hunters seeking a new challenge. For years, the wild boar have held their own, outlasting the grizzly, outnumbering the cougars and bobcats, and outsmarting the resident human population. Today the wild boar is well established here, its natural enemies vanished or scarce.

The Big Sur boars are nocturnal, feeding at twilight on bulbs and roots. A rangy, swaybacked sow is capable of plowing up a hundred square yards of meadow in one night, a feat that doesn't garner the boars much support from environmentalists or anybody else. Wild boars are quiet, swift, and hefty (weighing more than 300 pounds), with treacherous razor-sharp tusks that can exceed six inches. There have been many nasty encounters between these mammals and hunters and their horses, or the occasional hiker unlucky enough to accidentally corner or appear to threaten a sow with babies.

Boar's piglets are dropped in March or April, often as many as a dozen in a litter, after a four-month gestation. Piglets are striped with light brown, but soon lose the endearing quality inherent in most of nature's young to become just as primitively scraggly and ugly as their parents. The California Department of Fish and Game estimates that about 600 wild pigs are shot annually, many in these mountains. Still, many remain. Look and listen.

Watery Rainbows

The jewellike colors of Big Sur's water are among its most beautiful environmental features. Often the water changes from a deep, reflective blue at sea, to a startling turquoise, baby blue, green, or sometimes golden shade inland.

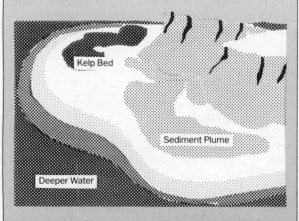

The color of a patch of ocean results from the scattering of sunlight by water molecules. The purer the water, the deeper the color. Deep ocean water, almost void of organic content, is usually quite dark—but Big Sur's waters are teeming with life and its colors reflect that life.

Plumes of yellow, brown, and green indicate the mouth of a stream or creek tumbling Santa Lucia silt into the Pacific. The ancient and colorful metamorphosed lava beds that make up Point Sur and other sites account for the rainbow shades there, and extensive kelp beds turn spots of blue to a deep green. The icy light blue and some of the turquoise shades along the cliffs are caused by wave action as air is forced into the surface water.

Andrew Molera State Park

Andrew Molera is a magnificent state park, a recent acquisition that has not been overdeveloped in line with the Department of Parks' contemporary park planning approach that attempts to portray the natural environment on its own terms.

Most significant about the park, however, is that it provides entry to Big Sur's longest beach—four miles of northern California beach maintained in wild ocean grandeur. This is a beach to be walked and explored without preconceptions, an

adventure in seaside sensuality.

After Andrew Molera, Highway 1 regains a more officious identity, lying straight and wide like a highway with a destination. Point Sur Rock, the granite spiritual comrade of Morro Rock, embraces the shoreline with formality and dignity, topped by a flashing light station and a group of Gothic buildings straight out of *Wuthering Heights*.

At Little Sur River informal trails lead to another superb beach. North of Little Sur, Highway 1 climbs again, accompanied by postcard vista points along the road. Next is Bixby Creek Bridge.

Big Sur Books

There are many guides and histories dedicated to Big Sur. Here are a few that will provide a solid base of information for enjoying Big Sur's present, as well as understanding its past.

BIG SUR: A BATTLE FOR THE WILDERNESS 1869-1981
John Woolfenden
The Boxwood Press,
Pacific Grove, 1981.

A story of the first white settlers in Big Sur, why they came and how they survived. Woolfenden carries his theme into the present, detailing the major land use and development issues today, and describing with the eyes of an insider the concerns of local Big Sur residents.

MAKING THE MOST OF THE MONTEREY PENINSULA AND BIG SUR
Maxine Knox and Mary Rodriguez
Presidio Press,
San Rafael. 1978.

A good, basic guide to Big Sur and Monterey, complete with a detailed events list and sightseeing services.

LARSON'S DIRECTORY & MAP OF BIG SUR, THE SOUTH COAST, AND LOS PADRES NATIONAL FOREST
R. E. Larson
Big Sur.

The information on this easy to carry map could fill a guide book. A very handy resource.

WALK THIS WAY PLEASE: ON FOOT ON THE MONTEREY PENINSULA, CARMEL, CARMEL VALLEY AND BIG SUR
Irene Gaasch
Hummbird Press,
Carmel. 1984.

A book for the hiker, written by a nature lover whose bent is describing the seasons, history, and the natural environment. Included is a survey of all the major parks and trail systems of Big Sur.

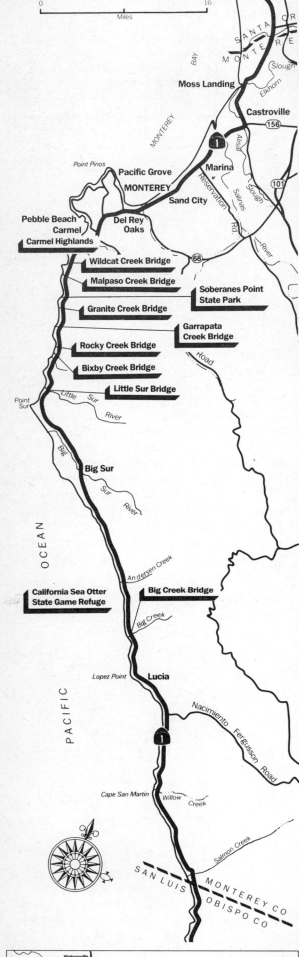

The Final Barrier

Not all of Big Sur's chasms were bridged. Some, like the gaping mouth at Partington Canyon, were filled by exploding the solid granite cliffside into a more or less level topography. At Partington "coyote holes" were drilled into the side of the canyon and loaded with 6,500 pounds of black powder. The explosions blew loose thousands of cubic yards to fill the 300-foot wide canyon.

In 1934 the two prison gangs working toward each other met south of Anderson Creek and removed the final barrier to the through road from Carmel to San Simeon. A few official cars were driven through to commemorate the occasion, although much of the road was wide enough only for one vehicle to pass. Several bridges were still incomplete, so the cars had to make their own way down and back up various steep canyons.

With the completion of the remaining construction in 1937, a colorful pageant was presented to celebrate the opening of the new highway that had cost nearly $10 million and taken 18 years to build. Costumed performers depicted the history of Big Sur, and the governor lit a fuse to a dynamite charge that exploded a symbolic boulder in the center of the road.

Dignitaries congratulated themselves while they ate barbeque and discussed the miraculous engineering accomplishment. The occasion also marked the dedication of the Pfeiffer Redwood Grove, which permanently protected more than 700 acres of staggeringly beautiful Big Sur landscape.

The Bridges of Big Sur

While convict crews slaved to move millions of cubic yards of earth for the new highway, other contracted crews labored to construct the 32 bridges required to cross the streams and canyons on the edge of the ocean. The uncertain chasms of Big Sur's wilds presented unique engineering challenges: great arches were built across Granite, Garrapata, Malpaso, and Wildcat Creeks. At Big Creek a 500-foot long span had to be supported from its center arches rather than its end spans due to the extreme instability of the ground.

Bixby Creek Bridge

Most renowned of the Big Sur Bridges is the Bixby Creek Bridge, which has become a worldwide symbol of the California coast. Bixby Creek is Big Sur's longest bridge—714 feet—and when constructed in 1932 it was the longest arch in the West. The bridge, which cost $200,000, carries the roadway 270 feet above the ocean.

The original plan for spanning Bixby Creek called for an 890-foot tunnel to bore through the cliffside and connect to a shorter span considerably inland from the site of the present bridge. The present location was chosen primarily for its spectacular scenic qualities, and its breath-taking perspective of the Pacific at Big Sur. To the natural shoreline grandeur, the bridge contributes its own elegantly stated single white arch.

The broad open exposure to high winds from the ocean made building the bridge an exceptionally tricky undertaking. Workers balanced on platforms and slings suspended from a highline cable 300 feet above the water were buffeted by sudden ocean gales that swung them like wind socks. When the wind blew too fiercely, work simply had to be stopped.

Rocky Creek Bridge

Construction of the Bixby Creek Bridge eclipsed the completion of another concrete arch at nearby Rocky Creek. Beautiful in its own right, the 497-foot Rocky Creek Bridge was built from concrete mixed at Bixby Creek and transported the half-mile north by highline. Rocky Creek Bridge cost approximately $60,000 to build.

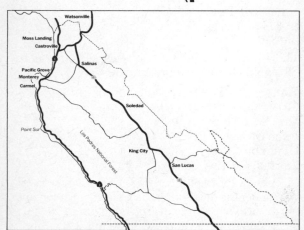

The Southern California Sea Otter

The Big Sur and Monterey County coast is the place to see the lovable antics of the Southern California sea otter. Members of the weasel family, sea otters have a slim body, high hips, broad head, and short fully furred tail. The typical male weighs 80 pounds and is 5 feet long; the female is slightly smaller. The otter lacks webbing in its feet, but it has heavy pads and semiretractable claws that function almost like hands—to open shells, wield a rock as a tool, and even shade its eyes on a sunny day. This creature with the cartoon-silly whiskers lives comfortably in the ocean surf. Mothers have to teach their babies to swim down in order to gather their food from the ocean's floor.

Hundreds of thousands of northern sea otters live along the Alaskan coast, but in the early 20th century the southern sea otter was thought to be extinct in California waters. Then, in 1938, a herd of some hundred of these endearing animals was discovered south of Carmel, and since that time the otter has become one of the most zealously protected and intensely studied wild animals in

this country. Today a state sea otter game refuge stretches from Santa Rosa Creek in San Luis Obispo to the Carmel River in Monterey County. The population numbers in the thousands, with the heaviest concentration along Big Sur's coastline.

The range of the sea otter is restricted by its food sources: mussels, sea urchins, and abalone—sea creatures that live on the kelp beds and rocky shores in shallow offshore waters. The otters congregate in groups (called *rafts*) within about a mile from shore, seldom in water more than 100 feet deep and seldom coming to land. Their heads are often indistinguishable from the floating bulbs of the bull kelp, which protects them from the powerful surge of the surf and hides them from their most feared enemy, the great white shark.

Although many environmentalists applaud the protection of otters, others now worry that the otters are encroaching on commercial abalone grounds and the natural reserve of abalone along the central coast. Still, even with legal protection against the hunters who once valued their furs, otters are unlikely to ever regain their original numbers. Their preferred offshore habitat zone is precisely that part of the ocean most subject to the adverse effects of human activity: pollution, toxic waste, and refuse.

Bixby Bridge

North of Bixby Creek Bridge lies Rocky Creek Bridge, similar in design to Bixby and uniquely attractive. Just north is the Rocky Point Restaurant, which may be the best view restaurant on the coast. From the window you may be able to spot the natural arches just to the south. Serving charcoal-broiled meats in a casually elegant atmosphere, Rocky Creek Restaurant is the proper transition between Big Sur and Carmel.

A series of informal trails from Highway 1 to the beach mark much of the shoreline from Rocky Point to the Carmel highlands. Most of this area is now being purchased by the State to form Garrapata State Beach. At Soberanes Point, a spectacular trail along the headlands affords close-up views of the edge of paradise.

Carmel Highlands

At Carmel Highlands the character of the landscape becomes refined. The terrain's rough edges are smoothed into a prettified expanse of neatly placed trees and rocks, and the surf seems intent on furnishing opulent vistas for residents of the

expensive new houses that dot the seashore.

No place is truer to the heart of Carmel Highlands than the Highlands Inn, which proffers the most serene of elegant Monterey coast overnight accommodations. The Inn's understated good taste and well-designed features nobly complement and enhance the Ansel Adams views of the Pacific Ocean. The Highlands Inn is an expensive resort, to be sure, but one that graciously outclasses other expensive resorts.

Friends of the Sea Otter

3750 The Barnyard, Carmel.
625-3290

Open daily from 11am to 3 pm and run by volunteers, this shop offers any and everything you can imagine related to sea otters as well as free literature, maps of spots for otter watching, and general nature resources. Sales support the Friends.

What Is a California Sea Otter?

Written by
Jack A. Graves

Illustrated by
Ralph W. Cooke III

THE CALIFORNIA SEA OTTER—SAVED OR DOOMED?
John Woolfenden
The Boxwood Press.
Pacific Grove. 1984

All the conflicting viewpoints about the sea otter's past, present, and future are presented here, including those of commercial abalone collectors and sport divers, university otter and abalone specialists, State Fish and Game biologists, mariculture experts, kelp-cutters, and member of Friends of the Sea Otter. This is an excellent, informative, and well-illustrated volume.

WHAT IS A CALIFORNIA SEA OTTER?
Jack A. Graves and Ralph W. Cooke III
The Boxwood Press, Pacific Grove. 1977.

The world of the otter for children of all ages with text by Graves and drawings by Cooke.

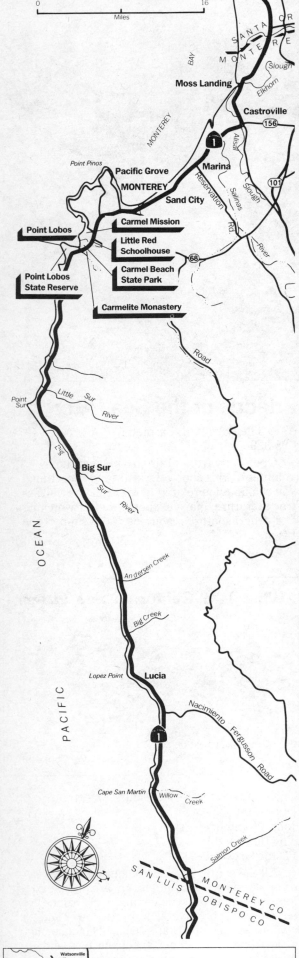

From Quarry to Reserve: Point Lobos

Among Monterey County's most sublime coastal treasures is Point Lobos, a state reserve that could have easily become a privately exploited enclave subject to a variety of permanently damaging land uses.

As it was, the beautiful land was treated extremely roughly in its early days. Point Lobos was once a granite quarry from which stone slabs were sent for the construction of the San Francisco Mint. Afterwards the point became a shorewhaling outpost where Portuguese sailors chased whales in small boats and

boiled whale blubber on the beach in cauldrons. One 90-foot whale skeleton remained on the shore until the 1950s.

Later Point Lobos became a mining port. Coal was taken out of the ground and shunted aboard ships, an extremely indelicate enterprise that was abruptly curtailed in 1896 when a mine cave-in killed 10 Chinese workers. While the mine was in operation, its owners, the Carmel Land and Coal Company, attempted to subdivide portions of the area into 25-foot-wide lots that would form the new town of Point Lobos City, later Carmelito.

In 1897 Gennosuke Kodaní initiated another unique use of the land at Point Lobos when he opened an abalone cannery. No small operation, the cannery spanned several large buildings and for 25 years supplied scores of California restaurants and exported tons of canned abalone to Japan.

In the early part of this century visitors' interest in the remarkable shoreline began to show itself, and people traveled for miles to explore and ramble. After Alexander Allen bought 640 acres at Point Lobos from the Carmelo Mining Company and started buying up and retiring the 25-foot subdivision lots, interest shifted to preserving the uniquely beautiful spot.

In 1925 the Save the Redwoods Association proposed including Point Lobos in the state park system. An evaluation of the land was conducted by Frederick Law Olmstead, America's most revered 19th-century

landscape architect and designer of New York's Central Park. Olmstead recommended purchase of the site, which was, in his words, "the most outstanding example on the coast of California of picturesque rock and surf scenery in combination with unique vegetation, including typical Monterey cypress."

In 1933 the State Department of Parks completed the transfer of the first 400 acres into public ownership. Eventually other acquisitions increased the size of the State Reserve at Point Lobos to 1,250 acres, permanently protecting one of the world's most scenic seascapes.

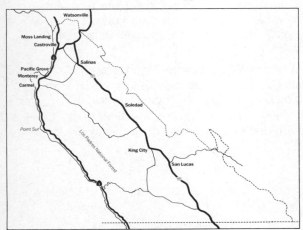

Environment	Roadside Attractions	Resources

Abalone

The red abalone is the sea otter's favorite meal, and human diners have also been long-fond of this tasty mollusc. Abalone once was harvested commercially on the Monterey coast and it was a bountiful harvest. In the 1930s, great piles of discarded red abalone shells lined the road between Monterey and Castroville, refuse from the processing plant at Cannery Row, where the abalone was second only to the sardine. At that time, the annual abalone harvest here was over 3 million pounds. But the commercial collection of abalone from natural beds has ceased in Monterey and on the central coast, where once hundreds of abalone boats harbored, though a few commercial collectors still work out of Santa Barbara and ports farther south. Today abalone aquaculture is slowly advancing in technology and profit.

The world's oceans are home to about 100 species of abalone, but only in the Pacific do they attain large sizes. The red abalone is the largest, growing up to 13 inches long. It is distinguished from the other seven American abalone by the bright red margin along the growing edge of its shell and by its thick, jet-black tentacles. Despite

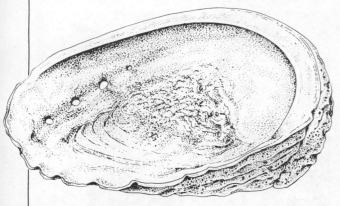

the halting of commercial harvesting, recreational diving and near-shore collection of red abalone are popular. There are legal season, size, and bag limits, and some muscle is needed to pry an abalone loose from the rocks, but the taste of a thinly sliced, well tenderized abalone steak is worth it.

The Eco-History of a Mollusk

The history of most marine species is intricately tied to human activities, as the fate of the abalone illustrates. When the Monterey shores were inhabited by Native Americans (some called *Ohlone*, "abalone people"), and the waters by the sea otter, the abalone populations remained fairly even.

With the coming of Europeans, Indians disappeared from the coast, and the abalone were undisturbed by the Spanish, who preferred beef and agricultural products to seafood. Later, when hunters slaughtered the sea otter populations for their fur, the abalone populations flourished. Nineteenth-century reports describe abalone clustered against one another, sometimes on top of each other, for miles along the coastal rocks.

Such abundance made harvesting easy, and soon an abalone industry developed. But within about three decades around the turn of this century, the abalone had been severely thinned out. As Ed Ricketts notes, because a lucrative industry was at stake, people "took notice" and began to study the lives and habitats of the abalone. Today, with proper management and some protected areas, abalone have begun to repopulate the coast, although it will be a long time before they regain their earlier abundance, if ever.

Point Lobos State Reserve

Point Lobos Natural History Association
Route 1, Box 62, Carmel 93923.
624-4909

The crown jewel of the California State System, Point Lobos State Reserve was christened "the greatest meeting of land and water in the world" by landscape artist Francis McComas. That's close.

The Reserve covers 554 acres of headland, coves, and rolling meadows plus 750 submerged acres that were added in 1960, creating the nation's first underwater reserve. Hours are 9 to 5, sometime later on long summer days. An entrance fee is charged for vehicles. Walk-ins are encouraged to relieve accumulated auto impacts (check with the ranger on fees, in any). Drivers must obtain permits at the Ranger Station to explore the 100-foot-high kelp forests and other wonders of Whalers and Bluefish Coves. Divers must be paired and show proof of certification.

Over 300,000 people come to Point Lobos each year, but the rangers enforce a limit of about 450 visitors at a given time, a capacity intended to protect the natural environment and also provide a quality experience for visitors. When this capacity is reached, rangers close the gate. However, you can park in a waiting line to be admitted on a one-in/one-out basis if you have the time and patience.

Write the Reserve for a mail-order list of publications (enclose SASE) that incudes brochures, maps, walker's guide, booklets on flowers and birds, and all sorts of specialized guides and information sheets.

Enter Point Lobos State Reserve at the Ranger Station off Highway 1 and drive to one of four parking areas to begin a walk along your choice of more than a dozen spectacular trails. You will be rewarded with some of the most breathtaking and fascinating sights, sounds, and smells along the California coast.

Carmel River

South of the Carmel River at San Jose Creek, Highway 1 passes close by Monastery Beach (Carmel Beach State Park), a tame beach across from the entrance to the Carmelite Monastery.

Just here is the site of the Little Red Schoolhouse, which has heard the uninterrupted song and shouts of children since 1879. For years the school housed eight grades in one room, but since 1957 it has been used by the Carmel Unified School District as a cooperative nursery.

Despite floods, termites, and hardships, the Little Red Schoolhouse has survived through dedicated community effort (including the endeavors of Joan Baez) to maintain a beautifully instructive place for kids to learn about nature.

Rio Road leads to Carmel Mission; Ocean Avenue to the center of Carmel.

POINT LOBOS: AN ILLUSTRATED WALKER'S HANDBOOK
Frances Thompson
Inkstone Books
Carmel. 1984.

Published in coöperation with the Point Lobos Natural History Association, Thompson's text and brush paintings and line drawings provide a sensitive, informative companion for a walk through Point Lobos. Each drawing depicts the view from a specific trail vantage point and the text identifies the sights. Five of Point Lobos' best-loved trails are covered.

Trails at Point Lobos

For detailed descriptions of these trails, obtain the *Natural History Map* and the *Walker's Guide:*

Trail Name	Length (miles)/ Time*	Major Parking Access Point	Highlights
Perimeter Hike	6.0/3–5 hours	Ranger St.	Includes all shore trails
Cypress Grove	0.8/30 mins.	Sea Lion Pt.	The favorite, through the trees
Sea Lion Pt.	0.6/30 mins.	Sea Lion Pt.	Sea lions & coves, wheelchair access
Bird Island	0.8/30 mins.	Southern	Cormorants, otters, seals, beaches
North Shore	1.4/40 mins.**	Whalers Cove & Sea Lion Point	Diverse cliffs, trees, lot & lots of birds
Whalers Knoll	0.5/25 mins.	Entrance Road & North Shore	Ascends to 180 feet through woods to vistas
Lace Lichen	0.5/10 mins.	Ranger St.	Meadow, mushrooms, lichen
South Shore	1.0/40 mins.**	Sea Lion Point	Cliffs' edge, pebble beaches
Carmelo Meadow	0.1/5 mins.	Ranger St.	Wildflowers, owls, coyotes
Moss Cove	0.6/30 mins.	Granite Point	Open to field rocky beach
Granite Point	1.3/60 mins.	Whalers Cottage	Meadow, woods, views, seals
Pine Ridge	0.7/20 mins.	Piney Woods	Monterey pine, deer, woods.

*Distance and time for round trip except those marked ** for one-way.

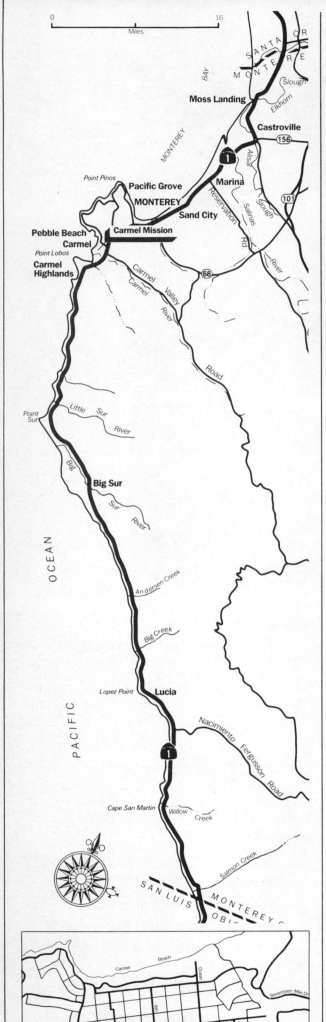

Real Estate, Religious Retreats, and Subdivisions

Not many had considered the profit potential of a California mission before S. J. Duckworth went into the real estate business in Carmel in the 1880s. After witnessing the success of the nearby Methodist resort at Pacific Grove, Duckworth became excited about the possibilities for a similar resort at Carmel. Duckworth's resort, however, would be a Catholic religious retreat and subdivision, with a historic Spanish mission as its central attraction.

Duckworth watched the restoration of Carmel Mission advance from the efforts of Father Casanova and Mrs. Leland Stanford. Great publicity attended the workers' discovery of the remains of Father Junípero Serra and three other padres. Encouraged, Duckworth purchased a large parcel of land in 1888 and laid out a town, Carmel City. Duckworth tried advertising and even built a hotel and a glass bathhouse to entice customers. But the intractable road from Monterey prevented Carmel City from gaining immediate popularity, and most of the lots went unsold.

Carmel by the Sea

In 1902 or so, James Devendorf and Frank Powers, two developers with more experience than Duckworth, formed the Carmel Development Company and filed a plat for a new subdivision to be called Carmel by the Sea. Devendorf and Power's special talent was providing extra attentions to their customers. Lots were sold for as little as $5 down and $5 a month, with more generous terms available. And to counter the harshness of the journey from Monterey, prospective buyers were met at the depot and brought by carriage over the rough road to Carmel.

Some sort of road from Monterey had existed since the earliest days of the mission, but the torturous route climbed over Carmel Hill at such a severe incline that carriage passengers had to walk much of the distance to save the horses from exhaustion.

Yet despite the difficulties in reaching Carmel, Devendorf and Power's graciousness won the day, and Carmel began to draw enough residents to resemble a town. Attractive little wooden houses were built at the end of narrow trails amid the pines, and the place began to resemble a kind of fantasy land where friendly people lived in enchanted cottages, partaking in the gratifications of a kind and affectionate natural world.

The Presence of the Tourist at Carmel by the Sea

Carmel by the Sea is not like other places. No place could be as quaint. Take a stroll on Cinderella Lane, look at the dollhouse architecture, note the garbage cans garbed in wooden overcoats with drawings of squirrels and cypress trees, and contemplate this place that could have been spun from the imagination of an extremely well-behaved child after reading *Heidi, Daughter of the Alps.*

Carmelites have always been adamant about protecting their town's unique charm. In 1925 stables and "obnoxious industries" were excluded from the town as alcohol had been banned earlier. In the 1960s Carmel passed stringent ordinances to protect trees—even cutting a branch requires a permit.

In recent years the very charm of Carmel has created the town's biggest threat as multitudes of voracious tourists have journeyed to Carmel's shops and restaurants in a manner frequently likened to the descent of locusts. So many tourists crowd Carmel on a summer day that appreciation of its subtle charms is sometimes impossible.

Indeed, the tourist has become both the curse and the blessing of Carmel's retail economy. Residents worry that perhaps the 90-odd souvenir shops, 72 galleries, 66 restaurants, and 39 hairdressers—all of which cater mainly to tourists—may have overwhelmed the town. At what point does Carmel's quaintness turn to ticky-tacky, they wonder.

For years Carmel controlled its destiny and preserved its charming appeal through municipal zoning laws. Recently, however, new pressures from Carmel's business community for less strict zoning controls has created a schism in the town.

In 1984 the Carmel City Council adopted new city zoning ordinances that restricted certain kinds of commercial uses on some downtown blocks. A backlash developed among members of Carmel's business community who thought the council had gone too far. Though the ordinance applied only to *changes* in commercial use, business owners were concerned that the rules would limit the future value of their holdings. Feelings ran so intensely that an organization to push for the council's recall was formed, although not many Carmelites could imagine a way to limit the effects of tourism other than strict zoning controls.

Environment

Roadside Attractions

Resources

Monterey Pine

No western conifer has been so widely planted as an ornamental as the Monterey pine. Its beauty is a familiar sight in cities, towns, and gardens all over America and Europe. In South Africa and Australia it is cultivated as a valuable timber tree as well.

The Monterey is native to only four small areas of the earth, however, and the most famous is here on the Monterey peninsula between the town of Monterey, the interior hills, and Carmel. The southernmost growth of natives is 90 miles south at Cambria; the northernmost around Point Año Nuevo on the Santa Cruz–San Mateo coastline.

Unlike other trees, the Monterey pine lives longest (30 to 40 years) and grows tallest (to 80 feet) away from its native setting, so you may not even recognize it here. Like the cypress, the Monterey pine often drips with the misnamed Spanish moss. But unlike cypress, it seldom perches on rocks within the salt spray of high-tide areas. Specimens that do grow along the coast are apt to appear twisted and gnarled like cypress; but inland, out of the fog and with plenty of soil and space, individual trees can shoot up to 100 feet high.

The timber of the Monterey pine is hard and durable, qualities that have not gone unnoticed by the timber industry. As late as 1947, an annual 3 million board feet of Monterey pine was felled on the peninsula. Today all the stands except the one at Point Lobos State Park are still privately owned.

Metamorphosis of a Monarch

The monarch is the best known, most easily recognized, and among the most beautiful of winged insects. If you observe the populations of monarchs clinging to the trees of Monterey, you'll easily understand the saying that the number of insects on an acre of land can exceed the billions of humans on the entire planet. If all insects were monarchs, that axiom would not be so unsettling.

Between October and April of each year thousands and thousands of monarchs arrive in Monterey to winter in semihibernation. The monarch lays its eggs on the underside of leaves, most often leaves of milkweed, a poisonous plant. A caterpillar emerges within a week or two, feeding on the leaves that supported its former home. The milkweed's poison provides a natural immunity against predatory birds, making the soon-to-be butterfly itself poisonous. (Don't ever try to eat

one.) Soon the full-grown larva, having molted a few times, selects a protected location to once again shed its skin. Then the chrysalis rests for about two weeks as the insect metamorphoses into a monarch, which then emerges, shakes its wings, and takes to the air.

Once transformed into butterflies, the winged beauties disperse in seeming disarray to the north, until at some instinctive future date they rise and gather by the thousands to migrate south and winter in "butterfly trees" in Monterey and other coastal counties.

Carmel's Imagemakers: Adams, Genthe, Weston

Carmel and its surrounds are famous for one of the most photographed and reproduced shoreline images in the world. Everyone recognizes the trees, rocks, and waves that have become almost a photographer's emblem for "oceanside beauty," just as the reproduced image of the Mona Lisa has become a signpost of "great art."

The definitive quality of Carmel's beautiful-ocean image was created and circulated by the photographers who developed their craft into an advanced art at the same time that they made certain photographic images more commonplace than the places they depict. Three of the nation's most influental photographers lived in or near Carmel.

Although Ansel Adams photographed much of the West's natural environment, it was next to the sea at Carmel Highlands where he spent most of his life. Adams, who holds the distinction of being the wealthiest photographer in history, was also extremely well liked. So striking are his high-contrast studies of California's most scenic areas that many travelers familiar with his work express disappointment when they view the real thing.

Arnold Genthe, famous for his soft-focused photographs that evoke romantic seaside fog, lived in Carmel in the early part of the century as part of George Sterling's crowd of seacoast Bohemians. After gaining the attention of the rich and powerful, and becoming a society photographer, Genthe moved to New York and later served as photographer to two sitting presidents.

Edward Weston lived in Carmel until 1958, photographing abstract forms and landscapes and maintaining himself as the center of Carmel's F-64 group (f-64 is the lens opening for the sharpest images). An avid follower of the occult and an ardent pursuer of beautiful women, Weston sported an elegant cape while conducting his art in Carmel under the sign "Unretouched Photos." Weston's *California and the West* (1940) is one of the best books of California images.

Carmel by the Sea

Once Carmel by the Sea was a storybook village that existed without notoriety. It was a time when California was more innocent, and tourism conducted itself less aggressively. Carmel was a perfect honeymoon spot, romantic enough to ensure the stability and permanence of any marriage consummated under the eaves of one of its Hansel-and-Gretel fairy-tale inns.

Today, although some of Carmel's enchanted charm is tempered by evidence of its tourist economy, it is still an oftentimes engaging hamlet with a fanciful character. Fanciful enough to have a pastry shop on nearly every block: L'Amandine, Wisharts Bakery, and Hector DeSmets' Carmel Purity Bakery, in addition to the Patisserie Boissiers that is a fancy pastry shop plus.

Carmel has two excellent bookstores—Books Inc. and the Thunderbird, an unbelievable book emporium at the Barnyard.

And certainly no place other than Carmel could offer overnight accomodations like the Lamp Lighter's Inn, where guests luxuriate within the confines of storybook architecture while living out their favorite Grimms's fairy tale. Is it necessary to mention that the Lamp Lighter's most popular room is the Hansel and Gretel Cottage?

Should you be a more contemporary fantasist, or should your brand of fairy tale run to movies or movie stars, you may wish to investigate the Hog's Breath Inn and Tavern, owned by Walter Becker and Clint Eastwood. Although there is probably no more genuine fool's errand in Carmel than to strike out to the Hog's Breath in search of Clint Eastwood, the landscaped open-air courtyard and fireplaces just might make your day.

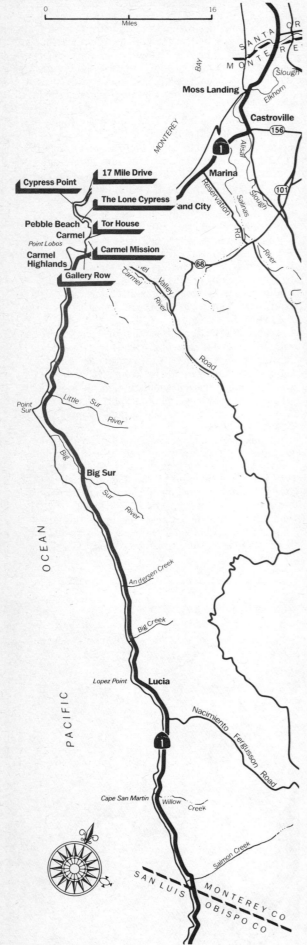

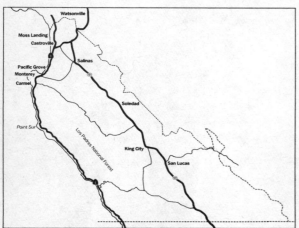

The Lure of Enchantment

Carmel's enchantment captivated the poet George Sterling and the novelist Mary Austin, who in the summer of 1905 journeyed together to Carmel from San Francisco for a few days of enrapture beside the blue Pacific. Carmel was at its romantic best, scenting the wind with airs of the sensual sea and filling the nights with love. Sterling fell in love with Carmel and Austin fell in love with Sterling and Carmel. Both vowed to return.

Sterling moved to Carmel first, with his wife, to

write poetry, farm, and entertain in the high celebratory style he had enjoyed while carousing through San Francisco's Barbary Coast with his friend Jack London. A few months later Austin followed, moving into a log cabin and writing in a treetop studio she called her "wik-i-up." There, dressed in flowing Grecian robes, she found inspiration among the twittering birds.

Soon Sterling and Austin became the center of a Bohemian artists' colony that included writer Jimmy Hopper, poet Nora May French, photographer Arnold Genthe, and Xavier Martinez, an artist, in addition to several university dons from Stanford and Berkeley. Jack London was a frequent guest, at times a continual one, and Joaquin Miller often stayed at Sterling's house. Another guest of Sterling's was Upton Sinclair. Despite his compatible politics, Sinclair proved to be far too priggish in matters of diet and drink to participate in the group's epicurean excesses; he left Carmel less welcome that when he arrived.

Within a few years a great deal of the passion that enlivened Carmel's early days had subsided. Gone were the moonlit mussel roasts and abalone feasts when free-flowing wine stimulated discussions of art and life. And gone were the fresh discoveries that sharpened insights and nourished new sensibilities. By 1914 Carmel was becoming too staid to be thought of as very Bohemian anymore. During that year George Sterling moved to Greenwich Village, and Mary Austin abandoned Carmel except for occasional visits.

The Abalone Song

Some live on hope and some on dope
And some on alimony,
But bring me in a pail of gin
And a tub of abalone.

Anonymous guest at one of
George Sterling's abalone barbeques.

In the Land of Seven Golf Courses

If, as the Greeks believed, the first roads were made by the wanderings of the gods, then it is not so improbable that at least a few deities might have wandered up the California coastline. Those who came upon the Monterey peninsula might have even rambled around the shoreline long enough to put their mark on the scenery in some fashion.

Sometime after the disappearance of the gods, boundaries were set upon Monterey's peninsula landscape. At first these boundaries were *inclusive,* transforming wilderness to forest and commons used by all members of the nearby settlements: "Property in land begins with possession in Common," observes Jacob Grimm, "the forest in which I picked an apple, the meadow where I grace my cattle, belongs to *us.* The land which we defend against enemies, belongs to *us;* soil and earth, the air in which we live—no one can own even a fragment of these for himself. They are owned in common; like fire and water they belong to all."

But soon enough the boundaries became *exclusive,* consecrating the ground to the god of enclo-

sure. In 1890 Charles Crocker purchased 7,000 acres on the peninsula, which he later sold to Samuel F. B. Morse, inventor of the code. Morse in turn subdivided the acreage into ever-smaller lots, each establishing ever-narrower boundaries, each marked out to isolate, protect, and exclude. The road that had been laid out through the forest and along the shoreline became in itself a boundary, demarking not only the roadside landscape as private property but also the entire domain as the personal reserve of a private, powerful, wealthy gentry.

A road is the great conduit of public life. But at 17-Mile Drive the road has been restricted to a carefully controlled promenade where the less well-off are permitted brief passage through an area of unrelieved, stupendous wealth. Which gods would pass this way again?

Environment

Dante's Trees: The Monterey Cypress

On the Monterey peninsula you will see one of the world's most mysterious trees, the wind-twisted and fog-nourished Monterey cypress. The Monterey cypress is suggestively depicted by Robert Louis Stevenson in his *Travels and Essays* as a conifer that stands "without change in a circle of the nether hell as Dante pictured it."

There are only two native stands of Monterey cypress in the world, both in Monterey County.

The main grove at Cypress Point has over 7,500 trees (its extension along 17-Mile Drive through Pebble Beach another 2,700); the second native grove is at Point Lobos. From these two stands are descended all the other specimens in the world, including the ones planted as agricultural windbreaks or ornamentals in parks, gardens, and yards along Highway 1 to the north. Untold numbers of seeds have been exported to Europe, Australia, New Zealand, and South America.

The bark of the Monterey cypress is dark red brown in young trees, thick ashy gray on older trunks. The leaves are short, only half an inch long, and bright green. Like the Monterey pine, the cypress is closed-cone, its small cones having six to eight pairs of shield-shaped scales, each containing about 140 seeds. The eerily beautiful cypress thrives only in a salt-sprayed, foggy, cool coastal environment. The same marine environment accounts for the tortured, twisted shapes of the trunks as they bend away from the elements. The bewitched wind-sculptured tops of these trees can reach 100 feet up, often tilting drastically on craggy trunks.

The overall effect of coastal mystery is heightened by long trailing beards of moss attached to the cypress leaves. Named "Spanish moss," but actually a lichen, this foliage eventually smothers and kills the tree. But in so doing, it provides decades of shelter to a variety of birds which use the lichen for nests and windbreaks from the harsh coastal climate. Many of the cypress host another perching plant that, like the lichen, merely resides on the tree, taking nourishment from the foggy moist air, not the tree itself. The distinctive orange glow around the tip of some of the branches is a filamentous alga, which is sometimes so prevalent that orange becomes the dominant color of the entire tree.

Roadside Attractions

Carmel Mission

There is a peculiar beauty in the simple, rather heavy building that I could not easily explain to myself. I think it lies in the perfect balance which has been kept between solidity and ornament. The tower is a model of proportion, and the facade is only broken by one star window of simple but beautiful design. The star is a little out of the symmetrical, as is also the cupola of the tower, but the variation is too slight to be jarring, and, if anything, adds a pleasing and humane touch to the modest building, as a token of the artless sincerity of the poorly skilled workmen.
J. Smeaton Chase

John Robinson Jeffers (1867-1962)

No California writer has ever been more deeply rooted in a specific region than Robinson Jeffers, whose absorption with the northern California shoreline reached mythical proportions. The son of a classical scholar and Presbyterian minister, Jeffers lived for most of his life at Carmel's Mission Point. Here he built a tower of stones gathered from all over the world and lived a life "straight out of ancient sagas" with his wife Una Kunstler.

Deeply serious and committed to the natural world, Jeffers first won acclaim with *Tamar and Other Poems* (1924) and *Roan Stallion* (1925). Since his death, Jeffers has gained wide appeal chiefly for his stirring descriptions of the natural landscape, almost eradicating the controversy caused by his unpopular philosophical outlook.

Preoccupied with violent action ("Old violence is not too old to beget new values"), Jeffers maintained that humanity was a "mold to break away from," eventually choosing the term "in-humanism" to describe a mode of belief and conduct requiring cruelty to survive.

However misanthropic, Jeffers was a poet of unmatched skill whose strong vision and sharp images created a body of work that is often as dramatic, forceful, and compelling as the seascape where he lived.

Resources

Carmel's Gallery Row

1. The Artist's Gallery
2. Gallery Who's Who in Art
3. Rose Rock Gallery
4. Landell Galleries (4 & 5 upstairs)
5. Lindsey Gallery
6. Saar-Jarvis Gallery
7. Carmel Art Association Galleries
8. Douglas Purdy Gallery
9. James Peter Cost Gallery
10. First Impressions
11. Atelier Galerie
12. Winters Gallery
13. The Fireside Gallery (behind Bill Dodge Gallery)
14. Bill W. Dodge Gallery
15. Loran Speck Art Gallery

Robinson Jeffers Tor House Foundation

P.O. Box 1887, Carmel 93921.
624-1813.

Founded in 1978, the nonprofit foundation purchased Tor House to save it from proposed real estate development. Eventually the preserved house, Hawk Tower, and gardens will host a research center for scholars and writers, and the foundation will sponsor workshops and grants for new writers. For now, volunteers lead hourly tours every Friday and Saturday. Reservations are advised. The Docent Room at Tor House offers material relating to Jeffers.

Events

The Monterey Jazz Festival and Laguna Seca Races are world famous. Here is a list of some other annual events. Contact the Visitor Assistance resource organizations for more details:

January	Spalding Pro-Am Golf Tournament
February	Bing Crosby Pro-Am Golf Championship
March	National Rugby Tournament
April	Monterey Adobe Tour
May	Laguna Seca—IMSA Premier Road Racing Series
June	Stuart Haldorn Sailboat Regatta
	Monterey Merienda
	California State Amateur Golf Championship
	Laguna Seca—Racing Series
July	Carmel Bach Festival
	Japanese Obon Festival
	Pacific Grove Feast of Lanterns Festival
	Monterey National Horse Show
	Scottish Highland Games
August	Laguna Seca—Historic Automobile Races
	Pebble Beach Concours d'Elegance
	Monterey County Fair
September	Monterey Jazz Festival
	Santa Rosalia Festival
	Carmel Mission Fiesta
October	Laguna Seca—SCAA Can-Am Championship Races
	Carmel Beach Sand Castle Contest
	Monterey Winery Wine Stomp
November	Monterey Symphony Concerts
	Hidden Valley Musical Theatre
	Golden Domino Tournament
December	California Wine Festival
	Monterey Festival of the Trees
	Pastorela Pageant

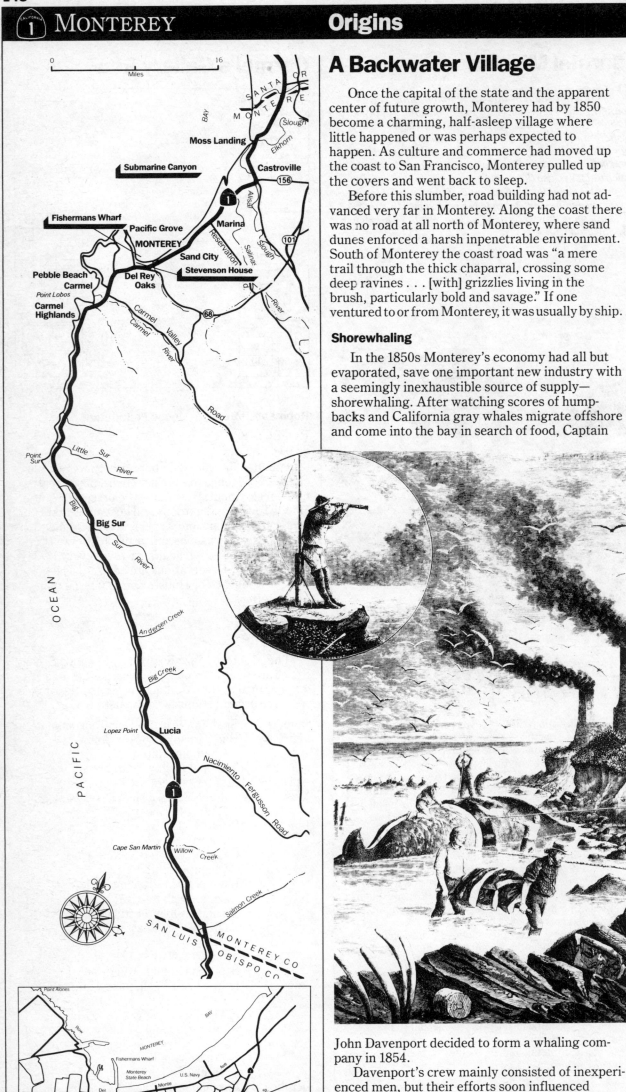

A Backwater Village

Once the capital of the state and the apparent center of future growth, Monterey had by 1850 become a charming, half-asleep village where little happened or was perhaps expected to happen. As culture and commerce had moved up the coast to San Francisco, Monterey pulled up the covers and went back to sleep.

Before this slumber, road building had not advanced very far in Monterey. Along the coast there was no road at all north of Monterey, where sand dunes enforced a harsh inpenetrable environment. South of Monterey the coast road was "a mere trail through the thick chaparral, crossing some deep ravines . . . [with] grizzlies living in the brush, particularly bold and savage." If one ventured to or from Monterey, it was usually by ship.

Shorewhaling

In the 1850s Monterey's economy had all but evaporated, save one important new industry with a seemingly inexhaustible source of supply—shorewhaling. After watching scores of humpbacks and California gray whales migrate offshore and come into the bay in search of food, Captain

John Davenport decided to form a whaling company in 1854.

Davenport's crew mainly consisted of inexperienced men, but their efforts soon influenced others to hunt the great-sized mammals. By 1861 Monterey boasted four whaling companies, among them a group of Portuguese whalers, who became known as the "Old Company," and the Carmel Company, which moved to Point Lobos in 1862.

The Monterey whaling companies prospered for about 20 years. Thousands of barrels of whale oil were produced annually, and thousands of California grays and humpbacks were slaughtered.

Conflict of Cultures on Monterey Bay

Monterey Bay may seem like a relatively large body of water, but it may not be large enough for two groups whose use of its waters have engendered serious conflict. The two groups are American and Vietnamese fishermen, and their conflict centers on methods of fishing the bay and adjacent waters, though there are strong racial and territorial aspects to the dispute.

Some Anglo fishermen at Monterey and Moss Landing believe the Vietnamese are responsible for a reduction in the size of their catch. They are also strongly aggrieved by the methods the Southeast Asian fishermen use—stringing mile-long gill nets that occasionally bring in salmon, which the Vietnamese are not licensed to catch, and sometimes become entangled with American hook-and-line fishing gear.

A Very Explosive Situation

So intense are feelings in the dispute that nets have been slashed, water poured in gas tanks, and boats set on fire. "We're talking about a very

How Gill Nets Work

Gill nets are ancient marine tools, used by many cultures throughout the world. The nets share a common design, but vary in length and mesh size. Length is usually from .25 miles to over 1 mile, and mesh size in California corresponds to three target fish: halibut, rock fish, and white croakers.

The gill nets are suspended like giant curtains, held up by floats and weighted to depths of about 12 feet into the ocean. When a fish swims into the net, its head can pass through but nothing else. As the fish struggles to escape, its gills catch in the mesh, and soon it dies.

This system is efficient, but wholly indiscriminate. Any animal of the right size can become fatally entangled, including nontarget fish such as hake, shark, and skates, as well as crabs, marine mammals, and seabirds. The loss can be staggering; for example, in 1983 gill nets were blamed for the deaths of 25,000 common murres, 28% of the central California murre breeding population.

tense, very explosive situation," said an investigator from the Monterey County Sheriff's Department.

Despite the fears of American fishermen, the Vietnamese are but a small threat to their livelihood, according to Fish and Game officials. The Vietnamese have such inferior equipment—usually rebuilt cabin cruisers converted to fishing boats—that all the Vietnamese fishers on Monterey Bay combined catch only about 100,000 to 150,000 pounds of rockfish and kingfish a month, compared to the millions of tons of fish that American fishermen bring in each month.

Although some Anglos may continue to blame every poor fishing season on the Vietnamese, disputes over fishing methods and territories seem to be lessening, as both groups learn the practicality of simply trying to stay out of each other's way.

Monterey Bay

Monterey Bay forms a westward facing crescent between Santa Cruz and the town of Monterey. In waters thousands of feet deep live more than 25 marine mammal species, including the sperm, gray, humpback, blue, and minke whales. Here are forests of giant kelp, the largest kelp in the world, and sea otters, abalone, clams, fish, and thousands of other marine organisms. Instead of a uniformly muddy or sandy bottom, Monterey Bay has reefs, rocks, and underwater granite volcanic cliffs. The Bay harbors fishing fleets and commercial fishing grounds, and provides some of the central coast's best beaches for surfing, swimming, and diving.

The Submarine Canyon

Unlike the shallower San Francisco Bay, with its average depths of about 10 feet, Monterey Bay is slashed along its bed by one of the world's largest submarine canyons. Only a half mile from shore, it drops more than 300 feet, reaching over 4,000 feet below sea level at its head. The Grand Canyon would easily fit inside.

One of 27 submarine canyons on the California coast, Monterey's canyon exerts significant biological and geographical influence over the entire Monterey Bay region. Here on the edge of the continental shelf, rich nutrients accumulated over centuries are caught in the upwelling of deep ocean waters and thrown toward the surface and inland to nourish a rich and diverse marine community. The canyon also affects the shore's geography by swallowing up entire beaches of sand that arrive on northern and southern littoral currents.

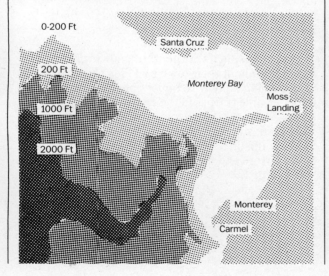

Monterey

Highway 1's most exalted presence is not expressed through its temporary disguises as a California freeway. In Monterey the redwood trim that outlines the giant green road signs does not alter the fact that the irreducible quality of freeway is destination, ends justifying means in eight-lane concrete spectacle. The Fisherman's Wharf exit leads to Monterey's tourist ghetto.

Say That You Love Me, Fanny Osbourne

Among the countless love affairs—literary and otherwise—along the California cosast, few evoke such strong feelings of tenderness, sympathy, and desire as the passion of Robert Louis Stevenson and Fanny Osbourne.

Fanny Vandergrift Osbourne from Oakland, California met Robert Louis Stevenson in Paris, where Osbourne had taken her two children after separating from her husband. Stevenson was attracted to this woman ten years his senior for a variety of reasons: her keen intelligence enlivened their dialogues, her high-strung temperament matched his own, and her beauty shone from her dark hair and soft eyes.

For two years Stevenson and Osbourne continued their Parisian dalliance; he lived off an allowance from his father, she with an allowance from her husband. But when Osbourne's husband cut off her stipend, she was forced to return to California.

For months Stevenson moped around Paris, disconsolate. When news came that Fanny was ill—a nervous disorder, it was said—Stevenson borrowed money and sailed for Monterey, where Osbourne was recuperating.

When the two lovers reunited in California, the very birds seemed to sing from the trees in approval. Robert and Fanny rolled in each other's arms. Every afternoon, Stevenson would read his morning's work to her and revise according to her criticism.

The four months Stevenson spent in Monterey, however, were hardly his most joyous days. Sick with a bronchial ailment and skin disease, Stevenson was evicted from one rooming house after another because of his unsightly condition. And his emotional well-being plunged as Osbourne equivocated about her divorce. "It is a strange thing to lie awake in nineteenth century America and hear one of those old heartbreaking Spanish love songs mount into the night air," he wrote.

Finally Osbourne divorced, committing herself to Stevenson though he had become so sick she didn't know if he would survive. Soon the two were free of Monterey, where the sickly Scots writer and the unusual woman with short hair, cigarets, and a younger lover had left a trail of scandal. The lovers married and, with Osbourne's son Sam along, honeymooned in a cabin at an abandoned silver mine in Mount St. Helena in Napa County. They left the U.S. in 1880.

Natural and Literary History of Monterey

MONTEREY BAY AREA: NATURAL HISTORY AND CULTURAL IMPRINTS
Burton L. Gordon
The Boxwood Press.
Pacific Grove. 1979.

The revised text of the author's field course, "Human Ecology of the Monterey Bay Area," prepared for graduate students at Moss Landing Marine Laboratories. The diverse elements of the natural environment of the area are described, but the book's real value is in its interpretation and critical explanations of the impact of humans, development, and natural change over time.

BETWEEN PACIFIC TIDES
Edward F. Ricketts, Jack Calvin, and Joel W. Hedgepeth
5th edition, revised by David W. Phillips
Stanford University Press,
Palo Alto. 1985.

Steinbeck's introduction to the 1939 edition of his friend's book best describes this classic, cherished by professionals and laypersons alike and having as its main purpose, "to stimulate curiosity, not to answer finally questions which are only temporarily answerable." If you read one book about tidal life on California's coast, this should be it.

JOHN STEINBECK: THE CALIFORNIA YEARS
Brian St. Pierre
Chronicle Books
San Francisco. 1983.

ROBERT LOUIS STEVENSON IN CALIFORNIA: A REMARKABLE COURTSHIP
Roy Nickerson
Chronicle Books
San Francisco. 1982.

These two books are part of Chronicle Book's excellent Literary West Series. They tell not only of the man, and his literary and personal passions, but also of the Monterey coast, its places and people.

Building Monuments

Matching the impulse to build monuments with practical business expertise, Charles Crocker spent $1 million in 1880 to construct "the most elegant seaside establishment in the world." The Del Monte Hotel, a magically grandiose Swiss Gothic structure, inaugurated a century of high-deck local tourism.

Grand and eloquent, the Del Monte stunned the sensibilities of visitors from San Francisco, who could not have anticipated its lavishness or imagined its daunting scale. On 7,000 acres purchased for $5 an acre, Crocker created a new world that combined elegance and fantasy in mythic proportions.

The exotic turreted and towered main building was situated in the middle of a garden of natural and landscaped wonders where color and exotica entreated the eye. Gaslights and mirrors made images flash, and a 7-foot high maze rambled for acres near the hotel, lending a pleasant mystification to the surrounding grounds.

Varied Pleasures

Elegantly turned-out men and women jour-

neyed from San Francisco on twice daily trains to take part in the Del Monte's varied pleasures. Grand balls and extravagant banquets were frequently held amid the grandeur of the hotel's confines. Tasteful lavishness was the order of the day, and opulence the accompanying theme.

The well-off traveler of the 1880s found the Hotel Del Monte with its highly touted cuisine and genteel appurtenances a fitting rival to five-star hotels in San Francisco and New York. As the Del Monte garnered an international reputation for sophistication and splendor, publicity crowned it as "the queen of American watering places"—until 1887, when it burned to the ground in a single hour.

A year later the Del Monte was rebuilt to grander proportions yet, with a polo field, race track, and golf course. A sense of economic optimism returned to the bay city. The reborn hotel was not the sole contributor to Monterey's economic resurgence, but it testified to the faith of big investors like Crocker, and it brought thousands of tourists to spend their dollars in other parts of town. Although tourism in Monterey continued to grow, influencing the town's shape and character, a quite different industry was to perform the major economic miracle at the turn of the 20th century.

How Many Hotels?

In one sudden explosion of interest, Monterey has become the hotest new tourist destination on the coast. Almost 2 million visitors a year descend on this historic fishing city with a population of 29,000. As a result, serious questions arise concerning Monterey's capability to survive with its identity intact.

The focus of Monterey's burgeoning appeal is the Monterey Aquarium, which has exceeded all expectations of popularity, bringing throngs of visitors to an area generally unprepared to accommodate them. Most significantly, Monterey's waterfront area is undergoing a rapid physical transition as several hotel developers rush to cash in on the arrival of so many tourists. These new projects have been recently completed or soon will be:

★ The Monterey Sheraton, 350 rooms, $44 million;

★ The Monterey Plaza on Cannery Row, 291 rooms, $41 million;

★ The Rohr Hotel at Cannery Row, 212 rooms, $40 million;

★ Expansion of the Hyatt Del Monte Hotel, 170 rooms, $25 million.

In addition, a new indoor shopping center—the Tin Cannery (156,000 square feet, $25 million)—was recently completed at Cannery Row, further transforming the sleepy seven block area into what is being called by eager Cannery Row developers "the Riviera of the West." Said one new restaurant owner in the area, "This is the place that's growing economically. We expect Monterey to rival Disneyland."

Not all residents of Monterey, however, are as optimistic about their town's sudden popularity after dealing daily with impossible parking and impenetrable traffic. In the face of the tourist boom, Monterey has elected a new mayor, Clyde Roberson, whose first major action was to place a moratorium on new construction on the waterfront. "More and more people," said Roberson, "are killing the goose that laid the golden egg."

Sardines

The California or Pacific sardine is a soft-rayed, bony fish, in the same family as the Pacific herring, the California round herring, the bonefish, the American shad, and the Pacific ladyfish. The sardine has an elongated body, compressed head with no teeth, a small single dorsal fin slightly forward of the middle of its back, and a line of oblong black spots on both sides of its body. When mature, the fish is about a foot long and its color is greenish to dark blue on the back, fading

to silver on the belly. Young sardines are nick-named "firecrackers" by coastal anglers, although they seldom see these fish anymore.

When Cannery Row was—to use Ed Rickett's term—in "its palmiest days," around the mid-1930s, millions of tons of sardines were processed in Monterey each year. At the industry's peak in 1936, some 1.5 billion pounds of processed fish left Monterey in large oval tins for grocery shelves across America. But mindless, greedy overfishing combined with a global period of low natural productivity caused production to decline, not only in California but Brittany, Portugal, and Morocco as well. By 1962 Cannery Row was silent.

Fisherman's Wharf

Monterey's Fisherman's Wharf proves the thesis that a tourist attraction can be totally delightful, entertaining, and joyfully engaging merely by being a tourist attraction. Unlike many tourist spots, there is nothing self-conscious about Fisherman's Wharf—it is merely what it is—a good-hearted collection of unelaborate seaside pleasures and distractions that wastes no time on affectations. If you are light-hearted enough to be corny, you could even say it is more fun than a barrel of monkeys.

At the start of the Wharf, the Harbor House Gift Shop announces the district's decorative style and image of make-believe with a 1940s-era miniature pink lighthouse. A few doors down the Carousel Candy Store commemorates small-town American pleasures in an aura of shine and fancy. You may purchase what tastes like the world's best sugar jellies, pastelles, and rock candy, or you may merely delight in their bright multicolored array under the polished chrome and glass display cases.

A passel of good fish markets do business on Fisherman's Wharf, as befits anyplace so named. Cavaliere's Fish Company, Peninsula Fish Com-

pany, and Liberty Fish Company all dispense fresh-caught fish: salmon, rock cod, squid, crab, and their kin, as seasonably available from Monterey's abundant waters.

You may take a deep-sea fishing cruise (Monterey Sport Fishing) or a bay cruise (Princess Monterey), or may take a dive to the bottom of the Bay in the *Sea Garden Diving Bell.*

At the end of the pier, you can have a fine meal and enjoy an excellent view at Rappas, which boasts that it serves more people than any eatery in Monterey. Or you can pick up an order of squid and chips at Albonetti's take-out stand or dine inside.

In addition to any number of souvenir shops, Fisherman's Wharf also has a bookstore, an art gallery, and the Wharf Theatre, where Richard Boone got his start, contrary to what you might have believed about the man who seems to have been born as Paladin.

History

Monterey deserves its sobriquet: "The Most Historic City in California." You may enjoy that history by partaking of a walking tour that includes a sidewalk made of whalebone, ten State-designated historic buildings and sites, the streets that inspired Stevenson, and many more sites and structures of historic romance and interest. For more information:

649-2836   The Old Monterey Council
372-2608   Monterey History and Art Association
373-6454   California Heritage Guides
373-2103   Monterey State Historical Park

The Dramatic Story of Its Past
by Augusta Fink

MONTEREY COUNTY: THE DRAMATIC STORY OF ITS PAST
Augusta Fink
Western Tanager Press.
Santa Cruz. 1982.

Bringing the romance and reality of Monterey's historical heritage to life, Fink offers an authentic and comprehensive account of the history of Monterey, the land where California began. This book was first published in 1972 under the title *Monterey: The Presence of the Past* (Chronicle) and was awarded the California Silver Medal as part of the Commonwealth Club of California's 42 Annual Literature Awards. This is the best local history of the county.

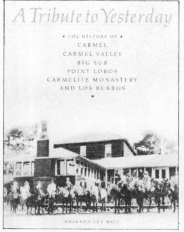 

A TRIBUTE TO YESTERDAY:
Sharron Lee Hale
Valley Publishers, Santa Cruz. 1980.

The culmination of ten years' research, interviews, and writing, this fine local history of Carmel and its surrounds offers exhaustive historical detail and hundreds of photographs.

GHOST TOWN PRODUCTIONS, CARMEL
Books by Randall A. Reinstedt
Incredible Ghosts of Old Monterey's Hotel Del Monte, Incredible Ghosts of the Big Sur Coast, Ghosts, Bandits & Legends of Old Monterey, Ghostly Tales and Mysterious Happenings of Old Monterey, Mysterious Sea Monsters of California's Central Coast, Tales, Treasures and Pirates of Old Monterey, Monterey's Mother Lode, Shipwrecks and Sea Monsters of California's Central Coast, and *Where Have All the Sardines Gone?*

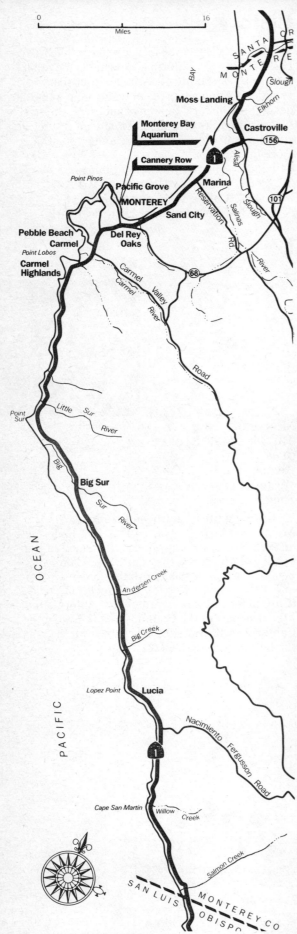

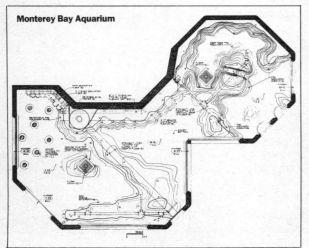

Monterey Bay Aquarium

Economic Prosperity

Sardines. Once Monterey had such an abundant supply that the water glistened silver from the sun's reflection on the backs of the small fish that swam freely just beneath the surface. The Bay was alive with sardines, and with the advent of the sardine industry, Monterey became alive with new economic prosperity.

At first the catching and canning were carried out by rudimentary methods: sardines were caught from sailboats with gill nets and carried in wicker baskets by hand. But soon came improvements in fishing and canning that increased production a thousandfold—most significant was the lampara net, modeled after nets used by Italian fishermen on the Mediterranean. The lampara, (signifying 'lightning') allowed a very fast cast and haul.

Wealth From the Sea

By 1918 Cannery Row hosted 27 sardine plants, and some 4 million cases of sardines were shipped that year. Production continued apace as Monterey ascended to the position of the world's third largest fishing port, by tonnage. There seemed no end to the wealth to be gained from the sea.

But by the mid 1940s the sardine catch began to seriously decline. Within a few years there were not more sardines at all, victims of overfishing, pollution, and unlucky climatic alterations. The golden harvest of the silver fish had ended.

Cannery Row in Monterey in California is a poem, a stink, a grating noise, a quality of light, a tone, a habit, a nostalgia, a dream. Cannery Row is the gathered and scattered, tin and iron and rust and splintered wood, chipped pavement and weedy lots and junk heaps, sardine canneries of corrugated iron, honky tonks, restaurants and whore houses, and little crowded groceries, and laboratories and flophouses. Its inhabitants are, as the man once said, "whores, pimps, gamblers, and sons of bitches," by which he meant Everybody. Had the man looked through another peephole he might have said "Saints and angels and martyrs and holy men," and he would have meant the same thing.
John Steinbeck, *Cannery Row*

How Literature Determines Land Use At Cannery Row

Only outside California would it seem unusual that a realistic novel inspired by a seaport could become so famous that the seaport would wind up imitating its own image in the novel. Such is the case at Cannery Row where life imitates art that imitates life.

There is perhaps no more glaring irony in California literature than today's bull market in John

Steinbeck's reputation and stock. Once the plague of Monterey's bibliophobic chamber of commerce, Steinbeck has become the very darling of the area's present day promoters of tourism.

Steinbeck's first novel, *Tortilla Flat* (1935) met with almost superstitious reaction from those worried about its effect on tourism. *The Grapes of Wrath* (1939) sent many of the same people nearly into apoplexy over its unsanitized account of California social and economic injustice. *Cannery Row* (1945) unbelievably shocked a great many Monterey residents, who regarded it as extremely harmful to the city's image. In 1945 California's first Nobel Prize winner gave up on the provincialism of his home state and moved to New York City.

Within a few years of his death in 1968, however, northern California radically revised its perception of the native son who had earned more antipathy in one region than most literary figures garner worldwide. Salinas, Steinbeck's birthplace, wooed the tourist dollar by renaming its library, and Monterey could not do enough to capitalize on the public image of a literary lion whom they had held in undisguised contempt a few short years before. Today dozens of shops are named for John Steinbeck and the characters from *Cannery Row*, and an entire section of town advances and prospers from the re-creation of a literary identity.

Underwater Forests

Kelp are the "trees" of a marine "forest." Under their floating boughs live thousands of plants and entire kingdoms of marine creatures, large and small. These swaying underwater forests attach themselves to rocks, cliffs, and the ocean's floor, breathing life from the cold seawater and powerful surf that supplies a constant stream of dissolved nutrients to fuel photosynthesis.

Giant Kelp

Giant kelp is the largest kelp in the world and

Canopy

Flotation Spheres

Fronds

Stipe

the most common around Monterey's coastline. Its tough stem, or stipe, ascends more than 100 feet from the ocean floor, supporting flat, golden-brown fronds held afloat by small, gas-filled bulbs.

Bull Kelp

A second common kelp is the rubbery nerocystis, or bull kelp, an annual plant distinguished by air bladders at the base of each blade. In late summer and early winter storms, bull kelp withers and breaks from its anchor or holdfast, piling up on Big Sur and Monterey beaches to decay and shelter millions of sand hoppers, themselves food for the sandpipers.

Doc Ricketts

His mind had no horizon —and his sympathy had no warp.
John Steinbeck

Edward F. Ricketts ("Doc" Ricketts) was all Steinbeck ascribed to him in *Cannery Row,* and much more. A born naturalist from the streets of Chicago's westside, Ricketts was a thorough, and self-taught, biologist who could never get enough of marine life, tide pools, laboratory notations, good music, literature, cars, or women. A handsome man whose appearance was held together by safety pins poked through tattered shirts, he ran his biological supply business out of Cannery Row almost as a sideline to his real purpose—living.

Development of an Amazing Aquarium

MONTEREY BAY AQUARIUM, 886 Cannery Row, Monterey 93940.
649-6466.

The Monterey Bay Aquarium was first conceived in 1978 by a group of marine scientists, residents, and members of the Packard Foundation who dedicated themselves to building a facility to expand public interest, enjoyment, and knowledge of ocean life, but especially of ocean life within Monterey Bay.

The group soon formed a foundation and obtained the site of the old Hovden Cannery on Cannery Row, financed by a gift from the Packards. The aquarium is just west of Ed Ricketts's lab, on the oceanfront side of the Hovden Cannery, which was built in 1916. Once the largest sardine cannery on the row, the Hovden met with hard times and was abandoned in the late 1960s, at which time Stanford University obtained it. They sold it to the Aquarium Foundation, and Cannery Row will never be the same.

Designed by Esherick, Homsey, Dodge and Davis, the building combines parts of the original Hovden Cannery and new construction that includes 60,000 square feet of interior public exhibit areas and 20,000 square feet of exterior decks, overlooks, and public walkways. Support facilities take up another 90,000 square feet. The tanks are supplied by a circulating seawater system designed to pump 2,000 gallons of seawater a minute from Monterey Bay.

Every exhibit presents its own challenges of construction, operations, and maintenance. For example, consider the kelp tank, one of the largest but simplest of the exhibits. When no U.S. manufacturer could provide panels of the strength needed to withstand pressure of 1,800 pounds per square foot and still meet the standards necessary for easy viewing, the 2.73-ton windows were requisitioned from Mitsubishi in Japan. Once the shell of this tank was in place, a method was needed to clean out the organisms that entered through the computer-controlled seawater intake system. The solution: ask volunteer amateur divers to serve as janitors for the kelp. But the biggest problem of construction for this tank was how to keep water moving constantly enough so that the life-sustaining nutrients on which the kelp depend would move across the plants' blades. Designers concluded that the 300,000 gallons of water could be kept in gentle motion by a mechanism hooked up to a tiny 3-horsepower motor.

And that was just to design one exhibit.

The restoration of the Hovden Cannery is as authentic as the new construction is high-tech futuristic. The original Hovden boiler house remains on its original site in an open brick courtyard and is open free to the public. Inside, the Historical Museum depicts the technological history of the local canning and fishing industries, and of the Hovden Cannery especially.

During the restoration, help flowed in from an enthusiastic community. The original welder offered his services, and the former plant foreman located an old promotional film that documents the canning process in start-to-finish detail. Original photos of the interior and an original water-testing kit materialized, and even the original whistle is back in place.

Construction on the Aquarium began in 1981 and ended in 1984, on time and within its budget of $32 million.

Programs and Exhibits

All living exhibits at the Aquarium come from local waters and are displayed in natural associations, comprehensive "ecosystems" that would warm the holistic heart of Ed Ricketts. No exotic man-eating monsters from oceans afar. The near-marine environment is exotic enough. Here is a summary of some of what you may expect to find:

THE MONTEREY BAY TANK. This 90-foot-long, 17-foot-deep tank, with an average width of 25 feet, engages observers in a fantasy of an underwater dive in the bay. Inshore wharf pilings (made from real pilings collected from the bottom of the bay) support all the tidal communities and crustaceans of that zone. Then shale outcroppings appear with their hundreds of fish and invertebrates. Above in the water column swim the open-water pelagic fishes of Monterey Bay: bonito, albacore, salmon, striped bass, and several species of sharks. At the edge looms the deep granitic reef that is Monterey Bay's submarine canyon.

THE KELP FOREST TANK. This large tank houses living giant kelp, which rise 24 feet to a canopy open to the sky at the third floor level of the Aquarium. All the creatures of the kelp forest reside here, invertebrates, algae, and fishes.

TIDAL BASIN. A subtidal area below the Aquarium provides views of the natural rocky shoreline community of Monterey Bay, including tidepool life, free-roaming harbor seals, and the marine birds that frequent the shoreline.

THE HABITAT GALLERIES. More than 100 individual small aquariums, graphic exhibits, and interpretive areas surround the central tanks.

EXHIBITS. Major exhibits include a shoreline exhibit, with a working model of tidal action, and the marine mammal exhibit for viewing the southern Sea Otter above and under the water level.

All this is complemented by an educational program, a 300-seat auditorium, two laboratory classrooms, a scientific resource program, and an army of docents who lead guided tours. The coffee shop serves lunch and snacks, and an excellent book and gift store focuses on items associated with the natural history of Monterey Bay and the history of Cannery Row.

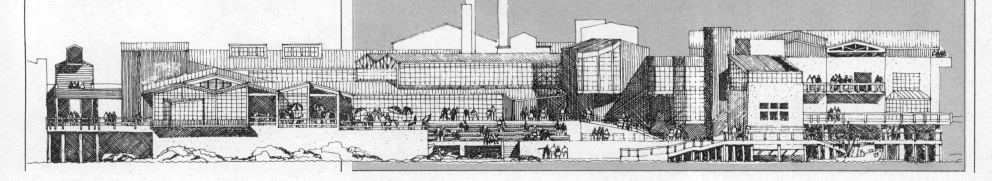

A Road Deep in Sand

North of Monterey, the coast road's original route was slow to develop. While the blue waters of the crescent-shaped bay offered the same appeal as in the town of Monterey, northward huge shifting sand dunes slowed any practical development of a road or settlement until into the 20th century.

Chase recounts from his 1913 journey: "We took the 'Sand Hills' road near the coast . . . on my left was the wide blue bay of Monterey, blue as the word can mean, backed by faint purple mountains where it curved round to the north the sea was soon buried from sight by dunes of sand, but hour after hour its soft thunder accompanied us as we tolled along a road deep in the sand and through a day and almost uninhabited country."

Embryo City

Along his way, Chase encountered the "embryo city" of Seaside, "Where avenues and broadways have been laid out in readiness for a handsome population." Seaside was founded by the same Dr. John Roberts who originally proposed the Carmel–San Simeon Coast Road through Big Sur; his success with Seaside, however, was less apparent.

During the Depression, Seaside parcels were of such small value that lots could be purchased for $1 each. A number of lots were given away free by the *San Francisco Examiner* as an inducement to subscribe to the newspaper. Not until World War II, when Fort Ord swelled with 50,000 recruits, did Seaside even become a town. The sudden influx of military personnel combined with rampant speculation, substandard construction, and poor planning left Seaside in a state of unarrested chaos for years.

Sand Mining, Mock War, and Misguided RVs: The Fate of Monterey's Sand Dunes

Highway 1 north of Monterey is lined by a ribbon of sand dunes, the only remains of the largest dune system on the West Coast, which once extended for miles inland. The remaining "river" is not always a scenic one, and these dunes have not been protected like San Luis Obispo's Nipomo Dunes have. Many people with many conflicting interests have looked to these mountains of sand.

Sand Mining

Monterey's sand is prized worldwide and has great commercial value in industry as well as in recreational beach replenishment programs. The exceptionally fine-grained sand is marketed for grinding, aerator filtration, sandblasting, and the manufacture of glass. The sand business is among the largest on the coast.

Expansive sand-mining operations stretch from Seaside, past the aptly named Sand City, and north of Fort Ord to Marina. Railroad cars transport tons of sand daily to destinations around the county. The mining occurs both within the surf zone and inland on the dunes themselves.

Most of Monterey's sand-mining operations were in business long before the Coastal Act of 1972. Thus, unless operators apply for a development permit for new construction, they are exempt from most land-use controls, including requirements for inland dune restoration programs and development of safe public accessways to the beaches. While these issues remain unresolved, the County is contending with new evidence that surf-zone mining here may have long-term effects on the beaches and the shore south along Monterey Bay.

Fort Ord

Monterey's dunes are subject to another use as well. The acres owned by Fort Ord are used for training operations and military mock maneuvers. A fence surrounds most of this dune area, and warning signs are prominent. The military use precludes public access, of course, but also visually impairs the coastline with its barricaded presence and introduces the noise and sights of helicopters and planes swooping from the skies while troops with live ammunition swarm along target practice sites.

Marina State Beach

One can reach the coast at Marina State Beach without danger of being shot, arrested for trespass, or swooped up in a sand suction machine. However, here 200 acres of sand dunes have suffered tragically from uncontrolled recreational vehicular use. The State has increased its ranger protection and the City of Marina patrols the dunes, but the large area resists easy surveillance, and the ecology here shows the serious effects of misuse and mismanagement.

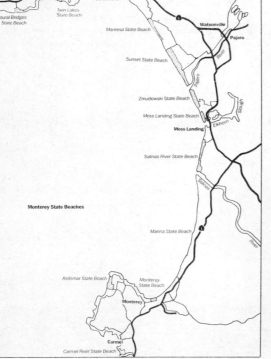

The Story of the Salinas River

Three major rivers empty into Monterey Bay—the Salinas, the San Lorenzo in Santa Cruz, and the Pajaro—and deliver most of the sand to Monterey's beaches.

Today the Salinas empties into the Bay at a point several miles south of its natural path. Once the river flowed naturally up to Elkhorn Slough, reaching the ocean at Moss Landing and depositing its sands north of the Bay's submarine canyon. But in the winter of 1909 local residents redirected

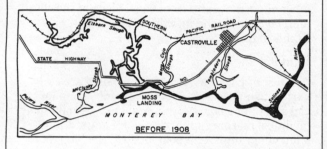

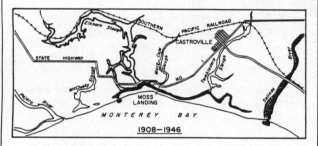

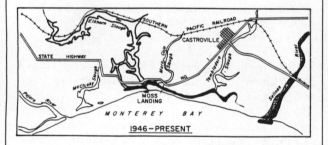

the river, which flooded annually during the rainy season, by excavating a channel through the sand dunes. In doing so, the residents were able to reclaim the old riverbed to the north for agricultural use.

The alteration soon became permanent, and in 1955 an earthen dike was built to forever close off the original channel. As a result, the Salinas River now deposits its heavy load of sediment south of the Monterey submarine canyon, rather than north of the canyon as it once did. Although beaches south of the mouth of the river have benefited from the change, Elkhorn Slough has not, because the Salinas was its major source of fresh water. After redirection, Elkhorn was no longer a true estuary, but instead became an important saltwater marsh and habitat.

Freeway North

The Aguajito exit from Highway 1 leads to the U.S. Naval Postgraduate School, which in an earlier incarnation was the Del Monte Hotel. Since 1948 the once magnificent Del Monte has been held captive within the military compound, its elegant strut disciplined by the rigors of Navy training.

Visitors are allowed to view the remains of the Del Monte, but be prepared to be disappointed by the saddest induction into military service since Elvis Presley was drafted into the Army in 1959.

Sand City's huge conceptual art piece of industrial machinery does have a purpose beyond its showy ornamental character and wry commentary on American industrial arrangements. Even though this is California, the machinery is actually machinery, and its purpose is to "mine" sand, an industry that in many ways seems no less absurd for its obviousness.

Seaside lies between Sand City and Fort Ord, and principally distinguishes itself by the strong presence of soldiers who live, trade, and relax in the area. Founded by Dr. John L. D. Roberts, who first proposed threading a road through Big Sur, Seaside has two unusual attractions: a Buddhist temple with carp-filled ponds, and the local K-Mart, where low prices and fascinating merchandise are set against a form of tragicomic consumer theater.

In Marina you may "learn to fly on the soft sands of Marina Beach," an invitation extended by Kitty Hawk Kites, a hang-glider center off Reservation Road that will help you fulfill your winged desires or give you a view of others sailing like Icarus over the shining Marina Dunes.

Hang Gliding

Thousands of people from all over the world each year try their wings at Marina State Beach, a designated hang gliding training area for the nation. The constant wind and take-off points of varying difficulties have lured at least three national hang gliding schools here. Lessons are usually given every day, and a variety of packages are offered. Beginning courses generally start around $50, which includes five flights. Kitty Hawk Kites will provide details; stop by their shop on Reservation Road and Highway 1, just west of the highway, or write or call (Box 828, Marina 93933; 384-2622). String kites and other flying toys can be obtained here also, should you wish to remain on the ground and send a surrogate into the wild blue.

The Artichoke Capital of the World

First, Southern Pacific Railroad was rerouted to bypass Castroville, and then in the 1970s Highway 1 became a freeway that heaped insult on injury when it too bypassed the place.

But Castroville endures, and does so because of its thistle-like hardiness that flowers despite adversity. In Castroville the artichoke is sovereign, and there is no better place to purchase them in eager quantity or to enjoy them already prepared in a myriad of ways. A bag full of french fried artichokes to-go from the Giant Artichoke and a couple of bottles of beer will leave Castroville fondly imprinted in your heart forever.

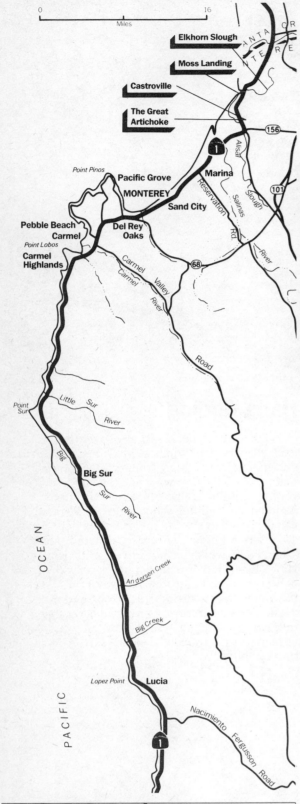

The City of St. Paul

The route of the early coast road in northern Monterey County was largely determined by both features of the terrain and certain economic imperatives. North of Castroville, the presence of sloughs and lagoons directed the coast road back toward the ocean where a small settlement had sprung up around 1860.

At the original mouth of the Salinas River (before the entrance to the sea was shifted in 1908), Paul Lezer operated a ferry across Elkhorn Slough. The ferry was operated by a windlass and a horse, or by hand when loads were light. Lezer had bought 300 acres at the river mouth at $1 an acre and had dreams of creating a new town, the City of St. Paul.

Long on dreams and short on practical evaluation, Lezer failed to realize the economic prospects for a port near his ferry. The Salinas River was the perfect conduit for carrying wheat and barley out from the Salinas Valley, and Lezer's property at the river's mouth the perfect location for a wharf.

To Charles Moss, a New England sea captain who arrived a few years later, the Salinas' potential was unmistakable. With alacrity, Moss built a wharf and began a steamship service to San Francisco. Soon there were warehouses next to the landing and river barges loaded with grains waiting to unload. For a time and until 1865, Captain Davenport had a lucrative shorewhaling enterprise at the location. Instead of the City of St. Paul, the place became the Landing of Charles Moss.

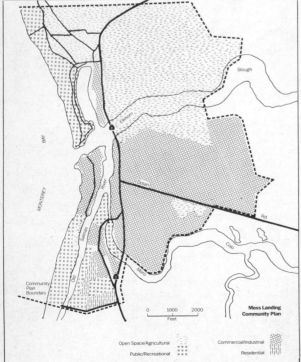

Moss Landing: Coastal-Dependent Industry

Moss Landing, Monterey's most intensive industrial corridor, exemplifies how coastal-dependent industry coexists in relative harmony with sensitive natural resources and public access.

Moss Landing's industry is bounded by Salinas River State Beach on the south and Moss Landing State Beach on the north, two important public access points. Industrial uses also come right to the edge of Elkhorn Slough, one of the nation's most important estuarine areas. Some of the commercial uses extend into the mud and waters of Elkhorn itself.

Light Industry

West of Highway 1 at Moss Landing are canneries, fish-processing companies, 600 commercial and public boat berths, boat storage and repair facilities, marine supply stores, fueling stations, launching ramps, and boat lots. Up the Slough, more than 30 acres of wetland are used for private aquaculture and several aquaculture companies maintain offices, laboratories, indoor growing tanks, and processing equipment.

Heavy Industry

Moss Landing's two major heavy industries are located east of Highway 1: Kaiser Refractories and the mammoth PG&E station. Kaiser, constructed in 1942, produces magnesia and refractory brick using magnesium extracted from seawater and dolomite taken from the Natividad Quarry near Salinas, 13 miles away.

The PG&E thermal electric plant opened in 1952. Two cooling water-intake structures are located in the east branch of the harbor at the outlet of Moro Cojo Slough. Thermal discharges are made into Elkhorn Slough at the north and the Pacific Ocean to the west. The plant is fueled by natural gas and oil, which is delivered by tankers off-loaded about three-fourths of a mile offshore. Seven steam turbine units produced about 2,113 megawatts in 1982.

Public Management

All of these industries are an important part of the local economy, providing critical services, goods, and jobs and representing land uses that predate current public policies concerning the environmental management of coastal resources. In order to remain commercially competitive, these industries need to expand and cooperative planning by public agencies addresses this need.

County policies encourage industrial expansion provided that new development is restricted to areas already zoned for such uses. This, the new thermal-unit expansion at PG&E will be infilled on the present plant site, and construction of new dormitory housing for fishermen, new cafes, and new services, as well as expanded harbor support facilities, will soon take place in Moss Landing on land already in use or zoned for these purposes. All ongoing industrial operations and any expansions are also subject to strict standards, conditions, and environmental monitoring.

Moss Landing demonstrates that coastal-dependent industry can coexist peacefully in an environmentally sensitive locale and that industry need not conflict with public use and access. At Moss Landing, the favorable intermingling of uses has yielded widespread public benefit that exceeds the sum of its parts.

Environment	Roadside Attractions	Resources

Elkhorn Slough

Monterey County suckles the sea at Elkhorn Slough, 2,500 acres of water, marsh, and mud uninspiring to the eye but awe inspiring to the contemplative mind. Wetlands are truly life centers, nurseries for creatures of sea, shore, and air and for growing things of all shapes, sizes, and dispositions.

Named after its pronged shape, Elkhorn Slough is a tidal embayment about 7.5 miles long, extending from the midpoint of Monterey Bay's crescent at Moss Landing Harbor inland toward

Watsonville. The channel is about 700 feet wide and 15 feet deep at the mouth, narrowing to 20 feet wide, 3 feet deep at its head. The channel covers some 350 acres; salt ponds, 190 acres; salt marsh 1,440 acres; and intertidal mudflats, 420 acres.

The slickly smooth surface of the mudflats conceals thriving, crawling, and writhing underwater communities of diverse invertebrates such as worms, clams, sea hares, and snails. These muddwellers feed the hundreds of thousands of shorebirds—more than 250 species—that reside at and migrate to Elkhorn. Nearby eelgrass beds harbor the surfperch and pipefish, greatest of pretenders in the adaptive wetland world. The mimic pipefish takes the long, slender shape of eelgrass as well as its chartreuse coloring. The fish even spends most of its life swaying in grasslike undulating motions.

But it is the salt marsh of a wetland that is among the most productive of the world's natural systems. Elkhorn Slough's salt marshes produce as much as 5 tons of organic matter per acre each year. By comparison, a Kansas wheat field produces about 1.5 tons per acre a year.

The California Clapper Rail

The California clapper rail was first identified at Elkhorn by Silliman in 1915. The bird is best described as resembling a small thin chicken. Its bill is proportionally long, about two inches. A brown bird with a tawny breast, striped sides, and short upturned tail, the clapper is largest of the California rails. Seldom seen very far from salt marshes, the endangered clapper rail has a secretive nature and highly specialized characteristics that make it unable to adapt to even subtle environmental changes.

Moss Landing

Moss Landing is one of the most unique and unspoiled spots between San Francisco and Big Sur. Tirelessly romantic, it maintains an enduring seaside charm. Moss Landing is all heart, an authentic California seaport of a type worthy of imitation in New England.

Gaining vitality from diversity, Moss Landing is a jumble of a place with a one lane bridge and T-shaped harbor, and a $13 million dollar fishing industry that brings in salmon, tuna, and

albacore aboard small commercial fishing vessels. There are pleasure craft and pleasure boats, antique shops and flea markets, as well as markets that sell fresh produce and fish. The Harbor Restaurant with excellent food overlooks the entire hodgepoge and provides its own seaside romance to an appealing locale.

Just before the county line, appears one of Highway 1's most unusual examples of roadside

architecture: the California vernacular castle, representing unknown personal visions of its owners. This spectacular monument to California eccentricity completes Highway 1's journey south to north through Monterey County, from Big Sur to a residential castle with aluminum windows, or

from
the sublime
to the
ridiculous.

Resources

Elkhorn • Slough
NEWSLETTER
FALL/WINTER 1984

The Elkhorn Slough Estuarine Sanctuary
The Elkhorn Slough Foundation

1454 Elkhorn Road, Watsonville 95076.   728-0560.

The newly founded Elkhorn Slough Foundation can answer all questions about the resources here. The Foundation is a nonprofit support group whose purpose is to plan and operate education and research programs in the Slough and to assist the California Department of Fish and Game, managers of the sanctuary, in its long-standing docent interpretive and public information programs. Contact the Sanctuary or Foundation for a current checklist of birds, maps, and other assistance.

The National Estuarine Sanctuary Program
Federal Office of Coastal Zone Management

3300 Whitehaven Street, N.W., Washington, D.C. 20235. (202) 653-7301.

Elkhorn is one of 15 estuarine sanctuaries around the nation, so designated to be preserved in perpetuity for education and research on the importance of wetlands to the world's health. To find out more about the federal program, contact Elkhorn Slough or the national office.

Moss Landing Marine Laboratory

An educational and research facility, the "laboratory" consists of a collection of trailers, converted cannery sheds and assorted structures, along with a 79-foot boat, the *Cayuse*. Moss Landing Marine Lab is operated by a consortium of six major marine biology programs from colleges and universities across the state. The 200 or so students host an annual open house and are available for certain technical and field assistance. Call for more details.

Moss Landing Harbor District
Box 102, Moss Landing 95039
633-2461

For a complete list of services, including availability of slips, dry storage, fuel and boat ramps, pumpout station, yacht club, restaurants, shops, and charter tours, contact the Harbor district.

Visitor Assistance

Monterey Peninsula Visitors and Convention Bureau
380 Alvarado, Monterey 93940
649-3200

Carmel Business Association
P.O. Box 4444, Carmel 93922
624-2522

SANTA CRUZ

HIGHWAY 1'S ROUTE through Santa Cruz County begins at the Pajaro Valley farmlands and stretches northward for 45 miles to Waddell Bluffs. Much of the roadside panorama is composed of the Santa Cruz Mountains and the crashing blue Pacific.

At the City of Santa Cruz, Highway 1 changes from a freeway into a city street for a sometimes congested journey through town. Nearby is the Santa Cruz Boardwalk, California's last seaside amusement park, and Pacific Garden Mall. The University of California, Santa Cruz is just north of town.

Santa Cruz County has an abundance of excellent public beaches from one end to the other. Along Monterey Bay are a series of well developed and maintained beaches, including Capitola, the location of California's first seaside resort. North of Point Santa Cruz, the seacoast is wilder, more dramatic, with beautiful untamed beaches.

Beyond the City of Santa Cruz, Highway 1 eases into a comfortable two-lane stretch of country roadway, in sight of the shore to the county line. Along the way are Brussels sprouts and an always available ocean.

The Seductive Appeal of the Pajaro Valley

Despite the dangers of retaliative Indians and assaultive grizzly bears, the lush bottom lands of the Pajaro River Valley held a seductive appeal for early settlers in Santa Cruz County. Within a few years after the Gold Rush, word spread of the rich soil next to the Pajaro, and squatters came in droves to live on and plant portions of the gigantic *ranchos* that divided up the land.

As the land offered up a bounty of barley, wheat, and potatoes—and later the famous Pajaro apples—shipping arrangements were made and transportation networks developed. At the head of Elkhorn Slough was Watsonville Landing, four miles from the town of Watsonville, where Goodall & Perkins Shipping Company landed to take crops to market in San Francisco aboard the *Kilburn,* an elegantly outfitted steamer, whose upper passenger deck had 458 staterooms. The steamer made the run to Mission Creek in San Francisco in four hours.

At Pajaro Landing was a large warehouse for storing grain and produce. Near the turn of the century the short-lived Port Rogers had a brief

fling with a shipping and recreational venture that included a dance pavilion and racetrack in addition to piers that extended a quarter mile into the sea.

Travel by Land

Land transportation was far less economical than transportation by sea. The road from Monterey, such as it was, was only temporary—built only to accomodate *carretas* loaded with hides—and usually washed out in winter. (The entire Pajaro Valley was, at times, a lake.) The local roads sufficed for a sparse population and barter system, but a market economy demanded greater efficiency. The location of roads became more defined, with the coast thoroughfare entering the Valley from the south, running straight to the Pajaro River, crossing the big *ranchos* at Los Corralitos and San Andreas, and eventually leading to Santa Cruz.

Santa Cruz's Sister City

As the agricultural economy of the Pajaro Valley continued to grow, Watsonville became more of a city, referring to itself as "Santa Cruz's Sister City." In 1868 Watsonville was incorporated and soon confirmed its new urbanity by outlawing the riding of horses on the city's plank sidewalks.

In 1876 Frederick A. Hihn inaugurated railroad service between Watsonville and Santa Cruz. The rails supplanted the exhausting stagecoach ride between the two cities and ensured wholesale changes in the lives of Pajaro Valley residents.

Preserving the Pajaro

The fertile fields of the Pajaro Valley insisted on their cultivation. Few places on earth are as naturally abundant, and few places have so well supported an agriculturally based economy. Today, however, the Pajaro Valley faces the possibility of a future that threatens to replace the farms with business parks, shopping centers, and suburbs.

Growth Pressures

The problem is that Watsonville is growing and needs more land. The town's population, now about 25,000, has almost doubled over the last decade, which has created a strong demand for new housing. And the half dozen high-technology plants that moved here within the last few years are casting eyes toward the relatively cheap land in the city and around it. Although Watsonville encourages new agricultural industries, the lure of high-technology plants, with a higher tax base, is extremely compelling to the expanding city.

From Farm to Backyard

To meet the demand for new land, Watsonville is looking beyond its town limits to the adjacent open agricultural fields. Municipal annexation of agricultural lands for new housing is becoming public policy, and the County can do little to prevent conversion even though its general plan designates the land for agricultural use. Annexation of unincorporated county land by a city is controlled by the Local Agency Formation Council in Santa Cruz, which has so far approved all requests by Watsonville to annex new territory.

Impact of Conversion

The most important industry in the Pajaro Valley is agriculture, which provides over 15,000 jobs in the fields, as well as thousands of jobs related to food-processing plants, the wholesale trade, and transportation industries. For every acre of land converted from productive agriculture use to a residential subdivision or a high-tech plant, the chain of economic impacts extends far beyond the field worker. Often the effect is especially severe since the displaced workers are hard-pressed to find new jobs in their literally shrinking fields of employment.

County Profile

Geographic

Land Area (acres)	280,960
Land Area (sq. miles)	439.0
Water Area (acres)	400
Water Area (sq. miles)	0.6
Acres in Public Ownership	35,528.26
Percent in Public Ownership	12.65
Miles of Public Roads	* 1,075
County Seat	Santa Cruz

Demographic

Population	200,300
State Rank by Population	23
Projected 1990 Population	225,000
Unemployment Rate (state avg. = 9.9)	11.3
Per Capita Personal Income	$11,004
State Rank by Income	14
Total Assessed Property Value	$5,583,449,740

The Pajaro Valley

The Pajaro Valley marks the boundary between Monterey and Santa Cruz counties. To the north, Highway 1 passes through some 120 square miles of rolling hills within a valley that is one of the most fertile agricultural regions in California. Former floodplains of the Pajaro River have created soils of unusual richness. Farmers here pay respect to this natural fertility by allowing periodic reversion of fields to native grasslands and by aerial seeding of ryegrass, which improves the natural pasturages.

The 15-mile long and 7-mile wide Pajaro agricultural fields embrace the town of Watsonville on three sides, making agriculture and its infrastructure the town's number-one industry. The area also leads the nation in frozen-food processing. Along the eastern edge of the valley run the Santa Cruz Mountains, where European explorers sighted their first redwood tree. The redwood grove at Logan Quarry near the south bank of the Pajaro marks the first stand of these trees outside the Santa Lucia Mountains in Big Sur.

Crops of the Pajaro

The combination of fertile soils and a stable, warm in-coastal climate produces a multitude of crops whose total annual yield exceeds $16 million. Among the valley's riches are cauliflower, celery, corn, lettuce, mushrooms, prunes, squash, tomatoes, artichokes, greenbeans, broccoli, brussels sprouts, cabbage, and grain. But even such abundance is secondary to the area's single most valuable crop—apples, which cover over 8,500 acres and yield over $10 million a year. The Pajaro Valley leads the state in the production of apples, bushberries, and Brussels sprouts and is the world leader in strawberry production.

County Line

The Pajaro River marks the start of southern Santa Cruz County, where fecund farmland defines the landscape and sustains the region's economy.

Watsonville

Although Watsonville's city limits embrace Highway 1, the city's center is to the east, where it rests free from all discernible characteristics of contemporary coastal California.

At the center of town is the plaza, a model of classical American town squares circa 1875. Watsonville's town plaza is a one-block square park that contains all the exemplary accoutrements of a 19th-century small-town square: a fountain, cannons, and a domed central bandstand with six Girandole lamps.

Looming above the plaza in its own anachronistic splendor is the Odd Fellows Building, a proud 1893 structure with a noble, four-sided clock tower. Although no men with bowlers and canes or women with bonnets or parasols stroll through the park, they would not be conspicuous in such a setting.

Heart of the City

Watsonville's town square dates from 1860 and has since then served as the physical heart of the city, if no longer its most vibrant center. In Watsonville the public social function of a town square as the focal point for civic activities has largely been lost to changing contemporary land-use arrangements, but the indelible charm of its downtown park remains.

On Main Street, in front of the plaza, is the restored Mansion House, built in 1871. Across the street the venerable Ford's, founded in 1852, endures as California's oldest department store. Down the street the Pajaro Bakery makes superb French bread, pastries, and donuts. The Hotel Resetar hangs on with solemn dignity.

There is, of course, another Watsonville, one uninspirited by history's ghosts. Spread out along the town's traffic arteries in leapfrog fashion is the Watsonville of contemporary goods and services, but this is not the Watsonville with a heart.

AREA CODE: 408

Rules of the Road

Highway 1 through Santa Cruz County offers easy driving past rolling agriculture plains, through the mild metropolis of the City of Santa Cruz, and north along low coastal bluffs with good visibility and gentle curves. Keep an eye out for the prevalent bikers and hikers.

Public Transportation

872-7245	Amtrack (800)
426-5520	Care A Van
425-2776	County Bicycle Coordinator
429-POOL	County Carpool
423-1800	Greyhound Bus
524-1558	Lift Line
423-1800	Peerless Stages
425-8688	S.C. Cycling Club
425-8600	SCMTD Information

Climate

Average temperatures in Santa Cruz range from a high of about 69° to a low of about 44°. Coastal temperatures seldom exceed 80°, even in August and September, the hottest time of year. Rain falls from December through March, averaging around 30 inches per year. Many people consider California's central coast to have the best of both weather worlds: warm days in which to enjoy the beaches tempered by invigorating cool sea breezes and romantic, rolling fog.

Harvest Time

If you are in the valley during harvest season, join in these celebrations. Check *Bay Views,* a bimonthly newspaper for a complete year-round listing of events in Watsonville and the Pajaro Valley.

Farmerama. Organized tours of local farms and food-processing plants, luncheons and lectures on valley agriculture take place in September each year.

Apple Annual. September and October host a queen's pageant, parade on Main Street, international food bazaar, softball tournaments, poster contests, and apple recipe contests—all in honor of the fall apple crop.

Santa Cruz County Fair. Agriculture, horticulture, floriculture, livestock, poultry and pigeons, horseshows, fireworks, midway amusements, and many exhibits and demonstrations make up the county fair held each September in Watsonville.

Also in Watsonville. The Antique Fly-In is sponsored by the Northern California Antique Aircraft Association. Air shows, aerobatics, contests, balloon launches, antique aircraft, and commercial booth displays delight and amaze each May. Watsonville Municipal Airport.

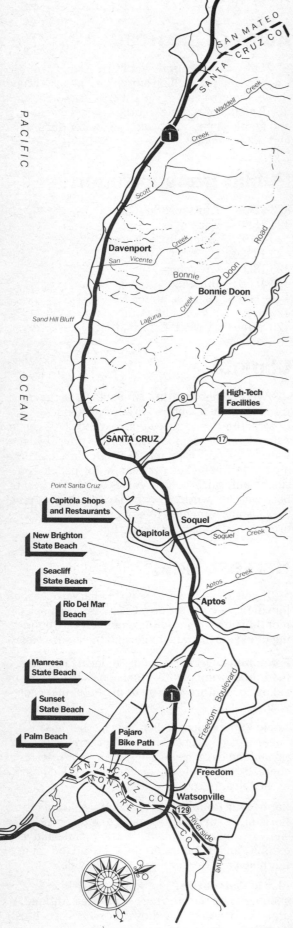

The Rich and the Powerful

Frederick Hihn's Watsonville–to–Santa Cruz Railway brought new life and activity to the towns located along its route. At Soquel, Hihn donated a 10-acre site to Claus Spreckels, the sugar monopolist who had a nearby country estate. Spreckels's refinery became Soquel's dominant industry throughout the 1870s.

Hihn and Spreckels controlled most of Soquel, Santa Cruz County's third township, which for a while included Aptos. Capitola, originally called Soquel Landing, was connected to Soquel both by the road between the two settlements and by controlling economic interests.

Santa Cruz's First "European Watering Place"

It has been said of Frederick Hihn that he "once owned a sixth of all the land in Santa Cruz County and had mortgages on most of the rest." In 1869 he laid out the resort town he called Camp Capitola, where he sought to build a sophisticated beach resort on the model of "European watering places." Capitola, California's first planned seaside resort, was a natural attraction with a beautiful sheltered beach.

The first tourists to arrive in Capitola came by horse-drawn cars and rented tents or small cottages that Hihn built on the sand close to the water. Men and women in full-body swimsuits approached the calm surf with restraint, smiling to each other as they met the pleasureful waves.

When the railroad came though in the 1870s, Hihn's lots attracted eager buyers who sought seaside romance on the installment plan. Capitola reached its height of appeal in 1896, when Hihn built the famous Capitola Hotel. Its Victorian seaside stateliness endured for 35 years, the landmark of Capitola and a charming comfort to families on a beach vacation.

The Siliconization of Santa Cruz County

Santa Cruz County shares its eastern boundary with Santa Clara County, home to Silicon Valley, the nation's capital for computer chip high technology. And Santa Cruz residents worry that their county is about to become "siliconized."

Although many counties envy Silicon Valley's growth, Santa Cruz does not. County and municipal officials here are not bedazzled by high-tech's growth, which has forced working-class families out of Silicon Valley and brough skyrocketing housing costs, gridlocked traffic, and toxic wastes in their place.

City and County Growth Controls

Santa Cruz County has made serious efforts to control growth. A 1978 county ordinance limits annual growth to 2.1%. The County also uses special zoning designations—agricultural, timber, open space, and recreational—to control development, and district zones clearly separate urban and rural land-use areas.

The City of Santa Cruz also has strong growth-control ordinances and looks closely at proposed new development projects. The last high-tech plant to be approved in Santa Cruz was okayed in 1982; the project provided 500 new jobs and was subject to a variety of conditions, including construction of a small public park.

Plants and Parking Lots

Successful countywide growth management, however, requires the participation of all of a county's jurisdictions, but all of Santa Cruz's localities are not of the same mind. Scott's Valley, for example, has allowed high-tech facilities, and many new plants have been built along Highway 17, which links Highway 1 to Santa Clara County. Among the unexpected consequences are housing shortages, water and sewer service problems, transportation headaches, and industrial waste pollution.

Nor does the burden of these impacts fall totally on Scott's Valley. Nearby jurisdictions also witness the prices of their housing soar and their roads and services stretched beyond capacity. Although the tax benefits from the newly recruited industries fall solely to the local jurisdictions, the entire county pays the price. A final solution thus seems to await a regional planning approach.

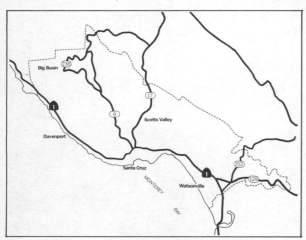

| **Environment** | **Roadside Attractions** | **Resources** |

Life In an Artichoke Field

Artichokes, those delicious and highly nutritious thistles imported from Italy, are grown in profusion along Highway 1 in the Pajaro Valley. But artichokes are not the only things growing in these profitable fields.

The tiny brown meadow mouse is always present in artichoke fields. Unlike other mice, this species survives solely on plant leaves and stems, and the leafy, thick-stemmed artichoke plant is a favorite. The Valley's artichoke fields are home to at least 3,000 meadow mice per acre. Once established, the mice quickly reproduce: females bear litters of 15 young as often as six times a year.

During the last few decades Santa Cruz County's meadow mice population has reached critical levels. The worst recent infestation occurred in 1968 when some growers lost almost half their crops. The control program required 20,000 pounds of rolled oats treated with zinc phosphide to be spread by air over 7,000 acres.

The mice do have natural predators, including hawks, owls, crows, and gulls. On a good day as many as 100 whitetail kites feed on the mice, as do many gulls, especially after the fields have been cleared in preparation for new planting. Vultures abound then also, cleaning out the thousands of limp bodies massacred by the thrashing machines. If an occasional crow catches a meadow mouse, the unlucky fellow is immediately besieged by sea gulls until it drops its squirming catch. The gulls don't care about the mouse; they just don't like crows.

Endangered

The tiny reptile known as the Santa Cruz long-toed salamander has unfortunately crept its way on to the Department of Interior's list of endangered species. Its habitats are few: one is near Aptos around Valencia Lagoon; another is Elkhorn Slough in Monterey County. Though researchers have undertaken many studies, little is known about the evasive salamander except that the salamander's demise is related to the filling in of ponds where the reptile breeds and might live. Most of the fill results from natural siltation or excavation to accommodate new construction and development. Potential salamander habitat is now regularly considered during the County's environmental review process for evaluating proposed new development.

North of Watsonville

North of Watsonville, the freeway highballs into Santa Cruz with little attention to views of the ocean or the Monterey Bay shoreline. West of the freeway, however, a string of beaches distinguish themselves for their wide sandy shorefronts and excellent swimming:

Palm Beach. The county's southernmost beach runs to the Pajaro River's mouth, an excellent spot for fishing. There are picnic facilities and a par course. The nearby shorefront development is the exclusive Pajaro Dunes luxury second-home subdivision, where

Capitola

Capitola is California's oldest seaside resort, and probably the state's most floral: ruby, pink, and white begonias explode in florid array between June and November. Go to Antonelli Brothers Begonia Gardens and expect to be overwhelmed.

Capitola is also distinctive because it favors pedestrians. The best way to visit this pleasurable resort town is to leave your car and take the shuttle bus near Highway 1.

The town embraces the beach on both sides of Soquel Creek with an assemblage of youth-oriented shops—craft shops, art galleries, gift shops—whose merchandise speaks of a different class sensibility (and commands higher prices) than many places in Santa Cruz.

The beach at Capitola is pleasurable despite the presence of rock jetties placed to restore the sand that disappeared after expansion of the Santa Cruz Harbor interfered with the natural flow of littoral currents. Today there is plenty of sand on the beach as well as a marvelous natural attraction for kids—Soquel Creek, which cuts across the beach and makes a magic swath of warm water and child-sized waves across the sand.

Beyond the beach, an abundance of activity—music, dancing, and dining—in an area scaled for walkers makes it a pleasure to stroll from place to place.

San Francisco's Mayor Dianne Feinstein spends much of her leisure time. 724-1266.

Sunset State Beach. This picturesque 3.5-mile beach differentiates itself from nearby beaches by its blazing springtime display of blossoming lupine and poppies in adjacent meadows. There are 90 campsites and plenty of secluded spots along the beach. 724-1266.

Manresa State Beach. The road to Manresa passes a big KOA campground on its way to this fine, wide beach. There is an outdoor shower and, reportedly, plenty of Pismo clams. Adjacent are tiny La Selva Beach and Trestle Beach, both accessible only from Manresa or by stealth. 688-3241

Seacliff State Beach and Rio Del Mar. Seacliff is one of the most popular swimming beaches around Santa Cruz. Seacliff's unique attribute is a 435-foot offshore cement ship, the *Palo Alto*, which now serves as a fishing pier after once enjoying two celebrated years as an amusement pier with a dance floor on deck. Seacliff also has campsites. Adjacent is Rio Del Mar, a nice beach with hot dog stands. 688-3222.

New Brighton State Beach. Another superb beach for swimming, New Brighton has several interpretive nature trails that are equally compelling. And birds: red-tailed hawks, valley quail, western meadowlarks, and goldfinches. From spring to late summer the grunion are running. Campsites. 475-4850.

Bike the Pajaro Path

A peaceful 10 + miles of bike path stretches aside the Pajaro River on the Monterey–Santa Cruz County line. You can pick up the bike path at Highway 1 and ride to the sea.

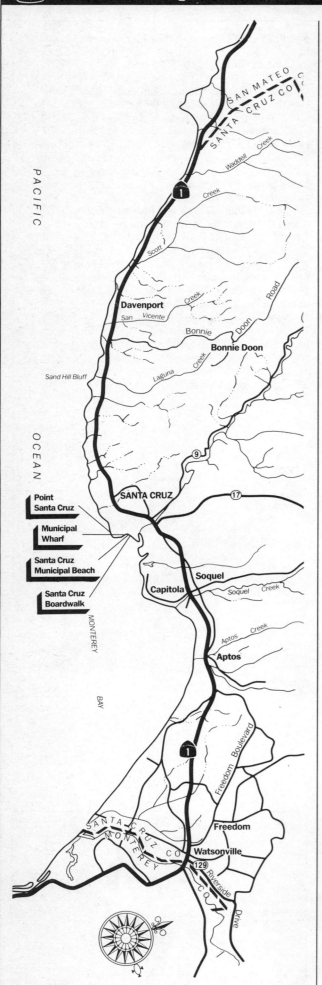

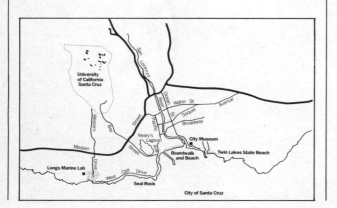

Santa Cruz: The Beginning of a Resort Town

By the end of the 1880s the City of Santa Cruz had established a statewide identity as a major coastal resort city. The town's economy prospered as new arrivals, drawn by the pleasant climate and seaside charm, bought land and spent money. Santa Cruz also attracted more and more vacationers, who stayed at new resorts like the Neptune Baths close to the Liebrandt Bathhouses, or the Old Pope House. On the beach, a huge new resort, the Sea Beach Hotel, was under construction.

An Electric Future

To early Santa Cruzans prosperity had arrived. Optimism prevailed, the town's vitality seemed almost charged, and the future appeared luminous. Indeed, to Fred W. Swanton, Santa Cruz's future was electric.

In 1889 Swanton joined in partnership with Dr. H.H. Clark to form an electric light business that would make gigantic profits at the flip of a switch. Swanton rightly anticipated that Santa Cruzans would want to keep their city up to date by installing electric lights. By 1892 Swanton and his partner had turned a $7,500 initial investment into a $100,000 electrical business. This shining success allowed Swanton to invest in other projects and design other electric schemes.

In 1891 Swanton's creative aspirations led him to form a company for the purpose of building an "electrical road" to carry open-bench railway cars from Santa Cruz's north boundary to the beach. In June 1891 the City's Common Council granted franchises for the new company, giving Swanton a virtual electric-transit monopoly.

Within months the new transit company had laid new tracks, built trestles, erected a car barn, and taken delivery from Stockton of the new cars, trucks, and motors. On opening day the first car of the electric railroad rolled up to Vue de Leau Chalet for a celebration and community barbeque. Newspapers called it "a gala day," and few people failed to note that getting to the beach could now be done in matchless swift high style.

California's Last Seaside Amusement Park

Once California's coast glittered with the showy "gilt and plush" of numerous seaside amusement parks. Fantasy and illusion had a gaudier image then, as flashing lights, whirligig motion, and exaggerated detail combined to temporarily extricate visitors from landlocked reality.

But now pleasure taking along California's coastline is marked by less flamboyance and gaudery, and the only seaside amusement park that remains is the Boardwalk at Santa Cruz. If it was the allure of the exotic, the larger than life, and the thrill-a-minute that once stimulated the creation of seaside amusement parks, then it has become the bottom-line reality of coastal land-use economics that has meant their disappearance.

Why They Disappeared

Up and down the coast California's amusement parks cashed in their chips. Several factors account for their demise:

LAND VALUE. The escalating value of coastal property has pushed many owners to convert the

parks to more profitable commercial or residential uses. Owners of marginally profitable private enterprises became eager to sell or convert when their land seemed far more valuable without the amusement park on it.

INCREASED COMPETITION. A new era of Disneyland-type theme parks, located away from the coast where land is cheaper, has brought about insurmountable competition. The simple rollercoaster and carousel were no match for the newest advanced-technology superrides.

REHABILITATION COSTS. Whether to modernize rides or replace rotting piers, rehabilitation in many cases required a far greater investment than investors could justify.

CLASS STIGMA. In some instances, amusement parks were closed because they had begun to attract "the wrong elements," visitors with limited disposable income who spent less freely than upwardly mobile visitors.

Santa Cruz's boardwalk has felt the lash of each of these conditions but has survived because the town's highly focused tourist economy recognizes that the boardwalk is a primary component of overall tourist appeal. The boardwalk, the identifiable emblem of Santa Cruz's seaside enjoyments, draws attention to the entire area.

Santa Cruz promotes the boardwalk and the boardwalk promotes Santa Cruz: 90% of Santa Cruz's 1.5 million annual tourist visitors spend some portion of their stay at the boardwalk or municipal wharf. The boardwalk continues to prosper.

Santa Cruz Municipal Beach

The mile long cresent-shaped beach in front of the Santa Cruz Boardwalk is almost always in sunshine. The beach faces due south, embraced on both ends by steep bluffs that catch and deflect the prevalent fog banks of Monterey Bay.

The expansive sandy beach is replenished each year by the San Lorenzo River, which reaches the sea just downcoast from the Boardwalk. An estimated average of 100,000 cubic yards of sediment flow through the mouth of the river each year, more than 20% of it sand eroded from the Santa Cruz Mountains far inland.

A walk north along Santa Cruz Municipal Beach leads to the Wharf where sea lions are often seen resting on the beams under the pier and where starfish, barnacles, and mussels cling to the pilings.

Point Santa Cruz

Point Santa Cruz marks the northern boundary between the Pacific Ocean and Monterey Bay. It is also the location of one of California's best big-wave surfing spots. Deep water off the Point allows ocean swells to arrive with unaltered energy across Steamer Lane, as the underwater ocean bottom here is called. This, coupled with the orientation of the coast, creates ideal conditions for formation of long-crested, plunging waves, a surfer's delight.

Santa Cruz

Santa Cruz's heart beats to the rhythm of the amusement park calliope. There is no sense in trying to make it otherwise. Though Santa Cruz trifles with Northern California restraint and flirts with the notion of becoming a Berkeley south, the city sustains itself on its love of entertainment. Even while its eyes look seriously to the problems presented by growth and transition, its feet want to dance.

Tourism has always been Santa Cruz's livelihood, which perhaps explains how it has learned to pursue the tourist dollar while maintaining its integrity. Defining itself as California's most inviting seaside resort, it has pitched to the dreams of Californians for a century and endured with a showman's optimism toward the performance. To its praise, it has preserved one of California's most special roadside attractions.

The Boardwalk

From a distance the Boardwalk shines in the sun like a bannered emporium of gladness that seems as capable of resting on cloudtops as its unlikely position on the white sands of Santa Cruz's seashore. The Boardwalk is a rare miracle of fantasy that appeals to all ages across class and racial lines. Few seaside entertainments in contemporary California are so well shared by a diversity of people. At the Boardwalk, like the circus, foolish pleasures mean more than foolish differences.

The Arcade

Underneath the pleasure dome is an arcade rare and fanciful: 80 years of games and distractions are scattered about the place yearning to be played. Grandma the Fortune Teller sits enigmatically inside a glass booth ready to tell, if not all, at least some part of what prescient figures have always apprehended.

There are movieolas and shooting galleries, oak and glass cases filled with exotic but worthless treasures waiting to be grabbed with miniature polished silver cranes. For a quarter, who knows what you might retrieve?

For a few quarters more you can move into contemporary game playing with video games animated and up to date. For the Highway 1 motorist nothing rivals the drive-yourself electronic racecourse games.

The Wharf and Boardwalk

SANTA CRUZ BEACH BOARDWALK
400 Beach Street, Santa Cruz 95060.
423-5590   Boardwalk General Information
462-RIDE   Casino Arcade
423-2053   Coconut Grove Box Office
423-5590   Group Discounts and Programs

Admission to the Boardwalk is free, ride tickets may be purchased individually or in a variety of packets. The Boardwalk is open Memorial Day to Labor Day, weekends the rest of the year. The Casino Arcade is open year round. Sunday champagne brunch is usually served in the spectacular glass-domed Sun Room at the Coconut Grove, and big band dances are held there on weekends. Along the Boardwalk you will find 20 rides, 3 arcades, 26 games of skill, 15 refreshment stands, 5 restaurants, a shooting gallery, and 13 gift shops. Have fun at California's last seaside amusement park.

SANTA CRUZ WHARF
Santa Cruz 95060.
423-1739

The Wharf cuts a perpendicular line to a mile-long white sandy beach. Cars and people can travel its half-mile length. There are ramps, boat rentals, shops and restaurants, and, of course, fishing.

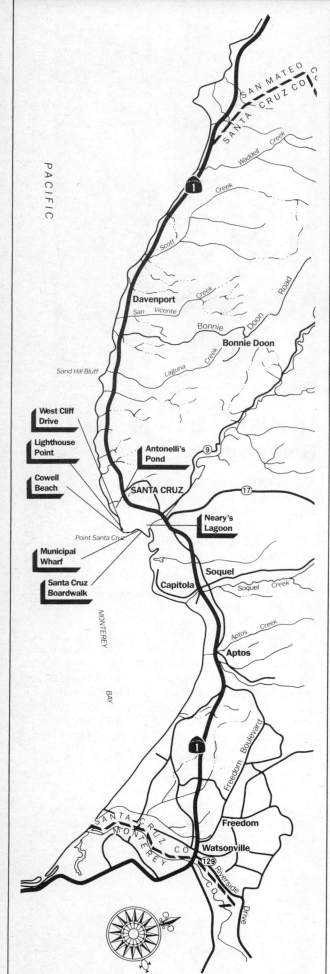

An Improbable Vision of Baghdad

The discovery of unique investment opportunities was becoming Fred Swanton's special talent as he continued to prosper in prosperous Santa Cruz. Tourism seemed an obvious choice, so in 1903 Swanton bought the Miller and Leibrandt Bathhouse and converted it to Swanton's Tent City, from which sprung, in 1904, Neptune's Casino, a magnificent Moorish fantasy with a boardwalk and "electric pier."

Swanton publicized his extravagant beach resorts with the same enthusiasm with which he created them. He visited towns all over California, peddling the gospel of Santa Cruz from the back of a five-coach special train provided by Southern Pacific. Two brass bands and a congregation of advertising men accompanied the pilgrim of progress.

While Swanton was on one such trip in 1906, the Casino at the beach burned to the ground. Undeterred, he formed a new company and rebuilt the structure more elaborately than ever. Michael Angelo Garibaldi made statues for the Casino's roof and natatorium, where "the plunge" quickly became the Casino's most popular attraction. The hotel's new bar was modeled after the bar at the Waldorf Astoria. And there were private dining rooms, a dancing pavilion, a convention hall, and a theater that "brought opera stars and other famous personalities to Santa Cruz." Despite many remodelings and a change in ownership, Swanton's Casino still graces the Santa Cruz Boardwalk.

The Saga of the Self-Service Gas Station

Less far away than you might imagine is a future world in which people are no longer seen because it is safer. Few cars pass on nighttime highways because the threat is too severe. The night has become a terrifying domain, illuminated only by darkly harrowing mercury vapor streetlights, populated only by motorists in seach of what no longer exists, guarded over by *the machine,* which has supplanted the service station as the traveler's sanctuary. But no one is certain of what darkly sinister things *the machine* is capable.

Behind this plot is, of course, the major oil companies, which are increasingly requiring service station operators to convert to self-serving gas stations. The Santa Cruz Board of Supervisors considers the consequences of this changeover to be serious enough that is has discussed enforcing a moratorium on such conversions.

Who Controls What

Most gas stations are run by operators who lease their facility from a major oil company, which controls major elements of individual station's operating policy. Converting to "pumpers" (kiosk-only stations) seems to be the oil companies' latest scheme for boosting the profitability of individual stations: lower labor costs mean higher profits.

In Santa Cruz County the number of full-service gas stations has dropped from 65 in 1983 to 18 in 1984. Local station owners fear that nonautomated stations could completely disappear from the county—and with them would go public services such as restrooms and motorist assistance.

Most severely affected, station owners point out, would be the elderly and the handicapped who are unable to pump their own gasoline. Motorists needing a quick minor repair or a new tire could be stranded on the highway many miles from spare parts and assistance.

Exactly who benefits from self-service gas stations? Certainly not the consumer—it's been a long time since self-service stations sold gas cheaper than anywhere else. Certainly not the employees being replaced by kiosks, nor the station operator who makes money from services, products, and repairs. Certainly not the community, which loses the measure of safety provided by pairs of roadside eyes.

A New Era

From the *Santa Cruz Sentinel* when the boardwalk reopened after a fire in 1907:

A new epoch, a new era, greater prosperity—all these thoughts were ringing in the minds of the people. They were all happy and at one time, for each citizen felt that the buildings were his buildings, that they belonged to all the people as a whole, and he realized that they would be a means of uniting all the people more closely together in the common cause of making Santa Cruz a great city.

0 ————— 8
Miles

Environment

Roadside Attractions

Resources

Freshwater Lagoons and Dabbling Ducks

An unusual number of fresh water lagoons lay between Highway 1 and the ocean within the City of Santa Cruz, including Moran Lake, Corcoran Lagoon, Schwan Lagoon, Neary's Lagoon, Natural Bridges Ponds, Antonelli's Pond, and Younger's Lagoon. Most of these pockets of fresh water have trails around them, some have beaches and parks, and all are excellent places for birdwatching, particularly brilliantly colored migrating waterfowl, including several varieties of "dabbling," or "puddle" ducks such as pintails, mallards, and gadwalls.

Pintail

Pintail ducks are probably the most abundant waterfowl in California and the most widely distributed duck in North America. They follow a complex migration and breeding pattern, and are seen in large flocks during winter on lakes, ponds and bays. The pintail is easy to distinguish in flight by its slender body and long pointed tail feathers, and at rest by the male's white underparts and dark brown head and black protruding tail. Pintails call with a short whistling sound.

Mallard

The unmistakeable green head of a male mallard is almost as common a sight in California as the Pintail's tail. Annual mallard populations in the Central Valley alone exceed a million individuals. Its head, framed by a white neck band, rusty breast and bluish purple wing patch, add to the distinctive attire of the male. The sound a mallard makes is a classic duck's "quack-quack."

Godwall

Godwalls are much less common than mallards and pintails, but they are still sometimes seen in Santa Cruz, frequently among a flock of pintails. The male godwall has an unusually common brown head and black beak, but very distinctive grey, brown, black and white chests and wing patterns.

Dressed for Success

The brilliant coloring of male ducks is no accident. As with other species in the world, colors and patterns aid in distinguishing the species and protect the ducks from interbreeding. Mallards and pintail males, for example, are aggressive breeders and will woo any female duck around. It is up to the female to make the distinction between specific species and she does so by color and pattern recognition.

Sunshine Pleasures

Next to the arcade is the Coconut Grove Dance Casino, where old-time bands still play and old-time rituals like the Miss California Pageant are still enacted.

Outside the arcade the promenade accommodates sunshine pleasures of every shade: a candy shop with candy apples and a bandstand on the sand, bumper cars and Fascination, hot dogs on a stick (and otherwise). You may ride through the air above the Boardwalk or stroll along and eat yourself blind. You can do anything or nothing, but passing up a ride on the merry-go-round is like turning your back on life.

The Merry-Go-Round

The merry-go-round at the Boardwalk is magic by design. Hand-carved and handsome, the 62-horse carousel spins to the music of a 324-pipe Ruth Bank organ made in Germany in 1894. Designed by Charles Loof, who hand-built the merry-go-round at Coney Island in 1875, the carousel sports horses made of Japanese white pine with horsehair tails that whirl through a mirrored world with lights-a-plenty.

And yes, riders on these aristocratic steeds may grab for rings of brass. A successful ring toss through the clown's gaping mouth sets his eyes to flashing and bells to ringing. If you doubt the cheer of the merry-go-round, watch the faces of the riders, child to adult—everybody smiles.

Rides, both traditional and newfangled high-tech, adorn the boardwalk from end to end. There is a logger's revenge that could have come from Marriot's Great America, and a pirate ship swings back and forth in a giant arch as part of a complicated maritime fantasy.

The Giant Dipper

But nothing eclipses the Giant Dipper, a 1924 wooden roller coaster that is the oldest full-sized roller coaster on the West Coast and one of the few wooden rides still swirling on any of the nation's coastlines. The Giant Dipper is a thrill-a-second attraction that still clacks and groans with the nobility of its true-excitement roller-coaster bearing.

And what is to be said of the eloquent ferris wheel, save that from what other vantage point does California's last seaside amusement park so well shine?

The Land Trust of Santa Cruz County
P.O. Box 1287
Santa Cruz 95061

The Land Trust of Santa Cruz County operates behind the scenes and at public hearings to find swift, non-confrontational solutions to the county's complex land use problems. Among its most notable successes is the protection of Antonelli's Pond, a freshwater system just inland from Natural Bridges State Park. Contact the Trust for information on environmental issues and resources, and for a copy of their booklet *The Landowner's Options: A Guide to Voluntary Protection of Land in California.*

The Atlantic City of the West

Among the myriad ways that Santa Cruz promoted itself in the early 20th century was by staging the Miss California Pageant, organized by the Chamber of Commerce to broadcast the image of Santa Cruz as "the Atlantic City of the West."

The town's first beauty pageant was held in 1924, and Mary Black was chosen as Miss Santa Cruz. In June of the same year, 19-year-old Faye Lanphier was crowned Miss California, and became the first Miss California to become Miss America. In a grotesque mix of symbolic significance, the pageant's parade from Pacific Avenue to the beach was led by the knights of the Ku Klux Klan, who marched in white robes and hoods.

But headlines carried Lanphier's "classic" 35-26-37 measurements as proof of her worthiness to represent the state of California and American womanhood. Lanphier, known as the "Blonde Venus," was treated to a tickertape parade in New York, but her greatest moment of exaltation was her trip from Atlantic City to New York, which she made in Calvin Coolidge's private railroad car.

After her reign, Lanphier became a California housewife.

Historic Preservation in Santa Cruz

Preservation of historical structures is a high priority in the City of Santa Cruz. Few other cities in the county have as thorough and stringent historical protection ordinances.

About a dozen years ago, the City was persuaded by local citizens, students, and historical organizations to protect its architectural heritage. An increase in demolition of some of Santa Cruz's oldest structures prompted the move.

The City responded by commissioning the San Francisco firm of Charles Hall Page to undertake a comprehensive inventory of all residential and commercial structures in the town. When the inventory was completed, an ordinance was passed requiring that any changes to a structure listed as historically significant must be reviewed by the newly created Historic Preservation Commission. Commission members include local citizens and architectural and historical experts, and their recommendations are presented to the city's planning commission before any development permits are approved. The rule of thumb has been that an owner of a historically significant structure may paint the exterior and make any interior changes desired, but any other alterations require design review and approval. Proposed demolition of a historic structure to allow new construction is extremely unlikely to gain approval.

Santa Cruz takes historical preservation one step further than design review for individual buildings of significance. The City has mapped out several districts that have a concentration of historically important structures. Within these historical overlay districts, *all* development is subject to design review, whether the individual building is itself important or not. The rule of thumb here is that new construction or conversion must complement, not distract from, the architectural historical integrity of the district.

Santa Cruz used two other tools to ensure that its historical buildings are preserved. City staff offer individual assistance to owners of private property who wish to protect their buildings by obtaining national register status. The major downtown commercial area, the Pacific Garden Mall, has its own special design district, enforced by the zoning commission, although it is not exempt from the Historic Preservation Commission's review for individually important buildings.

Movie Magic on Pacific Avenue

In its time, Pacific Avenue has seen the life span of several theaters that helped shape Santa Cruz's romantic dream lives. In 1904 a 700-seat vaudeville house, the Unique Theater, was opened. Shortly afterward Mark Swain, who later became Charlie Chaplin's film accomplice, converted the Unique into a playhouse for drama; *Sidewalks of New York* was the first production. The theater was again converted, this time into a movie house, but finally demolished in 1936.

The same year that Swain's theater was razed, the Del Mar Theater was built next door. Six usherettes and three ushers seated moviegoers to view Warner Brothers' *China Clipper,* starring Pat O'Brien, as the Zigzag Moderne building began its inaugural run as Santa Cruz's premier movie palace. Still operating today, the Del Mar has maintained its splendidly festive facade with tall electric sign and marquee. Inside, the lobby ceiling and star-adorned frosted lamps continue to evoke movie magic, although the theater has been multiplexed into four ill-fitted screening rooms that have considerably damaged its pride.

The New Santa Cruz Theater, which became the

Santa Cruz after the Del Mar opened, was designed by Reid Bros. of San Francisco, who also designed the Hotel Del Coronado in San Diego and the Fairmont in San Francisco. This theater opened in 1920 with the Mack Sennett comedy *Back in the Kitchen.* Twenty years later a heraldic Moderne tower with cut-out stars and moons were added. In 1976-77 the theater was again remodeled and the extraordinary tower destroyed.

Environment

Shoreline Geology

The Santa Cruz shoreline is largely composed of low vertical bluffs of shale and sandstone backed inland by a series of marine terraces about 100 feet above sea level. These terraces line the northern portion of Monterey Bay's crescent from the Pajaro Valley to north of the town of Santa Cruz.

Along this geologically soft shore, a natural process called differential erosion has etched a landscape of diverse sea caves, sea stacks, and outstanding offshore formations. Differential erosion is the process by which the abrasive action of waves and sand wear away less resistant materials that once covered the sandstone edge of the continent here. This process both formed the original arched bridges and caves at Natural Bridges in Santa Cruz, and eventually caused the arches to collapse. Much of the eroded sediment becomes beach sand; the rest finds its way to the bottom of the ocean as new sediment in the Monterey submarine canyon to the south.

The powerful erosive action of the Santa Cruz shoreline combines with the soft, vulnerable geological makeup of the coastal cliffs to produce constant sloughing along the shoreline. The many rubble revetments, large stone structures stacked against the cliff face, that make up the shore are intended to absorb the wave action and protect the base of the sandstone cliffs from the relentless forces of differential erosion.

Natural Bridges

The stunning profiles of Santa Cruz's three natural sandstone bridges once graced postcards and tourist brochures, and brought thousands of visitors to Santa Cruz to marvel at nature's wonders.

Two of the bridges have since fallen into the sea, the last in January 1980, when it was duly mourned by a public wake. But the third bridge remains and a new one is being formed, though it won't be completed for another two or three centuries.

In addition to the sandstone bridges and sea caves, there are excellent tide pools, a gentle nature walk from the parking area to the beach, and a freshwater lagoon. The sight that sets everyone aquiver, however, is the grove of butterfly trees. Recently declared a state nature preserve, a 10-acre segment of the park contains hundreds of eucalyptus trees on which, in season, perch hundreds of thousands of monarch butterflies. These beauties arrive in September, and depart in March. Within the last few years this preserve has become the second-largest gathering place of monarchs in the entire world.

Roadside Attractions

Pacific Garden Mall

It resembled a pot, it was almost a pot, but it was not a pot of which one could say, Pot, Pot, and be comforted.
Samuel Beckett

Like Beckett's pot, Santa Cruz's Pacific Avenue Mall resembles a mall, is almost a mall, but is not a mall. On this winding street the usual relationship between automobile and pedestrian has been reversed, so that the pedestrian comes out on top. Cars are still permitted, but only on an underprivileged basis.

Once a traditional American main street, Pacific Avenue has been transformed by extensive landscaping and enough twists and curls to give the urban explorer a sense of discovery around every curvy turn. The avenue has lots of shops, but it is also a swell place to hang out, and many do, imparting to the street a sense of peopled vitality.

Amid the flower boxes, ornamental trees, and passing parade of bums, street people, squares, and ordinary folk, several places stand out. In addition to the Catalyst, which offers a restaurant and name musical acts (Ry Cooder, Tito Fuente), there are three excellent bookstores: Plaza Books, Logos Books (and Records), and Bookshop Santa Cruz.

The Saint George Hotel is a splendid old structure with a romantic garden court, stamped metal ceilings in quatrefoil designs, and garlanded art nouveau seashells. The Saint George, which functions as a sort of Santa Cruz version of New York's Chelsea Hotel, provides inexpensive overnight accommodations.

Resources

Santa Cruz's Architecture and History

Together, the four books recommended here provide an excellent introduction to Santa Cruz's past and present.

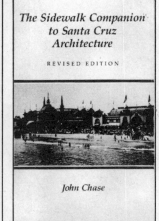 

THE SIDEWALK COMPANION TO SANTA CRUZ ARCHITECTURE
John Chase
Western Tanager Press
Santa Cruz. 1981.

THE WALK AROUND SANTA CRUZ BOOK
Margaret Koch
Valley Publishers
Fresno. 1978.

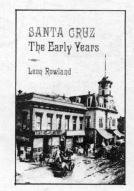

SANTA CRUZ: THE EARLY YEARS
Leon Rowland
Paper Vision Press
Santa Cruz. 1980.

SANTA CRUZ COUNTY: PARADE OF THE PAST
Margaret Koch
Western Tanager Press
Santa Cruz. 1981.

Events

Here are some annual events offered in the County of Santa Cruz. Contact the Visitors Bureau for more detail on these and others.

February	ANNUAL CLAM CHOWDER COOK-OFF, Santa Cruz Boardwalk.
March	KITE FESTIVAL, Capitola Esplanade Beach.
April	CRITERIUM BICYCLE RACES, Capitola, Watsonville, UC Santa Cruz.
May	ANNUAL WATSONVILLE FLY-IN, Watsonville.
June	HARBOR FESTIVAL AND BOAT SHOW, Santa Cruz. MISS CALIFORNIA PAGEANT, Santa Cruz. GRAND INTERNATIONAL CRAWDAD CRAWL, Santa Cruz.
July	BEACH STREET REVIVAL, Santa Cruz. APPLE ANNUAL, Watsonville.
October	SANTA CRUZ MISSION FIESTA & PARADE, Santa Cruz. WINE FESTIVAL, Santa Cruz. SANTA CRUZ WHEELCHAIR TOURNAMENT, Santa Cruz.
November	TURKEY TROT 10K Run, Santa Cruz.
December	NATIONAL CYCLOCROSS BICYCLE CHAMPIONSHIP, Santa Cruz.

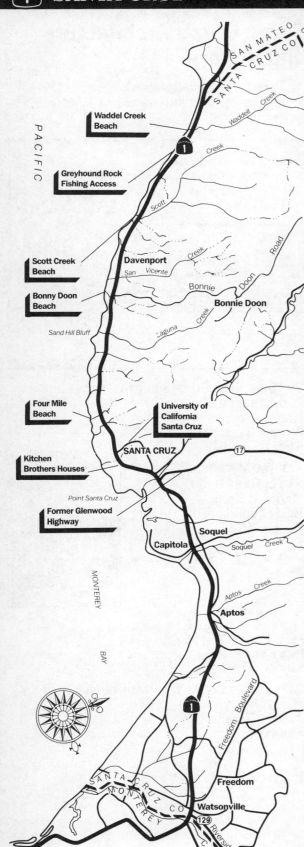

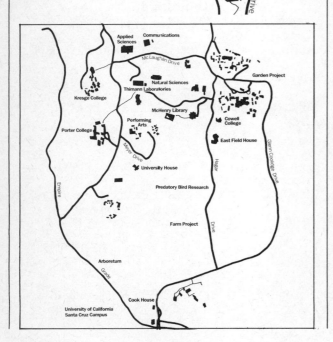

Automobiles and Tourism

When the automobile came to Santa Cruz County—in increasing numbers after 1915—the town's character changed once again. The city's beaches and resorts needed no longer to depend on mass transportation, and automobiles created new recreational opportunities. Santa Cruz's reputation as a seacoast resort had continued to spread as new tourist attractions were built. This reputation soon surpassed that of Long Beach, where the discovery of oil at Signal Hill had

shifted economic attention, and Santa Monica, where the advent of the motion picture industry and urban sprawl varied the economic outlook.

In Santa Cruz recreation remained sovereign. To accommodate the tourist's automobiles, roads were built or improved. Attention was given to the thoroughfare leading east from town through the enchanted trees that connected to better transportation and greater populations inland. But no one proposed roads up the coast, where untamed beaches and giant coastal ranches seemed less appealing to builders than the close-in beaches and magnificent redwoods on the coastal ridge.

In August 1921 the Glenwood Highway, now State Highway 17, was opened, and Santa Cruzans had a new scenic road to motor over. The logic was irresistible: a new road meant new visitors, and new visitors meant more tourist dollars.

Auto-Camps ar Motorlogues

In the 1920s several auto-camps were established to accomodate the new motoring tourist. After a pleasant journey through the country, young families who found the old resort hotels too stuffy or too expensive could stop at El Río Auto-Camp or Mac's Auto-Camp, whose brochure promised a unique dream of leisure at a site "where wife takes her ease and where hubby does the family wash."

Santa Cruz had been one of the first coastal resorts to promote tourism, and the intense promotion continued. One favorite method was the "motorlogue," large newspaper ads that featured photos of shiny new cars parked at scenic Santa Cruz locales. In effect, the Chamber of Commerce, the automobile dealers, and the newspaper publishers combined their pitches to promote Santa Cruz. The automobile dealers would send photographers in new cars to shoot scenic spots. The dealers then purchased big spreads of advertising in newspapers to publish the results, which provided good publicity for the automobile dealers and Santa Cruz. The newspapers profited handsomely from the sale of advertising space, but printed the motorlogues as though they were merely honest discoveries of scenic travel spots.

After witnessing years of popularity for the Glenwood Highway, the County Board of Supervisors passed a resolution on May 27, 1927, declaring the construction of the coast highway to be in the public interest. But State authorization for construction was still a few years away.

The University of California at Santa Cruz

Since the first ground breaking, UC Santa Cruz has had a dramatic effect on the city and county of Santa Cruz, determining land use and public policy that extends far beyond the confines of the bucolic campus.

In the mid 1800s UC Santa Cruz land was the site of a lime-quarrying operation. Later it became the Cowell Ranch, and in 1961 the ranch was selected by the State as the spot for its next campus. Original plans called for a campus like Berkeley's or UCLA's, with approximately 30,000 students and major professional graduate schools in business and engineering. During the early 1960s, however, student demand for those fields declined, and the plans for Santa Cruz were redefined. School enrollment was set at 7,500 and undergraduate liberal arts became the academic focus.

Santa Cruz Students, Consumers—and Voters

At first Santa Cruz's business community was pleased by the arrival of the well-heeled students, who brought new dollars and intellectual prestige to the small coastal resort town best known as the home of the Miss California beauty contest. The opening of the professional schools was expected to bring new industry to the town, and expectations ran so high that a major portion of Santa Cruz's downtown core was converted into a mall specifically aimed at the student consumer.

But as more than one observer has noted, the city's expectations were exceeded in unexpected ways. Instead of business administration graduates, the campus' new curriculum drew an extremely idealistic student body that was attracted by the informal learning environment and politically liberal atmosphere. UC Santa Cruz was

strongly perceived as the exception to "establishment" education. A large portion of the student body came to learn how to create change, and the entire city became their laboratory.

To this day, the student body at Santa Cruz often votes in a 90% block on local land-use and social issues, and many graduates and dropouts stay on to become permanent local residents. As a result, the City of Santa Cruz has become one of the most liberal-voting cities in California. Politicians are elected on feminist, gay rights, environmental, and socialist platforms. Student influence in Santa Cruz remains responsible for many liberal municipal programs, and even while UC Santa Cruz struggles to find a new and contemporary self-definition, its initial educational philosophy continues to influence the community.

Environment

Roadside Attractions

Resources

Agroecology

The agricultural wheel is being reinvented at the University of California, Santa Cruz. The concept of self-sustainable agriculture, a process understood by other cultures for centuries, is being studied here and refined for practical application by America's farmers. On the sloping hills of the campus, students, apprentices, and faculty work daily at a model farm that marries traditional agricultural knowledge and the principles of ecology. As optimistically reported by Harold Gilliam, environmental reporter for the *San Francisco Chronicle*, herein lies "the beginning of a great search for a culture consonant with the natural systems of the Earth."

Corn-Bean-Squash Polyculture

Stephen Gliessman, director of the program, gives an example of self-sustainable agriculture—Mexican farmers' practice of planting corn, beans, and squash crops together. When researchers tested this traditional combination, they found the corn yield was 50% greater than when corn was planted alone. The beans stimulate corn growth because bacteria in the bean root fixes nitrogen,

which is transferred to the corn. The corn reciprocates by stimulating greater nitrogen-fixing ability in the beans and by providing a convenient stalk for the beans to climb. Squash, the third member of the commune, spreads across the ground, shading it, preserving water, and producing a good microclimate for soil organisms, as well as crowding out weeds.

The Measure of Success

This method of multiple planting won't produce per-acre yields comparable to those of the highly-engineered corn fields in Kansas. But, if the two yields are compared in terms of energy used—including energy required to manufacture, transport, and apply fertilizers, insecticides, herbicides, and fungicides and to pump water and fuel machinery—the yield in Kansas is much smaller. High-tech agriculture is further disadvantaged by the requirement for ever-increasing amounts of fertilizers, of insects that develop resistance to chemicals, and damage to the soil by erosion and poor water practices.

Agroecology prefers to evaluate efficiency by measuring the costs of energy as well as the bushel output. By this measure it is a true success. Experiments at Santa Cruz continue with combinations of plants that fertilize each other, repel insects, control weeds, and conserve water. The basic concept was simply expressed by John Muir: "Everything is hitched to everything else."

UC Santa Cruz Architecture

From its inception, UC Santa Cruz was meant to be different, an emphasis that has achieved stunning architectural results.

The basic concept of the campus's design is to maintain several independent clusters of structures, grouped in such a way to minimize their obtrusiveness. Most of the buildings have been built in bunches and hidden within a redwood grove. The open grass–covered fields that slope toward the sea for the most part remain undeveloped. Views, and most of the historical

structures remaining from the site's lime quarry and ranching days, have been preserved.

The UC Santa Cruz campus has had the benefit of many distinguished designers, beginning with John Carl Warnecke and Thomas Church, who prepared the original site plan, and including Moore, Lyndon, Turnbull, and Whitaker, and several nationally and internationally known architects. Some of the most interesting structures are:

Cowell College, 1967 (Ernest Kump and Associates)
Adlai Stevenson College, 1967 (Joseph Esherick and Associates; Lawrence Halprin, Landscape Architect)
Merrill College, 1968-9 (Campbell and Wong)

North of Santa Cruz

Before Highway 1 (Mission Street) departs from Santa Cruz on the north side of town, it is crossed by Fair Street, the location of two of Santa Cruz's most unique roadside attractions, both built by the Kitchen brothers.

At 1211 Fair is a bulbous-domed, abalone shelled office building that is a superb example of absurdist architecture. A few blocks down the street (519 Fair) is another structure also built by the Kitchens, the Saint Elias Orthodox Church.

Built as a Yogi Temple in 1946, this tile and abalone shell structure features an entrance arch that originally contained a moon and star, the alignment of which was believed to signal the end of the world.

From Santa Cruz to Davenport a number of excellent beaches are accessible from Highway 1. Monterey Bay ends at Point Santa Cruz, and the shoreline north is much more rugged and oftentimes spectacular.

Kresge College, 1966-73 (Moore and Turnbull – MLTW)
Central Science Building, 1965 (Ernest J. Kump Associates)
Field House, 1965 (Callister, Payne, and Rosse)
National Science Buildings, 1965, 1969 (Anshen and Allen)
University Library, 1968 (John Carl Warnecke)
Outdoor Theater, 1968 (Royston, Hanamoto, Beck, and Abey)
Communications Building, 1968 (Spencer, Lee, and Busse)
Cowell Student Health Center, 1970 (John Funk)
Student Apartments, 1971 (Ratcliff, Slama, Cadwalader)
Performing Arts Center, 1971 (Reid and Tarics)
Applied Science, 1971 (Reid and Tarics)
Class Room Unit #1, 1972 (Marquis and Stoller)
College V, 1969-70 (Hugh Stubbins, Jr.)

In addition the the new buildings, great care has been taken to preserve or adapt all the original ranch structures on the campus. Among these are the 1864 Jordan House at 10001 High Street—an old horse barn that is now a 207-seat theater—ranch cabins, the lime kilns and blacksmith's shop, a bull barn, carriage house and powder house, as well as the original ranch slaughter house.

University of California
SANTA CRUZ
General Catalog 1984-85

University of California at Santa Cruz

429-0111

The UC Santa Cruz campus offers surprises and delights for almost any taste. One can spend an hour here, days, or academic years. Visitors information in provided at the booth at the campus entrance, including maps, brochures, and current events. Pick up a campus phone and dial 4409 to hear a daily taped calendar of events. The school newspaper, *The City on a Hill,* also lists events, shows, and lectures.

Long Marine Lab
429-4087

The Joseph M. Long Marine Laboratory is a research and instructional facility of the Santa Cruz campus of the University of California. Open to the public during most afternoon hours, the lab contains an aquarium, touch tanks, exhibits, and an 85 foot long skeleton of a blue whale. Docent tours are available.

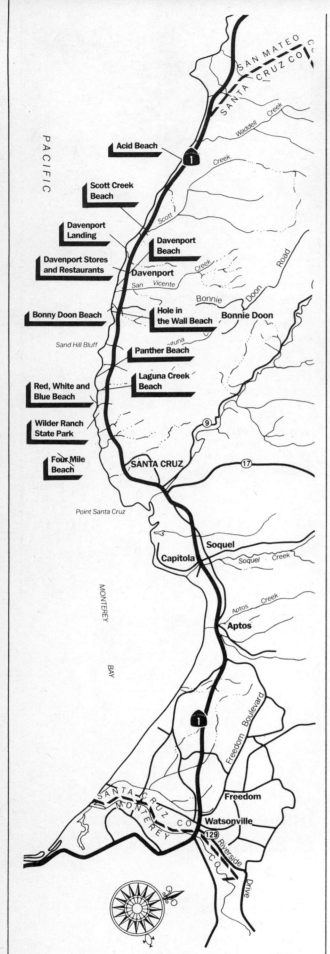

When Davenport Thrived

North of Santa Cruz the only real coastal settlement was at Davenport, where Captain John Pope Davenport had moved in 1867 to begin a shorewhaling enterprise similar to those he had conducted at Monterey Bay and Moss Landing. Throughout its early years, the town of Davenport relied heavily on the sea owing to the unreliability of the coast road north and south.

Shorewhaling at Davenport was especially productive because the whales came close to land, attracted to near-shore rocks against which they scraped off skin-clinging barnacles and parasites. Davenport also built a 450-foot wharf to ship out redwood from the coastal forests and lime from the mountains. Up until the end of the century, Davenport was enough of a town to have three hotels, stores, and blacksmith shops.

But when the whaling and lumber industries declined, Davenport began a steady descent. In the 1890s the post office was moved inland to Laurel Grove (later Swanton), and in 1906 most of the land around Davenport was sold to the newly incorporated Santa Cruz Portland Cement Company. Apart from a few small flings of excitement during prohibition, when Davenport Landing, like its coastal neighbors to the north, was a secret port of entry for illegal booze, the spot has lain relatively still in the 20th century.

From New Town to No Town at Wilder Ranch

Wilder Ranch, 5,000 acres on both sides of Highway 1 in northern Santa Cruz County, is in agricultural use today just as it has been for 100 years. Eventually it will be a developed state park, but it might have been something quite different.

In 1972, the Canadian firm that owned Wilder Ranch announced plans, four years in the making, for an oceanfront development of 33,000 houses that would be annexed to the City of Santa Cruz. A new highway was planned to parallel Highway 1 and to bring the public and residents to the new town's shopping centers and retail areas.

When residents of Santa Cruz heard about the plan, they raised their voices in shocked protest, taking out full-page advertisements against the project and gaining legal ammunition from the passage of the California Coastal Act. The strength and adamance of public opinion convinced the developer to confer with public agencies and citizen's groups to seek other alternatives for Wilder Ranch.

From Park to Peril

Eventually the California Department of Recreation was induced to consider purchasing the ranch for the state park system. The State noted the ranch's special scenic qualities and historical significance—the Castro adobe, which dates from 1781, is located on the site—and the property was purchased for public use. While planning for the new state park progressed, the property was leased for continued agricultural use.

But the State soon found itself with a park it could not open. Tests revealed unsafe residues of dangerous chemical pesticides that had been sprayed for years on the local brussels sprouts fields.

An integrated pest management program was developed for the park land, and after three years of phased-in application, it appears to efficiently and economically control pests with less chemical pollution. Even so, public use of the park is years away.

Meanwhile, crowds of beach goers "unofficially" use Wilder Ranch's beaches despite the possible danger and despite the neglect of beach maintenance by the Department of Parks and Recreation, which awaits the results of more tests.

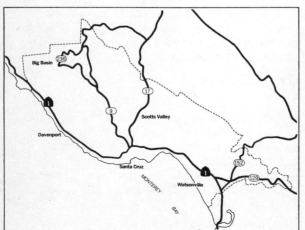

Blacktop for the State

Bitumen chopped from the ground around Wilder Ranch provided blacktop for roads and streets throughout California and as far away as South America. Market Street in San Francisco was first paved with bitumen broken from a "petroleum mine" here that contained an asphalt layer 20-feet thick under 90 feet of sandstone and chalk. Men with sharp iron bars worked 10-hour days for 15¢ an hour to break out thousands of tons of the heavy substance, which was then loaded on wagons or ships to pave the way for progress.

Tanbark Oak

The California tanbark oak, an evergreen also known under the names of tan chestnut, peach, bur or sovereign oak, is among the most handsome of all the hardwoods. The leaves of this tree produce a dazzling, glittering sight with their dark-green tops and silvery-white undersides. The flower is white, perched on long catkins, and the fruit is an elongated, dark acorn with a brushed polished sheen.

The tanbark defies the traditional oak form by growing from one central, straight trunk that reaches heights of 70 to 90 feet, topped by a long and narrow crown of foliage within forested areas. In more open territory, the tanbark spreads out lower on its trunk and sports more luxuriant foliage, but still centers on one primary trunk.

The bark of the tanbark oak is high in tannin, the key substance used in tanning hides (the process named after the natural element of the bark). The high tannin content of the thick, firmly crisscrossed gray bark gives the tree its name, but was also almost its undoing in the 1880s and 90s when Santa Cruz County became the nation's largest tanning center, processing more than 5,000 cords of bark in 1886 alone.

Within only a few decades the tanning industry had almost exhausted the supply of oak, and by 1918 over three-quarters of the tanbark in Santa Cruz County had been peeled. In the 1920s the shortage of trees and the importation of cheaper tanning materials from abroad brought an end to the tanning industry on the Santa Cruz and Big Sur coasts. Today the trees have reestablished themselves in great abundance.

The tanbark follows the coastal redwoods into their forests, growing in scattered sites rather than clustered groves. Individual trees, left undis-

turbed, have a life span of about 500 years. Their lucky habit of intermingling with other species has made the tanbark too expensive to harvest for its wood, which is hard and lovely but cannot be gathered economically. You can enjoy the sight of this stately hardwood in Santa Cruz and further north through California's redwood belt.

The Loganberry

The popular loganberry has its origins in Santa Cruz County. John H. Logan arrived in Santa Cruz in 1880 and soon became one of the area's most prominent judges. He was also a passionate horticulturist. One day while working in his garden he noticed a strange hybrid that appeared to be a cross between the native blackberry sport (Auginbaugh) and the red antwerp raspberry he had planted here. The Judge immediately sent a sample of the new plant to experts in Salem, Oregon, where it was declared a major find and officially named in honor of its discoverer.

Once the scandal of seashore communities from Black Point to Point George, nude bathing gains daily in social acceptance and is generally tolerated by most Californians. Each year sees more and more bathers at clothing optional beaches. Rarely are citations issued, particularly in Northern California where nudity at the beach is usually ignored by authorities. (Department of Park and Recreation's policy is not to issue citations at State Beaches without a specific complaint made by an offended party. Usually a warning precedes a citation.)

For the most part nude beaches are quiet, easy going places where people find uncomplicated pleasure in nature. In Santa Cruz County most clothing optional beaches are located north of Monterey Bay, although there is some nude bathing at Manressa and Sunset Beaches. Below is a list of Santa Cruz County clothing optional beaches.

Four Mile Beach: Four miles north of the City of Santa Cruz at Baldwin Creek; surfing too.

Bonny Doon: Across Highway 1 from Bonny Doon Rd., large beach with caves.

Davenport

Davenport is about a mile north of Bonny Doon Road, which leads to Felton and State Route 9. The shorewhaling industry that once distinguished the community has now disappeared, but many descendents of the Portuguese whalers still live here. Several roadside pullouts provide prime areas for viewing the migration of the gray whales, which are now protected from slaughter.

Davenport has a gas station, saloon, several shops displaying local art, a classic county jail, and the Davenport Cash Store, a 1950's replica of what was once the social and economic nucleus of the town. North of Davenport is the Davenport Cement Plant, which still thrives thanks to rich deposits of limestone nearby and the successful curbing of a pollution problem that once dusted houses and fields for miles around with gray smoke.

Clothing Optional Beaches

Red, White, and Blue Beach: Six miles north of the City of Santa Cruz, marked with red, white, and blue mailbox with numbers 5021 Highway 1. Excellent facilities. Fee.

Laguna Creek Beach: Approximately .7 miles north of Red, White, and Blue Mailbox at Laguna Creek; uncrowded but frequently windy.

Panther Beach: Approximately 7.5 miles north of City of Santa Cruz, one of the most beautiful beaches along this part of the coast; uncrowded.

Hole in the Wall Beach: Accessible from Bonny Doon Beach through a hole in the wall; fine beach with large granite outcroppings.

Davenport Beach: Just south of Davenport, with clothing optional at sheltered end.

Scott Creek Beach: About 12 miles north of Santa Cruz at Scott Creek, fine sand.

Acid Beach: Just south of Greyhound Rock, Acid Beach is named for the discovery of a large cache of LSD once left by a philanthropic donor.

County Guides

COMBING THE COAST 2: SANTA CRUZ TO CARMEL
Ruth A. Jackson
Chronicle Books
San Francisco. 1982.

COASTAL VISITORS GUIDE
P.O. Box 1139
Santa Cruz 95061
429-0151

The second in a series of coastal guides, *Coast 2*, is lively and full of facts, lore, and legend about the Santa Cruz Area and south. The first of Jackson's guides covers from Santa Cruz to San Francisco. The *Coastal Visitors Guide* is a free bi-weekly tabloid of things to do and places to go on the Santa Cruz coast. Available in local stores and stands, or write directly.

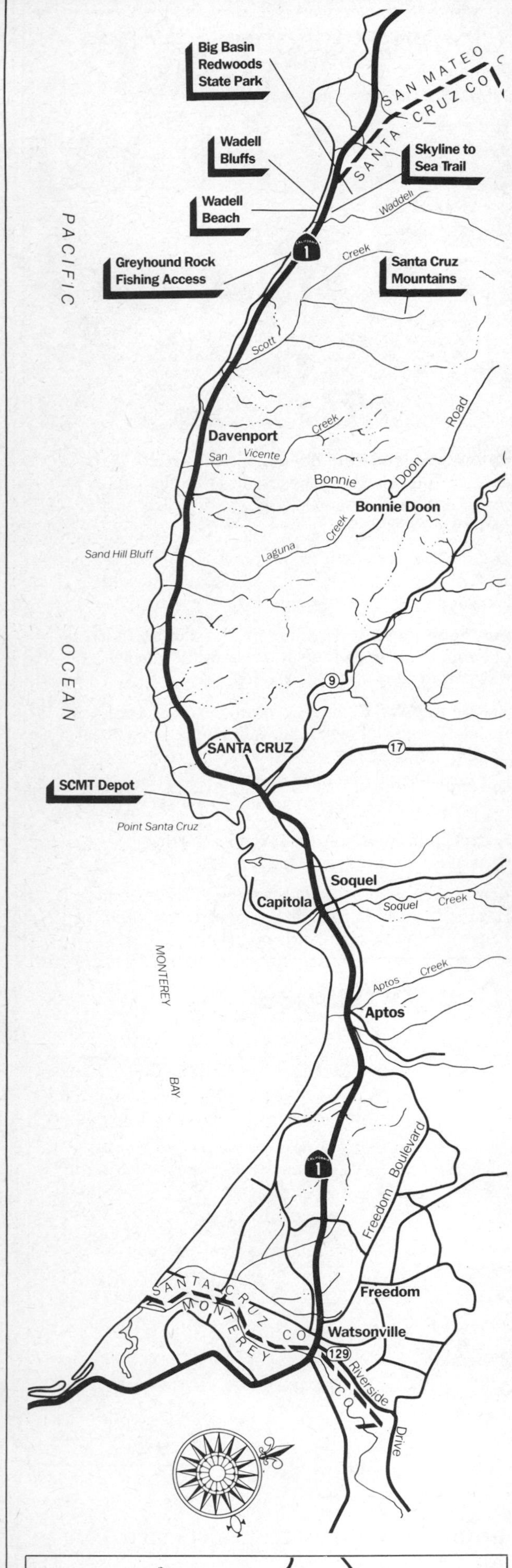
Big Basin Redwoods State Park
Wadell Bluffs
Skyline to Sea Trail
Wadell Beach
Greyhound Rock Fishing Access
Santa Cruz Mountains
PACIFIC
OCEAN
SAN MATEO
SANTA CRUZ CO
Waddell
Creek
Scott
Davenport
San Vicente
Creek
Road
Bonnie
Doon
Bonnie Doon
Laguna
Creek
Sand Hill Bluff
9
SANTA CRUZ
17
SCMT Depot
Point Santa Cruz
Soquel
Capitola
Soquel Creek
MONTEREY
BAY
Aptos Creek
Aptos
1
Freedom Boulevard
Freedom
SANTA CRUZ CO
MONTEREY CO
Watsonville
129
Riverside Drive

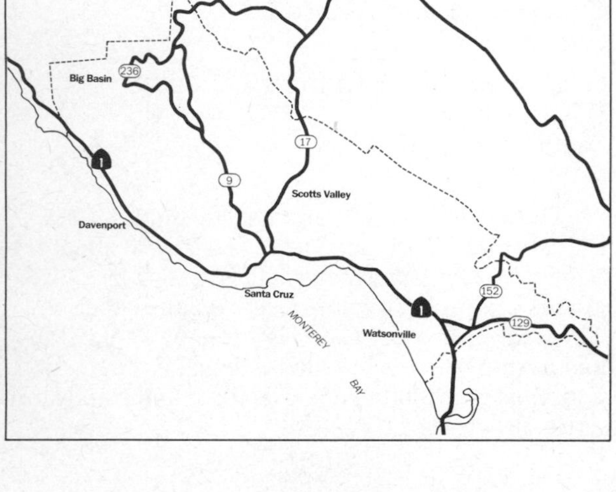
Big Basin
236
1
9
17
Scotts Valley
Davenport
Santa Cruz
152
129
Watsonville
MONTEREY
BAY

Ocean Shore Highway

North of Davenport the coast road had, since 1852, made a precarious way over unsettled terrain. Its serpentine route wound inland almost to the county line to avoid the oceanfront perils of sudden slides and erosion. At Waddell Creek the old road returned to the ocean, where it clung uncertainly to the toe of Waddell Bluffs between falling rocks and the shining sea.

Popular Support

For years the Waddell Bluffs had been unpredictably treacherous: stages were often forced to take to the sandy beach to negotiate the distance. But by the late 1930s the notion of a coast road had become sufficiently linked to possibilities for tourism and land development that it gained strong popular support. Since 1927, local residents had been petitioning the State to build a modern highway north of Santa Cruz along the ocean. In May 1939 construction began.

The route of the reconstructed highway was angled across a wide bench of Monterey shale that extended from the base of the Santa Cruz Mountains to the bluffs along the shore. Because the highly eroded bench was deeply trenched by streams with headwaters in the Ben Lomond Mountains, extensive fill and grading were required; but because the stream sheds were narrow, bridging was necessary only at two locations.

This section of the coast road extending north from Santa Cruz into San Mateo County became known as the Ocean Shore Highway in partial recognition of the never-completed Ocean Shore Railway planned to run from San Francisco to Santa Cruz along the ocean's edge. The railroad's tracks extended from San Francisco only to Tunitas in San Mateo County, where an auto-stage carried passengers over the old coast road to Swanton. At Swanton, tracks resumed into Santa Cruz—until the railroad ceased operations in 1920.

By the end of 1939, Santa Cruz had a new modern highway along the coast. Residents called it the Ocean Shore Road, but it was officially designated as State Sign Route Number 1. Soon after, completion of right-of-way acquisition and construction of a remaining link in southern San Mateo County created a handsome new highway that coursed along the edge of the vivid blue sea from Santa Cruz all the way to San Francisco.

Transit for the Masses

Most of America's mass transit systems are designed to get commuters to cental-city jobs or shoppers to centralized retail areas. Santa Cruz's mass transit serves these users but also gives equal attention to other groups, including students, recreationists, the disabled, the elderly, and the rural resident. In this Santa Cruz is unique.

SCMTD: Not Just Another Bus Company

All mass transit in the county is provided by a single agency, the Santa Cruz Metropolitan Transit District (SCMTD), which services 440 square miles and some 200,300 residents. The district's 95 buses run 43 routes from 6:30 am to 9:00 pm, some until 11:00 pm, seven days a week.

Nine of the routes have buses with lift-equipment for wheelchairs, and the SCMTD works closely with other "paratransit" agencies, such as the County Food and Nutrition Services, to meet the needs of the nonmobile population. A subsidized taxicab program is administered by the district through private cab companies to help users make the final connection between bus stop and medical or shopping centers and home. The elderly, disabled, or sick can call in advance to have a cab waiting for them. SCMTD also runs a flexible shuttle bus system during peak hours and seasons, and the district is developing an aggressive bike and ride program.

SCMTD offers its rainbow of transit services without spilling any red ink. The citizens of the county instituted a 0.5% sales tax, which accounts for about half of SCMTD's $20-million budget. State, federal, and local grants and passenger fares make up the rest.

The Rural Connection

The population of Santa Cruz County's unincorporated areas is greater than the combined population of its four cities, which creates a special need for transit planning. Five or six buses make daily runs along Highway 1 and other rural routes. During the tourist season special shuttles often run between trailheads, beaches, parks, and other recreational destinations.

These services allow bicyclists to make a challenging day trip in one direction and then return by bus. Hikers may leave their cars at one trailhead, enjoy a long walk, and catch a bus back from the other end. Students, residents, and visitors alike find it often cheaper and more enjoyable to catch the bus to the beach rather than drive a private automobile. Few counties in California are as conscious of their transit responsibility to the masses.

Environment

Roadside Attractions

Resources

The Santa Cruz Mountains

About ten million years ago the Santa Cruz Mountains were born after lying beneath the ocean for eons. During the time of the Miocene upheavals the 80-mile long mountain range that runs from the Pajaro Valley to San Bruno Mountain arose from the sea, spewing forth igneous rock to declare itself.

Although marked by deep earthquake faults—the largest being the San Andreas—the Santa Cruz Mountains soon settled down into relative quiet. Eventually, vegetation began to take root, aided by the moist marine climate and the Mountains' volcanic nutrients. Redwood trees began to spring up on the north facing slopes and in the canyons where more moisture was available out of the sun's drying rays.

As the redwoods grew to magnificent heights, a special shaded world was created on the seaward side of the mountains, creating a cool verdancy that evoked the Garden of Eden. Ferns, sorels, and wild ginger grew as the plants of paradise.

On the ridgetops, where the sun shown brightest, oaks and madrones created another world yet, higher and drier. Chanise, sage, manzanita and scruboak decorated the Mountains with a warm colored beauty, creating a home for mountain lions, bobcats, gray foxes, coyotes, and skunks, participants in a complex ecological balance.

Greyhound Rock

About six miles north of Davenport sits a smooth, gray sandstone mass that resembles nothing so much as a beached whale. This is Greyhouse Rock, a state fish and game reserve. An icy wind often blows here, but neither the divers seeking treasure and game in the clear turbulent

waters nor the rock fishers who scale Greyhound in huge numbers seem to mind.

Greyhound Rock is connected to the mainland by a tombolo (a natural sand bridge) on a nice sandy beach nestled at the bottom of one of northern Santa Cruz County's typically high bluffs.

What Is a Tombolo?

A tombolo is a naturally formed sand or gravel bridge that connects a near-shore island or rock formation to the mainland. Tombolos are created by wave action, most notably by wave diffraction and refraction. Diffracted waves from various directions bend around the island of rock, depositing sediments between the island and the mainland. If the process continues for many years, a tombolo similar to the one at Greyhound Rock is created. Some geologists predict that a tombolo will eventually reconnect Año Nuevo island to the mainland. This would, in effect, reverse the erosion process that originally separated the two.

Big Basin Redwoods State Park

338-6132

The first California State Park, and the largest park in the Santa Cruz Mountains, Big Basin Redwoods State Park contains more than 35 miles of trails that interweave through a beautiful forested semi-wilderness. Ancient redwoods have been protected in Big Basin since 1901 when members of the newly-formed Sempervirens Fund saved them from unrestricted logging.

From Highway 1 access to Big Basin is gained by the "Big Basin to the Sea" trail, which begins at Waddell Creek and winds its way through chapparal, pine, and redwoods for more than 10 miles to Big Basin Park Headquarters. Much of the trail follows Waddell Creek, paralleling an open canyon once used by the Ohlone Indians as a conduit from the coast, where they fished, to the mountains, where they hunted game.

Along the trail are 3 trailcamps: Alder Trailcamp, Camp Herbert, and Twin Redwoods Trailcamp. Big Basin Redwoods State Park has numerous facilities, including a grocery store and nature museum. Car camping is also available. Reservations may be obtained by calling Park Headquarters. Ground fires are not permitted.

The Big Basin to the Sea Trail is part of the longer "Skyline to the Sea" trail, the main artery in a network of trails through the Santa Cruz Mountains. The "Skyline to the Sea" trail was built by volunteers and the Sempervirens Organization in 1969 and connects a series of adjoining parks and open spaces beyond Big Basin headquarters at Castle Rock State Park and Saratoga gap. The distance from Saratoga Gap to the ocean is approximately 28 miles.

In addition to pristine stands of trees, Big Basin Redwoods offer an amazing variety of wildlife including foxes, bobcats, possums, raccoons, deer, and coy-

otes, as well as being an extremely valuable nesting site for birds. One first growth redwood called the Eagle Tree is uniquely regarded for once sheltering an eagle nest.

The Skyline to the Sea trail offers hikers a magnificent opportunity to explore the unspoiled qualities of Big Basin and the Santa Cruz Mountains without distraction. A variety of trails accommodate short distance and longer distance walkers. Due to infrequent water supplies on some trails during the summer, hikers are advised to carry water.

An excellent topographic map of the "Skyline to the Sea" trail is available for 35 cents (stamped self-addressed envelope) from the Sempervirens Fund, P.O. Box 1141
Los Altos, California 94022

Waddell Creek

North of Davenport are excellent beaches at Scott Creek and Greyhound Rock Fishing Access. Just south of Waddell Creek is the shorefront estate owned by the Hoover family, relatives of the former president.

Waddell Creek Beach, on the southeast corner of Big Basin Redwoods State Park, is noted for good surfing and is a favorite of windsurfers. The shoreline at Waddell Bluffs has been in a constant state of erosion since waves met the shore. Offshore

and south of the beach is a harbor seal rookery.

The bluffs at Waddell Creek end Santa Cruz county with a geologic flourish, setting a majestic stone backdrop against the blue ocean.

Exploring the Santa Cruz Mountains

Pick up these two guides, which will enhance any visit from Highway 1 inland to the beauty and drama of the Santa Cruz Mountains. The *Trail Book* is essential and authoritative, and the *Visitors Guide* is a free seasonal tabloid listing up to date information on events and features.

SANTA CRUZ MOUNTAINS VISITORS GUIDE
The Valley Press and Scotts Valley Banner
Free at Area Newstands or Visitor Centers

THE EXPANDED SANTA CRUZ MOUNTAINS
TRAIL BOOK
Tom Taber

Visitor Assistance

SANTA CRUZ COUNTY CONVENTION AND VISITORS BUREAU
P.O. Box 1476
Santa Cruz 95061. 423-6927.

CAPITOLA CHAMBER OF COMMERCE
410 Capitola Avenue
Capitola 95010. 475-6522.

WATSONVILLE CHAMBER OF COMMERCE AND AGRICULTURE
444 Main Street
P.O. Box 470
Watsonville 95076. 724-3849.

SAN MATEO

Highway 1's route through San Mateo County traverses a distance that begins with pastoral landscapes and ends with suburban subdivisions, a span that evolves over 55 miles of varied, often magnificent coastline.

Highway 1 enters the county from the south at Año Nuevo State Reserve, where elephant seals cavort in one of coastal California's most unique habitats. Shortly afterward begins a series of northern California's most pleasurable beaches—Gazos Creek, Pescadero, Pomponio, San Gregorio—with golden sand and china blue waves.

South of Half Moon Bay, Highway 1's route is marked by agriculture—fields of flowers, broccoli, and pumpkins, which preserve the roadside's bucolic character. Agriculture, the area's traditional principal economic activity, is also one of its most scenically gratifying.

At Half Moon Bay, the effects of increasing urbanization begin to show themselves until Montara Mountain rises up a few miles north. Passage over the mountain is by way of Devil's Slide, Highway 1's most notorious corridor.

San Mateo's Coastside ends in suburban solemnity at Pacifica, where Highway 1 transforms into a freeway for a quick jaunt to Daly City and the county line.

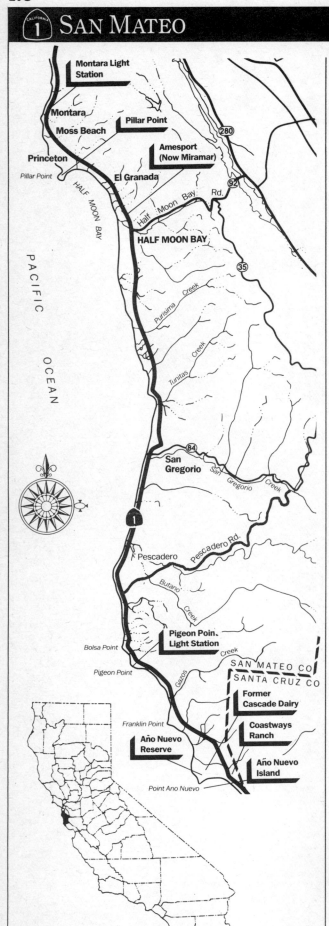

The Isolated Coast

Prior to 1905, San Mateo's coast was cut off and at a far remove from most of the outside world. Straight–up hillsides and plunging gorges kept the early residents of Point Año Nuevo, Pescadero, San Gregorio, and Purisima strangers to the expanding world 40 miles northward in San Francisco.

Early roads, such as they were, only confirmed the area's isolation by their unreliability and frequent impassability. The only road at all in 1855 ran from the town of San Mateo on the bayside to Half Moon Bay, more frequently referred to as Spanishtown. Afterward another route was built along the coast south of Montara Mountain to Tunitas Creek, but it was hardly even a passageway. From San Francisco, there was no road along the coast "other than the wet sand."

Between Año Nuevo and south of Half Moon Bay, the land offered an abundant soil that made produce grow to magical proportions. There was rich grass to fatten calves, and the trees scraped the sky—even though there was no way to get the produce, the calves, or the trees to market.

Early Shipping

So as the land rewarded and confined, the early Coastside residents turned to the sea to find a way out. If goods couldn't be carried overland to the markets, they would be shipped. Unfortunately, the sea held its own difficulties: deep water was far offshore and there were few natural harbors where ships could anchor safely. To reach the deeper water, long wharves were built at Amesport (now Miramar), Pillar Point, and Point Año Nuevo. At Point Año Nuevo some protection was gained from the offshore island, enabling a 700-foot wharf to be built. At Pillar Point, natural protection existed on the north side of the harbor, but on the south side—

San Mateo's Lighthouses

The San Mateo coast is distinguished by its lighthouses and decorated by their presence. Three of the structures were perched on this rugged shore during the 1870s, at Año Nuevo Island, Pigeon Point, and Point Montara.

The Año Nuevo Lightstation was retired from service in 1948 and now stands abandoned and in scenic disrepair, occupied only by resident seals and sea lions. Time has been kinder to the Point Montara and Pigeon Point Lighthouses, which are now youth hostels.

The Pigeon Point Lighthouse is particularly distinctive for its historic lens constructed of 1,008 pieces of highly polished glass. The structure was built in 1872 from bricks shipped around Cape Horn from Norfolk, Virginia, and it is a state historical landmark, as well as being on the National Register of Historic Places and the Historic American Building Survey.

County Profile

Geographic

Land Area (acres)	290,560
Land Area (sq. miles)	454.0
Water Area (acres)	49,130
Water Area (sq. miles)	76.8
Acres in Public Ownership	53,537.24
Percent in Public Ownership	18.43
Miles of Public Roads	1,975
County Seat	Redwood City

Demographic

Population	593,500
State Rank by Population	11
Projected 1990 Population	630,800
Unemployment Rate (state avg. = 9.9)	6.7
Per Capita Personal Income	$16,206
State Rank by Income	3
Total Assessed Property Value	$22,126,905,480

the direction of the most frequent and dangerous storms—the harbor was vulnerable to disaster.

The difficulties of loading the ships, caused by precarious wharves and dangerous seas, affected the types of goods that could be shipped. The most easily loaded and transported products were butter and cheese. Consequently, dairies along the coast thrived, such as the Steele Family's Cascade dairy, which became famous for making a 2,000-pound cylinder of cheese that was sold for a dollar a pound in San Francisco, the first slice having been sent to President Lincoln.

Ecological Succession on Display at Año Nuevo

The open fields at Año Nuevo State Reserve, with their waving coastal grasses, wild flowers, and shrubs, once supported a different crop. Before 1971, the fields were neatly plowed rows where brussels sprout after brussels sprout grew. Following public management of the area, the agricultural lands were allowed to simply revert to their wild state with no further human interference. The result is a display of the process of eco-

logical succession: the natural relationship of one species as it establishes itself, grows, and is eventually replaced by another, more adapted species.

The grasses are the first invaders, or pioneer species, typical of coastal terraces. These include field mustard, with its bright yellow spring flowers, wild oats, poison hemlock, and thistles. These annuals are now well established in the former brussels sprout fields, perpetuating themselves with their habit of speedy germination and profuse supply of seeds, and providing protection for their shadows in the parade of ecological succession, the slower-growing perennials.

Woody shrubs have now gained a foothold, along with other ground-clinging perennials like lizard tail or coyote bush, as these species move in to redecorate the original homes of the pioneer species to their own tastes. Local naturalists speculate that the next stage in ecological succession here will include the growth of taller forms of bushes and small trees. The encroaching Douglas fir and Monterey cypress seedlings close to the parking field area corroborate this theory.

County Line

Here we go to San Mateo: across the southern county line beyond the redoubtable Waddell Cliffs, begins San Mateo County, 55 miles long with 75,000 residents and its own self-christened sobriquet, Coastside.

North of marker 2.77 is Coastway's Ranch, a fine introduction to a county that finds its most beautiful expression in a combination of coastal farms and the sea. Coastway's Ranch is open to the public and you may pick your own Olallie blackberries in June while you experience a serenity that is rapidly vanishing in San Mateo County, as in other places, as the family farm goes the way of the drive-in theater.

Año Nuevo

Next stop Año Nuevo. Turn left at New Year's Creek Road. Año Nuevo is an astonishment of a roadside attraction. Here the Highway 1 traveler can view an extraordinary sample of natural coastline with a miraculous diversity of habitats for marine mammals, birds, and plant species. There is nothing like Año Nuevo on the entire coast.

AREA CODE: 415

Rules of the Road

Highway 1 in San Mateo County offers luxuriously easy driving through rolling coastal plains, fronted on the west by low cliffs and on the east by productive agricultural lands. The easy driving continues through the south and mid-county until open vistas give way to the short-lived, but intense driving thrill of Devil's Slide.

Public Transportation

871-2200   SamTrans (north)
348-8858   SamTrans (central)
367-1500   SamTrans (south)
726-5541   SamTrans (Half Moon Bay)
343-3222   SamTrans (Hearing Impaired)

Climate

Year-round temperatures on Coastside are consistently moderate, with a mean annual maximum temperature of about 66° and a mean annual minimum temperature of about 48°. The two basic seasons are delineated by fog and rainfall. The rainy season runs from December through March with an average 32 inches of rain a year. Summer months are characterized by frequent fog. September and October are the warmest months.

Coastside

San Mateo's natural barrier of mountains and hills dissects the county longitudinally, isolating the coastal region from the land area of the San Francisco bayside. From early days, the western edge has been called "Coastside" to distinguish it from the rest of the county. The name sticks today.

Año Nuevo Reserve

Punta del Año Nuevo was named in honor of New Year's Day, 1603 when Sebastián Vizcaíno sailed by and his expedition's diarist and chaplain, Father Antonio de la Ascensión, wrote the name down on his map. Today the State Reserve extends over a 700-acre stretch of bluffs, sand dunes, beaches and coastal mesa. The 13-acre Año Nuevo Island sits about one half of a treacherous mile off the tip of the Point.

If you stop here, you may join a unique tour led by trained volunteer docents. As you walk along the paths on dunes and bluffs, the docents describe the geology of the Point, the ecology of the dune vegetation systems, the presence of visible earthquake faults, birds, mammals, intertidal life, and the dynamics of the ocean.

The tours last about two hours, covering several miles. Your destination is the other side of the dunes, where you may find yourself disturbingly close to a harem of 2,000-pound elephant seals guarded by a bull weighing over three tons. During the early season, you may watch the vicious and bloody fights between these huge mammals as they establish territory. At another time you may look into the innocent eyes of a newborn pup or weaner.

The season for visiting Año Nuevo splits into winter and summer segments. During the winter breeding season (December through March) tours are in high demand; about thirty tours are conducted each day. Tickets are cheap, but must be purchased through a ticket agency in advance. If you can't get a ticket for your day, check the public transportation programs that assure you of a spot on a tour besides driving you to the Reserve.

During the summer season there are still plenty of pinnipeds around, and the docent program is a little less structured. Some days may have guided tours on other days visitors can enjoy a roving naturalist program that allows you to stroll along the paths to the habitat areas, there to be met by a ranger for more formal instruction.

Spanishtown

Despite the difficulties of moving goods to market (or receiving them), towns grew up and prospered. Spanishtown, as Half Moon Bay was called, expanded at a fast enough clip to have a population of 1,000 by 1892, becoming the third largest town in the entire county. Although some witnesses saw the town as possessing only "whiskey and blacksmiths," it was important as the area's commercial and transportation center.

Half Moon Bay was the crossroads for the San Mateo Stage, which ran the alternately dusty or muddy route from the county seat to the coast. The adventuresome quality of the ride was assured by colorful characters like Buckskin Bob, whose fame was evidenced by his ability to turn a fully loaded stage on two wheels in front of the Occidental Hotel.

Gordon's Chute

The demand for lumber brought men with axes to the lush redwood forests that filled the canyons. The tall trees were cut ignominiously into railroad ties and shingles, requiring new loading methods to get the lumber to the boats. Slides, hawsers, chutes, and slings were put to use to make ports where no real ports could have been. At Pigeon Point an offshore rock supported a cable that slung goods in and out of ships, at least when the seas were calm enough to allow it. And at Tunitas Point, Alexander Gordon erected the famous Gordon's Chute, which, in its creator's mind, was to solve the Coastside's shipping problems while making him a rich man.

Ships' captains questioned the plausibility of Gordon's shipping scheme, and predictably, perhaps, the chute was washed away to sea in a storm in 1882 after having seen only infrequent use.

Cascade Ranch

Cascade Ranch is a 4,000 acre area of dunes, forest, and farmland that lies adjacent to Año Nuevo State Reserve. The ranch, which takes its name from a stunning 30-foot waterfall on the land, is a magnificent expression of the original San Mateo landscape.

Cascade Ranch is also the focal point for San Mateo's most significant coastal land use conflict. At issue is the appropriateness of dividing the area into hundreds of "ranchettes," as its current owner proposes, versus the alternative of creating a new coastal park and maintaining the area as protected open space to serve as a buffer to Año Nuevo State Reserve.

Those who support the purchase of Cascade Ranch for public open space point to the intense demand for parkland in the area. Año Nuevo attracts 120,000 visitors a year, a number that must be limited because of the size and sensitivity of the area. Cascade Ranch is the logical place to look for the Reserve's expansion, they maintain.

In its relatively undeveloped state, Cascade Ranch has always served as a buffer for the sensitive habitats at Año Nuevo. If development is allowed, not only will an unusual opportunity for park expansion be lost, but Año Nuevo's rare ecology could be made vulnerable, its fragile watershed threatened.

Two groups have been working diligently to preserve Cascade Ranch as protected open space. In 1983, the Sierra Club Legal Defense Fund sued to halt the development of the project based on San Mateo's Local Coastal Program, which requires preservation of agricultural areas. Later the same year the Trust for Public Land (TPL), a non-profit organization that acts as an interim agent for the protection of endangered land, entered the scene. TPL hopes to facilitate the transfer of Cascade Ranch to the State Department of Parks, an action that faces funding uncertainties and uncertain support from the governor.

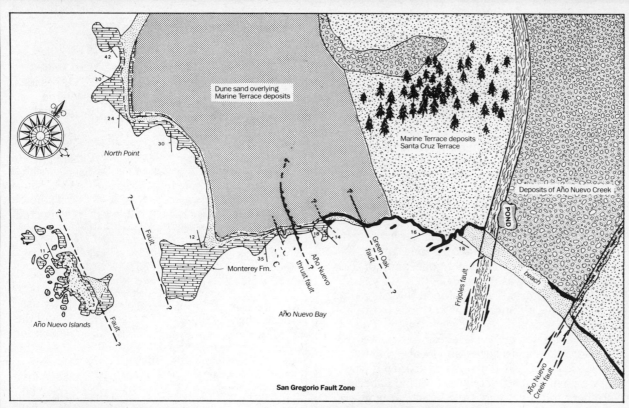

Map labels: Dune sand overlying Marine Terrace deposits; North Point; Marine Terrace deposits Santa Cruz Terrace; Deposits of Año Nuevo Creek; POND; Año Nuevo Islands; Monterey Fm.; Año Nuevo thrust fault; Green Oak fault; Frijoles fault; beach; Año Nuevo Bay; Fault; Año Nuevo Creek fault; **San Gregorio Fault Zone**

Exploring Año Nuevo

THE NATURAL HISTORY OF AÑO NUEVO
Burney J. Le Boeuf and Stephanie Kaza
The Boxwood Press, Pacific Grove. 1981.

This is the best available local book on San Mateo's natural environment. Within its pages are authoritative treatises on Coastside weather, geology, land and marine plants, shore and marine mammals, intertidal life, and birds. Although the book focuses on Año Nuevo's environment, most of the information applies to the entire San Mateo coast.

Earthquake Faults at Año Nuevo

Point Año Nuevo is beautiful and fascinating, but it has some distinctly obvious faults: at least seven, in fact. The point lies astride one of the major active earthquake fault zones in the state, the San Gregorio fault zone, which branches off the San Andreas fault at Bolinas Lagoon, north of San Francisco, and extends at least as far south as Point Sur, south of Monterey. The San Gregorio fault zone has experienced about 70 miles of horizontal movement in the past 15 million years, which means that Point Año Nuevo was once somewhere south, around Big Sur.

Today southern San Mateo County is one of only two places where this zone comes ashore, extending from the base of the Santa Cruz Mountains to Año Nuevo Island, a width of between 1.6 and 2 miles. The pedestrian trail at Año Nuevo takes you over three of the seven individual faults in the zone, and the other four are visible, especially if you take the ranger tours. The faults slice across the Santa Cruz marine terrace, which forms the geological base for the point. Here marine terrace deposits were left over 105,000 years ago, pounded by the surf and eventually uplifted through earthquake motion to their present position above sea level.

Beach Unconformity

Southern San Mateo's coast is listed among the county's inventory of cultural resources. Here at beach level, on the south side of a point of land extending westward into the sea, horizontal beds of sandstone and conglomerates of Oligocene age rest on vertical sandstone and shales of the Pigeon Point Formation from the Late Cretaceous age. Approximately 50 million years of geological record are missing at the contact, or "unconformity," between the two units. During this time span, geologists theorize that the Pigeon Point Formation was uplifted from the ocean floor and the rocks were beveled before the deposition of the much younger sandstones and conglomerates. The site is one of the most important to the geological history of the Coastside.

Cascade Ranch

North of the entrance to Año Nuevo is what is left of the Cascade Ranch. The Cascade Ranch was the original occupant of practically all of the Coastside from Pescadero to the present county line. At one time, there were 11 dairies in the area owned or leased by R. E. Steele, the ranch's founder.

The Cascade Ranch is not only a reminder of Coastside's past but also an emblem of its future. Pay attention to the next cultural artifact: the for-sale sign for 5-acre coastal ranchettes. Such signs represent the economic competition for coastal land in southern San Mateo County. Like the remains of Cascade Ranch, the pastoral farms that give this section of the coast much of its roadside attractiveness are in serious danger from such more profitable land uses.

Gazos Creek

At Gazos Creek there is a splendid beach and (on the east side of the Highway) a restaurant bar at the Gazos Creek Beach House. Stop here for your first immersion into San Mateo County cultural life amid the yellow leatherette booths and brown-swirl shag carpeting. There's good food, a large friendly bar, and dancing on the weekends. No one here is out of place.

Across the road is the beach. From the parking lot follow a short smooth path down to the nice sandy beach. Go south (north is more crowded, less open) beyond where the shallow creek finds its way across the sand to the tide. Notice the elegant striations cut through the sand by the creek.

South 300 yards and low sandstone cliffs jut out to the edge of high tide. These soft crumbly rocks have been intricately eroded by the tides into a series of tiny pockets with golden sand at the bottom and silver sun flooding from the sky. Should you decide to avail yourself of one of these enchanted spots for a picnic, a sunbath, or a commune with the sea, you will be amazed at the ornately etched sandstone that surrounds you.

North of Gazos Creek the roadside maintains most of its agricultural character as the road sprints for Pigeon Point. On the east side of the Highway is Pacific Mushroom Farm, a different type of nonfield agriculture that thrives on the low evaporation and high moisture of San Mateo's coast. Across the road, on the ocean terrace, small-scale coastal farming proceeds quietly and in harmony with its surroundings. Brussels sprouts.

Interpretative Tours at Ano Nuevo

DURING THE WINTER SEASON
(roughly December through March):

Obtain tickets through Ticketron ticket agency for $3 before arriving to ensure a spot on the tour, or arrive on a bus tour that includes your Año Nuevo ticket (about $5). Inquire about schedules:

SAMTRANS
400 S. El Camino, San Mateo 94402.
348-SEAL.

SANTA CRUZ METROPOLITAN TRANSIT
230 Walnut Street, Santa Cruz 95060.
(408) 425-8600.

During the summer season, check with the ranger: 879-0227, 879-0228, 879-0595.

For more information, a selection of other books and pamphlets, and a wonderful coloring book for children, stop by the Reserve or contact:

AÑO NUEVO INTERPRETIVE ASSOCIATION
95 Kelly Avenue, Half Moon Bay 94019.

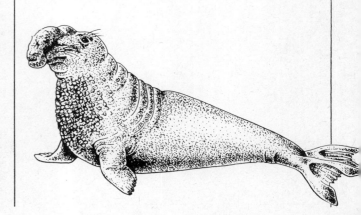

The Coast Stage

Once it arrived in Half Moon Bay, the stage turned south on the coast to Pescadero and proceeded through colorful towns like Purisima ('the purest'), which lay along Purisima Creek. It was here that Redwood City promoter and politician Ben Lathrop invested in an 800-acre ranch with several mineral springs. Lathrop, banking on the springs' popularity with tourists and health seekers, promoted them as the Purisima White Sulphur Springs—"The first medicinal waters in California!" But Lathrop's expectations, like those of many to follow, were never realized. Purisima remained only a half-aware outpost for logging the giant stands of redwoods in Purisima Canyon. Within 50 years the trees were gone, and, for the most part, so too was Purisima.

At San Gregorio, the Half Moon Bay Stage met the Redwood City Stage at the entrance to the Coastside's widest and most scenic valley. The fertile soil drained by San Gregorio Creek created a rich farmland and a successful local economy. The soil also nourished plants and attracted wildlife, which in turn attracted hunters and fishermen who spent freely in town. In 1878 San Gregorio was enough of a town to possess a post office, a livery stable, a meat market, a school, two churches, a saloon, and a resort hotel, the San Gregorio House.

Although never an equal in size to Half Moon Bay or Pescadero, San Gregorio's quiet charm and beautiful environment sustained well those who lived there, until the coast road, signifying modern times, moved in a different direction.

The final stop of the Half Moon Bay Stage was Pescadero. Millionaires like the Crockers and the Floods came all the way from San Francisco to this romantic place with quiet New England seaside appeal. With others they came for the abun-

dant trout in the streams, enchantment in the redwoods, and, at nearby Pebble Beach, the magnificent stones—opals, cat's-eyes, and carnelians—that sparkled in the sand like the jewels of Fatima. The favored hotel in those days was the nationally known Swanton House, which mixed graceful hospitality with rural charm.

Pescadero in the last of the 19th century was *the* resort town along San Mateo's Coastside, a function it balanced well with its basically agricultural economy. Soon, improved roads created new resort towns up and down the shoreline, not all with the simplicity and style of the town named for the ample fish in its streams.

Property Is Theft

The public's right to access and use of the California shoreline has a long, heated, and often theatrical history. Nowhere along the coast did the public agitate more turbulently for access to the shore than at San Mateo's Pebble Beach in the 1890s.

The story begins in 1872 when Loren Coburn bought land at Pebble Beach. When the County dedicated the Coast Road through his land, Coburn put up fences on both sides, with a gate and a sign that read "Pebble Beach Private Driveway." Then in 1891, he locked the gate, completely shutting off the only access to the area's most popular beach, famous for its crystalline gems and valuable to merchants as Pescadero's principal tourist attraction.

Coburn's neighbors, accustomed to a lifetime of use of the beach, were angered and outraged. They assembled in Pescadero's town square and stormed the beach, holding a riotous picnic and hanging Loren Coburn in effigy. Coburn responded by barricading the gate more securely.

Meanwhile, Supervisor Henry B. Adair declared the road to the beach a public highway. Still Coburn kept the gate locked, refortifying it each time it was knocked down by the local citizenry, and building a hotel and a stable in 1892. When the state legislature attempted to resolve the conflict in 1893 by passing an act that set aside for public use beach lands from Pescadero Creek to Bean Hollow, Coburn responded by digging a deep ditch across the road. Local residents would fill it and Coburn would redig it. Back and forth they went, with Coburn sometimes placing animal carcasses at the bottom of the ditch to add to the animosity of the battle. Finally, Coburn brought suit in the federal courts, where he received a favorable ruling based on the public's loss of prescriptive rights when Coburn put up his private sign 17 years earlier.

Coburn had his beach for himself, but his hotel never prospered and he was ostracized by the entire community. After a series of bizarre and violent events, Loren Coburn died in 1917, in enmity.

Design Standards With a Reason

Throughout history, architectural style and urban design developed based on either a functional or demonstrative premise. In Pescadero, the predominate existence of white building after white building is an example of a very functional occurrence. In 1897 a boat named the *Columbia* was wrecked off the coast of Pigeon Point, and its cargo drifted ashore. The cargo was white lead, which was easily converted into enough white paint to maintain Pescadero as the most spotless town on the Coastside for years.

Map labels:

SAN FRANCISCO CO / SAN MATEO CO

DALY CITY
Colma
PACIFICA
35
280
82
101
SAN FRANCISCO BAY
Point San Pedro
Devil's Slide
Montara
Moss Beach
Princeton
Pillar Point
El Granada
280
Half Moon Bay Rd.
92
HALF MOON BAY
35
Purisima Creek
Purisima
Tunitas Creek
San Gregorio
84
San Gregorio
San Gregorio Creek
Pescadero
Pescadero Rd.
Pebble Beach
Bean Hollow Beach
Pescadero
Butano Creek
Flower Fields
Pigeon Point Lightstation
American Youth Hostel
Bolsa Point
Gazos Creek
Pigeon Point
SAN MATEO CO / SANTA CRUZ CO
Franklin Point
Año Nuevo Reserve
Point Año Nuevo
PACIFIC OCEAN
HALF MOON BAY

0   8
Miles

Environment	Roadside Attractions	Resources

Marine Mammals at Año Nuevo

Four species of pinnipeds (aquatic mammals having flippers) are found year-round at Año Nuevo: northern elephant seals, harbor seals, Steller sea lions and California sea lions.

Pinnipeds were once terrestrial carnivores (land animals that eat meat). Like the whale, they eventually took a distinctively individual adaptive action and left the land to enter a life at sea. Pinnipeds got a much later start than the whale, however, having splashed into the surf only about 25 million years ago. Not yet totally adapted, they still come ashore to rest, mate, and have their babies. When they leave the water though, they become less agile and they prefer the shelter of offshore islands free from predatory and human interference. This is why they like Año Nuevo Island and why it has become the major pinniped rookery in Northern California. Año Nuevo Island's proximity to land, its rich feeding grounds, and its gently contoured rocks and beaches provide a safe and comfortable resting and breeding place.

California Sea Lions

The dark-brown California sea lion is familiar to most coastal residents and travelers. Although sea lions are usually seen on the shore only if sick, a view through binoculars toward Año Nuevo Island in September or October might reveal up to 13,000 exhausted males basking on the rock island, taking a well-deserved respite in their migration north in search of food. This is their recuperation time from the strains of breeding rituals in Southern California, Baja California, and the west coast of Mexico.

The California sea lion is dark brown when wet; brown or ochre when dry. The male weighs between 700 and 1,000 pounds; the smaller, lighter female averages 100–200 pounds. Although you are unlikely to see the female here, you know her— she is the circus seal or the most familiar pinniped resident in your local zoo. In the 1920s these animals were hunted or killed (often just for sport), and the population declined to a mere 940 individuals statewide.

Today over 50,000 sea lions live off the California coast, providing cautious evidence for the survival of this species—cautious because a new, potentially more dangerous enemy is beginning to take its toll on pinniped life. Scientists are only now starting to gauge the effects of decades of human waste products, such as DDT, which have been dumped into the sea in great quantities or which continue to run off or seep into the coastal zone from inland areas.

Pigeon Point

Pigeon Point is one of the coast's most stately-looking and easily accessible lightstations. Although there are tours only on Sunday from 10 am to 3 pm (closed for lunch), from Highway 1 the lighthouse is an easy-off, easy-on for a closer look anytime. The most significant feature of the handsome tower is its 9-foot in diameter Fresnel lens built by Henri Le Paute of Paris in the 1850s.

Adjacent to the tower is an American Youth Hostel, where visitors of any age can stay overnight in one of American hosteling's most spectacular settings. Despite the aura of privacy, you neither have to be a member nor have a reservation to stay, although as with any overnight accommodation, space is limited and reservations are helpful.

Beside the lightstation and the hostel, there is also a shellfish stand, open in the summer from 10 am to 5 pm. Pigeon Point oysters (which, some people say, rival the elegant blue point) and a bottle of white wine make gratifying companions for an afternoon on the beach.

Beyond Pigeon Point are signs of abandoned agricultural use on the coastal terraces with intervening residential construction of the 1960s. On the east side of the Highway at Marker 15.75 is the first evidence of the coastside's flower culture. Behind the gates forcefully marked "Wholesale Only" lies an example of Coastside's largest agricultural industry, growing flowers. Should you desire to purchase some flowers or greenery, on the same side of the road adjacent to the flower farm a nursery opens after April first.

Bean Hollow

Bean Hollow Beach has a small cove that looks to be too close to the highway but has a tame surf if you want to exercise a small child and don't have much time to seek out other places. More interestingly, however, is the coastal trail that leads from Bean Hollow to Pebble Beach, about a mile north.

Despite its closeness to the road, the trail offers an easy opportunity to view rich tidepools, birds, and seals. Small footbridges make the trail easily negotiable as it winds through patches of wild strawberries and checkerbloom. Above, you may spot red-billed oyster catchers, cormorants, killdeer, or pelicans. Aside the trail are fascinating tidepools within the fragile intertidal zone; they contain hundreds of barnacles, urchins, sponges, snails, starfish, and creatures unnamed and unknown. As the path winds further through lizard tail and wild buckwheat, keep an eye peeled toward the offshore rocks for harbor seals enjoying themselves in the California sun.

History

HALF MOON BAY MEMORIES: THE COASTSIDE'S COLORFUL PAST
June Morrall
Moonbeam Press, El Granada. 1979.

June Morrall has filled this book with text and photographs that depict almost every outlaw, bootlegger, artist, rascal, family, dreamer, lost soul, thrill seeker, bear fighter, and farmer who dared to seek fortune or fame on the isolated Coastside of San Mateo County.

THE LAST WHISTLE (OCEAN SHORE RAILROAD)
Jack R. Wagner
Howell-North Books, Berkeley. 1974.

The Last Whistle is an elaborately illustrated and fascinating tribute to a magical dream that was too grandiose to come true.

COASTSIDE CULTURAL RESOURCES OF SAN MATEO COUNTY, CALIFORNIA
Department of Environmental Management
San Mateo County, Redwood City. 1980.

Describes San Mateo's history and explains how the protection of its important sites can co-exist with continuing development. A site-by-site inventory includes detailed maps and photographs. The book ends with a proposed protection program for development of scenic corridors along Highway 1.

FROM FRONTIER TO SUBURB: THE STORY OF THE SAN MATEO PENINSULA
Alan Hynding
Star Publishing Company, Belmont. 1982.

Citing newspapers, census data, voter registers, and local monographs, Hynding traces the entire course of Peninsula history, paying special attention to the last half century, when the Peninsula was often dismissed as a traffic corridor between San Francisco and points south—"a nowhere land of uncertain geography, without political identity."

For more information on Coastside's history, contact:

SAN MATEO COUNTY HISTORICAL ASSOCIATION (Museum, Library, Bookstore & Photo Collection)
College of San Mateo Campus
1700 West Hillsdale Blvd., San Mateo 94402.
574-6441.

JOHNSTON HOUSE FOUNDATION
Box 689, Half Moon Bay 94019.
726-4708.

SPANISHTOWN HISTORICAL SOCIETY
Box 62, Half Moon Bay 94019.
726-4707.

The Ocean Shore Railroad

Soon after the turn of the century, Coastside found an answer to its remove from the outside world—"A double-track, highspeed electric railroad running along the very edge of the Pacific!"

Though there had been talk of a railroad in San Mateo for years, the idea remained a phantasm until a group of San Francisco millionaire capitalists launched the Ocean Shore Railway Company on May 18, 1905. The route was to follow the ocean shoreline from a terminal in San Francisco along the length of San Mateo County to the beach at Santa Cruz, a distance of 80.26 miles over a course that eventually became Highway 1.

The way would not be clear, however, and the going would not be easy. The topography that had isolated Coastside for centuries was no more accommodating to a railroad than it had been to trails or wagon roads.

The Plan for Paradise

The plan was a grand one. Once finished, the railway would open up pleasure palaces and seaside enchantments to stir the heart of Ozymandias. Paradise would be gained on an iron horse: casinos, exotic hotels, bathhouses, iron piers, tennis courts, and golf courses were envisioned. Visitors would come with stars in their eyes with the opportunity to buy their own portion of paradise. The purpose of the railroad was singular: to make money for its San Francisco backers by dividing up and selling coastal real estate.

Promoters laid out lots on the bare sand dunes and christened them with romantic-sounding names like Edgemar, Brighton, Rockaway Beach, Vallemar, Moss Beach, Arleta Park, and El Granada. There were fortunes to be made, new worlds to be gained. The Ocean Shore Investment Company had money, lots of it, and enough political influence to raise the specter of scandal for years.

By April 1906, some 4,000 workers were working like mad on the line—blasting out rock, grading, building trestles, laying track. They expected to be finished in September. A couple of months later, grading was nearly completed over the most difficult sections. Rails had been laid from San Francisco to Mussel Rock—the point where the San Andreas Fault returns to land from the ocean.

Subdivisions Made of Paper

The early subdivision of San Mateo's coastside by speculators like the Ocean Shore Development Company never materialized according to expectations. Most of the subdivisions that were drawn up were only partly sold, and those that were sold were usually not developed. These fragmented ownership patterns have caused a miasma of land use difficulties that continue to confound county planning and development.

Since the passage of the California Coastal Act, which set standards for coastal development, the owners of coastal property in "paper subdivisions"—those platted, but not yet individually sold or developed—have been in the unfortunate position of owning property that is often unbuildable because it may block views, harm a sensitive habitat or block off access to a beach.

Solution: Lot Consolidation and Restoration

One solution to this confused situation is to recombine the old subdivided lots into sizes more practical for legal development while at the same time separating developed portions from public access corridors or important habitat areas. Ideally, such "lot consolidation" allows both the maximum development practical for an area and maximum amount of protection for natural areas and open space.

In the City of Half Moon Bay there are an abundance of unbuilt paper subdivisions. Developments that were divided in 1906, with names like Redondo View, Bernardo Station, and Lipton By-The-Sea, exist only as ghosts along the coastal portion of Half Moon Bay. Just inside the city's southern boundary, on either side of the Ocean Colony, lies a group of subdivisions that may eventually be recombined by the State of California, through its Coastal Conservancy, to achieve the development of new housing, the restoration of degraded nature areas, as well as the creation of new coastal access for recreational users.

The Coastal Conservancy's ambition is to buy up all these lots and recombine and restore them, eventually building up to 1,000 appropriately clustered residential units, an RV campground, public improvements, and maybe even a golf course, while at the same time restoring degraded areas, maintaining significant open space, and possibly using project revenues to preserve prime agricultural lands nearby.

Environment

Northern Elephant Seals

Earthquake faults, geological formations, a brilliant diversity of plant, animal, bird, and shoreline life—all these attractions at Año Nuevo pale in comparison to the main star of this show: the northern elephant seal, without a doubt among the most unlikely of life forms following its genetic imperative on this planet.

Start with the body: a whalelike mass weighing around three tons in the average mature male and reaching lengths of over 16 feet. Follow this hulk to its improbable frontal conclusion: two circular eyes, set farther apart than would seem to permit successful vision; a wide, low mouth forever transfixed in a smile that can only be called goofy; and, in between, a pendulous proboscis, or trunk, whose existence argues beyond a shadow of a doubt that nature does have a sense of humor.

The humor is only skin deep, however. These animals are serious, deadly serious, about the business that brings them to the San Mateo coast: that most important natural motive—reproduction. Everything the seals do (from bloody fights, to female behavior in the harems, to survival clustering of the pups or weaners) can be understood

as "an adaptation, an adjustment, a strategy to maximize individual reproductive success."

Elephant seal bulls engage in serious and often bloody battles to determine dominance and harem territories. During a single breeding season, only about 30% of all the males present emerge as maters. The top 5% usually impregnate about 80% of the females, and a single bull will sire over 50 pups in a single year.

Newborn pups, or weaners, are adorable to look at, a stage that lasts only a short time. Their early life is a dangerous time, as they are threatened by drowning during coastal storms; by the effects of overcrowding, which include being crushed to death at the rookery by adult bulls who don't bother to go around them, but move their massive bodies over the tiny pups instead; and by vicious attack from unfriendly females into whose territories they stray.

Roadside Attractions

Pebble Beach

At Pebble Beach there actually are pebbles, millions and millions. In a simpler time tourists came from near and far to collect these magnificent stones that were imbued with a sense of glamour. Now the pebbles may seem tame compared to store-bought stones that shine in our ready-to-purchase minds. It isn't the pebbles that have changed.

The Pebbles at Pebble Beach

Living up to the name it earned over a century ago, Pebble Beach today still provides visitors with an abundant collage of colorful pebbles and rocks. An offshore quartz reef supplies the raw materials for the beach sediment, which is eternally polished and smoothed by the matchless artisan touch of the sea. Fragments of moss-agate, carnelian, and jasper are common, but one can always look for the rubies, amethysts, emeralds, garnets, opals, and aquamarines, which were claimed to have come ashore in the 1860s, and which were familiar products in jewelry stores in San Francisco during the 1880s.

Pescadero

Directly north of Pebble Beach is the cutoff for Pescadero. Pescadero has always been one of Coastside's most interesting resort towns and remains so, quietly, today. Most celebrated attraction: the unimpeachable Duarte's, which has the world's best artichoke soup and a hearty menu that includes unmatched fresh berry pies.

Five Beaches

Between the cutoff for Pescadero and the cutoff for San Gregorio lie five of Coastside's best beaches:

Pescadero State Beach: Accessible by two entrances, the northern portion is the more interesting. East of Highway 1 is the Pescadero Marsh Natural Preserve, the largest coastal marsh (555 acres) between Monterey and San Francisco. Birds.

Unsigned Turnout, Marker 27.35: This public beach is owned but undeveloped by State Parks. A short even trail takes you to the cliff's edge, steep and dangerous at its end. Glorious beach with lots of privacy.

Pomponio State Beach: Bigger than it appears. If you turn south from the parking lot and proceed 400+ yards past the point, you will come to a special world of high cliffs with outcroppings that hold a series of deep caves. The biggest is the Cave of Pomponio, one-time home of a Native American who led a group of desperados and heroically evaded for years the long arm of arbitrary Spanish law by skill and derring-do.

San Gregorio State Beach: Connected to a small estuary on both sides of the highway, San Gregorio has a beautiful large sandy cove and high bluffs similar to Pomponio.

Resources

California Marine Mammal Center

Marin Headlands, Golden Gate National Recreation Area, Fort Cronkite, California 331-SEAL.

The California Marine Mammal Center is a non-profit organization licensed to rescue, treat, and study distressed marine mammals that become stranded along the California coast. Since incorporation in 1975, the Center has treated hundreds of stranded marine mammals, always with the mission of returning the animal, healthy and wild, to its natural habitat. Call them immediately should you come across a stranded or sick marine mammal anywhere on the coast.

Parks and Beaches

Consult the *Coastal Access Guide* (see Index) or call the local ranger for more information on these San Mateo parks and beaches.

879-0227	Año Nuevo State Reserve
879-0227	Gazos Creek State Beach
879-0633	Pigeon Point Lighthouse Hostel
726-6238	Bean Hollow State Beach
726-6238	Pescadero Marsh Natural Preserve
726-6238	Pescadero State Beach
726-6238	Pomponio State Beach
726-6238	San Gregorio State Beach
726-9943	Martin's Beach
726-6238	Francis Beach
726-9871	Venice Beach
726-9871	Dunes Beach
726-1382	Pillar Point Harbor
728-3584	James Fitzgerald Marine Reserve
728-7177	Montara Lighthouse Hostel
726-6238	Gray Whale Cove State Beach

San Gregorio Nude Beach: North of San Gregorio State Beach is a nude beach that was at one time the most famous in northern California. (Fee entry through white gate .4 mi. north of State Beach.) Since clothing-optional beaches have become so commonplace in Northern California, however, distinctions mean less and San Gregorio has rather faded into the (undraped) background.

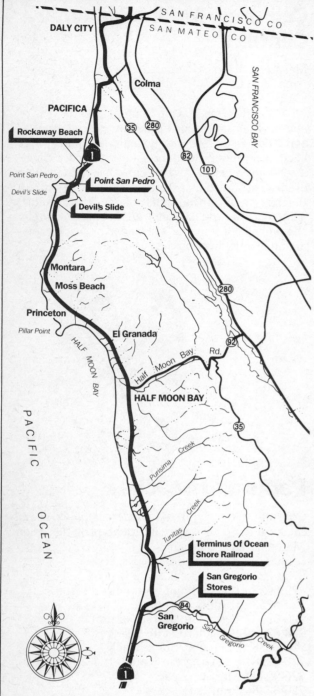

Disaster

On June 17 1906, the early morning brought a rumble and a crack from inside the earth, and the land's edge pitched the Ocean Shore Railroad into the sea in the way that large animals dispatch small bugs with unconcerned twitches. Rolling stock, construction equipment, and 4,000 feet of railroad track slid into the ocean. Entire grades disappeared or were reformed in a new topography. In San Francisco, a city had been demolished; on San Mateo's Coastside, the Ocean Shore Railway was stopped before it began.

But the railway began again, this time with less financial backing—the earthquake had cost the Ocean Shore's investors millions. To save money, the proposed two-track electric railway was replaced by a plan for a single-track steam line. Construction was resumed, and by September 1907 rails extended as far as Rockaway Beach.

Obstacles and Efforts

One of the line's most difficult obstacles waited at Point San Pedro, where not only did a ledge have to be constructed out of a cliff face, but a tunnel had to be bored through the point itself. Even to get supplies and materials to the site was a challenge—from a ship anchored offshore, they were transported by an aerial tramway. Workers had it the worst of all. They found themselves suspended by ropes in midair over the cliff face in order to plant blasting powder in the mountain's side.

At Devil's Slide 3,500 tons of mountainside were blasted to smithereens to make a level grade at Saddle Rock for the new railway. Nine tons of black powder were stuffed into a 70-foot tunnel, turning the top of the mountain into a bomb that when ignited exploded to the heavens, leaving a gradable surface.

By 1907, the tracks were down and trains started operating, but not all the way to Santa Cruz. The new railway stopped at Tunitas, where an auto stage met the embarking passengers and carried them over a dirt road to Swanton. From there, the Ocean Shore resumed to Santa Cruz.

The frantic effort to build a railroad was now matched by a frantic effort to subdivide and develop the adjacent lands. Eager San Franciscans rode the rails to barren coastal mesas to be met by fast-talking salesmen with free lunches and brass bands. Festivity prevailed; sales were made; and new towns were born.

Greenhouse Floriculture

Like other coastal counties, San Mateo encourages protection of its agricultural lands. This effort is complicated by recent changes in floriculture, the business of growing flowers, the county's major crop. In San Mateo, floriculture takes two forms: outdoor field production and greenhouse production. Both depend on the county's rich soils, consistent temperatures, availability of experienced workers, and proximity to the Bay Area's high-demand markets for fresh-cut flowers.

Out of the Fields and onto the Racks

Greenhouse floriculture is on the rise in San Mateo as more farmers remove their crops from the open fields and set up more manageable and profitable greenhouse environments on their land. This conversion trend raises several issues: What happens to the existing prime soil? What happens to the view across the fields? And how is the Coastside's limited water supply affected by greenhouse floriculture?

The greenhouses you see from Highway 1 may or may not be using the prime soil on which they sit. In either soil or non-soil-dependent facilities, there is always some paving for paths, storage and parking areas on previously open land. Planners are concerned with this conversion which is considered fairly permanent since it costs a farmer up to $12,000 an acre to restore land covered with a greenhouse back to prime conditions.

Besides the effect on the soil, there is an obvious visual difference between a field of flowers and an agricultural mesa with a cluster (some say "clutter") of greenhouses on it. View impacts can be cut down by appropriate siting away from cut slopes or visible grade changes, landscaping, stag-

gered setbacks and clustering of facilities. Still, many people consider greenhouses to be development, not agriculture.

Water is the final concern. Floriculture has always been at odds with potential residential development that would consume much less water per acre. Planners fear that by covering the land with nonpervious development that diverts the uniform distribution of moisture from rain and fog, the new greenhouses may have a long-term effect on the cumulative groundwater recharge besides using more water than an irrigated field.

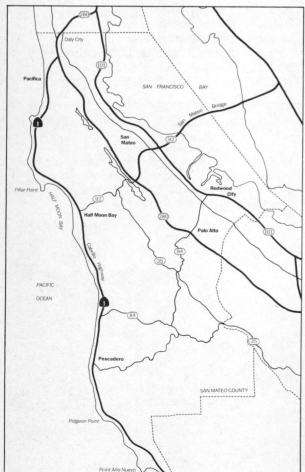

Environment	**Roadside Attractions**	**Resources**

Fields of Flowers

Along Highway 1 in San Mateo you will see flowers, lots and lots of them, both cultivated and wild.

A 1916 account describes San Mateo County "in its entirety, from northern to southern boundary, from Bay to Ocean, [as] one extensive flower garden." The county supplied 75% of the cutflowers used in San Francisco at the time, and shipped orchids to the King of England and the Queen of Holland. The north coast of San Mateo cultivated violets, roses, orchids, chrysanthemums, and carnations.

The inspiration for cultivated flowers seems a natural consequence of San Mateo's abundant fields of wild flowers. The county was famous for its many varieties, enjoying, according to local boosters: "the unchallenged reputation of growing more wild varieties than any other county in the state." In one 1905 Coastside competition, a boy entered 96 varieties of locally picked wild flowers, including several kinds of wild orchids.

Exotic Whites

The rein orchid is still seen on the bluffs and rocky cliffs of the Coastside. Its ample leaves surround a long and graceful stalk or spike of white (sometimes tending toward green) flowers. The spurs of the blossoms are about half an inch long and are easily recognized as being of the orchid family. Look for them from July through September.

Bitterroot is a dazzling little white flower that sprouts out from rocky edges where the Coastal Range joins the mesa although it is most common in the northern Rockies (it is the state flower of Montana). Native Americans, early settlers, and explorers relied on this white beauty for nourishment; its root is white, fleshy, and full of starch.

The western azalea joins the display of lush white flowers in San Mateo. Its whitish flowers have a central spot of pink or salmon. This member of the rhododendron family stands from 3 to 12 feet tall, flourishing in moist spots along the coast.

San Gregorio

At San Gregorio Creek a one-mile cutoff leads to the historic town of San Gregorio, one of Coastside's most sagacious early villages. Today practically all that remains is the Peterson and Alsford General Store, a one-floor emporium with a full bar with liar's dice on one side and a fine selection of country-flavored merchandise throughout. The store also has an interesting selection of books. If you're hungry, there is deli food. Across the street in San Gregorio is a stage stop converted into a gas station, but just barely.

North of San Gregorio Valley Highway 1 climbs up and out of the deep lush valley carved through the coastal foothills until another valley appears at Tunitas Creek. Beneath the great sheared cliffs was the site of Gordon's Chute. The chute's eyebolts are still visible in offshore rocks at low tide. A sea monster is said to exist in the cave south of the creek, but if you expect to search out the monster do so with great stealth—the beach at Tunitas Creek is controlled by a private landowner who forbids entry.

Harvest Trails: Fresh Produce at Coastside Farms

Approximate harvest dates in San Mateo County are listed below. These dates, provided by the County Farm Bureau, are approximate only; dates of maturity vary from year to year and place to place.

	JAN	FEB	MAR	APR	MAY	JUN	JUL	AUG	SEP	OCT	NOV	DEC
APPLES									▓	▓		
ARTICHOKES	▓	▓	▓	▓	▓					▓	▓	▓
BRUSSELS SPROUTS	▓	▓	▓							▓	▓	▓
CHRISTMAS TREES												▓
NURSERY PLANTS	▓	▓	▓	▓	▓	▓	▓	▓	▓	▓	▓	▓
OLALLIE BLACKBERRIES						▓	▓					
PUMPKINS									▓	▓		
TOMATOES						▓	▓	▓	▓			
VEGETABLES	▓	▓	▓	▓	▓	▓	▓	▓	▓	▓	▓	▓

Bicycling

The San Mateo coast provides easy pedaling for the biking enthusiast. You will have to arrive on your bike, have it in your car, or rent one in San Francisco or Santa Cruz, however, since Coastside has no commercial bike rental shops. The Montara Lighthouse Hostel usually has a few for day rental (for a tax-deductible contribution to AYH) and can offer bike repairs and services, all part of their campaign to encourage nonmotorized transportation. The Pacific Coast Bikecentennial Route runs along here, and Joan Jackson's book describes the joys of a "Coast Ride: Fifty Miles of Beach" from Santa Cruz to Half Moon Bay.

50 BIKING HOLIDAYS: FROM OLD MONTEREY TO
THE GOLDEN GATE
Joan Jackson
Valley Publishers/Western Tanager Press,
Santa Cruz. 1977.

COAST BIKECENTENNIAL ROUTE MAPS
& INFORMATION
Caltrans, Division of Highways
6002 Folsom Blvd., Sacramento CA 95819.
Public Information Officer (916) 445-4616.

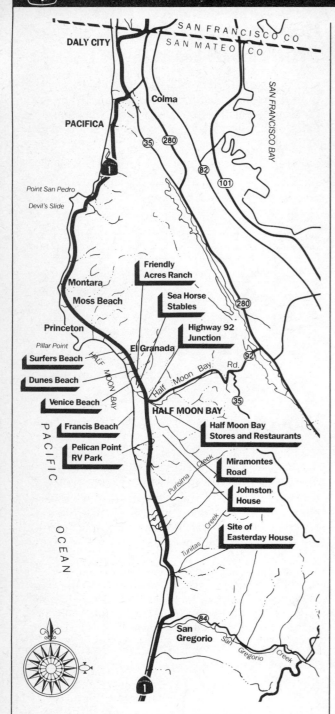

Rails to Roads

The intense suburban migration envisioned by the speculators never did come to pass, although substantial growth occurred on the bayside of San Mateo County, which was more accessible to San Francisco and had warmer, dryer, and clearer weather.

The Ocean Shore Railroad finally pulled up its tracks in 1922, putting quietly to sleep the day-dream of new town development on San Mateo's coastside. For all the hoopla, the coastside remained what it had been before the railroad—a 45-mile stretch of mainly agricultural coastal farms, broken by small towns and an occasional seaside resort. Nobody was getting rich.

The advent of the automobile added to the Ocean Shore's problems. Just as the railroad was trying to build up its freight business, new roads were being constructed that allowed much of the area's freight to be shipped over the coastal hills by truck. In 1913, San Mateo voted a bond issue of $1.25 million to build new roads in the county. Part of this money financed a new coastal road that linked Half Moon Bay and the coastal settlements and farms with markets in San Francisco. In 1914 construction was completed on an unbelievably serpentine route over the summit of San Pedro Mountain, a few miles inland. Coastside residents had another way over the mountain besides the train.

The new road didn't bring a great many visitors to the area—it was far too steep, narrow, and dangerous to be negotiated easily—but it did allow a lot of artichokes and brussels sprouts to be shipped out; and once Prohibition began, it became the main route in San Mateo County's legendary bootleg trade.

Restoration of the James Johnston House

The Johnston House is a saltbox-style structure, built in 1853. One of the few examples of this typically Atlantic-seaboard design in California, it is among the oldest houses in the Bay Area. The preservation of the site, however, has hardly been easy.

In 1972 local citizens around Half Moon Bay organized a foundation to attempt to restore the house, and in 1976 restoration began. One side of

the frame structure was removed as part of the construction, but this proved an unlucky strategy. A typical Coastside storm hit that night, and by the next morning the entire house was just so much old wood scattered over the surrounding artichoke and broccoli fields.

Local residents interested in historical preservation came quickly to the rescue, obtaining grants and consultant assistance from the Smithsonian Institution. Almost all the materials were salvaged and reassembled using the original mortise-and-tenon construction. The house was accepted to the National Register and is now respected as an important memento of California's coastal history.

Sybil Easterday

Sybil Easterday was an iconoclastic, world-famous sculptor with come-hither looks who lived in Coastside from 1905 until her death in 1960. She lived near Tunitas Creek (south of Half Moon Bay) as a recluse who had abandoned her art and her fame to seclude herself in a cabin on property where she had camped as a child. Some said it was a failed romance that drove her there.

Early in her career, Sybil Easterday scandalized the nation by shunning "femmine fripperies" and wearing men's clothes. Judged a "traitor to her sex" for her frequent attire of white duck trousers, white flannel shirt, and low-cut shoes, she patiently explained to her blue-nosed critics: "I only wear this suit while working in my studio and I do it to be free and comfortable."

She shared her life at Tunitas only with her parents, who moved to the area and built a house at the creek: Meticulous landscaping hid the house from all but invited outsiders. Inside, the house was adorned with Sybil's paintings, her sculpture, and a set of ornate stair railings that she elaborately hand-carved.

After more than ten years, Easterday's Emily Dickinson world was finally penetrated by Louis Charles Paulsen, a young and wealthy playboy, whom she married during World War I. Paulsen opened a tavern near the Ocean Shore Railway Station, and love blossomed. Then, three months after their wedding, Paulsen was fatally shot during a drinking party. Sybil retreated further, sharing her world only with her mother and venturing out seldom, except to sell chickens, ducks, and eggs in downtown Half Moon Bay.

In 1960, nine years after the death of her mother, Easterday received notice from the State Highway Department that she would have to move from her Tunitas home—a new crossing was to be built where Highway 1 spanned Tunitas Creek. Move she did, surrendering her sanctuary without a fight. In a few months Sybil Easterday became seriously ill and died. The house she had been evicted from at Tunitas Creek burned to the ground.

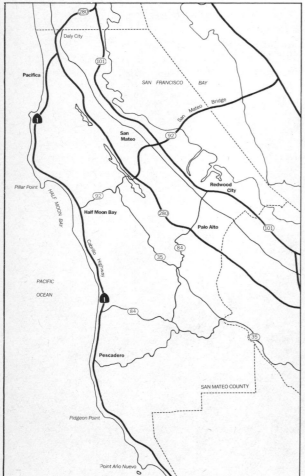

Environment

Hooked Bays and Beach Cusps

Before construction of the breakwaters, Half Moon Bay was a classic hooked bay, the granitic, nonerosive rock of the headlands creating a clearly hooked shoreline.

Hooked bays are also called crescent or crenulate bays. They are created when waves approaching predominantly from one direction refract and diffract, or bend, around an erosion-resistant feature such as a rocky headland, and erode the

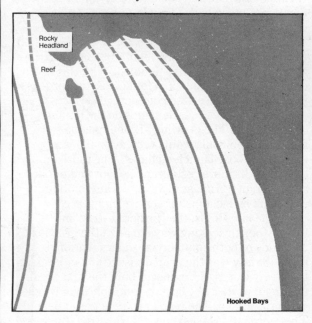

Rocky Headland

Reef

Hooked Bays

less-resistant downcoast shoreline.

The coast curves sharply inward immediately downcoast of the headland, then gradually straightens as the influence of wave refraction becomes less pronounced. The well-defined hooked shape mirrors the refraction pattern of the waves as they pass around the headland. The crenulate beach is typically stable, exhibiting only minor seasonal variations.

Beach cusps arise from many of the same forces of wind and waves as do bays, but on a much smaller scale. Beach cusps are evenly spaced, crescent-shaped depressions found on the seaward edge of beaches like those common in San Mateo. The cusps vary in length from a few inches to hundreds of feet. Beach cusps are informative places to watch the delivery of new sand to

a beach.

The process is always the same: A swash of water heavy with suspended sand rushes up the face of the beach. The points between the cusp deflect the force of the wave, causing some of the suspended sand to drop out on the inner beach. Gravity pulls the water back into the ocean along the steepest path, maintaining a central channel within each cusp. The outgoing waves stop new incoming ones, forcing them to unload their sand at the horns of the cusp.

Roadside Attractions

Half Moon Bay

Beyond Martin's Beach roadside field agriculture intensifies until the town of Half Moon Bay appears to the north. There is still some field agriculture within the city limits and plenty of flower houses, marking the landscape almost to the center of town. Much of the undeveloped land in Half Moon Bay represents unbuildable paper subdivisions.

The first landmark over the southern city limits is the tall brown-and-yellow sign for Pelican Point

RV Park (turn left at Miramontes Road). Inexpensive facilities and personable operators. Next is Ocean Colony Subdivision, a luxury locked-gate community with a mix of suburban American architectural styles sometimes verging on parody. Adjacent are the Half Moon Bay Golf Links. The golf pro's name is Moon Mullins.

Highway 1 reaches the cutoff for Half Moon Bay's central business district at Kelly Avenue. A few doors down Kelly is the Carriage House Café, a fine comfortable, unpretentious eating place with daily specials and peanut butter–and–jelly sandwiches for kids (75¢). The Carriage House Café also has a rack of reading material and a supply of board games.

West on Kelly Avenue takes you to Francis Beach, but you may want to stop at the vegetable stand .5 miles west of Highway 1, one of the most interesting in the area. Within the town limits of Half Moon Bay are five main beaches, all connected: Miramontes Road, Francis Beach, Venice Beach, Dunes, and Surfers.

Highway 92 Junction

Beyond its juncture with Highway 92, the main inland artery, Highway 1 changes again in character. Just north of town on the Highway is another fine vegetable stand, Niagris. For the rest of the route through Coastsisde into San Francisco, Highway 1 is significantly more marked by development sprawl and roadside residential subdivisions than is the portion south of Half Moon Bay. What is lost in rural attractiveness, however, is gained in more diverse roadside attractions.

For example, immediately north of Half Moon Bay are Sea Horse Stables and Friendly Acres Ranch, both of which rent ponies and horses on an individual basis. These stables are among the few places on the coast where you don't have to follow a string of horses on a trail ride. You are free to take a horse to the nearby equestrian trail from Dunes Beach to Francis Beach, or on the other side of Francis Beach, onto the beach itself.

The Costanoans

San Mateo's Native Americans were called Costanoans, ("coastal people"). The sea provided most of their food, although they did hunt onshore with bow and arrows. And the mild Coastside climate and dense forests provided a comfortable environment for these migratory people. Like other tribes in California, the Costanoans were doomed by the arrival of the Europeans. Mission life and diseases introduced by the Europeans soon sealed the fate of this several-thousand-year-old civilization, and no Costanoans are known to exist today.

Resources

Two Coastside Events

The Great Pumpkin Festival

In October the coastal mesas around Half Moon Bay become dotted with brilliant orange. It is the season of the pumpkin and Half Moon Bay is the pumpkin capital of the world.

During the annual Great Pumpkin Festival, Highway 1 becomes clogged with costumed children and adults. Pumpkins are king: witness a pumpkin parade down Main Street, a pumpkin-carving contest, a pumpkin-decorating contest, a pumpkin-eating contest, and a pumpkin recipe contest. Mimes, musicians, arts and crafts displays, a haunted house, rides on a real 1868 stagecoach, and helicopter hops over the orange fields complete the celebration.

Since the first festival in 1970, the main event has been the Great Pumpkin Weigh-Off for the largest pumpkin grown in the United States. (Windsor, Nova Scotia is Canada's weigh-off point.) On the Monday of Columbus Day weekend, farmers come from all over to compete—the winner usually tops the scales at over 350 pounds (and is often not from Coastside). The full Great Pumpkin Festival cuts loose the weekend after the Weigh-Off.

The Chamarita, Festival of the Holy Ghost

The Portuguese heritage of Coastside is reflected in the pageantry of the annual Chamarita Festival. The event, which has been celebrated in Pescadero and Half Moon Bay for over 100 years, has its origins in a miracle that occurred long ago in the Portuguese Azores.

The people of one of the islands were starving; neither sea nor land produced nourishment. Then, as the legend goes, a ship appeared on the misty ocean, loaded with food that was given freely to the dying people. The mysterious captain refused reward and sailed away after unloading his precious cargo. The people of the island were saved, and Queen Isabella of Portugal arrived to lead a joyous parade through the streets of the villages to celebrate the miracle attributed to intervention by the Holy Ghost.

Today, on the sixth Sunday after Easter in Pescadero and on the seventh Sunday in Half Moon Bay, a reenactment of Isabella's procession takes place. A queen with an ornate velvet train and a silver crown made from melted silver dollars parades through town. Many other queens—past, present, and future—and their costumed companies join the parade for a spectacular show. Both weekends host dances, bands, horse shows, and lots of food—some of it free in honor of the Portuguese day of salvation by the Holy Ghost.

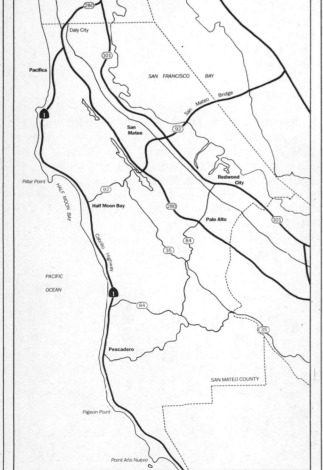

Coastside's Seamy Side

The isolation that was reimposed on San Mateo's coastside after the final demise of the Ocean Shore Railroad became a perfect cover for many illicit activities. By the early 1920s the coastside was a haven for rumrunning, bootlegging, speakeasies, and prostitution. Quite apart from the Ocean Shore promoters' depiction of an untroubled seaside paradise, there was another, seamier side to the area, one that enthusiastically mixed all varieties of vice.

Fast-living San Francisco provided the best of black markets, the coastal fog provided secrecy, and the hard-drinking populace in consort with numerous corrupt politicians and civic leaders provided social (and often legal) legitimacy. In 1923 local newspapers claimed that nearly 75,000 cases of whiskey (with a value of $6 million) had been sneaked in at Half Moon Bay and San Pedro.

So much illegal booze was being brought in that the smugglers' methods sometimes became bizarre, like the time rumrunners seized the lighthouse at Pigeon Point and used the light to signal in an offshore supply ship. Submarines, it was rumored, were used by bootleggers as rum carriers.

At Princeton, John Patroni used the pier adjacent to his speakeasy to smuggle in booze, at least until the evening a Coast Guard cutter, in pursuit of escaping bootleggers, fired a gaping hole through his wharf. A few miles up the coast, Jack Mori used a fleet of small boats, an automobile engine, and a contrivance of cable and buoys to haul in countless cases of illicit booze. In 1923 authorities confiscated 24,000 cases of Scotch, worth more than $2 million, from his farm.

Combined with all the bootlegging was a flourishing local moonshining industry that provided 150-proof whiskey for $4 a gallon to Coastside speakeasies. Like bootlegging, moonshining sustained many Depression-era Coastside residents who would otherwise have been out of work. In the first six years of Prohibition, over 70 stills were raided in the county, hardly scratching the surface of what was an extensive countywide cottage industry.

Pillar Point: Harbor or Marina?

Development plans at Pillar Point Harbor have caused prolonged controversy, pitting commercial fishers against recreational boaters, environmentalists against engineers, and public agencies against each other.

Pillar Point Harbor has always been important to the local commercial fishing industry. Catches coming ashore here include salmon, crab, abalone, rockfish, flatfish, and squid (roughly in that order of volume and value). The salmon season runs begin off the San Mateo coast and if the "bite is in" the opening of the season will see 300 to 400 boats tied up around the harbor. Between 1969 and 1975 the average catch more than doubled. With this has come an increased demand for berths, fish-processing facilities and related commercial services.

But there are other demands on the limited resources here. The growing affluent population along the Peninsula wants recreational boating berths and boat-launch facilities. The tourist industry seeks more restaurants, shops and public access points. And, as always, the automobile makes its own claims for service and space.

In the late 1950s, the Harbor District and County began seeking ways to meet the growing demands of both commercial and recreational users. Safety was the primary issue and in 1959-60 the Army Corps of Engineers built the first breakwaters to protect the harbor from southern winds and storm tides. The results were not as expected. The redirected waves, now entering from the west, hit an offshore reef causing new swells into the harbor on the calmest of days. Several sandy beaches disappeared as the 2,600- and 1,440-foot breakwaters diverted the natural littoral drift, the process by which sand moves along the coast and replenishes beaches. To further complicate things, siltation from inland water runoff could not wash out of the harbor, obstructed by the breakwaters. The harbor began to fill with silt.

In the mid-1970s the Harbor District announced elaborate new plans to expand Pillar Point from a small-craft harbor catering solely to the commercial fishing industry into a marina with both commercial and recreational boating slips. Besides trying to satisfy these two interests (which some say is impossible), the plans include a rock dam to redirect sediment flows and a new breakwater to reduce the swells. Riprap along the shore will protect Highway 1 and provide public access, and there are plans to replenish some of the lost sandy beach area. Onshore improvements such as restaurants, shops, and much more parking are underway.

In its elaborate and controversial development, Pillar Point Harbor is attempting a delicate balance between commercial fishing, recreational boating and environmental protection. The future will tell whether all of these masters can be served equally.

Environment

Roadside Attractions

Resources

Miramar

The next town north is Miramar, most of which is inside Half Moon Bay's city limits. Most evident from Highway 1 is the Miramar Beach Inn, formerly one of Coastside's most popular speakeasies. Today it caters to a college-age crowd, serving dinners and providing dancing to live bands after 9:30 pm (earlier on Sundays).

Just south on Mirada Road is the Douglas House, where the Bach Dancing & Dynamite Society provides one of the best Sunday afternoon jazz

James V. Fitzgerald Marine Reserve

728-3584 or 573-2595.

The three-mile long reserve has some of the coast's most productive tide pools. Guided tours and walks are provided daily by marine biologists, and visitors can picnic in the cypress grove and explore a series of bluff-top trails. All tidal life in the reserve is protected and should not be disturbed.

On the Wing at Fitzgerald Marine Reserve

The 32-acre Fitzgerald Reserve at Moss Beach provides fertile opportunities for birders. Depending on the season, you will see the long-necked cormorants, diving murres, willets, brown pelicans, and a multitude of other shorebirds along the tidal flats. Local rangers can provide a current list.

Cormorants

Some people consider cormorants rather grotesque-looking creatures. Certainly their appearance distinguishes them from other shorebirds. These muddy-black and deep-green slender birds with snaky necks can be seen at their nesting sites along the San Mateo Coastside. The smaller, thin-billed pelagic cormorant has a dull-red throat pouch and a downward tip to its beak. The pelagic nests along the sheer cliffs while the larger Brant's cormorant will be seen near its two-egg nests on the flat nearshore rocks off the reserve's shore, usually gathered in large colonies. The Brant has a blue throat pocket outlined by a dull yellow margin.

Cormorants are underwater feeders, diving for fish and swimming submerged for two to three minutes. However, unlike many divers, these birds lack oil glands on their wings, so you will see them perched on the rocks after a dive with wings outstretched so that the wind and sun may blow-dry them before they can fly or dive again. Cormorants are of interest to birders in California, but in Peru, they are an important part of the economy, their guano serving as the base of a lucrative fertilizer industry. This "crop" provided by nature is gathered at the cormorant and boobie colony on Peru's offshore islands, the home of the largest bird colony in the world, numbering over 10 million individuals.

shows in the San Francisco Bay Area. Name jazz artists and hot newcomers make every show distinctive and exciting. Of equally high quality is their series of candlelight-dinner concerts of classical music on Friday nights. The Bach Dancing & Dynamite Society is a nonprofit organization "devoted to the musical arts" that has achieved the rare feat of presenting beautiful music in surroundings worthy of the sounds. A five-star attraction.

Close by a few doors south is The New Age Center, which shows that despite its general common-sense outlook and down-to-earth attitudes, San Mateo County is still a part of Northern California. The star-shaped structure, an exotic variation on a Californian new-age coastal fantasy, is all wood, some salvaged, some found on the beach. The effect resembles a psilocybin-induced adventure among the kingdom of the driftwood people. There is nothing like this in Omaha.

Pillar Point Harbor

#1 Johnson Pier, Half Moon Bay 94019. 726-4382.

The Harbor offers the following resources: fuel dock, 24-hour launch ramp and small-skiff storage, public restrooms, public pier for fishing or hoisting crab traps, commercial and sport fishing boat tours, whale-watching tours (in season), a 24-hour RV parking area with fresh water and restrooms (no hookups and a 14-day limit), fresh seafood, and shops and restaurants. The Harbor Master's office is open 24 hours a day for information and assistance.

Pelican Point RV Park

P.O. Box 65, Half Moon Bay 94019. 726-9100

This is the only full hook-up RV park between Pacifica and Santa Cruz and is at Pelican Point, just south of Half Moon Bay on Miramontes Point Road past the golf course. The park has 76 sites, many with ocean views and within walking distance to a sandy beach. Hot showers, laundry, storage, cable TV, a store, propane, and dump station are available.

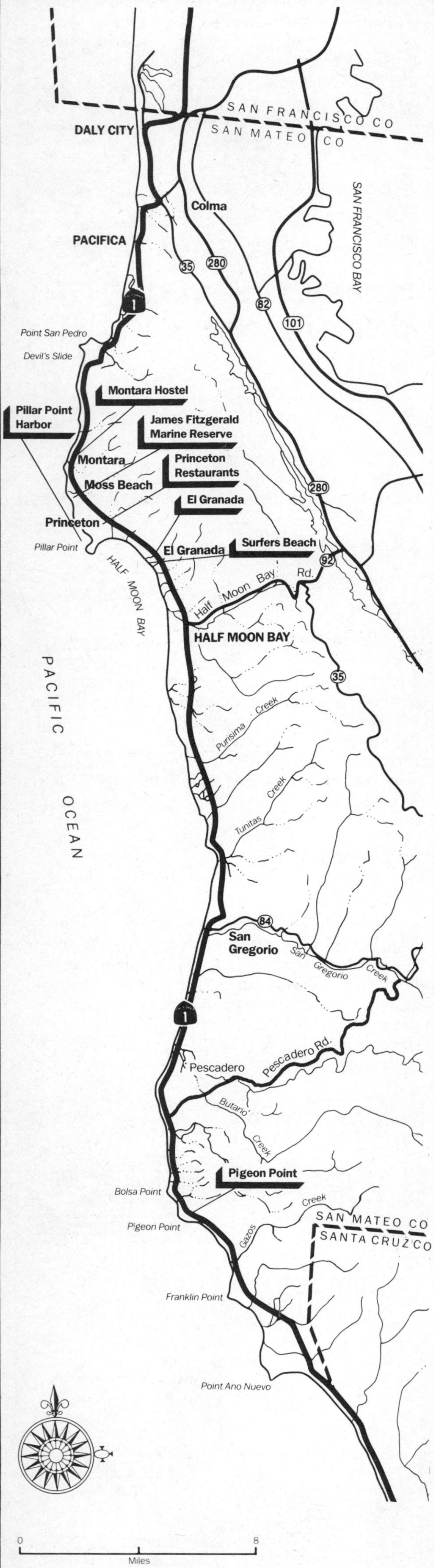

Map labels (left column):

SAN FRANCISCO CO
SAN MATEO CO
DALY CITY
Colma
PACIFICA
35 280
82
101
① 1
Point San Pedro
Devil's Slide
Montara Hostel
Pillar Point Harbor
James Fitzgerald Marine Reserve
Montara
Princeton Restaurants
Moss Beach
El Granada
Princeton
280
Pillar Point
El Granada   Surfers Beach
HALF MOON BAY
Half Moon Bay Rd.
92
35
Purisima Creek
Tunitas Creek
San Gregorio   84
San Gregorio Creek
Pescadero Rd.
① 1
Pescadero
Butano Creek
Pigeon Point
Bolsa Point   Creek
Pigeon Point   SAN MATEO CO
SANTA CRUZ CO
Carol Creek
Franklin Point
Point Ano Nuevo

PACIFIC OCEAN
HALF MOON BAY

0   Miles   8

The New Highway

After the Ocean Shore Railroad's "rather spectacular failure," its right-of-way, skirting the shore and carved out of high cliffs, became the sought-after prize of numerous investors who envisioned buying the old roadbeds and starting a new railroad that would freight out the valuable crops and trees. But continuous litigation prevented any activity on these plans.

In the early 1930s the State of California entered the scene, expressing interest in the Ocean Shore's roadbeds for the construction of a new highway to run astride the cliffs and aside the shore. Originally called the Ocean Shore Highway, the road was later renamed California State Highway 1.

A few years before, a joint highway district (JHD 9) had been established among the counties of Santa Cruz, San Mateo, and San Francisco for the purpose of constructing a coast road from Santa Cruz to San Francisco "as closely as possible to the shoreline of the Pacific Ocean." Several eminent domain (condemnation) suits were filed, including one for the state's acquisition of the notorious Devil's Slide. And so, the road went ahead: a new roadbed was cut in the cliffs, this one just bypassing the old right-of-way at Pedro Point and above it on the sheer side of Montara Mountain.

The Beach Nobody Wants

The narrow strip of beach west of Highway 1 between El Granada and Miramar is all that is left of a once-sandy stretch of beautiful beachfront. The construction of the Pillar Point breakwater effectively destroyed the area for practically all but the many surfers who value the ocean's waves, regardless of the condition of the beach. Once this was El Granada beach, dreamed of as the Coney Island of the West; now it is referred to as "Surfers."

The property was first owned by the County, which offered it to the State in the early 1970s. The State wasn't interested in developing the then-expansive 5-acre beach, but the city of Half Moon Bay was happy to accept it because a local developer envisioned building a restaurant there. Shortly after the city obtained title, however, the sand began to disappear. The beach was soon half its original size, with barely enough room for parking on the edge. The developer lost interest and the city looked for a new buyer (or, failing that, a taker).

The Harbor District, which owns all property north, is not interested in the beach; San Mateo County is not interested; the State is not interested. Caltrans is beginning to worry because breakers spill over onto Highway 1 during storms and high tides, and erosion and undercutting of their road are becoming serious—but the agency has no interest in acquiring what is left of the beach. In the meantime, local surfers and teenagers park along the highway and edge; maintenance and garbage clean-up are haphazard, with no effective management; and no solution is in sight.

If you've always had a desire to own coastal property with an ocean view, this may be your chance, but you better act now while the property is still there.

El Granada

Of the early new towns created by speculators the grandest was El Granada—advertised as "The Coney Island of the West." Not only vacation homes were to be built here, but a dazzling casino, hotel, and bathing pavilion were promised. The Ocean Shore Company had selected this spot above all others—"aside the most remarkable stretch of clean, sandy, safe beach in the world"—for a seaside resort town that would weave spells and seduce the most resistant lot-buyer.

To design the new town, the Ocean Shore Investment Company had the unlikely fortune of hiring Daniel Burnham, one of the most influential of American city planners. Burnham was patriarch of the City Beautiful movement; originator of comprehensive urban planning in America; author of plans for Chicago, Washington, Cleveland, San Francisco, and Manila; and the architect of world-class buildings such as the Flatiron Building in New York and the Reliance Building in Chicago. Burnham, whose chosen motto

was "Make no small plans," made a very small plan for El Granada while finishing his draft of the never-used San Francisco plan.

But Burnham's plan for El Granada was used, at least to lay out the street pattern. Its main features—curvalinear streets, broad boulevards, central open spaces, and interspersed parks are City Beautiful conventions that lent themselves conveniently to real estate speculation before any structures were built.

El Granada, so grand in conception and so promising in expectation, never materialized as the "Coney Island of the West." Although various roadhouses came and went, there never would be an El Granada in reality to equal the El Granada of dreams.

Once the original promotional to-do ended, few lots were sold and fewer homes built. Most of the lots that were sold, for as little as $10 down, were foreclosed as the dream faded and the railroad's demise became inevitable. Although the Ocean Shore Investment Company maintained the lush Burnham landscaping for a while, eventually El Granada deteriorated into a near–ghost town until the 1950s.

Environment

Geological Formations and Tidepools at Fitzgerald Marine Reserve

The James V. Fitzgerald Marine Reserve extends along the seaward side of the bluffs and into the ocean for about .5 miles just north of Pillar Point. The reserve is designated an area of special biological significance by the State and is managed by the County of San Mateo.

The tidal areas at the reserve provide brilliant examples of sedimentary formations, including graded and crossbedding, scour and fill structures and a small, but complete, syncline that is visible in the intertidal and shallow-water zone at low tide. The predominant rock type here is from the Upper Pliocene-Merced Formation. The San Gregorio earthquake fault zone is clearly visible from the Reserve near the Seal Cove cliffs, making this a nationally significant site for geologists wishing to study the rare but easily accessible phenomenon of sedimentary rocks faulted against granitic basement rock. The county provides a guided tour of the protected tidal areas during low tides, or you can explore for yourself.

Tide Pool Formation

About seven million years ago, the area that is now James V. Fitzgerald Marine Reserve was an immense mudflat that extended for miles. Over geologic time, the mud was compressed into shale as other marine sediments were deposited. Later materials were uplifted by movements of the earth's crust. The exposed shale was then slowly eroded by waves, leaving the channels, crevices, cracks, and ledges that form today's tide pools.

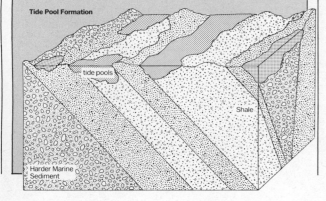

Tide Pool Formation

Roadside Attractions

Princeton

After passing through El Granada, a 1950s subdivision based on Daniel Burnham's street plan for the Coney Island of the West, Highway 1 arrives at Pillar Point, where a cutoff leads to Princeton-by-the-Sea. Contrary to its high-sounding name and its showy entry boulevard, Princeton is an authentic place, in keeping with Coastside's eschewment of extravagant adornment or pretentious sophistication.

First of all there is the harbor. Its authenticity

derives from its commercial orientation. Although an inner breakwater and recreational slips have been added, the harbor is not yet the St. Francis Yacht Club, nor likely will it become so. Two fish markets sell locally caught crab, salmon, shark (eat him before he eats you), and shellfish, as seasonally available.

In the same row of stores are a couple of cafés and several spots where you can charter a fishing boat, although fishing on the pier is free and excellent. Captain John's Fishing has daily excursions from 6 am, as well as whale-watching expeditions and trips to the Farallon Islands to study birds and sea mammals. At Pillar Point Fishing Trips you can arrange for most of the trips offered by Captain John, including, should you so desire, burial at sea.

Up from the harbor area an orangish ramshackle structure with blue-tinted glass sits out over the harbor on stilts. Sea gulls and brown pelicans fly about the place frantically as if seeking entrance and a break from the unrelenting effort of animal life. Or they may just know a good restaurant featuring one of the best beer collections on the coast when they see it. The name of the place is the Fishtrap; their grilled fish is first-rate, and fried calamari is a local favorite.

Across the street, the Shorebird also serves excellent food in a less proletarian atmosphere. The ambience suggests Cape Cod (of all places) and the quality of the menu is on a par with many San Francisco restaurants.

Princeton, like a lot of Coastside towns, has a colorful past of rumrunning, gambling, and prostitution. The Princeton Inn (a National Heritage Building), once the site of a variety of dramatic forms of vice, now sedately concentrates on the tour-bus crowd. Other places in town nod to Princeton's past, but more evident is the contemporary vitality that surrounds activities like boat building and commercial fishing, which exemplify Princeton's straightforward maritime livelihood.

Resources

The California Coastal Hostel Chain

Although hosteling is 75 years old in Europe, it is only beginning to leave its mark in this country as an alternative to motels, hotels, or tents for travelers of all ages.

San Mateo brings you to one of the original links in a planned hostel chain that may eventually provide overnight accommodations, each one-day's bike ride apart, from Oregon to Mexico.

American Youth Hostels

Golden Gate Council
680 Beach Street #396, San Francisco 94109.
771-4646.

Write AYH for information on the more than 30 hostels in California, and 300 in the United States. AYH also publishes a hostel guide and newsletters, and provides travel information.

Pigeon Point Lighthouse Hostel

Pigeon Point Road and Highway 1,
Pescadero 94060.
879-0633.

This hostel is particularly favored by photographers for its dramatic lighttower (one of the tallest in the U.S.). It is only 50 miles from here to San Francisco and only a few miles to Año Nuevo, to tidepools, beaches, and redwood forests.

Montara Lighthouse Hostel

16th Street/Cabrillo Highway (Highway 1)
Montara 94037.
728-7177.

Here you will find two fully equipped kitchens, dining room, common room, laundry, community room with wood-burning fireplace, a volleyball court, outdoor hot tub on the grounds, bicycles to rent and facilities to repair your own, beaches, and room for 35 guests. By public transportation from San Francisco, take Muni or BART south to the Daly City BART station, then transfer to SamTrans bus #1A or #1H southbound (weekdays until 5:50 pm, Saturdays until 6:15 pm, Sundays and holidays until 5:15 pm). Ask the bus driver to let you off at the 14th Street Montara stop. Bus service to San Francisco airport is also available from the hostel.

Roadbuilding Heroics

The effort to cut the road was likened to the effort to construct cliffside portions of Highway 1 at Big Sur. At Montara's summit the cut for the new highway was 465 feet above the ocean. The 5.9-mile road required 28 curves and a total rise and fall in grade of 1,225 feet. The effort was further complicated by extremely unstable soils, which necessitated excavating to a depth of 40 feet below grade and refilling the cut with large rock anchored to the mountainside. Overall, 1.5 million cubic yards of soil and rock were excavated.

The unstable soils also caused slide after slide while construction crews worked. Sudden slides would unexpectedly hurl thousands of tons of rock and earth down the mountain, burying steam shovels, road cats, and equipment. Contractors considered themselves lucky that only one worker was killed. The men who balanced upon the cliffs were heroically regarded by each other, by the local community who knew firsthand the perils of Devil's Slide, and by the State Department of Transportation, which in its June 1937 issue of *California Highways and Public Works* said, "The location of the highway along the cliff face re-

quired men with the agility of mountain goats, courage, experience, and complete lack of nerves. One false step meant a tumble into the breakers."

On Armistice Day, November 11, 1937, the road was opened to public use, providing some of the most stunning vistas and vantage points on the whole coast and enabling travelers improved access to the beaches and the redwoods. The new road also established the long-sought market artery for Coastside's expanding agricultural industry.

The problems that cursed the road's construction, however—the slides, washaways, and sloughing—would continue to devil its existence to the present day, perhaps foreordaining a replacement road, and lending a prophetic irony to the comments of the Department of Highway's district engineer who, in 1937, anticipated that "considerable trouble may be experienced by our maintenance forces."

Women and the Good Roads Movement

Ben Blow, Manager of the Good Roads Bureau of the California State Automobile Association, dedicates his *California Highways* (1920) to "The Women of California who have helped more than any other agency in the fight for good roads." Here, as in many of the most important social and environmental struggles in this country, women were prime movers.

The records of meetings organized and conducted by women in San Mateo County justifies Blow's perception. Women organized presentations on the needs and advantages of better roads in schoolhouses and halls with parent-teacher associations, mother's clubs, granges and farm bureau centers. Here they would stir local sentiment in favor of highway improvements. Then they would send an elected delegation to the local board of supervisors to generate a plan for road locations and development. Finally, the women would work tirelessly to secure the necessary two-thirds majority vote needed for a local bond issue to finance construction.

Women wrote articles and sent in comments for newspapers, providing facts on accidents and travel times that affected the local economy. They presented lantern slides of mishaps and pictures of children slipping and sliding through knee-deep mud on their daily walks to and from local schools, and compared these roads to paved highways in other locations. These meetings usually were followed by a "draw" such as a rented reel of a Fairbanks, Arbuckle, or Chaplin movie—always shown after the pitch for better roads, of course.

During election campaigns, women repeatedly canvassed local citizens on the telephone and door-to-door, converting nonbelievers and, when necessary, getting voters to the polls on election day. Women in the remote country areas wrote to urban women who had led successful campaigns, asking them "[as] sisters to help get good roads from farm to town." Evidence documents Blow's conclusion that "in most instances [it was] the women who have been interested in the [Good Roads] campaign, working harder than the men and almost invariably recording a larger percentage of the vote."

Map labels

SAN FRANCISCO CO
SAN MATEO CO
DALY CITY
Colma
PACIFICA
35
280
82
101
Devil's Slide
Point San Pedro
Devil's Slide
Gray Whale Cove State Beach
Montara Hostel
Moss Beach Restaurants
Montara
Moss Beach
Princeton
Pillar Point
El Granada
Half Moon Bay Rd.
92
280
HALF MOON BAY
35
Half Moon Bay
Purisima Creek
Creek
Tunitas Creek
PACIFIC OCEAN
SAN FRANCISCO BAY
84
San Gregorio
San Gregorio Creek
Pescadero Rd.
Pescadero
Butano Creek
Bolsa Point
Pigeon Point
Creek
Gazos Creek
SAN MATEO CO
SANTA CRUZ CO
Franklin Point
Año Nuevo Rookery
Point Año Nuevo

0   Miles   8

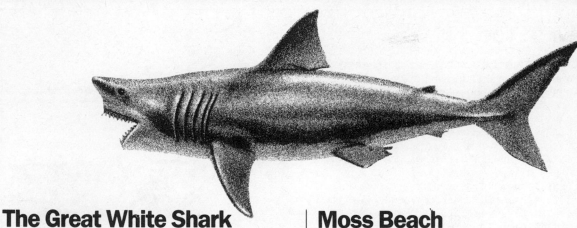

The Great White Shark

Seals and sea lions now flourish along the central coast of California; likewise these pinnipeds' major predator: the great white shark. Since 1955 more shark attacks on human beings have occurred along the stretch of California's coast that encompasses the Año Nuevo Rookery than anywhere else in the world. The responsible party is the great white shark.

Sharks are among the oldest of vertebrate life forms. Fossils date sharklike fish to the middle Devonian period, over 300 million years ago. By the time of the early Tertiary (60 million years ago) all 250 to 350 species of living sharks had developed and they remain pretty much the same today. Sharks' command of their watery world is made possible by physical characteristics that inspire awe and an instinctive fear in the human species: multiple rows of regenerating teeth set in powerful hinged jaws capable of swallowing anything half the shark's size in one bite; skin equipped with dermal denticles rather than scales, making sharkskin as abrasive as some shark's teeth; and a hydrodynamically efficient body with a well-developed olfactory sense capable of detecting minute dilutions of blood in water over a quarter of a mile away.

The great white shark is a member of the shark suborder *Galeoidei,* which includes the most aggressive of these torpedo-shaped, five-gilled creatures. The great white is as big as it is mean, attaining lengths of over 25 feet although there are undocumented reports of larger individuals, such as the white in Australian waters that measured over 36.5 feet. Like all sharks, the great white never sleeps. Since sharks don't have air bladders (the gland that keeps most fish afloat) they must constantly move their pectoral fins to keep floating; if they didn't, they would sink. Another characteristic shared with all shark members is the great white's frantic approach to its food. There have been cases of sharks pursuing their prey upon the shore, and in feeding frenzies they have been known to eat their own bodies as they twist and turn to secure their meal. Sharks also apparently have no sense of pain, and generally keep functioning, attacking and devouring, even when disemboweled.

Moss Beach

Among Coastside's three or four outstanding restaurants is the Moss Beach Distillery. Take the signed cutoff from Highway 1 all the way to the ocean. Another artifact of Coastside's bootlegging past, the Distillery serves excellent seafood and beef to complement the stunning ocean views. You can order a full dinner in the dining room or hors d'oeuvres (oysters, clams, ribs) in the oyster bar. Full bar. The Distillery looks down upon the ocean reef that makes up Fitzgerald Marine Reserve.

Moss Beach also hosts the peculiar Nyes Reefs II, only occasionally open. Once a freewheeling resort frequented by Luther Burbank and Jack London, today it is almost a tavern museum, open on weekends, but not always.

Should you desire overnight accommodations, inquire for vacancies at the Farallone Hotel, a simple-looking little place with a spectacular ocean setting. Or consider spending an evening at the Montara Lighthouse Hostel just north of Moss Beach. (The hostel can accommodate families in private rooms.) Beyond the lighthouse the best beach in 25 miles shows up at Montara. Access can be gained on either side of the large restaurant. Just before Devil's Slide is another nude beach. Gray Whale Cove State Beach.

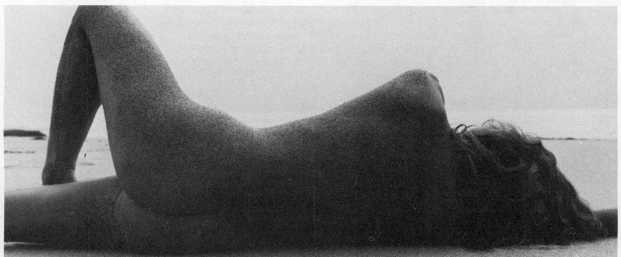

How To Protect Yourself Against Sharks

★ **Avoid wearing strong contrasting colors** (e.g., a white swimsuit if the skin is deeply tanned), and remember that sharks can more easily see strong contrasts such as a swimmer in a dark suit swimming above a white sand bottom.

★ **Remove jewelry before swimming;** the bright flash of metal attracts sharks. Don't wear luminous bathing suits.

★ **Carry an object at least three feet in length** that you can use to prod a shark in an emergency.

★ **Try not to swim or dive alone.** Post a lookout if you must swim for a boat.

★ **Don't swim or dive at night** (when sharks feed) or in dirty or murky water during the daytime—even in a harbor or a bay.

★ **Keep your face underwater** so that you can always look down.

★ **Don't splash or make loud noises** that attract sharks; swim smoothly.

★ **Leave the water if you are even slightly cut;** some sharks are able to detect very small concentrations of blood in the water. Spear fishermen should get their catches quickly into the boat, as the blood of the wounded fish may attract sharks.

★ **Get out of the water** as calmly and quickly as possible if you spot a shark. Don't attempt to tease it or ride its back, or any other foolhardy act (as some divers have). Swim or walk to the shore rapidly but in as steady and quiet a manner as possible.

★ **If you can't leave the water, keep calm** and never let the shark out of your sight—sharks rarely attack humans facing them.

★ **If a shark should appear** to be readying itself for an attack, scream at it. This has worked for some divers, frightening sharks off.

★ **Other divers tell** of swimming directly at belligerent sharks to scare them off, while still others have pounded their snouts and gills with their fists or whatever weapons were available.

SHARKS
Wildlife Education, Ltd.
930 West Washington Street
San Diego 92103.

The Wildlife Education *Zoobooks* series offer excellent introductions to a variety of species, in a format that is accessible to many ages. The *Sharks* publication is especially helpful, including color photos and illustrations, and a full bibliography for more reading for both children and adults, including *The Natural History of Sharks,* published by J. B. Lippincott, and *The Book of Sharks,* published by Grosset and Dunlap.

Land Sharks Came First

Sharks of the sea take their name from land sharks, rather than the other way around, which is the usual order of things. *Shark* derives from the German *Schurke,* meaning "greedy parasite," the name German sailors applied to the sea creature with the "land shark" (a shore-dwelling person who swindles sailors) in mind. English sailors imported the word in about 1569, when John Hawkins, the first English mariner to be engaged in the African slave trade, exhibited a huge shark in London. The word was quickly adopted to describe the "killer fish."

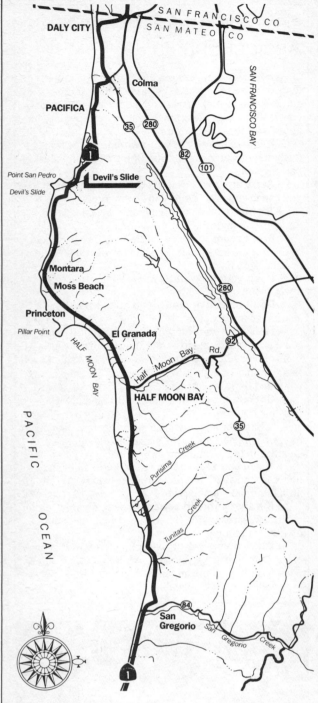

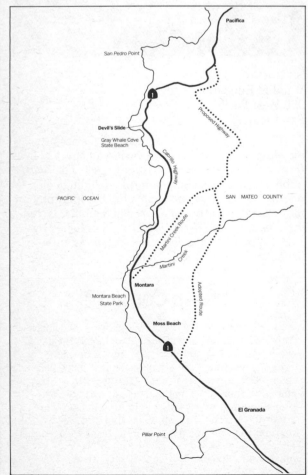

Devil's Slide Bypass

In what may or may not be a Faustian reversal, the fate of Devil's Slide is in the hands of the California Department of Transportation (Caltrans). After nearly half a century of slides, slippages, and winter closings, the State, backed by advocates of the Coastside's growth, has decided to correct once and for all the Devil's Slide portion of Highway 1. The impacts loom as large as anything that has ever happened on the San Mateo Coastside.

For years the State has been trying to build an inland bypass around Devil's Slide. When they originally proposed the bypass, in the early 1970s, the project was halted at the last minute by a Sierra Club lawsuit claiming that Caltrans had not filed an adequate environmental impact statement. Now, as attitudes toward the environment change with the times, the idea of the bypass is again gaining currency.

For and Against

The prospect of the bypass divides Coastside communities along a strict line between pro-growth and no-growth advocates. Those who favor the bypass, which would bisect McNee State Reserve inland from the coast, see it as a permanent solution to the numerous closings of Highway 1 at Devil's Slide, tiveness. Without question, a new road that would speed residents to San Francisco and expanding job centers on the bay side of the Peninsula—where the housing shortage has reached frantic proportions—will induce more potential growth than anywhere along the north or central coast.

which seriously hurt local businesses. The bypass would also significantly increase the convenience of driving to Bay Area work places, which would consequently stimulate local real estate values to skyrocket.

No-growth advocates, who favor a reconstruction of Highway 1 through Devil's Slide to decrease the frequency of road closures but still restrain access to the area, fear that the bypass would create so much fast growth along the Coastside that much of its scenic beauty would be lost forever. Also lost would be the vistas from Highway 1 over Devil's Slide itself, which provide one of the most stunning visual entrances to any section of the coast. So strong is sentiment on the issue that Harold Gilliam, a well-respected author, has called the bypass "a freeway pointed at the heart of this open wonderland like a dagger of death."

The Impact of Growth

The proposed bypass or the reconstruction of Highway 1 would each entail serious environmental impacts, but they would be secondary to the effects of population growth. The proximity of San Mateo's Coastside to expanding population centers on the bay side of the Peninsula has already brought about a rapid spate of growth that has strained the Coastside's water supply, sewage capacities, and scenic attrac-

And beyond the question of the Coastside's capability to manage such fast growth lies the issue of what *type* of growth might occur. Because of the economic incentive to expand further and further from population centers (remote land is cheaper), a new faster highway often results in dispersed development and scattered-lot construction. In-fill development, which consolidates impacts, fosters neighborhood communication, and preserves open space, appears unnecessarily expensive if a cheaper lot or subdivision can be developed just a few minutes down the road. But such scattershot development increases automobile traffic and changes vast stretches of countryside into a pocked landscape.

Beauty and Excitement

In addition to the loss of much of the Coastside's scenic beauty, the bypass would mean the loss of the Devil's Slide road itself. No accounting of costs or benefits accurately measures the emotional and aesthetic value of one of the most magnificent stretches of road in Northern California. The experience of driving over Devil's Slide is unique: at once exhilarating and inspiring in the intensity of its beauty and excitement. The loss of this stretch of road, foreordained by the bypass, removes permanently these rare qualities from San Mateo's Coastside.

| **Environment** | **Roadside Attractions** | **Resources** |

Geology of Montara Mountain and Devil's Slide

The Devil's Slide section of Highway 1 is cut out of the side of Montara Mountain, which towers inland to a height of over 1,900 feet above sea level, forming a dramatic backdrop for the communities of Montara, Moss Beach, and El Granada. The exposed road cuts reveal tightly folded, thin-bedded Cretaceous sandstone and shale along with granitic rocks (primarily quartz diorite) deposited beneath the ocean during the last half of

the Mesozoic era, about 100 million years ago. At other points, cuts expose early Cenozoic shale and sandstone, a sedimentary rock dating back about 60 million years.

The softer, relatively unconsolidated shale and sandstone are subject to a severe erosion and are easily broken down by heavy rains that flow through the porous openings in the earth. Such a geological terrain responds to moisture above (fog and rain) and wave attack below, to contribute to the frequent landslides in the area.

The slides, a natural occurrence along the relatively young coastal cliffs in San Mateo, once would have instigated little notice. Today, they take on a new meaning and present a new challenge to the human beings who have their own ideas for use of this mountainside.

The Fatal Attraction of Devil's Slide

*How paltry is the Devil's power
to destroy compared to what can momentarily be.*
Jack Gilbert

Devil's Slide has always had a far-reaching reputation for sudden mysterious death, and for good reason. Many an unsuspecting motorist has roared off the narrow curves at the road's height and flipped into a sea-bound somersault. Nine went in one car in 1944, five more a year later. In 1949 the growing death toll led the county deputy sheriff to put up warning signs along the edge. Whenever the slide claimed another victim, a black cross was painted on one large sign to warn others. But soon enough this practice was curtailed, the sign having become an illegible jumble of black crosses.

Since its opening in 1936 Devil's Slide has witnessed more than 100 deaths. Many have been suicides like the case of one 37-year-old distraught woman from San Francisco who parked her car at the top of Devil's Slide in the middle of the night and jumped to her death, taking her nine-year-old daughter and ten-year-old son with her. And there have been murders: victims pushed and countless bodies dumped. During one period in the early 1970s there were so many bodies showing up at the bottom of the cliffs that rescue crews worked overtime.

In some people's minds there is a curse on the Slide that compels death. Witnesses continually testify to the audacity of the mountain to seduce the living over its edge and into the sea. Rescue workers wonder about the frequency with which helicopter rotors are dashed against the cliff wall, about the many rescue boats that are broken upon the rocks.

Indeed, tragedy always seems to strike when least expected at Devil's Slide. In 1955 Van Earl Terrall posed against the ocean background as his honeymoon bride took a snapshot of him. "Just a little step back, honey." The newlyweds suddenly found that an unexpected chasm had opened between them.

Environmental Action

Pacifica, City of Suburbs

If there is any one distinguishing physical feature of the contemporary American landscape, it is the sprawl of suburbs over the countryside. Yet it is probably the most maligned neighborhood form there is, despite being preferred by most people as a place to live. In San Mateo County this preference has garnered famous ridicule by Malvina Reynolds, a songwriter from Berkeley, who took one look at Harold Doelger's Daly City subdivision and wrote *Little Boxes*, in which "ticky tacky" houses symbolize mass conformity and the banality of middle class existence.

Suburbs and More Suburbs

The same explosion of suburban expansion that transformed Daly City also created a new suburban settlement at Pacifica in the years after World War II. The entire northern portion of the San Mateo Coastside had lain more or less dormant after the unsuccessful tries by the Ocean Shore Railway to create seaside resort towns at Brighton, Rockaway Beach, and Valle-mar. But in 1953 Andrew Oddstad took a clue from Harold Doelger's miracle of cookie-cutter houses in Daly City and began building several thousand tract homes in Coastside's Linda Mar. He purchased land for his new subdivision from another speculator who had obtained giant tracts from the Ocean Shore Railway.

Subdivisions soon began to spread northward from Linda Mar along Highway 1. Although much of the land was barren and without usable water, subdivisions began popping up nearly overnight in Sharp Park, Vallemar, Rockaway Beach, Edgemar, and Pacific Manor. The population of the Pacifica subdivisions increased from fewer than 5,000 inhabitants in 1950 to more than 15,000 in 1955.

What the Planners Forgot

Unfortunately, the rapid expansion occurred without any comprehensive plan to accommodate the inhabitants of the Coastside's new subdivisions. In a rush to subdivide and sell as many new homes as possible, developers ignored making provisions for water, schools, and sewage. Residents were obliged to create their own water district, and schools had to be carried on in makeshift classrooms and conducted on double shifts.

In response to the general lack of services for the Coastside subdivisions, homeowner associations were formed to obtain what poor planning had ignored. By 1957 these groups (along with PTA groups, business associations, realtors, and local builders) prevailed in a local election to incorporate all the subdivision settlements into the new town of Pacifica. As a city, Pacifica was able to more effectively obtain improved public services, and great strides were made in utility service, schools, and police protection.

Incorporation did not bring total unification, however. The separation of the scattered communities has always made agreement on planning and development issues difficult. With a growing population that today exceeds 40,000 and a bedroom-community economy that has brought about some of the highest property taxes in the country, Pacifica faces a new set of suburban growth issues.

Planning Disaster Adverted: Flooding Valleys to Water Lawns

Development pressure on Coastside is evidenced in a multitude of plans, some realized and others dropped or altered from their original grand scope. In the 1960s and early 1970s the possibilities for big dreaming to accommodate a projected San Mateo coast population of 200,000 residents seemed endless. Such was the spirit that encouraged the Army Corps of Engineers to propose in 1969 to dam Pescadero Creek, thereby creating a 725-acre reservoir to furnish water for the projected future Coastside population.

The Corps' plans not only called for inundation of a major portion of Portola State Park but also gave new authorization for commercial logging in the area. Conservationists, who were becoming increasingly sophisticated in understanding and responding to development plans, attacked the project with a vigor that surprised the Corps and local politicians. The plans were withdrawn, and the lovely woods of Portola State Park continue to provide breathing space for Bay Area residents. Today, water supply remains one of the major constraints on otherwise unbridled Coastside sprawl.

Map labels:

SAN FRANCISCO CO
SAN MATEO CO

DALY CITY

Pacifica Municipal Pier

Pacifica Stores and Shops

Colma

Sharp Park

PACIFICA

Rockaway Beach

Linda Mar

Point San Pedro

Point Pedro Restaurants, Shops

Devil's Slide

SAN FRANCISCO BAY

Montara

Moss Beach

Princeton

Pillar Point

El Granada

HALF MOON BAY

Half Moon Bay Rd.

PACIFIC OCEAN

Purisima Creek

Tunitas Creek

San Gregorio

San Gregorio Creek

Pescadero Creek

Pescadero

Pescadero Rd.

Butano Creek

Bolsa Point

Pigeon Point

Gazos Creek

SAN MATEO CO
SANTA CRUZ CO

Point Ano Nuevo

Potential Coastal Hostel Sites

Environment

Roadside Attractions

Resources

Rare and Endangered in San Mateo

Ten known endangered, rare, or threatened animals and eight rare plants call the Coastside their home, at least temporarily. Among the animals are the San Francisco garter snake, the California least tern, the California brown pelican, the San Bruno elfin butterfly, and the Guadalupe fur seal. Some of the more "common" of the rare plants are Davy's bush lupine, San Francisco wallflower, and yellow meadow foam.

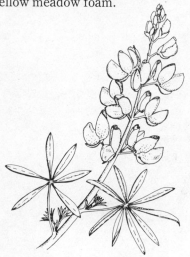

The San Francisco Garter Snake

Although rare, if a San Francisco garter snake is anywhere near your path, you are likely to see it. The uniquely beautiful snake sports marks of red, white, and blue on its back, joined by a brilliant turquoise on its underside. Its beauty, along with the fact that it is nonpoisonous and unaggressive, has contributed to its swift demise from the natural environment to the collector's shelf (or jar) because very little is known about this snake, its prime habitats, or ecological restrictions. This makes protection hard, but county policy requires any developer to make "sufficiently detailed analyses of any construction that could impair the potential or existing migration routes of the San Francisco garter snake" and prohibits development on the few known riparian or wetland habitat locations in the county. The State Department of Fish and Game, the county, and local conservationists are working against the clock to learn more about this snake in order to better encourage its survival.

The Pacific Ocean

The word *pacific* derives from the Latin *pacificus,* 'making or tending to make peace.' The ocean named by Magellan after its tranquil appearance is the largest of the earth's oceans, stretching between Asia and the American continents for an area of about 63.75 million square miles. Here in Southern California, you may indeed see the Pacific as a peaceful force; more often you will be amazed by its roaring strength as it merges with the shoreline, rearranging tons of rock and earth over the ages. As Conrad said: "An elemental force is ruthlessly frank."

Pacifica

Immediately north of Devil's Slide, the promised land of Pacifica comes into view. Pacifica is the largest town on San Mateo's Coastside with 40,000 inhabitants spread over 12.6 square miles. Despite the derision of urban sophisticates from San Francisco who find the town too provincial, Pacifica's heart still beats true.

Pacifica was formed in 1957 from a group of suburban subdivisions, most of which had been hastily thrown up after World War II. Point Pedro, the southernmost community in Pacifica, precedes the other settlements and is the most interesting. Turn west on San Pedro Avenue toward the Point. There are two decent restaurants before a right turn on Danman brings you past the Sea Urchin Crafts Store, the Point Surf (Surfers' Store) and the Pacific Arts Center (classes and sometimes concerts). At the end of the road stands a private house that was once a terminal for the Ocean Shore Railroad. The view here is stunning. The cliff-face parking area was the railroad's track bed as it climbed up and around Point Pedro before slicing across Devil's Slide. Imagining its route can induce vertigo.

South of Point Pedro on the ocean side of the Highway is one of the most distinctive-looking fast-food restaurants on the California coast: the A&W Hamburger stand at Rockaway Beach. The structure owes more than a little to the influence of the respected architectural style developed at Sea Ranch in Sonoma County by Moore, Lyndon, and Turnbull. Its modern redwood exterior and a dauntless mix of tall open interior space and panoramic ocean views give the place an immediate appeal.

Pacifica also has a superb bowling alley (Pacifica Coast Lanes) and a castle that once was a speakeasy, then a coast guard station, and now a private residence. From the Pacifica Municipal Pier, which goes 1,000 feet into the surf, the fishing and whale viewing are excellent. North of Pacifica the freeway leads through Daly City into San Francisco.

> After
> suburbs
> comes
> the city.

Visitor Information Guides

The Curious Traveler's Guide to Pescadero, San Gregorio, Loma Lar, and Gazos Creek
The Studio Press,
P.O. Box 207
Pescadero. 94060.

Combing the Coast:
San Francisco to Santa Cruz,
A Lively Guide to Beaches, Backroads, Parks, Historic Sites and Towns
Ruth A. Jackson
Chronicle Books, San Francisco. 1981.

The ongoing narrative in *Combing the Coast* describes sights and stops along San Mateo's coastside from San Francisco almost to Santa Cruz. This excellent guide is pleasureful, thorough and very accessible. *The Curious Traveler* is much more specialized but also recommended as an insiders guide.

The San Mateo County Convention and Visitors' Bureau
888 Airport Blvd., Burlingame 94010.
347-7004

Pacifica Chamber of Commerce
80 Eureka Square, Suite 117, Pacifica 94044.
355-4122

Half Moon Bay Chamber of Commerce
The Caboose, 225 S. Cabrillo Highway,
Half Moon Bay 94019.
726-5202

Coastside Publishers & Printers
(for the *Coastside Directory*)
537 Main Street, Half Moon Bay 94019.
726-6662

In Case of Emergency

Highway Patrol: Ask Operator for Zenith 1-2000

Sheriff (unincorporated county areas):
726-4435 or 364-1811

Pillar Point Harbor Master: 726-4382

Police, Fire, or Accident: 911 or
726-2211   Half Moon Bay
726-4422   El Granada
728-5500   Point Montara & Moss Beach
355-4151   Pacifica

Hospital Emergency and Medics:
728-3921   St. Catherine Hospital, Moss Beach
364-1313   Medevac, Inc.

Poison Control Center: 800-792-0720 (toll free)

Animals in Distress:
573-3785   Peninsula Humane Society
494-SAVE   Wildlife Rescue, Inc.

SAN FRANCISCO

HIGHWAY 1 goes through San Francisco in almost understated fashion, skirting the city edge along 19th Avenue and Park Presidio Drive, barely noticed but highlighting one of America's largest and most beautiful urban parks and the world's most famous bridge.

The Highway 1 traveler gains a unique perspective on "the cool gray city of love," bounded by water on three of its sides. Although there are no cable cars on its route, few Victorian houses, and not many steep hills, Highway 1 strikes through the heart of what makes San Francisco San Francisco—its neighborhoods. To the north and south of Golden Gate Park lie the city's two largest neighborhoods, the Richmond and Sunset districts.

It is the neighborhoods, with their heterogeneity of people, their diversity of interests, shops, restaurants and lifestyles, and their variety of architecture that create what has been described as "a kind of urbanity that exists nowhere else in this country." Each neighborhood contributes significantly to the cultural richness, ethnic variety and social vitality of this unique and exciting city and county.

The Great Sand Waste

Distinctly different from the San Francisco that developed adjacent to the Bay shoreline and grew up overnight in the Gold Rush frenzy of the 1840s and 1850s, the western portion of the city experienced a more gradual, less exuberant pace of development. Instead of plank streets that were hurriedly constructed, attached buildings jammed wherever they would fit, and throngs of stargazing get-rich-quick adventurers who caroused through the gold dust night, the area now referred to as the Sunset was a nearly unbroken plain of sand dunes. Not even recognized as a part of San Francisco, when referred to at all, the area was called the Great Sand Waste.

The Outside Lands

In the 1850s and 1860s the developed portion of San Francisco ended near Divisadero Street. Beyond Divisadero lay the area officially designated the "Outside Lands," which consisted of 13,765 acres of wind-blown sand dunes. The few residents of the Outside Lands included a scattered group of squatters who homesteaded in the sand and fought with the city over rightful ownership to the land. The dispute was marked by angry confrontations at City Hall and torchlit parades.

Few roads led through the Outside Lands, making the area almost inaccessible by horse-and-carriage. Only the Point Lobos Toll Road (now Geary Boulevard) and the Ocean House Road interdicted the miles of blowing sand. The Ocean House Road, which began at about Eddy and Divisadero Streets and ran through the dunes to the ocean, was the original precedent to the 19th Avenue stretch of Highway 1 in San Francisco.

The Gridiron Streets of San Francisco

The grid street pattern is so commonplace in American cities that one seldom gives it a second thought. In San Francisco, however, its presence is distinctive because of its incongruity with the city's hilly topography.

In 1845, a surveyor named Jasper O'Farrell drew up San Francisco's most influential platt map, outlining streets and blocks that were cleanly standardized, uniformly measured, and neatly laid down in rectangular form. This scheme has become known as the gridiron street pattern, or as Lewis Mumford calls this influential urban land-use concept: the "speculative ground plan."

The principle of the gridiron is simple: street widths, lot sizes, and block sizes are standardized in a repetitive rectangular format. The underlying concept is just as simple: a standard unit of land is most swiftly reduced to a standard price for purchase, sale, and development. In short, the potential for private profit is greater. This system lends itself to endless repetition by city founders anxious to accommodate new development at a city's edge.

There are problems with such a limited utilitarian approach urban development, however. Frederick Law Olmsted warned San Franciscans in 1865 that the gridiron system paid no attention to their city's unique local topography, its hills, valleys, and potential for stunning views and vistas. Daniel Burnham's 1905 San Francisco plan noted the same: "Where [cutting into hills] follows a well-defined plan of terrain and improvements, it might be permitted, but where it is done simply for immediate commercial gain, it constitutes an affront to public taste and an infringement of public rights which should be strictly prohibited."

The City largely ignored both men, however, and proceeded to develop the streets according to the original grid map. As a result, early San Francisco incurred huge grading, filling, paving, and maintenance costs for streets rammed over hills in straight lines rather than in forms dictated by nature.

Blind application of the gridiron pattern instead of an intelligently platted street system in San Francisco may be a particular misfortune. Entire neighborhoods were built with no regard for the classical considerations of construction: maximum exposure to sun, orientation to accommodate prevailing winds, and enhancement of natural views and landscaping.

County Profile

Geographic

Land Area (acres)	28,800
Land Area (sq. miles)	46.38
Water Area (acres)	29,500
Water Area (sq. miles)	46.1
Acres in Public Ownership	14,009.16
Percent in Public Ownership	48.64
Miles of Public Roads	887
County Seat	San Francisco

Demographic

Population	705,700
State Rank by Population	10
Projected 1990 Population	667,500
Unemployment Rate (state avg. = 9.9)	8.9
Per Capita Personal Income	$15,533
State Rank by Income	4
Total Assessed Property Value	$22,734,915,937

Environment

Roadside Attractions

Resources

Seasons in San Francisco

As you drive up Highway 1 into San Francisco, if you don't like the weather in the first neighborhood, the Sunset, wait until you get to the Park; if you don't like it there, drive a few blocks to the Richmond or the Park Presidio District. If you are still displeased, try any seven blocks in any direction.

The San Francisco Bay Area has weather like

none in the world. Climatologists say that it is unlikely that there exists a populated area anywhere on earth that simultaneously displays as many varieties of weather.

A combination of unique geographical features is responsible for one San Francisco block being blanketed in fog; the next glowing under brilliant sunshine. The city sits at the tip of a rugged peninsula, its elevation ranging from sea level to 938 feet within an area of only 46.38 square miles. The rivers and mountains across the East Bay, the huge inland body of water called San Francisco Bay, and an eclectic mix of land topography here meet the natural forces of the Pacific Ocean. At the continent's edge, an erratic battle constantly rages as continental and oceanic forces collide. The effect on the weather is spectacular.

Spring in San Francisco is characterized by swirling mystical fog, blown in and away often in a matter of minutes or hours by west winds of the Pacific High. During the summer months, the wind and fog pick up in tempo, producing often-predictable cycles of hourly change. The skies sparkle clear at sunrise, and the atmosphere is charged with blowing clouds and fog by noon. Later, the totally fogged-in city warms for a romantic evening.

As the fall months bring changes to other parts of the state and country, San Francisco's warmest period arrives. These are the months you can count on a clear warm day for a picnic in Golden Gate Park, a walk or run over the Golden Gate Bridge, or an afternoon at the beach. September and October are usually the warmest months of the year, with temperatures sometimes reaching to the 80s. Then the clouds come and San Francisco has its rainy season (winter) interspersed with often balmy days until spring arrives again, sometimes as early as March, with its brilliant air and occasional fog.

Where the Freeway Ends

San Francisco begins where the freeway ends. Approached from the south, San Francisco takes Highway 1's route over Interstate 280 and turns it into Juniper Serra Boulevard. Even at its southern edge, the image of San Francisco clearly enforces itself; you'll immediately notice the abrupt change in scale and density from Daly City's sprawl to San Francisco's compactness.

Around the first curve, Juniper Serra gives way to 19th Avenue for a straight course across

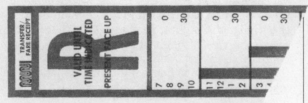

the Sunset District to Golden Gate Park. The streetcar tracks that divide 19th Avenue are those of the M Ocean View Line, which runs all the way to downtown. The M line's light-rail vehicles that operate in some places as a streetcar, in others as a subway, are part of San Francisco's latest addition to its municipal transportation network (Muni), the Muni Metro.

At this early juncture you may want to park your automobile, while parking is still possible, and board the Muni Metro for downtown to discover for yourself why Frank Sinatra said of San Francisco, "Now there's a grown-up swinging town."

AREA CODE: 415

Rules of the Road

Cable cars, electric streetcars, and buses in San Francisco always have the right-of-way. If you park your car on a hill you must set your brake and turn the wheels in against the curb to prevent rolling, or you will find a ticket on your vehicle when you return. Some neighborhoods have restricted parking rules that give preference to residents, so you can only stay in one spot for two hours at a time. Read the curbside signs and watch out for the city's notorious metermaids.

Public Transportation

673-MUNI	San Francisco Muni
788-BART	BART (City and East Bay)
839-2882	AC Transit (to East Bay)
332-6600	Golden Gate Transit (to Marin)
761-7000	SamTrans (to San Mateo)
938-7654	Central Contra Costa
433-1500	Greyhound Bus (all points)
495-4546	Caltrans/Southern Pacific

THE SAN FRANCISCO BAY AREA REGIONAL TRANSIT GUIDE
The Metropolitan Transportation Commission Hotel Claremont, Berkeley 94705. 1983.

The Bay Area is fairly accessible by public transit. The *Guide,* the result of a coordinated effort of the region's transit systems, provides all the basic information and maps you need, as well as route maps, transfer diagrams, and detailed service information.

Hard Cases and Dynamite Factories

So isolated was the land adjacent to 19th Avenue that it was suited for very little. One enterprise was able to take advantage of the desolation, however—dynamite factories. At least two thrived in the area, one on 19th Avenue. The dynamite factories worked overtime to supply the mining operations that were feverishly blasting for gold in the Mother Lode. Had one of the dynamite factories accidently blown up, no one would have even been around to hear.

The district was inhabited by some of the hardest cases in Gold Rush San Francisco. Gruesome types who had been exiled to the Outside Lands by the Vigilance Committee as being too tough for one of the West's toughest towns, found a compatible environment among the isolation of the Outside Lands. There men with explosive instincts could cause no more harm than a dynamite factory.

Few people were brave or desperate enough to live in the Great Sand Waste, although many came for recreation. Among the several roadhouses of notorious repute, none was better known than the Trocadero Inn, an early-day gambling casino that was a popular stop on the Ocean House Road. The Trocadero was located on the homestead of George M. Greene, Jr., today the site of Stern Grove. And the Trocadero still stands; it is known now as the Stern Grove Recreation Hall.

Although Golden Gate Park was marked off in 1870, after a report of the Outside Lands Commission in 1869, its influence on the development of the Outside Lands was minimal until the opening of the Midwinter Exposition in 1894. Many of the Park's earliest workers lived in the Sunset (as the southern portion of the Outside Lands was called after 1887) while they were converting the dunes to green park land, but their numbers were not large. As late as the 1890s there were only 20 or so residences and a couple of dairies in the entire area south of the Park to the ocean.

STAR: Park Merced's Short-Term Auto Rental

The 9,600-unit Park Merced Apartment complex is testing a plan that, if successful, may alter the driving habits of many urban residents and their concept of the private automobile. Under the unique plan, the first in the country, Park Merced residents are being enticed away from two-car ownership and, in some cases, single private-car ownership altogether.

The privately funded program, called "short-term auto rental" (STAR), seeks to free urban residents from the expense and burden of owning a car while allowing them to maintain the freedom of use and choice that public transportation denies.

STAR members pay an annual $25 fee (set off the first year with $25 worth of coupons as part of the promotion campaign). In return, they can check out a car from a centrally located garage at Park Merced. Members receive monthly bills: the rental charge is 60¢ an hour for a subcompact and 14¢ a mile, $5 daily maximum, which includes gas and insurance. A full-sized car costs 90¢ an hour, 18¢ a mile, $9 maximum. The demand so far has been greatest for compacts and wagons.

STAR is based on the economic concept of shared fixed cost. Since the cars are shared, fewer cars are needed overall, and overhead is spread out more effectively. Ownership headaches of repairs, monthly payments, annual insurance, and even gas lines are also eliminated. The idea has been well received at Park Merced. During its first months of operation in 1984, STAR exceeded its required projected-used figures, all with no advertising other than an initial letter, word-of-mouth, and press coverage.

Several Park Merced car owners have already sold their cars, and others have deferred purchase of second cars or new ones. For many people STAR provides an appealing alternative to keeping a car for occasional use and driving it just because it is there.

Doelger City

Most of the houses east and west of 19th Avenue in the Sunset were built after World War II, although the district was originally named in 1887 by Aurelius E. Buckingham and development was first spurred by the arrival of the streetcar in 1918. Best known of the Sunset's developers are Henry and Frank Doelger, who built so many houses in the area that an entire section came to be known as Doelger City.

Building at a rate of two houses a day, the Doelgers became the biggest developers in the nation between 1934 and 1941. The pair made millions from their quick-built houses that came to dot the landscape from the Sunset to Half Moon Bay like points in a Seurat painting. Although the Doelgers' main consideration was never architectural, and many of the houses were shoddily constructed, they did provide a ready supply of affordable housing to an expanding population.

The styles of the houses are also more varied than is apparent from a distance. Mixing French Provincial styles with English Cottage, Colonial Regency, and

International Style Modern, the Doelgers attempted to avoid visual monotony, but the uniform lot sizes (25 ft. by 100 ft.) and construction techniques enforce the impression of sameness. The Doelgers could have done worse; the builders were more responsible to neighborhood planning than strict profit incentives required. For example, they undergrounded utilities and made efforts to provide neighborhood commercial services for the new homeowners.

Environment

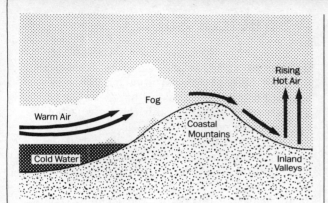

Fog

Highway 1 into San Francisco provides stunning vistas, and often the vibrant coastal weather actively contributes to the view. Sometimes, in fact, the weather may *be* the view. Such is often the case in the Sunset, which locals call the neighborhood where "the fog meets the fog."

Fog, symbol of coastal mystery and romance (or, at least, decreased road visibility), develops as a result of differences in temperature and moisture content between marine air and the air over land masses. In the summer especially, the Pacific High induces a steady flow of northwesterly air toward the Bay Area. On its journey over the open sea, the air close to the ocean surface becomes saturated, dense, and cool, kept next to the surface by a higher inversion layer of warm, lighter air. While the heavy moist air approaches the shore, the water beneath it is rapidly changing temperature as subsurface cold waters are thrust upward by the intruding land. These icy waters meet the already saturated air, condense, and create fog on the ocean surface. Whether the fog stays on shore or rises somewhat to become a low stratus cover ("high fog" to San Franciscans) depends on the force and direction of the surface winds, and on shoreline temperature and topography.

Spring provides the most spectacular fog patterns on the Bay in San Francisco's neighborhoods. At this time of year, as much as a million gallons of water an hour float through the Golden Gate as vapor. This heavily laden moist air meets the warm surface of the Bay, condenses into fog and, thanks to the spring winds from the Pacific High, often moves around the city and Bay in beautiful swirls and patterns as it collides with and caresses the peaks and valleys of the local landscape.

Like all other elements of coastal weather, fog is subject to sudden change—moving out to sea, burning off, or lifting within a short time. It is a unique Northern California attribute and part of the road. Enjoy it.

Roadside Attractions

Neo-Corbusian Architecture and An Epochal Shopping Mall

Immediately past the Park Merced Apartments (built in 1951 by the Metropolitan Life Insurance Company and favoring the strictest rental requirements of any middle-income apartments in San Francisco) lies San Francisco State University. San Francisco State offers a variety of cultural resources—you can sign up for a weekend extension course, or browse through the college bookstore in the student union building. The building, completed in 1980, features elements of updated Corbusian architecture: its exterior is defined by two gigantic pyramids, one of which contains an elevated outdoor ampitheater that seems to be contemplating flight.

Almost adjacent to San Francisco State is the Stonestown Shopping Center, built in 1952 and one of America's first double-anchor shopping malls. (A double-anchor shopping mall uses two

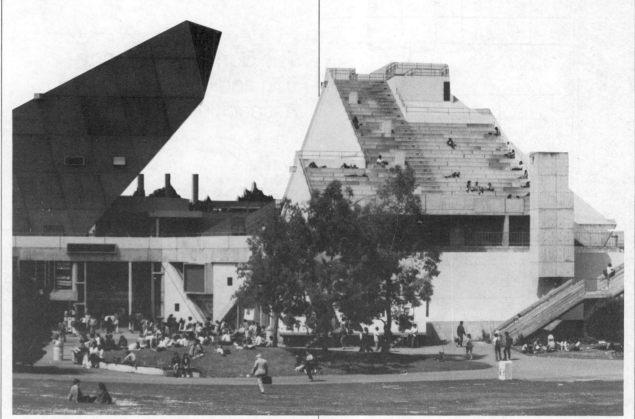

major department stores to "weight" or ensure its economic livelihood and define the ends of interior malls.) Apart from its sociological interest, Stonestown may not be much by current shopping mall standards (although it is being remodeled in 1985), but it is almost all there is of suburban mall shopping in San Francisco, a city where small specialty stores thrive in a pedestrian-oriented environment.

At Taraval, Highway 1 intersects one of the many commercial strips that sprung up aside streetcar routes in the Sunset (in this case the L Taraval streetcar). West of 19th, one may view a surprising vista of the Pacific Ocean thirty blocks away or take in a movie at the Parkside, a repertory house that shows anything from D. W. Griffith to John Cassavetes. East of 19th is the last low-cost motel for miles and miles (Sunset Motel). And to evidence the Sunset's residents' obvious pleasure in kicking up their heels, two dance studios in one block: Arthur Murray's and the Avenue Ballroom, whose offerings include fitness classes, lessons in 1950s jitterbugging, and Greek and Balkan folk-dancing. A few blocks north of Taraval is Ortega and the home of the San Francisco Conservatory of Music.

Resources

San Francisco State

San Francisco State University
1600 Holloway Avenue, San Francisco 94132.

San Francisco State maintains its diverse urban character and the independent spirit that gained it national attention in 1968–69 (when the entire student body went on strike in support of the right to free speech of a radical group whose public address system had been unplugged by then–university president S. I. Hayakawa).

Today you can enroll in classes at the School of Ethnic Studies, which was founded as a compromise to end the strike, attend one-day or weekend seminars or workshops on a variety of contemporary subjects, or enjoy one of a series of lectures, music, and films sponsored by the Associated Students Performing Arts organization. The monthly campus newspaper, *The Golden Gater*, is an award winner. Stop by or write for catalogues and announcements of events.

1st Seal of San Francisco
Adopted Nov. 4th, 1852.   H. Blair

The Sunset

I was given blood tests, aptitude tests, physical co-ordination tests, and Rorschachs, then on a blissful day I was hired as the first Negro on the San Francisco streetcars.

Mother gave me the money to have my blue serge suit tailored, and I learned to fill out work cards, operate the money changer and punch transfers. The time crowded together and at an End of Days I was swinging on the back of the rackety trolley, smiling sweetly and persuading my charges to "step forward in the car, please."

For one whole semester the streetcars and I shimmied up and scooted down the sheer hills of San Francisco. I lost some of my need for the Black ghetto's shielding-sponge quality, as I clanged and cleared my way down Market Street with its honky-tonk homes for homeless sailors, past the quiet retreat of Golden Gate Park and along closed undwelled-in-looking dwellings of the Sunset District.

Maya Angelou

The Sunset Transportation and Development Association

The Sunset Transportation and Development Association (STDA) was organized in March 1921 to "work for the advancement of the Sunset District and the general welfare of San Francisco." Its history both tells a great deal about the aspirations of early Sunset residents and exemplifies the racist attitudes of the early neighborhood.

From its inception the STDA worked hard to bring improved public transportation to the Sunset, realizing that its economic health was tied to the streetcar. The organization worked diligently to secure city approval for a new carline through Duboce Tunnel, which was predicted to enhance immeasurably growth in the Sunset. After much testimony before the Public Utilities Commission, in 1925 the tunnel was approved.

The STDA also petitioned the Board of Supervisors for improved traffic control and the construction of new roadways. They were concerned about humorous matters, such as "the nuisance of autos driving over and above the sidewalks," and more serious ones, like care of the elderly and education. They founded playgrounds and closed down dance halls, complained to the Board of Health about "promiscuous dumping" and worked tirelessly to beautify the Sunset.

But like many early suburban groups, one of their stated fundamental purposes was to "rid the Sunset of undesirables," by which they meant all nonwhites. To prohibit black families from moving in and to "Keep The Sunset White," the STDA hired a land company, and all sales contracts had restrictive clauses—a common practice in early American suburban development that became illegal in 1948.

A Streetcar Suburb

Suburban development is in all cases tied to transportation. In the physical evolution of cities, the availability of transportation has defined the shape of outward expansion from the urban core. The advent of the streetcar in the early part of the century made possible the development of one of San Francisco's earliest suburbs, the Sunset, transforming it from a literal backwash into a near-uniform grid of single-family detached suburban homes.

In the early 20th century, the declining cost of materials and the increased supply of electricity stimulated the expansion of streetcar service. The new electric cars were cheaper to run per passenger mile than their predecessor, the horsecar, and much faster, particularly in outlying areas.

The Tunnel to the Future

Development of the outlying areas of San Francisco as distant as the Sunset did not really begin until 1918, when a group of local land speculators pressured City Hall into constructing a tunnel through Twin Peaks. The tunnel brought streetcar service to the outer Sunset for the first time and

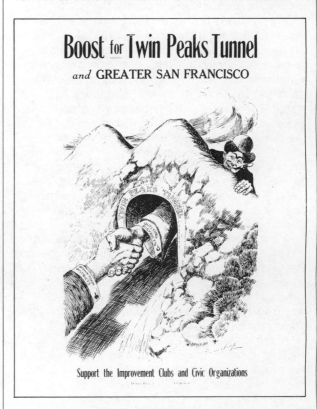

Boost for Twin Peaks Tunnel
and GREATER SAN FRANCISCO

Support the Improvement Clubs and Civic Organizations

linked it to the downtown area. Constructed with funding obtained through a $3 million tax assessment, the Twin Peaks Tunnel was built for a small sum compared to the millions that were made by the construction companies that followed, building house after house on the former sand dunes.

The Commercial Strip

Characteristic of the Sunset's "streetcar suburb" form are the commercial strips that follow along the main transportation lines of the original streetcars. Taraval, Irving, Judah, and parts of 19th Avenue all reflect their origins as strips of shops and services that sprung up alongside the streetcar routes and prospered as the centers of activity for the area.

The streetcar strip became the dominant form of commercial activity until the automobile generally replaced the streetcar after World War II, bringing about the automobile commercial strip and the development of the shopping center. The streetcar was more than the lifeline that sped the new suburbanites to their downtown jobs—it also became the focus of activity for much of their lives, determining sometimes how, and usually where, activities took place.

San Francisco's Hills

San Francisco's 46.38 square miles stretch from sea level to 938 feet above the ocean. In between, the peninsular city provides an eclectic profile of hill and valley, making this one of the most geographically diverse cities in the world.

Many people think that San Francisco, like her spiritual sister Rome, has seven hills. The names that come to mind are Telegraph Hill, Nob Hill, Rincon Hill, Twin Peaks, Russian Hill, Lone Mountain, and Mt. Davidson. The city actually has many more hills—at least 43, many of which exceed 500 feet in height.

This proliferation of hill and valley in so small an area is result of the relatively young, unstable base of this geologically turbulent city. The Franciscan Formation, comprised mostly of sandstone (graywacke type), shale, and volcanic rock provides the foundation of San Francisco. It is one of the world's most erodible and unstable geological foundations in a metropolitan area, but it makes for a beautiful city.

Heights of the Hills

225'	Alamo Heights	448'	Lone Mountain
260'	Anza Hill	515'	McLaren Ridge
325'	Bernal Heights	500'	Merced Heights
569'	Buena Vista Heights	938'	Mt. Davidson
500'	Candlestick Point	570'	Mt. Olympus
407'	Castro Hill	250'	Mt. St. Joseph
206'	Cathedral Hill	918'	Mt. Sutro
350'	City College Hill	376'	Nob Hill
200'	College Hill	370'	Pacific Heights
510'	Corona Heights	400'	Parnassus Heights
360'	Dolores Heights	300'	Potrero Hill
600'	Edgehill Heights	370'	Presidio Heights
315'	Excelsior Heights	689'	Red Rock Hill
700'	Forest Hill	120'	Rincon Hill
679'	Gold Mine Hill	294'	Russian Hill
274'	Holly Hill	412'	Strawberry Hill
275'	Hunters Point Ridge	200'	Sutro Heights
250'	Irish Hill	284'	Telegraph Hill
378'	Lafayette Heights	903'	Twin Peaks (North)
725'	Larsen Peak	910'	Twin Peaks (South)
264'	Laurel Hill	265'	University Mound
380'	Lincoln Heights	260'	Washington Heights

The City of St. Francis

The City and County of San Francisco bears the name of its patron saint, Saint Francis, among the most famous and best loved of all saints. Born in 1182 at Assisi, Italy, his father was a wealthy merchant who changed his son's name from John Bernardone to Francisco. Francis of Assisi founded the order of Friars Minor in 1208 and died in 1226 at the age of 45.

Stern Grove

P.O. Box 44690, San Francisco 94114, or call: 398-6551.

At 19th and Sloat is the entrance to Stern Grove, where the Trocadero Inn used to fete the social elite and its aspirants in early San Francisco. The building still stands after a 1930s remodeling by Bernard Maybeck and is available for rental for almost any purpose at a modest fee. The pungent eucalyptus that cover the entire grove also contain a magnificent natural amphitheater that offers free Sunday concerts in the summertime, a tradition since 1938.

A typical summer program at the Grove runs from June through August. Sunday fare ranges from New Orleans jazz to Midsummer Mozart conducted by George Cleve, or a program of country western music, or another prepared for the Grove's stage by the San Francisco Ballet. All shows begin at 2:00 pm and are free.

Fire Hydrants

To learn all about San Francisco's renowned fire department, and even more about the fire hydrants you may spot along the road, visit the Fire Department Museum (558-3981). If you can't make it, you will want to at least know these colorful facts about the city's hydrants:

Large white hydrants are connected to a special high-pressure water supply that is separate from other city water supplies. Large hydrants with red tops are connected to a tank that is effective for fighting fires at elevations of 150 feet. Large hydrants with blue tops are connected to a tank whose pressure is effective only at targets under 150 feet. Standard street-corner hydrants with green tops indicate proximity to one of 150 underground cisterns holding 75,000 gallons of water—these reserves can be pumped out by special high-suction fire hoses should something go wrong with the water supply to the hydrant.

The San Francisco Conservatory of Music

1201 Ortega Street, San Francisco 94122. 564-8086.

The Conservatory of music is a unique Highway 1 resource, offering extension programs for adults, preparatory instruction to Bay Area children, and a master class program in which nationally renowned musicians work individually with the Conservatory's most promising students before a public audience. Stop by for the daily program or write or call for the season's schedule.

THE PEOPLE'S RAILWAY: THE HISTORY OF THE MUNICIPAL RAILWAY OF SAN FRANCISCO
Anthony Perles
Interurban Press, Glendale. 1981.

Muni is unique among the world's transit systems, simultaneously operating streetcars, a light-rail subway, electric trolley coaches, motor coaches, and cable cars. The political battles, physical challenges, and city-shaping decisions made during development of this system formed the city we know today. *The People's Railroad* tells this story in words, charts, photographs, maps, blueprints, and engineer's drawings.

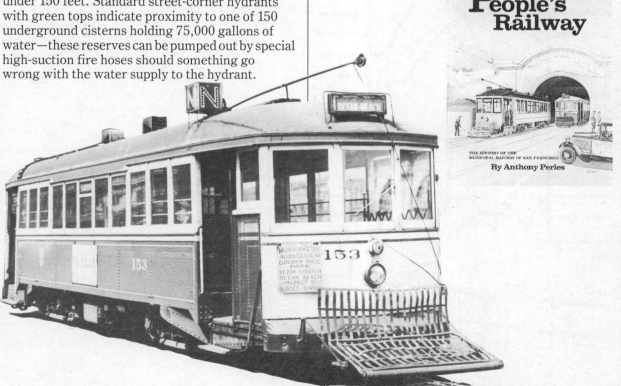

The People's Railway

THE HISTORY OF THE MUNICIPAL RAILWAY OF SAN FRANCISCO
By Anthony Perles

The Beginnings of Golden Gate Park

When Golden Gate Park was marked off amid the desolation of the Outside Lands in 1870, a lot of people thought the decision was insane: A park in the middle of the Great Sand Waste?

When the first topographical survey of the Park was prepared, the area was still a Sahara, inaccessible and barren. For more than 10 years after work had begun, the closest transportation was a horsecar that stopped well short of the Park's entrance. Getting to the Park required both the physical dexterity needed to negotiate the mud and sand by foot and the courage to brave one of the toughest sections of the Outside Lands, where hooligans and desperados often lay in wait.

In 1871 William Hammond Hall began the formidable task of reclaiming arable land from the dunes. Hall's plan was to start from the ocean and work eastward to the better soils, a scheme that required the construction of a road to the Park's western edge and then the construction of a barrier to fend off the blowing wind and sand. The North Ridge Road was built in record time for half the cost of municipal streets and gave the Park its first interior definition.

Beyond expectations, the Park became an extremely popular attraction, particularly for well-heeled San Franciscans who sought an arcadian alternative to the city's rough-and-tumble street life. The Park was ordered, landscaped, and relatively well mannered, and bespoke a sense of civilization unavailable amid the griminess of the burgeoning city. Since the absence of public transportation effectively prevented the poor from getting there, the Park became the near-exclusive domain of those wealthy enough to ride to the Park in two-horse phaetons with shiny leather harnesses and brass adornments or in silk-lined family carriages that had room enough inside for the children's nurse.

And still the Park grew in popularity. By 1886, three streetcar lines to the Park were finally completed and more than 47,000 streetcar riders joined the hundreds of visitors in carriages and on horseback. After 100 iron settees were placed in discreet spots, the Park became the preferred alternative to chaperoned front parlors for young lovers, who kissed and squeezed beneath an approving moon. Newspapers clucked at the phenomenon and older citizens, perhaps unconsciously envious, talked about how the settees were undermining the morals of the city's youth.

The Making of the Park

There is not a full-grown tree of beautiful proportions near San Francisco, nor have I seen any young trees that promised fairly, except perhaps, of certain compact, clumpy forms of evergreens, wholly wanting in grace and cheerfulness. It would not be wise nor safe to undertake to form a park upon any plan which assumed as a certainty that trees which would delight the eye can be made to grow near San Francisco.

Frederick Law Olmsted, 1865

Many agreed with Olmsted in 1866. No intelligent person would dream of a major park or even of many trees in San Francisco, especially in the desolate, blowing sand dunes of the Outside Lands. Within a decade, however, William Hammond Hall had proved differently. All the trees, shrubs, flowers, grasses—everything that grows in Golden Gate Park—are the descendants of plants placed here sheltered and nourished by human hands and the human heart.

Forestation of the Dunes

Hall's forestation of the sand dunes was an environmental feat of grand proportions, and one unlikely to be duplicated. (The conventional ecological wisdom of the 1980s calls for restoring sand dunes, not for landscaping them with non-indigenous plants.)

Hall was not interested in restoring sand dunes; he wanted to cover them with lush landscaping so that people could walk among the flowers and lie upon the grass rather than brace themselves against whipping, stinging sand.

Forestating the Outside Lands presented three major challenges: (1) stabilization of large hills and valleys of blowing sand for a long enough time to allow vegetation to root in wind-protected segments; (2) selection and growth of seedlings of the appropriate plants and trees; and (3) protection, nourishment, and coaxing of newly planted seedlings until they could hold their own against the harsh environment.

Stabilization of the Hills

Hall's landscape architect's eye saw beyond the surface of the sand of the Outside Lands. He could trace the scattered rock outcroppings and vague lines of subsand hills and valleys. Through these natural features, he laid out the main roads whose existence may have been mandated by the economic and political pressures of getting people to the beaches, but whose character

was determined by a basic landscaping rationale. The width of the roads and their serpentine pattern were designed to break the force of the winds over the bare sands. They remain today much as he planned them.

The drifting dunes on the park's western edge were soon brought under control by a method now commonly used for snowdrift management. Posts were placed at close intervals, and boards, lupine, and brush were stretched between them to catch the blowing sand. As the barrier was topped, more boards and brush were laid, creating a perpetual haven on the inland side. While these exercises continued, the sand in the park's interior was constantly mixed with street sweepings, humus, peat, and imported soils.

Selection of Trees and Plants

The task of identifying and obtaining trees and shrubs for the park led Hall to some unorthodox decisions and unusual methods. He risked the wrath of local nurserymen by developing all his seedlings himself at the new park nursery. Spurning traditional East Coast "park trees" like the elm, chestnut, or live oak, Hall looked to species that understood and thrived in the harsh coastal environment. The nursery soon held seedlings of tough Monterey cypress and pine, which rooted elsewhere on coastal cliffs, rock, and sand. They were joined by young blue gums called eucalyptus, brought from Australia and found to be stubborn to wind and drought. In addition to these three pioneer trees, Hall gathered specimens of a variety of natural beach grasses and bushy shrubs such as the coastal lupine and European beach grass.

Nourishment of Newly Planted Seedlings

Several different accounts describe the circumstances under which the first plants took root in the new park. One story recounts a crew of frustrated gardeners who happened to notice that quickly germinating barley had fallen from their horses' burlap feedbags into the sand and was sprouting up around the horses' feet. Another credits the burlap itself, claiming that a rotten piece of the porous material fell on top of the spilled barley, providing a screen from the elements while the grain took hold. Yet another source describes eager crews of young boys scrambling hills and beaches for lupine seeds and beach grasses, these to be planted in the thousands until a few could take hold.

Whenever the moment of conception, some grass or grain eventually sprouted in enough abundance and vitality to allow the chain of ecological succession to begin, one pioneer plant providing temporary shelter for another to get a roothold, and that one protecting another and another. The park began to bloom. Forestation worked and the result was a "green oasis in the arid desert of business and dissipation."

Golden Gate Park

No city has anything like Golden Gate Park, the most enchanted of urban places in an enchanted city. This is where the scarecrow found his brains, the tinman his heart, the lion his courage, and where Dorothy, that intrepid urban adventurer, discovered that she could never go back to Kansas again.

It is not too much to say that there is more to do in Golden Gate Park than one could ever imagine. Sweep away images of parks that lie moribund beneath the backsides of tired picnickers—Golden Gate Park is one of the most lively urban spaces in the world. Its splendorous beauty means less than its ebullience, its vigor, its convivial heart.

The most predictable joys to be had in Golden Gate Park derive from its unpredictable pleasures. The park is full of surprises, and it contains them just carefully enough to spring them jack-in-the-box-style when the moment is ripest. Allow yourself the opportunity to wander, even get lost, and be surprised by events and attractions that you would never have dreamed.

The Fathers of Golden Gate Park

William Hammond Hall was Golden Gate Park's first superintendent and engineer. Hall surveyed and laid down the initial plans for the park, which were adopted by the Board of Park Commissioners in December 1871.

John McLaren was superintendent of Golden Gate Park from 1873 to 1943. Thought by many to be a horticultural genius, McLaren devoted his professional life to realizing Hall's initial vision and plans for the park. Under McLaren's guidance and protection, the park matured and withstood many attempts to overdevelop it with structures and monuments.

Park Information

Golden Gate Park
558-3706

Headquarters for the Recreation and Parks Department of the City and County of San Francisco are located in Golden Gate Park at McLaren Lodge. Open Monday through Friday during business hours; general information and maps available.

Friends of Recreation and Parks
221-1310

The Friends are a nonprofit organization dedicated to the support and enhancement of San Francisco's parks and recreation programs, one of the most comprehensive neighborhood-serving programs in the nation. At Golden Gate Park, the Friends were responsible for the renovation of the children's playground, the purchase of benches for the music concourse, improvements to the Tea Garden and Lily Lake, and the acquisition of a van for use by the Senior Citizens' Center. Members conduct free walking tours throughout the park as well as the city.

Helen Crocker Russell Library of Horticulture
661-1514

This library is located near the main entrance across from the general information kiosk (where you can pick up self-guided tours and maps of the gardens). Open daily from 10 am to 4 pm, the collection includes over 10,000 titles and 100 periodicals devoted to horticulture and related subjects. There is also a smaller collection of nursery catalogues, rare botanical books, and slide photographs.

Hall of Flowers
558-3623

On a given day as many as four or five different events may take place at the Hall of Flowers. Write or call for the month's calendar of events.

PACIFIC OCEAN

[Map of Golden Gate Park with labeled features including: Great Highway, Murphy Windmill, Dutch Windmill, La Playa, 48th Ave., 47th Ave., Beroit Equitation Field, Chain of Lakes Dr. West, Chain of Lakes Dr. East, North Lake, South Lake, Buffalo Paddock, Fly Casting Pool, Middle Lake, Spreckels Lake, Golden Gate Park Stadium, Metson Lake, Lincoln Way, Mallard Lake, Elk Glen Lake, Lloyd Lake, Kennedy, Stow Lake, Stow Lake Drive, Japanese Tea Garden, Spreckles Bandshell, De Young Museum, Shakespeare's Garden, Music Concourse, African Hall Planetarium Aquarium, California Academy of Sciences, Nursery, Lily Pond, Conservatory, Middle Dr., Bowling Greens, Tennis Courts, McLaren Lodge, Kezar Stadium, Alvord Lake, streets: 41st Ave., 43rd Ave., 36th Ave., 30th Ave., 25th Ave., 19th Ave., 10th Ave., 9th Ave., 8th Ave., 7th Ave., 6th Ave., 3rd Ave., Arguello, Frederick St., Stanyan St., Page St., Hayes St., Grove St., Sunset Blvd., Kezar, Keokuk, Stanyan]

The Speed Road

In 1886 the San Francisco Bridge Company was awarded a contract to construct a track for "speeding" horses. The road ran near what is now Highway 1 as it intersects Golden Gate Park. But it was always controversial, particularly to those park users who preferred more sedate recreation and saw the speed track as being chiefly for those wealthy enough to own expensive horses.

Construction was interrupted by a severe storm in December 1889 that seriously damaged the Speed Road. The fierce gales also caused widespread unemployment throughout the state, which moved the Archbishop of San Francisco to establish a $30,000 fund to hire the jobless. The fund helped pay for more than 1,000 workers receiving $1 a day to complete the Speed Road and the South Drive to Ocean Beach. Once completed, the Speed Road became one of the Park's major attractions, a place where showy equestrians could parade their blooded horses and demonstrate their talents in front of admiring eyes.

The Social Vitality of a Park

The best urban parks reflect the best features of the city of which they are a part, socially, culturally, and historically. Like cities, urban parks generally thrive or stagnate according to their capability to attract a mixture of users for a variety of activities.

Parks that show the greatest vitality are places where, in Jane Jacobs's words, people visit "for different reasons at different times, sometimes to sit tiredly, sometimes to play or watch a game, sometimes to read or walk, sometimes to show off, sometimes to fall in love, sometimes to keep

an appointment, sometimes to savor the hustle of the city from a retreat, sometimes in the hope of finding acquaintances, sometimes to get closer to a bit of nature, sometimes to keep a child occupied, sometimes simply to see what offers, and almost always to be entertained by the sight of other people."

More than all the green grass and trees, it is people that define a park's environment. Golden Gate Park, like America's best urban open spaces, attains a strong sense of vitality because of its crazy quilt of park visitors who are always engaged in a variety of activities as diverse as the law allows.

On any given day, Golden Gate Park teems with people from a mix of races, nationalities, and economic backgrounds. All of this leads to the most beneficial of arrangements, in which a public space is vitalized by human activity, at the same time that we as social beings are enlivened by our connection to others.

De Young and Spreckels: Just a Shot Away

The namesakes of two of Golden Gate Park's most enduring attractions—de Young Museum and

Spreckels Bandshell—figured prominently in wild west San Francisco. The two were also involved in a personal animosity that culminated in Adolph Spreckels shooting his rival Michael de Young.

De Young came from a family that was no stranger to violence nor to character assassination. After staircasing the *Chronicle* into a large-circulation daily newspaper attended by numerous libel suits and allegations of blackmail, the de Youngs incurred the wrath of Isaac Kalloch, a Baptist minister elected mayor in 1879. Kalloch parried the *Chronicle's* attacks by accusing de Young's mother of running a whorehouse and his brother Gustavius of being an inmate in an insane asylum. Brother Charles de Young responded by shooting and nearly killing Kalloch. Shortly afterward, Kalloch's son shot and killed Charles.

The son of another notorious California bloodline, Adolph Spreckels ran the family business in San Francisco that included the *San Francisco Call*. The newspaper had been acquired by the Spreckels to fight the annexation of Hawaii, which threatened their sugar empire, then operating as a virtual monopoly.

In 1884, the *Chronicle* alleged that Adolph Spreckels had been involved in stock fraud; in return Spreckels shot Michael de Young. De Young recovered, later to become a prominent conservative Republican who promoted the Midwinter Fair in 1894 and donated the de Young Museum to the city. Today the park monuments named after de Young and Spreckels sit within pistol range of each other, expressing a deceptive dignity for two men whose reputations have been sanitized by time.

Environment

Urban Birds

Birds, like people, have preferred places of residence. Some seek solitude in wilderness areas and along remote coastal shores. Others stake out their territory in densely populated areas. In this category are the earthern brown towhees, colorful scrubjays, fussy titmice, fleeting hummingbirds, and more than a hundred other species of birds that populate San Francisco's neighborhoods and parks. And, of course, there are the pigeons.

Pigeons

The common urban pigeon is really a rock dove, a species introduced from Europe. They are seen moving on short legs across a park or plaza, feeding furiously on seeds and scraps, always more anxious to walk than to fly. Few statues are unadorned by commemorative pigeon droppings.

There are more than 290 species of pigeons and rock doves in the world, many of them spectacularly colored. But the ones in U.S. cities are usually gray, brown, or dirty white. And, although babies, dogs, and some bench sitters enjoy watching them, many other people consider them pests.

Even the most ardent bird lovers express disdain

Why Don't You Ever See a Baby Pigeon?

It is not true that pigeons clone themselves at adult size. Rather, baby pigeons remain well hidden in nests high in trees or under eaves of buildings. For an unusually long infancy, they stay there, nurtured by "pigeon milk" provided by both parents. This urban adaptation protects the hapless squabs until they are able to handle the stress of adult pigeon life.

for this urban resident. Because pigeons displace native bird species, wreak aesthetic havoc with buildings and public plazas, and spread diseases, cities like San Francisco conduct extensive pigeon population control programs, relying on the distribution of pigeon birth control pellets, among other methods.

Roadside Attractions

Two Gardens

Beyond the park buildings are attractions that surprise and delight. Close by the concourse is the Japanese Tea Garden, one of the few surviving features of the 1894 Exposition and the Park's most popular attraction. Within its three acres are wonderful expressions of Oriental serenity that strive for the Buddhist ideal of unification of the human and the natural. Through the bonsai and cherry blossoms and aside reflective pools, the paths lead to the giant Buddha. Along the way are exquisite granite lanterns, a teahouse, a moonbridge, and benches for contemplation and meditation. If you are attentive, and if you have chosen a time when the crowds are not too great, you may gain something from your expedition beyond the mundane.

WILL POWER

Behind the Academy of Sciences Building is another park treasure—the Garden of Shakespeare's Flowers. Here you'll find more than 150 varieties of flowers mentioned in the works of Shakespeare, who certainly knew his daffodils and daisies:

> *When daisies pied and violets blue*
> *And lady-smocks all silver-white*
> *And cuckoo-buds of yellow hue*
> *Do paint the meadows with delight.*

Love's Labor's Lost *V,*2

Within a locked box is a bronze bust of Shakespeare cast from a 1623 carving thought to have been modeled by the Bard. Shakespeare's Garden is one of the loveliest spots in the park, an unsurpassed location to spend a few hours with a good book or to discover how easily "one touch of nature makes the whole world kin."

Indoor Park Resources

Many buildings in the park offer programs of interest to the Highway 1 traveler, guided docent interpretative tours, and a multitude of special events. Consult any of the guides, books, and maps listed or call the number given.

Asian Art Museum of San Francisco.
387-5922.
Houses the internationally renowned Avery Brundage Collection as well as over 10,000 art objects from China, Japan, India, and other Asian cultures.

California Academy of Sciences and the Morrison Planetarium.
752-8268.
Includes the Steinhart Aquarium, a dizzying fish roundabout, touchable tidepool, anthropological exhibits, and discovery room for children. Bookstore.

Resources

A Park History and Guide

THE MAKING OF GOLDEN GATE PARK: 1865–1906
Raymond H. Clary
A California Living Book, San Francisco. 1980.

Details the story of one of the world's great urban parks, from sand waste to cherished gem, tracing the political, engineering, economical, social, and cultural history of the Park and thereby revealing much about the history of San Francisco as well. The book is elaborately illustrated with the author's personal collection of rare historical photographs.

The Making of Golden Gate Park
The Early Years: 1865-1906

Raymond H. Clary

GOLDEN GATE PARK AT YOUR FEET
Margot Patterson Doss
Presidio Press, San Rafael. 1978.

Margo Patterson Doss is the Bay Area's best-known walker and author of several books about the region. This volume on the park is among her best. The reader is taken on the "Walk McLaren Loved," "A Stroll in Rhododendron Row," and a "Walk in the Bard's Garden," among the 43 strolls in the book.

M.H. de Young Memorial Museum.
752-5561.
Hosts internationally significant exhibitions and maintains a respected collection representative of the history of Western art from ancient Egypt, Greece, and Rome through the present. Museum Society Bookstore includes Asian, de Young, and city resources.

Spreckles Temple of Music.
Free shows on almost any summer weekend in this 1900 bandshell. Home of the Golden Gate Park Band, the oldest continuously operating municipal band in the United States.

Senior Citizen's Center.
751-4926.
Open every day since 1965, the center conducts a major program of events and activities.

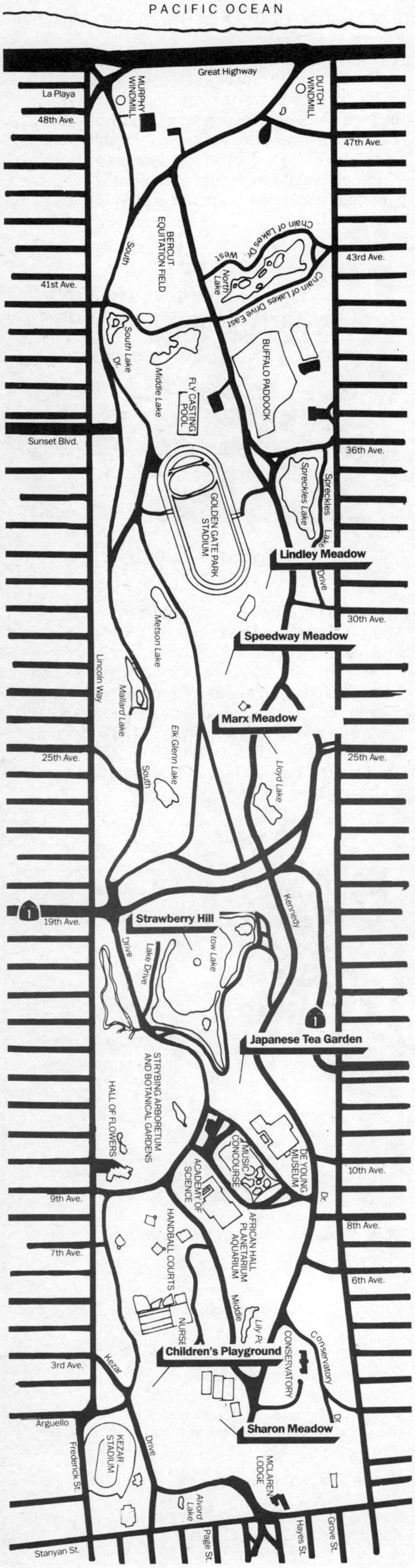

PACIFIC OCEAN

[Map of Golden Gate Park with labeled features including: La Playa, 48th Ave., Great Highway, 47th Ave., Murphy Windmill, Dutch Windmill, Chain of Lakes West, North Lake, 43rd Ave., Berout Equitation Field, South, 41st Ave., Middle Lake, South Lake Dr., Buffalo Paddock, Fly Casting Pool, Sunset Blvd., 36th Ave., Spreckles Lake, Spreckles Lake Dr., Golden Gate Park Stadium, Lindley Meadow, 30th Ave., Speedway Meadow, Metson Lake, Lincoln Way, Mallard Lake, Elk Glenn Lake, South, Lloyd Lake, Marx Meadow, 25th Ave., Kennedy Dr., Strawberry Hill, Low Lake, Lake Drive, 19th Ave., Japanese Tea Garden, Stryking Arboretum and Botanical Gardens, Hall of Flowers, Music Concourse, Academy of Science, De Young Museum, 10th Ave., African Hall Planetarium Aquarium, 9th Ave., Handball Courts, 8th Ave., 7th Ave., Nurse Lily Pt., Middle Dr., Conservatory, 6th Ave., Children's Playground, 3rd Ave., Conservatory Dr., Kezar Dr., Arguello, Kezar Stadium, Sharon Meadow, McLaren Lodge, Frederick St., Stanyan St., Alvord Lake, Page St., Hayes St., Grove St.]

The Midwinter Fair

*So twice five miles of fertile ground
With walls and towers were girdled round:
And there were gardens bright with sinuous rills,
Where blossomed many an incense-bearing tree.*

Coleridge

The most certain early enchantment in Golden Gate Park was the Midwinter Fair of 1894. The Fair was "a miracle of rare device" that brought new attention to the Park and adjacent neighborhoods, and marked the moment from which the

entire area began to be considered as part of San Francisco.

The Fair was conceived during a period of national economic hardship when many local banks had failed and unemployment was soaring. Noting the stimulating effect of the Columbian Exposition in Chicago on that city's business climate, a group of San Franciscans led by M. H. de Young decided that a similar extravaganza might aid San Francisco's troubled economy. The Fair was held in the middle of winter to demonstrate to the world—particularly to the snowbound East Coast—the appeal of San Francisco's salubrious climate.

The Fair was located on over 200 acres just east of Strawberry Hill, which now overlooks Highway 1's route through Golden Gate Park, and the site today hosts the De Young Museum, the Academy of Sciences, and the Music Concourse. South Drive was used for the Fair's midway or fun zone.

Groundbreaking ceremonies in August 1883 produced the largest parade crowd ever gathered on the Pacific. Schools, businesses, banks, and municipal offices closed for the opening-day festivities, and thousands rushed to the city's western edge to see what wizardry had produced at the Midwinter Fair.

Restoration of the Children's Playground

The first Children's Playground at Golden Gate Park was dedicated in 1888, a Victorian wonder consisting of game yards, a maypole, wooden slides, and homemade swings (one set for girls, one for boys). At the center was the new Sharon Building, named for park donor Senator William P. Sharon. This Richardson Romanesque structure housed water fountains, ice cream fountains, soda stands, dairy rooms, storerooms, and stables for goats. There were also six bicycles, six tricycles, six baby carriages, two donkeys, and three croquet sets. The first playground was an immediate success with visitors to the park, and there have been several major restoration projects in the almost 100 years since.

The Mary B. Connolly Children's Playground

The most recent restoration of the playground was completed in 1978. New mazes of up-to-date play equipment and climbing structures now cover the old play yards, and a series of long bumpy slides are set into the steep bankment at the south end. The restoration also reinstalled a lost, but loved entertainment, the Farmyard with its goats, chickens, sheep, and ducks.

The Golden Gate Carousel

The Children's Playground at Golden Gate Park has what is surely among America's most wonderful carousels. The Noah's Ark merry-go-round consists of 62 figures, 2 chariots, 36 interpictorials, murals, glass, brass, and organ music to bring out even the most submerged child in us all.

This carousel first arrived in the Park in 1939 after service at the World's Fair on Treasure Island. It was carved in upper New York State around 1912 by the Herschell-Spillman Company. Declared unsafe in 1977, the carousel was closed and a CETA-funded restoration project began. Eventually funds for the $800,000 job were raised by citizens and allocated from other public programs. Twelve artisans worked more than 200 hours on each animal during the seven-year project, applying three coats of primer and six to eight layers of paint to the reconstructed, repaired, and often recarved animals. The work is of such quality that individual pieces were exhibited in museums and public galleries throughout the Bay Area during the restoration period.

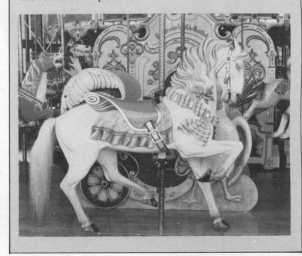

Environment

Flowers of All Colors

Golden Gate Park is a floral field that lends truth to the popular 1920s saying that "Los Angeles may be California's diamond stomache, but San Francisco is the poppies in her hair." The Park provides a stunning year-round floral spectacle, with the main show in the spring and summer.

Rhododendrons—including descendants from a plant imported from Kew Gardens and another from the Himalayas—bloom throughout the Park in splendid ranges from pure white to cream, pink,

San Francisco's Flower

The dahlia partakes essentially of the character of our beloved city, in birth, breeding, and habit, for it was originally Mexican, carried thence to Spain, to France and England in turn, being changed in the process from a simple daisylike wild flower to a cosmopolitan beauty.

Board of Supervisors, Resolution #26244, October 4, 1926, making the dahlia the official city flower.

rose, lavender, wine, and blood red. Azaleas abound next to bedded masses of daffodils, jonquils, waxy rosettes of cream and pink and rose camellias, magnolia, and tulip trees. The western rose garden offers over 60 varieties, many of them under study or just being developed by the American Rose Society. The Conservatory of Flowers, the oldest remaining building in the Park, and a replica of Kew Gardens, offers spectacular tropical displays.

Golden Gate Park has a wealth of specialized gardens, many within the Strybing Aboretum. One unique spot is the Garden of Fragrance, designed for the enjoyment of the blind with Braille plaques identifying the distinctive-smelling plants. The nearby Biblical Garden features only plants mentioned in the Old Testament. There is a succulent garden around one path, a Japanese moon-viewing garden around another. An Opera Garden aims at eventually containing all the plants mentioned in the world's greatest operas.

When you pull off on Highway 1 for a walk through San Francisco's Golden Gate Park, you have the opportunity to indulge almost any floral, herbal, arboreal, or sylvan desire you ever dreamt of.

Roadside Attractions

Meadows: Marx, Sharon, Lindley, and Speedway

Within Golden Gate Park are also several large meadows that resemble parks within a park. Each of these lush green expanses was used at one time or another for free rock concerts during the salad days of rock and roll, when groups like the Jefferson Airplane, Quicksilver Messenger Service, Big Brother and the Holding Company, and It's a Beautiful Day performed to a devoted audience with shared cultural ideals.

Theater in the Parks: Legacy of the San Francisco Mime Troupe

On any given weekend one is likely to find live theater and performances in San Francisco's parks and public plazas. This is the legacy of the San Francisco Mime Troupe, the city's oldest theater company. The Mime Troupe has never been based in any one indoor theater, but performs instead on a movable stage in parks, plazas, or wherever the people are. The collective enjoys local, national, and international respect, earned after 25 years literally on the streets.

The Mime Troupe was founded in 1959 by R. G. (Ronnie) Davis, not as a white-faced mime group in the silent traditional style; rather, as Davis explained, "Mime is the point of departure of our style in which words sharpen and refine, but substance of meaning is in action." Posing political alternatives and encouraging people to act on them is the consistent theme of their work, and free public appearances (passing the hat) has been their enduring method.

The streets were not always open, however. In 1965 Davis was arrested and began a harsh legal battle to gain the right to perform on public property in San Francisco. The American Civil Liberties Union's defense was successful, and benefits by the Jefferson Airplane, Grateful Dead, and others not only supported the Troupe's free shows but also

launched its then-producer Bill Graham on his career as czar of the outdoor rock concert.

Today city officials cooperate with these and other artists to make San Francisco one of the world's leaders in outdoor performances. For the Mime Troupe's current schedule call 285-1717.

Today there are no more such concerts in the park. Rock and roll music has become a billion-dollar industry whose performers have little interest in free concerts, and obtaining a city permit for such large gatherings has become a virtual impossibility. The meadows—Speedway Meadow, Sharon Meadow, Lindley Meadow, and Marx Meadow (not named for Karl but Johanna, a park fund contributor)—still endure, however, and they are fine places to attend. And the meadows are probably somewhat better off minus the large crowds that trampled them under, even if a miraculous ceremony of innocence has been lost.

The Fortune Cookie

The fortune cookie forms the indispensable conclusion to any Chinese restaurant meal in America. It is almost impossible to imagine the fortune cookie as anything but Chinese in origin and traditional in use. Well, like television wrestling and chop suey, fortune cookies are less authentic than one might believe.

The fortune cookie was, in fact, invented in Golden Gate Park and its inventor was Japanese, not Chinese. Makato Hagiwara, who managed the Tea Garden before he was deported in 1942, introduced his creation to an eager public in 1901. Kimono-clad women served the new cookies with tea to a fascinated clientele for 10¢. No reports describe what fortunes were involved.

So popular did fortune cookies become that eventually they were exported to China, perhaps for use at restaurants featuring American cuisine.

Resources

Outdoor Park Resources

Recreation

Here is a partial list of outdoor activities in the Park. Consult the Reineck & Reineck map and guide for more information, or call the Park.

Archery: Range near 47th Avenue with bales; bring your own equipment.

Baseball: Two hardball and two softball diamonds.

Basketball: Free play practice courts on the Panhandle.

Bicycling: 7.5 miles of bike trails; racing track at the Polo Fields.

Boating: Stow Lake offers rowboats, pedal and electric boats for rent.

Cards: Two card shelters with space for hundreds of players.

Carriage Rides: Horse-drawn rides throughout the park.

Fly Casting: Casting pools near Anglers' Lodge; bring equipment.

Football: Playfield may be reserved at the Polo Field.

Golf: Nine-hole course with par 3 holes; green fee.

Handball: Two indoor and two outdoor courts.

Horseback Riding: Rental stables and 27 miles of bridle paths; lessons available.

Jogging: Jogging trails, parcourses, and a senior citizens' exercise course.

Lawn Bowling: Free lessons and green south of the tennis courts.

Model Yacht Sailing: Wind and motor-powered models on Spreckles Lake.

Petanque: Court opposite 38th Avenue.

Picnics: Groups of 25 or more should reserve space; all others free.

Playgrounds: Mary B. Connolly Children's Playground (see feature).

Soccer: Three soccer pitches.

Tennis: 21 tennis courts opposite Conservatory of Flowers; make reservations.

Map

PACIFIC OCEAN

Great Highway
Murphy Windmill (Unrestored) **Dutch Windmill (Restored)**

La Playa
48th Ave.
41st Ave.
Sunset Blvd.
25th Ave.
19th Ave.
9th Ave.
7th Ave.
3rd Ave.
Arguello
Frederick St.
Stanyan St.

43rd Ave.
36th Ave.
30th Ave.
25th Ave.
10th Ave.
8th Ave.
6th Ave.

BERCUT EQUITATION FIELD

Buffalo Paddock
Fly Casting Pools

Chain of Lakes Dr. West
North Lake
Chain of Lakes Drive East

GOLDEN GATE PARK STADIUM

Lloyd Lake
Metson Lake
Mallard Lake
Elk Glen Lake
Spreckels Lake
Lake

South Dr.
Lincoln Way
Kennedy
Stow Lake Drive
Middle Dr.

Stow Lake

Strybing Arboretum

HALL OF FLOWERS

MUSIC CONCOURSE
DE YOUNG MUSEUM
ACADEMY OF SCIENCE
AFRICAN HALL
PLANETARIUM
AQUARIUM
HANDBALL COURTS
NURSERY
CONSERVATORY
Lily Pond
BOWLING
TENNIS
KEZAR STADIUM
Kezar Dr.

Alvord Bridge
Alvord Lake
Page St.
Grove St.
Hayes St.

A Magical City

And wizardry it was. In only a few months a magical city had been raised with such monumentality that it stunned the eye and dazzled the mind. The exhibits at the Fair invited enchantment: gold and silver ores from California, glassware and ivory from Nevada, exotic foods from east and west; from Chicago, the design for the new Ferris wheel, and always the sound of music that poured from the magical heart of the Fair. At the center of the fairground was the billiantly lighted electric tower, "the most powerful searchlight in the world." Atop the restaurant and three observation landings was a revolving light, whose designers claimed would offer enough illumination for reading a newspaper eight miles away.

There were perfumes from the East and a Japanese tea garden with bonsai trees, flowers, and imported roosters with rainbow tail feathers 16 feet long. At Colonel Boone's wild animal arena trained pigs performed tricks and trained birds waved American flags in rhythm to the national anthem. There, too, a lion named Parnell one day lived up to his billing as a "man-eating lion" by eating his trainer. There were camel rides on Cairo Street, and the mirror maze and Dante's Inferno on the Fair's midway. And there was Little Egypt, who made her San Francisco debut at the Fair, seducing and scandalizing the crowds with her writhing undulations of bare skin and silk.

After the Fair

By the end of the 1890s San Franciscans were beginning to see more and more of an unusual phenomenon—the horseless carriage. Within months of the Fair's end the entire city was caught in the advance of a technological change that would completely and permanently alter the lives of San Franciscans.

By March 1900, automobile traffic had grown so rapidly that the Park Commission felt obliged to prohibit all automobiles (except electric cars) from using any of the Park roads or the avenue in the Panhandle. Eventually the prohibition was relaxed for certain portions of the Park, but requirements were stiff—a driver's license was mandatory for Park driving even before the State required a license. To pass the driving test, motorists had to drive the Park's engineer over a portion of the Park in a safe manner, and react appropriately when his assistant, hiding in the bushes, threw a dummy into the middle of the road. Running over the dummy disqualified the applicant.

The Great San Francisco Freeway Revolt

Had the Great San Francisco Freeway Revolt never happened, Highway 1 through San Francisco would have been an express freeway—four to six lanes of elevated fast road that would have displaced housing, transformed the landscape, and changed permanently the character of two of San Francisco's largest neighborhoods.

In the 1950s, California joined the rest of America with plans to bulldoze entire neighborhoods and pave open spaces to build highways that would link expanding suburbs to downtowns. For San Francisco, the State Department of Highways devised a new freeway system to speed Marin and San Mateo residents to the central city.

When the state announced its plans, local reaction was loud, united, and negative. Hearings were held, protesters marched, editorials appeared, and one resident chained herself to a tree in the park at the place where the freeway would have sliced it. On a showdown vote, the Board of Supervisors and the Mayor blocked the state's plan in a rare use of municipal veto power.

As a result of San Francisco's Freeway Revolt, the Panhandle and Golden Gate freeways never left the drawing board, thereby preserving the northeastern edge of the park, the entire Panhandle, and the lusciously landscaped Park Presidio Blvd. Construction of the third link, the Embarcadero Freeway, was stopped in midair.

The local action had national repercussions as well, causing other cities to at least pause to consider the wisdom of large-scale freeway building within their limits. In the analysis of Harold Gilliam, conservation writer for the *San Francisco Chronicle*: "Golden Gate Park and the northern waterfront were saved from the bulldozers by mass action—nonviolent but otherwise in the best tradition of Lexington and Concord. From here a chain reaction of freeway insurrections spread across the country."

| **Environment** | **Roadside Attractions** | **Resources** |

Trees in Golden Gate Park

There are over 4,000 varieties of trees in the 1,000 acres of Golden Gate Park. The oldest, hardiest, and most numerous include the three species that first provided the stabilized dune cover for subsequent species: cypress (8 varieties), pines (22 varieties), and eucalyptus (more than 100 varieties from Australia, New Zealand, and the Orient). Redwood, cedar, spruce, elm, oak, maple, and ash are prominent among the hundreds of other species. Samples of San Francisco's few indigenous

stands are also represented in the park—the arroya, yellow willows, and the cat-wax myrtle.

The Strybing Arboretum

The 70-acre Strybing Arboretum is the first place to go in Golden Gate Park to view its trees. The Arboretum was begun with a collection of pioneer plants developed by John McLaren during his half-century reign as Superintendent of Parks and is world famous for its number and varieties of plants native to this hemisphere. It is also full of clearly marked and described trees from all over the world, including China, Japan, the Himalayas, South America, Central America, Australia, Burma, New Zealand, and South Africa. Among the most rare of the trees here are the dove tree (*Davidia involcrata*), the *Magnolia campbellii*, and the *Michelia doltsopa*.

Park Potpourri

Among Golden Gate Park's unique attractions are two windmills at its western edge. One, Dutch Windmill, has been restored to its original glory as a dignified and majestic machine that graces the landscape. Built in 1902 to pump water for park irrigation, the windmill has a 150-foot wingspan, which was the largest in the world for its time.

The park also has lawn bowling, indoor and outdoor handball courts, two shelters for playing cards, chess, checkers or mah-jongg. Near the

Haight Street entrance is the oldest reinforced concrete bridge in America (Alvord Bridge, built in 1889). At the other end of the park are fly-casting pools built by the WPA in 1936 (400 x 180 feet), as well as a dog training field and a pitch-and-putt golf course. At Stow Lake you may rent a pedal boat or a small motorized yacht. The lake's boating concession was the attraction that prompted park founder William Hammond Hall to resign in the 1890s, claiming that the park was being made into a "Coney Island."

But the Park's most peculiar attraction is certainly the buffalo paddock, where a herd of buffalo reside and stare blankly at tourists who take their photos as if they were nature's most important creation. The buffalo, who have had nothing but a hard time of it for an extremely long while, seem resigned to their role as foil for the stupidities of the dominant two-legged species.

Strybing Arboretum and Botanical Gardens

9th Ave. & Lincoln Way
San Francisco, California 94122

Location: To reach by public transportation, take MUNI Metro N (Judah) at any Metro station on Market Street; get off at 9th Avenue and Irving, walk one block north on 9th. Or call MUNI for information: (415) 673-6864.

SPECIAL GARDENS TO VISIT:
1. Arthur Menzies Garden of California Native Plants.
2. Biblical Garden
3. Demonstration Gardens
4. Eric Walther Succulent Garden
5. Garden of Fragrance
6. James Noble Conifer Garden
7. Jennie B. Zellerbach Garden
8. Moon-viewing Garden
9. Redwood Trail

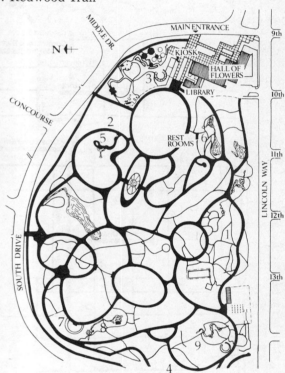

City Guides

558-3981

Several times a week trained volunteers lead free 90-minute tours of San Francisco's neighborhoods, highlighting history, architecture, and culture. The tours, which are sponsored by the Friends of the San Francisco Public Library, include City Hall, Coit Tower, Gold Rush City, North Beach, Historic Market Street, Golden Gate Park, and the Presidio Museum. Call for current schedule and topics.

Stanyan Street and Other Sorrows

History's best-selling poet got his start on the street that runs along the eastern edge of Golden Gate Park. In commemoration, Rod McKuen called his first book *Stanyan Street and Other Sorrows.*

McKuen, originally named Rodney Hooper, saw his career take off in a way that few who heard his early poetry readings would have imagined possible. Soon he was accompanying his poetry with music and parlaying a singing career and more books into a multimillion-dollar income.

Blatantly sentimental and bereft of usual poetic interest, McKuen's poetry perhaps says more about America's expectations from art than it does about the emotional life of a man who gave up a brief career as a B-movie replica of Tab Hunter to become America's poet-laureate of popular verse.

The Earthquake

In the spring of 1906 an event took place that made all the automobile regulations insignificant: on April 18 the San Francisco earthquake and fire completely wiped out entire sections of the city in the most disastrous natural catastrophe ever to hit a large American metropolis. Four hundred and fifty lives were lost, and tens of thousands of homeless people sought refuge in Golden Gate Park.

Shortly after the earthquake and fire, reports estimated that more than 200,000 of the homeless were encamped in Golden Gate Park. Public agencies and charitable organizations rushed to provide help, and within weeks tents and barracks had been set up throughout the Park. Two refugee camps were built, one of them atop the old Speed Road.

Another more permanent barracks camp of 2,400 apartments was built on land immediately west of the Park, on what is now Park Presidio Drive/Highway 1. This section of the present road, between Golden Gate Park and the Presidio, became the city's principal refugee camp, particularly after January 1907 when the last of the refugees in Golden Gate Park were transferred out and workers undertook the plowing and reseeding of the Park's evacuation camps.

1907 to 1936

Between 1907 and 1936 the road that was to become the San Francisco section of Highway 1 was gradually defined. As the 19th Avenue section was first covered in macadam and then asphalt, it was transformed into a bustling thoroughfare, with development increasing on both sides. By

1923, the road was catering to "a parade of automobiles [that] goes on day and night." In 1933 the State took over jurisdiction from the City of San Francisco in preparation for State Highway 1.

Completing the Links

But the road was still incomplete, lacking a connection at Golden Gate Park and one through the Presidio. Construction of the remaining links began in 1936, when the 19th Avenue–Park Presidio (Cross Over Drive) connection was cut across the Park. Park advocate and author Ramond Clary considers the wide concrete road to have been horribly misconceived: "It would have been . . . very simple to dig a trench wide enough for a road, build a concrete tunnel, and cover it over with soil, trees, and shrubs."

Unlike the Cross Over connection, the final segment through the Presidio of San Francisco did rely on a tunnel—in order to preserve the military's golf course. The 1,300-foot four-lane tunnel, which took four years to build, completed the last significant link in the Coast Highway, giving travelers a straight route from the Peninsula, through San Francisco, to the Golden Gate Bridge.

San Francisco's Housing Crisis

Highway 1's route through San Francisco darts across two of the largest neighborhoods, the Sunset and the Richmond districts. Because of the city's housing crisis, would-be residents have found it increasingly difficult to locate housing in the Sunset, the Richmond, or practically any other San Francisco neighborhood. Many have given up looking and moved out of the city entirely, forgoing the benefits and pleasures of urban life.

The shortage of housing has created a strong demand for any housing at any price. And things are getting worse: just to keep pace with present demand would require the construction of about 20,000 new units a year. Nothing like this is being built and those new units that are being constructed are primarily luxury units.

Unlike other San Francisco neighborhoods, the Sunset has a high proportion of single-family residences and most of these are owned by their occupants. Although the Sunset has always been a comfortable, unpretentious, mainly middle-income neighborhood, skyrocketing housing costs are closing all but wealthy individuals out of the market. To illustrate: San Francisco's average family income is about $26,000, which by standard bank measures qualifies a purchaser for about $75,000 worth of housing, disregarding down payment. For $75,000 one is about half way to the minimum purchase price of a substandard Sunset home.

Unaffordably high purchase prices have forced many middle-income residents from the city, raising the possibility of a future San Francisco inhabited only by those wealthy enough to afford high-cost housing. Sky-high purchase prices have also forced many homeowners into the rental market, aggravating the imbalance in the city's housing stock.

The Richmond district has a higher percentage of renters than does the Sunset, but affordable housing is no easier to locate. Available rentals are often passed on by word-of-mouth and usually snatched up even before the former occupant has moved out. When an apartment is advertised, landlords in some cases have 50 or more applicants to choose from. The cost of an average apartment rental in San Francisco is as high as any urban area in the nation with few exceptions.

To counter the untethered rise in rental costs, the City of San Francisco was forced to invoke a rent-stabilization law after several stronger ballot initiatives almost passed. The law, which limits rent increases to between 4% and 7% a year, has one glaring loophole: controls are temporarily suspended when an apartment is vacated, thereby enabling a landlord to reset rents to the maximum rate the market will bear. As a result, the eviction rate has increased and landlords have become more interested in renting to shorter-term tenants, a trend that further frustrates families in their search for affordable housing.

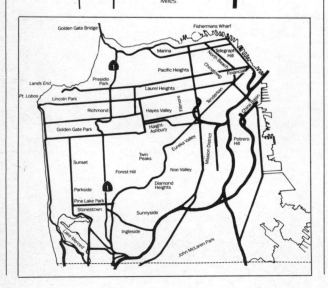

| **Environment** | **Roadside Attractions** | **Resources** |

Lungs of a City

Since the middle of the nineteenth century, urban open spaces have been thought of as "lungs of the city," places at which a city's spoiled and begrimed air is replenished. This pleasant thesis, however, isn't accurate.

In fact, forested or landscaped areas absorb so little carbon dioxide that their capacity to improve the air is minuscule. Three acres of greenery absorb only about as much carbon dioxide as four people expend in normal activity. As Jane Jacobs explains, it is "the oceans of air circulating about us, not parks, that keep cities from suffocating."

Why All the Bay Windows?

Practically every structure in San Francisco, regardless of architectural style, avails itself of the near-total use of bay windows. Why is this so? Could it be that everybody in San Francisco is trying to get a better look at the bay? Are the views so exciting that everyone goes to elaborate ends to have big windows? No, these romantic notions do not explain the phenomenon.

The reason there are so many bay windows in San Francisco is that the city zoning law allows a 36-inch overhang beyond the owner's property line for windows above the ground floor. Thus, in effect, a building with bay windows receives a gift of an extra 36 inches per front room per floor. Few builders fail to take advantage of the extra free space.

Out of the Park

You may still be in the park after thinking yourself out. Presidio Parkway, which resumes Highway 1's journey northward, is actually part of Golden Gate Park. For nearly a mile through the Richmond District, Park Presidio Drive extends Golden Gate Park and connects it to the Presidio. Although continuous expansions of the roadway have substantially diminished the width of the promenade, it still provides a much needed green strip and practical shield from traffic noise and unsightliness for nearby residents.

The handsomely planted strip also makes for a beautiful roadway that serves as an intermediary between the Park and the nonverdant world. Soon Geary Boulevard intersects Park Presidio Drive with the longest and widest commercial strip in San Francisco. One block north of Geary is Clement, one of San Francisco's most interesting commercial areas.

Clement Street

Clement (accent on second syllable) is a street that is characteristically San Francisco—a city of mostly small shops often run by families or individuals. The stores reflect personal tastes, talents, and skills, as well as personal idiosyncrasies, and they tend to be as unusual as the people who run them.

At 17th and Clement, for example, is San Francisco Flyfishers Supply, offering "fine tackle and clothing for the western angler." Across the street is Fairy Lake Aquarium, which sells goldfish and tropical fish. Down the street is one of the city's best medium-priced restaurants, Alejandro's, which serves great-tasting Spanish, Peruvian, and Mexican seafood. In one small stretch of Clement

Street, the Highway 1 traveler who favors fish has the opportunity to outfit himself to catch one, have one for dinner, or take one home for a pet.

East of Park Presidio Drive, Clement Street offers shops, restaurants, and bookstores of every description. The best bookstore is Green Apple Books (new and used books). The best restaurant, among many excellent ones, is Ocean Restaurant, one of the outstanding Cantonese eateries in San Francisco, a city with scores of good Chinese restaurants.

Architecture and History

Architectural historian Roger Olmstead once said that a city is more than its collective architecture, but its architecture generally manages to reflect its character. The bold beauty, the proud independence, the great diversity, and the whimsical self-indulgence of San Francisco's architecture support his statement. In recent years, lots of good books have been written about the city's architecture, some from a historical or guidebook perspective and some with the intent to inform and protect San Francisco's architectural resources from loss to newer construction. Here are three of the best.

HERE TODAY: SAN FRANCISCO'S ARCHITECTURAL HERITAGE
Roger Olmsted and T. H. Watkins (Text), Morley Baer (Photos)
Chronicle Books/A Prism Edition, San Francisco. 1978

ARCHITECTURE OF SAN FRANCISCO
Sally Woodbridge and John Woodbridge
101 Productions, San Francisco. 1982.

A GUIDE TO ARCHITECTURE IN SAN FRANCISCO & NORTHERN CALIFORNIA
David Gebhard, Roger Montgomery, Robert Winter, John Woodbridge, Sally Woodbridge
Peregrine Smith, Inc., Santa Barbara. 1976.

SAN FRANCISCO ALMANAC
Gladys Hansen
Presidio Press, San Rafael. 1980.

The *San Francisco Almanac* is written by the archivist of the City and County of San Francisco. It includes information on a wide range of local subjects, from history to the arts. For more information, photographs, maps, and expert assistance on subjects concerning the history of San Francisco or the state, contact the California Historical Society (567-1848).

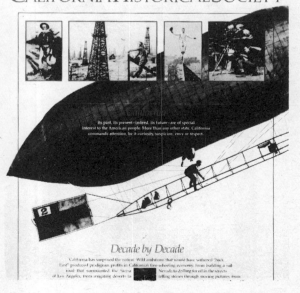

Decade by Decade

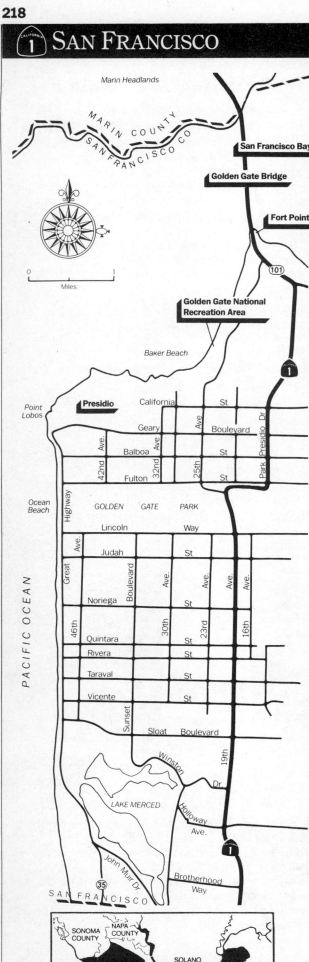

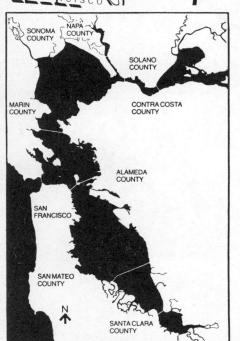

The World's Most Famous Bridge

From its beginnings, San Francisco developed in an improbable fashion. Characteristically, perhaps, the Golden Gate Bridge began as an utter improbability, deriving from an idea originally proposed by a madman.

Madmen and Others

Joshua Abraham Norton was a local eccentric who, after declaring himself Emperor of the United States and (for good measure) Protector of Mexico, garnered the bemused attention of San Francisco with his colorful plumed and uniformed presence and his deranged pronouncements. Norton had gambled on rice futures— and lost it all.

Emperor Norton was famous for his pronouncements of dementia: for usurping his authority, he ordered by declaration the death of Mexico's Maximillian. And so that he might have imperial headquarters (instead of a small corner in an inexpensive rooming house), he commanded the seizure of the opulent Palace Hotel. In 1869, Emperor Norton ordered that a suspension bridge be built across San Francisco Bay. Like Norton's other decrees, this proposal was met with tolerant disregard.

But three years later Charles Crocker presented plans for a suspension bridge between Marin and San Francisco to the Marin County Board of Supervisors. Crocker soon abandoned the idea, but four decades later James Wilkins, a newspaper writer who had attended Crocker's presentation to Marin County, began an editorial campaign in the *San Francisco Bulletin* pushing for construction of the bridge. Wilkins' editorials caught the attention of Joseph Strauss, who was in town to design drawbridges in China Basin. Riveted by the idea, Strauss quickly delivered a working blueprint for the construction of a bridge across the Bay at its deepest point. He estimated that the project would cost $25 million to $30 million, a fraction of what most imagined possible.

Strauss was a romantic who used to unconsciously pencil lines of verse in the margins of his plans. He had already built more than 400 bridges, including one at the Winter Palace of the Tsar of Russia that was stormed by rebellious peasants in the Revolution of 1917. The Golden Gate Bridge would become the crown of his lifetime's effort, but 15 years of political manipulation and financial maneuvering delayed the start of construction.

Guns and Parks: The Military's Role in Preservation of Open Space

Your drive along Highway 1 in San Francisco winds through another parklike open space north of Golden Gate Park. This is The Presidio of San Francisco, a U.S. military base. Here on prime real estate surrounded by exclusive neighborhoods, national defense has prevailed over the prerogative and pressures of private development capital. In so doing, the military has inadvertently become the single most important force in preserving open space on the San Francisco headlands.

Like the Outside Lands, this area at the tip of the San Francisco Peninsula once consisted of rolling sand dunes and desolate windswept hills. The military initiated a forestation program in 1883 and today continues lush landscaping and grounds maintenance with visible success. During the 1880s, some 60,000 trees were planted here, mostly from seedlings obtained from the nursery at Golden Gate Park.

By the 1960s, the expense of maintaining the

post was questioned by members of a new military guard whose national defense systems did not need cannons on headlands or continental staging areas for troops. Luckily, by this time, the public had discovered The Presidio's unique urban open spaces and history.

In 1963 the entire post became a registered National Historic Landmark. When the Army decided that some of its coastal property between Fort Point and Fort Mason was unnecessary for national defense, these lands became part of the Golden Gate National Recreation Area (GGNRA), forever preserved for public use.

Bridge Books

The drama of the construction of the Golden Gate Bridge makes a good story. These three books tell that story, each factually complete and gloriously illustrated.

SPANNING THE GATE
Stephen Cassady (text) and Clyde Winters (design)
Squarebooks, Mill Valley. 1979.

HIGH STEEL: BUILDING THE BRIDGES ACROSS SAN FRANCISCO BAY
Richard Dillon (text), Don DeNevi and Thomas Moulin (design)
Celestial Arts, Berkeley. 1979.

SUPERSPAN: THE GOLDEN GATE BRIDGE
Baron Wolman (photography), Tom Horton (text), and Georgia Gillfillan and Phil Carroll (design)
Chronicle Books, San Francisco. 1983.

San Francisco Bay

San Francisco Bay is the most important and best-known estuary on the west coast. Although the Bay no longer covers the 680 square miles it did in the 1880s, its size remains impressive: 450 square miles of water, rimmed by over 1,100 miles of shoreline, extending inland south almost 40 miles from its golden mouth in a graceful butterfly shape. Its massive surface area, coupled with its relatively constant water temperature, moderates extremes of heat and cold in the surrounding lands; its surface condensation and surface currents significantly affect local weather patterns.

What is called San Francisco Bay actually encompasses eight separate bays: San Francisco, San Pablo, Honker, Richardson, San Rafael, San Leandro, Grizzly, and Suisun. Ten islands protrude from its waters. Seven major bridges cross it, and more than 300 lights, buoys, beacons, and other aids to navigation sparkle in its waters.

Every day a diverse fleet of commercial ships, including giant oil tankers, container ships, and freighters, enter the Bay's shipping channels, which extend as deep as 36 fathoms (216 feet). The Bay is a port of call for many national and inter-

national luxury liners, and military vessels from all nations find port here. Commercial fishing boats work the Bay waters or head to the open ocean from their berths. On any weekend, the Bay is alive with hundreds of pleasure boats, sailboats, ferries, rowboats, rafts—almost anything that will float. People jog and sun along its shores, fish from its piers, and sometimes swim in its relatively cold waters. The Bay defines much of San Francisco's economic, transportation, and recreational life.

Golden Gate Bridge

Through the bound cable strands, the arching path upward, veering with light, the flight of strings,—

Hart Crane

The Golden Gate Bridge is one of the most beautiful structures in the world and it is archetypically so: this is what bridges should look like for all time. It soars above the ocean with such splendor, pride, and monumentality that a viewer's appreciation may touch exaltation.

To drive the bridge is one of the great driving pleasures of the California coast. Regardless of the type of vehicle you are in, the well-spaced side rails are low enough to permit excellent views of the Bay, the islands, the city, or the ocean. The

height of the roadway—260 feet above the ocean—provides vistas that are dizzying in perspective and stunning in composition. There are no equivalent vantage points save those gained by flight.

And what sights: to the northbound traveler the San Francisco Bay inland side of the bridge is a fascination of blue water, green and brown islands, and a white city. On weekends the bay may be filled with so many white-sailed boats that it looks to be swarming with flocks of sea-top butterflies.

On the ocean side of the bridge, the stretch of blue water arches toward Cathay. From this height one's vista on a clear day may reach 80 miles.

The Presidio

Department of the Army, Public Affairs Office
Headquarters, Presidio of San Francisco
Presidio of San Francisco 94129. 561-5187

The Presidio of San Francisco is an open post with most of its 1,400 acres available for your use and enjoyment. Two maps are helpful, "The Historic Trail Guide," which features historic and scenic points at 22 stops, and the "Environment Trail Guide," a tour through the natural areas of the post that identifies plants, trees, and birds. The Presidio also has an Army Museum.

Fort Point

P.O. Box 29333, Presidio of San Francisco 94129.
556-1693 or 556-2857

Beneath Golden Gate Bridge is Fort Point, which was constructed between 1853 and 1861 to guard San Francisco from hostile fleets entering the Bay, though none ever arrived. The towering walls of the massive fort average eight feet in thickness and there are 30 gun rooms on each of three floors. There is a museum, a bookstore, and various displays and exhibitions as well as a staff of volunteers and rangers in full Civil War regalia who conduct tours and retell the stories of this dramatic place. Free.

THE GOLDEN GATE BRIDGE
SAN FRANCISCO, CAL.

PROJECT REPORT OF CHIEF ENGINEER
SEPTEMBER 30, 1937

**MAIN BRIDGE
PLAN AND ELEVATION**

Construction Begins

Construction of the Bridge began on January 5, 1933, when two steam shovels started excavation on the shore. During the 15 years that had elapsed since Strauss proposed his plan for a semicantilevered structure, advances in steel composition enabled the present-day graceful design. Other changes included the abandonment of elaborations that Strauss's assistant, Clifford Paine (who would ultimately bear more responsibility for the Bridge than Strauss) felt unnecessary: a masonry toll

plaza, gilded wrought-iron gates, and a glass public observation elevator.

Construction of the Bridge's anchorages—the huge concrete structures that would hold taut the cables—required blasting into the cliffs and slopes on both sides of the Bay. Excavations were cut to building-size depths and filled with triply reinforced concrete blocks that could withstand millions of pounds of pull.

The anchorages were built with relative ease, although special accommodation had to be made for the preservation of Fort Scott (Fort Point) on the San Francisco side. This dry land construction demanded nothing so complex or dangerous as the sinking in mid-ocean of the piers that would hold the span from deep inside the bedrock of the ocean's floor.

For the first time in the history of bridge construction, cement piers were to be sunk in the open sea. On the San Francisco side, 1,160 feet from shore, the south pier had to be sunk to a depth of more than 1,100 feet amid the raging ocean. Here the water churned with force enough to engage the heart of Charybdis.

To build the San Francisco pier the ocean floor had to be excavated more than 40 feet below the channel bottom. The digging was accomplished with 20-foot cylindrical bombs, each filled with 200 pounds of blasting powder, that were dropped through hollow pipes to blast out the solid rock sea floor. Divers, who had been brought to San Francisco from the Columbia River, swam to the bottom of the ocean to connect wire detonators.

Construction of the south pier involved underwater heroics by the divers who braved the surging Bay depths; their efforts enabled a bridge to be set in an ocean passage deeper and more turbulent than any which had ever been spanned by a bridge.

Traffic on the Bridge

Besides being one of the loveliest urban art pieces in San Francisco, the Golden Gate Bridge also provides weekday entry to about 25,000 cars and 40,000 commuters who drive from Marin County and points north to workplaces in San Francisco. Use of the Bridge is steadily increasing along with the numbers of downtown office workers, most of whom commute from out of town to the growing skyscraper community downtown. Already, during peak hours, traffic on the bridge sometimes exceeds capacity. If traffic continues to multiply, soon commuters to work may meet commuters returning from work at midspan.

The Golden Gate Highway District has tried a

number of solutions to decrease traffic on the Bridge, including the operation of ferries from Marin. The one-direction toll was first introduced here. Other solutions, such as no tolls for carpools during rush hour and traffic-free bus lanes have helped in managing rush-hour traffic atrocities, but have had little overall success in reducing traffic on the bridge.

Among the most extreme of solutions that have been considered is adding a second deck, effectively doubling the number of cars that the Bridge could carry. Although some consideration was given to the idea of a lower deck that would carry a two-track interurban line, the idea lost currency when Marin residents heavily voted against inclusion in the BART system.

The automobile-only second deck would have consisted of a 60-foot wide five-lane roadway with sidewalks and suicide barriers on each side. Traffic on the bottom deck would have run northward, southward on the upper deck. A new approach ramp was to be built on the south side and new approach spans were envisioned on the north approach.

The second-deck idea never went very far. Most Bay Area residents revere the postcard appearance of their bridge and any proposals to alter it are met with utmost apprehension and suspicion. (The ongoing debate over adding a suicide barrier hinges on visual impact). Despite such concerns, the District continues to be pressured by northern counties to pursue feasibility studies for a new deck.

Increasing bridge capacity, however, would only shift the inevitable constraints of automobile commuting from Marin to San Francisco, either to the limited capacity of the freeway or to the city's streets. Other constraints as well (air quality, parking, and safety) are also critical. The problem remains beyond the solutions of a single, technological "fix."

Environment

Life in the Bay

About 70% of the entire San Francisco Bay is only 12 feet deep or less, providing along its edge remarkably rich marshes, tidal shallows, and mudflats. These are the estuarine sanctuaries, key to aquatic (and much shore) life on our planet. It is said that if the earth is perceived as having a nest, its estuaries are that nest; if California is conceived likewise, then San Francisco Bay is its birthing place.

The impressive waters of the Sacramento and San Joaquin Rivers combine around Suisun Bay, flowing into the huge backwater of the San Francisco Bay around Carquinez Strait. Together these two river systems pour over 3 million acre-feet of fresh water into the Bay during winter months. Sheltered ocean saltwater mixes with fresh water from the rivers and stirs a cauldron of life.

Over 1,000 types of fish abound in the Bay, feeding on the tiny bay shrimp and bottom life. Steelhead trout and striped bass thrive in the salt and freshwater mix. Each year millions of salmon make a ceremonial exit from the freshwater rivers into the Bay and out to sea through the Golden Gate.

The Bay is a major stopover for birds traveling the Pacific Flyway from Canada to Mexico. Millions of individual birds and hundreds of species rest or live on the Bay. Among them are the rare brown pelican, the white pelican, avocets, clapper rails, black-necked stilts, and the endangered least tern.

Reber's Dam Folly

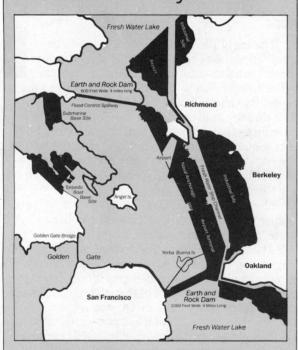

John Reber was a teacher and playwright. He was also a visionary with a plan for San Francisco Bay. He would "save" it, becoming the Bay's "stage manager," in what was to be the "greatest pageant on earth."

Reber arrived in San Francisco in 1907, and by the mid 1920s he had envisioned his life's work: dam San Francisco Bay to transform it into two enormous freshwater lakes. Trains, light-rail vehicles, and 40 lanes of freeway traffic would have solid-ground passage atop two earthen dams between San Francisco, the East Bay, and Marin County. Agriculture and seaside tourist attractions would flourish.

As audacious as Reber's plan seems today, the intelligent and charismatic actor carried it to the public, to Sacramento, and finally to Washington, where in 1949 Congress approved a $2.5 million study to address technical problems posed by the plan. If the Korean War and lesser engineering dreams like the Richmond–San Rafael Bridge had not intervened, today the Bay might have been the Lake. Reber's Dam Folly, as it came to be called, was officially declared infeasible by the Army Corps of Engineers in July 1963.

Roadside Attractions

"Double Exposure"

Photography develops in tandem with one of the most characteristic of modern activities: tourism. For the first time in history, large numbers of people regularly travel out of their habitual environments for short periods of time. It seems positively unnatural to travel for pleasure without taking a camera along. Photographs will offer indisputable evidence that the trip was made, that the program was carried out, that fun was had.

A way of certifying experience, taking photographs is also a way of refusing it—by limiting experience to a search for the photogenic, by converting experience into an image, a souvenir. Travel becomes a strategy for accumulating photographs. The very activity of taking pictures is soothing, and assuages general feelings of disorientation that are likely to be exacerbated by travel. Most tourists feel compelled to put the camera between themselves and whatever is remarkable that they encounter. Unsure of other responses, they take a picture. This gives shape to experience: stop, take a photograph, and move on. The method especially appeals to people handicapped by a ruthless work ethic—Germans, Japanese, and Americans. Using a camera appeases the anxiety which the work-driven feel about not working when they are on vacation and supposed to be having fun. They have something to do that is like a friendly imitation of work: they can take pictures.

Susan Sontag, *On Photography*

What You See From the Bridge

On the San Francisco Bay side the most distinguishing land mass is, of course, San Francisco, which curves from the bridge's anchorage all the way around the end of the peninsula. The Marina District, Fisherman's Wharf, and the Ferry Building stand out on the water's edge. Close to the bridge it's easy to spot the elaborate red dome of Bernard Maybeck's Palace of Fine Arts. The Financial District, with the tallest buildings, is also conspicuous. The huge red tower is Sutro Tower, sometimes said to appear as the mast of a ghost ship sailing through the fog, other times called the most intrusive blight on the horizon.

There are three main islands in the Bay: the largest is Angel Island, which is a state park accessible by ferry from San Francisco's Fisherman's Wharf or from Tiburon in Marin County. The smaller island in the middle of the Bay is Alcatraz, famous for its guests and cruel formidability (accessible by ferry from Fisherman's Wharf). The other principal island is Yerba Buena, which hinges the San Francisco/Oakland Bay Bridge and attaches to Treasure Island, an artificial land mass created for the 1939 World's Fair and, like Yerba Buena, today controlled by the military.

On the ocean side of the Golden Gate Bridge you can easily view the Marin Headlands. On a clear day you may be able to see the Point Bonita Lighthouse on the tip of the headlands, or the Farallons, 25 miles out to sea due west, which is a bird sanctuary and one of the few federally protected marine sanctuaries on the California coast.

Resources

Bay Area Environment

UC Natural History Guides

For the best overall introduction to the Bay Area's natural environment, pick up one or all of the books in the University of California's Natural History series. Smith's *Introduction to the Natural History of the San Francisco Bay Region* (1959) was the very first of this respected basic resource series. Gilliam's *Weather of the San Francisco Bay Region* and Hedgpeth's *Introduction to Seashore Life of the San Francisco Bay Region* are two more of immediate interest. Others in the Bay series include *Butterflies* (Tilden), *Evolution of Landscape* (Howard), *Mammals* (Berry), *Mushrooms* (Orr), *Native Shrubs* (Ferris), *Native Trees* (Metcalf), *Reptiles and Amphibians* (Stebbins), *Rocks and Minerals* (Bowen), and *Spring Wildflowers* (Sharsmith).

Environmental Events Hotline
474-4848

A daily message of environmental events, including classes, workshops, hearings, and meetings. Presented by the Environment Action Clearinghouse at Fort Mason (474-5080), which also provides referral and resources services, job, internships and volunteer opportunities.

San Francisco is Washing Away

Every 100 years, San Francisco loses about 1.25% of its shoreline land mass to the Pacific ocean, which rises 0.1 feet per year.

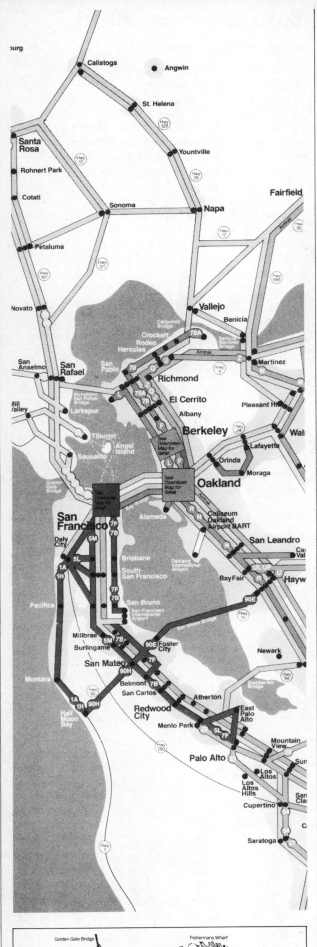

Raising the Towers

From the first the height of the towers was emphasized both as an engineering requirement, needed to maintain the massive sweep of a suspension bridge over so wide a distance, and as an aesthetic feature that would dramatically emphasize the Bridge's majestic presence across the Golden Gate. The towers were to rise 690 feet above the cement piers, 746 feet above the water line. No edifice in San Francisco came—or comes—close to this height.

Bethlehem Steel was in charge of the towers' construction, bringing to the job its own bridgemen, who were uniquely unafraid, and who, in the words of Stephen Cassady, "were generally excited by the acrobatics of high steel labor. The risk of death was real, but for the most part dismissed as the price they paid for working adventurous jobs all over the world at premium salaries." The north tower was erected in 10 months; the south tower in 101 days.

Spanning the Bridge

On August 2, 1935, a 5,000-foot length of wire rope was dragged across the Bay, then slowly hoisted out of the water and across the towers' tops to become the first of 25 foundation ropes put in place to span the 420 feet between towers. Once the foundation ropes were in place, wooden catwalks were tied onto the ropes, enabling workers to string the cables. But placing the planks required the workmen to straddle the preliminary ropes hundreds of feet above the water and to balance between the swinging strands.

The catwalks, constructed of redwood planking, were extremely uncertain-looking propositions, although to the acrobatic cable-workers they became as reliable as city streets. Ahead of schedule, the cable workers hung the 7,650-foot–long, 36.5-inch–diameter cables, each containing 27,000 strands of wire. In barely six months they hung more than 80,000 miles of wire, enough to circle the globe three times.

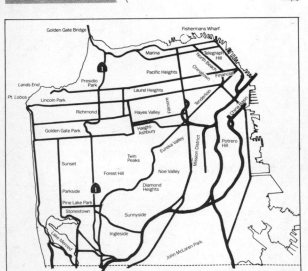

Regional Planning in California: ABAG and BCDC

Some land-use problems cannot be solved by any one city or county alone. The San Francisco Bay Area has 92 cities and nine counties, each affected by the policies of the others on issues like development of the Bay shoreline, control of air and water quality and dumping of chemical wastes. California leads the nation in bringing cities and counties together to study, understand and try to resolve such issues of mutual concern.

This approach is called regional planning and it takes two forms, both originally developed in model programs in the San Francisco Bay Area. One is a voluntary approach wherein advisory groups known as COGs (councils of governments) fund studies and make recommendations on issues. The other approach is a statutory one, in which the regional body has the power of law to define and enforce its policies.

ABAG

The first COG in California was established here in 1961, the Association of Bay Area Governments (ABAG). Its purpose is "the permanent establishment of a forum for discussion and study of metopolitan area problems of mutual interest and concern . . . and for the development of policy and action recommendations." ABAG, like its sister SCAG (Southern California Association of Governments) reviews new development proposals that have regional impacts and seeks cooperative resolution to conflicts.

BCDC .

The early 1960s ushered in a building boom that had almost every city on the Bay filling its mudflats to accommodate new luxury housing and office towers. Since 1850 the original water area of the Bay had shrunk from 787 square miles to 550, and demand and technology were quickly accelerating that rate. Although this land-use conflict required swift, informed, and effective action, the sanctity of private property and the huge profits of fill prevented local jurisdictions from meeting the challenge.

The San Francisco Bay Conservation and Development Commission (BCDC) was established by state law in 1965 after local citizens failed to get ABAG members to adopt an effective plan for voluntary control of fill. BCDC's initial task was to develop a plan for controlled growth, and then to regulate implementation of that plan through the permit process. By 1974 BCDC was responsible for restoring or reclaiming as open water more of the Bay area than it allowed to be filled thereby not only stopping, but reversing, the trend to fill in the Bay.

BCDC was the model for Proposition 20 and the resulting State Coastal Commission and inspired successful regional planning agencies throughout the nation. Like all government bodies, however, BCDC's effectiveness lies in the hands of legislators and an informed public whose support is needed to ensure the agency's survival, particularly in times of shift toward local control and away from collective responsible action.

Environment	Roadside Attractions	Resources

A Drowned River Mouth

The San Francisco Bay is really a drowned river mouth. The Sacramento River long ago reached the ocean at the Golden Gate, cutting its path through the Coastal Range and, aided by earthquakes, separating forever the Marin and San Francisco peninsulas. About 10,000 years ago, the sea level rose around 300 feet during the melting of the great ice caps, and the mouth of the Sacramento was submerged as the sea encroached on its inland territory through the Golden Gate.

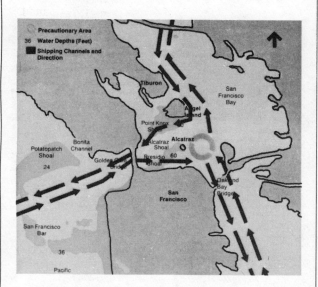

Highway 1 sweeps above the turbulent five-mile gash that is the Golden Gate. The channel itself is only about a mile wide and is a treacherous passage even in the best of circumstances. This narrow passage provides the only exit for the masses of fresh water that flow into the Bay from over 40% of the entire state's watersheds, and it is the only entry for the powerful Pacific, whose tides crash through and exit twice daily.

Walking the Bridge

On both ends of the bridge for the northbound traveler are vista points. The northern one has better views, particularly looking back to San Francisco, but the southern point has a souvenir shop open on weekends and a closer view of the toll booths and bridge buildings.

The most rewarding way to experience the Golden Gate Bridge is to walk it. The beauty and exhilaration of the structure are far enhanced by hiking across its pedestrian way, regardless of the weather (almost always cold and sometimes foggy). It's less than a mile each way and there are two great walking options.

The first is to walk the bayside of the Bridge across, then walk under the roadway north of the Marin Vista Point, and return on the ocean side. This route gives you the best of both views, but you can only do it on weekends because the ocean-side walkway is closed during the week. During the week simply return the way you came.

A second route is to walk the bayside of the Bridge past the north vista point, but rather than returning by reversing direction, keep going down Alexander Drive into Sausalito. It's only about another mile or so and almost all downhill. In Sausalito, have a light snack and catch the ferry back to San Francisco. From the Ferry Building you can take Muni back to the Bridge to retrieve your car.

Events

Highway 1 in San Francisco leads to an ecclectic array of events and entertainment. A sample:

The Exploratorium
563-3200

San Francisco's artful museum of science and human perception, housed in the Palace of Fine Arts, consists almost solely of exhibits to be touched, operated, or otherwise manipulated. A nationally recognized and one-of-a-kind attraction, always full of amazed participants of all ages. Free.

San Francisco International Film Festival
221-9055

The most eclectic, far-ranging, and prestigious film festival in the country, the San Francisco International takes place each spring (usually in April). The festival is also the country's oldest, established in 1956. It is based at the Palace of Fine Arts.

Bay to Breakers
777-7770

The Bay to Breakers is northern California's

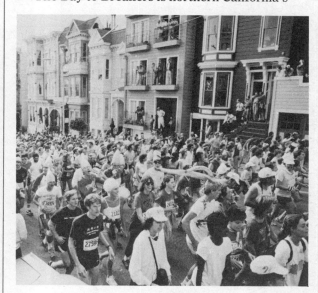

most famous footrace. The 7.6 meter run from the downtown bay waterfront, over the hills to the ocean, is sponsored by the *San Francisco Examiner* as a benefit for the Red Cross. Each May more than 25,000 runners dress in only-in–San Francisco running attire (as a bunny, a building, a spaceship) and participate in this for-fun-only run.

Pickle Family Circus
441-5705

For three days around each Fourth of July, San Francisco's renowned Pickle Family Circus dazzles the eye and gladdens the heart of young and old in a traditional circus performance outside on the green at Fort Mason. No animals, just the most delightful acrobats, clowns, trapeze artists, and jugglers. The Pickles also run a circus school that offers novice through professional training in the circus arts, and the circus tours each season. Call for schedule.

The Urban Fair
557-8758

San Francisco is the state's only city-county. As such it conducts one of the nation's most unusual county fairs. Instead of livestock, pie contests, and square dancing, the San Francisco Fair presents stand-up comedy, street theater, wine tasting, ice cream scooping contests, waiter/waitress races, breakdancing, and a citywide race to find legal parking spaces in designated neighborhoods. Labor unions, nonprofit groups, local businesses, and San Francisco's diverse neighborhood organizations sponsor exhibit booths and events. Mid-June.

Highway 1 On the Bottom of the Ocean

When the EPA warned about the Greenhouse effect and the rising of the seas in 1983, people laughed. When the dams overflowed in 2014, Nob Hill became an island.

"The Day San Francisco Drowned," *SF Chronicle/Examiner*

In 1983 the Environmental Protection Agency issued a report entitled "Can We Delay a Greenhouse Warming?" The little-noticed report predicted that major climatic changes would take place by the year 1990 or 2000, when a thermal blanket of gases trapped in the upper atmosphere would cause average temperatures to increase by as much as 27 degrees. Such a change would, of course, have significant consequences for most of the world's population. For San Francisco, sitting on a peninsula formed by a drowned river mouth, the consequences would be more than significant. Most of the city would go under.

Oceanographers agree that a greenhouse warming could melt the two remaining continental land mass ice shields, Greenland and the Antarctic. A total melt would mean a 300-foot rise in sea level. Even a partial melt, combined with 100-year flood conditions such as freak tides, a sudden melt-off of a record snowpack in the Sierra Mountains, and an unusually wet coastal storm, would result in the sea level rising by as much as 200 feet.

In such a situation, Highway 1 would sit on the shoreline of a new city, submerged in several places in the Sunset and on the approach to The Presidio. The Golden Gate Bridge would be underwater and the former peninsula would become several islands (about seven).

If a total melt occurred, there would be no islands and no Highway 1, and not much of anything else would remain above water.

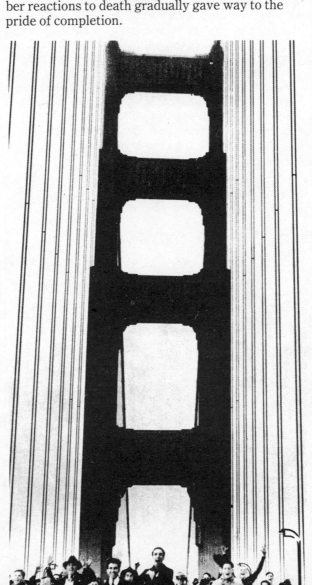

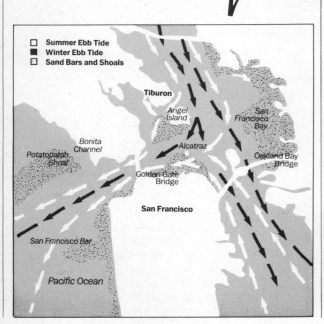

Setting the Roadway

The laying of the roadway was the last major element and the most dangerous. To build the floor, workers had to balance on 6- to 8-inch girders without walkways, without handrails, and always but one false step from doom.

So precarious was this phase of construction that a steel net was hung beneath the bridge to catch falling workers. Up until this step in the construction no one had fallen, but such good luck was becoming too improbable to hold. The San Francisco–Oakland Bay Bridge, six months from completion, had already lost 22 workers from its lofty heights. As the Golden Gate's roadway was laid, the net proved a needed lifesaver, sparing 19 men from the certain watery grave that waited below. Their individual brushes with death created a camaraderie among the victims of imbalance, giving rise to the "Halfway to Hell Club," an affiliation of the fallen who had been saved.

The net did not save them all, however. On February 17, 1937, when most of the construction was nearly complete, 12 men were pulling off wooden forms from the newly laid concrete on the Bridge's underside. They fell into the net when their scaffolding collapsed, but the scaffolding tore the net, then ripped it from its mooring, wrapping the workers in a shroud and plunging them into the deep ocean. Two of the men miraculously survived.

Within a few weeks the net was replaced and final construction resumed. On April 19, 1937, the Bridge was finished, and the bridge builders' somber reactions to death gradually gave way to the pride of completion.

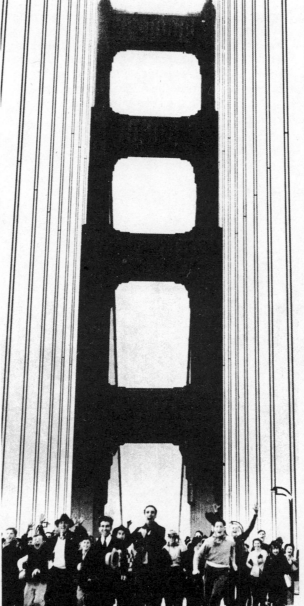

Painting the Bridge

Every day of the year that the weather permits, the Golden Gate Bridge is being painted. The brutal corrosive salt air, wind, and rain make quick work of the steel structure's protective coating and it must be constantly restored. When the bridge was young, workers chipped off the old paint and rust with air guns and applied new orange paint by hand, but that method was soon abandoned. Today the surface is sandblasted, undercoated with a gray, zinc primer (which

remains for 90 days to cure, marring the uniform color of the bridge in spots), and covered with two coats of international orange vinyl paint. This is a job with unusual thrills and extreme danger. Two workers lost their lives in the last decade as they fell from scaffolds, and many can't take the free-swinging 400-foot heights and widely fluctuating weather. But to most of the workers in the crew of 31, painting the Golden Gate Bridge is a one-of-a-kind Herculean labor of love.

Flying Saucer City

The inevitable practicality of flying saucers led Alexander G. Weygers in 1941 to conceive of San Francisco's most high-flying urban transportation plan. In Weygers's San Francisco of tomorrow "discopters" (his patented invention) were to whirl through the sky and land on rooftops, eliminating automobile congestion and easing downtown traffic.

Weygers's plan called for various-sized flying saucers that would be available much as private automobiles and public buses are available today. At the Bay's edge, larger flying saucers were to be docked like ocean liners with bars, promenade decks, and shuffleboard facilities.

Several decades have passed since Weygers introduced his plan for San Francisco's harbor, but the appeal of his idea has grown no less evident with the passage of time.

Picking Up Good Vibrations: Harmonic Oscillation

Harmony with the natural environment is a design tenet that necessarily influences architects and planners. In bridge building, however, one harmony is fastidiously avoided: too much of it at the wrong time can set in motion the phenomenon of harmonic oscillation, which can twist a bridge from its moorings in a matter of minutes.

All things, including bridges, have a natural frequency of vibration. When your fist hits a table,

for example, the vibrations of the table respond with a clash describing the impact of incompatible vibrations. Sometimes, however, you may strike something (even gently) and notice that its vibrations continue and even increase or seem to build upon themselves. This is harmonic oscillation caused by resonance.

Physicists often describe harmonic oscillation by using another common experience: as a young child, you may have discovered that pushing a friend in a swing higher and higher was not so much a matter of strength as it was of timing. Even small pushes, if delivered in rhythm with the frequency of the swinging motion, ultimately produce a larger amplitude.

This same thing can happen with bridges. On opening days, parade troops are warned to break step and not march in unison across the new bridge since their collective vibrations may induce resonance and cause damage to the structure. Resonance can be induced through other forces, however, including the wind—which does not obey orders.

Wind-induced resonance is the fear of all bridge engineers. A gale blowing at the correct frequency for a long enough time can induce a harmonic oscillation pattern that, like an accelerating wave on the ocean surface, can roll the length of a bridge, double back upon itself, and roll in the opposite direction with increasing power until the bridge literally vibrates itself to pieces.

This occurred in November 1940 at the Tacoma Narrows Bridge in the State of Washington. The graceful suspension bridge was only four months old when a mild gale blowing through the narrows hit it and caused a slight fluctuating force to ripple throughout the structure. As the bridge continued to absorb and amplify the vibrations of the gale, a self-perpetuating wave moved across its surface and continued until the bridge collapsed. In 1951, a similar episode threatened the Golden Gate Bridge when a gale with winds of 70 mph blasted through the Gate. At the height of the rippling, one side of the span was pitching 11 feet higher than the other side, and the Bridge was closed for the first time. It has been closed many times since, often for high-wind conditions. After the 1951 scare, a series of criss-crossed girders was installed under the roadway to help dissipate energy.

Getting Away from It All

Not everybody who uses the Golden Gate Bridge does so to get from San Francisco to Marin or from Marin to San Francisco. A great many people use the bridge to dash themselves to death by jumping from its heights. By 1984 more than 850 bridge visitors had decided to take the short way home, making the Golden Gate Bridge the number 1 suicide attraction in the world. Nowhere else even comes close.

Harold Wobber was the first. Less than three months after the Bridge was opened, Harold went from center span and fought off a bystander who tried to detain him. Since then, they have come by car, by foot, by bus and by taxi to follow Harold Wobber's historic lead.

Death is a 98% certainty for the leapers, but it is a far messier proposition than most people imagine. Travelling at over 75 mph leaves one violently disfigured upon impact with the water. Only about a dozen have survived.

In the past two decades the number of leapers has increased almost every year. And the jumpers are getting younger, with their average age declining from the early 50's to early 20's.

Statistics disprove a commonly held explanation for bridge suicides. It is often said that the Golden Gate Bridge is a magnet for troubled souls who have reached the edge of the continent with no place left to go. So they jump. But as Tom Horton points out in *Superspan*, 80% of the recovered bodies are those of Bay Area residents, not recent arrivals.

Another incorrect supposition holds that almost everyone who jumps leaps to the Bay side out of love or disappointment associated with San Francisco. But the reason most people jump toward San Francisco is simply that the oceanside pedestrian way is open only on weekends.

Proposals to erect a suicide barrier have been hotly debated for years. Other famous monuments that have conflated beauty and death have barriers—the Eiffel Tower, the Empire State Building. Beyond question, a barrier would save lives, but the public at large opposes the idea. The most frequent objections—that a barrier would mar the Bridge's beauty or that potential suicides would only go somewhere else—seem rather weak compared to the reality of so many people dead.

Guides

SAN FRANCISCO FREE & EASY:
THE NATIVE'S GUIDEBOOK
William Ristow, *editor and chief writer*
Downwind Publications, A Bay Guardian Book
San Francsico. 1980.

Winner of *The New York Times*'s best guidebook award for San Francisco (May 1982). Hotels, inns, motels, restaurants, bars, a chapter for kids and parents, trips, ethnic music, the gay scene, grassroots politics, arts, an after-midnight guide, nude beaches, and the "Native's Yellow Pages."

THE OTHER GUIDE TO SAN FRANCISCO
(OR 105 THINGS TO DO AFTER YOU'VE TAKEN A CABLE CAR TO FISHERMAN'S WHARF)
Jay Hansen
Chronicle Books, San Francisco. 1980.

This book is for visitors who prefer to become involved in the day-to-day life of the city rather than merely to hit all the required sights. Includes "Odysseys and Pilgrimages," which trace in brief summary a few of the city's important cultural episodes (Barbary Coast, Beat Generation, Haight-Ashbury, *Rolling Stone,* and Lenny Bruce).

GUIDE TO SAN FRANCISCO FOR SELF-PROPELLED PEOPLE and MAP OF SAN FRANCISCO STREET GRADES FOR THE BICYCLIST AND PEDESTRIAN
W. S. Chase
2001 Grove Street, San Francisco 94117.

For cyclists, runners, walkers, joggers, skaters, the old and the young, the fit and the less-than-fit. Both maps show every street grade in San Francisco by a color-coded system. The first publication includes more information, such as suggested routes according to challenge, location of bicycle shops, and bridge and ferry access to the city. If you plan to depart from the gentle slope of Highway 1, you will be interested in these maps.

Visitor Center

SAN FRANCISCO CONVENTION & VISITORS BUREAU
1390 Market Street, San Francisco 94102.
391-2000 (recorded message of daily events).

Located at Powell and Market Streets (take the BART or MUNI Metro to the Powell Street stop), the Bureau was established in 1909 as a clearinghouse for all visitor-serving information. Write or visit to pick up multilingual maps, shopping guides, restaurant and nightlife guides, and lists of lodging, events, and tours.

MARIN

LIKE A CALIFORNIA movie star, Marin County is rich and beautiful. The state's most affluent county, it is also luxuriously scenic.

There is nothing ordinary about Marin County. Embraced by bay and ocean and capped by the Bay area's stateliest mountain, the county offers nearly every natural amenity imaginable. Highway 1's route passes through the heart of Marin's most sublime scenic attractions.

Beginning at the Golden Gate Bridge, Highway 1 streaks northward over Waldo Grade just above tourist-oriented Sausalito with shops, restaurants, and various brandishments of upscale consumerism. Shortly after Highway 1 separates from Freeway 101, it turns toward Marin's seaward side and 40 miles of California's best protected shoreline. Along the way are Muir Woods, Mount Tamalpais State Park, Stinson Beach, Point Reyes National Seashore, and Tomales Bay, all of which exist in unmarred and unthreatened splendor.

West Marin offers many quintessential Highway 1 scenic pleasures. There are crashing waves, and mountain edge cliffs north of Muir Beach, a wide sandy beach at Stinson, and fantastic vistas and abundant wildlife everywhere.

Waldo Tunnel

Construction of the Marin approach to the Golden Gate Bridge required a different type of complex engineering and construction skills than had been required by the Bridge. Workers had to build what was essentially a mountain road over an earthquake fault and highly unstable soils. The design of the $2 million road required inspired ingenuity and was one of the largest individual projects undertaken up to that time by the Department of Highways.

Road construction at Waldo Grade was similar to Devil's Slide. To reach earth stable enough to hold a road in place on the side of the sweeping hills, soils had to be removed to a depth of 40 feet, then refilled with rock back-fill to increase stability. Continual slides during construction aggravated the difficulties; more than 2 million yards of material were excavated and refilled before the project was over.

The boring of Waldo Tunnel was less of a problem: tunneling through the hillside took only about six months, much of it done by hand with jackhammers. Despite the unsteady soils, the three main excavations were accomplished without a major slide. Even before the concrete was set, the timbers used to stabilize the inside of the 42-foot–wide tunnel were never challenged by slides or cave-ins. When the bridge was ready, so too was the new road, its newly invented sodium-vapor lights twinkling in the afterglow.

Before the Bridge

Before the completion of the bridge to San Francisco, Marin County was sparsely populated, heavily rural, and fully reliant on its ferry for access to San Francisco, which sometimes seemed as far away as the locations in the *Tales of Arabian Nights*. Before there was a ferry, there was hardly a Marin at all, save the one divided into *rancheros* from land often stolen from the trusting Miwoks.

All the land that Highway 1 now intersects between Sausalito and the ocean was part of the Rancho Sausalito, which eventually came under the ownership of Samuel R. Throckmorton. In 1868, Throckmorton, "the undisputed Lord of Sausalito" sold 1,200 acres on Richardson Bay to the Sausalito Land and Ferry Company, which then laid out the town and started selling off lots. Prospective customers were brought by ferry aboard the steamer *Princess,* a near-antique that trundled passengers from Meiggs Wharf on San Francisco's North Beach for a fare of 25 cents. The town boomed.

Marin City Public Housing

As you drive north on Highway 1 down the Waldo Grade, you will notice a cluster of houses nestled into the hills on your left. These red tile–roofed buildings are Marin City, a public housing project built in the 1960s. The project provides housing for about 600 families, many of whom were residents of the first "Marin City" on this site.

A Wartime Settlement

In 1942 the federal government condemned 202 waterfront and hillside acres at Sausalito to provide a temporary shipbuilding facility, Marinship. Housing was thrown up wherever possible, and people, many of them poor rural minorities, flocked to the area. When the yard closed in 1945 the people remained, unemployed and living in temporary pre-fab housing that rapidly deteriorated into a slum. In the late 1950s the Marin Housing Authority purchased one of these housing enclaves for $900,000. The site, called Marin City, comprised 350 acres of condemned farmland and marsh and still housed a large part of its 6,000 wartime inhabitants.

Distinguished Public Housing

The County designed, built, and manages the Marin City that you see today. The architectural style of this public housing project has been nationally acclaimed and its design proposed as a model. Lawrence Halprin designed the landscape, architects John Warnecke and Aaron Green designed the pre-unit budget allocated buildings. Marin City is an exception to a great deal of subsidized housing in this country, which is often intentionally built to be unappealing.

County Profile

Geographic

Land Area (acres)	332,800
Land Area (sq. miles)	520.0
Water Area (acres)	43,500
Water Area (sq. miles)	68.0
Acres in Public Ownership	46,691.11
Percent in Public Ownership	14.03
Miles of Public Roads	1,190
County Seat	San Rafael

Demographic

Population	223,800
State Rank by Population	22
Projected 1990 Population	227,200
Unemployment Rate (state avg. = 9.9)	6.0
Per Capita Personal Income	$17,428
State Rank by Income	1
Total Assessed Property Value	$8,548,794,201

Environment

Hawk Hill

Every fall an extraordinary procession soars over the Golden Gate. More than 10 species of hawks, including kestrels, sharp-shins, Coopers, red-tails, and the rare peregrine falcon join the procession, congregating in flight above the Marin headlands to catch powerful northwest thermal winds. (The heavy-bodied hawks can't swim, and they take special precautions over dangerous waterways like the Golden Gate.)

The hawk migration, which begins in August

and ends in November, peaks at the autumnal equinox. The ridge above Point Diablo on Marin's north shore, west of the bridge, has become known as Hawk Hill and it is the only known major hawk lookout in western North America. On most days during the migration, several hundred hawks can be seen. On September 21, 1984, enthralled observers counted an astounding 2,833.

Roadside Attractions

On the Other Side of the Rainbow

Marin County begins on the Golden Gate Bridge, which it shares with San Francisco. The Bridge's north vista point offers fantastic views of San Francisco Bay, but the personality of Marin doesn't appear until after you pass through the Waldo Tunnel, whose rainbow entrance announces what is probably the most unselfconscious opinion that any California county holds of itself.

Just before the exit for Stinson Beach stands Marin City and houseboats at Sausalito's Gates Five and Six. Marin City, on the west side of the road, holds a huge weekend flea market.

Highway 1 separates from US 101 after their short conjunction in Northern California at the exit for Stinson Beach. On the frontage road is Commodore Seaplanes offering 25-minute seaplane rides for $20 a person. The ride takes off and lands on the San Francisco Bay and passes close over the water, with flyovers of San Francisco and the Golden Gate Bridge. This is a five-star attraction.

The Rainbow Tunnel

The rainbow tunnel originated as a whimsical notepad sketch by the Cal Trans engineer charged with repainting the entrance to Marin County. His light-hearted primer paint job stole the hearts of Marin's commuters and the rainbows stayed. The entrance to the tunnel going the other direction—out of Marin—is a drab green.

Resources

AREA CODE: 415

Rules of the Road

Highway 1 enters Marin County as a wide freeway, the number of traffic lanes in each direction varying according to commuter peak hours when buses and commuter diamond lanes are in effect. Soon, however, the road twists and turns its way in two-lane glory to the edge of the Pacific. Be prepared for 180° switchbacks at dizzying heights, and watch for rock slides and road repair crews. If traveling leisurely, use roadside turnouts. Travelers relying on public transit should know that service to west Marin is very limited, so plan ahead.

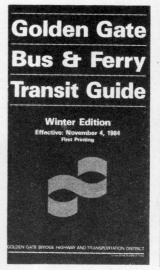

Public Transportation

453-2100 Golden Gate Bus & Ferry
433-1500 Greyhound Bus
454-0964 Marin Senior Council
457-7080 Travelers Transit, San Rafael
861-POOL Van or Carpool Information
453-2100 Special Events Transit
921-5858 Golden Gate Bridge, Highway and Transportation District

Tide Tables

Free tide tables issued by one of several public agencies or Chambers of Commerce are often available in stores along Highway 1. For a unique daily depiction of Bay Area tides, pick up Pacific Publishers Tidelog (924-6352). The Tidelog, which can also be used as an appointment calendar, is based on predictions by the National Ocean Service. The illustration is Escher's 1926 woodcut, "Second Day of Creation."

Climate

Marin's climate is typical Mediterranean style. Temperatures seldom exceed 80 and rarely drop below 50. The rainy season is roughly October to March. Dry season is roughly April to September. Summer fog is common as are highly variable winds. Call GGNRA Park Headquarters (663-1092) for daily conditions.

The North Pacific Railroad

Soon the railroad came to Sausalito to further boost its growth. More ferries from San Francisco brought hordes of tourists who picnicked and danced at the Wildwood Inn or searched for treasure amid a shorefront Indian mound that yielded arrowheads, pottery, and human bones for souvenirs.

The North Pacific Railroad was established in 1875 to allow the hauling out of newly cut redwoods above the Russian River. Its route ran north

from Sausalito, angling west through San Anselmo, Fairfax to the Ocean, then north to the Russian River. Above Olema, Highway 1 now follows much of the railroad's original route. The picturesque coaches steamed through some of California's most beautiful landscape, spurring development and providing glimpsed moments of enchantment to travelers. In 1889 a spur line was established from Sausalito to Mill Valley for the purpose of selling homesteads at the foot of Mount Tamalpais to San Franciscans anxious for suburban living. Mill Valley was inaugurated with a picnic and auction sale within weeks of the arrival of the North Pacific Spur. On the first day alone $69,000 worth of small lots were sold.

Sausalito's Most Experienced Mayor

Sally Stanford was a successful businesswoman on both sides of the San Francisco Bay before being elected Mayor of Sausalito in 1976. In 1950 she opened one of Sausalito's most successful restaurants, the Valhalla.

Prior to her move to Sausalito, Stanford earned the respect of all who knew her for her keen business sense in running a number of San Francisco's finest whorehouses. Stanford, who took her name from a sports-page headline ("Stanford Wins"), prided herself on always providing her customers with "the best of everything" at her famous bordellos on San Francisco's Nob and Russian Hills.

At one time Stanford managed four houses in San Francisco, each more elegant than the last. One had a glass-roofed court, another was famous for its exotic marble bathtub.

She was elegant and she had a heart of gold, devoting countless hours to the cause of saving Caryl Chessman from the electric chair (despite his background as a red-light bandit) and opposing the killing of California deer. Her election successes in Sausalito demonstrated a unique example of electorate good sense.

Sausalito's Houseboats

Over 300 houseboats are moored on Sausalito's waterfront, descendants of an era when houseboat living was conducted in a far different environment than that of contemporary Sausalito.

In the 1960s the abandoned piers of Marinship became the perfect rent-free location for a Bay Area artist community that sprung up on a motley collection of floating houses on the Sausalito waterfront. The houses were imaginatively constructed on practically anything that would float —tugboats, skiffs, even anti-aircraft balloon barges. They became an expression of personal creativity and ingenuity, and within the community, a sense of group regard thrived.

Alan Watts, who lived with painter Jean Varda at Gate Five on the converted ferry *Vallejo*, imparted a sense of good-natured California Zen to the houseboat community's residents. Nearby, artist Piro Caro lived on another converted ferry, *The Issaquah*. Gate Five became the spiritual and philosophical center of the San Francisco hip scene: Allen Ginsberg and Aldous and Laura Huxley were frequent visitors, and Duke Ellington once gave a performance on *The Vallejo*. Today

the boat is home to the Alan Watts Society for Comparative Philosophy.

Apart from Watt's old houseboat and several elaborately handcrafted and decorated vessels, little remains of Sausalito's original houseboat community. Strict enforcement of county building codes as well as increased concern for unconventional sewage arrangements have transformed the community after years of struggle against public agencies. Once primitive conditions were modernized, Sausalito's waterfront became prime real estate. Enter the inartistic affluent, exit the unaffluent artistic.

San Francisco Bay Model

U.S. Army Corps of Engineers, 2100 Bridgeway, Sausalito 94965. 332-3870.

Covering two acres, this working model is a hydraulic scale replica of the entire San Francisco Bay that enables researchers to analyze impacts of fill, pollution, freshwater flows, and saltwater intrusion. The visitor's center, open Monday through Friday from 9 am to 5 pm, offers displays, a theater, amphitheater, library, and overlooks of the model.

The San Andreas Fault

Highway 1 in Marin County provides a fine opportunity to view, touch, and understand the San Andreas Fault, perhaps the most famous geological feature in California. Here, the road straddles the fault zone for most of its inland route. You are driving along one of the most seismically active stretches of highway in the world. When the road reaches Olema, it is at the epicenter of the 1906 quake, which caused surface displacement here of over 20 feet.

The San Andreas fault ravages the coast for more than 600 miles from Mexico to Cape Mendocino. The fault zone varies from 100 yards in width to over a mile, with a multitude of minor veins branching off along its route. Over 60 million years ago, action in the fault zone wrenched away from the mainland what is now Baja California, creating the Gulf of California. This agitation carved the Imperial Valley, formed the Coast Range, split open the Golden Gate, and laid the beds for Bolinas and Tomales Bays.

Sausalito

Sausalito's most interesting attractions are still related to its maritime character. Near the center of town—adjacent to the Vina del Mar Plaza (named for Sausalito's Chilean sister city) with a fountain and elephants designed by McKim, Meade, and White—is the dock for the ferry to San Francisco. The *Golden Gate Ferry* is the most economical way to experience San Francisco Bay. With a close-up approach of Alcatraz, an on-ship bar, sociable fellow travelers, and an entourage of

following seagulls, the Sausalito ferry is a beautiful way to enjoy a beautiful day.

Another way to enjoy the entire Bay at once is to visit the model of San Francisco Bay, which provides historical and geographical information.

Golden Gate National Recreation Area

The GGNRA is one of the world's most spectacular urban area parks and Highway 1 takes you there. Begin your journey with one of these guides.

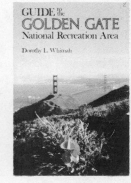

THE COMPLETE GUIDE TO THE GOLDEN GATE NATIONAL RECREATION AREA
Karen Liberatore, produced by Goodchild and Jacobsen
Chronicle Books, San Francisco. 1982.

Written with the voice and knowledge of a user and lover of the GGNRA, extremely accessible and gifted with insights not usually found in guide books. All parts of the GGNRA are covered, as well as many neighboring areas, including Point Reyes National Seashore and Audubon Canyon Ranch.

GUIDE TO THE GOLDEN GATE NATIONAL RECREATION AREA
Dorothy L. Whitnah, Wilderness Press. 1978.

Comprehensive and a good companion to Whitnah's book on the Point Reyes National Seashore. The introductory history on the citizens' movement to acquire land and establish the GGNRA is particularly informative.

Alan Watts

Alan Watts was a longtime resident of Marin County during a period in which the quiet verdancy of the county north of San Francisco seemed to speak in particularly strong spiritual terms to the aspirations of a generation on a quest. From the 1950s Watts lived alternately on a converted ferryboat, *The Vallejo*, in Sausalito and in a small house on Mount Tamalpais. He was a man of wit and irreverence who became a spokesperson for an influential spiritual philosophy largely based on Zen but incorporating features of California good-time sensuality. Watt's approach was to replace "stone-buddha" asceticism with a more pleasurable and less up-tight "active zen."

About himself Watts said in his 1972 autobiography: "My vocation in life is to wonder about the nature of the universe. This leads me into philosophy, psychology, religion and mysticism, not only as subjects to be discussed but also as things to be experienced. . . . Some people expect me to be their guru or Messiah or exemplar, and are extremely disconcerted when they discover my 'wayward spirit' or element of irreducible rascality, and say to their friends, 'How could he possibly be a genuine mystic and be so addicted to nicotine and alcohol?' or have occasional

shudders of anxiety? or be sexually interested in women? or lack enthusiasm for physical exercise?"

In the *Divine Comedy,* Dante likens the song of the angels to the laughter of the universe, a comparison Watts appreciated and in some ways represented.

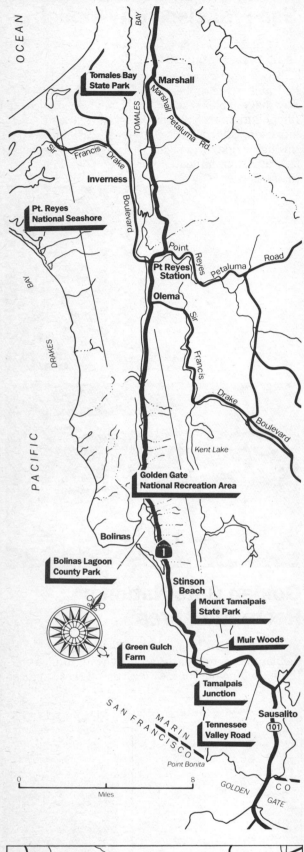
Marin's Land Preservation Movement

In 1907 William Kent donated the first 300 acres to the federal government for what was to become Muir Woods, and thereby inaugurated a course of action that continues to define the county's evolution. Kent's motives may have been less than altruistic—he saw the original donation principally as a means to appreciate the value of his adjoining property—but the ensuing land conservation ethic has shaped the appearance and quality of the west Marin countryside more than any single land use and influenced attitudes toward the preservation of scenic areas throughout California and the nation.

Kent's gift was a marvel of generosity from a man with some of the strongest personal ambitions and land-trading acumen in the state. His donation of Redwood Canyon to the national government was heralded as an act of supreme significance by John Muir who said, "This is the best tree lovers monument that could be found in all the forests of the world." And indeed it was, not only for the magnificent first-growth redwoods that it preserved but also for the impetus it gave to the ideal of scenic preservation in Marin County.

Mt. Tam and Point Reyes

In the 1930s, after years of pressuring the state legislature to act, the Tamalpais Conservation Club succeeded in having Mount Tamalpais designated a state park. The club also raised more than $50,000 to assist the state in the purchase (and condemnation) of the lands for Mount Tamalpais State Park.

As early as 1935 local conservationists were agitating for the preservation of the spectacularly unique Point Reyes Peninsula. Their influence resulted in a recommendation from the National Park Service for the purchase of 53,000 acres of Point Reyes (total price: $2.4 million). When the U.S. Congress failed to act, preservationists persevered on the county level and succeeded in obtaining Drakes Beach in 1938 and

McClures Beach in 1942; and the state acquired the major portion of Tomales Bay State Park in 1945. After World War II, logging operations and subdivision lot lines began to appear with increasing frequency. Conservationists, aided by Congressman Clem Miller and California Senator Clair Engel, finally succeeded in having the entire 53,000 acres authorized for acquisition by the Kennedy administration in 1962. Lady Bird Johnson presided at opening day celebrations on September 20, 1966.

No Marina Del Rey

In 1957 the California state legislature created Bolinas Harbor District, and architect Norman Gilroy

was enlisted to create a lagoon plan. His proposal called for the development of a Marina del Rey North: a pleasure boat marina for 1,600 yachts with cafés, motels, a shopping mall, and heliport. Conservationists led by the Marin County Audubon Society insisted that the lagoon—a particularly sensitive portion of Marin's natural environment—be preserved against such indelicate treatment, and they held sway. (In 1961 the Marin Audubon Society entered into an agreement for purchase of a 506-acre heron and egret rookery at the ranch, saving it from subdivision into 20-acre parcels.) The Bolinas Harbor plans were scrapped and after

years of back-and-forth with Governor Reagan's administration, jurisdiction was given to Marin County, which created the 840-acre Bolinas Lagoon County Park and committed itself to maintain the park in accord with recommendations from the National Conservation Foundation.

What Almost Happened

In 1949 the State Department of Highways proposed a new six-lane freeway along Sausalito's waterfront. Residents reacted with horror and organized opposition—stopping implementation of the plan and preserving Sausalito's intimate relationship to the water's edge. Their protests signaled a new era of community attitudes toward freeways. In 1962 another freeway proposal would have replaced Highway 1 along the ocean and transformed western Marin by destroying countless natural habitats. Again, conservationists prevailed, as they did in 1966 when Balboa Shores, a super-development with 5,000 homes, an air strip, shopping center, and condominiums was halted by conservationists led by the Sierra Club.

Often it appeared that the forces of chance were on the side of conservationists as well, such as in the case of Marincello, a planned housing development for 20,000 people on 2,000 acres of Golden Gate headlands financed by the Gulf Oil Company. After years of opposition, the development finally won enough approvals to proceed with construction only to be stopped at the last moment when the developer suffered a heart attack.

The Golden Gate National Recreation Area

Most spectacular of all conservation achievements has been the creation of the Golden Gate National Recreation Area (GGNRA), 35,000 acres of protected parkland unique to any public open space in the world. The acquisition was coordinated by the People for a Golden Gate National Recreation Area, a grassroots conservation organization that harnessed 65 years of local land-preservation consciousness to bring about the protection of a major portion of Marin's shoreline.

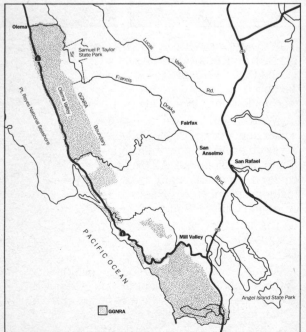

Environment

Roadside Geology: The Franciscan Formation and the Salinian Block

The edge of the North American plate is to your right as you drive along the bed of the San Andreas fault. The geological base here is of Franciscan rocks. The Franciscan Formation consists of mostly large, muddy, dark sandstone that has been crushed, folded, and mauled over the centuries by the onslaught of the continental plates at their meeting. The brave outcroppings visible in fields along Highway 1, surrounded by crushed fragments, are Franciscan Formation, as are the rocks forming the ridges of the Coastal Range.

Geologists are particularly unfond of Franciscan sediments as the rock is usually a monotonous mash, thousands of feet thick, so folded and merged that it is next to impossible to distinguish one layer from another, or to identify fossils—both activities that are basic to dating and understanding the origins of geological formations. As a result, this part of the coast and the Coast Range will always protect some of its geological secrets.

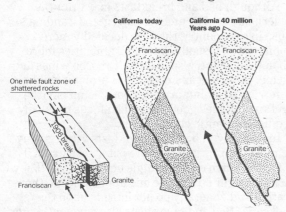

The land west of Highway 1 and the San Andreas fault is comprised of a granite base known as the Salinian Block, a base which to geologists is hopelessly out of place in Northern California, bearing no similarity at all to the inland formations. As it turns out, the Salinian Block *doesn't* belong here; it is a geological transient in Marin, having hitched a ride along the San Andreas at a rate of about two inches per year.

The point of origin of the Salinian Block is a surprising 350 miles to the south. Geologists have matched its granite base with that in the southern edge of the Sierra Nevada. According to this theory, the land that now forms the Pt. Reyes Peninsula was severed from the Sierra Nevada some 35–40 million years ago.

Roadside Attractions

Tam Junction

From here north, Highway 1 is signed as the Shoreline Highway.

After circling back under the freeway, Highway 1 is soon crossed by Tennesse Valley Road, where a left turn at the vegetable stand will take you to the trailhead for the Tennessee Valley Trail. From the trailhead it's a level 2-mile hike through a bucolic valley to the ocean.

On the other side of Highway 1 at Tennessee Valley Road is Le Camembert, a fine French restaurant that is not too expensive. Its real attraction, however, is a small deli that sells inexpensive gourmet food and desserts. Example: a truffle pâté on a large baguette for about the price of a Big Mac and a shake.

Highway 1 turns west at Tamalpais Junction to regain the sea. In a short distance its character becomes rural, with a giant stand of eucalyptus trees accompanying the road past the cutoff for Mount Tamalpais and Muir Woods. If your destination is Muir Woods, however, you may prefer to wait a few miles for the Muir Beach entrance to the woods; that approach is a bit shorter and affords the opportunity to continue on Highway 1 along Green Gulch until it meets the ocean.

A short distance past the Mt. Tam cutoff, Highway 1 bends into an S curve that opens up a startling vista of Green Gulch to the blue ocean beyond. The Miwok Trail intersects the road at this juncture and in a few hundred yards is the entrance to Green Gulch Farm.

Muir Woods

Muir Woods Visitor Center.
388-2595.

Muir Woods is open from 8 am to dusk every day. You will find a snack bar, gift shop, bookstore, restrooms, parking, self-guided nature trails, sensory and Braille trails for the visually impaired, and handicapped-accessible facilities. The main attraction, of course, are the *Sequoia sempervirens*, the only stand of virgin redwoods located within a major urban area.

Six miles of trails wind through the 550 acres of Muir Woods, some connecting with other GGNRA and Point Reyes National Seashore Trails and trails into Mount Tamalpais State Park. The 400- to 800-year-old redwoods receive over 2 million visitors a year. If you go be sure to look for the albino baby redwood, a rare, small tree with silvery white shimmering leaves, attached forever to its mother's roots on which it depends for chlorophyll, the stuff of its young (only a few hundred years) life.

Mount Tamalpais State Park

801 Panoramic Highway, Mill Valley 94941.
388-2070.

The state park at Mount Tamalpais encompasses 6,200 acres. On clear days views to the east can exceed 200 miles, to the crests of the Sierra Nevada and Cascade Ranges across the Sacramento River Delta. The park opens for day use an hour before sunrise and closes half an hour after sunset. There are two picnic

Resources

Using the GGNRA

Headquarters
Building 201, Fort Mason, San Francisco 94123.

The main offices of the GGNRA are open weekdays from 8 am to 5 pm. Maps and brochures are available here as well as at most rangers' offices in park locations. Useful phone numbers:

556-0560	General Information
556-7940	Park Police
556-6030	Weather Information
921-9529	Community Gardens
556-4462	Special Programs
556-3535	Interpretation Office

Headlands Ranger Station and Visitor Center
Building 1050, Marin Headlands, Sausalito 94965. 331-1540.

Open 8:30 am to 5:00 pm daily for information and brochures on portions of the GGNRA within Marin. Other numbers at the Marin Center are:

331-2777	American Youth Hostel
331-SEAL	California Marine Mammal Center
331-9622	YMCA Point Bonita Outdoor Center
332-5771	Yosemite Institute of the Headlands
332-8200	Golden Gate Energy Center

GGNRA Ranger Stations Outside the Headlands

383-7717	Tennessee Valley
388-2595	Muir Woods
868-0942	Muir and Stinson Beaches Ranger
868-1922	Weather Information
663-1092	Olema Valley

areas with tables, stoves, piped drinking water, and restrooms; individual family overnight campsites for tent-style camping (first-come, first-served); and a group camp for up to 40 people (reservations required, open April 15 through November 15).

The trails on Mount Tam are the best developed and maintained in the Bay Area, with a history of use that dates to the 19th century. About 30 miles of park trails link up to the extensive 200-mile-long network of trails through Muir Woods, the GGNRA, and the Marin Municipal Water District's watershed lands. One of the trails leads to a natural amphitheater that offers excellent acoustics for shows and an impressive scenic backdrop 2,000 feet above sea level on the eastern slope of the mountain. Contact the park ranger staff for more information and maps of facilities and trails.

The Stage Road

In 1869 the County Board of Supervisors approved a 12-mile stage road from Sausalito to the Ocean and along the shore northward, first establishing the route of present-day Highway 1 in Marin. The State Legislature allocated $14,000 to help pay for the road, $3,000 of which went to Samuel Throckmorton for purchase of the right-of-way through his land. The unsurfaced road was quickly built, in an amazing 13 weeks, and completed on November 1, 1870.

The rapid completion was the result of hard work by the men who cleared the path. The road crew, most of whom were Chinese, slaved with small reward, racing to finish the project before the onslaught of winter rains made the work all the more miserable. The 15 white men on the crew were paid $2 a day; the 100 Chinese men, half that amount.

Anti-Chinese feeling ran high in Marin: in appreciation for constructing practically all the county's wagon roads and railroad lines—not to mention caring for the gardens and children of the rich—the Chinese were attacked, set-upon, and exploited. In 1886 informal racism was channeled into the establishment of the Anti-Chinese League, with groups in Sausalito and Tomales.

When the road was completed, the presence of the stage along the coast altered habits and changed lives. On the ocean side, the stagecoach replaced the schooner as the principal means of transportation. Farm produce went cheaper and quicker by wagon, and travelers found a new romance in the unexplored countryside, despite the roughness of the road and the obstruction of gates thrown up across the road by "The Lord of Sausalito," out of petty spite.

The Crookedest Railroad in the World

Within a few years after the North Pacific Railroad was established another small railroad was started from Mill Valley up the face of the half-mile-high Mount Tamalpais. The Mount Tamalpais and Muir Woods Railway was to go only to the top of the mountain, but for thousands of passengers the marvelously serpentine route and magnificent vistas made the short route the most exciting excursion in Northern California. For the mountaintop offered unmatched views of the coastal range, San Francisco Bay, the city, and the ocean: "Ships under full majestic sail passing through the Golden Gate looked like toy boats from [the] imposing height."

Open gravity cars holding 30 people each sped the non-faint-of-heart down the side of the mountain, whipping them around the "double bow knot" and through the redwoods in roller-coaster fashion. They screamed and they laughed, and when the cars seemed most certain to jump the track, they grabbed the arm of the "gravity man," who held the brake-handle between his legs, and pleaded for mock mercy.

When a side line was built to Redwood Canyon (later

Bed and Breakfast Inns

One of the most significant recent occurences on the Northern California coast has been the emergence of numerous bed and breakfast inns. Many charming old houses along the roadside, which once only nodded graciously to the passing traveler, have been converted into small overnight accommodations, now the traveler's destination.

The bed and breakfast phenomenon originated in Europe, but has found an extremely receptive greeting in California. A major appeal of bed and breakfasts is their strong evocation of place, affording a reasonably close experience of what it is like to live in the area, an experience not generally available at larger-scale chain motels.

The presence of so many bed and breakfasts along the coast is the direct result of the California Coastal Commission, which has generally prevented the development of large motels along the north coast because of their incompatability with the environment. In the face of an expanding north coast tourist industry, bed and breakfasts have sprung up to accommodate the tourist in search of a place to spend the night.

Although bed and breakfasts may offer the modern day replacement for a visit to Grandma's house in the country, they are decidedly more sophisticated, usually providing amenities more urban than country, such as well-chosen wines and cuisine. Most bed and breakfasts prohibit children, preferring to maintain an almost solemn environment that exudes good taste. The focus is usually on quiet, romantic charm.

In their favor, bed and breakfasts are arguably the most appropriate type of visitor serving facility for the north coast's fragile environment. They are usually suited in scale and appearance to their location and generally do not intrude upon the landscape. Bed and breakfasts also frequently preserve significant historical architecture, in addition to benefitting the local economy because they are generally owned by small-scale entrepreneurs who spend their receipts where they live.

Muir Woods), the attraction became more popular yet. Rolling through the redwoods, passengers with their heads back could watch the sunlight break through the tops of the tall trees. Then they would disembark at Muir Inn to enjoy lunch and pre-Prohibition pleasures.

For years, the operation of the Mount Tamalpais and Muir Woods Railway went on apace, but soon a new auto road provided another access to Muir Woods, and when Tamalpais Tavern was reopened after a fire, the new building included a parking lot. Eventually, sightseeing buses sought the top of Mount Tamalpais and jammed into Muir Woods with eager visitors whose modern minds had not even considered the train.

Environment

Plate Tectonics

The San Andreas fault zone is the meeting place of two of the great floating geological masses that make up the earth's surface. According to the theory of plate tectonics, huge floating plates, called *lithosphere*, compose the outer layer of the earth, kept afloat by a core *asthenosphere* of hot molten material hundreds of miles thick.

As these crusts or plates bob around on the earth's surface, two kinds of events take place. When two plates meet, one will override the other,

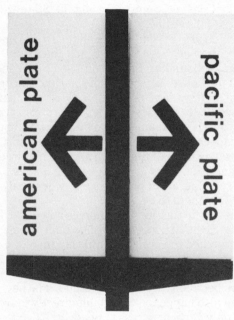

which then melts and dives down toward the asthenosphere. When plates are moving away from each other, they create a ridge of molten material rising from below.

In the San Andreas fault zone, the first case applies. The fault line on the map represents the meeting place of the Pacific plate on the west and the North American plate on the east. Geologists estimate that the Pacific plate moves about two inches a year in a northwesterly direction relative to the North American plate, which forms our continent. There are exceptions, of course—such as 1906 when it moved over 20 feet in a matter of minutes.

These movements are called earthquakes and their cause is explained by the theory of elastic rebound.

Elastic Rebound

As the Pacific and North American plates rub shoulders along the San Andreas fault, they tend to push each other into an armlock. Each plate has a certain amount of elasticity in its geological makeup, enabling it to dig in and absorb more and more tension as it rubs against the other. Eventually, however, the strain becomes too much, and instead of gently slipping past each other, the locked edges abruptly break their hold, shattering the edge in the process, as the opposing plates part ways.

This slippage is referred to as *elastic rebound* and is the cause of what we call earthquakes. Scientists further distinguish two types of earthquakes: *shallow-focus quakes*, which are the result of slippage of plates as they move laterally (most typical in California and the West), and *deep-focus quakes*, which occur when one plate is forced directly under the other in a head-on collision (more typical in South America, such as Peru in 1970). Shallow quakes extend up to 10 miles into the earth's surface and are often more intense and more destructive within a smaller area; deep-focus earthquakes come from as far down as 25 miles and tend to be felt much further away, but with relatively less force as the shock waves dissipate on their journey up to the surface.

Roadside Attractions

Green Gulch Farm and Zen Center

*It's not because it is.
It's not because it isn't.
It is because it is
because it's not at all.*
James Broughton, "Those Old Zen Blues"

Green Gulch Farm and Green Dragon Zen Temple are part of the San Francisco Zen Center. The Farm covers 110 acres of a ranch once owned by George Wheelwright, a physicist and inventor who came to California with his society wife, Hope Livermore, after co–inventing the Polaroid Camera at the Land—Wheelwright Labs in Boston.

Today about 50 Zen students live at the center, meditating and performing the work of the world by raising flowers, herbs, and the organic vegetables that are served at Greens, the Zen Center's highly regarded restaurant at Fort Mason. The students, who spend only a brief sojourn at Green Gulch, just one of the San Francisco Zen Center's outposts, work hard and give significance to the Zen proverb: Before enlightenment, chop wood, carry water—after enlightenment, chop wood, carry water.

The Zen Center's public trails, which cut through Green Gulch, are open at all times. The Sunday morning public program includes meditation instruction, a lecture, discussion, and lunch. You can skip the meditation instruction (beginning at 8:30) and arrive for just the lecture (10:00) and stay on for the discussion and lunch.

Muir Beach

Just north of Green Gulch is Muir Beach, where Redwood Creek finds its way to the ocean. At this fine beach nude bathing is unofficially sanctioned at the north end.

By the turnoff to Muir Beach a white-sided English Pub and small inn, the Pelican Inn, serves excellent English beers and Irish ale on tap (Watney's, John Courage, and Guinness), as well as providing satisfying pub food, better tasting than what you might find in England. Often there

is music and sometimes skits from Shakespeare. The pub is authentic and very warming on a foggy day, its great-sized fireplace providing needed comfort. On the wall is a quotation: "A night with Venus, a lifetime with Mercury"—which loses none of its poetic interest when you realize that mercury was a standard English remedy for venereal disease.

Past the Pelican Inn is the exit to Muir Woods.

Resources

Geology

Your appreciation of Marin's roadside geology will be enhanced by these books.

GUIDE TO POINT REYES PENINSULA AND THE SAN ANDREAS FAULT ZONE
Field Trip A, Bulletin 190, Alan J. Galloway
California Division of Mines and Geology.

This guide, one of a set of seven, takes the reader on a mile-by-mile itinerary from the south end of the Golden Gate Bridge to Stinson Beach, Olema, Bear Valley, Inverness, Drakes Beach, Point Reyes Lighthouse, Samuel P. Taylor State Park, Greenbrae, and back to San Francisco. Descriptions are technical but clear, and photos helpful.

PEACE OF MIND IN EARTHQUAKE COUNTRY: HOW TO SAVE YOUR HOME AND LIFE
Peter Yanev
Chronicle Books, San Francisco. 1980.

The author, an engineer who specializes in seismic hazards, wrote this do-it-yourself handbook to help residents of Earthquake Country understand the causes of quakes and minimize the dangers of living near an active fault.

ROADSIDE GEOLOGY OF NORTHERN CALIFORNIA
David D. Alt and Donald W. Hyndman
Mountain Press Publishing Co., Missoula, Montana. 1981.

This unique book tells a lot about a complicated subject in a simple manner. Written by geologists for their friends and other people eager to understand rocks, mountains, and sea cliffs without taking a technical scientific course of study, the book truly meets the authors' intention: it's informative but never indigestible.

West Marin Bed and Breakfast Inns

383-6000	Pelican Inn, Muir Beach
868-1757	Grand Hotel, Bolinas
868-1430	Wharf Road, Bolinas
663-8441	Olema Inn, Olema
663-1554	Holly Tree Inn, Point Reyes
663-1709	Thirty-Nine Cypress Road, Point Reyes
669-1244	The Gray Whale, Inverness
669-7392	MacLean House, Inverness
663-8621	Blackthorne Inn, Inverness
669-1648	Ten Inverness Way, Inverness
878-9992	Randall Guest House, Tomales (707)

In Case of Earthquake

Experts claim that most people in a moving car do not even realize when an earthquake is taking place. Should evidence convince you otherwise, their advice is to pull over and stay in the car. Try not to park under electrical lines or wires or culverts, bridges or elevated roads. Remember that the quake itself lasts only about 30 seconds at the most. The road ahead may be damaged, but if you are close to the shoreline try to move slowly on—unless you wish to witness another natural phenomenon, a tsunami.

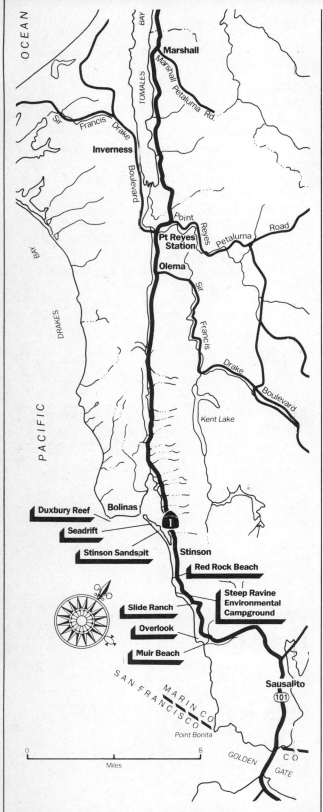

Easkoot's Beach

Mount Tamalpais and Muir Woods were not the only places that attracted travelers in search of outdoor pleasures. Easkoot's (now Stinson) Beach, beneath Mount Tamalpais on the ocean side and up the Sausalito stage road from Muir Woods, offered a long, white sand beach that shined in the eyes of travelers and investors alike. Entrepreneur after entrepreneur came to the place, each more certain than the last that there was money to be made. The beach was too large and too beautiful not to become a major attraction.

The popularity of Mount Tam and Muir Woods also seemed to foreordain the popularity of the wide, even beach with the white rolling combers. The stage stopped there; soon enough, so would visitors aplenty from San Francisco and elsewhere.

Shortly after the completion of the State Road from Sausalito (1871), Alfred Easkoot, a Marin County surveyor who had played a part in getting the stage road built, bought several scattered parcels and moved to the beach. "Captain" Easkoot was once a sailor and he retained a colorful maritime manner. With him came Amelia, his young wife from Philadelphia, dark haired, intelligent, and resourceful.

Soon enough, Easkoot set up a tent resort on the sand, his spellbinding stories and colorful personality lending a sense of shipdeck fantasy to early visitors' seaside excursions. When Easkoot would bluster about his sea adventures, often brandishing a ship's periscope to make his point, Amelia would look on, bemused and tolerant.

Jack Mason describes the resort: "By 1879 there were 20 family tents at Easkoot's Beach, each big enough to sleep five, with canvas dressing rooms for men and women. The Captain collected fees for tent platforms and restrooms,

took fishing parties to sea in his boat *The Margaret*, laid bonfires on the beach at night, hosted candy pulls, games and song fests."

Easkoot kept the resort a lively, charming place that seemed the perfect world for his rolling, gregarious personality and sea-captain charm. Then, Amelia suddenly died. Easkoot became a changed man and the vitality of the place turned sullen, ending a magical time.

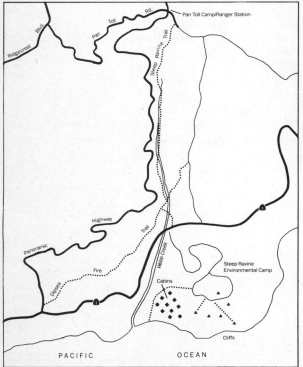

Gates and Seawalls at Seadrift

For years residents of the exclusive Seadrift subdivision at the northern end of Stinson Beach have contested public use of the area. They have built high walls with locked gates that can be opened only with the electromagnetic passes possessively guarded by their owners. They have put up signs declaring the area to be a private beach—it is not. And they have spent thousands of dollars and many years of effort negotiating the matter with the Coastal Commission and the State Attorney General's Office.

Particularly at issue has been the lateral line of demarcation between public beach and private property, a boundary that is confused by the location of the houses on the beach sand and the presence of shifting sand dunes. In 1983 a new element weighed on the impasse when severe storms carried away the sand dunes along with several Seadrift houses. Floodtides and storm-driven surf swept away most of the beach and did hundreds of thousands of dollars in damage to the homes located so vulnerably upon the sand, where only folly dictated them to be.

Fearing further losses of homes and more damage, the Seadrift property owners built a seawall that stretched the entire 1.5 mile length of the subdivision. Constructed from boulders, the seawall cost each of the approximately 110 oceanfront lot owners between $7,000 and $10,000. The new seawall also happened to be built directly in front of the only vertical access at Seadrift.

The Trouble With Seawalls

Unfortunately, seawalls generate an entire realm of problems that may be far worse than the ones they are designed to address. Rock and con-

crete seawalls are particularly poor dissipaters of energy; instead of dissipating the waves' energy like sloping beaches and sand dunes do, hard seawalls reflect the waves back, which scours away the sand on the beach. The end effect can be the total loss of a beach, such as happened in Miami Beach, Florida, when several beachfront condominiums built seawalls that caused the beach to wash away.

Seawalls also have unpredictable effects on nearby beach areas. The neighbor of a seawall owner may have his beachfront seriously eroded or otherwise harmed by the increased velocity of wave action redirected to his portion of the beach.

In March 1984 the County of Marin, realizing the potential for the Seadrift seawall to degrade the beach, ordered a limited environmental impact report to determine its overall effects. Potentially the seawall could be ordered removed. At the same time, the County began steps to tie the resolution of the seawall issue to Seadrift's commitment to improve public access to the beach.

Environment	Roadside Attractions	Resources

Duxbury Reef

Duxbury Reef is the largest intertidal reef on the West Coast and the largest shale reef in the entire United States. At minus tides, the exposed reef stretches half a mile off the Bolinas Peninsula shore. The 66-acre intertidal reef supports unusual and large populations of California mussel, rockboring invertebrates, sea stars, crabs, eels (monkey-face, rock, and wolf), and other marine organisms. Duxbury Reef can be clearly seen from Highway 1 off to the northwest extending south

and west from Bolinas Point. Look for the long stretch of white breakers.

Because the reef is so easy to reach from the Bolinas area, unthinking human visitors have left their mark. Rockclammers leveled the soft shale with their climbing and chipping, while educational groups all too often took their observations home with them. In response to the alarming decline in marine life at Duxbury, the State Water Resources Control Board in 1972 designated Duxbury Reef a marine life reserve. This protective label assures that only certain regulated harvesting can take place—for example, market crabs, rock crabs, abalone, and marine fish, all of which are subject to size, season, and bag limits in California. Since the reserve was established, life has returned to this important aquarian metropolis.

The Stinson Sandspit

The Stinson Beach Sandspit is a 1.5-mile long barrier beach separating Bolinas Lagoon from the Pacific Ocean. The height and width of the dunes were artificially increased when the Seadrift subdivision was built atop them. It is hard to imagine a less appropriate place for development anywhere along the coast than on the Stinson Sandspit.

The Ocean's Ledge

From Muir Beach, Highway 1 climbs back up to the ocean's ledge. There is a sensational view from Muir Beach Overlook Drive, where a short trail climbs out to a rocky outcropping and observation point for the spectacular Marin coastline and San Francisco to the south. This spot was originally a base end station; the concrete bunkers were used as observation points and rangefinders for coastal defense artillery batteries located around the entrance to San Francisco Bay.

Across the road from the overlook is a hillside crop of purple heather, particularly spectacular in the early fall, which is grown on State Park property in a lease-back arrangement with a private rancher. (Almost all the coast from Muir Beach to Stinson Beach lies within Mount Tamalpais State Park.)

Past Slide Ranch are several turnouts with trails that lead to wonderful cliffside vista points with unbelievable views down the coast—and sometimes, but not often, to small sandless beaches. Remember, this is all public property, so you are free to make your way—as freely as the dangerous cliffs allow.

After Steep Ravine Environmental Campground (by reservation only), Red Rock Beach appears at Marker 11.35. Red Rock was one of the proposed state-operated clothing-optional beaches suggested by Director of State Parks Russel Cahill in 1976. The proposal garnered fierce controversy even though almost all the beach areas Cahill named were already clothing-optional areas. Red Rock endures as Marin County's most popular nude beach.

Slide Ranch

Star Route 304, Muir Beach 94965.
383-0358.

Frontier Arts Institute at Slide Ranch is a small farm located 18 miles north of San Francisco off Highway 1. The ranch, once a dairy farm and now within GGNRA, has offered educational programs to children and adults since 1969. Most of the one- to three-day programs are designed for urban children who otherwise might never know the coastal headlands so close to their home.

Facilities at the 134-acre site include a goat barn where participants try their hand at milking, large organic gardens and compost areas, a nature museum, observation beehive and paths to the tide pools. Overnight groups sleep in tents or in a geodesic dome. Contact the ranch in advance since schedules are filled with structured programs and drop-ins are hard to handle.

Steep Ravine Environmental Campground

Steep Ravine Environmental Campground is one of the state's newest coastal parks. Ten primitive cabins and six tent sites sit on the edge of one of Marin's most dramatic coastal bluffs. The cabins have wood-burning stoves and plywood platforms for carry-in bedding. Outside are running water and chemical toilets. The cabins were built more than 50 years ago by William Kent for the enjoyment of his friends and guests. Today Steep Ravine is undoubtedly the cheapest California coastal resort: cabins rent for only $12 a night. Call (800) 952-5580 for reservations (try 393-6914 for last minute availability).

Dipsea Trail Foot Race

388-5496

In June each year determined runners gather to take part in what may be California's most demanding footrace. The Dipsea trail is only 7.1 miles long, but it goes from sea level to sea level with a mountain in between. The second-oldest footrace in the United States (1910)—after the Boston Marathon—the Dipsea is not for the faint of heart.

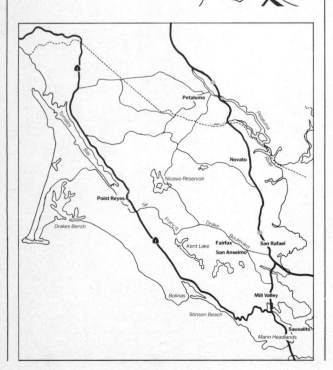

Nathan Stinson's Resort

In 1880 Nathan Stinson, witnessing the popularity of Captain Easkoot's tent resort, opened up one of his own right down the beach. Stinson set up tents on the beach and built a dance floor in the willow woods, where marked paths with names like Tippecanoe Lane directed visitors to their tents. Stinson envisioned his enterprise as a kind of health resort, but no specific amenities were offered save an abundance of water faucets in the wooded area. In supposition, it was the sea air that was to work natural miracles, and who knows but that it did? An advertisement from 1880 may not have exaggerated at all when it declared: "So exhilarating are the air and water that ladies crossing the beach are seen to flip a handspring."

By the early part of the century, the Stinson Beach resorts had become so popular that Langford and Crane's Sausalito stages were jammed during good weather. But what men like Easkoot and Stinson were banking on most was the arrival of the railroad; they had seen the prosperity that accompanied the arrival of the North Pacific Railroad miles up the coast. A railroad had even been planned to connect Stinson's Beach with the

Mount Tamalpais Scenic Railway—the tracks were to come down Steep Ravine to the beach and then run along the sandspit past Bolinas. Among many others who expected the railroad to increase their fortunes were William Kent, who bought huge portions of oceanfront property in anticipation of the railroad, and William Neuman, who built the Dipsea Inn on the sandspit that was to become the railroad's depot.

But the railroad never came. Even as its planners and promoters were ruminating, the new railroad was displaced by the automobile. In 1911 Langford and Crane replaced their horse-and-wagon stage with a new white steamer auto-stage, and soon enough Studebakers, Stutzes, and new REO Speedwagons were making the twisting climb over the coast road from Sausalito to the increasingly popular Stinson Beach.

Environmental Protection at Audubon Canyon Ranch

Protection of the egrets and herons at Audubon is a constant struggle against natural and human threats, past, present, and future.

In the early 1900s, the decorative plumes (aigrettes) sported by female and male egrets during mating season brought a high price on the market as fashionable additions to women's hats. Widespread slaughter of the birds for their plumes al-

most destroyed the species, and to stop the killing the nation's first Audubon Society was organized. It took years and lots of local political pressure, but the Society and others eventually leveraged Congressional legislation that banned the killing of egrets and set a national precedent for wildlife protection laws.

Today the egret and heron populations at Audubon Canyon are seriously threatened by yet another predator, natural but abetted by humans. Tree-hopping raccoons plundered nearly all the early spring laying of egret and heron eggs at the Ranch in 1983, and nesting was off 50% in 1984. The raccoons scamper through the rookery from branch to branch, needing only one access point up the 100-foot redwoods to reach all the nests.

Raccoons have adapted well to urban-fringe life and they do very well in Marin, with its no-firearms laws and friendly rural residents who feed the cute critters on backdoor handouts, garbage, and pet food.

Until recently, the coast was also a relocation point for raccoons captured elsewhere in the county. Most of the raccoons caught in traps at Audubon Canyon bore the tags of the Marin Humane Society and Wildlife Center's relocation program. The relocation program has been suspended and Ranch personnel are looking for new ways to control the raccoons and protect the precious bird eggs.

The third threat to the birds has its roots in the past and present, but its real effect will be felt into the future. Tissue analysis of adult birds that die near the Audubon heronry have begun to reveal high concentrations of pesticides, levels many times higher than considered normal or safe. When carnivorous species begin to record dangerous levels of synthetic chemicals, serious concern arises about the presence of these chemicals in the human food chain. (We eat the same fish the birds do.) No organization, national legislation, or citizen movement now exists to monitor, seek controls, or even fully understand this final and most lethal threat to the birds at Audubon, and, ultimately, to us all.

| |

Bolinas: Bay, Estuary, and Lagoon

Just north of Stinson Beach, the San Andreas fault cradles its first Marin inland waterway. Bolinas Bay marks the mouth of the severed earth as the fault comes ashore. Bolinas Lagoon, divided from Bolinas Bay by the Stinson sandspit, unfolds to the north along the west side of Highway 1.

Bolinas Lagoon is a 1,400-acre estuarine area composed of salt water, mudflats, marshlands, and sandbars. About 1,000 acres are subject to tidal action. Two freshwater sources drain into the water system, providing rich spawning habitats for salmon and steelhead trout. Pine Gulch Creek contributes about one-half of the fresh water inflow from the north, and Redwood Creek joins other run-off waterways on the eastern slopes providing the other half.

Bolinas Lagoon is actually a lagoon in the summer, when the freshwater inflow from Pine Gulch and Redwood is almost nil, and an estuary in the winter, when the rainy season raises the interchange action between fresh and salt waters.

The shallow Bolinas Lagoon supports popula-

tions of marsh grasses and seaweed, diverse families of benthic invertebrates, over 25 species of fish, and substantial populations of migratory shorebirds, waterfowl, and gulls. In the spring and summer the surface of the lagoon is dotted with the graceful bodies of the great blue heron, great egret, and an occasional snowy egret as they hunt the deeper channels in search of fish and crabs. Other shore and sea animals abound in this small lagoon, including the harbor seal, which uses Kent Island at the southwest corner as a haul-out and pupping site.

When is a bay a bay, an estuary an estuary, and a lagoon a lagoon?

An *estuary* is a confined coastal body of water with an open connection to the sea that contains measurable quantities of salt in its water. A *bay* is a large estuary with a very high degree of tidal action or flushing. A *lagoon* is a shallow estuary with very limited tidal action or exchange with sea waters and no significant freshwater inflow.

In California, the term *wetland* is often used to refer to an entire lagoon-type estuary, including the channels, creeks, and other small adjacent bodies of water. Ecologists generally use the rule-of-thumb of 50% to determine whether a body of water is a wetland or an estuary: a system with more than 50% open water (outside the marsh) is an estuary, one with less than 50% open water is a wetland.

The Stinson Sea Serpent

Loch Ness is not the only place with water monsters—legend has it that Stinson Beach possesses a sea serpent of its very own. The creature has been seen several times during the past decade, usually in August, September, or October.

One sighting occurred in 1983, when six Cal Trans crew members working on Highway 1 noticed a slithering, rolling mass offshore. The startled crew members took out their binoculars and watched something, which one later described as a "giant snake or a dragon with a mouth like an alligator's," swim from Bolinas Point to Stinson and then turn out to sea, moving at the snappy pace of about 60 miles per hour. The episode made national news.

Over the years, several visitors and residents have seen the Stinson Sea Serpent. One Bolinas artist-priest has seen it twice, making him the leading expert on the subject. He leads serpent-watching trips, interviews other people who have seen the monster, collects data from other areas and makes wood sculptures of the serpent.

After every sighting, marine mammal experts are quick to point out that dolphins and sea lions often swim in single file in a synchronized fashion, one diving just as the next rises out of the water, so that they could be mistaken for one long continuous animal. Other experts talk about ocean glare and wave action. People like the men and women on the Cal Trans crew, however, know what they saw—they talk about sea serpents.

Stinson Beach

The town of Stinson Beach stands out from other towns in coastal Marin because of its greater activity and undisguised recreational character. Always a resort town, Stinson Beach is colorful, appealing and, on summer weekends, busy.

In the center of town are an art gallery and a surf shop, indicative of Stinson's two moods, contemplative and sportive. You'll also find an excellent bookstore (Stinson Beach Books), a pottery and tile shop, and two restaurants. The Sand Dollar Restaurant has a full bar and extensive wine list, while Jackson's Bungalow offers live jazz on Saturday 5 to 7. On the north end of town is Ed's Superette, a good place to stop for groceries, refreshment, or the local newspaper.

The heart of Stinson Beach's resort life has always been its long wide beach with a fine rolling surf. This is a traditional California recreational beach, rare north of San Francisco. There are lifeguards in the summer, a refreshment stand, people making sandcastles, and children carrying sand buckets. Stinson attracts the most unsnooty crowd this side of San Francisco's Ocean Beach.

Audubon Canyon Ranch

4900 Shoreline Highway, Stinson Beach 94970. 383-1644.

Audubon Canyon Ranch is a nonprofit organization sponsored by the Marin, Golden Gate, and Sequoia Audubon Societies. It is open to the public from March 1 through July 4. You may stop by on any weekend or holiday between 10 am and 4 pm to walk the self-guided trails for views of the rookery, to visit the display hall and bookstore, or to picnic on the grounds. Nature tours led by

Audubon Canyon Ranch

Spring 1984

trained docents are offered on most weekends; check with the registration table for time and place or call ahead. Admission on weekends is free, donation requested.

The Ranch is closed on Monday, but open by appointment Tuesday through Friday for schools, groups, and researchers. Seminars, some one- and some two-day, are offered for modest fees as part of the Volunteer Canyon program. Subjects on the spring 1984 calendar included spring wildflowers, various photographers' workshops, the 9th Annual Butterfly Count, and, of course, a weekend on egrets and herons. Optional overnight lodgings during the seminars are available at the dormitory at the Hubbard Center on the Ranch. Call 868-0611 or the Ranch for seminar and other educational schedules.

If it is absolutely impossible for you to visit on a weekend and you don't want to miss the experience of viewing this unique area, call the Ranch and see what they can arrange. The staff and volunteers are flexible, helpful, and dedicated to expanding public awareness of Marin's fragile natural environment.

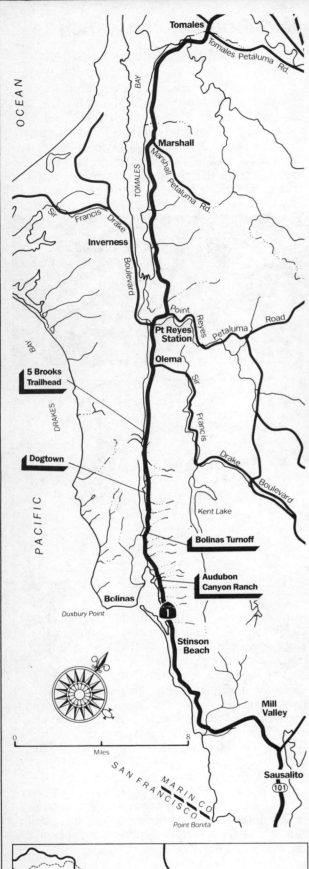

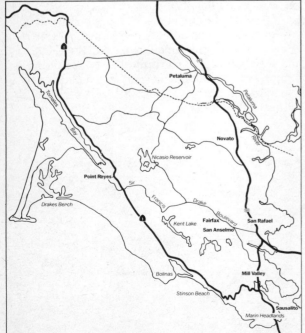

Bad Road at Bolinas

Beyond Stinson Beach, the new autos were stymied by bad roads. The road north of Stinson Beach was no sort of a road at all—travelers heading north along the course of today's Highway 1 had to wait for low tide and negotiate the mud flats. A pole south of the lagoon indicated the status of the tides further north. Passengers in the auto-stages heading up the coast were ferried across the lagoon in a launch with a one-cylinder "Frisco Standard" engine, *The Alice F.* Eventually,

in 1921, Marin County brought in enough rock fill to define a year-round thoroughfare on the edge of Bolinas Bay.

The road from Bolinas to Olema, first surveyed by the County in 1871, had always been treacherous. In 1872 the Olema to Bolinas Stage was washed into Olema Creek, its driver, John Nelson, nearly drowned. Whenever slides washed out the roads, Bolinas was totally cut off, and frequently the road was so deep in mud that passage was ridiculously slow or impossible. And dangerous: it was deep mud that broke the neck of Joseph Adams's horse when his team mired down in the slop in 1880.

But by the 1920s the automobile dictated the need for better roads along Marin's coast. The appeal of the new machines had become pervasive. Even the old Langford and Crane Sausalito Stage, sold in 1920, now sported in addition to five white auto-stages, a ten passenger Packard, two Stanley Steamers, and several Studebakers.

No Growth in Eden

The unbelievable inattention paid to west Marin during the 1930s, 40s, and 50s preserved its splendorous environment and left the small towns along Highway 1 to an easy slumber. But by the 1960s things began to change—west Marin became a kind of perfected model of spiritual pastoralness and new arrivals flooded in. And almost as quickly as the latest urban refugee arrived, he or she joined in ardent support of the view that further growth should be stopped lest Eden be ruined.

The most significant land use consequence of this popular attitude was a near total moratorium on new construction of any kind. This policy was principally accomplished not through zoning, but by a total restriction on new public services.

At one time or another over the last 15 years, practically every community in west Marin has for a period imposed a complete moratorium on new construction. Stinson Beach enacted a moratorium based on water and septic system limitations that lasted for over a year, while Inverness has prohibited any new development for most of the past eight years. And Bolinas, which upholds a national reputation for aggressive insularity, has maintained a complete moratorium for 15 years based on its continuing "water crisis."

In 1983, the Bolinas moratorium became the subject of a federal suit brought by the Pacific Legal Foundation against the Bolinas Community Public Utility District. The suit charged that Bolinas has made no effort to resolve its water crisis and that its prolonged moratorium, which has precluded the development of the town's unbuilt lots, amounts to the taking of the undeveloped property without compensation.

The suit, initiated by a law firm known for its persistence in challenging government land-use regulations and environmental protection, cuts both ways against liberal and conservative political views. On the one hand, resistance to growth is often seen as a progressive principle by its supporters who sometimes miss the implicit issues of discrimination, privilege, and exclusion. On the other hand, those who seek to do away with the moratoriums to stimulate unbridled development may overlook the fact that land-use zoning, as practiced in coastal Marin, can be equally as stringent in its efforts to protect the environment as any moratorium, without so roughly treating important social principles of equity and fairness.

Sign Wars

For the past decade, the turnoff to Bolinas has been the only main intersection on Highway 1 not officially marked by a Cal Trans sign. The Department gave up maintaining a Bolinas marker in the 1970s, since every time a sign went up, within 24 hours it was down—chainsawed or otherwise demolished by one of the 350 or so residents of the small town that prefers to remain in coastal oblivion. This isolationist attitude, however, is being challenged in the 1980s. In 1984 a local attorney and business owner commissioned his own road sign, hired guards to watch it on weekends, and vowed to replace and repair the sign as needed. It was soon needed. The sign was disfigured, the watchers threatened. For the time being, at least, the way to Bolinas remains without a sign.

Environment

The Egrets and Herons at Audubon Canyon Ranch

Egrets and herons return to Audubon Canyon each year, arriving in early January and lingering into July. Here, among a redwood grove adjacent to Highway 1, these beautiful birds engage in a colorful ritual of courtship, nest building, procreation, and rearing of their young. About 30 pairs of great blue herons and about 130 pairs of great egrets return to the Ranch each year. The birds are members of the heron family, which includes over 62 species of herons, egrets, and bitterns. Other family members, including the black-crowned night heron and the little snowy egret, often stop over as well.

The great blue heron is the second-largest long-legged bird in the West and the largest heron of North America, standing up to five feet tall with a wingspan of almost six feet. The smaller great egret has a span of roughly four and a half feet. Trails through Audubon Canyon Ranch lead to an overlook where the activities of the birds in the treetop nests of the rookery may be discreetly observed. Courtship of both species evolves around a magnificent dance between the decked-out birds that culminates in the selection of mates. Nest building continues through the spring at a staggered pace as new birds arrive, select mates, and choose nesting sites. The egrets and herons feed peacefully side-by-side in the Bolinas Lagoon, but in the rookery they engage in long pecking battles over the best nesting sites.

Roadside Attractions

Bolinas Lagoon North

Stinson Beach is actually a sandspit attached to Bolinas Lagoon, which Highway 1 runs behind on its inland side. Adjacent to the lagoon is the Audubon Canyon Ranch. Immediately past Bolinas Lagoon at Marker 17.01 is the cutoff for the town of Bolinas. For years, residents of Bolinas have chosen to remove the signs on Highway 1 that mark their town—their disinterest in the outside world and fear of its encroachment are legendary.

From Bolinas to Olema, Highway 1 follows the spine of the San Andreas Fault, which carved the Olema Valley to Tomales Bay. The drive is fast along the cracked valley floor. Along the way you'll spot the intersection for the Olema Valley Trail and Marin's most colorfully named settlement, Dogtown. Dogtown was named in the 1850s for the town's dogs, reputed to be tougher than the local bears. Residents changed the town's official name in 1868 to the more genteel Woodville in the hopes of attracting marriageable female residents, but Dogtown stuck. Five Brooks appears next, both the stables and the trailhead.

Marin Trails

Five Brooks Trailhead

About 5 miles beyond the turnoff to Bolinas, on the left is the trailhead to Five Brooks, access to many of the most scenic trails in the Point Reyes National Seashore. There are toilets and a few picnic tables at the trailhead. Some of the trails here lead along Olema Creek and Pine Gulch Creek (which run parallel to one another about 1,500 feet apart but flow in opposite directions); others lead along Inverness Ridge. Gain access to the trails by circling counterclockwise around the duck pond near the parking lot, look for signs for Firtop (via Stewart), Greenpicker Trail (which goes along the edge of the Vedanta Society's retreat), Palomarin (on the left), or Bear Valley (to the right).

Trails from the Visitor's Center include the Rift Zone Trail, Bear Valley, Sky Meadow, and Horse. The Bear Valley Trail is the most popular in the park, 4.3 miles to the coast ending at Arch Rock and passing through forests, Divide Meadow and a lovely creek. Views are staggering and a sea tunnel at the end of the trail is an exciting diversion (especially when the tide is coming in). Allow about five hours round-trip for this walk unless you plan to turn around before reaching the coast.

Almost a mile north of Horseshoe Hill Road look for the sign west of Highway 1 that announces the Olema Valley Trail. This is the trailhead for a fine 5-mile walk up to Five Brooks, fording several creeks and meandering through oaks and bays alternating with grassy glades.

Just across Highway 1 to the East is GGNRA land, and the McCurdy Trail going up Bolinas Ridge crosses here to link with the National Seashore system.

Resources

Marin Birds

Audubon Canyon Ranch (383-1644) produces brochures on Marin's shore and land birds, and the gift shop sells all the best bird guides, including the Audubon Field Guides. Another excellent resource for birders is the Point Reyes Bird Observatory (868-1221), an independent, scientific research organization which also sponsors an unusual and extensive public education program. PRBO's offices are on Highway 1 just north of Stinson Beach.

FIELD CHECKLIST OF THE BIRDS OF MARIN COUNTY, ALTA CALIFORNIA
Compiled by David Shuford,
Point Reyes Bird Observatory,
4990 Shoreline Highway, Stinson Beach 94970.
Revised edition, 1982.

Lists 411 species of native birds and 4 introduced species, all documented to have occurred within the county confines or offshore waters to a contour line 10 miles west of the continental shelf.

TO WALK WITH A QUIET MIND
Nancy Olmsted with Stephen Whitney
Sierra Club Books, San Francisco. 1975.

This Sierra Club "tote book" describes 27 hikes in the 200,000 acres of public land open to hiking in the San Francisco Bay Area. The book is written for hikers who love to explore, not those who try to travel long distances in the shortest time. Detail is given to trailside flora and fauna and to reflective insights on the fragile meaning of nature in a major urban area. Some of the best walks are those at Mount Tamalpais and Point Reyes, especially the one to Duxbury Reef.

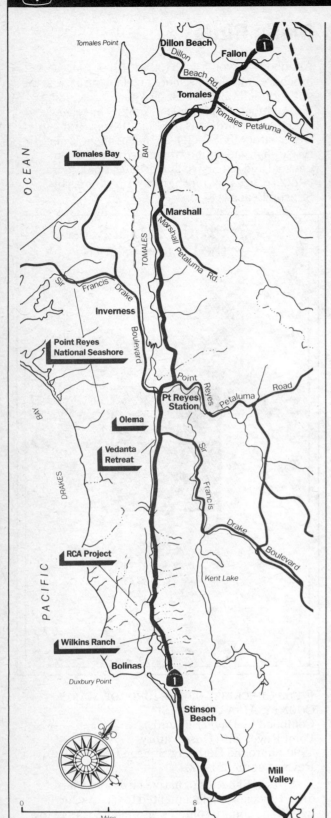

Drunken Loafers at Olema

Travelers to the town of Olema in the early days were usually either repulsed or attracted by its unsavory reputation. West Marin was never a very prim or proper place—numerous taverns, gambling spots, and whorehouses stood all along the Coast Road. Olema, though, had the most heralded reputation for drinking and debauchery.

Rowdiness at Olema was the talk of Marin: tongues wagged from San Rafael to Sausalito about the "drunken loafers" who caroused the night away in Olema. The number of saloons that lined Olema's streets were in part intended to compensate for the lack of drinking places in nearby Point Reyes Station. Because of Galen Burdell's deed restrictions, Point Reyes Station had only one saloon prior to 1907, and Olema received the full spillover of its thirsty inhabitants.

Such a major aspect of the town's identity was linked to drinking and hellraising that local temperance societies such as the Olema Sons of Temperance were organized to eradicate the menace. But their attempts to eliminate drinking and associated indecorous behavior had little overall effect, except perhaps to heighten alcohol's appeal by forbidding its use.

Olema's position along the Coast Road in west Marin was almost, but not quite, far enough north to protect its stake in the future. When the North Pacific Coast Railroad was extended into the new town of Point Reyes Station (not so named then) a few miles north, Olema's future dimmed. Although a short stage ride connected the two places, Point Reyes's growth was in many ways at the expense of Olema's. In 1914 the telephone switchboard moved to Point Reyes Station, followed by a steady stream of Olema's residents.

Olema in Washington, D.C.

After years of inattention, Olema was finally discovered in 1967 when scouts for the Smithsonian Institution came upon Olema and found Joe Gambioni's 1900 butcher shop to be worthy of preservation as an authentic illustration of American life. The store's small façade was cut down and transported to Washington, D.C. There it resides, for the ages, in the Hall of Everyday Life in the American Past.

Private Purchase with a Public Purpose

Much of Marin's public land was first purchased by the Trust for Public Land (TPL), usually at substantial public savings and often when the only alternative was private development.

This highly-regarded national land trust first became involved in pre-acquisition for national recreation areas in 1973 when it purchased the Wilkins Ranch, 1,300 acres fronting on Bolinas Lagoon next to Highway 1 at the junction of the road to Bolinas. The owner, a speculator who needed fast cash for his land, responded to TPL's ability to purchase an option, eventually selling the property to the Trust, which resold it to the federal government when funds became available. By the time the transaction was complete, TPL had saved the public at least $99,000 in carrying and appraisal costs, establishing a lasting relationship with the National Parks Service, local property owners and Marin conservationists.

One of the best-known of many TPL projects in Marin is the RCA project, negotiated between

1975 and 1979. RCA Global Communications owned 2,241 acres in two parcels fronting on the Marin coast adjacent to the National Seashore. Originally the site of their trans-Pacific radio facility, the land had become surplus to the corporation—communication satellites don't need land. The property has panoramic views, sandy beaches, tidal reefs, stands of Douglas fir, estuaries, and streams. Private development was an option and several developers were in the wings, but RCA was receptive to a complex proposal put together by TPL to purchase the property for eventual inclusion in the National Seashore.

TPL convinced the corporation, raised the funds, and resolved many local issues. The measure of TPL's ultimate success was expressed by Eugene F. Murphy, president of RCA Global Communications: "[Their] unique skills created an opportunity for RCA to achieve a prompt sale of surplus land . . . in a manner beneficial to both the public at large and the company. This is a fine example of a partnership between the private and nonprofit sectors for the public good."

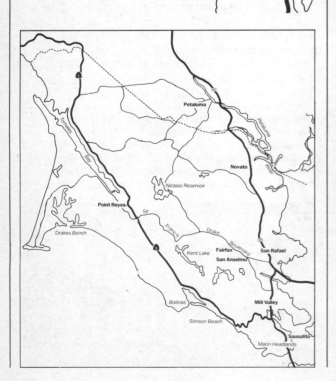

Environment | Roadside Attractions | Resources

Tomales Bay

Tomales Bay is Marin's most important marine resource. The long, narrow bay follows the San Andreas fault as it dips below sea level north of Point Reyes Station, and Highway 1 runs aside the bay's eastern edge for most of its 12.5 miles in length. The Bay is very narrow, from 0.4 to 1.5 miles wide, and its water area at mean low tide is about 11 square miles with depths averaging from 12 to 60 feet in the channel.

By 1970, about 500 acres of salt marsh on the south end of the Bay had been diked and drained, and converted to agriculture use, but this practice ended with the passage of the Coastal Act. About 70% of the fresh water inflow to this important estuarine system comes from two creeks: Lagunitas to the south and Wilder to the north. The total watershed of the Bay, famous as one of the cleanest urban bays in the world, is about 220 square miles.

The Bay's marine environment offers a rich habitat for over 1,000 species of invertebrates and an enormous variety of fishlife, including herring, crab, perch, halibut, jacksmelt, striped bass, and greenlings. Oysters are grown commercially and

over a half dozen resident species of clams encourage constant recreational clamming. Sharks and rays spawn in the Bay's waters, while harbor seals haul out on Hog Island.

Common Baylands Invertebrates

California horn snail	Giant clam worm
Oyster drill	Lugworm
Mud snail	Brine shrimp
Ribbed or horse mussel	Burrowing pill bug
Bay mussel	Oriental shrimp
Olympia oyster	Bay shrimp
Atlantic oyster	Blue mud shrimp
Pacific oyster	Ghost shrimp
Gem clam	Hermit crab
Japanese littleneck clam	Mud crab
Littleneck clam	Salt marsh water boatman
Soft-shell clam	Salt marsh mosquito
Bent-nosed clam	Salt marsh flies
Baltic clam	Brine fly
Clam worm	Pigmy blue butterfly

Common Baylands Plants

Cat-tail	Fat hen
Salt Grass	Russian thistle
Cordgrass	Alkali heath
Tule or bullrush	Marsh rosemary
Alkali bullrush	Salt marsh dodder
Curly dock	Gum plant
Pickleweed	Jaumea
Beet or swiss chard	Brass buttons
Australian saltbush	Arrow-grass

Olema

At the northern end of Olema Valley sits the town of Olema. Upon entering the town you see a small sign marking Vedanta Retreat—this is the entrance to what was once the showplace mansion of Olema, the Oaks, where the Shafter family built a magnificent home and racetrack in 1869. The house has been preserved by the Vedanta Society, which purchased the grounds for a spiritual retreat. The public is invited to use the trails that cross the Vedanta Society's property.

Tiny Olema also contains the Olema Store and the Olema Inn, a restored hotel of Shaker Design that is perhaps the only such building in California. The Inn's dining room is light and airy and there is a wide deck outside for balmy days. Across Highway 1 is Jerry's farmhouse, Olema's friendliest gathering spot.

Between Olema and the Olema Campground is the cutoff for the Point Reyes National Seashore.

The Point Reyes National Seashore

The Point Reyes National Seashore has been rightfully called one of the most stunning ocean parks in the world. Park headquarters and the visitor center are about one mile off Highway 1 at Olema, a side trip worth taking.

At the center one can view a film of the Seashore, see museum displays and exhibits of natural life, and take a walk along Earthquake Trail, which follows the San Andreas fault. Maps, books, and rangers are available to help you select which of the miles of trails to walk, or which of the many beaches to explore. A nonprofit educational program offers short field trips and classes on all aspects of the Point Reyes environment and culture (Point Reyes Field Seminars, 663-1200). Within the Seashore are a hostel, a remote lighthouse, whale-watching overlooks, horseback riding stables, a replica of a Coast Miwok Village, and the Highway 1 traveler's first taste of the raw beauty of the northern California coast.

Vedanta Society of Northern California

2323 Vallejo Street, San Francisco 94123. 922-2323.

From the Vedanta Society's office in San Francisco you may obtain a road map of the Olema retreat as well as general information on the Society's spiritual principles, based on the belief that all religions lead to the same goal and that the essence of all beings and all things—from the blade of grass to the personal god—is Spirit, infinite and eternal.

Trust for Public Land

87 Second Street, San Francisco 94105. 495-4014.

TPL was established in the early 1970s in San Francisco and now has regional offices in New York, Florida, Washington, and New Mexico. A private nonprofit organization, TPL cooperates with urban and rural groups and public agencies to acquire and preserve open space to serve human needs, to share information about nonprofit land acquisition processes, and to pioneer methods of land conservation and environmentally sound land use. Contact TPL for its publications lists, description of programs and services, and any issue concerning private land conservation in America.

The National Seashore

663-1092

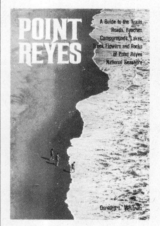 

POINT REYES, A GUIDE
Dorothy L. Whitnah
Wilderness Press, Berkeley. 1981.

A companion to the author's *Guide to the Golden Gate National Recreation Area.* Whitnah offers clear and comprehensive descriptions of principal trails for hikers, backpackers, bicyclists, and equestrians. Fully illustrated.

PICTORIAL LANDFORM MAP OF THE POINT REYES NATIONAL SEASHORE AND THE SAN ANDREAS FAULT, CALIFORNIA
Dee Molenaar
Wilderness Press, Berkeley. 1982.

Light, easy to carry and to read, this pictorial map names towns, communities, parks, campgrounds, backcountry campsites, visitor centers, topographic and shoreline features, streams, lakes and reservoirs, roads, and trails.

POINT REYES FIELD SEMINARS
663-1200.

This self-supporting nonprofit educational program is sponsored by the Coastal Parks Association in cooperation with the Point Reyes National Seashore. A sample of the spring 1984 catalogue: tidepooling at Duxbury Reef, the sexual life of plants and animals, horseback riding, and a family exploration of Drake's Beach.

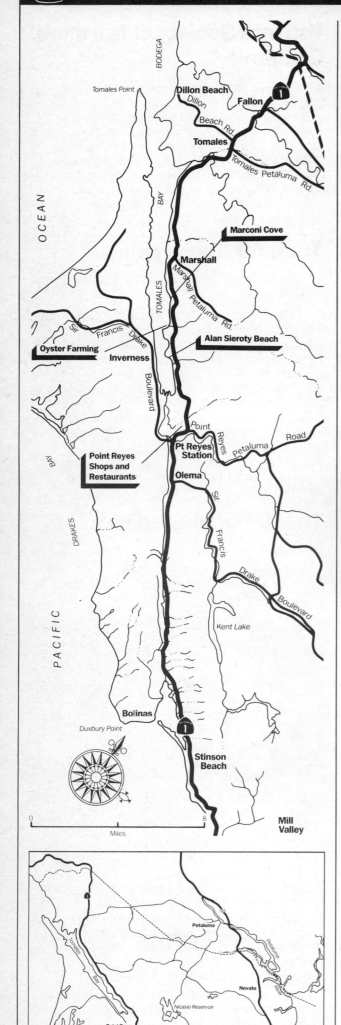

Excitement at Point Reyes Station

In the fall of 1874 the North Pacific Railroad reached Point Reyes Station from Sausalito and San Quentin Landing via San Anselmo and Fairfax. The new railroad was built primarily by Chinese laborers for slave wages; its purpose was to haul out the newly cut redwood forests near the Russian River and Cazadero.

But the train was nothing if not colorful; the coaches, painted a bright buttercup yellow, sported battened sides, arched window frames, and iron guardrails. Inside the coaches were a marvel of polished and varnished natural woods and elegant velvet seats. Coal-oil ceiling lamps illuminated the coaches' interiors in the evening, and a pot-bellied caboose stove offered varying degrees of warmth. Along with the passenger coaches and freight cars was usually a smoking car: "This section had conventional passenger-car windows but bench seats ran lengthwise on each side. This was the car for drunks, anglers, and hunters (who might be placed in the same category, after imbibing all day from a pocket flask while

in field or stream). Tunnel smoke penetrated their compartment with difficulty, for the air already was thick with tobacco smoke and whiskey fumes. Jokes and tall tales bandied about were as stale as the air, but always brought uproarious laughter."

A train's arrival at Point Reyes Station was always an event. The sound of the locomotive whistle brought a rush of excitement from the outside world to the town's residents. "Even placid farm horses hitched to waiting vehicles entered into the general excitement by cutting capers," writes A. Bray Dickinson. The train caused gaity to bloom in Point Reyes Station as the town gradually became the shipping point and supply center for the area's expanding dairies and farms.

For years Point Reyes Station was controlled by one man, Galen Burdell, a dentist who ran the town's only hotel and saloon. Burdell, in fact, owned the entire town until 1906. Among the many people who were economically dependent on Burdell (as Burdell was dependent on the railroad) were the "drummers," or traveling salesmen, who rented Burdell's horses and rigs to carry them over the barely apparent roads to sell their wares to dairy owners.

Environmental Living at Marconi Cove

The road to your right after you pass Marconi Cove and the site of the Marina development leads to the Marconi Conference Center, a 64-acre site, formerly Synanon's headquarters. The parcel was purchased in 1981 by the San Francisco Foundation, along with the nearby Walker Creek Ranch for $6.4 million. The money came from the foundation's Buck Trust.

New development on this site has been of much concern to local residents. Would the buildings eventually house another private retreat, a bed-and-breakfast complex, a hotel, or a commercial mall? After considering several proposals, the San Francisco Foundation accepted the one put forth by the California State Parks Foundation, a nonprofit organization committed to improving the state park system.

The State Parks Foundation proposal is to turn the buildings into a conference center that could accommodate 200 visitors in the environmentally luxurious style of Asilomar in Montery County. William Penn Mott, Director of the State Parks Foundation, and a local private developer from Dillon Beach plan to add a dining facility and recreation area to refurbish existing living accommodations on the land. The developed property would be deeded to the state park system as soon as the center becomes self-sufficient. Funds will come from the State Parks Foundation, the San Francisco Foundation, and private sources.

The proposed Marconi Conference Center has found favor with most west Marin residents, who are thankful for the business and who also appreciate the controlled clientele that a conference center will assure.

The Buck Trust

Marin is the most blatant example of the rich giving to the rich we have ever seen.
The Nation Institute 1983.

Marin County is the home to what is quickly becoming America's most famous endowment in support of the poor and needy. In 1975, Mrs. Leonard Buck, long-time resident of Marin, bequeathed to the San Francisco Foundation her 7% share of the Belridge Oil Company. She attached on stipulation to the gift: that it be used for nonprofit purposes in Marin County only.

When Mrs. Buck wrote her will, the value of her gift was about $7 million. But in 1979 Belridge Oil was purchased by Shell Oil and the gift's value soared to $300 million. The San Francisco Foundation suddenly became the 11th largest foundation in the country with over 70% of its assets in the Buck Trust, and all of that earmarked for Marin, the wealthiest county in the state. The Foundation is obligated to disburse about $25 million in Marin each year.

Environment

Acid Fog in Marin

Southern California is not the only area threatened with acid fog, a phenomenon even more devastating than its more well-known cousin, acid rain. Alarming levels of acidity are now showing up in the frequent fog at Point Reyes and west Marin.

Environmental engineering students from the California Institute of Technology recently collected 50 fog samples during a five-day experiment near the Point Reyes Lighthouse. Several samples were extremely acidic; their pH content averaged 4.0, which is 60 times more acidic than normal. Potentially more potent than acid rain, the acid fog involves small amounts of water combined with large amounts of dry acid deposition, which makes it much more efficient than rain in scavenging acid particles and acid-forming gases from the air.

Acidic air pollutants from power plants and industrial sources—such as those in Richmond, Antioch, and Pittsburg, less than 40 miles away—and from automobile and shipping lanes are among the suspected sources of west Marin's acid fog. A solution is not at hand: both acid fog on the golden shores of Marin and acid rain in the industrial wastelands of the East Coast resist simple remedies.

Don't Eat the Berries

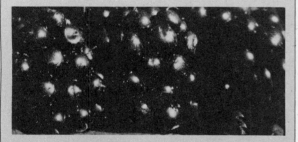

Poison oak and other obnoxious weeds pose continuous problems to maintenance crews along the sides of the narrow west Marin Highway 1. In recent years Cal Trans has tackled the problem with periodic sprayings of a herbicide called Roundup,® marketed by Monsanto Chemical Company and one of the best-known roadside herbicides in the country. This solution has created a few problems of its own.

Also growing along the highway are generous crops of blackberries. And, in many cases, local private gardens are located within the windshed of the Highway's shoulder. Concern among residents about Roundup's effect on these crops, cultivated and natural, has paralleled increasing use of the spray. Several residents claim to have had adverse effects after eating berries gathered along the road, a common practice by tourists and residents alike during berry season. Even some workers applying the chemical complain about side effects when the wind is blowing in the wrong direction.

Cal Trans, the State Food and Drug Administration, Monsanto, and others argue that the cure justifies the means and that Roundup produces no dangerous effects. Locals respond by demanding hearings and notices of times and location of all sprayings; one angry local parked her car in the path of a Cal Trans truck that was spraying the controversial herbicide. The battle lines are drawn, but until this one is resolved, think twice before eating the berries.

Roadside Attractions

Point Reyes Station

Point Reyes Station caters less to the tourist than other towns in coastal Marin, which only improves the quality of its attractions. In Point Reyes Station there is an Old West bar (the Western), an excellent restaurant for breakfasts, lunches, and dinners (the Station House Café), and a Pulitzer Prize–winning local newspaper (The *Point Reyes Light*). You can also find good natural foods at Papermill Natural Foods and enjoyable reading at Point Reyes Book Store. At John's Truck Stop a

scene from the movie *Shoot the Moon* was filmed.

At Point Reyes Bikes you can rent high-quality mountain bikes for the day to pedal the trails of Point Reyes Peninsula. These 18-gear high-tech machines are an excellent way to experience the magnificent terrain beyond Highway 1. Adjacent to the bike shop is Gallery Route One, a cooperative featuring works of west Marin artists.

Tomales Bay

North of Point Reyes Station, Highway 1 runs adjacent to Tomales Bay almost to the ocean. Tomales Bay is over 16 miles long and has water that is almost ten degrees warmer than the Pacific, making it an excellent place to swim. An interesting spot to walk along Tomales Bay is Alan Sieroty Beach on Millerton Point. The fine facilities here—picnic tables, grills, restrooms —were built by local residents to raise money for school programs.

Next to the state-owned property at Millerton Point is Tomales Bay Oyster Company, part of the thriving local shellfish industry that produces about 20% of California's commercial oyster crop. Tony's Seafood and Nick's Cove (north on Highway 1) both specialize in barbecuing the excellent local oysters.

Resources

Mountain Biking

Mountain biking, the latest national athletic craze, originated in Marin County in 1974 when Gary Fisher souped up his old Schwinn Excelsior (a classic fat-tired "paperboy's bike") with derailleur gearing and powerful handbrakes so he could maneuver the rocky slopes of Mt. Tamalpais. In 1976 Joe Breeze, also of Marin, built the Breezer, which had frame angles like the Schwinn but was constructed of strong, light space-age chrome-moly tubing. By the early 1980s, the Japanese

began mass-producing mountain bikes, also called fat-tire, off-road, all-terrain, or cross-country bikes. Each year since, sales have more than doubled, as fat-tire fever spreads over trails, roads, and city streets.

Point Reyes Bikes
11431 Highway One, Point Reyes 94956. 663-1768.

To obtain any information on biking in west Marin, contact these people. Although their business is renting and selling mountain bikes, they provide a full range of informational services.

Oyster Farming

Oyster farming is an important mariculture activity on Tomales Bay. The frames of oyster beds are visible at several spots along the road. Growing oysters in the bay began in 1875 when two farmers laid out 17 freight cars of East Coast oysters in Millerton's tidelands. The industry's fate has ebbed and flowed, but local demand for fresh seafood is now on the rise. Most operators import Pacific seed oysters, which hang on racks in the shallow waters until they are mature at about 18 months. Some of the growers also freshen and maintain Maine lobsters and blue point oysters from the East Coast in large, filtered-seawater tanks off the bay's shore. The farming is regulated through permits issued by the California Fish and Game Department.

When the Railroad Reached Tomales

The railroad continued to define life in Point Reyes Station until 1930s, when the abandonment of the railroad and the advent of the Depression plunged the town into quiet darkness. To the north, Tomales met the same fate.

Tomales was another hard-drinking coastal town where whoring and carousing were among the most visible civic activities. Once Tomales was an active seaport situated on Keys Creek, but stream siltation caused by the town's development soon closed off access to the ocean.

The railroad saved the town from extinction when it came through in 1875. Tomales's predominantly Irish-Catholic inhabitants may or may not have seen the arrival of the railroad as a sign of providence, but they certainly saw it as an opportunity to celebrate. Drunkenness of historical proportion lasted through the night, accompanied by a feast of chicken, broiled turkey, beef, and homemade pies and cakes. Ladies of the evening accompanied ladies from the church in riotous singing, and noise was made to dim an Irish wake. The evening concluded with a free-for-all at the Continental Hotel, but not before James McMillan Shafter summed up the wisdom of the evening, as told by Jack Mason: "There is a better place to build a railroad, but it don't lead to Olema or Tomales, and that is the reason it is here."

Native Americans, Marconi Wireless, and Synanon

Even into the 20th century, an Indian settlement built on pilings over the water at Tomales Bay straddled two civilizations, white and Native American. Between Point Reyes Station and Tomales where Highway 1 runs along the Bay, was the settlement known as Fishermens. The North Pacific Railroad made scheduled stops there to take on Tomales fish and clams caught in nets by members of the Tamallos tribe. Later, automobiles started making their way up the coast road were met by the Tamallos from Fishermens, peddling clams by the sack.

The Tamallos were suddenly dispatched to history in 1913 when the Marconi Wireless Company bought 1,127 acres of Bay frontage to build a trans-Pacific receiving station. Elaborate facilities were installed, including a collection of Mediterranean-style buildings, a two-story hotel with a front-length veranda, machine shops, steam plants, and towering steel poles that caught radio beams from China and Tokyo. Eventually, the Marconi facilities became obsolete, as did the smaller RCA facilities that followed at the location.

In 1964 a portion of the land was sold to Charles Dederich for the headquarters of Synanon, his expanding west Marin therapeutic empire that at one time included more than 600 members who lived on almost 4,000 acres. Dederich, who based his organization on the principles of encounter therapy for the rehabilitation of drug users, was transfigured into a cult leader of lost souls. In the late 1970s Synanon was shattered by Dederich's egomanical excesses, which sometimes approached violence. For their brilliant series of investigative reports on Synanon's dark decline, David Mitchell and Catherine Mitchell, then owners of the *Point Reyes Light*, won a Pulitzer Prize in 1979. Synanon's properties were turned over to the San Francisco Foundation in 1981 after the organization's bankruptcy.

MALT

Agricultural land in Marin County is subject to some of the most intense development pressure of any area along Highway 1. The existing agricultural land is productive and valuable; but houses, hotels, and other development in Marin County would be many times more profitable. Preservation of existing agricultural uses presents a formidable challenge.

Marin County's local coastal program and general plan encourage the preservation of agricultural

land. Since 1972, Marin's zoning ordinance for agricultural parcels has allowed only one structure per 60 acres. This restriction works fairly well to preserve open space, but it is pretty much a failure in preserving viable agricultural uses. Sixty acres is just too small a parcel for a productive farm.

Parcel Consolidation and Partial Development

One way in which MALT is helping farmers maintain their operations is by sponsoring development proposals based on parcel consolidation in conjunction with limited revenue-generating uses. In a sample project, several parcels are joined together into one larger master-planning unit. Their cumulative development potential (1 site per 60 acres) is clustered together at an appropriate spot, say next to Highway 1 or another public road. Plans are drawn for development of a bed-and-breakfast inn, conference facility, or other appropriate structure. The rest of the land is now one large parcel, protected by easement and productive for agricultural uses.

MALT has been working for three years on such a project in the town of Marshall, where three large agricultural tracts, subject to subdivision into 60-acre parcels, were on the market. One of the tracts crosses Highway 1 and fronts on Tomales Bay at the site of the old marina just south of town. Here local plans allow new visitor-serving facilities and a small new marina complex.

MALT helped the three parcel owners form a limited partnership and consolidate the land. MALT's proposal is to develop the Marshall site to the degree allowed under current planning. Revenue from the project and the more than $1 million MALT has raised in state and local funds will go toward the purchase of a conservation easement on the agricultural land. The agricultural lands will be protected and badly needed development will come to Marshall.

Environment | ## Roadside Attractions | ## Resources

Blue Blossoms

Baby blue eyes is an early actor in the annual Marin County coastal floral show. The flower's five united petals sport tiny light-blue veins or dots that blend out from a broad, open corolla to a seductive dark-blue edge. Baby blue eyes can be seen as early as February in moist valley slopes or on protected hillsides. The blossoms are supported by slender stems that reach a height of up to 18 inches.

Another Marin wildflower that mirrors the

early spring's icy-blue sky and sea is the Douglas iris, or mountain iris. The shape of this three-part flower is very similar to the iris seen in domestic gardens, making the Douglas among the most commonly recognized of wildflowers. The Marin iris may vary in color from the usual blue-purple to lavender or cream. You will see them in sturdy clumps next to the road, standing up to 2 feet high and surrounded by their glossy moss-green thick leaves.

Blue dicks are yet another early blue bloomer. The flower head has between four and ten separate blossoms, surrounded at the base by small shiny purple bracts. (A *bract* is a specialized leaf or petal that encloses or embraces a group of flowers.) The blue dick is a lovely bluish-purple and its bulb is edible, raw, boiled, or roasted.

Exotic Deer

Because so much of west Marin is protected public land where hunting is restricted, the deer population is healthy and very visible. Native black-tails are common, but two exotic species may also appear in front of your car around the next curve. Fallow deer, a white (sometimes brownish) deer, were introduced in the 1940's by a local rancher who also introduced the unusual spotted axis deer. Spotted axis are native to India and Ceylon, and fallow deer are natives of Mediterranean lands. The species do not interbreed but coexist peacefully.

Marshall

Just before Tony's Seafood begins the lovely town of Marshall, spread along the east shore of Tomales Bay. Marshall is maritime in character, both quaint and authentic, with most of its houses built out over the water on piers. Several boatworks unselfconsciously go on about the business of building and repairing small commercial vessels. Marshall also has a crafts jeweler and a gallery.

Between Marshall and Tomales are two fishing access points—Miller Point and Walker (formerly Keyes) Creek. Miller Point is located on Tomales Bay, and Walker Creek on a small tributary of the Bay that once connected the town of Tomales to the water. As you wind north into town along Walker Creek, its evolution from creek to meadow, where sheep now graze, is evident; siltation from early development hastened the process.

Tomales

Tomales is a quiet place with interesting architecture. Our Lady of Assumption Church, of elaborate Victorian Gothic design, dates from 1860. Another early railroad town, like Point Reyes Station although older, Tomales still has a general store—Diekman's—that would not look out of place in the 19th century and is a fine stopover point for food and supplies.

The land north of Tomales is almost entirely sheep and cattle country as Highway 1 delays for a few miles its return to the shoreline. Try Wally's Fix-It Shop, at the intersection of Highway 1 and Whitaker Bluff Road (left .25 miles), should you need to repair before leaving the county.

History of Marin

DISCOVERING MARIN
Louis Teather, Mallette Dean (engravings).
A. Philpott, The Tamal Land Press, Fairfax. 1974.

This lovely small guide, with stunning engravings by Mallette Dean, includes a full bibliography, museums, and historical landmarks.

SAUSALITO: MOMENTS IN TIME
Jack Tracy
Windgate Press, Sausalito. 1984.

The story of Sausalito is one of rugged individuality mixed with a cosmopolitan small-town self-image, and this is the book that tells it.

BEN'S AUTO STAGE (1967)
POINT REYES: THE SOLEMN LAND (1970)
EARLY MARIN (1971)
LAST STAGE FOR BOLINAS (1973)
SUMMER TOWN (1974)
THE MAKING OF MARIN 1850–1975 (1975)
EARTHQUAKE BAY (1976)
Jack Mason
North Shore Books, Inverness.

Jack Mason was West Marin's most prolific historian. His colorful local histories are based on thorough original research, oral histories, and a love of the communities about which he wrote.

BROKEN SHORE: THE MARIN PENINSULA
Arthur Quinn
Peregrine Smith, Inc., Salt Lake City. 1981.

Poet and Nobel laureate Czeslaw Milosz christened this book "the Ecclesiastes of the West Coast"; and Kevin Starr praised Quinn for having sought "what is perhaps the most subtle and elusive harvest of historical investigation: the interaction among place, people, event, and moral meaning."

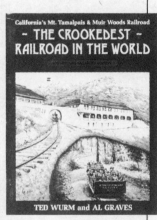

NARROW GAUGE TO THE REDWOODS
A. Bray Dickinson
Trans-Anglo Books/Interurban Press, Glendale. 1981.

THE CROOKEDEST RAILROAD IN THE WORLD
Ted Wurm and Al Graves
Trans-Anglo Books/Interurban Press, Glendale. 1983.

In these two volumes, informative prose and rare nostalgic photos tell the tale of California's narrow-gauge North Pacific Coast Railroad, its paddle-wheel ferry line, and one of the best loved railroad endeavors in history.

Visitor Information

Marin County Chamber of Commerce
30 N. San Pedro Road, Suite 150
San Rafael, 94903. 472-7470.

Marin Coast Chamber of Commerce
P.O. Box 94
Olema, 94950. 663-1244.

SONOMA

QUIET AND PASTORAL, the Sonoma Coast displays some of the most pleasing shorefront vistas in the state. From Valley Ford, a slight town with honest charm, to the sprawling Sea Ranch, Highway 1 glides along a picturesque panorama, almost always in sight of the sea.

There are actually two Sonoma Coasts, with the Russian River serving as the line of division. South of the river the coastal landscape is flatter, with dune remnants and greater activity—particularly near the town of Bodega Bay, where an active maritime industry colors the goings-on. The popular Sonoma Coast beaches, nearby, offer an uninterrupted string of convenient facilities along an easily accessible shoreline.

North of the Russian River, the Sonoma Coast changes character, with a wilder landscape and fewer traces of human habitation to interrupt the sweeping coastal hills. The town of Jenner marks the entry to this beautiful kingdom. North of Jenner, Highway 1 ascends to dizzying, awe-inspiring heights along the unmatched Jenner cliffs.

After Fort Ross, where a large settlement of Russian colonists and fur traders held forth for more than 30 years, Highway 1 winds along the rocky shoreline until it reaches the 10-mile long luxury subdivision, Sea Ranch, just before the county line.

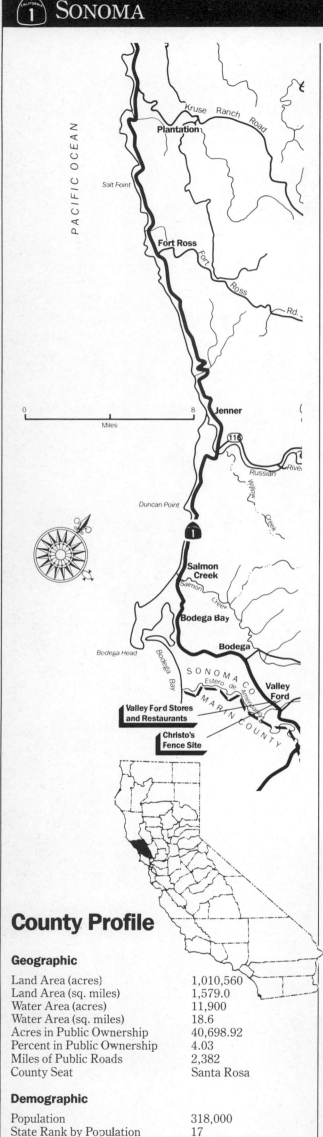

The Russian Road

The earliest roads along the Sonoma coast were built by a colony of Russians who first arrived in 1808 aboard the ship *Kodiak,* sailing into Bodega Bay from the north. Ivan A. Kuskov, a one-legged Russian adventurer, captained the ship sent from Sitka by the Russian-American Fur Company to seek out otter pelts and establish a trading base near San Francisco Bay.

When Kuskov reached Bodega (called Port Romanzov) the only inhabitants were a group of outlaw sea otter hunters hiding out from Spanish authorities. For eight months Kuskov and his party of 40 Russians and 150 Aleuts hunted sea otters before returning to Sitka with evidence of the otters' plentitude. Four years later Kuskov was granted authority by the Russian government to establish a colony.

The Russian Colony

For three blankets, three pairs of breeches, three horses, two axes, and some beads, Kuskov leased the village known as Mad Shui Nui from a Pomo Indian tribe and established a settlement 13 miles north of the Slavianka (Russian) River. Located 110 feet above the ocean with an uninterrupted range of fire for its cannons, the fort called Ross (derived from Russia) was well protected from Spanish attacks.

Within a short period the Russian colonists succeeded in establishing a varied economy: engaging in lumbering, brick making, tanning, and metalwork, in addition to raising livestock and starting a dairy. With Indian labor they cultivated fields and raised crops of barley, flax, rye, buckwheat, and maze. To accommodate their varied activities, ranches were established at Bodega, near Jenner, and Freestone. Between these locations roads were built to facilitate harvests and planting that followed the contours of the land. First marked off in 1811, the main artery of the Russian settlement from Fort Ross to Fort Romanzov on Bodega Bay was essentially the same route that Highway 1 follows today.

The Return of the Coyote

The lonesome howl of the coyote, which once echoed the wild isolation of the western night, is being heard again in Sonoma County. During the past two years, so many of the wily predators have reestablished themselves in western Sonoma that residents and ranchers are growing seriously alarmed.

The coyote is not just a benign member of the animal kingdom who howls to lend atmosphere to the night. Coyotes kill sheep. And in coastal Sonoma County, where sheep ranching is a major part of the local economy and a major contributor to the preservation of open space, the coyote is seen as an enemy by sheep ranchers and environmentalists alike.

Coyotes were almost completely eradicated during the 1930s by a major federal program that poisoned thousands of coyotes throughout the West. But so adaptable are the animals that they have returned, and threated to reestablish themselves in even larger numbers because of fewer natural controls and a federal ban on poisoning coyotes. Coyotes are so adaptable—even able to thrive quite well along urban fringes—that some people say they may survive to the end of the earth.

Leroy Erickson, a sheep rancher in Valley Ford, lost 35 sheep in the first few months of 1984. "I go out every day to see how many have been killed," he told a San Francisco newspaper. Sonoma County has hired three permanent trappers in an attempt to gain control of the situation, but without noticeable success.

Two possible solutions have been proposed: one is to develop a repellent to make the sheep less appetizing; the other is to obtain Pyrenee or Komondor sheep dogs to guard the sheep. But no effective answer has yet been put into practice.

County Profile

Geographic

Land Area (acres)	1,010,560
Land Area (sq. miles)	1,579.0
Water Area (acres)	11,900
Water Area (sq. miles)	18.6
Acres in Public Ownership	40,698.92
Percent in Public Ownership	4.03
Miles of Public Roads	2,382
County Seat	Santa Rosa

Demographic

Population	318,000
State Rank by Population	17
Projected 1990 Population	387,700
Unemployment Rate (state avg. = 9.9)	9.6
Per Capita Personal Income	$10,610
State Rank by Income	20
Total Assessed Property Value	$10,206,579,437

Golden Waves of Grain

A bouquet of Sonoma County coastal wild grasses offers pleasures in texture, shades, and diversity to match even the most colorful bunch of wildflowers. Especially in the summer and fall months, Sonoma's open meadows are often covered with softly waving stalks of annual grasses, among them wild oats, soft chess, goatgrasses, mouse barley, wild ryes, bluegrasses, and some needlegrasses. All of these plants are highly adapted to survival along the coast. Most of them

are able to produce huge numbers of seeds even under the most adverse weather conditions and despite grazing by sheep and deer.

Curly Dock

Many of the coastal grasses are golden, but curly dock features a distinctive tall rust-colored stalk that bears hundreds of polygon-shaped rust or brown seeds. Curly dock is becoming more and more common on the California coast, its seeds having the advantage of sporting wings to travel further on the winds. This wild grass is extremely high in vitamins A and C, as well as iron. Like many coast grasses, curly dock has a wide variety of medicinal and dietary uses, its seeds being a good substitute for buckwheat flour and its roots and stems delicious when cooked like asparagus.

County Line

Highway 1's route along the highly scenic Sonoma coast offers one of the most pleasurable drives anywhere. Approached from the south, the county begins with an idealized landscape that shows whitewashed barns and rolling hills decorated with spotted cows and arcadian flocks of sheep. A quiet beauty pervades everything about the place.

Just before Valley Ford, a roadside pasture offers further evidence of coastal Sonoma's exceptionability—a family of llamas whose improbable presence contributes to the wonderland character of their surrounds.

Valley Ford

Named for the ancient Indian and Spanish trail that crossed the Estero Americano, Valley Ford has been a quiet spot on the side of the road for almost its entire existence. Except for its single moment in the sun, when the internationally known artist Christo strung an undulating white fabric fence across the nearby rolling countryside for 22 miles to the sea in 1976, Valley Ford has remained relatively unnoticed.

In the center of town a mural atop the Valley Ford Market commemorates Christo's fence, an event that garnered more controversy with the California Coastal Commission than local residents, who tended to appreciate the sheer spectacle of event.

In addition to its few moments of international art-world glamour, Valley Ford has an excellent Italian family-style restaurant—Dinuccis—that continues to proudly endure, a fine nursery, a sandwich and bake store and a shop called the Happy Hooker (bait shop and deli).

AREA CODE: 707

Public Transportation

884-3723 Mendocino Transit Authority (MTA Coast Vans run from Jenner to Gualala; flag the van at any safe pull off).

Climate

Southern Sonoma enjoys moderate weather year round. The north coast tends to be a bit cooler. Average annual rainfall is 30 inches, with January usually being the wettest month. Expect morning and evening fog during the summer. The warmest months are September, October, November. For weather and driving conditions, phone 875-3596 (south coast) or 847-3222 (north coast).

Leash Laws

Pet control is serious business in Sonoma where an across-the-board leash law is operative 24 hours a day, every day, at all places outside the dog owner's property. Even at home, the property must be enclosed or the dog constrained. Thousands of dollars of livestock are lost in Sonoma each year due to dogs. The Northbay Woolgrowers Association and County Animal Regulation Department issues a pet owner's "Welcome to Sonoma County," which warns that livestock owners shoot on sight any dogs on their property. It's best to leave Fido home. For more information, call 527-2471.

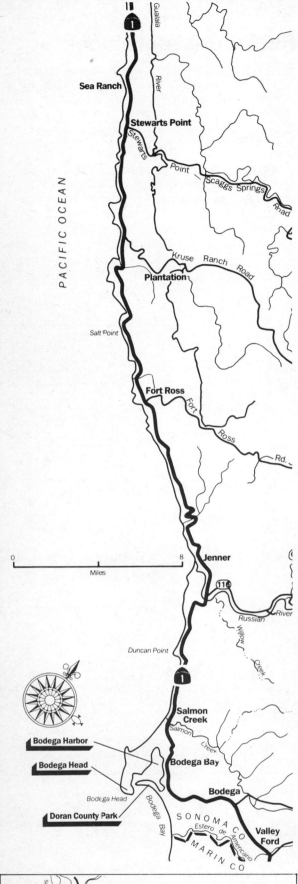

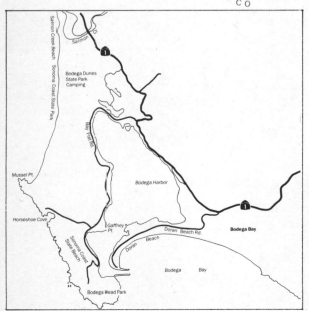

Nikolai and Conception

Long beside the deep embrasures, where the brazen cannon are,
Did she wait her promised bridegroom and answer of the czar;
Watched the harbor-head with longing, half in faith and half in doubt,
Every day some hope was kindled, flickered, faded and went out.

Bret Harte

This is the story of Nikolai Rezanov, a Russian explorer, and Conception Arguello, daughter of the commandante of Spanish San Francisco, who met one day in 1806 and had six weeks of love that lasted a lifetime.

When Rezanov landed at Bodega with a ship full of treasure, his first mission was to seek out San Francisco's Spanish commandant, José Arguello, for an exemption to foreign trade restrictions. The Russians needed to be able to trade to sustain their Sonoma coast colony.

Rezanov was a traveled man who had been an adventurer, Czarist Ambassador to Japan, and now head of the Russian-American Fur Company. But when his eyes fell on José Arguellos' 16-year-old

daughter, Conception, his heart overwhelmed him. Conception, for her part, saw the tall noble-looking Russian through enamored eyes that made their meeting bloom into love, despite the consternation she caused her father. For six weeks, Nikolai and Conception trafficked in the cargo of the heart while all those about the two lovers implored them to separate.

Then Rezanov sailed for Russia, alone, to obtain the permission of the Czar to marry his beloved. Conception waited while he docked at Sitka and began his way across Siberia by horseback. But on the journey to Saint Petersburg his horse threw him. Rezanov waited restlessly for his injuries to mend.

Had he waited longer, love might have had another day, but his impatience to reach Saint Petersburg forced a relapse. Rezanov died on the road, never getting to the Russian capital.

It was years before Conception received the news, though all the while she waited, confident of her lover's return and the strength of their bond. Without her intended bridegroom, Conception chose solitude, finally joining the Order of the Sisters of Visitacíon, and devoting her life to good works.

Red Right Returning

All shipping channels, including those at Bodega, are marked by a federally-designated system of buoys and beacons. These navigation aids exhibit varying light patterns, shapes and colors to warn mariners of danger, obstructions or changes in the channel bottom. Numbers are painted on buoys lining a channel's boundaries. The numbers increase in sequence as one approaches port. Even numbers are always placed on the right sides of the channel; odd numbers on the left. The buoys are also distinguished in shape and color. A boat traveling into port should find red buoys on the starboard (right) side, and black buoys on the port (left) side, thus the old seafarers expression "red right returning." The starboard buoys are called nuns, and are cone-topped, while the port buoys are can-shaped with flat tops.

A day beacon is a fixed navigation aid, usually mounted on piles along a channel. The center of a channel is designated by a floating black-and-white striped buoy. At a junction where a shipping channel branches to the right and left, a black-and-red horizontally banded buoy will be found. If the buoy has a red band on the top, the preferred channel is to the left. One with a black top band indicates that the preferred channel is to the right.

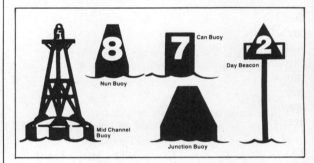

The World's Most Expensive Duck Pond

It is hard to imagine that Bodega Head was once the proposed site for what was to be the largest nuclear power plant of its kind in North America. In 1962, plans had proceeded as far as to begin actual massive excavation on the head's harbor side. Frightened and outraged citizens demanded public hearings as the hole grew larger and larger. Local fishermen began to discuss interference with marine radio communications caused by proposed power lines. A few environmentalists and engineers also pointed out to backers of the project that they were building a nuclear power plant on a rock that arrived here after millions of years of seismic action on the San Andreas Fault directly below. Finally, construction was halted and the hole began to fill with water. Locals who remember one of California's earliest coastal land use battles now refer to the site as "the world's most expensive duck pond."

Environment

Bodega Harbor: A Natural and Engineered Marvel

Bodega Harbor, also called Inner Bodega Bay, is 8,000 feet wide and 9,000 feet long. Its 840 acres include more than 500 acres of mudflats, 70 acres of salt marsh and a 100-foot wide, 16,000-foot long shipping channel protected by two jetties (south jetty is 1,650 feet long, and north jetty is 1,130 feet long). The harbor also depends on a bulkhead that protects the long sand spit on the ocean side, as well as several harbor turning basins, all constructed and maintained by the Army Corps of Engineers.

The complex engineering in Bodega Harbor is necessary due to the "depositing" state of the harbor floor. The sand dunes and adjacent unstable hills provide a constant supply of sediment carried into the harbor by wind, tidal currents and rain runoff. By the 1940's the harbor was almost completely filled in, and would be so again today were it not for a massive 1943 dredging and engineering project that continues today.

The harbor engineering has not interfered too much with the rest of the natural environment here, however. Bodega's mudflats, salt marshes, open water, sub-tidal channels, freshwater streams, and freshwater marshes nourish an outstanding array of bird and marine life: more than 200 species of invertebrates, 36 species of clams, 20 species of crab, and at least 315 species of birds, 82 mammals, 17 reptiles, 12 amphibial species, and hundreds of fish species.

Bodega Head

Bodega Head forms the southern oceanside entrance to Bodega Harbor, and marks the northern hook of the gently sloping Bodega Bay, which extends crescent-shaped all the way south to Dillon Beach in Marin County. The Head is a rounded granitic monolith, rising about 250 feet above the ocean. It is connected to the mainland by an isthmus whose sand dunes range up to 100 feet in height.

The Head also marks the northernmost portion of the Point Reyes granitic block, a geological mass that originated hundreds of miles south and arrived at its present location along a conveyor belt of seismic San Andreas fault activity. At Bodega Head, three major geological boundaries are visible: the Head is part of the Pacific Plate, Bodega Bay indicates the presence of the San Andreas Fault Zone, an the Sonoma hills to the east of Highway 1 are the western edge of the Continental Plate.

Roadside Attractions

Bodega

Through long lanes of eucalyptus trees and clusters of cypress, Highway 1 winds generally westward, seeking the ocean at Bodega Bay.

Just inland is the tiny Victorian town of Bodega, with a weaving studio, antique store, bar, cemetery, and hand-carved wooden statues. The Church of St. Teresa of Avila, a simple gothic revival structure, is a state historical landmark that has been preserved for 135 years.

As Highway 1 approaches Bodega Bay, signs of

California second-home living present themselves. At Bodega Harbors, large single-family residences dominate the landscape; Doran Beach Road marks the entrance to Doran County Park.

Doran County Park

Doran County Park is located on the sand spit that separates Bodega Bay from Bodega Harbor and provides access to almost the entire Bodega Bay shorefront. This is an excellent county park in a county of excellent parks.

A superb place to view shorebirds, surf cast, or stroll the long shoreline, Doran Beach also has top-notch facilities for the camper and fisher. Choose from 138 camping spaces near the water's edge, picnic areas, boat launch facilities, and a fishing pier and fish-cleaning station.

Resources

Bodega Dunes Campground

875-3382

Bodega Dunes Campground is a part of Sonoma Coast State Beach. The campground is located on the northern edge of the town of Bodega Bay, bordered by Bodega Harbor, the Pacific Ocean, and Highway 1. Access to the beach is either by hiking trail or by a short drive inside the facility to a boardwalk designed for handicapped use. There are some 100 campsites here, fully developed with picnic tables, food lockers,

and fire rings. The campground also has restrooms with hot showers, overflow parking areas for extra vehicles, and a campfire center. Reservations strongly recommended.

Sonoma Coastal Parks

875-3540	Doran County Park
875-3540	Westside County Park
875-3550	Porto Bodega
875-3382	Bodega Dunes Campground
875-3483	Sonoma Coast State Beaches

865-2573	Duncan Mills Campground
847-3286	Fort Ross State Park
847-3278	Timber Cove Campgrounds
847-3245	Stillwater Cove Park
847-3221	Salt Point State Park
847-2391	Kruse Rhododendron State Reserve
785-2377	Gualala Point Regional Park

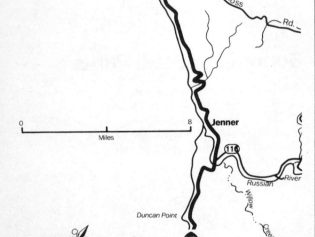

After the Russians

By January 1842, the Russian colony at Sonoma gave up on its American outpost after 30 years and returned to the northland. Any possibility of expansion had been foreclosed by a treaty in 1842. In addition, the sea otter population had become seriously depleted, no longer offering economic sustenance, and a series of crop failures convinced the Russian-American Fur Company to withdraw its California settlement.

Near the time of the Russians' departure, other white settlers began arriving in the area, the most prosperous of whom was Steven Smith, who took over the town the Russians built at Bodega and followed their practice of exploiting Indian labor in the fields to great economic success. In addition to his agricultural enterprises, Smith raised cattle, built a sawmill, ran a general store, operated a distillery, a tannery, a flour mill, a hotel, and a bowling alley.

So bad were the roads that almost all goods were shipped by boat from the Port of Bodega, a trip that took seven or eight hours from San Francisco. And within a generation of the American occupation of Bodega, unsound farming and building

methods caused the headwaters of the bay to fill with sand and mud, throwing the local economy into serious decline.

Edens Found and Lost

In the latter 19th century, when utopian experiments flourished all over California, Sonoma County had more utopian colonies than anywhere else in the state.

The best known was spiritualist-poet Thomas Lake Harris's Fountain Grove Colony, a theocratic community built on esoteric sexual practices, a supernatural method of breathing called Respirationism, and conversations with angels. Harris, a man who was read by Nathaniel Hawthorne and called "America's best known mystic" by William James, was finally driven from the gates of Eden by sexual scandal, allegations of fraud, and lawsuits, one of which settled $90,000 on Laurence Cliphant, who had been required by Harris to remain celibate, at least until his wife's bridal dowry was surrendered to the brotherhood.

Another utopian colony was established in 1881 on the banks of the Russian River—the Icara Speranza Commune, called the French Colony for its embrace of French socialist utopian philosophy and its mainly French-speaking members. In 1894, devoted readers of William Dean Howells's novel *A Traveler from Altruia* established a utopian colony based on the book. Others, such as Emily Preston (Madame Preston), variously enlisted the dedication of utopian-minded followers to create a new heaven on earth amid the edenesque inspiration of Sonoma County.

The 1960s ushered a revival of utopian communities in Sonoma. Best known was the Morning Star Ranch, near Graton, a few miles inland from Highway 1. Morning Star Ranch was established on a former Dominican retreat of 31 acres, purchased in 1962 by Lou Gottlieb, a former member of the Limelighters, a pop-folksinging group whose popularity in the late 1950s and early 1960s was exceeded only by the Kingston Trio and the Weavers.

Sometime in the mid 1960s, Gottlieb underwent "a change of consciousness" and began practicing a spiritual ethic that called for the abolishment of private property. This led him in 1969 to deed his redwood-covered Morning Star Ranch to God, with the idea of opening the land to all people, several of whom came to live on the land and explore new communal relations.

In response to Gottlieb's action, a woman filed suit in county court to gain Morning Star Ranch from its new owner, claiming that "God, also known as diety, also known as Jehovah, also known as creator" acted with malice and ill will when he caused lighting to strike her house in 1960 and owed her uncollected damages. Shortly afterward, a San Quentin prisoner claimed he was God and thus the land now belonged to him.

Eventually a Superior Court Judge ruled that God cannot own land in Sonoma County. Enforcement of health and sanitation laws was stepped up, forcing out many of the new-age pioneers, although remnants held on for years.

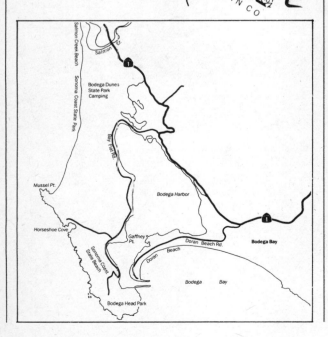

Environment	**Roadside Attractions**	**Resources**

The Birds

The birds at Bodega are abundant and conspicuous. There are more than 315 species of shore and water fowl to be seen here on beaches, jetties, headlands, mudflats, and marshes. The bird population peaks during fall and spring migration when flocks pass over Sonoma's coast along the Pacific flyway. The Bay is also a popular destination for many birds that disperse after the breeding season, including the endangered brown pelican.

Brown pelicans arrive in northern California from their nesting sites on islands off the south coast. Pelicans were once numerous in California, but their numbers declined drastically over the last decade because pesticides in the food chain caused pelican eggshells to thin, and infant mortality soared. The pelicans are making a comeback, however, and more and more are coming back each year to Bodega.

Brown pelicans are brown only when young. As they mature their bodies turn grayish, with white around the head. Their most distinctive features are a large grasping bill and a neck pouch, used to hold their catch. Brown pelicans have wingspans that may exceed six feet, making their

flight one of strong, slow wing beats with long glides. Flying in a long line or loose V, they present a spectactular sight when they drop into a glorious 60-foot plunge-dive with feet neatly tucked back to scoop up their marine catch.

When the pelican takes off from the water, it suffers a few indignant moments of clumsy effort, but once the large bird is aloft its style shows through. You may also spy the brown pelican along the shores of the bay moving into the interior protected marshes for roosting. These visitors are most numerous from mid-August to mid-November; most leave by January.

Bodega Bay

Bodega Bay, the most active commercial seaport between San Francisco and Fort Bragg, maintains its exceptional maritime vitality along with a growing visitor economy. At Tides Wharf, tourist and commercial fishing activities successfully combine in a constant panorama of real-life seaport goings-on, without affectation or imitation.

Though recently expanded, the wharf area has lost none of its vigor, thanks to a sensitive treatment by ROMA Associates. At any given time, Tides Wharf is astir and animated as dock crews hurry to unload full catches of shining fish from salmon boats beneath a sky of fluttering gulls. Trawlers with tall delicate masts glide in and out of dock set to a choreography of fish-to-market enterprise.

The Tides Restaurant, immortalized in Alfred Hitchcock's *The Birds*, provides a superb vantage point for watching the wharf activity, either from its pleasant dining room or convivial bar. The wharf area also offers a bait shop, a fresh-fish stand, a gift shop, and a 1,000-pound whale skull found offshore in 1965.

North of Tides Wharf, between Highway 1 and

the Harbor several fish companies are interspersed with charming redwood cottages that hang precariously above the water. On the way out of town are several roadside crab stands—the Crab Pot and Winston's Crab Shack—and a red-and-white striped saltwater taffy stand (Patrick's) that looks as good as its wares taste.

Maritime Bodega

Spud Point Marina

P.O. Box 339
Bodega Bay 94923
875-3535

The north coast's newest marina, Spud Point is primarily for commercial fishermen. It offers a 300″ floating service dock, 12″ wide fisherman's work platform, fuel and ice, pump-out and waste oil disposal facilities, laundromat, shower, coffee shop, and a three ton hoist. of the 250 berths, 80% are for commercial use and 20% recreational. There are plenty of places to sit and watch the Bodega commercial fleet in action.

The Tides

P.O. Box 518
Bodega Bay 94923
875-3595

The major Highway 1 center for Bodega Bay maritime activity, The Tides has a restaurant, bait shop, fish cleaning facilities, commercial fishing operations, and services for recreational and fishing boat rentals.

Partyboats Out of Bodega Bay

Bodega Bay offers Sonoma's only opportunities to rent a partyboat for a day at sea. Boats leave from Tides Wharf before sunrise, returning in mid-afternoon when the ocean often begins to get rough. Basic gear (rod, star draft reel with 40-pound test monofilament line) can be rented at the harbor. Rock cod up to 30–40 pounds are often brought in, as well as many other catches from wolf eels to cabezon. Two popular boats are the *Crystal C* (875-3595) and the *Bodega Bear* (875-3595). Prices for a day trip (food and equipment rental extra) are around $30. Reservations advised.

The Fisherman's Festival

In April the annual Blessing of the Fleet climaxes a weekend Fishermen's Festival at Bodega Bay. Arts and crafts, games of skill and chance, bath tub races in the bay, fresh fish dishes, and a boat parade are among the festivities.

Duncan's Mills

Despite Bodega's early economic doldrums, its population increased to 1,407 by the 1870s. In 1877 the North Pacific Coast Railroad was completed to Duncan's Mills (later Duncan Mills), drawing even more business away from the stagnant seaport.

With fast rail access from forest to market, logging quickly boomed on both sides of the Russian River, where stands of virgin redwoods were cut to pieces and converted to exhorbitant profits for timber speculators.

Mills sprung up all along the new rail line. To reach the untouched redwood groves along Austin Creek north of the Russian River, Alexander Duncan persuaded the North Pacific Coast to locate its terminal nearby, then moved his mill lock, stock, and barrel by floating it across the river on rafts.

The route of the North Pacific Coast was one of the most scenic and spectacular in 19th-century coastal California, a trip that could be completed from San Francisco to the end of the line at Duncan's Mill in six hours. Said the San Francisco *Argonaut,* "There is not an inch of the way that is not beautiful."

Entering Sonoma County at Estero Americana,

the narrow-gauge trains rolled through the high valley lands, stopping at Valley Ford, then Bodega Road, then Freestone, a pretty town settled by the Spanish to halt the spread of the Russian colony. North of Freestone, the great coast redwoods began to appear in abundance up and down the sides of gorges that took great bridges to cross. Above Brown's Canyon, near Salmon Creek, was the highest bridge west of the Mississippi, 137 feet above the canyon floor.

By the time the trains reached Howard's Station (later Occidental) the stands of redwoods were so thick they blotted out the sky. Finally arriving at Duncan's Mills over the Russian River on a 400-foot-long bridge, passengers would alight at Julian's Hotel, one of the most highly regarded resorts in 19th-century California. Nearby were excellent trout and game in unmatched natural settings. Said the *Pacific Tourist* in the 1870s, "considering the unequalled variety of beautiful scenery on the line of so short a road, and the charming picturesque region in which the road terminates, and amusements to be had in the vicinity, no spot deserves to be more favored by the tourist."

Cluttering Up the Roadside

The colorful roadside vendors along Sonoma's coast highway, who for years dispensed smoked salmon, flowers, and oranges to passing motorists, may have seen their last days. In 1985, the vendors were zoned out of existence along Highway 1 by a tough new ordinance that prohibits them from scenic county roadways.

The ordinance brings to focus two differing ideas of just what a "scenic roadway" is. Although many people see the bright-signed vendors as being a scenic addition to the roadside, a mark of small-scale commercial ornamentation that does no harm, others view Sonoma's scenic landscape to be too fragile to bear the weight of any commercial additions, colorful or not.

Unfair Competition

Also at issue, of course, is the economic competition the stands create for less temporary businesses that rely on the same motoring clientele. "We had a lot of complaints from merchants about the vendors undercutting prices," Sonoma County Supervisor Nick Espositi told a San Francisco newspaper. "And besides, we can't have peo-

ple cluttering up our scenic roadways."

The final smoked salmon has not necessarily been sold by the side of the road in Sonoma, however. Modifications to the complete prohibition of roadside stands are probable, and though the stands will undoubtedly be more closely regulated than they were in the past, roadside vendors in Sonoma will likely have another day.

Environment	Roadside Attractions	Resources

The Russian River

The Russian River is 110 miles long. Its basin drains over 1,400 square miles of land, including most of Northern California's richest agricultural area. In its course, the river runs from the Eastern Highlands of the state toward San Francisco Bay, making a 90° turn to the sea just below Healdsburg. The abrupt detour prompts speculation that the river once ran all the way to the Bay, but was diverted by seismic activity ages ago.

Today the river's mouth is partially enclosed by

a wide sand spit creating an inland estuary of unusual diversity. The once-variable location of the mouth was stabilized in the late 1920's by a concrete and rubblemound jetty constructed by the Army Corps. The rubblemound revetment visible on the downcoast bank was built to aid in now-defunct commercial excavation of the River's gravel deposits.

Penny Island sits in the middle of the River's inland estuary, a major haul-out point for harbor seals and California sea lions when the mouth of the river is open to the sea. Just offshore is Goat Rock, which was once much larger. Its size was reduced by extensive quarrying in the early part of this century. The causeway connecting Goat Rock to the mainland was built to support a 36-inch gauge industrial railway used in the quarrying operation. The jetty at the River's mouth is made up totally from Goat Rock rock. The golden color of the Russian River's water reflects its extremely high sediment content, shale and sand is carried from the highly erodable sandstone along inland banks until it is eventually deposited on the many pocket beaches in southern Sonoma County.

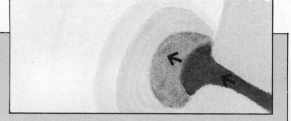

When River Meets the Sea

Strong-flowing rivers like the Russian River can affect the size and shape of ocean waves and may cause dramatic visual effects called freshwater plumes.

When the Russian River flows vigorously (especially during the rainy season), the ocean at its mouth becomes extremely turbulent. Surface waves, caused by the collision of the fast-flowing river current with the approaching ocean waves, are noticeably different from those on nearby beaches.

A second effect of a river's flow to the ocean is that of freshwater plumes. Freshwater is lighter than salt water, so when the river enters the sea, it overrides the ocean for a time until the waters mix enough to settle down through the water column. Since the Russian River has such a high sediment content, its golden brown plume is usually very visible, sometimes extending more than 100 miles offshore.

Sonoma Coast Beaches

North of Bodega Bay a string of popular beaches adjacent to the roadway attract thousands of visitors each year. Within this 13-mile stretch from Bodega Head to the Russian River, 17 state beaches are immediately accessible from Highway 1—broad open beaches, secluded coves, sculpted headlands, tidepools, and offshore arches. All have strong surf and sudden ground swells.

Salmon Creek Beach: A popular spot for families because of the creek provides a shallow swimming area. Much of the year the creek is closed by sand, forming a lagoon. The nearby sand dune stabilization area was created in 1951 to keep the harbor navigable by controlling drifting sand between Salmon Creek and Bodega Harbor.

Portuguese Beach: A fine sandy beach with rocky headlands. Surf fishing and rock fishing are popular activities. In the spring the headlands dazzle with Indian paintbrush and sand verbena.

Duncan's Landing: This former day landing for lumber and food products is also known as Death Rock because its treacherous, rocky headland has claimed many lives.

Wright Beach: A 30-site campground and an attractive beach lure many beachcombers and picnickers. Wildflowers.

Shell Beach: Noted for its excellent tide pools that also serve as outdoor classrooms for local schools. Good fishing.

Goat Rock: Quite different from its southern neighbors because of its proximity to the Russian River, Goat Rock Beach provides access to beaches on the ocean and on the river. Abundant bird life, fresh and salt-water fishing, and magnificent views south and north.

Jenner by the Sea

At the Russian River, Highway 1 assumes one of its most glorious personas against a backdrop of sweeping river and primeval sea. From Jenner northward, Highway 1's route seems to exist in another time as it carves through a 100-mile stretch of scenically stunning shorelands.

Jenner by the Sea, an appropriate point of departure, could be the entry post for the kingdom of Ecotopia, Ernest Callenbach's fictional Northern California land of perfected ecological order. With its cliff-hanging cottages and stunning offshore sea stacks, Jenner makes a magnificent tableau of unmanicured seaside charm. The River's End serves food suited to the scenery: boneless quail filled with roasted juniper berries, dates, nuts, and figs.

North of Jenner, Highway 1 climbs through a series of switchbacks to the heights of road-driving exaltation. Winding more than 700 feet above the ocean on the edge of sheer precipices, the road along the Jenner cliffs makes a sacrament of the distance between sky and sea.

Sonoma State Beach

RUSSIAN RIVER AREA
Department of Parks and Recreation
P.O. Box 385
Guerneville 95446
869-2221

Write for detailed information at the more than 30 developed campgrounds in the 13 mile long Sonoma State Beach chain. Camping is limited to a seven day stay in summer, 30 days the rest of the year. Park Headquarters are located about a mile north of Bodega Bay at Salmon Lagoon. Maps and several interpretative brochures are also available here. Reservations for campsites may be made through Ticketron.

Up the Russian River

Just past the Russian River Bridge, the River Road (State Highway 116) leads east to northern California's most popular summer playground where water carnivals, fishing, good food, and festivities abound. The tiny restored community of Duncan Mills is about three miles inland from Highway 1. The resort communities of Monte Rio, Guerneville, Rio Nido, and Forestville are a little further.

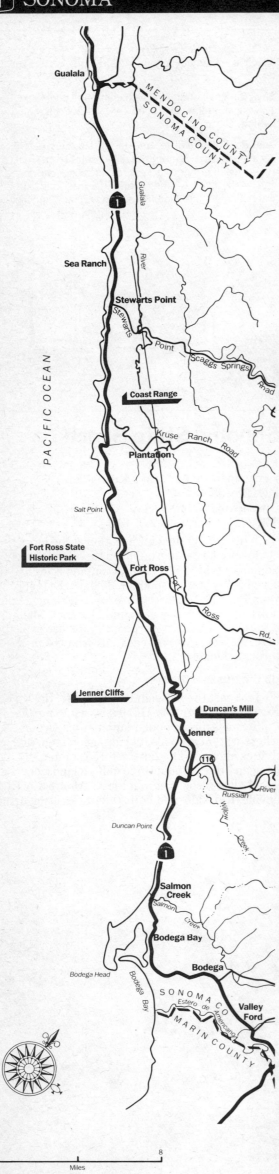

Call's Ranch

Beyond the North Pacific Coast Railroad's terminus at Duncan's Mill, the Sonoma coast existed as near wilderness until well into the 20th century. To be sure, logging operations were prevalent, but settlement in any conventional fashion was slow to arrive, and transportation remained an arduous nightmare.

At Fort Ross the settlement built by the Russians passed into the hands of John Sutter, while more than 200 Indians and half-breeds continued

to live at the fort. By 1898 Fort Ross had been transferred to George Washington Call, whose descendents still live in the area. Call previously had achieved a certain amount of fame in San Francisco as Mountain Man Grizzly Adams' partner in their wild-west animal menagerie.

A Unique Jobs Program

The California Conservation Corps (CCC) was begun in 1976 to provide jobs and training for young men and women, many of them from central city areas where youth unemployment is high. The jobs are different from those in other job programs because they aim at improving or protecting the natural resources and environment of California.

Members of the CCC "enlist" for a certain period, are trained, and then placed in work camps throughout the state, usually far from home and in

a totally different environment. The rules are strict and strictly enforced, the pay is just adequate, and the work can be backbreaking. Still, the waiting list to join the Corps is long, and the skills and experience a member obtains on the job can be of significant value.

Typical projects of the CCC include developing parks, trails, and public facilities, clearing streams, planting trees, restoring historical areas, and protecting and improving wildlife habitats. About 20% of the CCC's time is spent fighting floods and forest fires.

Russian Sleds and Ships at Fort Ross

Few places could have been more desolate than the high cliffs above the sea 13 miles north of the Slavianka River where Ivan Kuskov returned with his colony in 1812. But no place offered better protection from invasion.

With no harbor at Fort Ross, the Russians continued to rely on Bodega Bay for shipping and related activities. But the unevenness of the terrain made transportation between the two locations extremely difficult.

To connect the two places, a road was cut in solid rock bluff face at Fort Ross that led to the narrow beach hundreds of feet below. Wharf timbers were layed at lengths and bolted to the rocks, making a connecting track down the cliffs and along the nearby beach. On this timber track goods and produce were transported to Bodega in large Siberian sleds that

were dragged along the water's edge.

The Russians also constructed several ships on the beach beneath the high cliffs, although their unfamiliarity with native woods caused many problems. The Spanish, who kept Russian California under surveillance, were amazed by the Russians' industry and enterprise. In 1818, workers at the Fort Ross colony launched the 160-ton *Roumintzov*, built of native oak, which took two years to construct and proved utterly useless. In 1820 the *Buidakov* was launched, a 200-ton copper-bottomed ship also made of oak, which lasted only a few years. Two other boats were tried using other types of woods—pine, cedar, and perhaps redwood.

The *Volga,* launched in 1823 and pronounced unseaworthy four years later, and the 200-ton *Krakhta,* launched in 1824, lasted longer than any of the others—but not long enough to indicate much success at combining the Russians' native skills with the available materials of their new environment.

Environment | **Roadside Attractions** | **Resources**

Sonoma's Geology

The Russian River divides Sonoma into two distinct geological districts. From the Marin County line to the river, Highway 1 sits atop low coastal cliffs backed to the east by the rolling, vegetated foothills of the Coastal Range. On the north side of the river, the road rises to spectacular 700 foot heights as the Coastal Range meets the sea at Jenner. This eleven mile ascent along the Jenner cliffs is stunningly beautiful—more beautiful, some say, than Big Sur.

Highway 1 levels off on the north side of the Jenner grade. Here the road perches atop moderately-high rocky cliffs with broad coastal terraces extending to the sea from inland wooded hills. There are few sandy beaches north of Jenner. Instead, the traveler is rewarded by some of the most interesting rock formations and richest tide pools along the California coast.

The Coast Range

The geological province called the Coast Range extends more than 400 miles from the Transverse Ranges in Santa Barbara County to the Oregon Border. The range has an average width of about 50 miles, and seldom exceeds 8,000 feet in height. The northern section, which includes Sonoma County, is marked by the San Andreas fault on the west and the northern tip of the central valley on the east. Highly-erodable shale and sandstone of the Franciscan formation dominate the geological landscape.

From the Russian River, the Mendocino Highlands section of the Coast Range stretches more than 180 miles to the north. These relatively young mountains are believed to have been uplifted from an inland sea that once stretched west from the Sierra Nevada to the lost continent of Salinia. They are a mere million years old.

Fort Ross

Back down to earth (or almost there), Highway 1 winds through the remains of the old 15,000-acre Call Ranch to Fort Ross. Once the road levels off, a few paths to the ocean present themselves. Do not, however, confuse them with sheep trails, particularly in elevated areas. A magnificent rocky beach runs beneath the cliffs, access to which may be gained by fee at the campground 1.5 miles south of Fort Ross (or by determined exploration on the publicly owned lands adjacent to the fee parking area).

Fort Ross State Historical Park is one of the coast's most fascinating treasures. Restoration has created a visitors' attraction that masterfully evokes and describes one of California's strangest historical events, the occupation of the area around the Russian River by a colony of Russian settlers for some 30 years beginning in 1812.

Until 1972, Highway 1 ran through the center of the compound built by the Russians, later converted to a hotel and saloon, and eventually acquired by the State in 1906 for preservation and restoration. Since the 1970s the State Department of Parks and Recreation has undertaken a long-term project to restore much of the settlement to its original character.

The commandante's house was probably built in 1836 by Alexander Rotchev, the last commandante of Fort Ross. Rotchev was a poet, writer, traveler, and translator of seven languages. He lived in the house with Princess Helena Gagarin, who had forsaken Russian society and endured financial disinheritance to marry Rotchev.

The Russian Orthodox Chapel across the compound was first erected in 1824, but collapsed in the 1906 earthquake. Restored for the third time in 1974, the chapel is the compound's most architecturally interesting structure, symbol of the Russians' hardy spiritualism and strong determination to survive.

Also inside the compound are the restored stockade and blockhouse. Made of hand-hewn redwood timbers set as deep as six feet in the ground, the stockade uses some materials from the original structure. The blockhouses, which contained brass and iron cannons that protected the fort from Spanish invasion, now display exhibits depicting aspects of the Russian colony's difficult life at Fort Ross.

Fort Ross State Historic Park

19005 Coast Highway 1
Jenner 95450
847-3286

The Commandant's House holds interpretive exhibits and sells publications and artifacts related to the history and natural history of Fort Ross. A new visitor's center will soon expand these services. Members of the Fort Ross Interpretative Association are often available to answer questions,

and there is also a self-guided historical tour narrated by recording wands available on the grounds. Personal guided tours may also be requested. Once a year, on Living History Day, fully costumed volunteers act out the normal events of 1836, including musket drills, arrival of Mexican officials from Monterey, daily chores, and a Slavyanka chorus. The park also conducts an environmental education program for elementary classes. The children spend weeks in the classroom preparing for an overnight visit to the fort during which they participate in all functions of the 1800 era.

State Symbols

Nickname	The Golden State
Motto	*Eureka* (I Have Found It)
Colors	Blue & Gold
Animal	California Grizzly Bear
Bird	California Valley Quail

CALIFORNIA REPUBLIC

Fish	California Golden Trout
Flower	Golden Poppy
Fossil	Saber-Toothed Cat
Insect	California Dog-Face Butterfly
Marine-Mammal	California Gray Whale
Mineral	Native Gold
Reptile	California Desert Tortoise
Song	*I Love You, California*
Stone	Serpentine
Theatre	Pasadena Community Playhouse
Tree	California Redwood

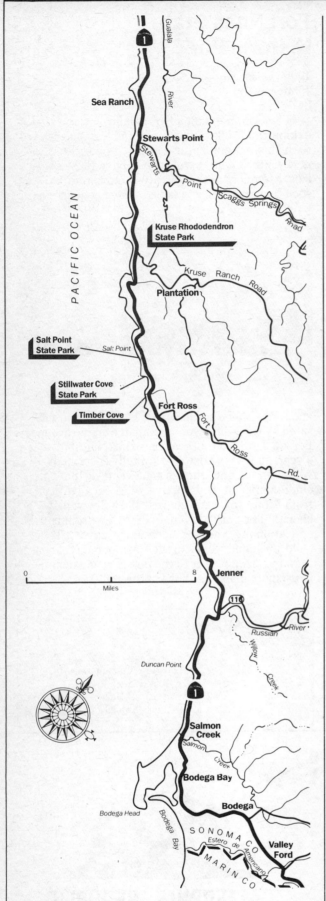

A Road in Place of a Trail

For most of its history, life along the Sonoma coast was lived in usually brutal, and often brawling, hard-drinking, hell-raising fashion. The only economy to prosper in the area was timbering, which attracted a type of personality more suited to the wildness of Gold Rush California than to the settling down of community life.

Consequently, for years there was little incentive to build or improve roads as any mark of civic or community betterment. The lumber produced

was shipped to San Francisco, mainly by sea from Timber Cove, Stewart's Point, Fisherman's Bay, or Black Point until the mills were shut down by the Depression in the 1930s.

Original construction of the coast road was initiated by Lew Miller, a stageline owner who wanted to extend passenger and mail service up the Sonoma coast from Duncan Mill to Gualala. In 1868 Miller took the entire Sonoma County Board of Supervisors on a tour of the Sonoma coast frontier and convinced them to build a road in place of the rough Pomo and pioneer trails that stuttered across the countryside.

Four years later there was a semblance of a road along the North Sonoma coast, and although it still took 12.5 hours to negotiate the distance from Jenner to Gualala, it was a proper enough passageway to be described in 1873 by historian C. A. Menefee as a "moderately good stage road running up the coast."

A "moderately good road" in the 1870s, however, left more than a little to be desired. Unpaved, the road was quickly transformed into a quagmire during winter rains. Although much of the Sonoma coast road ran along the relatively wide and well-drained marine terrace, parts of it became impassable after storms, and stage travel often had to be suspended.

In some of the most frequently muddy spots the roadbed was reconstructed with redwood timbers. Not without some justification, stories frequently circulated about the sudden disappearance of entire wagon teams into bottomless mudholes.

Stillwater Cove: Public Access for the Disabled

The public accessway at Stillwater Cove is one of the few coastal access facilities on the coast that is specially designed for people with physical disabilities. A special parking area, paved wheelchair accessible trail, and accessible public facilities make the beach area unique. Such improvements will become increasingly available, however, at many state parks where a new program is retrofitting 16 parks a year for disabled use.

California's national leadership in this field arose from a obvious necessity. About 80% of the state's population lives within 30 miles of the coast, and the total number of disabled people within that range approaches five million. Add all those people "temporarily" disabled or impaired through injury or age (the very young and very old), and availability of access to the coast becomes all the more important.

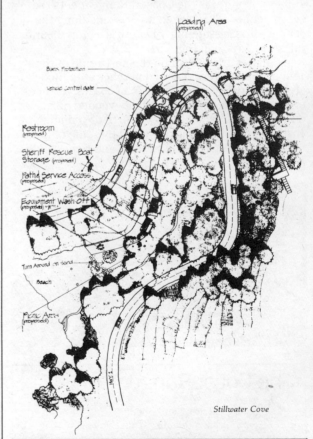

Stillwater Cove

A Mysterious Mirage

Most years, usually in the fall, a mysterious mirage appears about a mile offshore north of Bodega Bay. Those who have seen it agree that it is a "stupendous sight, best described as a Wizard of Oz City, hovering above the ocean, complete with fantastic towers, minarets, the whole thing." In September of 1984, local residents, park rangers, tourists and others were awed by a visit from the mysterious city, which floated offshore for several days. As the Bodega Bay Postmistress put it, "Most of us old-timers have seen it off and on for years. Only nobody knows what it is."

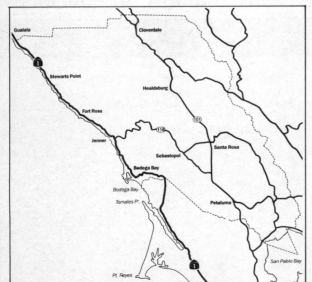

The Remarkable Rhododendron

Of the several hundred varieties of rhododendron, most are descendants of Oriental or European species, and several grow native to the California coast. The rhododendron plant may creep along the ground, stand as a foot-tall shrub, or reach tree-like proportions of up to 30 feet in height.

Rhododendron's glossy leaves make them lovely year round, but from April to June, when

the flowers appear, their beauty is unsurpassed. The clustered flowers come in every color and shade, including pure white, cream, pink, crimson, lavendar, orange, yellow, blue and purple. Many of the species are dramatically spotted or toned in splendid variations of a prime color.

The rhododendron thrives along the northern California coastal slopes, which provide limited sun and protection from exposure to winds. Larger trees like the pine and redwood offer filtered shade and a constant mulch of needles for the wild beauties, and the distinctly acid, moist Sonoma soil provides appropriate nourishment.

The two most common members of the rhododendron family on the coast are the California rhododendron, and the western azalea. The California rhododendron, or rose bay, is an evergreen that usually grows as a three to 12 foot-tall shrub. Here, however, it may reach heights of more than 20 feet, sometimes 30 feet. The especially dark green leathery leaves of the rose bay contrast beautifully with the gentle rose-purple or rose-pink of the clustered flowers. Western azaleas (*Rhododendron macrophylum*) are usually about three to 12 feet high, their smaller flowers sporting variations of shades from white to rose or from pink to an orange flush.

Timber Cove

Just up the road from Fort Ross Store (1870) and Lodge is Timber Cove, with boat launching and camping aside the rocky shore. The nearby Timber Cove Inn is a latter-day lodge and land sales venture that was built without public access to the shore just prior to the establishment of the Coastal Commission. Despite its snootiness, the Timber Cove Inn has its amenities—a gigantic warming fireplace and civilized bar, a carefully selected program of pre-recorded classical and experimental music, and occasional recitals.

Stillwater Cove and Salt Point

Between Timber Cove and Stewart's Point the roadside landscape becomes tighter in scale with sudden curves and crests and the closeby presence of redwood-stake fences textured with moss and lichen. The road races past richly green shrubs and wind-carved trees adjacent to the intermittently visible ocean.

Next is Stillwater Cove Regional Park, a fine county park with camping on the east side of the highway and excellent skin-diving facilities (accessible to the disabled) at the cove itself.

North of Ocean Cove Store (fee access to beach) begins Salt Point, a 400-acre shorefront park with spectacular tidepools, small coves, and beautifully eroded sandstone cliffs.

Benny Bufano at Timber Cove

Sonoma County's most evident coastal art piece is the Bufano totem pole that stands behind the Timber Cove Inn, gracing the cliffside with a pleasing mix of primitive and modern art elements. The totem pole is the work of San Francisco's best known sculptor Benny Bufano, who created the piece out of a special fondness for the Sonoma coast and its unique spiritual and aesthetic qualities.

Bufano was an ardent opponent of museums as repositories of art, which he denounced as tombs while speaking up strongly for free public art. An elegant tribute to the beauty of the shore land on which it sits, Bufano's sculpture is also a satisfying monument to his ideal of unfettered, free public art.

North Coast Diving

Sonoma's shore from Bodega Bay to the Russian River and from Fort Ross to Stewarts Point harbors some of the best diving spots in California. Calm water, ease of access, and the Russian River transportation corridor make this area very popular with divers who come to gather abalone, spear fish, participate in diving instruction, or indulge in underwater nature study, photography, and exploration.

CALIFORNIA SPORT DIVING CHART
Pacific Publishing Company
3871 Piedmont Avenue
Oakland 94701

This map marks and describes more than 50 diving spots from Bodega Bay north, including excellent references for Stillwater Cove and Salt Point State Park. The information includes water temperature ranges, access fees, supplies, services, and natural environment at each site. For more information on diving in Northern California, contact the California Council of Diving Clubs, Inc. (P.O. Box 779, Daly City, 94017).

Stillwater Cove

Access: Highway 1 for unloading west of the highway, parking on east side of highway. 847-3245.

Salt Point State Park

Access: Highway 1 at several signed entrances and the ranger station. 847-3221

Kruse Rhododendron State Park

Access: Take Kruse Ranch Road, 2.6 miles north of the main Salt Point access area. A map of the park is available at the park's parking lot. 865-2391

Stillwater Cove, Salt Point, and Kruse Rhododendron State Park are almost adjacent to one another, offering an excellent chance to camp, dive in protected coves or open surf, explore tide pools, and hike along miles of trails that twist through redwood, fir, and 20-foot high rhododendron plants. Gerstle Cove at Salt Point a designated area of special biological significance. In using Sonoma's tidal areas, please keep in mind that a current California sportfishing license is necessary to take legal invertebrates, and their take is restricted by seasons, bag and size limits.

The Gualala Highway

A great deal of travel along what came to be called the Gualala Highway, the traillike road that established Highway 1's course between Jenner and the town of Gualala just over the county line, took place on horseback. Well suited to the near-wilderness conditions of the coast above the Russian River, the horse remained a regular mode of transportation even up until World War II. In 1913 Joseph Smeaton Chase passed along the Gualala Highway upon his noble horse Anton en route up the coast:

"The road was over a bracken-covered moorland with a sprinkling of small oaks and madroños, and broken by frequent canyons dark with twisted and tousled redwoods. This tree has a way of throwing out, when stunted, a thatch of foliage so close and matted as to be quite impervious to light. The effect of a company of these freakish individuals, under conditions of storm or half-light, is weird in the extreme."

From about the 1870s the most frequently used form of transportation, besides the horse and the occasional stage, was the "spring wagon," so called because of its metal springs intended to iron out the roughness of the road.

Drawn by a span of horses, the spring wagon was the usual conveyance for families, who squeezed into the two wide seats, often fitting youngsters on boxes in between.

The spring wagon was the proudest and most colorful possession of many pioneer families. The wagons' bright green bodies with fancy black, white, or red scrollwork and sharply contrasting vermillion wheels cut a handsome path along the edge of the bright blue Pacific.

Less stylish than the spring wagon was the go-cart, a springless, one-horse hard-riding wagon that often pitched its riders out of their seats and onto the side of the road when encountering a hump or hollow at speed. In the soft mud, however, the go-cart was at its best, performing well when moving slowly.

Several livery stables marked the Gualala Highway until the automobile finally put the carriage out of business. Young men and women with romantic destinations in mind could rent a canopy top to carry them in high style along the ocean road.

Public Access at Sea Ranch

The question was whether or not ten miles of spectacular coastline would become a private beach, and for more than a decade it remained unresolved while generating more controversy than any land use issue on the north coast. Eventually, after years of costly litigation, a federal court decision affirmed the public's right to use the shoreline at Sea Ranch, and a special state legislative bill implemented the solution.

The conflict dates from the early 1970s when public sentiment against the increasing loss of public beach areas became a major contributing factor in the passage of proposition 20, which established a legal process to protect access and coastal resources.

Proposition 20 established the Coastal Commission, which refused to issue development permits at Sea Ranch without conditions to provide coastal access. Lot owners were enraged and argued that the Commission's authority did not extend to Sea Ranch because it had been planned without public access before there was any state permit authority, and that individual lot owners could not fulfill public access requirements anyway because the land required for dedication was owned in common under the Homeowners Association. The Homeowner's Association filed suits against the Coastal Commission on these grounds as well as challenging the Commission's overall authority to regulate public access on private property, which they maintained was a taking without just compensation.

In 1981 a federal district court ruled in favor of the Coastal Commission, upholding the legality of all public access requirements. Said the court, "It is clear the Commission would be in violation of the policies and duties spelled out under the Coastal Act if it had not imposed the challenged conditions," otherwise "ten miles of the California coastline would become a private beach."

After the court's ruling, a special Assembly Bill, which had been passed in 1980, paved the way for the transfer of access easements to a public agency by authorizing the payment of $500,000 to the Sea Ranch Homeowners Association. Eventually, the County of Sonoma accepted the easements and, with assistance from the State Coastal Conservancy, set out to construct the trails and facilities that will allow the public the chance to use a major portion of Sonoma's magnificent coast for the first time in nearly 20 years.

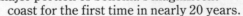

Environment

Roadside Attractions

Resources

Life on the Rocky Edge

Honeycombed sandstone rocks, offshore reefs full of tidal life, and protected coves for dividing make Salt Point State Park a major attraction for north coast naturalists. The perpetual eroding action of northern Sonoma's powerful waves has pocked the sandstone marine terrace at Salt Point in truely unearthly fashion. A network of paths along barren edges leads to intertidal reefs, which —depending on the tide level—reveal the startling diversity of life in the tidepools.

Sea Palms

Even when high tides obscure most nearshore life, one resident of the mid–littoral zone is likely to be visible. Sea palms cluster in tiny foot–high forests, clinging to the rocks with incredibly strong "holdfasts" or bundles of small fibers that tightly grip the rock.

Sea palms are really a type of algae that grow only where surf is continuous and high like it is along Sonoma's coast. The tiny palms wage a continuing battle with powerful forces of wind and wave. The sea palms absorb the natural energy through movement of a flexible, rubbery stalk that supports it nourishment–gathering head of waving foilage. The palms also provide protection for animals that could not otherwise survive the turbulent environment, such as the brown and white-shelled limpet.

Giant Green Anemone

The giant green anemone is almost as common and as easily-recognized a form of tidepool life as is the sea palm. The green color of this solitary animal comes from a symbiotic green algae that lives in the anemone's tissue. Its waving tentacles are covered with tiny stingers called *nematocysts* that emit a poison to grasp, sting, paralyze, and eventually kill tiny prey washed by on the tidal currents. The poison, which is also highly effective in discouraging predators, is barely felt by a human hand.

Sea Ranch

Stewart's Point and its surrounds offer a nearly unchanged portrait of the northern Sonoma coast for the last 75 years. So, too, the Stewart's Point Store is from another time, dispensing general store items such as cast-iron stoves and axe handles as readily as picnic supplies for the 20th-century tourist.

Three miles up the road, however, modern life shows itself much less reticently—this is Sea Ranch, which has been both Northern California's

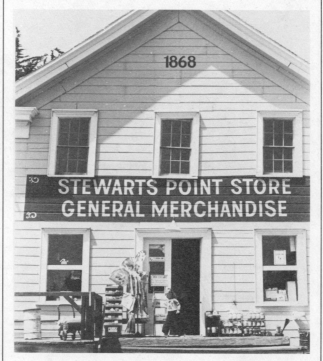

most controversial second-home development and an international model for contemporary shore-front architecture.

Based on a master land-use plan created in 1964 by Lawrence Halprin, Sea Ranch is a large-scale, luxury second-home development originally intended as a low-density urban residential community. Halprin sought to preserve viewsheds and the natural character of the land by leaving considerable portions of open land along the bare coastal plane and allowing only unobtrusive "clustered" development. Unfortunately, Halprin's original concept has been largely replaced by a land-use program that relies on tasteful architecture with not much restraint for where it is placed.

Sea Ranch's most celebrated structure is Condominium I ("The most written about building erected in Northern California during the last 25 years") designed by Moore, Lyndon, Turnbull and Whitaker. The structure relates well to the Sonoma coastal environment without dominating it, and does so with dramatic style. Moore and Turnbull also designed a number of other single residences throughout Sea Ranch that have gained deserved recognition, as have several structures by Joseph Esherick, contributing to Sea Ranch's reputation "the California architectural monument of the 1960s."

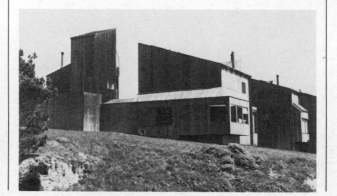

Public Access at the Sea Ranch

Use these trails to reach the public beaches and bluffs at Sea Ranch. Look for informational signs or call the County Parks Department for full description of facilities 527-2041.

Blackpoint Beach Trail: Trailhead near marker 50.85 on Highway 1, just north of the lodge.

Pebble Beach Trail: Trailhead near marker 52.21, south of Navigator's Reach Road.

Pocket Beaches Access: Trailhead near marker 53.96, just north of the stables.

Shell Beach Trail: Trailhead just south of Whalebone Reach.

Walk-On Beach Trail: Use the Blufftop Trail, or the trailhead north of Leeward Road, near marker 56.76.

Salal Trail: Trailhead located on Highway 1 and in the Gualala Point Regional Park.

Sea Ranch Blufftop Trail: Trailhead at the park, or at several intersections with other trails.

Shoreline Highway

When the automobile came to the Sonoma coast, its influence was not great at first. Until well after the Depression, most of the autos to be seen on the coast highway were owned by tourists making their was slowly from San Francisco, and there were not many of them. Sonoma was a Good Roads Movement county, however, and took road-building seriously. By the mid-20s a decent road ran from the Russian River to Gualala, despite some sections having toll gates across private property.

On October 10, 1926, the county celebrated the opening of a fine road from Bodega Road to the ferry at the Russian River, following the route made by the Russians in 1811, and composed of "only the best crushed rock and other materials." The "popular celebration" included a dedication of a large warning sign at Death Rock on Wright's Beach where 14 fishermen had been swept out to sea by large waves.

Russian River Bridge

On October 4, 1931, more than 10,000 persons showed up to celebrate the opening of the Russian River Bridge, probably the best-attended celebration in coastal Sonoma's history. The new bridge was christened by "Miss Shoreline Highway," who broke a bottle of Sonoma mineral water over the new structure.

For 60 years a small rickety ferry had been the only way across the river. With a new bridge finally completed, a pasteboard replica of the old ferry was towed out into the middle of the river, blown up, and burned as the dedication ceremony ended.

Meeting the Expectations of the Land

The sudden appearance of Gualala Point Regional Park after ten miles of Sea Ranch second homes illustrates by contrast an unavoidable reality of coastal land use economics: few free market incentives exist for the preservation of scenic open space. Given current land use patterns, the day may eventually dawn on the north coast when all the areas not marked off as public parkland will be built on and closed off from view, establishing a coastal landscape that is essentially suburban in nature.

Gualala Point Park and Sea Ranch were once part of the giant Rancho de Herman, a 5,000 acre sheep ranch that preserved the scenic qualities of the land while maintaining a quiet compatibility with the isolated character of the Sonoma Coast. Unfortunately, scenic preservation has no value in a market economy and development potential does. Once its value for development increased by many times its agricultural value, its future was foreordained.

Subdivisions and Hotcakes

For much of the nation's history, scenic rural areas were protected by the existence of small farms and agricultural operations. In effect, the free market supplied a means to maintain the countryside, at the same time it supplied independent livelihoods, rewarded individual initiative, and strengthened community relations. But modern land use economics now often reward the conversion of agricultural areas to more intense development such as subdivisions, particularly along the California coast where real estate sells like hot cakes. The free market dances with another partner.

There has been much success against the tide of conversion of scenic areas on the north coast. The California Coastal Commission has significantly slowed the rate at which scenic lands are disappearing through regulation of development permits, although the Commission's influence has been weakened in the 1980s. The State Coastal Conservancy maintains several programs to help protect scenic coastal lands by means other than regulation and has shown the capability for innovative action. Several land trusts—both local and national—have had major success in preserving scenic lands. But the task is monumental, and many people disagree entirely with a land use ethic that restrains private profit.

The Gualala River

The Gualala is not as important a waterway as the Russian River to the south, but it is comparable in the beauty of its setting. It also has a few unusual attributes of its own, including a double sand spit at its mouth and a north–south flow line.

Although most northern California rivers flow east to west, the Gualala follows the bed of the San Andreas fault zone in a north to south direction. The phenomenon of a double sandspit like the one that typically forms at the mouth of the river is also somewhat unusual. During fall months until early spring, northern movement of sand by the offshore current called littoral drift establishes the southern sand spit. But after the winter storms subside the wind and currents often change direction to the southeast, creating a northern sand spit. Both the spits, which are also fed by sediments transported inland by the river, build until the mouth closes, then open up again as the power of the river swells with winter rains.

The southern banks of the Gualala River front on the flat grassy marine terrace that forms Gualala Point Park. The beach on this side is well known for the beauty and abundance of its driftwood. On the northern side of the River (in Mendocino County) sandstone bluffs drop huge slabs to the waterline, forming an effective natural revetment armor along the shore.

Driftwood

Driftwood is plentiful on north coast beaches for several reasons. Some of the pieces are remnants of old logging operations closed decades ago. The cut pieces have been softened, their edges sculptured by water, waves, sun, and time. Most of the wood, however, comes from the inland wooded shores of rivers. The wood floats downstream, eventually coming to rest along the south side of the river's mouth, or moving out to sea for transport to another beach. The location of the largest piles of driftwood on Sonoma and Mendocino beaches marks the highest point of ocean wave uprush during annual north coast storms.

Gualala Point Park

Sea Ranch extends almost to the county line at the Gualala River, but not quite. Between Sea Ranch and the River is Sonoma's finest coastal park.

Gualala Point Regional Park is a worthy complement to the natural coastal environment; little has been done to transform the original landscape into a "park." Understated facilities (restrooms and interpretive center) are perched high and away from the trails, the river, and the ocean. This is a magnificent open space to walk in, through,

and over.

Gualala Point sits along and south of the Gualala River, on both sides of Highway 1. On the west side of the road is the day-use park, where three trails take you to the ocean cliffs and a magnificent sandy beach at the terminus of the Gualala River, and Gualala Point itself, a sandstone promentory that juts proudly into the ocean meeting the sea's full force with its own elemental dignity.

On the east side of the Highway, in a protected redwood grove adjacent to the usually still river, is the overnight camping facility (168 spaces). The day-use facility is primarily open coastal terrace with grasses and lupine and wind.

Viewed from just above the Gualala Bridge, the splendid river is much as it has always been, although the mills that smoked the air and muddied the water at the turn of the century are gone. Now the unraveling road spins past and over the water with only a smattering of remains from the Gualala Mill and the Gualala ferry.

Protecting Open Space and Agricultural Lands

Contact the following organizations for comprehensive information on Sonoma County's efforts to protect its open space and agricultural lands.

AMERICAN FARMLAND TRUST
512 Second Street
San Francisco 94107.
543-2098.

AFT works to bring together agriculturists and conservationists, business people and scholars, and public officials and private citizens to achieve protection of farmland and farming opportunities in California and the nation.

PEOPLE FOR OPEN SPACE
512 Second Street
San Francisco 94107.
543-4291

POS is one of the leading Bay Area specialists on open space and agricultural preservation, including Sonoma County. They publish a newsletter, numerous technical reports and studies on Bay Area farmland and housing/open space issues, and work to achieve a Bay Area greenbelt of agricultural land within which appropriate development could occur. Contact for publication list.

SONOMA LAND TRUST
Box 1211
Sonoma 95476.
545-7572.

The primary purpose of the Sonoma Land Trust is to protect the remaining agricultural lands in the county. Write for brochure and newsletter.

Problems and Solutions

THE UNSETTLING OF AMERICA
Wendell Berry
Avon Books
New York. 1978.

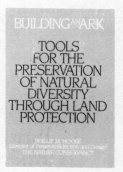

GAINING GROUND: THE RENEWAL OF AMERICA'S SMALL FARMS
J. Tevere MacFadyen
Holt, Rinehart & Winston
New York. 1984.

MEETING THE EXPECTATIONS OF THE LAND
Wes Jackson, Wendell Berry, and Bruce Colman, Editors
North Point Press
Berkeley. 1985.

LAND SAVING ACTION
Brenneman and Bates, Editors
Island Press
Covelo. 1984.

BUILDING AN ARK
Phillip M. Hoose
Island Press
Covelo. 1981.

MENDOCINO

HIGHWAY 1'S NORTHBOUND route through Mendocino County begins at the Gualala River and ambles along the ocean's edge to just beyond Westport where it abruptly turns inland, ending at the juncture of U.S. 101 at Leggett. Along the way are stretches of unbelievably dramatic scenery and a series of tiny one-time timber towns that fit snugly into river mouth clearings between the forest and sea.

North of Gualala, Highway 1 runs astride the rugged shoreline to Point Arena where a 200-foot lighthouse lends dignity to the coast landscape. Just beyond, whistling swans rest on the Garcia River plain.

From Elk to the town of Mendocino, Highway 1 is dotted with nearly half a hundred of California's most romantic bed and breakfast inns. The historically preserved town of Mendocino offers restaurants, shops, and a pleasing pedestrian ambience.

After Fort Bragg, coastal Mendocino's most urbanized population center, Highway 1 stretches toward oblivion, escaping the influence of the free-spending tourist and most marks of 20th century civilization.

Westport

① Inglenook

Cleone

Pudding Creek

FORT BRAGG

Caspar

20

Mendocino

Little River

Comptche

Albion

Flynn Creek Rd.

Elk

Greenwood Creek

Elk Creek

128

①

Alder Creek

Manchester

Brush Creek

Mountain View

Point Arena

Point Arena

Ten Mile Road

Fish Rock

Old Stage

Gualala Stores and Restaurants

MENDOCINO

Gualala River

Gualala

PACIFIC OCEAN

Branscombe Road

County Profile

Geographic

Land Area (acres)	2,244,480
Land Area (sq. miles)	3,507.0
Water Area (acres)	2,360
Water Area (sq. miles)	3.7
Acres in Public Ownership	392,634
Percent in Public Ownership	17.49
Miles of Public Roads	2,219
County Seat	Ukiah

Demographic

Population	70,400
State Rank by Population	35
Projected 1990 Population	77,700
Unemployment Rate (state avg. = 9.9)	13.3
Per Capita Personal Income	$9,250
State Rank by Income	38
Total Assessed Property Value	$1,973,771,876

The Banner County for Bad Roads

Highway 1's development through Mendocino is the story of a wild, inhospitable terrain that was eventually cajoled to permit a road.

Until early in the 20th century, the principal means of travel for residents along the Mendocino coast was not by road, but by sea. Schooners, first sail-powered, then steam-powered, provided the chief link to the outside world as they brought in supplies and shipped out lumber to market from the many mill towns between Gualala and Mendocino. Roads that connected these early mill towns were slow to develop, and for years after the establishment of the first mills, coast travel was either by sea or horseback.

Once roads were established, they were extremely uncertain propositions: the topography was brutally rough, broken every mile or two by steep ravines and gulches, and cut in many places by rivers too deep to ford easily without long detours. The thick stands of timber, the original motive for the mill towns, also formed a barrier to decent roads. Together these factors made the

Mendocino coast one of the most isolated sections of California, and the roads as bad as any. A correspondent for the *Daily Alta* wrote in 1870: "I have travelled over rough roads during my 19 years on this coast, but must accord to Mendocino County my fullest recognition as the banner county for bad roads."

The earliest record of a coast road dates from 1870, when a wagon road was built from Point Arena to Mendocino along old Indian trails used by valley Indians to reach the ocean's store of shellfish and kelp. Here the terrain was flatter, less uncertain, but always extremely unreliable. Dusty in summer, muddy in winter, tree-strewn in any season, the roads were the cause of frequent accidents and constant delay. During the winter rains redwood bark or logs were often used as a roadbed, when deep mud didn't require that operation to be suspended entirely. A traveler from San Francisco may have only slightly exaggerated when he described the road as being "in horrible condition, with the depth of mud varying from six inches to six feet—more or less."

Mendocino Marijuana

The most profitable land use in Mendocino County is growing marijuana. Mendocino is the home of the lauded sinsemilla plant, considered to be the Maserati of marijuana among connoisseurs. So much pot is being grown in hidden patches in the mountains and woods that Mendocino marijuana has become its major export. Mendocino is one of the state's major overall producers of a crop that last year was the nation's second most valuable and ranked above grapes and cotton as California's largest agricultural product.

In a county with the lowest per capita income in the state, the economic impacts of such a high-profit activity are significant. California leads the nation in marijuana production with an estimated $2 billion a year crop, and a lot of this money finds its way into Mendocino's economy. The traditional industries of the county—timber, fishing, dairy farming, and ranching—are in serious decline, and without marijuana, many of the county's residents could not make a living.

Because of its increasing significance to the north coast's overall economy, many local officials take a milder attitude toward the drug than they once did. Yet, the State Attorney General's office, which last year spent $2 million on a paramilitary Campaign Against Marijuana (CAMP), disputes any local economic benefits from the drug in north coast counties like Mendocino. At a hearing before the state Senate Judiciary Committee in 1984, Attorney General John Van de Kamp claimed that most marijuana growers are transients who take their short-term (untaxed) profits elsewhere.

Others take a different view of marijuana's economic influence. The National Organization for Reform of Marijuana Laws (NORML), which advocates the legalization of marijuana, contends that most marijuana growers are local residents who make less than $30,000 a year and spend most of their profits locally, creating a ripple effect for the area's grocers, clothing stores, and automobile dealers. One thing for certain is that growing marijuana for a living in Mendocino has a wider respectibility than most places. Many residents, in fact, judge its influence to be beneficial to the community. One Mendocino County proprietor told a San Francisco newspaper, "I would say that most of the growers are good people. They shop here and they raise families. It's not a Mafia-type thing."

Steelhead and Salmon

The Gualala River has attracted steelhead and salmon enthusiasts from the days when the only way to reach the area was by ship. Today, the Gualala fish run has diminished, but populations are now holding steady, and programs are underway to increase the runs. There are still plenty of salmon, as well as steelhead trout.

Salmon and steelhead are anadromous fish, meaning that they move from salt water to inland waterways to breed. The adaptations of steelhead are par-

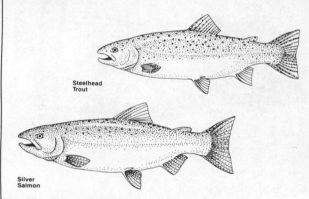

ticularly impressive: these fish find their way back each year from the open to the exact stream in which they were born, often journeying hundreds of miles in the process.

The fish arrive each year around mid-summer and continue running until fall at an average spawning weight of 20 pounds for the King (Chinook) and 7-12 pounds for the silver. The young steelhead stay in the fresh water for one or two seasons prior to migrating to sea. Unlike salmon, steelhead may spawn for several seasons before they die.

The Advantages of Being Anadromous

An anadromous fish is one that spends most of its life in salt water, but returns each year to fresh water to spawn. In order to do this, anadromous fish have learned to absorb water through their gills like all fresh water fish, but they also can drink through their mouths and use their gills to excrete salt like salt water fish do. There are many theories on how this versatility was developed, but no one is really sure why fish that first lived in the ocean eventually found their way to fresh water systems.

County Line

Twelve miles, and I came to a handsome stream, deep, slow, wide, and green, the Gualala River. The little town of the same name, on the north bank, was depressed and depressing, most of its buildings closed and decaying. Five years ago the lumber-mill, which was the be-all and end-all of the place, was burned down, and Gualala threw up its hands and sank into despair. The barber-postmaster-shoemaker, with whom I had business in his official capacity, observed as he lathered a gloomy patron that this was the last time: he had "had enough of this derned place." and was going to "light out for some liver burg." When I inquired where he meant to go, he paused a moment with suspended razor to consider: then answered, with sardonic emphasis, that he guessed he would go to Greenland.
J. Smeaton Chase

Contrary to J. Smeaton Chase's observation in 1913, the town did recover from its economic despair. Not as a result of logging, which never saw the return of the glory days of 1870–1910, but from the conversion of the Rancho de Herman sheep ranch into Sea Ranch. The town is actually

booming, with a new supermarket, several bed and breakfasts, a bank, and southern Mendocino's construction and lumber center facilities, all of them derived mainly through the "neighborhood effect" of nearby Sea Ranch.

Since before the last ocean trading mill closed, life in Gualala has usually ignored the ocean in favor of the river. One cannot even reach the ocean from the central portion of Gualala, although there was, until recently, a rope ferry behind the Surf Motel that crossed the river and enabled access to the wide beach below Gualala. An unsigned public stairway there will take you to the river's edge and a stunning view of the meeting of the ocean and the river. The other best vantage point is at the Sea Gull, a snack place as you enter town, which has an open deck above the river that shows off the ocean and river to miraculous advantage. They also serve OK pizza and happy-hour beer, and provide binoculars for whale watching.

The Gualala River has always been the town's main attraction and it continues to inspire with its wild, untamed beauty. There are campgrounds on both sides and plenty of fat fish in its waters. One of the Mendocino coast's only nude swimming beaches lies approximately 1.8 miles upstream.

Area Code: 707

Public Transportation

964-0167	Mendocino Stage
884-3723	MTA Coast Van
882-2137	South Coast Senior Center
964-0877	Ft. Bragg Greyhound
964-9574	B&H Transportation

Rules of the Road

Highway 1 in Mendocino County is often clogged with a procession of slow-moving recreational vehicles and tourists. Use roadside pullouts. Watch out for deer, rocks, and mudslides, as well as the surprising and sudden appearance of enormous logging trucks around the next bend.

Climate

Mendocino's is a typical Mediterranean maritime climate, characterized by moderate temperatures and rainfall. The mean seasonal temperatures fall within a narrow range, from 48°F in winter to 56°F in summer. Annual rainfall is between 50 to 80 inches, most occuring from October to April. Summers are cool and often foggy.

A Treasure Trove of Trees

"The redwood grows tall and straight and big beyond the belief of an eastern man," wrote Charles Nordhoff in 1874. The majesty of the redwood was undoubtedly equally impressive to the first loggers who arrived in Mendocino County during the time of the Gold Rush. Filled with more ambition than exaltation, they contemplated the world's tallest trees only briefly before chopping them to the ground and milling them into manageable, marketable sizes.

Down the coast, San Francisco had created an insatiable demand for the soft dark wood cut from ancient stands; Mendocino County held a treasure trove of trees that promised reward beyond imagination. At Gualala an instant town was created aside the fine, fast-running river that flowed through the giant trees to the sea. One by one the trees were cut, then pulled over wet timber skids by 1,500-pound bulls to the river's edge, where they awaited a *freshet,* a sudden surge of the river brought about by a storm or damming, that would take the logs downstream to the mill.

Because of the great stands of redwoods and the accommodating river, Gualala prospered, and soon hotels like Big Bert's, Gualala House, and the Gualala Hotel sprang up to house loggers and offer wild-west hospitality to travelers who had received word of a north coast fishing paradise.

A place of primitive beauty, Gualala has always been a town that likes to carouse through the darkening night, typified by the Gualala Hotel, where since 1903 from "rooms behind the balcony, the rhythmic beat of the surf soothed guests into slumber almost as quickly as the parties downstairs woke them up."

Timber Management

Management of Mendocino's coastal timber raises difficult land use issues in a county where commercial timberland outside state parks covers 26% of the land mass. The forest products industry is the county's largest employer, accounting for about 2,000 jobs in 1984. At the same time, protection of the beauty of the county is critical to a growing tourist industry, and a strong environmentally-conscious populace must grapple with issues of protection of private land while still accommodating urgently needed commercial and

residential development.

Some redwoods have been growing for more than 2,000 years, but they can be felled in less than two hours. Thus, policies regulating rates and methods of cutting must balance new growth and plantings. Miles of new logging roads winding through the forests are necessary for cutting and moving timber, but they can cause packing of soil and erosion that may endanger nearby stands and abort efforts at reforestation.

These are important issues in areas where timber cutting has been deemed appropriate. But how are "appropriate" areas defined in the first place? What makes for for a "commercial timber" stand. Is it one of 5, 50, 500 acres? How should "commerical" stands be regulated to prevent their over-logging or conversion to development such as housing and new visitor-serving development? How can commercial and non-commercial land uses coexist in good health and peace?

In a declining timber market and growing tourist economy, timber-residential conflicts are more likely to be amplified. Visual effects, noise, dust, traffic, water supply, and access impacts of commerical cutting are often of serious concern to people catering to tourist-serving and residential land uses.

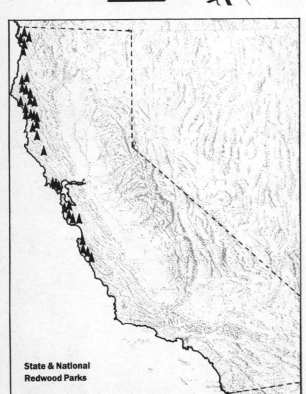

State & National Redwood Parks

Long Walker and the Famous Walker Drive

Long Walker was a legendary figure in the logging camps between Gualala and Mendocino. He wielded a magic axe and was considered the fastest axeman on the coast with either the old poleaxe or the new California or double-bitted axe. He always worked alone.

Long Walker would chop trees all week, but never let a tree fall until Saturday afternoon. Then, finally, he would chop one tree so that it fell and hit the next, bringing it down, and so on the next and the next. Once started, a week's worth of partially cut trees would be on the ground within minutes. His well-calculated aims became known as the "Walker Drive," much to the awe and amazement of local loggers.

Environment

Redwood Trees

Coast redwoods first appear adjacent to Highway 1 in Big Sur, and again in spots of Santa Cruz and Marin County, but Mendocino marks the gateway to the north coast's remaining virgin stands.

Almost everything about the coast redwood is notable, but the tree's renowned strength and ability to survive may be most impressive. Many 300 foot tall virgin redwoods have lived for 2,000 years because only the most radical assaults (such as a chain saw) can kill them.

A Forest of Ferns

The foggy coastal watershed that nourishes redwoods also produces an abundance of ferns on the forest floor. There are more than 10,000 species of ferns in the world, about 86 species native to California. Those found in the north coast region include the lady, coast wood, western, sword, giant chain, five finger, deer, licorice, and maidenhair ferns.

Unseasonal cold or drought may damage these moisture-dependent titans, but usually the tree survives, regenerating itself around its wounds. Neither the two types of fungi, nor the one beetle that associates with the redwood, can do fatal harm, and floods pose little threat.

Fire, the most dangerous threat, may leave scars and hollow bases, but seldom topples a mature redwood, which lacks the highly-flammable resin common to other trees, and which is shielded by unusually thick, protective bark. Even when fire succeeds in destroying a trunk, the tree often reaches into the depths of its ancient core, transforming any remaining sparks of life into new sprouts that rise bravely from the charred trunk.

Unfortunately it is these very qualities—straightness of grain, impressive heights, an absence of resin, and a natural immunity to insects and fungi—that add to the value of the tree's harvested timber, and marks its demise, not from the forces of nature, but from those of the marketplace.

Redwood, 368'   Douglas Fir, 302'

Roadside Attractions

The Gualala Hotel

The Gualala Hotel today may not be much like the days when loggers contested their skill at running up the walls in their spikes and the owner used to ride his horse into the lobby, but if you catch the place on Saturday night you may not be so sure. Saturday nights at the hotel's bar are a unique cultural phenomenon, rarely witnessed in nonpagan societies. The place is jammed with revelers dancing and drinking away nascent signs of north-coast cabin fever.

Built in 1903, the Gualala Hotel is one of the few pre-earthquake structures along this part of the coast. It has been the temporary residence of steelhead fishermen from Jack London to Earl Warren to Fred MacMurray, and still offers the most affordable oceanfront rooms (bath down the hall) to be found between San Francisco and Ft. Bragg. The dining room provides excellent, relatively inexpensive meals from morning to night, and the bar serves good, cheap booze.

Jack London in Gualala

A frequent visitor to Gualala, where he fished for steelhead and drank for immortality, Jack London typifies a major aspect of the town's enduring character. Gualala has always been a place that might have been the setting for one of his well-muscled tales, a place where men stand toe-to-toe with nature all day and indulge in unrestrained carousing all night.

London, who grew up in the Bay Area and died in Sonoma County, lived a life at least as freewheeling and adventurous as the rough-hewn loggers who worked in Gualala's redwood forests and drank in the Hotel Gualala bar. Dropping out of school at 13, London soon took to cavorting with oyster pirates on San Francisco Bay and riding the rails across the width of the county. By 21 he had ventured to Alaska for the Gold Rush while developing an appetite for Spencer, Huxley, Darwin, and Marx.

London's untimid grasp on life and literature led him to produce two and three novels a year and criticize the social and economic structure of his country. Called variously "the father of proletarian literature in the U.S." and "California's first native literary genius," Jack London has become an American myth larger than his literature whose heroic individualism ironically eclipses his strong advocacy for collective action and complete social and economic equality.

Resources

Redwood Resources

REDWOOD COUNTRY: A GUIDE THROUGH CALIFORNIA'S MAGNIFICENT REDWOOD FORESTS
Harriette E. Weaver
Chronicle Books, San Francisco. 1981.

Written by California's first woman park ranger, this guidebook describes every major stand of redwoods in the state, with detailed information on facilities and nearby attractions.

REDWOODS: THE WORLD'S LARGEST TREES
Jeremy Joan Hewes and Jon Goodchild
Rand McNally & Co., a Bison Book, London, 1981.

This is the best of many books on the redwoods. It tells the trees' story from the days when millions of forest acres dominated parts of the globe's landscape to today's fragile enclaves of protected trees and threatened commercial holdings. The photos and illustrations are stunning; the breadth of information is outstanding.

POCKET FLORA OF THE REDWOOD FOREST
Rudolf W. Becking
Island Press, Covelo. 1982.

FERNS AND FERN ALLIES OF CALIFORNIA
Steve J. Grillos
University of California Press, Berkeley. 1966

These two field guides provide complete illustration and description of ferns and related plants of the redwood forest. *Pocket Flora* is aided by color photographs, and the information is clear if somewhat technical. *Ferns,* part of the renown UC Press Natural History Series, may be of more help to the novice.

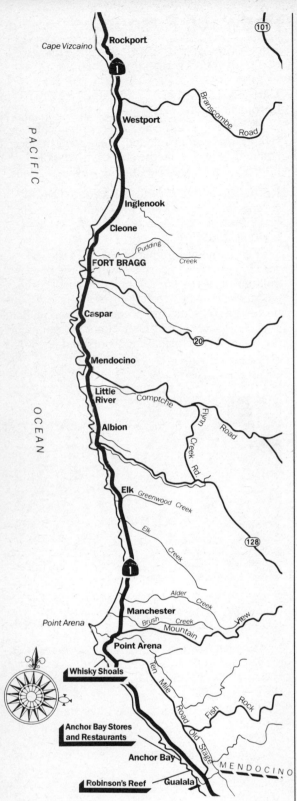

Doghole Ports

Across the numerous ravines, rivers, and gulches, bridges were required to enable land travel up the coast. Some bridges were built by private landowners whom the gulches were named after—Getchel, Robinson, Pedotti, St. Ores—others were constructed by the entire community out of common need, as was often the case in Gualala. "Before bridges, the road led down one side, crossed over with redwood timbers, then led up the other side. When bridges were built, the timbers were left the the gulches to make fill." So numerous were the gulches that between Gualala and Fish Rock, a four-mile distance, seven bridges were required—and not piddling ones either, but wood constructed to an average height of 60 feet.

But eventually, the coast road was able to link a succession of mill towns. Dependent on ships to get lumber to market, Mendocino's first mills were built on rivers close to coves or bays. The towns usually grew up around the shipping points, on the bluffs overlooking the ocean, while the mill was in the gulch of the stream flowing into the cove.

The bigger and better-protected coves, with a river to provide a means of bringing logs to the mill and a thick stand of nearby trees, became thriving lumber ports. The coves were referred to as dogholes: "bigger than a hole a dog might crawl into, squirm around and crawl out again—but not much."

North of Gualala, Bourne's Landing was the major local shipping point. Although better protected than most of Mendocino's anchorages, Bourne's was treacherous enough: numerous people were swept from the landing and drowned. Ships such as *Bill the Butcher* and the *California* were broken up on the rocks.

The most common method of loading the ships was to slide the lumber down a chute.
In the early days apron chutes of wood were used, to be later replaced by wire cable chutes. The apron chutes were built on the bluff over the anchorage, under which the small ships would maneuver to receive the lumber slid to the deck. A "clapper" was fitted to the end of the chute to slow the speeding lumber, operated by a "clapperman" whose responsibility it was to save the deck from the falling wood. The chute at Bourne's Landing was 30 inches wide and hinged at the middle to allow for the rise and fall of the tides. Rails were placed on the sides of the chute and a small car, controlled by a stationary engine, could be let down to the ship to bring up freight arriving from the city. Passengers also embarked this way. A box equipped with seats swung the passengers to and from the ship, although daring individuals often rode the lumber slings.

The Ghost of Whiskey Shoals

Whiskey Shoals, on the west side of the highway eight miles north of Anchor Bay, is an unbuilt subdivision that for years has sat ghostlike in the sun, the roaring wind as its only resident. Despite the plans of many, Whiskey Shoals remains unlikely to ever be anything more than an example of how not to build a coastal subdivision.

When Whiskey Shoals was originally proposed as a 72-lot second home subdivision, many buyers rushed to purchase lots. They soon found, however, that the Coastal Commission would not issue development permits to build on the bare headlands. The Commission maintained that the way the subdivision was laid out ignored the scenic

qualities of the area and seriously harmed the views toward the ocean from Highway 1. The development also closed public access to the beautiful sand beaches below.

A New Plan

In 1979 the State of California, acting through a new agency, the State Coastal Conservancy, undertook an ambitious plan to revise the proposed development in a manner what would satisfy the lot buyers, the scenic and environmental needs of the area, and the public who wanted to get to the beach. The plan was to cluster the lots in a less obtrusive manner to not block the viewshed between Highway 1 and the ocean and to allow the public two paths through the area to the beach. The size of the development was to be reduced to 55 lots and a scenic (conservation) easement placed over the unbuilt portion to prevent future expansion.

Since the Conservancy is not a management agency, a developer was to be brought in once the restoration plan was finished to complete the project. However, due to the smaller size of the subdivision and the high land costs, the only way the new development could proceed was to plan the vacation homes as time-share condominiums. Most of the local community resisted this idea.

In September, 1982, after a lengthy testimony by local residents, the Mendocino County Board of Supervisors rejected the Coastal Conservancy's lot restoration and time share condominium plan as being inadequate to protect the sensitive scenic and natural resources at Whiskey Shoals. The Coastal Conservancy, which had purchased most of the lots in the subdivision in anticipation of County approval, went back to the drawing board.

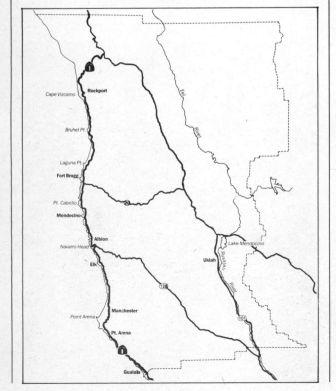

Tides

Tides are the rhythmic rise and fall of the earth's water, a gradual movement generated by the gravitational pull of the sun and moon. As these two heavenly bodies move around earth, the ocean waters form a bulge which moves like a giant wave slowly around the world and causes the water level to fluctuate where it meets the shoreline.

When the sun, earth, and moon are aligned with each other, the gravitational pull on the ocean is the greatest, and the difference in high and low tides is the

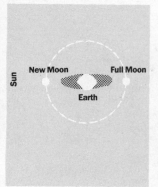

most extreme. These are the times of spring tides, which occur at each new and full moon. Neap tides have the lowest range, occuring at the halfway point between the spring tides. In California, the tidal cycle is generally twice daily; times and extremes can be predicted with great accuracy. Check local stores for tidal charts for each segment of the coast.

Killer Waves

The northern Pacific Ocean holds deadly surprises, particularly along Mendocino's western edge. Here, without warning, freak waves—called sneaker waves—claim lives almost every year. No one knows for sure what causes the occasional mammoth crests, but they are often associated with off-coast storm activity and local current changes, and they almost always occur on the outgoing tide. In November 1984, a giant sneaker broke 80-100 yards across a northern coast beach, submerging the entire beach and extending 15 feet up to an inland trail. Three hikers on the trail were knocked down, but managed to avoid being swept out to sea—one saved himself by clinging to the trail sign that warns "Dangerous Surf." A 40-foot-high wave at the same beach killed a man in 1978, and sneakers were blamed in many other northen California deaths. Never turn your back on the Pacific Ocean.

Anchor Bay

North of Gualala, Mendocino County begins to show itself in near-mystical, surreal beauty. The pines and cypress seem etched upon the landscape and the explosion of blue and white surf against dark rocks brings drama to an incomparable natural world. About 3.5 miles north of Gualala, west of Highway 1 about 1,100 feet, is a 10-acre peninsula parcel called Haven's Neck, of exceptional interest with unusual plant species and wind-sculptured rocks.

Off to the left, immediately offshore, is Robinson's Reef, a treacherous escarpment that surfaces here but runs for miles in a northwesterly direction. Cormorants, pelicans, and sea lions frequent the reef.

Just north are two exceptional bed-and-breakfast inns, the Old Milano and the St. Orres. The Old Milano has perhaps more real Victorian charm than any place south of Little River. Your choice from seven elegant bedrooms inside or an old renovated railroad caboose outside are not inexpensive, but charming. Children not allowed.

Across the road from the Milano, past the bluff-top private landing strip, is the most imposing landmark to be seen from Highway 1 in this area. The St. Orres Inn was built by local craftspeople and opened in 1977. Across from the St. Orres is a small pocket cove, not private.

Anchor Bay makes for a pleasant enough little stop on the side of the road above Anchor Bay Beach and Fish Rock (does it look like a fish?). The beach is famous as a haven for bootleggers during Prohibition, and as the location of the film *Blue Dolphin.* A dog-hole chute used to extend from the shore to Fish Rock, from which ships were loaded with lumber and bark. Today, access to the beach is controlled by the Anchor Bay Campground, which rents camping space for $5 a day and charges $1 to walk through the campground to the public beach.

Anchor Bay also has a fine General Store—short of fresh fish, meat, and produce, but long on Mendocino wines (Fish Rock Road runs between Anchor Bay and the Navarro Valley wineries). They also serve free coffee while you shop. In town you will find a laundromat, two restaurants and bars and a couple of uninspired shops. One of the restaurants, Rusty Anchor, has rock music on the weekends; the other, The Galley, is cheaper, more proletarian, and a good place to take kids.

County History

QH AWÁLA LI "WATER COMING DOWN PLACE": A HISTORY OF GUALALA, MENDOCINO COUNTY, CALIFORNIA.
Annette White Parks.
Freshcut Press
Ukiah. 1982.

One of the most loving and comprehensive community histories on the entire California coast, this book traces the people and natural history of the Gualala region from the Pomo Indians' time to the mid-twentieth century.

AN EVERYDAY HISTORY OF SOMEWHERE
Ray Raphael
Island Press
Covelo. 1974.

Written with a holistic concern for the humble details of the "somewhere" the author lives, this book begins one hundred million years ago when the coastal hills of northern California lay underwater, but moves quickly to the recent historical era, and into the present, telling in the process what a day was like in the life of a Native American, and a deer, and a Kodiak sea-otter hunter, and a modern-day homesteader.

For More on Mendocino History:

937-5791   Mendocino Historical Research, Inc.
937-5791   Kelly House Historical Museum
462-6969   Mendocino Historical Society

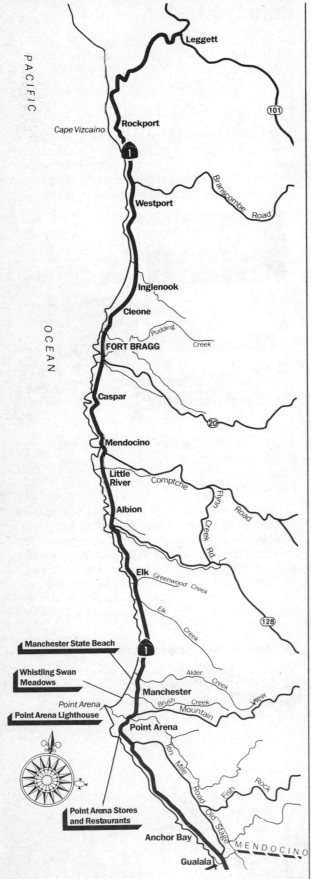

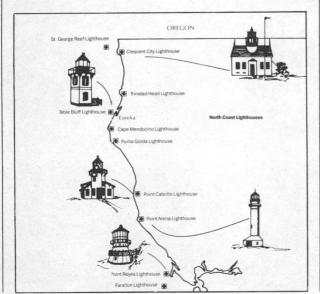

The Road from Point Arena

Beyond Bourne's Landing and Fish Rock, the focal point of the southern Mendocino coast's economic activity was Point Arena, the main shipping point for agriculture. Point Arena's economy was diverse enough to include a paper mill, a tannery, and several dairies; but like most of Mendocino's shipping ports, a brutal terrain and lack of a decent road separated it from other coast towns, particularly to the north.

Mail between Point Arena and Mendocino was carted over 300 miles, though the towns were only 30 miles apart. Before the construction of a bridge, the road twisted down into the bottom of Mal Paso and crawled treacherously up the bank on the other side—passable only when the road was not washed out, flooded, or covered in debris.

The ill-famed Mal Paso (Bad Pass), a steep ravine a few miles north of Point Arena with a high bluff on its southern side, was the most notorious obstacle to travel on the Mendocino coast: "Mal Paso split the earth in twain maybe eighty feet deep from far back in the woods to the ocean—a gulch so severe that even the hardiest dreaded to cross it." Favored with a bad reputation since the days when the Spanish had named it and made it the northern boundary of the Garcia land grant, Mal Paso seriously hindered travel and communication between Point Arena and Mendocino.

To cross the pass, wagons often had to be dismantled and carried down one side and up the other. Sometimes a pully was used to shuffle family members across one at a time, using a rope. This method entailed deadly risk: one woman with her infant in arms was thrown out of the buggy as it was being pulled across; both fell into the deep gorge below.

Protean Beauty

There was little economic motivation for road-building in the county, and despite the opening in 1904 of the Point Arena Hot Springs, which offered accommodations for 150 people and billed itself as a "first-class summer resort," there was not much tourist interest in the Mendocino coast. The Point Arena Hot Springs tried eagerly to attract a clientele similar to that just down the road in Sonoma, where the springs at Calistoga and Skaggs Place were attracting visitors from all over the nation.

Pamphlets were printed with seductive inducements that described Point Arena as the place "where the lover of nature can always find his gentle mistress in her most delightful moods. Nowhere is she more various in her whims, nowhere more rapturously charming as one surprises in different unsuspected retreats new phases of her protean beauty." Rates were from $8 to $12 a week, and the round trip fare from San Francisco, aboard the "fast Steam Schooner Albion River" was another $8, including stage fare to the springs.

Sentinels of the Coast

Lighthouses were among the first buildings on the California coastline. Since the 1850s, their brilliant beams have guided mariners through heavy storms and dense fog and warned of offshore shoals and submerged rocks.

The first lighthouses required as many as four full time keepers who were called "wiskies." Their job was to tend lamps that were fueled by whale oil and lard. The light in all of the lighthouses was reflected through sophisticated lenses created by Augustine

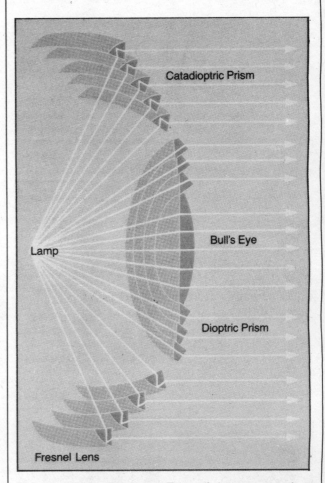

Fresnel, a French inventor. Fresnel's lenses created a maze of glass prisms, capable of throwing light up to twenty miles.

Today, north coast lighthouses are under the responsibility of the U.S. Coast Guard's 12th District, and, like all the remaining structures in California, they are fully automated.

The Point Arena Lighthouse

The first Point Arena Lighthouse, built to warn ships away from the projecting hidden reefs offshore, was destroyed in the 1906 earthquake. The present structure, somewhat less precariously placed, is a concrete tower that rises 156 feet to the lamp. The revolving white light pulses four flashes to the minute, each of five seconds duration, five seconds intermission, then twenty seconds intermission. On the rocks below the lighthouse reside a colony of sea lions.

At the Point Arena Lighthouse you are on the closest land point between mainland USA and Hawaii.

Environment

Ospreys

Ospreys are frequent visitors to the Mendocino coast, especially in the summertime. These strong, handsome birds are distinguished by their large size, wing spans of six feet or more, and white head with brown crown. In flight ospreys have a very distinctive crook in their wings, which are whitish with black patches underneath.

Often called a "fish hawk", the osprey is unique among birds of prey in that it feeds entirely on fish rather than small mammals. At hunt, it is also unique: circling high above the water for several minutes, then plunging talons first to capture its prey, often completely submerging itself in the swift, violent process.

Look for osprey nests of sticks high atop Mendocino trees. Like many coastal birds, ospreys are very sensitive to toxic wastes in the fish and water, and in recent years nesting success has decreased. But in a good year, an osprey will produce two to four buff eggs.

Whistling Swans

Each year for the past ten or 20 years, a flock of whistling swans have arrived at the Garcia River plain, adjacent to Highway 1. During the middle or end of November, the swans provide a magnificent site from the road as it descends just past the lighthouse turnoff. The birds come from their breeding habitat on the Arctic coast between the Bering Sea and Hudson Bay, and stay until the end of March. Then they return to their nesting grounds to breed and raise four or five cygnets (baby swans).

The swans are splendid birds: all white with a black bill and a yellow spot near the eye. They weigh anywhere from 14 to 20 pounds, are 47 to 48 inches in length, and have a wingspan of almost seven feet. In flight, the swans make a high-pitched and etherial whistling sound, midway between that of a snow goose and a trumpeter swan.

Roadside Attractions

Point Arena

Past Anchor Bay, Highway 1 meanders through windswept bishop pines, rhododendrons, madrone, and third-growth redwood until it opens up to stunning ocean views just north of Iverson Point, a partially built subdivision near the spot where a dog-hole port by the name of Rough and Ready was once ensconced. This section of the coast is well suited to either fast driving along the edge of California on some of its most magnificent roadway, or stopping to enjoy beaches on a par

with any in the world. At Galloway Creek several trails lead to Schooner Gulch Beach, a superb beach with a near-wilderness quality. North is Bowling Ball Beach with its unique clustering of round black rocks at the surfline.

Point Arena has an authentic coastal character that is without concern for charm or cuteness. Three restaurants serve good food in a non-tourist environment (Disotelle's, Giannini's, and Sign of the Whale). You'll also find a general store where you can purchase food, overalls, or apple barrels (Gillmans), and an honest-to-goodness soda fountain (Garcia Center). There are also three or four spots to get a drink cheaply, a natural foods store, a bowling alley, a movie theater and place to hear live music (on weekends), and a working wharf with an authentic (if slightly depressed) maritime character.

Immediately north of Point Arena, a sharp curve to the left takes you past the town cemetery to the cutoff for the Point Arena campground and the Point Arena Lighthouse.

Resources

West Coast Lighthouses

SENTINELS OF SOLITUDE: WEST COAST LIGHTHOUSES
Chad Ehlers, Photography
Jim Gibbs, Text
Graphic Arts Center Publishing Company
Portland, Oregon. 1981.

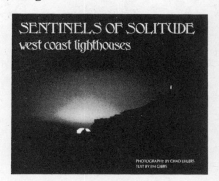

Informative histories, photographs, and maps of more than seventy lighthouses on the West Coast are presented in stunning detail in this book. This is an authoritative reference for all lovers of the solitary sentinels.

Manchester State Beach

937-5804

Just north of Point Arena, Alder Creek, Kinney, and Stoneboro Roads branch off to the left, leading to one of Mendocino County's finest beaches, Manchester State Beach. Here you may walk for hours along 972 acres of sandy beach and rolling sand dunes. Driftwood collecting is popular at Manchester, as is diving in the offshore underwater park. There is a 48-site campground off Kinney Road; small fee for use. No fee for day use of the beach.
Other Mendocino beaches include:

884-9923	Fish Rock Beach
937-5804	Greenwood/Elk State Beach
937-5707	Albion Flat
937-5804	Van Damme State Park
937-0273	Mendocino Headlands State Park
937-5804	Russian Gulch State Park
964-4630	Jug Handle State Reserve
937-9138	Mackerricher State Park
964-2964	Wages Creek Beach
937-5804	Westport-Union Landing State Beach

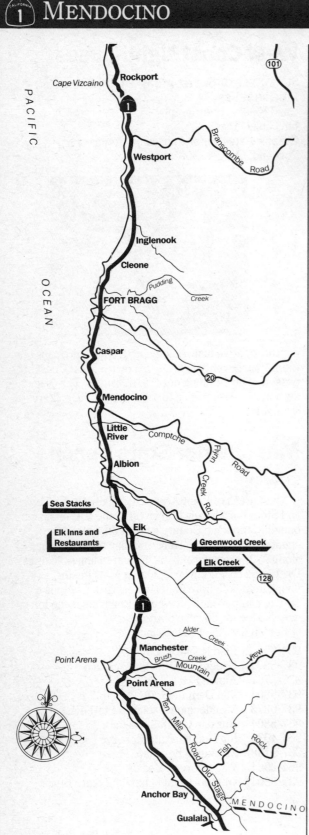

Schooner Villages

In their early days, Mendocino coast towns were boom-and-bust schooner villages where wild men and sometimes wilder women conducted their lives on the margins of convention. Lumber was the thing, as was back-breaking labor in the forests, hard living, and absolute faith that the tall trees could be cut down forever.

Mendocino coast towns followed the same pattern again and again: settled when the mill was built, growing slowly or rapidly depending on the luck of the times, the safety of the port, and the acumen of the mill owner; then almost disappearing when the mills eventually closed. Said a 19th-century history of the county: "The history of the towns is but the history of mill operations." Thus was the Mendocino coast settled by white culture. The elk and grizzly bear retreated into the hills, the Indians to reservations.

Albion

Some villages endured the rise and fall of the timber economy better than others. Albion, which had the benefit of a good port and river, maintained a busy presence with a mill, lumber yard,

store, and hotels and cabins on both sides of the river, joined by a drawbridge.

For years logging on the Albion, as on other coastal waterways, was done by river driving, which was subject to the occasional misfortune of uncontrollable crests that sent thousands of logs racing out to sea.

Tourism in Mendocino

Economic life and land use patterns on the Mendocino coast are increasingly shaped by the presence of the tourist, that free-spending pilgrim whose arrival stirs dread and desire in the hearts of local residents. Without the tourist, the Mendocino coast would face catastrophic unemployment and economic stagnation. But with the tourist the bargain may not be much better, as increased numbers of travelers create traffic, alter the area's rural character, and stimulate an economy based on marketable "charm" that transforms the landscape into a stage set.

Tourism is changing the face of Mendocino. Approximately 300,000 parties of visitors visit the area annually, and the number is increasing. Bed and breakfast inns have achieved such a ubiquitous presence along Highway 1 that practically any sized house with moderate charm is ripe for conversion. Demand for accommodations in bed and breakfast inns is so strong that most are fully booked during the summer and holiday weekends. Observers agree that the tourist season is expanding into the winter months.

The most beneficial effect of all of this attention is to provide a wide variety of jobs, particularly food service and lodging, as well as retail trade, which brings an estimated $16 million in wages to the area in sight of Highway 1 in Mendocino and Sonoma Counties. The nature of the jobs makes them almost equally available to men and women, distinct from the area's two other major industries, logging and fishing, which are both ebbing.

Tourism also contributes significant amounts of tax revenues, which reduces the individual burden for local residents and pays for better schools, streets and sewage systems. But none of these benefits are without cost. Mendocino has an inestimably fragile environment whose wild beauty could be eradicated in a generation by uncontrolled growth, its tiny shorefront towns cannibalized in a season.

Blessing or curse (or part of both), tourism is creating major change along the Mendocino Coast that requires close attention and planning. It won't go away.

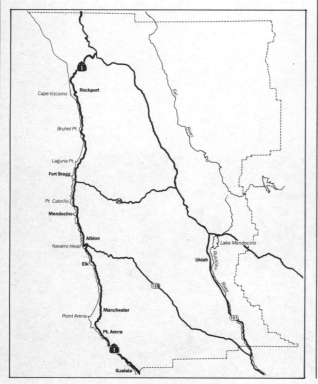

Coastal Geology

Mendocino's coastal shelf is part of a series of elevated, ancient terraces that extend inland several miles. There are at least five distinct ridges, the oldest uplifted more than a half million years ago. These old terraces now reach heights of 700 feet or more above sea level. Moving toward the sea, each marine terrace is about 100 feet lower and 100,000 years younger than its inland neighbor.

Most of Highway 1's route in Mendocino is perched along the youngest of these terraces. The

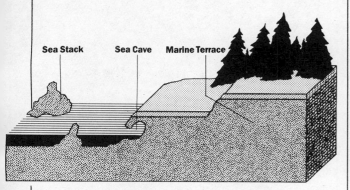

Sea Stack   Sea Cave   Marine Terrace

rock strata here on the edge is an eclectic mix of strong and weak rock types, including several types of sandstone and stronger shales of Cretaceous or Upper Jerassic formation.

Sculptured Beauty

This mixture of soft and hard rocks subjects the Mendocino coast to dramatic effects from the sculpturing hand of the elements. Weaker rocks are eroded away much more quickly than the hard ones, causing differential weathering to develop picturesque caves, arches, blowholes, and sinkholes.

The scores of sea stacks that add dramatic beauty to Elk's coastline were also caused by the process of differential erosion. The initial land mass was thrust up from the ocean as part of the ongoing terracing of the shoreline.
wind, rain, and surf ware away the softer stones, breaking down any land bridges, and eventually leaving only the free-standing island-like sea stacks.

Elk

The town of Elk is located not on Elk Creek but on Greenwood Creek. Actually, Elk used to be called Greenwood, but when the mill at the original Elk (on Elk Creek) went under, the name was shifted to Greenwood. (Cuffey's Cove also used to be within what is now called Elk, but that's another story.)

As you approach Elk, the first inland site, a thousand yards or so each of the road, is the remnants of the old Greenwood Mill. The mill was active until the late 1950s and is one of the few extant mill fossils in an area that once had perhaps more than a hundred small to large mills.

Elk is as picturesque as a town can be and still maintain its own integrity. It is a beautiful place, perhaps Mendocino's most beautiful coast town, and, despite its small size, is excellently outfitted for the Highway 1 journeyer. Amenities include a good, inexpensive cafe (Roundhouse Cafe), an excellent restaurant (Greenwood Cafe—5 stars), a lively bar (Greenwood Oasis), and four bed and breakfasts, all quite lovely. The beach is accessible from the center of town by a gently sloping trail that leads to a wide sandy crescent beach adjacent

to Greenwood Creek.

Elk is a delicately enchanting spot, made so by its unaffected Victorian architecture on soft rolling hills and Greenwood Creek. The creek defines a great deal of the place's richly verdant character, as it defined the town's economic existence in mill days. But it is the miraculous sea stacks located directly offshore that give Elk its mystery and enchantment. Characteristically Mendocino, this is a coastal site unmatched anywhere else along Highway 1.

Geology

ROADSIDE GEOLOGY OF NORTHERN CALIFORNIA
David Alt & Donald Hyndman
Mountain Press Publishing Company
Missoula, Montana. 1983.

One of an outstanding series, this is an invaluable handbook and guide to take on the road up Mendocino's coast. Describes in lay-persons terms advanced geological concepts and information. Fully illustrated with maps, drawings, and photos.

One Ocean, One World

The majestic meeting of ocean and shore in Mendocino County prompts reflection on the unity of the world's resources.

There are many books on global conservation and the challenges of planatary management. Two of the best are the classic *Whole Earth Catalog,* whose pages are filled with valuable resources, and the new *Gaia* (Greek Goddess of Earth), a stunning atlas of global conditions and a blueprint for survival.

GAIA: AN ATLAS OF PLANET MANAGEMENT
Dr. Norman Myers, Editor
Anchor Press/Doubleday
New York. 1984.

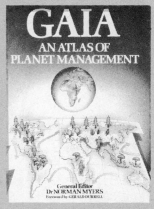

THE WHOLE EARTH CATALOG
Stewart Brand, Editor
Rand McNally/Random House
New York. 1980.

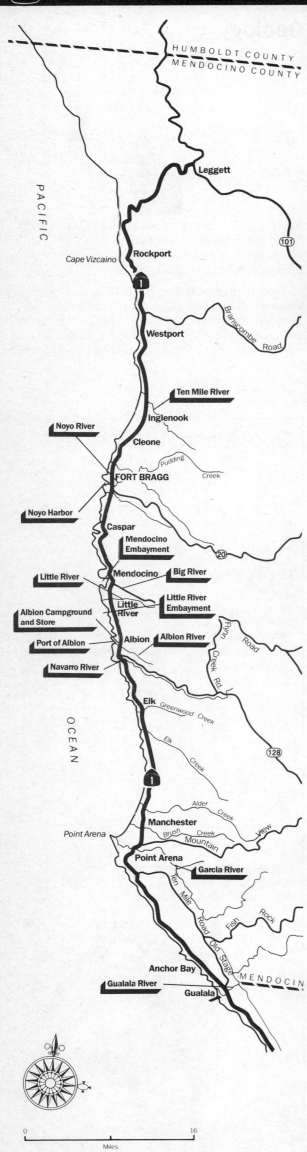

The Appearance of the Automobile

Greenwood (now Elk) was another active mill town that prospered from a combination of plentiful trees and a reasonably protected cove at the river mouth. But until well into the 20th century, land travel in Greenwood was nearly as primitive as it had been 50 years before.

By 1906 non–horse-drawn vehicles were beginning to make their appearance along the Mendocino coast, and an auto-stage was inaugurated

between Greenwood and the town of Mendocino. In 1915 Joe Halliday of Point Arena replaced his horse stage with a "Gramm-Bernstein truck, with six to eight seats and a baggage compartment in back." Besides passengers, the new auto stage also carried the local mail.

After 1915 the county of Mendocino began to formalize the "road up the coast" in response to the increasing presence of the automobile. A few years prior the county of Sonoma had done the same, extending the road from Jenner to the bridge leading to Gualala. Such road building was not specifically intended to aid the lumber industry. Indeed, motor transport of lumber to market did not replace sea transfer until years later, and throughout the first quarter of the century, logging interests steadfastly opposed development of any roads along the coast. As far as the mill owners were concerned, the forests were for cutting, the ocean for shipping, and the residents for complying with the owners' needs. Roads would only complicate matters.

Building Bridges

Eventually, issues of public safety prompted the County to pay for the construction of bridges at the Navarro, Garcia, and Gualala Rivers, in addition to crossings over Mike Finn Gulch, Irish Gulch, and Brushcreek. Most of the bridges were constructed of redwood planks and timbers. The bridges at Skunk Creek and Denman Creek, for example, were constructed of 16-plank redwood, wide enough for two carriages to pass at a time.

Bridge construction usually took place in the summer, when the rivers and creeks were tame. Often, however, some work was planned for winter—despite the heavy rains, muddy ground, and rampaging waters—to take advantage of the labor pool of loggers idled by the rainy season. On January 16, 1917, three workmen tying timber supports at the base of the new Navarro Bridge were standing on three-foot-wide scaffolding when the river unexpectedly surged toward them. The men, unable to grab onto the quickly receding shore, did manage to hold onto some debris, which became their raft as they were swept out the mouth of the river and into the ocean. Miraculously, the crew on a small steam schooner, the *Doris K.*, heard the men's shouts and, despite a rough ocean, was able to rescue them unharmed.

North Coast Anchorages

Mendocino's coast lacks protected anchorages for ships like those more prevalent to the south. This absence of safe land-locked harbors is compensated for by the use of river mouths, embayments, and coves for anchorage.

Embayments at Shelter Cove, Mendocino and Little River offer the possibility for anchorages, but they are safe only for the experienced seafarer. Both Shelter Cove and Mendocino's embayments are exposed to the brutal force of the open ocean when the weather is from the southwest, but offshore reefs break the powerful northwesterly surges. The best and most commonly-used north coast anchorages (particularly for small-craft) are deep coves like these at Russian Gulch and Casper. Both the Noyo and Albion Rivers offer year-round mooring sites, although during heavy seas the breakers and surges can make navigation into the river mouths very dangerous.

The Port of Albion

The Port of Albion sits near the mouth of the Albion River at Albion Cove, once a classic Mendocino doghole. Mooring Rock, topped by a light and fog signal, guides commercial and sports fishing traffic into

Albion

Between Elk and the Navarro River are some of Mendocino's most spectacular coastal headlands and two magnificent, if inaccessible, beaches.

At the Navarro River a county cutoff (south side) leads to a camping area where the river empties into the ocean. The road goes past the old Navarro River Inn (now closed) and a campground area for RVs and campers. Across the Navarro, Highway 1 is joined by State 128, whose function as a funneling artery from 101 to the coast radically alters the character of the coastal towns to the north, which become considerably more tourist-oriented.

Albion—named by Captain William H. Richardson after his homeland in Britian—is the last outpost of non-chic Mendocino until Fort Bragg. The town has one bed and breakfast (Albion River Inn), a general store that dates from 1910, a campground, a boat launch and rental service, a biological field station, a grocery-liquor store, and a post office next to the fishing marina on the flats below the bridge. The bridge here is of structural distinction; built for $350,000 in 1944, it was constructed from salvaged wood and materials because steel

and reinforced concrete were unavailable during the war.

Albion is a fine place, much favored by the two types of residents the town attracts: summer residents who live in the quaint hillside cottages on Albion Road overlooking the fishing activities below, and alternative culture habitants who reside along Albion Ridge. Both the town and the flats are off the side of the road, allowing the place to maintain a local feel.

Harbor Resources

Mendocino's two major harbors offer the opportunity to picnic in colorful maritime settings, buy fresh fish directly from the boats, camp, rent canoes, charter a fishing boat, and much more.

Noyo Harbor
964-9138

Colorful Noyo Harbor was once used in the film *The Russians Are Coming.* Here strung out along the estuary are marine hardware stores, restaurants, partyboat landings, motels, and fish-processing plants. When the seas are stormy, the port is packed with vessels of all kinds. There is a sandy ocean beach and a boat ramp on the south bank of the river at the end of Basin Street.

Albion Flat
937-5707

Just north of the Albion River bridge, a sharp right off Highway 1 leads down to the Albion Flat, a small settlement with a growing fleet of boats, both sport and commercial. There are also canoe rentals, boat launches, beaches, and camping and hookups at a private campground.

the heavily-used river mouth. Traffic is stopped often, however, during the winter storm seasons. Then the entrance to the Port must be closed as high energy waves stack up and break at the river mouth.

The docking piers at Albion Port are small and portable so they can be removed during high river flow and storms. The River itself is small compared to its north coast siblings, but it still serves as a fertile nursery for coho salmon, surf perch, smelt and steelhead trout, as well as a sanctuary for other fish and many birds.

Noyo Harbor

Noyo Harbor is one of the north coast's most important commercial and sportfishing centers. Seasonal catches include chinook and coho salmon, ling cod, black cod, rockfish, and more dungeness crab than any other northern California harbor. The natural embayment that forms the harbor reaches 400 yards inland to the mouth of the Noyo River. The 8.5 acre interior mooring basin is protected by an underwater offshore reef, a 345 foot long concrete and stone north jetty, a north wall rubble stone revetment, and a 234-foot-long concrete south wall. The channel itself is relatively shallow—only ten feet below mean low tide—and about 150 feet wide.

Rolling on the River

Mendocino's rivers lack the churning white waters of rivers to the north, but many of them offer the splendid satisfaction of canoe, kayak, or rubber raft trips into the solitary depths of the north coast wilderness.

The Gualala, Garcia, Noyo, Albion, and Navarro all are usually navigable, and many offer rental facilities on site. For a complete list of California groups which sponsor river training classes, and for more information on navigable inland waterways, write the California Department of Boating and Waterways, 1629 S. Street, Sacramento, CA 95814.

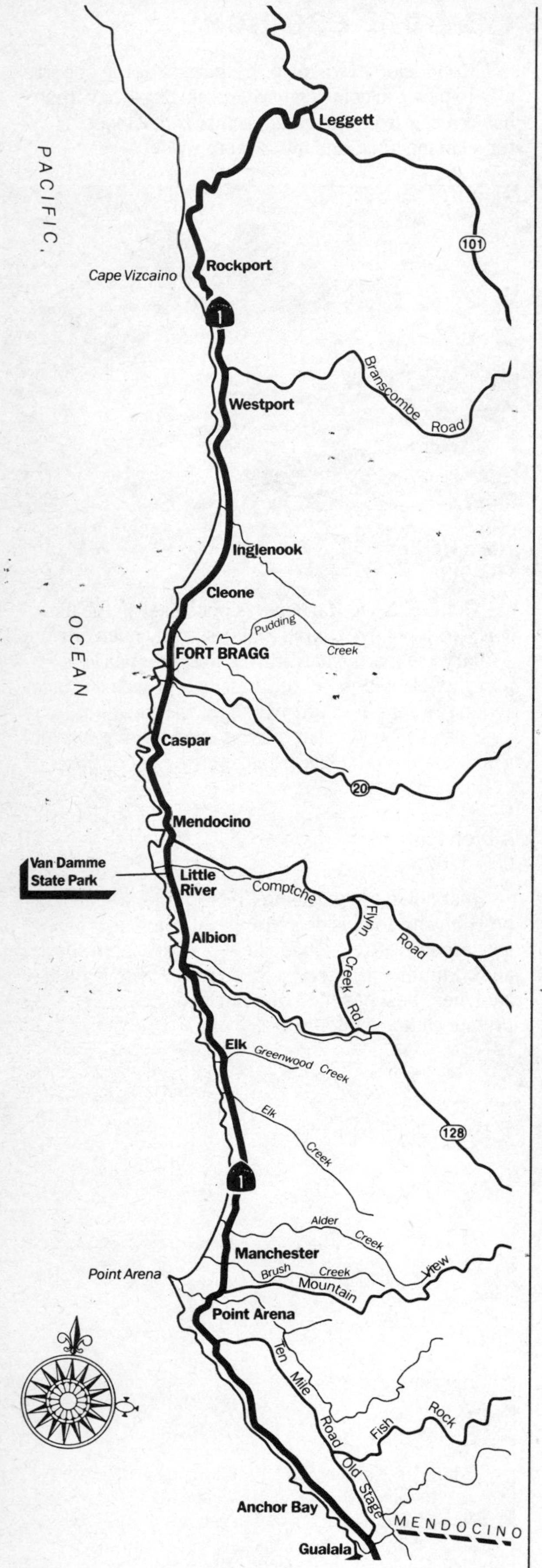

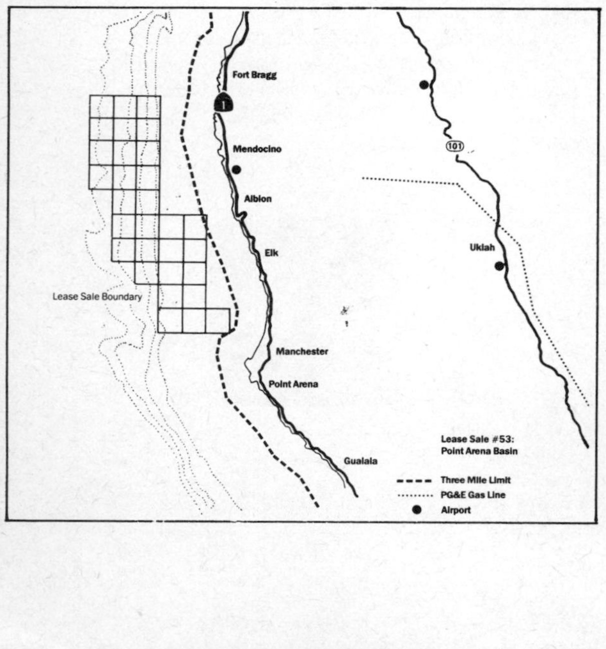

Map labels (left column):

PACIFIC

Leggett

Cape Vizcaino

Rockport

101

Branscombe Road

Westport

Inglenook

Cleone

Pudding Creek

FORT BRAGG

OCEAN

Caspar

20

Mendocino

Van Damme State Park

Little River

Comptche

Flynn Creek Road

Albion

Elk

Greenwood Creek

Elk Creek

128

Alder Creek

Manchester

Point Arena

Brush Creek

Mountain View

Point Arena

Ten Mile Road

Old Stage

Fish Rock

Anchor Bay

MENDOCINO

Gualala

Lease map labels (lower left):

Fort Bragg

Mendocino

101

Albion

Elk

Uklah

Lease Sale Boundary

Manchester

Point Arena

Gualala

Lease Sale #53: Point Arena Basin

—— Three Mile Limit

---- PG&E Gas Line

● Airport

Schooners: Sail and Steam

Despite the presence of a somewhat credible coast road after 1915, nearly all the lumber produced on the Mendocino coast continued to be shipped to San Francisco by sea until the mills were shut down by the Depression of the 1930s.

For many years Little River was the most reliable port of refuge on the Mendocino coast, and in the early days schooners were both built and repaired there. The most famous of the shipbuilders was Captain Thomas H. Peterson, who is reported to have built 20 ships at Little River. Navarro, Albion, and Point Arena were also sites of shipbuilding activity, and nearly every port at one time or another turned out at least one ship.

The ships that first carried the coast trade were small, efficient schooners. These were eventually replaced by steam schooners, a type of ship developed by the Pacific Coast lumber trade exclusively for the lumber business. A direct descendent of the sailing schooner, the steam schooner had as its main feature a large open deck space for stowing a huge load of lumber. The ships were small enough to enable access to windy doghole ports.

Sailing ships carried all the coastal sea trade before 1870, and until the mid-80s, they still carried much of the lumber; only after the turn of the century were these vessels completely supplanted by steam schooners. Although brigs were often used, the schooner was the most important sailing vessel in the lumber trade. Larger ships could safely enter only the largest of coves, and so were seldom seen, although Mendocino sent an occasional order to Tahiti, Mexico, or South America in a full-rigged ship. The appearances of such ships were great events, taken by the local newspapers as a certain sign that Mendocino was at last becoming a major Pacific port.

Most of the early steamers were merely converted schooners. Despite the objections of the skippers to the "tea kettles," ship owners understood the advantages of steam power, although sail was retained on the steamers, in modified form, for three decades after the first conversion. Coal fueled the earliest steamers, but by 1911 nearly all were burning oil.

Northcoast Drilling

Offshore oil drilling is an issue all along California's spectacularly beautiful coastline, but in Mendocino County, is raises special questions. Since 1979 when the U.S. Department of Interior first proposed OCS (outer continental shelf) Lease Sale #53, these questions have been hotly debated. If oil were discovered and drilling allowed, the effects could be stunning to the local environment and tourist economy.

Imagine, for example, as you travel north on Highway 1, that off to the left, far on the horizon, sit from one to ten oil rigs. Imagine further, as you pass small north coast towns, onshore service bases typically requiring between ten and 30 acres for buildings, storage, facilities, pipes, towers, compressors, parking, and buffer zones. Consider that in Manchester, onshore exploration for oil has been proposed for a 1,200 acre site adjacent to Highway 1 as an initial project leading to eventual offshore drilling.

Now, as you enjoy the switchback curves for which this segment of Highway 1 is famous, imagine that you are suddenly face to face with a tanker truck loaded with oil or gas, or with a semi hauling 50 foot lengths of pipes and supplies. Think about the visual effect of pipeline right-of-ways of approximately 300 to 900 acres during construction, exposed pipes during some seasons, and permanently exposed riprap protecting lines from the powerful northern California surf.

Consider further the daily activity of helicopters as they shuttle supplies and crews from land to platforms. As a worst case, imagine the possibility of a major oil spill (or the almost certain reality of "minor" spills) whose effects may last three years or more.

All of these concerns are being weighed against perceived national energy interests, and the potential for meaningful deposits offshore. For many years, environmentalists, locals and California coastal friends fought off federal drilling in the courts, but recent announcements by the Department of Interior have once again brought the issue to the foreground, and some "exploratory" drilling is quite likely to begin in the near future.

Environment | Roadside Attractions | Resources

California Poppy

The brilliant orange color of the California poppy lends it a distinction worthy of the state's official wildflower. A perennial, the poppy is prevalent along the coast, often adding a splash of sunshine to golden grassy meadows or rocky roadside shoulders. It is said that this beautiful flower once covered such huge areas that the brightly colored patches were landmarks for ships at sea.

The four petals of the poppy are fan-shaped, sometimes ranging from orange to yellow, and, rarely, to white. It blooms in spring with large flowers, and then again in summer with smaller, lighter colored flowers. The foliage is a silver green that when dried was once used to relieve toothache pain.

Lupine

Whether adorning the night stand in a quaint bed and breakfast inn, or splashing the roadside with brilliant color, the lupine is one of California's best known and most liked spring wildflowers. Lupines, like bluebonnets, are members of the pea family, and they come in many species and sizes, shapes, and colors. However, all lupines have palmately compound leaves with five or more leaflets, and the flowers of all species grow in whorls on the stems.

The annual or dove lupine is one of the smallest

species. It is bright blue and white, growing on stems about two feet high. The most common lupine in Mendocino is the *lupinus succulentus*. It is a coarser and bigger plant than dove lupine, and its flowers are dark blue to white. Joining the parade of these sweet smelling wildflowers is the yellow or bush lupine. This is the biggest and brightest of the species, occurring all along Highway 1 in fields and on hills. The bush lupine is a woody shrub that can produce dozens of very large bright yellow, blue, or purple flowers.

Little River

At Little River the landscape becomes greener, denser, tighter in scale, and almost too pretty. So many bed and breakfast inns dot the roadside that residential dwellings appear almost as a rarity.

Little River has a fine state park (Van Damme) with a small beach at the mouth of the river and 74 campsites on the east side of Highway 1. Several miles of trails lead through the fur and pine woods. The pygmy forest is accessible from the park's interior, 3 miles east of the Highway 1 entrance.

Mendocino Bed and Breakfast Inns

Coastal Mendocino County may have more bed and breakfast inns per capita than anywhere in the nation, and some of the most interesting and romantic are located between Elk and Mendocino. Because of their popularity, it is best to call ahead for reservations. Many of Mendocino's bed and breakfast inns do not take children.

Elk

ELK COVE INN 877-3321: Elegant and romantic, with excellent French dining served on formal china with silver service.
GREEN DOLPHIN INN 877-3342
GREENWOOD PIER INN 877-9997: Offers a variety of interesting rooms and suberb breakfasts. Greenwood Pier Cafe is one of coastal Mendocino's best.
GREENWOOD LODGE: 877-3422
HARBOR HOUSE 877-3203: Beautiful redwood design that is a larger replica of Charles Mullgurdt's model house at the 1915 Pan American Exposition in San Francisco.

Albion

NAVARRO RIDGE INN 937-4511: Former stage coach stop with a parlor, library, tavern, and special weekly concerts.
ALBION RIVER INN 937-4044: Full bar, restaurant, and oceanfront terrace.

Coastal Flowers

There are almost as many books on California coastal vegetation as there are types of flowers. Here is a recommended sample.

SHORE WILDFLOWERS OF CALIFORNIA, OREGON AND WASHINGTON
Philip A. Munz
University of California Press
Berkeley. 1964.

WILDFLOWERS OF THE WEST
Mabel Crittenden and Dorothy Telfer
Celestial Arts
Millbrae. 1975.

AN INTRODUCTION TO CALIFORNIA PLANT LIFE
Robert Ornduff
University of California Press
Berkeley. 1974.

PACIFIC COASTAL WILDLIFE REGION
Charles Yocom and Rey Dasmann
Naturgraph Publishers
Happy Camp. 1965.

Little River

HERITAGE HOUSE 937-5885: One of Mendocino's fanciest with excellent wines and gingerbread charm.
THE VICTORIAN FARMHOUSE: 937-0697 Originally built in 1877 and refurbished with private baths; breakfast served in rooms.
SEAFOAM LODGE 937-0615
SCHOOLHOUSE CREEK INN 937-5525
FOOLS RUSH INN 937-4323
LITTLE RIVER INN 937-5942: Dating from 1853; includes rooms in original structure, cottages, and a more modern motel unit; golf course.
RACHEL'S INN 937-0088
GLENDEVEN 937-0083

Mendocino

BREWERY GULCH INN 937-4752
BIG RIVER LODGE 937-5615
MENDOCINO HOTEL 937-0511
MENDOCINO VILLAGE INN 937-0246
1021 MAIN STREET 937-5150
SEARS HOUSE INN 937-4076
BLACKBERRY INN 937-5281
HEADLANDS INN 937-4431: Built in 1868, ocean view and fireplaces; homemade breads, fresh fruits.
SEA GULL INN 937-5204: Fairly priced, excellent food, children welcome.
WHITEGATE INN 937-4892: Dating from 1880, six rooms, ocean views, antiques.
HILL HOUSE INN 937-0554
JOSHUA GRINDLE INN 937-4143
McCALLUM HOUSE 937-0289
SEA ROCK BED AND BREAKFAST 937-5517
BLUE HERON INN 937-4323

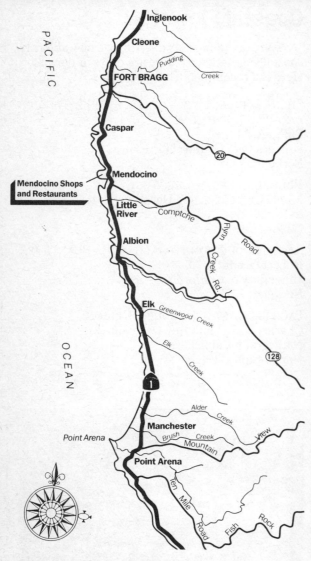

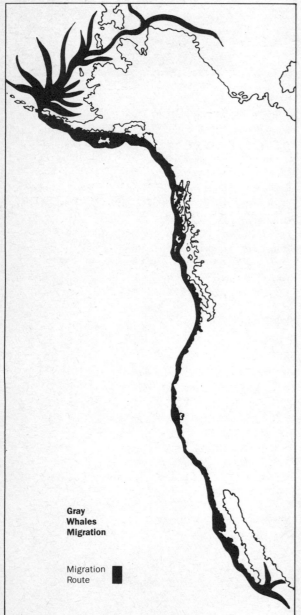

Gray
Whales
Migration

Migration
Route ■

Honest Harry Meiggs

Honest Harry Meiggs was a large, colorful, and gregarious man who saw fortune at every turn and, often enough, was able to grab enough for himself to become one of early California's most freewheeling entrepreneurs. Before his financial empire fell apart and he fled the country, Meiggs had made and lost a fortune, influenced the direction of development in San Francisco, and established the city of Mendocino.

Meiggs came to gold rush San Francisco in 1849 upon the packet ship *Albany* with his family and a load full of lumber. Seeing the gold rush hysteria as a ripe opportunity for practical riches, Meiggs sold his shipload of lumber at twenty times its cost to eager builders in the "instant city," making a quick $50,000 profit.

As San Francisco grew by leaps, Meiggs profited handsomely as its major lumber supplier, harvesting trees in Contra Costa County and buying up most of the land in San Francisco's North Beach, where he directed development by careful promotion. He built a 2,000 foot long wharf and established one of early San Francisco's most exotic and notorious bars at Meiggs' Landing.

In 1851, word came down the coast that a ship from China laden with silk and treasure had broken up on the rocks at Caspar Point, near the present town of Mendocino. With visions of shipwrecked treasure in his head, Meiggs sent J.B. Ford to the area with a pack horse to see what could be salvaged.

Spying Treasure

When Ford arrived at the shipwreck, he found no treasure. Most of the cargo had been sunk or washed to sea. Only a few items had been salvaged by the Indians, some of whom Ford noticed proudly garbed in Chinese silk. But Ford spied other treasure—trees taller than the eye could estimate, and in such profusion that it seemed they could be cut down forever to supply lumber to build hundreds of San Franciscos.

When Meiggs received the news of Mendocino's magnificent trees, he immediately set to work establishing a mill—which was bought on the east coast and shipped around the Horn already assembled and ready to be put in place. The mill and the adjacent settlement came to be called Mendocino, probably after Cape Mendocino, further north up the coast.

Although the mill in Mendocino thrived for years, Meiggs began to encounter financial difficulties shortly after Mendocino was established. Meiggs had incurred big debts and developed a bad habit of negotiating fraudulent city warrents to pay them off. During the middle of one dark night in 1854, Meiggs decided to make an unannounced departure for Valparaiso, Chile, one step ahead of the law.

From Chile, Meiggs soon migrated to Peru, where reports described him as having become even richer than his most profitable California days. However rich he once again became, it is clear that Meiggs was able to pay his California debts and buy shiploads of lumber from the Mendocino mill to build a railroad in Peru, which sustained Mendocino for years.

Even in exile Meiggs remained a well-liked man, to many people having committed no crime more serious than letting his ambitions fall victim to the era's boom mentality. Meiggs almost succeeded in having the indictments against him dismissed as well, receiving immunity for his crimes from the state legislature, which was vetoed at the last minute by Governor Newton Booth.

Environment

The Gray Whale

The sparkling plume of a whale's spout off-shore or the splash of a 12-foot-wide fluke is one of northern California's most exciting environmental sites. Whales migrate all along the California coast, but no county provides better vista points from Highway 1 than Mendocino County.

Whales, along with dolphins, and porpoises are of the order *cetaceans.* These mammals once roamed on land, but about 30 million years ago, some evolutionary call to adventure prompted

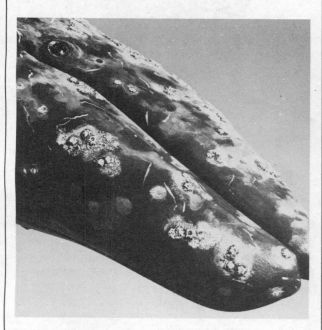

them to leave the shore and slip into the sea. Eventually the animals lost their hind legs and developed their forelegs into flippers, but they remain true mammals: air breathing, warm blooded, and milk nursing to live-born young.

Roadside Attractions

Mendocino

Like a make believe city perched upon the headland pretty and romantic, Mendocino endures as one of California's most appealing seaside communities. From a distance, the town shines all white-wooded and well dressed above a rolling ocean. Close up, small shops, walkways, and hand-crafted Victorian houses define an enchanting pedestrian environment.

Not just pretty, Mendocino has a wealth of visitor attractions that accommodate a wide range of inter-

ests. Most notable, perhaps, are those related to the town's reputation as an arts community. Four permanant theater companies offer everything from light opera to improvisational theater. A dozen galleries offer excellent paintings, woodworks, and ceramics, usually by local artists and artisans.

But the most basic pleasure in Mendocino is to walk its storybook streets and be surprised by unexpected pleasures. Along Main Street are numerous quality shops, interesting and appealing, and a collection of good restaurants, one of which has written a book about itself. There are mill site remains on the southwestern point of town, whale watching at Mendocino Headlands State Park, and ocean pleasures and Big River State Beach.

Resources

Whales

Many north coast environmental organizations and interpretive centers offer seminars, field trips by plane and boat, and whale watching programs during the migratory season. Others, like the reknown Greenpeace Foundation fight to stop global slaughter of whales and to promote their understanding. Two of the best known whale watching programs are run by the Oceanic Society and the Whale Center.

OCEANIC SOCIETY EXPEDITIONS
Fort Mason, Bldg. E
San Francisco 94123

THE WHALE CENTER
3929 Piedmont Avenue
Oakland 94611

GREENPEACE FOUNDATION
Building 240
Fort Mason
San Francisco

Whale Artists and Festival

The gray whale has inspired an entire generation of artists whose work is focused on the celebration

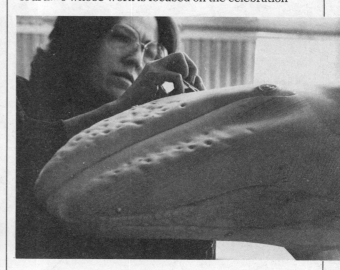

and understanding of these magnificent creatures. Painting, sculpture, jewelry, fabric, and printing are among the media embraced by these coastal artists, many of whom have achieved critical acclaim (such as artist Byrd Baker, sculptors Lynn and Wick Ahern, and painter George Sumner).

Many of California's whale artists converge in Mendocino each March, to participate in the annual Whale Festival. The Festival offers special gallery shows, films, fish and crab cook-offs, events, and guided Lighthouse and boat tours. Call 964-3153 for this year's Whale Festival schedule.

THE OCEANIC SOCIETY FIELD GUIDE TO THE GRAY WHALE
Legacy Publishing Company
San Francisco. 1983.

THE SIERRA CLUB HANDBOOK OF WHALES AND DOLPHINS
Stephen Leatherwood and Randall S. Reeves
Sierra Club Books
San Francisco. 1982.

WHALE PRIMER
Theodore J. Walker
Cabrillo Historical Society
Point Loma. 1975.

THE DELICATE ART
OF WHALE WATCHING
Joan McIntyre
Sierra Club Books
San Francisco. 1985.

Gray Whale Facts

SIZE: Mid-range 35–50 feet and 20–40 tons; females larger than males.

CALVES: Born live, average 14 feet 1,500 pounds at birth.

LIFE SPAN: Average 30–40 years, but up to 60.

BLOWHOLES: Paired as with all baleen whales; about eight inches long.

DORSAL RIDGE: No dorsal fin, instead a series of six to 12 small knuckles, or bumps.

FLUKES: Horizontal (compared to vertical fish tails), about 12 feet wide, 300–400 pounds of tissue and cartilage.

FLIPPERS: Range four to five feet long, supported by an internal skeleton evolved from land mammals forearms.

PREDATORS: Killer whales, large sharks and man.

PARASITES: Barnacles (up to several hundred pounds on an average male whale) and cyamid lice, which are orange lice that infest barnacle clusters.

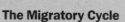

SWIMMING: Cruising speed two to four knots; top speed ten knots.

DIVING: Normal depth, 120 feet, maximum 500 feet (estimated); normal time 3-5 minutes, sometimes up to 15 minutes.

VOCALIZATION: Very low frequencies (less than 1,000 Hz), used to communicate, find way in darkness and in water with limited visibility.

The Migratory Cycle

APRIL—OCTOBER: Arctic feeding in the Chukchi and Bering Seas between Alaska and Siberia.

OCTOBER—FEBRUARY: Southern 6,000 mile migration of pregnant females, males, and in-season females who mate along the way.

DECEMBER—APRIL: Calves are born in the shallow backwaters of Baja's lagoons.

FEBRUARY—JULY: Northward migration, led by newly pregnant females, adult males, and juveniles, followed much later by new mothers and calves.

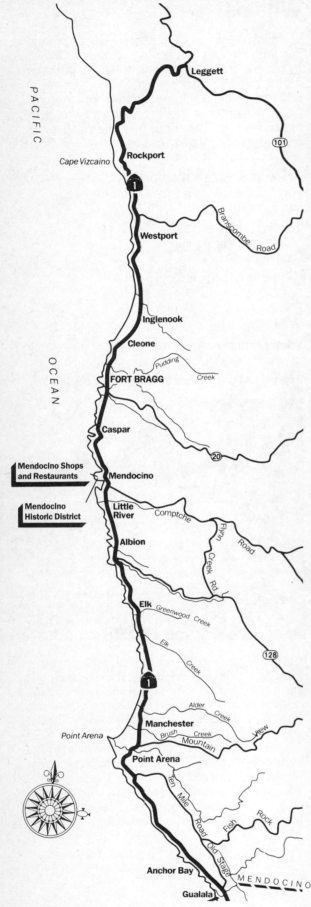

Historical Architecture

The town of Mendocino has a rich collection of early California Victorian houses that creates one of the most picturesque townscapes on the coast. Protected by a stringent historical preservation ordinance, these beautiful structures provide a compelling insight into historical Mendocino, many of them remaining from the days when Mendocino was a prosperous seaport and milltown.

Ford House (1855): Built by Mendocino's first white settler, now operated by Department of Parks and Recreation.

Presbyterian Church (1868): Main Street: A late example of Gothic Revival, now facing what was once the old coast highway, one of the first protestant churches in California.

Lansing House (1852): Built by one of Mendocino's original settlers from wood shipped from San Francisco.

Kelley House (1861): Main Street: Built by one of the town's original settlers, now a historical museum.

Joss House (1882): Once a Chinese shrine honoring a War Emperor-God, now a State Historical Landmark.

Mendocino Hotel (1878): The last of a string of milltown hotels that once lined Main Street.

Kasten-Hesser House (1852): Built by founder of *Mendocino Beacon* who also laid out many of town's streets.

Mendocino Beacon Building (1872): Home of Mendocino's most enduring newspaper (since 1877), originally built as a bank.

McCormack House (1882): Now the Mendocino Village Inn, the McCormack house was once the home of a succession of doctors, who resided here from 1882 to 1918, thus earning it the nickname, "House of the doctors."

Jarvis and Nichols Store (1877): Former general store.

Crown Hall (1901): Former Portuguese social hall.

Masonic Temple (1865): Nothing if not peculiar, cupola sculpture "Time and the Virgin" is based on Freemason symbolism.

Mendocino Arts Center (1885): Site of former Denison-Morgan-Preston mansion, which was the setting for *East of Eden* with James Dean filmed in 1954, 2 years before it burned down.

Spencer Hill House (1855): Gothic Revival Structure, once the main building of a 250 acre ranch.

Joshua Grindle House (1879): A one story Italianate cottage built for Alice Grindle who died in childbirth while house was under construction.

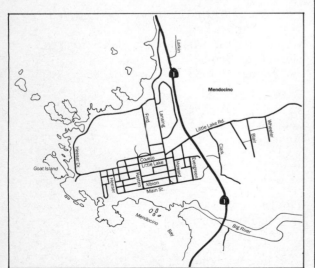

Dungeness Crabs

One of Mendocino's most important commercial catches is the big Dungeness crab, named for a Washington state area, but common from Alaska to Baja. One of more than 25,000 of the ocean's crustacean species, the Dungeness is most often found on sandy bottoms under 50 feet or more of water. This watery world supports the crab as it fleets along the bottom on the tips of three pairs of walking legs.

The crab's powerful front pincers catch and rip

apart small fish unlucky enough to be in the way. Then the crab stuffs the shredded morsels into its tooth-lined mouth in a gesture that would be frowned upon at most tables. Like all real crabs, the Dungeness' eyes are perched on movable stalks, which can be withdrawn into their sockets at will. Small, fine sensory hair coats the crab's body, assisting in locating food and filtering water near the gills. Like lobsters, crabs have the unusual ability to regenerate a severed or wounded pincher.

North coast fishermen catch crabs in bowl-shaped nets that are about three feet in diameter at the top and one foot at the bottom. The nets are baited with fish, and once a crab enters it, the net is quickly pulled to the surface to prevent escape of the wyly catch. Kept alive from boat to market, the Dungeness is highly prized (and, increasingly, highly priced) in California fish markets and restaurants.

Movie Making in Mendocino

Mendocino's photogenic charms have not been lost on California's moviemakers, many of whom have filmed features on the town's streets and in its preserved historical structures. Ironically, Mendocino is often represented as being on the Atlantic coast, with its Cape Cod architecture used to depict New England settings.

More than 15 major movies have been filmed in Mendocino, including 5 Oscar winners: *Frenchman's Creek* (made in 1943 with Joan Fontaine), *Johnny Belinda* (1947, Jane Wyman), *East of Eden* (1954, James Dean), *The Russians are Coming* (1965, Alan Arkin), and *The Summer of '42* (1970, Jennifer O'Neil). But for many people the presence of movie crews on Mendocino's streets only focuses one of the town's major problems—the marketing of Mendocino's quaintness for the tourist dollar. The issue has become a sensitive one for many residents of the town.

The presence of crews for movies, television, and commercials on Mendocino's streets has become an emblem of the town's increasing commercialization, which some local people maintain has become so intense that most remnants of everyday life have been displaced, threatening the very qualities that bring visitors here in the first place.

In addition to creating sidewalk congestion and sometimes blocking off streets, movie crews often create traffic and parking problems. Although motion picture and TV companies spend thousands of dollars locally on hotel rooms, restaurants, caterers, equipment, and other goods and services, not much direct publicity for the town is involved because Mendocino is usually portrayed as somewhere else. Many residents feel the disruptions are not worth the aggravation.

Other places would love to have Mendocino's problems. Many cities, including San Francisco, fall all over themselves trying to grab a portion of the $4 billion a year motion picture business. They pick movie crews up at airports, offer them tax rebates, free security, facilities and locations. Mendocino, however, remains dubious.

All the world may indeed be a stage, but in the town of Mendocino, many of its residents would prefer to see the movie version filmed somewhere else.

Galleries and Museums

937-0665	Ayers-Britton Gallery
937-4322	David Scott-Meier Studio
937-4538	Fine Line Gallery and Woodworks
937-5121	Gallery Fair
937-0214	Gallery Mendocino
937-4232	Goings on Gallery
937-5791	Kelly House Historical Museum
937-0453	Mayhew Wildlife Gallery
937-5818	Mendocino Art Center
937-5154	Ruth Carlson Gallery
937-5081	This Is Not Art?
937-5205	Zacha's Bay Window Gallery

Mendocino Events

There is a full calendar of special shows, celebrations, and other events available to the Mendocino traveler. Below is a sample from a recent year. Contact the Chamber of Commerce (964-3153) or the Mendocino Arts Center (937-5724) for the most recent listings. The Art Center also publishes a monthly magazine *Arts and Entertainment,* available free in local stores.

FEBRUARY	Mendocino Coast Music Celebration (937-5122). Mendocino Film Festival (937-5606
MARCH	Annual Whale Festival
APRIL	Rhododendron Festival, Botanical Gardens (964-0423)
MAY	Arts in Action (937-5818)
JUNE	Albion Beef BBQ (937-0276)
JULY	World's Largest Salmon BBQ
AUGUST	Annual Art in the Redwoods Festival (964-3153)
SEPTEMBER	Fuchsia Society Show (964-0429). Paul Bunyan Days (964-9376)
OCTOBER	Thanksgiving Fair (937-5818)

The Kelley House Museum and Library

Mendocino Historical Research, Inc.
45007 Albion Street, P.O. Box 922
Mendocino 95460.
937-5791.

Kelley House is the 1861 home of William H. Kelley, who came to Mendocino in 1852 on the brig which brought the men and machinery to set up the first lumber mill.

Today Kelley House is headquarters for an excellent museum and for Mendocino Historical Research, Inc., which publishes the *Mendocino Historical Review.* The grounds and the first floor are restored and display featured exhibits of local artifacts and private collections, as well as a permanant display of 1800's photos and architectural descriptions of the historic houses and buildings in Mendocino. There is a small gift shop and book store. A reference library is available for use by appointment. The musuem is open daily from 1:00 to 4:00 except in December and January when weekend-only hours are in effect.

The Liveliest Town in the County

The town of Mendocino remained the focal point of most travel along the coast once a road was established that linked all the mill towns. But from the 1890s, Fort Bragg became its fast-growing rival, and by 1914, had grown sufficiently to be regarded as "the livliest, busiest town in the county" with a population of almost 2,300.

A no-nonsense town that voted itself dry in the early part of the century, Fort Bragg had relied on

the timber industry for its economic welfare after the mill was moved from Ten Mile River in 1885. The town was literally carved out of a forest that surrounded a natural glade and afforded an excellent climate. But within only a few years, so many trees had been cut down that the climate changed, letting in considerably more fog and unbroken winds.

When the railroad came in 1911, connecting Fort Bragg to Willits, the town thrived with numerous stores, restaurants, banks, two moving-picture houses, a newspaper, a bottling works, and four school buildings. Although city streets remained unpaved, cement sidewalks lined the main part of town.

The Company People Love to Hate

A redwood deck is a thing of beauty forever.
Home Remodeling Advertisement

Timber cutting, the most influential land use activity in Mendocino County, is dominated by a single corporation, Georgia Pacific, whose sprawling processing plant occupies the major portion of Fort Bragg's shoreline and generally determines the health of the area's economy.

Locally, Georgia Pacific has achieved a reputation for insensitivity to the environment, which most people attribute to its size: the company accounts for 3% of the nation's lumber production, and owns 4.8 million acres of timberland in the U.S., Canada, and Brazil, with exclusive cutting rights to another 1.3 million acres.

With over $5.2 billion in annual sales and over 200 plants and mills throughout the world, Georgia Pacific ranks first in production of forest products and first in plywood production. It is the nation's third largest producer of lumber and gypsum. In 1972 the company became so gigantic, it was forced to seel off 20% of its stock, begetting Louisiana Pacific, the sixth largest lumber manufacturer in the country.

Georgia Pacific has not gained its position at the top of America's timber cutters through altruism. Say the authors of *Everybody's Business,* "Georgia Pacific is regarded as the tough guys in the forest products industry. They blame conservationists and government agencies for timber shortages. But they're beloved on Wall Street for their money making ability."

Established in 1927 by Owen Cheatham, a descendent of Benjamin Franklin who parried a $12,000 investment into a million dollar corporation, The Georgia Hardwood Lumber Company's first gigantic success resulted from recognizing the potential for plywood in homebuilding after World War II. Although it held no timber lands at all for more than 20 years, the company embarked on a ravenous land buying program in 1951, changing its name to Georgia Pacific and locating its headquarters in the west in 1953.

Besides being the area's largest job provider Georgia Pacific has also become the company that people love to hate. On more than one occasion Georgia Pacific has rushed to cut down virgin stands of redwoods of marginal economic value just hours before legislative action would have protected the trees.

Environment

Pygmy Forests

The area between the Navarro and Noyo Rivers offers the traveler a rare opportunity to explore a 500,000 year-old ecological anomaly called a pygmy forest.

Ecological Staircase

The Pygmy Forest Ecological Staircase is particularly visible near Jug Handle Creek where five level terraces comprise a geological and biological staircase that rises from sea level to 600

feet in elevation. Long ago, ocean waves carved the terraces into greywacke sandstone rock. Then, every 100,000 years or so, a new terrace was carved, slowly uplifting and pushing inland the one that preceeded it.

As each new terrace was lifted, coast conifer forest replaced grassland on the terrace above it. Eventually, however, the soils on the upper terraces became impoverished and strongly acidic. The conifer forest began to be replaced on the upper terraces by the stunted trees and acid-tolerant plants of the pygmy forest. The twisted, dwarf cypress, Bishop pine, Holander pine and manzanita that forest the area now stand in startling contrast to their fully-nourished and full-sized siblings visible on nearby slopes.

The Eye of the Beholder

The five terraces along Jug Handle Creek are recognized as the best preserved ecological showcase of coastal evolution in North America. Designated a Registered Natural Landmark, the forest fascinates scientists, geologists, and ecologists. However, the visitor who expects a "beautiful miniature rain forest in tiny elk, cute little Bambis and bonsai-style trees" is bound to share the disappointing view of one journalist who concluded that the Pygmy Forest is really "just a bunch of stunted little trees made runty by thousand of years of poor drainage, erosion, and the effects of salt-spray on the soil." A patient walk along the self-guided nature trail will soon dispell such an impression for most visitors.

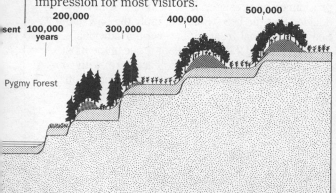

Roadside Attractions

Fort Bragg

North of the town of Mendocino, Highway 1 skirts the tiny town of Caspar, which is noteworthy as the location for the Caspar Inn, one of the area's most festive drinking and entertainment spots. Caspar also has a small crafts studio and gallery.

Back on Highway 1, just before the commercial clutter of Fort Bragg asserts itself, is Jughandle Farm, on the east side of the highway. Jughandle Farm has a public nature trail that leads through the ecological staircase (accessible to the disabled) and a small hostel housed in a pretty red Victorian. On the west side of Highway 1 is Jughandle State Reserve.

Just inside the Fort Bragg city limits is Mendocino Botanical Gardens, where a circuit of trails winds amid 10,000 varieties of plants that grow along the manicured headlands. The Botanical Gardens also has a garden cafe and a cliffhouse with a picnic area overlooking the ocean.

Noyo River

Noyo River is Mendocino's major fishing harbor, and it is loaded with excellent restaurants and fish stores. Several chartered fishing boat operations are based at Noyo, as well as whale watching expeditions and boat building enterprises. Full of color, Noyo harbor is active and vibrant, fascinating enough to capture anyone's attention for mounting hours.

Fort Bragg's most celebrated attraction is the Skunk Train, one of the best railroad adven-

tures remaining on the coast, despite the fact its steam locomotives have been replaced by more modern models.

Dowdy and unkempt, Fort Bragg has less chic appeal than most of contemporary coastal Mendocino, but it should not be too quickly passed by. See particularly downtown Fort Bragg, with authentic small town American gems like Daly's Department Store and Doug's True Value Hardware store on Franklin Street.

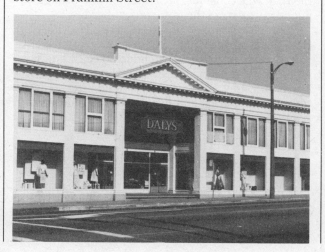

Resources

In and Around Fort Bragg

The Skunk. California Western Railroad
P.O. Box 907
Fort Bragg 95437.

Among Mendocino's most pleasurable attractions is the Skunk Railroad, a 40 mile trip into the past between Fort Bragg inland to Willits. The winding route crosses 31 bridges and trestles, passing through two deep mountain tunnels and redwood forests. Round trip tickets are available all the way to Willits, or to a halfway point in the redwoods. The replica

trains are powered by diesel logging locomotives featuring open observation cars. The original 1885 trains were nicknamed for their gas engines that prompted folks to note, "You can smell 'em before you can see 'em." Reservations needed.

Mendocino Coast Botanical Gardens
Highway 1, Two miles south of Fort Bragg
964-4352.

Covering 47 acres, this privately-run garden offers walks along winding paths through rhododendrons, azaleas, digitalis, heather, lillies, and many other cultivated flowers and native ferns. Paths end at scenic coastal headlands and a sandy beach. The Gardens offer picnic areas, a coffee house, a series of Sunday concerts, and special activities. Fee.

Jug Handle State Reserve
Jug Handle Farm and Nature Center
P.O. Box 17
Caspar 95420.
964-4630.

Stop at the signed parking lot on Highway 1 to pick up brochures at the ranger's station for Jug Handle State Reserve. The public reserve includes five miles of interpretive nature trails and a sandy beach at the mouth of the creek, accessible from the trails south of the Highway 1 overpass. The Farm and Nature Center adjacent to the reserve are owned and operated by a private, nonprofit organization. Cheap overnight accomodations are often available in the renovated farm house; call ahead.

The Redwood Empire Association
360 Post Street
San Francisco 94108.
(415) 421-6554

Since the 1920s, members of the Redwood Empire Association have worked to develop and maintain the roads of northern California, and to safeguard the environment while accommodating an expanding visitor serving industry. REA had a major role in unifying bickering local governments to develop the spectacular north coast road system, especially the scenic redwood highway (101), and, to a lesser degree, the Shoreline Highway (Highway 1). REA is an excellent resource for travelers and transportation buffs.

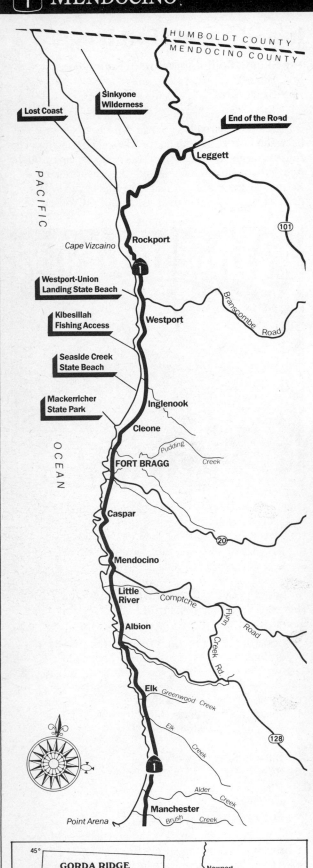

The Coast Road

Less committed to road building than practically any county in the state, Mendocino was finally required to expend some effort, if only to partially answer numerous complaints from newspapers like the *Pt. Arena Record* and *Mendocino Beacon,* which editorialized about the safety of the "ridiculous excuse for a road" that paralleled the coast.

Gradually the coast road was improved, usually by dint of horse-drawn rollers, which continued to be regarded more favorably than the steamroller, invented 50 years earlier in France. After about 1915 the introduction of the diesel engine for road construction in Mendocino brought about major improvements in grading and surfacing, but still not on a par with most other counties.

Coastal Mendocino County residents were slow to take to the automobile. Although many autos were seen after 1910, particularly in Fort Bragg and Mendocino, many residents continued to rely on horses even as late as the Depression.

In 1933 the State took over the Mendocino coast road, first coating it with dust oil and then paving it. But the paving was not very heavy, and stories passed among locals that any car could be

identified and tracked all the way down the coast by the wheel ruts left behind.

As the Depression closed Mendocino's mills one by one, the State tore out all the wooden bridges, bulldozing the gulches back to bedrock. New bridges were built over Schooner Gulch, Elk Creek, and the Navarro and Big rivers. In some places, such as the stretch between Gualala and Collins Landing, and just south of the town of Mendocino, the road was considerably realigned and brought inland, away from the more unstable edge.

Soon every mill on the coast save one at Fort Bragg ceased operation. But in a few years Highway 1 would bring to the Mendocino coast another import, whose influence, greater than all the mill towns and shipping schooners, would utterly transform the area: enter the motoring tourist.

Ocean Stripmining

Near the end of Highway 1 is the start of an offshore area destined for future controversy. This is the southern boundary of the proposed Gorda Ridge Lease Sale, a 70,000 square mile area extending from Cape Mendocino to Newport, Oregon. The Interior Department in 1984 supported a lease sale of this area, claiming that minerals called polymetallic sulfides are likely to exist beneath the ocean floor, and that mining of such minerals is necessary to expand the U.S. domestic supply.

The proposed lease brought immediate negative responses from environmentaltists and scientists, and a conflict that promises to be complex and long lasting.

The Gorda Ridge marks the collision point between the North American continent and the Pacific plate. As these land masses collide, massive pressure systems are created that force cold sea water downward where it is pushed back up by undersea volcanic activity, and released steaming into the ocean floor. The steaming vents are called "black smokers" and have been found to be surrounded by strange colonies of giant clams, enormous tube worms, white crabs, and previously unknown fish. Recent scientific discoveries at such sites are revolutionizing views of life

processes on the earth since the life forms survive not on the energy of the sun, but by a process tentatively called "chemosynthesis." The problem for the scientific researchers is that these vents are also where the ores, if they exist, are likely to be found.

While scientists argue that undersea stripmining would destroy valuable scientific evidence, and the government argues for the need for minerals, other critics claim that Gorda is merely a test site for the federal government to clearly establish its right to the minerals offshore for a 200 mile distance. Such a right, (called the "Exclusive Economic Zone") was proclaimed by President Reagan in 1983 when he decided that the U.S. would not ratify the Law of the Sea International Treaty. Whatever the individual motives, mining the ocean's floor is one of the most important issues in California's near future, with consequences as far reaching as those surrounding off shore oil drilling.

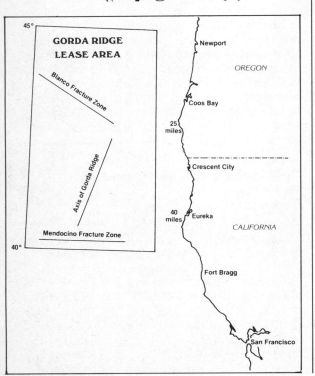

Ocean Seasons

Mendocino's ocean undergoes three very distinct seasons, each clearly identifiable by offshore current patterns. The Upwelling Period is the longest, stretching from February to July when the normal south-moving California current, the rotation of the earth, and seasonal winds cause upwelling. During this time surface waters flow away from shore, to be replaced by colder, nutrient-rich bottom water.

Between July and November, the seasonal Oce-

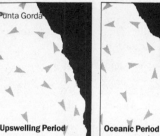

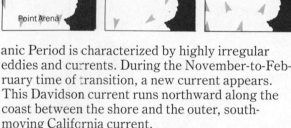

Ocean Seasons — Upswelling Period, Oceanic Period, Davidson Period

anic Period is characterized by highly irregular eddies and currents. During the November-to-February time of transition, a new current appears. This Davidson current runs northward along the coast between the shore and the outer, south-moving California current.

Westport to the Lost Coast

North of Fort Bragg, Highway 1 heads for one last moment of oceanfront exaltation before disappearing into the woods on its way to an inland merging with US 101 and extinction. Past one last gasp of Mendocino bed and breakfasts, Pudding Creek marks the entrance to MacKerricher State Park, six miles of beachland and dunes with a large campground, equestrian trail, and 15 acre fresh water lake with excellent fishing.

After MacKerricher are several fine beaches at Seaside Creek, South Kibesillah Gulch, Bruhel Point Bluff, Chadbourne Gulch, Wages Creek, and Westport Union Landing. The town of Westport has a smattering of places at which to stop over, including the Cobweb Palace (restaurant, inn, and bar) and a fine Mexican cafe (The Purple Rose.)

Beyond Westport, the road opens up across the coastal terrace before making an abrupt departure from the shoreline at Hollow Tree Road. Usal Road (unpaved), just after the turnoff, leads to the Sinkyone Wilderness and the Lost Coast, a far preferable alternative to US 101, 27 miles inland.

The End of the Road

Its merger with U.S. 101 at Leggett marks the northern end of Highway 1—but not quite. Another small stretch of road in Humboldt County is also designated as Route 1, between Ferndale and U.S. 101 near Eureka. The Ferndale section was designated Route 1 in anticipation of an extension through the Lost Coast, which would have connected the current Highway 1. If the extension is ever built, it will become, hands down, California's most scenic highway.

The Lost Coast

The best is last: just north of where Highway 1 turns inland to meet its demise, begins the Lost Coast, which includes Sinkyone Wilderness Park and King Range National Conservation Area, nearly 60,000 acres of the most stunning coastal wilderness in the 48 states.

Extremely steep and rocky terrain make the Lost Coast an isolated paradise. So rugged is the terrain that it was able to turn back Highway 1, a feat that Big Sur and the Santa Lucia Mountains were not able to do. (In fact, for years an extension of Highway 1 has been planned through the Lost Coast—even showing on many maps as "proposed route.")

Automobile travel through the Lost Coast is possible, however. Although rough going, a network of paved, gravel, and dirt roads allows access to most of the coastline and several mountain areas. Slides and washouts are frequent in winter.

The Beginning

The first residents of the Lost Coast were the Whilcut, Sinkyone, and Mattole Indians. For 2,000 years these tribes inhabited the area with little alteration to the land. Although they have been gone nearly 100 years, their cultural remnants still remain in the form of shell mounds, several of which are scattered along the deserted beaches and are protected by the Antiquities Act.

White settlers arrived in the 1850s and established farms and tanbark operations, primarily in the northern reaches of the area. The first oil well in California was drilled in 1861 in the tiny town of Petrolia, but production of the low quality petroleum proved unfeasible.

Throughout the 1950s and 60s, extensive timber cutting on private lands soon cleared off much of the unprotected forest. Some logging continues today on portions of BLM lands and private, unprotected lands to the south where public protest has been raised against the practice.

Lost in Time, Lost in Place

There is an incredible varied topography in the Lost Coast area: the King Range rises from sea level to 4,087 feet at the summit of Kings Peak so quickly as to be dizzying. On the western portion of the Kings Range, steep cliffs fall away abruptly to the ocean, creating rock slides and talus piles. A number of quick moving streams run directly down the severe slopes, undeterred on the precipitous journey to the ocean.

The Lost Coast's most certain glory is expressed in these areas where the King Mountains fall into the sea. The wilderness beaches in the conservation areas of the King Range are like no place on earth. At Punta Gorda is an abandoned lighthouse. In other stretches numerous relics of early shipwrecks show up along the beach, lending the shore a mood of being lost in time as well as lost in place.

But it is not only a place of expiration: an amazing variety of wildlife frequents the Lost Coast. Offshore rocks are inhabited by sea lions, seals, and marine birds. Black-tailed deer, mountain lions, and black bear populate the uplands, and river otter and mink are often seen. Valley quail, mountain quail, and blue grouse are also present in the area. Nowhere in California does the coastline achieve such primal forcefulness. The Lost Coast is a dramatic reminder of how well nature does when left alone. This is it.

All information in the county profiles (map column, first spread of each county) is from James S. Fay, Anne G. Loplow, Stephanie W. Fay, Editors, The California Almanac, 1984/1985 Edition, Novato: Presidio Press, 1984.

Orange County

Origins

14: Doris Walker, *Dana Point Harbor, Home Port for Romance,* Dana Point: To the Point Press, 1983. Quote is from Richard Henry Dana, *Two Years Before the Mast,* New York: Penguin Books, 1981.

16–20: Samuel Armor, *History of Orange County,* Los Angeles, 1911. Leo J. Frillis, *Orange County Through Four Centuries,* Santa Ana: Pioneer Press, 1965. Don Meadows, *Orange County Under Spain, Mexico, and the United States,* Los Angeles: Dawson's Book Shop, 1966. Charles E. Parker, *Orange County: Indians to Industry,* Santa Ana: Orange County Title Company, 1963. Mable Ramsey, Merle Ramsey, *Pioneer Days of Laguna Beach,* Laguna Beach, 1967. Ruth Ellen Taylor, editor, *Legacy: The Orange County Story,* Santa Ana: The Register, 1980. Quote on p.18 is from an undated brochure for the Hotel Laguna, Bancroft Library pamphlets; quote on p. 20 is from a 1922 Laguna Beach Chamber of Commerce pamphlet, Bancroft Library.

22: Robert G. Cleland, *Irvine Ranch,* San Marino: Huntington Library, 1962. Orange County Genealogical Society, *Saddleback Ancestors, Rancho Families of Orange County,* Orange, 1969. Quote is from Steve Oney's "All in the Family," *California Magazine,* November 1983.

24–30: Spencer Crump, *Ride the Big Red Cars,* Glendale: Trans-Anglo Books, 1983. Ellen K. Lee, *Newport Bay: A Pioneer History,* Fullerton: Sultana Press, 1973.

32: Kahanamoku's quote appears in Leonard Lueras's *Surfing: The Ultimate Pleasure,* New York: Workman Publishing, 1984.

34–36: *California Highways and Public Works,* January, 1927; March, 1927; December, 1927. Meadows, 1966. WPA, 1936. Quote on p.36 is from Armor, 1911.

Land Use

14: Jack Kerouac, *On the Road,* New York: Penguin Books, 1979. Thomas Pynchon, *The Crying of Lot 49,* New York: J.P. Lippincott, 1966. Whitman's quote is from "Song of the Open Road," contained in *Leaves of Grass,* New York: Random House, 1933. The quote from the Lewis and Clark expedition is contained in *The Journals of Lewis and Clark,* John Bakeless editor, New York: New American Library, 1964. Joan Didion's quote appears in *Play It As It Lays,* New York: Farrar, Straus & Giroux, 1970.

16: California Coastal Commission, South Coast District. Orange County Environmental Management Agency.

18: California Coastal Commission, San Francisco. *Protecting the Golden Shore,* Robert G. Hely, Washington D.C.: The Conservation Foundation, Stanley Scott, 1978. *Governing California's Coast,* Berkeley: UC Press, 1975. Quote is from Richard O'Reilly's "The California Coastal Commission: At the Crossroads," Los Angeles Times, 1981.

20: California Coastal Act of 1976, Title 14, Division 5.5.

24: "Showdown at Irvine Ranch," *California Magazine,* February 1982.

26: Charles Moore, Peter Becker, Regula Campbell, *The City Observed, Los Angeles,* New York: Random House, 1984.

30: Jane Addams quote appears in *Urban Open Spaces,* Lisa Taylor, editor, New York: Rizzolli, 1981. Keat's quote is from "On the Sea," which appears in *The Complete Poems of Keats and Shelley,* New York: Modern Library, 1982.

34: Quotes appear in *Everybody's Business,* Milton Moskowitz, editor, New York: Harper and Row, 1980.

36: Amigos de Bolsa Chica.

Environment

14: Elna Bakker, *An Island Called California: An Ecological Introduction to its Natural Communities,* Berkeley: U.C. Press, 1984. Walker, 1983. Quote is from Garcí Rodriguez Ordónez de Montaluvo, *Las Sergas de Esplandian,* circa 1510.

17: Allan Donley, Patton Caro, *Atlas of California,* Portland: Academic Book Center, 1979. David Hornbeck, *California Patterns: A Geographical and Historical Atlas,* Palo Alto:

Mayfield Publishing Company, 1983.

19: Elbert L. Little, *The Audubon Society Field Guide to Native American Trees: Western Region,* New York: Alfred A. Knopf, 1980. Howard E. McMinn and Evelyn Maino, *Pacific Coast Trees,* Berkeley: U.C. Press, 1981.

21: Bakker, 1984. Hornbeck, 1983.

23: Quote is from Carey McWilliams, *Southern California: An Island on the Land,* Salt Lake City: Peregrine Smith, 1983.

25: Orange County Local Coastal Plan.

27: U.S. Army Corps of Engineers.

31: Vinson Brown, *Handbook of California Birds,* Happy Camp: Naturegraph Publishers, Inc., 1979. Huntington Beach Least Tern Reserve.

33: Willard Bascom, *Waves and Beaches,* New York: Anchor Books, 1980. U.S. Army Corps of Engineers.

35: William Rintoul: *Drilling Ahead: Tapping California's Richest Oil Fields,* Santa Cruz: Valley Publishers, 1981.

37: Amigos de Bolsa Chica. Phylis Faber, *Common Wetland Plants of California,* Inverness: Pickleweed Press, 1982.

Roadside Attractions

25: Quote is from Steve Olney's, "Adventures in Paradise," *California Magazine,* November, 1983.

27: Quote is from Carol Dunlap's *California People,* Salt Lake: Peregrine Smith, 1982.

29: Dick Dale's quote appears in Lueras, 1984.

33: Quote is from Lueras, 1984.

Los Angeles County

Origins

40: Robert Fogelson, *The Fragmented Metropolis: Los Angeles 1850–1930,* Cambridge: Harvard University Press, 1967. Sidney C. Kendall, *Long Beach, the City By the Sea,* Long Beach, 1903. Joseph S. O'Flaherty, *Those Powerful Years: The South Coast and Los Angeles, 1887–1917,* Hicksville, N.Y.: Exposition Press, 1978. Quote is from McWilliams, 1983.

42: Stephen Brown, *The Pike (Past Its Peak),* Seal Beach: SCB Photographics, 1981.

44–48: Bowman, 1974. Fogelson, 1967. McWilliams, 1983. Crump, 1983. Steven Easlon, *The Los Angeles Railway through the Years,* Anaheim: Easlon Publications, 1973. Henry Huntington's quote on p.44 appears in Fogelson, 1967. Verse on p.46 appears in Dennis Shanahan's *Old Redondo: A Pictorial History of Redondo Beach,* Redondo Beach: Legends Press, 1982. Franklin Walker's quote on p.48 appears in John and La Ree Caughey's *Los Angeles: Biography of a City,* Berkeley: U.C. Press, 1976.

50: David Gebhard and Robert Winter, *A Guide to Architecture in Southern California,* Santa Barbara: Peregrine Smith, 1976. U.S. Army Corps of Engineers.

52: Tom Moran, Tom Sewell, *Fantasy By the Sea: A Visual History of the American Venice,* Culver City: Peace Press, 1980.

54–58: Fogelson, 1967. Bruce Henstell, *Sunshine and Wealth: Los Angeles in the Twenties and Thirties,* San Francisco: Chronicle Books, 1985. Luther A. Ingersoll, *Ingersoll's Century History, Santa Monica Bay Cities, Los Angeles,* 1908. O'Flaherty, 1978. Felix Riesenberg, *The Golden Road,* New York: McGraw Hill, 1962. Quote on p.54 is from *Santa Monica Evening Outlook,* Diamond Jubilee Edition, 1950. Lady Jeune's quote on p.56 appears in Gerald Silk's *Automobile and Culture,* New York: Harry N. Abrams, Inc., 1984; lower quote on same page is from the *Santa Monica Evening Outlook,* 1950, as is top quote on p.58. Bottom quote on p.58 is from Dunlap, 1982.

60: Gebhard, Winter, 1976. Moore, et al, 1984. Quote is from Dunlap, 1982.

62: W.W. Robinson, Lawrence C. Powell, *The Malibu,* Los Angeles, 1958.

64: Quote is from *California Highways and Public Works,* July, 1929.

Land Use

40: *New York Times,* "Drive-Ins Fade Into Yesteryear,"

May 30, 1982.

44: Source for Phineas Banning feature is Dunlap, 1982. Quote in Palos Verdes issue is from Fogelson, 1967.

46: Reynor Banham, Los Angeles, *The Architecture of Four Ecologies,* Penguin Books, New York: 1982.

48: Henstell, 1985. Dunlap, 1982.

50: Friends of Ballona Wetlands. Los Angeles County Local Coastal Plan. Jan Stevens, *Santa Monica Evening Outlook,* December 8, 1984.

54: Friends of the Santa Monica Pier. Santa Monica Convention and Visitors Bureau.

56: Robert Winter, *The California Bungalow.* Los Angeles: Hennessey and Ingalls, 1980.

58: The Mountains Restoration Trust. The Santa Monica National Recreation Area, National Parks Service.

60: Moore, et al, 1984. Gebhard and Winter, 1976.

64: Frank Bies, "Surf Wars," *California Magazine,* May, 1981.

Environment

41: B. Bailey, *Climate of Southern California,* Berkeley: U.C. Press, 1961. Crane S. Miller and Richard S. Hyslop, *California: The Geography of Diversity,* Palo Alto: Mayfield Publishing Company, 1983.

43: The Port of Long Beach. The Port of Los Angeles.

45: City of Long Beach. Robert P. Sharp, *Geological Field Guide to Coastal Southern California,* Dubuque: Kendall/ Hunt Publishing Company, 1978.

47: Sandra Blakeslee, "Strange Animals Thrive on Poison in Shallow Water," *New York Times,* February 28, 1984.

49: California Coastal Commission, South Coast office.

51: McWilliams, 1983. California Department of Water Resources.

53: Vinson Brown, 1979. Milos D. F. Udvardy, *The Audubon Society Field Guide to North American Birds,* Western Region. New York: Alfred A. Knopf, Inc., 1977.

55: Cabrillo Museum.

57: Santa Monica Mountains National Recreation Area. Huxley's quote appears in Dunlap, 1982.

59: David J. Parsons, "Chaparral," *Discovering California,* San Francisco: California Academy of Sciences, 1983.

61: Sharp, 1978.

63: Bayard Webster, *New York Times,* March 3, 1985.

65: Willard Bascom, *Waves and Beaches,* New York: Anchor Books, 1980. Source for the feature is the U.S. Army Corps of Engineers.

Roadside Attractions

41–45: Robert Venturi, Denise Scott Brown, Steven Izenour, *Learning from Las Vegas,* Cambridge: MIT Press, 1972.

47: Freeth quote appears in Lueras, 1984.

49: Quote is from Banham, 1982.

51: Dunlap, 1982.

53: Dunlap, 1982. Quote is from McWilliams, 1983.

61: Didion's quote is from *The White Album,* New York: Pocket Books, 1970. Jencks quote is from *The Language of Post Modern Architecture,* New York: Rizzoli, 1977.

65: Elaine Woo, *Los Angeles Times,* June 23, 1984.

Ventura County

Origins

68–70: Quote on page 68 is from *California Highways and Public Works,* March, 1913.

72: W.W. Robinson, *The Story of Ventura County,* Los Angeles, 1955. Quote is from Thompson and West, *History of Santa Barbara and Ventura Counties,* Berkeley: Santa Barbara Press, 1961.

74: Walter Bean, James Rauls, *California an Interpretive History,* New York: McGraw Hill, 1983. *Santa Paula Chronicle,* Greater Ventura County Edition, October, 1921. Sol N. Sheridan, *History of Ventura County, California,* Chicago, 1926.

76: *A Comprehensive Story of Ventura County, California,* Oxnard, 1979. Sheridan, 1926.

78: Robinson, 1955. *California Highways and Public Works,* March, 1913. Sheridan, 1926.

82: Bean, 1982. Caltrans. Dunlap, 1982.

Land Use

68: McWilliams, 1983. Robert V. Hine, *California Utopian Colonies,* Berkeley: U.C. Press, 1983.

70: Ventura County Planning Department.

72: Cletus E. Daniel, *Bitter Harvest: A History of California Farmworkers, 1870–1941,* Berkeley: U.C. Press, 1981. Paul Shinoff, "Whither the Eagle?" *San Francisco Examiner,* April 8, 1984. United Farm Workers.

74: Quote is from Stan Luxenberg, *Roadside Empires: How the Chains Franchised America,* New York: Viking Penguin Inc., 1985.

76: Taylor, 1981.

78: Moskowitz, 1980.

80 The Nature Conservancy, Santa Cruz Island Project Office. Channel Islands National Park.

82: Bruce Walter Barton, *The Tree at the Center of the World: A Story of the California Missions,* Santa Barbara: Ross-Erikson Publishers, Inc., 1980. Hornbeck, 1983.

69: Ventura County Planning Department. Condor feature source is Friends of the Earth.

71: John Perry and Jane Greverus Perry, *The Sierra Club Guide to the Natural Areas of California,* San Francisco: Sierra Club Books, 1983. Point Mugu State Park and Mugu Testing Center Public Affairs Office.

73: Dr. Norman Myers, General Editor, *Gaia: An Atlas of Planet Management,* New York: Anchor Books, 1984.

75: Ventura County Planning Department. Hornbeck, 1983.

77: Channel Islands Harbor District. U.S. Army Corps of Engineers.

79: David W. Lantis, *California: Land of Contrast,* Dubuque: Kendall/Hunt, 1981.

81: Channel Islands National Park.

83: Greater Ventura Visitor Bureau.

Roadside Attractions

75: Quote is from Didion, 1970.

77: Gardner's quote appears in *Two Bit Culture,* Boston: Houghton Mifflin, 1984.

Santa Barbara County

Origins (80–90)

86–90: Katherine M. Bell, *Swinging the Censer, Reminiscences of Old Santa Barabara,* Santa Barbara, 1931. Charles Lummis, *Stand Fast Santa Barbara,* Santa Barbara, 1927. Charles Nordhoff, *California for Health, Pleasure, and Residence; Book for Travelers and Settlers,* Berkeley: Ten Speed Press, 1973. Pamphlet Boxes, Bancroft Library. *Santa Barbara News Press,* Centennial Edition, April, 1954. Walker A. Tompkins, *Santa Barbara, Past and Present,* Santa Barbara: Tecolote Books, 1975. Quote on p.86 is from Santa Barbara Chamber of Commerce, "A Midsummer Paradise, Santa Barbara the Newport of the Pacific", which appears in *Santa Barbara By the Sea,* Rochelle Bookspan, editor, Santa Barbara: McNally & Loftin, 1982.

92: Pearl Chase, *Bernard Hoffman, Community Builder,* Santa Barbara, 1927. Bookspan, 1982.

94: Bookspan, 1982. Tompkins, 1975.

96–102: Marguerite Mildred Dart, *The History of the Lompoc Valley, California,* Master Thesis, University of California, 1937. Walker A. Tompkins, *Stagecoach Days in Santa Barbara County,* Santa Barbara: McNally & Loftin West, 1982. Works Project Administration Federal Writers' Project, *WPA Guide to California,* New York: Pantheon Books, 1984. Quotes on p.98 and 102 are from Nancy Lee Wilkinson's dissertation *Perpetual Frontiers of the Central Coast: the Lompoc and Santa Maria Valleys, Santa Barbara County, California,* University of Oregon, December, 1983.

Land Use

86: Allison Sky and Michelle Stone, *Unbuilt America,* New York: McGraw Hill, 1976.

88: Get Oil Out. Anne W. Simon, *The Thin Edge: Coast and Man in Crisis,* New York: Avon Books, 1978.

90: Bookspan, 1982.

92: Santa Barbara Department of City Planning.

94: Moira Johnston, "The Vanishing Land," *California Magazine,* August 1982.

96: J. B. Jackson, *Discovering the Venacular Landscape,* New Haven: Yale University Press, 1984. Quote is from William H. Whyte, *The Last Landscape,* New York: Doubleday, 1968.

100: Vandenberg Air Force Base

102: Carl Irving, *San Francisco Examiner,* February 11, 1985.

Environment

87: Bascom, 1980. Tomkins, 1975.

89: Point Reyes Bird Observatory.

91: Pauline J. Thompson, *Santa Barbara: How to Discover America's Eden,* Santa Barbara: Krickett Publications, 1984.

93: Santa Barbara Converence and Visitors' Bureau. Santa Barbara Museum of Natural History.

95 & 97: Lantis, 1981. Sharp, 1978.

99: Karen Pandell and Chris Stall, *Animal Tracks of the Pacific Northwest,* Seattle: The Mountaineers, 1981.

101: California Department of Water Resources. Source for the feature is Lantis, 1981.

103: Brown, 1979. Udvardy, 1977.

Roadside Attractions

87: Quote is from the Works Project Administration Southern California Writers Project's, *Santa Barbara, A Guide to the Channel and its Environs,* New York: Hastings House, 1936.

San Luis Obispo

Origins

106: Annie L. Morrison, *History of San Luis Obispo County and Environs,* Los Angeles, 1917. Quote is from Myron Angel's *History of San Luis Obispo County* (1883), Fresno: Valley Publishers, 1979.

108: Quote is from *San Luis Obispo Telegram Tribune, December 17, 1983.*

110: John Berger, Nuclear Power: *The Unviable Option,* New York: Dell Books, 1977. Virginia Brodine, *Radioactive Contamination,* New York: Harcourt, Brace, Javanovich, 1975. As well as various issues of the *San Francisco Examiner, Los Angeles Times,* and *It's About Times,* the newspaper of the Abalone Alliance. Quote is from "The 18-year War Against Truth," by Mark Evanoff, which first appeared in *Not Man Apart,* September 1981.

112–114: Angel, 1979. William H. Brewer, *Up and Down California* (1864), Berkeley: U.C. Press, 1966. Loren Nicholson, *Rails Across the Ranchos,* Santa Cruz: Western Tanager Press, 1980. Felix Reisenberg, *The Golden Road,* New York: McGraw Hill, 1962. *San Luis Obispo County Telegram-Tribune Centurama,* 1956.

116–118: Bancroft Library pamphlets. Dorothy L. Gates and Jane H. Baily, *Morro Bay's Yesterdays,* Morro Bay: El Moro Publications, 1982.

120–122: Thomas R. Aidala, *Hearst Castle: San Simeon,* New York: Hudson Hills Press, 1981. Oscar Lewis, *Fabulous San Simeon, A History of the Hearst Castle,* San Francisco: California Historical Society, 1958. W.B. Yeats quote from "Sailing to Byzantium," on p.120 appears in *The Collected Poems of W.B. Yeats,* New York: Macmillan Publishing Company, 1982; the other quote on p.120 is from W.A. Swanberg's *Citizen Hearst,* New York: Charles Scribner's Sons, 1961.

Land Use

106: State Department of Parks and Recreation. Natural History Association of San Luis Obispo Coast, Inc.

108: Chester Hartman, Jon Pynoos, Robert Schafer, *Housing Urban America.* Chicago: Aldine Publishing Company, 1973.

112: San Luis Obispo Environmental Center. San Luis Obispo County Land Conservancy.

114: Patricia J. Clark, *Mission Plaza,* San Luis Obispo, 1979.

116: Harold Wieman, *Morro Bay Meanderings,* San Luis Obispo: Padre Productions, 1975.

118: Michael Dileo and Eleanor Smith, *Two Californias,* Covelo: Island Press, 1983.

122: Dunlap, 1982. James D. Hart, *A Companion to California,* New York: Oxford University Press, 1978.

Environment

107: Bakker, 1984. Natural History Association of San Luis Obispo County.

109: Peter Howarth, *Foraging Along the California Coast,* Santa Barbara: Capra Press, 1977.

111: David E. Kaplin, *Nuclear California, An Investigative Report,* San Francisco: Greenpeace, 1982. Abalone Alliance, Friends of the Earth.

113: California State Parks Foundation Natural History Association of San Luis Obispo Coast, Inc. San Luis Obispo County Land Conservancy. California State Parks Foundation.

115: San Luis Obispo County Chamber of Commerce. Sierra Club, *San Luis Obispo County Trail Guide,* Santa Lucia Sierra Club, 1984.

117: American Littoral Society, *California Coastal Catalog,* New Jersey: ALS, 1980.

119: Jack Rudloe, *The Erotic Ocean,* New York: E. P. Dutton, Inc., 1984.

121–123: Aidala, 1981. Hearst San Simeon Historical Monument.

Roadside Attractions

121: Blake's quote is from *The Marriage of Heaven and Hell,* London: Oxford University Press, 1975.

Monterey County

126–130: Joseph Smeaton Chase, *California Coast Trails,* New York: Houghton Mifflin Company, 1913. James Miller Guinn, *History and Biographical Record of Monterey and San Benito Counties,* Los Angeles, 1910. John Woolfenden, *Big Sur: A Battle for the Wilderness 1869–1981,* Pacific Grove: Boxwood Press, 1981. Quote on p.128 is based on an account in Augusta Fink's, *Monterey County: The Dramatic Story of its Past,* Santa Cruz: Western Tanager Press, 1982.

132: Fink, 1982. Emil White's guides to Big Sur, published between 1954–1960, also provide a comprehensive description to the origins of tourism in the area. Published under several titles *(The Big Sur Yesterday, Today, Tomorrow; Monterey Peninsula and Big Sur, a Guide to Highway 1; Big Sur Guide to the Circle of Enchantment;* and *Big Sur Guide to the Hearst Castle).*

134–140: Fink, 1982. Woolfenden, 1981. Work Projects Administration (WPA) Writers Program, *Monterey Peninsula,* American Guide Series, 1941. Quote on p.138 is from *California Highways and Public Works,* June, 1924.

142: California State Parks Commission, *Point Lobos Reserve,* Berkeley: Save the Redwoods League, 1936. Fink, 1982. Vernon Aubrey Neasham, *Historical Background of Point Lobos Reserve,* Berkeley, 1937.

144–146: Dunlap, 1982. Fink, 1982. Pamphlet Boxes, Bancroft Library. Franklin Walker, *The Seacoast of Bohemia,* Santa Barbara: Peregrine Smith, 1973.

148–150: Henry Dwight Barrows, *A History of Coast Counties,* Chicago, 1893. Del Monte Properties Company, *Monterey Peninsula and Hotel Del Monte,* Monterey, 1924. Fink, 1982. Guinn, 1910. Monterey Foundation, *Old Monterey, Doorway to History,* San Francisco, 1951. WPA, 1941. Quote on p.148 is from Brewer, 1966.

152–156: Fink, 1982. *Monterey Peninsula Herald,* Centennial Edition, 1949. Randall Reinstedt, *Where Have All the Sardines Gone?,* Carmel: Ghost Town Productions, 1984. Quote on p.152 is from Chase, 1913.

Land Use

126: Big Sur Foundation. California Coastal Commission, State Office.

128: José Gómez-Ibáñez, *Autos Transit in the City,* Cambridge: Harvard University Press: 1981. Caltrans.

130: Gilliam's quote appears in *This World, San Francisco Examiner,* May 30, 1982. Trotter's quote appears in *San Francisco Chronicle,* January 30, 1984.

132: Big Sur Land Trust. Paul Denison, *Monterey Peninsula Herald,* October 4, 1979.

134: Big Sur Land Trust. California Coastal Commission. Harold Gilliam, "Private Property, Public Interest," *This World, San Francisco Examiner,* November 6, 1983.

136: Monterey County Planning Department. California State Coastal Conservancy.

138: Whyte, 1968. Caltrans.

140: *California Highway and Public Works,* various 1933 issues.

144: Carmel Business Association. *Carmel Pine Cone,* June 28, 1984.

146: Jacob Grimm's quote appears in Jackson, 1984.

148: Quote is from *San Francisco Chronicle,* September 10, 1983.

150: California Coastal Commission, Central District. City of Monterey Planning Department. Roberson's quote is from the *San Francisco Chronicle,* September 10 1983.

154: California Coastal Commission, Central District.

156: California Coastal Commission, Central District.

Environment

127: Floyd Schmoe, *The Big Sur,* San Francisco: Chronicle Books, 1975. Quote is from Jack Kerouac, *Big Sur,* New York: McGraw Hill, 1981.

129: WPA, 1941. Burr Snider, "Enraptured by the Beauty of Jade," *San Francisco Examiner,* June 15, 1984.

131: Woolfenden, 1981. Caltrans.

133: Jeremy Joan Hewes and Jon Goodchild, *Redwoods: The Worlds Largest Trees,* London: Rand McNally & Co., 1981.

135: Robert Ornduff, *An Introduction to California Plant Life,* Berkeley, U.C. Press, 1974.

137: Brown, 1979. Udvardy, 1977.

139: Source for the feature is the U.S. Army Corps of Engineers.

141: John Woolfenden, *The California Sea Otter—Saved or Doomed?* Pacific Grove, The Boxwood Press, 1984.

143: Peter C. Howorth, *The Abalone Book,* Happy Camp California: Naturegraph Publishers, Inc., 1978. Quote is from Edward F. Ricketts, *Between Pacific Tides,* Palo Alto: Stanford University Press, 1985.

145: Carmel Visitor Center. McMinn and Maino, 1981. Monterey Peninsula Visitors and Convention Bureau.

147: McMinn and Maino, 1981.

149: Burton L. Gordon, *Monterey Bay Area: Natural History and Cultural Imprints,* The Boxwood Press, Pacific Grove, 1979.

151: Randall A. Reinstedt, *Where Have All the Sardines Gone?,* Carmel: Ghost Town Productions, 1978. Quote is from Ricketts, 1985.

153: Steinbeck's quote appears in the introduction to Ricketts, 1985. The major source for the adjacent column on the aquarium is Mary Jo McConahay, "It's More Than Just Another Fish Tank," *San Francisco Examiner,* December 4, 1983.

155: Gordon, 1979. Monterey County Planning Department.

157: The Elkhorn Slough Foundation.

Roadside Attractions

131: Michael Murphy's quote appears in Walter Truett Anderson's *The Upstart Spring: Esalen and the American Awakening,* Monterey: Addison Wesley, 1984.

147: Carmel Mission quote is from Chase, 1913. Jeffers quote is from "The Bloody Sire," contained in *Be Angry at the Sun,* New York: Random House, 1941.

149: Stevenson's quote appears in Dunlap, 1982.

Santa Cruz County

Origins

160: F. W. Atkinson, *One Hundred Years in the Pajaro Valley,* Watsonville, 1934. Betty Lewis, *Watsonville: Memories That Linger,* Fresno: Valley Publishers, 1976.

162: Margaret Koch, *Santa Cruz County: Parade of the Past,* Fresno: Valley Publishers, 1977.

164–168: Book Club of California, *Coast and Valley Towns of Early California,* San Francisco, 1938. Koch, 1977. Charles S. McCaleb, *Surf, Sand, and Streetcars,* Glendale: Interurban Press, 1977. Pamphlets, Bancroft Library. Leon Rowland, *Santa Cruz, the Early Years,* Santa Cruz: Paper Vision Press, 1980. Source for the origin/land use feature on p.168 is John Chase, *The Sidewalk Companion to Santa Cruz Architecture* Santa Cruz: Western Tanager Press, 1981.

170: L. G. Olin, *The Development and Promotion of Santa Cruz Tourism,* Master Thesis, San Jose State University, 1967.

172–174: *California Highways and Public Works,* May, 1939, October, 1939. Koch, 1977. Rowland, 1980.

Land Use

160: California Coastal Commission, Central District. Santa Cruz.

162: California Coastal Commission, Central District. Santa Cruz County Planning Department.

164: Santa Cruz County. Santa Cruz Wharf.

166: Santa Cruz Board of Supervisors. *Santa Cruz Sentinel,* April 28, 1984.

168: Historic Preservation Ordinance, City of Santa Cruz. John Chase, *The Sidewalk Companion to Santa Cruz,* Santa Cruz: Western Tanager Press, 1981.

172: California Coastal Commission, Central District. Department of Parks and Recreation.

174: Santa Cruz Mountain Transit District.

Environment

161: Hornbeck, 1983. Lantis, 1981. Watsonville Chamber of Commerce.

163: Gordon, 1979. Santa Cruz County Planning Department.

165: Santa Cruz Wharf. U.S. Army Corps of Engineers.

167: Brown, 1979. Land Trust of Santa Cruz County.

169: Gordon, 1979. Natural Bridges State Park.

171: University of California at Santa Cruz. Quote is from Harold Gilliam, "Agroecology," *San Francisco Examiner,* April 5, 1985.

173: McMinn and Maino, 1981.

175: Sempervirons Fund. Source for the feature is U.S. Army Corps of Engineers.

Roadside Attractions

171: Gebhard, Montgomery, Winter, J. Woodbridge, S. Woodbridge, *A Guide to Architecture in San Francisco and Northern California,* Santa Barbara: Peregrine Smith: 1976.

San Mateo County

Origins

178–182: Philip W. Alexander, *History of San Mateo County,* Burlingame, 1916. Roy Walter Cloud, *History of San Mateo County,* Chicago, 1928. Elbert Hubbard, *A Little Journey to San Mateo County,* East Aurora, N.Y., 1915. Frank Merriman Stanger, *South from San Francisco,* San Mateo County Historical Association, 1963. Quotations on p.178, 180, 182 are from June Morrall's *Half Moon Bay Memories,* El Granada: Moonbeam Press 1979.

184–186: A. Bray Dickinson, *Narrow Gauge to the Redwoods,* Glendale: Interurban Press, 1983. Alan Hynding, *From Frontier to Suburb,* Belmont: Star Publishing Company, 1982. Ocean Shore Railroad Company, *Franchises and Permits, San Francisco, 1906.* Pamphlets, Bancroft Library. Quote on p.184 is from Jack R. Wagner's *The Last Whistle,* Berkeley: Howell North Books, 1974.

188–190: Hynding, 1982. Morrall, 1979.

192–194: Ben Blow, *California Highways,* San Francisco: Crocker Company, 1920. Panama–Pacific International Exposition Commission, *Road Book of Automobile Tours in San Mateo County,* San Francisco, 1915.

196: Devil's Slide Draft Environmental Impact Statement, November, 1983. Quote on p.196 is from *San Francisco Examiner,* February 26, 1984.

Land Use

178: Department of Environmental Management, *Coastside Cultural Resources of San Mateo County,* Redwood City: San Mateo County, 1980.

180: California Coastal Commission, Central District. California Department of Parks and Recreation. Trust for Public Land.

182: Morrall, 1979.

184: California Coastal Commission, Central District. State Coastal Conservancy. San Mateo County Department of Environmental Management.

186: California Coastal Commission, Central District. San Mateo County Local Coastal Program.

188: San Mateo County Department of Environmental Management. Johnston House Foundation.

190: Army Corps of Engineers, San Francisco District Office. California Coastal Commission, State Office. Pillar Point Harbor District.

192: *San Francisco Chronicle,* June 19, 1984.

194: Blow, 1920.

198: Hynding, 1982.

Environment

179–185: California Department of Parks and Recreation. Burney J. Le Boeuf and Stephanie Kaza, *The Natural History of Año Nuevo,* Pacific Grove: The Boxwood Press, 1981. Quote on page 185 is from Le Boeuf, 1981.

187: San Mateo County Historical Society. San Mateo County Local Coastal Plan. Quotes are from a working paper for the county local coastal plan.

189: San Mateo County. U.S. Army Corps of Engineers. The source for the adjacent feature on the Costanoans is R. F. Heizer and M. A. Whipple, *The California Indians,* Berkeley: U.C. Press, 1971.

191: James V. Fitzgerald Marine Reserve.

193: James V. Fitzgerald Marine Reserve.

195: *Sharks,* San Diego: Wildlife Education, Ltd., 1983. The feature on how to protect against sharks in the adjacent column is from Robert Hendrickson, *The Ocean Almanac,* New York: Doubleday and Co., 1984, as is the feature on land sharks.

197: Caltrans. San Mateo County Planning Department.

199: San Mateo County Department of Environmental Management.

Roadside Attractions

197: Jack Gilbert's quote is from "Prospero Without His Magic," which appears in *19 New American Poets of the Golden Gate,* New York: Harcourt Brace Jovanovich, 1984.

San Francisco

Origins

202-204: Raymond H. Clary, *The Making of Golden Gate Bridge,* San Francisco: California Living Books, 1980. Anita Day Hubbard, *Cities Within the City,* San Francisco: *San Francisco Bulletin,* 1924. Oscar Lewis, *Mission to Metropolis,* San Diego: Howell North Books, 1980. Charles Lockwood, *Suddenly San Francisco,* San Francisco: *San Francisco Examiner,* 1978. Roger Lotchin, *San Francisco, 1846-1856: From Hamlet to City,* Lincoln: University of Nebraska Press, 1979. Susan Shepard, *In the Neighborhoods,* San Francisco: Chronicle Books, 1981. Source for the feature on p. 204 is John Woodbridge, Sally Woodbridge, *Architecture in San Francisco,* San Francisco: 101 Productions, 1982.

206: Maya Angelou's quote is from *I Know Why the Caged Bird Sings,* New York: Random House, 1969. Sunset Transportation and Development Association quotes are from STDA papers at the California Historical Society.

208-216: Margot Patterson Doss, *Golden Gate Park at Your Feet,* San Francisco: Presidio Press, 1980. Guy Giffen, *The Story of Golden Gate Park,* San Francisco, 1949. Robert Johnson, *The Magic Park,* San Francisco, 1940. Herbet Pruett, *The Golden Gate Park,* Berkeley,: Pruett Mac-

Gregor, 1968. Coleridge's quote on p. 212 is from "Kubla Khan," contained in *Coleridge's Verse; A Selection,* edited by William Empsen and David Pine, New York: Shocken Books, 1973. Quote on p. 216 *(top)* is from Hubbard, 1924; quote on p. 216 *(bottom)* is from Clary, 1980.

218-224: Richard Dillon, *High Steel, Building the Bridges Across San Francisco Bay,* Berkeley: Celestial Arts, 1979. Golden Gate Bridge District, *The Golden Gate Bridge, Report of the Chief Engineer to the Board of Directors,* San Francisco, 1937. Tom Horton, *Superspan,* San Francisco: Chronicle Books, 1983. E.C. Mensch, *The Golden Gate Bridge, A Technical Description in Everyday Language,* San Francisco, 1935. Quote on p. 222 is from Stephen Cassady's *Spanning the Gate,* Mill Valley: Squarebooks, 1979.

Land Use

202: Lewis Mumford, *The City in History,* New York: Harcourt, Brace & World, Inc., 1961. Peter Wolf, *Land in America,* New York: Pantheon Books, 1981.

206: Sam Bass Warner, *Streetcar Suburbs,* Cambridge: Harvard University Press, 1962. Wolf, 1981.

208: Clary, 1980.

210: Quote is from Jane Jacobs, *The Life and Death of American Cities,* New York: Random House, 1961.

212: Friends of Golden Gate Park.

214: Quote appears in Lawrence Halprin, *Freeways,* New York: Reinhold Publishing Corporation, 1966.

216: San Francisco Department of City Planning. San Franciscans for Affordable Housing.

218: Golden Gate National Recreation Area. The Presidio of San Francisco.

220: The Golden Gate Bridge District. San Francisco Department of City Planning.

222: ABAG, BCDC.

224: Source for Flying Saucer feature is Joseph J. Corn and Brian Horrigan's *Yesterday's Tomorrows,* New York: Summit Books, 1984. Source for the painting feature is Horton, 1983.

Environment

203: S. Harold Gilliam, *Weather of the San Francisco Bay Region,* Berkeley: U.C. Press, 1983.

205: U.S. Army Corps of Engineers. Gilliam, 1983.

207: Gladys Hanson, *San Francisco Almanac,* San Rafael: Presidio Press, 1980.

211: Udvardy, 1977.

213: Elizabeth McClintock, "California's Botanical Gardens," *Discovering California,* San Francisco Academy of Sciences, 1983. Doss, 1980.

215: Strybing Arboretum and Botanical Gardens.

217: San Francisco Department of City Planning. Quote is from Jacobs, 1961.

219: Arthur C. Smith, *The Natural History of the San Francisco Bay Region,* Berkeley: U.C. Press, 1973. BCDC.

221: Smith, 1973. Source for the feature is Catherine M. Way, "Reber's Dam Folly," *Sunday San Francisco Examiner,* July 29, 1984.

223: BCDC. Source for the feature is Rick Rubin, "The Day San Francisco Drowned," *San Francisco Examiner,* April 8, 1984.

225: Paul G. Hewitt, *Conceptual Physics,* Boston: Little Brown and Company, 1971.

Roadside Attractions

219: Hart Crane's quote is from *The Bridge* contained in *The Complete Poems of Hart Crane,* New York: Doubleday, 1966.

221: Susan Sontag's quote is from *On Photography,* New York: Farrar, Straus and Giroux, 1973. Used with permission.

Marin County

Origins

228: Helen Bingham, *In Tamal Land,* San Francisco, 1906. *California Highways and Public Works.*

230: Dickinson, 1983. Dunlap, 1982. North Pacific Coast Railroad Company, *Prospectus,* undated.

232: Jack Mason, *The Making of Marin,* Inverness: North Shore Books, 1975. Sierra Club. Jack Tracy, *Sausalito, Moments in Time,* Sausalito: Wingate Press, 1984.

234: Jack Mason, *Last Stage for Bolinas,* Inverness: North Shore Books, 1973. Quote is from Ted Wurm and Al Grave's *The Crookedest Railroad in the World,* Glendale: Trans-Anglo Books/Interurban Press, 1983.

236-242: Marin County Historical Society, *Marin People,* Santa Rosa, 1971. Arthur Quinne, *Broken Shore: The Marin Peninsula,* Salt Lake City: Peregrine Smith, 1981. "A Century of Service, 1861-1961," *San Rafael Independent Journal.* Louise Teather, *Discovering Marin,* Fairfax: Tamal Land Press, 1974. Quote on p. 236 is from Mason, 1973.

244: Quotes are from Dickinson, 1981.

246: Mason, 1973. *Point Reyes Light,* various issues.

Land Use

228: Gebhard, et al, 1976.

230: Alan Watts Society for Comparative Philosophy.

234: California Coastal Commission, State Office.

236: California Coastal Commission, State Office.

238: Audubon Canyon Ranch.

240: Bolinas Community Public Utilities District. Marin County Planning Department.

242: Quote is from Trust for Public Land newsletter.

244: California State Parks Foundation. Quote is from Fred Powledge, "Marin County Legacy," *Nation Magazine,* May 14, 1983.

246: Marin Agricultural Land Trust.

Environment

229: Harold Gilliam, "A Procession of Hawks," *San Francisco Examiner,* October 28, 1984.

231-233: David D. Alt and Donald W. Hyndman, *Roadside Geology of Northern California,* Missoula: Mountain Press Publishing, 1981.

235: Point Reyes National Seashore. Peter Yanov, *Peace of Mind in Earthquake Country: How to Save Your Home and Life,* San Francisco: Chronicle Books, 1980. Alt, 1981.

237: Marin County Local Coastal Plan. State Water Resources Control Board.

239: Audubon Canyon Ranch. California Coastal Commission, State Office.

241: Audubon Canyon Ranch. Point Reyes Bird Observatory.

243: Conradson, 1982. Faber, 1982. Smith, 1973.

245: Point Reyes National Seashore. Caltrans.

247: Point Reyes National Seashore.

Roadside Attractions

235: James Broughton's quote appears in Alan Watts' *In My Own Way, An Autobiography,* New York: Random House, 1973.

Sonoma County

Origins

250-254: Alley Bowen and Company, *History of Sonoma County,* San Francisco, 1880. Thomas Gregory, *History of Sonoma County,* Los Angeles, 1911. Harvey J. Hansen, *Wild Oats in Eden,* Santa Rosa, 1962. Thomas C. Russell, *The Rezanov Voyage to Nueva California,* San Francisco, 1926. Honoria Tuomey, *History of Sonoma County,* Chicago, 1926. Bret Harte's quote on p. 252 is contained in *The Poetical Works of Bret Harte,* New York: Houghton Mifflin, 1898.

256-262: Richard Dillon, *The Story of Sea Ranch,* Oceanic Properties, 1965. Tuomey, 1926. San Francisco *Argonaut* quote and *Pacific Tourist* quote on p. 256 appear in Dickinson, 1983. C.A. Menefee's quote on p. 260 is from his *Historical and Descriptive Sketch Book of Napa, Sonoma, Lake, and Mendocino Counties, 1973.* Quote on p. 262 is from Chase, 1913.

264: Quote is from *California Highways and Public Works,* December, 1931.

Land Use

250: Erickson's comment appears in the *San Francisco Examiner,* June 20, 1984.

252: Bodega Bay Harbor District. The source for the feature on the nuclear power plant is Mike Hayden, *Exploring the North Coast,* San Francisco: Chronicle Books, 1976.

254: Hine, 1983. *Morning Star Scrapbook: In the Pursuit of Happiness,* Occidental: Morning Star Distributing Company, 1974.

256: Espositi's quote appears in the *San Francisco Examiner,* March 24, 1985.

258: California Conservation Corps.

260: State Coastal Conservancy.

262: California Coastal Commission, State Office.

264: Wolf, 1980.

Environment

251: Bakker, 1983. Robert Ornduff, *Introduction to California Plant Life,* Berkeley: U.C. Press, 1974.

253: Bodega Bay Harbor District.

255: Brown, 1979. Udvardy, 1977.

257: Sonoma State Beach, Russian River Area.

259: Alt and Hyndman, 1981. Miller and Hyslop, 1983.

261: Kruse Rhododendron State Park.

263: Ricketts, 1985.

265: Sonoma County Planning Department.

Roadside Attractions

261: Dunlap, 1982.

263: Quotes are from David Littlejohn, "Condo 1," *San Francisco Examiner,* June 3, 1984.

Mendocino County

Origins

268-272: A.O. Carpenter, *History of Mendocino and Lake Counties,* Los Angeles: 1914. Andrew M. Genzoil, *Redwood Frontier, Wilderness Defiant,* Eureka: Schooner Features, 1961. Menefee, 1973. Lyman L. Palmer, *History of Mendocino County,* San Francisco, 1880. Mendocino County Historical Society, *Logging in Mendocino County,* Fort Bragg, no date. *Daily Alta* quote on p. 158 (top) is contained in Margaret J. Brinzing's *Early History of the Mendocino Coast,* University of California (thesis), 1950; quote on 268 (bottom) is contained in Annette White Park's *Qh Awala Li, 'Water Coming Down Place,'* Ukiah: Freshcut Press, 1982.

274-280: Bruce Levene, *Mendocino County Remembered: An Oral History,* Fort Bragg: Mendocino County Historical Society, 1976. *Mendocino Coast Beacon,* Bicentennial Edition, 1976. David Ryder, *Memories of the Mendocino Coast,* San Francisco, 1948. Quote on p. 274 (top) is from Parks, 1982; (bottom) is from Bancroft Library pamphlet boxes. Quote on p. 276 is from Palmer, 1888. Quote on p. 278 is from Parks, 1982.

282: Dorothy Bear, *Mendocino* (Books 1, 2), Mendocino: Mendocino Historical Research, 1973. Carpenter, 1914.

284: Gebhard, et al, 1976.

286-288: Bonni Grapp, *Footprints: An Early History of Fort Bragg,* California, Fort Bragg, 1967. Parks, 1982. Palmer, 1888. Quote on p. 286 is from Carpenter, 1914.

Land Use

268: Paul Liberatore, *San Francisco Examiner,* September 19, 1984. *Ridge Review,* Spring 1984.

270: Mendocino County Local Coastal Program. California Coastal Commission, State Office.

272: Southern Mendocino County Action Committee, State Coastal Conservancy.

274: U.S. Army Corps of Engineers. Chad Eblers and Jim Gibbs, *Sentinels of Solitude: West Coast,* Portland: Graphic Arts Center Publishing Company, 1981.

276: Mendocino Chamber of Commerce. *Ridge Review,* Summer, 1984.

278: U.S. Army Corps of Engineers. Noyo Harbor District.

280: Abalone Alliance. California Coastal Commission, North Coast Office. Mendocino County Planning Department.

286: Moskowitz, 1980.

288: California Coastal Commission, State Office. Gorda Ridge Project, *A Citizen's Guide to Ocean Stripmining,* San Rafael, 1984.

Environment

269: Hayden, 1976. California Department of Fish and Game.

271: Hewes and Goodchild, 1981. Weaver, 1981.

273: Bascom, 1980. California Coastal Commission.

275: Brown, 1979. Mendocino County Department of Planning. Udvardy, 1977.

277: Alt and Hyndman, 1983. Jug Handle State Reserve.

281: Crittenden and Telfer, 1975.

283: *The Oceanic Society Field Guide to the Gray Whale,* San Francisco: Legacy Publishing Company, 1983. Stephen Leatherwood and Randall S. Reeves, *The Sierra Club Handbook of Whales and Dolphins,* San Francisco: Sierra Club Books, 1982. Theodore J. Walker, *Whale Primer,* Point Loma: Cabrillo Historical Society, 1975.

285: Hayden, 1976.

287: Jug Handle Farm and Nature Center. Jug Handle State Reserve.

289: U.S. Army Corps of Engineers. Source for feature is the Bureau of Land Management.

Roadside Attractions

269: Quote is from Chase, 1913.

271: London's quote appears in Dunlap, 1982.

Credits for photos and illustrations are listed below by county, column, and page number. Those photos credited "Bancroft Library" are courtesy of The Bancroft Library, University of California, Berkeley. Those credited "California Historical Society" are courtesy of The California Historical Society, San Francisco, unless otherwise noted. References to the "Corps" are from the U.S. Army Corps of Engineers. All photos not otherwise credited were taken by Rick Adams.

Key: *When more than one photo appears on a page in one column,* **(t), (m),** *and* **(b)** *indicate top, middle, bottom of the column. When two photos appear in the same column side-by-side,* **(l)** *and* **(r)** *indicate left and right.*

Introduction

3: Sonoma Coast. *Baron Wolman*

5: *I Love Lucy* publicity photo/Golden Gate Bridge composite. *Memory Shop West, Triad*

11: Devil's Slide, San Mateo County. *Baron Wolman*

Orange County

12: Huntington Harbor. *Baron Wolman*

Origins

14: Dana Point homesite advertisement. Reprinted by permission, from *Doris Walker, Dana Point Harbor: Home Port for Romance, To-the-Point Press, 1983*

16: Early campers at Laguna Beach. *Courtesy First American Title Insurance Company*

18: Hotel Laguna. *Courtesy First American Title Insurance Company*

20: Douglas Fairbanks and Mary Pickford at the opening of the Coast Road, Laguna Beach. *California Highways and Public Works*

22: Early views, Irvine Ranch. *Courtesy First American Title Insurance Company*

24: Corona Del Mar. *Courtesy Sherman Library*

26: Newport Beach car on the Pacific Electric Railway. *Courtesy First American Title Insurance Company*

28(t): Balboa Pavilion after arrival of Red Cars. *Courtesy First American Title Insurance Company*

28(b): Rendezvous Ballroom. *Courtesy Sherman Library*

30: Huntington Beach. *Courtesy First American Title Insurance Company*

32: California surfers circa 1950. *Courtesy Surfer Magazine*

34: Huntington Beach oil wells. *Works Projects Administration*

36(t): Seal Beach Joy Zone. *Courtesy First American Title Insurance Company*

36(b): Early Orange County beachgoers. *Courtesy First American Title Insurance Company*

Land Use

14: Highway 1 begins in Orange County

16: Open space in Orange County. *California Coastal Commission, David Miller*

26: Lovell Beach House, 1926. *Courtesy Architectural Drawing Collection, University of California, Santa Barbara*

30: A sunny day at Huntington Beach

32: Memorial bust of Duke Kahanamoku

Environment

15: Dana Point. *Courtesy Orange County Marine Institute*

17: *Triad, adapted from California Patterns illustration, 1983*

19(t): Laguna Beach

21: *Triad, adapted from Corps illustration*

25(t): *Triad, adapted from Corps illustration*

25(b): Newport Beach

27(t): Newport Beach groin field. *Corps*

27(b): *Triad, adapted from Corps illustration*

31: *Corps*

33(t): *Triad, adapted from Corps illustration*

33(m): *Corps*

35(t): *Corps*

35(b): *California Coastal Commission*

37: *Corps*

Roadside Attractions

17(t): South Laguna Beach

17(b): Aliso Pier

19: Beachgoers at Laguna

23(t): Orange Inn

23(b): PCH near Crystal Cove

25(t): Newport Dunes

25(b): Ferrari Dino

27: John Wayne, publicity photo. *Memory West Shop*

29: Balboa Pavilion

31(t): *Courtesy Surfer Magazine*

31(b): Huntington Beach. *Courtesy Surfer Magazine, Ker*

33: Surfing at Huntington Beach. *Courtesy Surfer Magazine*

35(t): Huntington Beach Pier. *Expression Classic, Tony Rowland*

37(b): Superman's telephone booth

Resources

15: The Pilgrim

17: *Triad, adapted from California Patterns, 1983*

19(b): Coastal Commission public hearing. *California Coastal Commission*

23(t): *Triad, adapted from Orange County Board of Supervisors illustration*

23(b): *Corps*

27(t): Newport Dory Fleet. *Corps*

27(b): Jetty at Newport Harbor. *Corps*

29(t): Balboa Island Ferry. *Corps*

29(b): Dick Dale's Surf's Up shop

33: Silver Surfer, ™&©1985 Marvel Comics Group. Used with permission

Los Angeles County

38: Pacific Coast Highway, Santa Monica. *Baron Wolman*

Origins

40: Redondo Beach Beauty Contestants. *Courtesy First American Title Insurance Company*

42: Amusement Zone at The Pike. *California Historical Society*

46: Redondo Beach. *California Historical Society, Los Angeles, Ticor Title Insurance Collection*

48: Passengers on the first Santa Monica trolley, 1896. *California Historical Society, Los Angeles, Ticor Title Insurance Trust Collecction*

50(t): Plane at LAX. *Corps*

50(b): Marina Del Rey Harbor, 1970. *California Historical Society, UPI*

52(t): Venice. *California Historical Society, Los Angeles, Ticor Title Insurance Collection*

52(b): Venice, Cabrillo Canal circa 1924. *California Historical Society, Los Angeles, Ticor Title Insurance Collection*

54: Swimmers, Santa Monica. *California Historical Society*

56: Santa Monica, Castle Rock from the north. *California Historical Society, Los Angeles, Ticor Title Insurance Collection*

58(b): Santa Monica, PCH. *California Historical Society*

60(b): Will Rogers. *Bancroft Library*

62(t): Malibu Colony, PCH. *California Historical Society, Trichnor Art Co., Los Angeles*

62(b): Coast road through Malibu. *California Historical Society, Los Angeles, Ticor Title Insurance Collection*

64(t): Opening of the Coast Highway from Santa Monica to Oxnard, 1929. *California Highways and Public Works*

64(b): San Juan Capistrano to Oxnard Highway. *California Highways and Public Works*

Land Use

40: Circle Drive-in marquee

42: East along the Pike, circa 1924. *California Historical Society, Los Angeles, Ticor Title Insurance Collection*

44(t): Ranchos Palace Verdes. *California Historical Society*

44(b): Phineas Banning at the reins. *Bancroft*

46: Surfurb

48: *Mr. Lucky,* 1943. *RKO*

50(t): Wetlands at the original Marina Del Rey site. *California Historical Society, United Press International*

50(b): Snowy egret in wetland. *Corps*

54: Santa Monica Pier carousel

56: California bungalow

60(t): Holiday House Motel, 1949. *Julius Shulman, used with permission*

Environment

43(t): Long Beach harbor. *Port of Los Angeles*

43(b): *Corps*

45(t): *Corps*

Credits

45(b): Cliffs of the Palos Verdes Peninsula. *Corps*
47: Pacific Shore. *National Parks Service*
49(t): *Corps*
49(b): *National Parks Service, Greg Gnesios*
51(b): Marina del Rey. *California Coastal Commission*
53(b): Western gull. *Corps*
57: *U.S. Forest Service*
59: Santa Monica Mountains. *National Parks Service*
61: *The Endless Summer,* 1964. *Cinema Distributing, Inc.*
63(t): Paradise Cove. *Corps*
63(b): Malibu Pier. *Corps*
65: *Triad, adapted from Corps illustration*

Roadside Attractions

43(t): *The Queen Mary* and dome housing the *Spruce Goose,* Port of Long Beach. *Courtesy Rather Port Properties*
45: Yummyburger stand, Long Beach
47(t): Veteran's Park, Redondo Beach
47(m): Redondo Horseshoe Pier
47(b): Monument to George Freeth, Redondo Beach
49(t): Hermosa Beach
49(b): Manhattan Beach Pier
51: Howard Hughes at the controls of the *Spruce Goose. Courtesy Rather Port Properties*
53(t): Muscle Beach. Venice
53(b): Aimee Semple McPherson. *Bancroft Library*
57: Santa Monica Place
59: Pallisades Park bench sitters
61(t): J. Paul Getty Museum Courtyard
61(b): The Getty Bronze. *Courtesy The Getty Museum*
63: Marilyn Monroe at LA city limits. *Courtesy The Kobal Collection, John Kobal*
65: *Gidget,* 1959. *Columbia Pictures Industries*

Resources

45(t): Ships in LA Harbor. *Corps*
45(b): *Courtesy Marineland*
47(t): Manhattan Beach surfers
47(b): Redondo Beach. *Corps*
51: LAX theme building
53: Manhattan Beach mural
55(t): Santa Monica carousel organ
55(b): Santa Monica Beach. *Corps*
57: Jane Golden mural, PCH, Santa Monica
65(t): Santa Monica Beach. *Corps*
65(b): *Illustration from Willard Bascom, 1980*

Ventura County

66: Northern Ventura Shoreline. *Baron Wolman*

Origins

68(t): Coast Highway cut around Point Mugu. *California Highways and Public Works*
68(b): Frank Lloyd Wright's Broadacre City. *Courtesy Frank Lloyd Wright Collection, Taliesin West*
70(t): Point Mugu. *Corps*
70(b): Model Missle
72: Stage negotiating surf. *Bancroft Library*
74: Oil pumps. *Ventura Chamber of Commerce*
76(t): Early Coast Road along Rincon. *California Highways and Public Works*
76(b): Construction of Coast Road at Rincon. *California Highways and Public Works*
78: Rincon Causeway. *California Highways and Public Works*
82(t): Cabrillo. *Bancroft Library*
82(b): Spanish Missionary and Native American. *Bancroft Library, Miguel Venega, 1739*

Land Use

72: Migrant farm families, 1933. *Bancroft Library*
74: Oxnard Avenue
80: Santa Cruz Island. *National Parks Service*

Environment

69: Juvenal condor. *Courtesy Museum of Vertebrate Zoology, Berkeley*
73: Citrus grove. *Corps*
75(b): *Triad*
77(t): Channel Islands Harbor. *Triad, adapted from Corps illustration*
77(b): Dredging at Channel Islands Harbor. *Corps*
79(t): Oxnard Plain
79(b): Ventura Promenade

81: *National Parks Service, Roy Murphy*
83: Ventura County Courthouse

Roadside Attractions

69(t): Neptune's Net
69(b): PCH Point Mugu
71: Ventura shoreline at Point Mugu. *Corps*
73(t): Channel Islands Harbor
73(m): *The Sheik,* Famous Players Laskey Corp. 1921
75: Oxnard Boulevard
77(t): Perry Mason, publicity photo. *Memory Shop West*
79: Wagon Wheel Restaurant
81(t)(m): Channel Island Visitor Center
81(b): *National Parks Service, Roy Murphy*
83: Downtown Ventura

Resources

69(t): California condor. *Courtesy Friends of the Earth*
69(b): *California Fish and Game*
71: Polaris Missile model
73: California farmworkers. *State Department of Agriculture*
79: Ventura Beach and Pier. *Corps*
81: *Courtesy Island Packer Cruises*
83: San Buenaventura Mission

Santa Barbara

84: Offshore oil platform, Santa Barbara Channel. *Baron Wolman*

Origins

86: Santa Barbara lithograph, 1877 *California Historical Society, E.S. Clover*
88(t): Muledrawn streetcar. *Bancroft Library*
88(b): West Beach: 1902. *Bancroft Library*
90: Arlington Hotel. *Bancroft Library*
92: Santa Barbara County Courthouse. *Santa Barbara Conference and Visitors Bureau*
94: Automobile tourists at Potter Hotel. *Bancroft Library*
96: Gaviota Pass. *Bancroft Library*
98(t): Lompoc "Drugstore." *Courtesy Lompoc Historical Society*
98(b): Fourth of July 1900: H Street and Ocean Avenue, Lompoc. *Courtesy Lompoc Historical Society*
100: Surf Depot. *Courtesy Lompoc Historical Society*
102: *The Ten Commandments,* 1923. *Paramount*

Land Use

86: La Parra Grande. *Architect and Engineer Magazine*
88: *Corps*
90: Fatty Arbuckle, publicity photo. *Memory Shop West*
92: Santa Barbara earthquake, 1925. *Bancroft Library*
94: WPA mural figure. *WPA, Clifford Wright*
100: Missle, Vandenberg Force Air Base. *Courtesy Lompoc Record*

Environment

87: Santa Barbara Channel. *Triad, adapted from Corps illustration*
89: Polluted waters. *California Coastal Plan, 1976*
91: Moreton bay fig tree. *Santa Barbara Conference and Visitors Bureau*
93(t): Oleander. *Triad*
95: Santa Ynez River. *U.S. Forest Service*
97: 1925 Santa Barbara earthquake. *Bancroft Library*
101: *State Department of Water Resources*
103: Bald eagle. *Courtesy Washington Zoo, 1944*

Roadside Attractions

87(t): Santa Barbara from Stearns Wharf
89: *Courtesy Stearns Wharf*
91: Roller skater, West Beach
93: Fox Theatre
95: *The Sign of Zorro,* Publicity still. *Walt Disney Productions*
97: Jalama County Beach Park. *Corps*
99(t): *Courtesy Lompoc Record*
99(m): *Courtesy Lompoc Record*
99(b): *Courtesy Lompoc Record*
101: WPA restoration of La Purisima Mission. *Department of Parks and Recreation*
103(t): Guadalupe Cemetary
103(b): Town clock, Guadalupe

Resources

89: *Courtesy Stearns Wharf*
91: Palm Park
93: *Courtesy Santa Barbara Zoo*
97: Windsurfer, Jalama Beach. *Courtesy Lompoc Record*
99: Lompoc Flower Festival. *Courtesy Lompoc Record*
101: La Purisima Mission. *La Purisima State Historic Park*
103: Amtrak Coast Starlight. *California Coastal Plan, 1976*

San Luis Obispo

104: Highway 1 and Hearst Castle. *Baron Wolman*

Origins

106(t): Early Pismo Beach. *Courtesy San Luis Obispo Historical Museum*
106(b): ATC at Pismo Beach
108: Map of Moy Mell. *The Dune Forum*
110: Diablo Canyon Power Plant. *Reprinted Courtesy Friends of the Earth from Not Man Apart 9–81*
112: *Bancroft Library*
114(t): Hotel Ramona *Courtesy San Luis Obispo Historical Museum*
114(b): Ah Louis Store
116: Morro Beach real estate promotion. *Bill Roy, 1981*
118: Highway 1 near Cambria
120(t): Citizen Kane, publicity still. *Memory Shop West*
122(t): *Courtesy Hearst San Simeon State Historical Monument*
122(b): *Courtesy Hearst San Simeon State Historical Monument*

Land Use

108: Mobile home, Oceano
110: Protesters, Diablo Canyon. *Reprinted courtesy Friends of the Earth from Not Man Apart*
112: San Luis Obispo mountain peak
114: Mission Plaza
116: Morro Bay. *Corps*
118: *Triad*
120(b): Marion Davies, publicity still
122: Julia Morgan. *Bancroft Library*

Environment

107: European beach grass. *Corps*
109(t): *Corps*
113: Madonna Inn. *Courtesy Madonna Inn*
115: *National Parks Service*
117: *Corps*
119: Mussels on piling. *Corps*
121: Neptune's Pool

Roadside Attractions

107(b): Highway 1, Nipomo mesa
109: Oceano
111: *The China Syndrome,* 1979. *Columbia Pictures Industries*
115(t): Fremont Theatre
115(b): San Luis Obispo Creek, Mission Plaza
117(t): Montana de Oro State Park
117(b): Morro Rock
119(t): Gull Cottage

Resources

107: Coastlines bus
119(b): Nitwit Ridge
121: Steps of Hearst Castle

Monterey County

124: Bixby Bridge, Big Sur. *Baron Wolman*

Origins

126: Early Trail. *Reprinted with permission, Boxwood Press, John Woolfenden*
128: *Bancroft Library*
130: Bixby Landing. *Pat Hathaway Collection*
132: Pfeiffer Resort, 1935. *Pat Hathaway Collection*
134: Highway 1 surveyor. *The Sun-Bulletin, April 12, 1984*
136(t): Construction, 1937. *Pat Hathaway Collection*
136(b): Construction. *Pat Hathaway Collection*

138: Convict Labor crew. *Pat Hathaway Collection*
140(t): Bixby Bridge construction, 1930. *Pat Hathaway Collection*
140(b): Bixby Bridge construction. *California Highways and Public Works*
142(t): Point Lobos. *Cara Moore*
142(b): Point Lobos. *Pat Hathaway Collection*
144(t): Ocean Avenue, Carmel, 1909. *Bancroft Library*
144(b): Early Carmel carriage travel. *Bancroft Library*
146: George Sterling. *Bancroft Library*
148: Shorewhaling. *San Francisco Maritime Museum*
150: Del Monte Hotel. *California Historical Society*
152: Cannery Row, 1947. *Pat Hathaway Collection*
154(b): Fort Ord, 1940. *California Historical Society*
156(t): Moss Landing. *Bancroft Library*
156(b): PG&E plant at Moss Landing. *Corps*

Land Use

128: Highway 1, Big Sur
130: 1983 slide. *The Sun-Bulletin, April 12, 1984*
134: Pico Blanco. *Pat Hathaway Collection*
142: View toward Point Lobos, *Pat Hathaway Collection*
146: Urizen creates the Finite Universe. *William Blake, Reprinted with permission, David Erdman, The Illuminated Blake, Doubleday, 1979*
148: Oiled murre. *Point Reyes Bird Observatory*
152: John Steinbeck. *Bancroft Library*

Environment

135: *Triad*
137: *The Sandpiper, 1963. Metro-Goldwyn-Mayer*
139: *Triad, adapted from Corps illustration*
141: *Martin Solberg, courtesy Greenwich Workshop*
143: *Corps*
145: *Triad*
147(b): *California Coastal Commission*
149(b): *Triad, adapted from Corps illustration*
151(t): *Pat Hathaway Collection*
153(t): *Corps*
153(b): Edward F. Ricketts. *Bancroft Library*
155(t): Historical changes in Salinas River. *Elkhorn Slough Foundation*
155(b): Fort Ord. *Corps*
157(t): Long-billed curlews. *Corps*
157(b): *Corps*

Roadside Attractions

131: Lucia. *Boxwood Press, John Woolfenden*
133: McVay waterfall. *Reprinted with permission, Boxwood Press, John Woolfenden*
135: Big Sur Inn
137: *Corps*
139(t): Big Sur coast, 1930. *Pat Hathaway Collection*
145: Ansel Adams. *Bancroft Library*
149(l): Robert Louis Stevenson. *Bancroft Library*
149(r): Fanny Osbourne. *Bancroft Library*
153: Monterey Bay Aquarium, February 1985. *Pat Hathaway Collection*
155: *Courtesy Kitty Hawk Kites*

Resources

131(t): *Courtesy Esalen, Kathy Thormod*
131(b): Courtesy Esalen
135: Nepenthe
147: *Triad, adapted from Carmel Gallery Guide*

Santa Cruz

158: Coastline north of the City of Santa Cruz. *Baron Wolman*

Origins

160: Watsonville, Main Street circa 1910. *California Historical Society*
162(t): Early Capitola. *California Historical Society, Ravnos*
162(b): Hotel Capitola. *California Historical Society, Pacific Novelty Company*
164: Seal Beach Hotel. *Bancroft Library*
166: Casino, Santa Cruz waterfront. *California Historical Society, Aydelotte*
168: Faye Lanphier, Miss Santa Cruz, 1924. *Courtesy Warren Littlefield Collection*
170: Tourists in the redwoods. *Courtesy Sempervirens Fund*
172: Early Davenport. *California Historical Society*

174: Coast road, 1939. *California Highways and Public Works*

Land Use

160: Watsonville, Oak Grove Berry Farm, circa 1925. *California Historical Society*
164: Santa Cruz Boardwalk and Beach. *Courtesy Santa Cruz Boardwalk*
168: Santa Cruz Theatre, 1930's. *Courtesy University California Santa Cruz, Special Collections*
170: *Courtesy University California Santa Cruz*

Environment

161(b): Watsonville Postcard. *California Historical Society*
165(t): The Casino, Santa Cruz Boardwalk. *Coutesy Santa Cruz Boardwalk*
165(b) Mouth of the San Lorenzo River. *Corps*
167: Northern pintails. *Triad*
169: Natural Bridges. *National Parks Service*
171: *Courtesy University of California Santa Cruz*
173: Tanbark oak. *Triad*
175: Greyhound rock. *Corps*

Roadside Attractions

161(b): Odd Fellows Building, Watsonville
163(t): New Brighton State Beach
163(b): Capitola Beach
167(t): Merry-go-round at the Boardwalk
167(b): The Giant Dipper. *Courtesy Santa Cruz Boardwalk*
171(t): *Courtesy University California Santa Cruz*
171(b): *Corps*
173(t): Beach Babies. *Courtesy Bart Dollhead, Dollhead Dezines*
173(b): Gray whale flukes. *Corps*
175: *Corps*

Resources

161: Parajo Valley
163(t): Seacliff State Beach. *Corps*
163(b): *Corps*
165: Fortune teller at the Boardwalk
167(t): Giant Dipper. *Courtesy Santa Cruz Boardwalk*
167(b): Antonelli's Pond. *Courtesy Land Trust of Santa Cruz County*
171: *Courtesy University of California Santa Cruz*
175: Redwood at Big Basin. *Courtesy Sempervirens Fund*

San Mateo County

177: Highway 1 at Devil's Slide. *Baron Wolman*

Origins

178: Pigeon Point loading chute. *California Historical Society, C.C. Johnson*
180(t): Half Moon Bay, 1903. *California Historical Society*
180(b): Gordon's Chute. *Courtesy San Mateo County Historical Society*
182: Early Pescadero. *California Historical Society*
184: Ocean Shore Railroad locomotive. *Bancroft Library*
186(t): Ocean Shore Railroad passenger cars. *Bancroft Library*
186(b): Ocean Shore Railroad construction. *Bancroft Library*
188(t): Early Coast Highway, San Mateo County. *Courtesy San Francisco City Archives*
188(b): Sybil Easterday. *Courtesy San Mateo County Historical Society*
190: Newly completed Highway 1, 1939. *California Highways and Public Works*
192(t): Coast Highway 1, 1939. *California Highways and Public Works*
192(b): Sidewalks to lots, Granada. *California Historical Society*
194: Highway 1 under construction at Devil's Slide. *California Highways and Public Works*
196: Devil's Slide
198: Pacifica. *Courtesy Pacifica Chamber of Commerce*

Land Use

178: Pigeon Point Lighthouse. *Corps*
188: Johnston House

Environment

179(t): *Reprinted with permission, Boxwood Press, F. Lanting, 1981*

181: San Gregorio Fault Zone. *Triad, adapted from Boxwood Press illustration*
183: Sea lion. *National Parks Service, Gary M. Nougues*
185: Male elephant seals. *National Parks Service, Eugene Fisher, Kenneth Parker*
187: Cultivated flower fields. *Corps*
189(t): *Triad, adapted from Corps illustration*
189(b): *Triad, adapted from Corps illustration*
191: Cormorant. *Corps*
193(t): Tidepools at Fitzgerald Marine Reserve. *Corps*
193(b): *Triad, adapted from Corps illustration*
195(t): Great white shark. Courtesy *Wildlife Education Ltd., San Diego*
195(b): Angela Beske
197(t): Montara Mountain. *Corps*
197(b): Stunt from *Portrait in Black. Peninsula Times Tribune, Rich McGovern*
199: Lupine. *Reprinted with permission, Boxwood Press, 1981*

Roadside Attractions

179(b): Point Año Nuevo. *Reprinted with permission, Boxwood Press, G. Weber, 1981*
183: Highway 1 in southern San Mateo County
187(t): San Gregorio service station
189: Half Moon Bay, southern city limits
191: (t and b) New Age Center
193: Pillar Point Harbor
195: Moss Beach
199: Daly City Freeway

Resources

181(m)): Tour at Año Nuevo. *Reprinted with permission, Boxwood Press, 1981*
181(b): Año Nuevo. *Reprinted with permission, Boxwood Press, 1981*
185(t): Harbor seal. Courtesy *California Marine Mammal Center, Ellen Blonder*
185(b): San Gregorio State Beach
187: Fresh Produce chart. *Triad, Adapted from San Mateo County Farm Bureau chart*
189(t): Picking pumpkins at Half Moon Bay. *Angela Beske*
189(b): Costanoans. *Bancroft Library*
191(t): James V. Fitzgerald Marine Reserve
193(b): Montara Lighthouse

San Francisco

200: Golden Gate Bridge looking toward Golden Gate Park. *Baron Wolman*

Origins

202: The Great Sand Waste. *Bancroft Library*
204: Vigilance Committee Seal. *Bancroft Library*
206: Early Sunset District. *California Historical Society, G. E. Russell*
208: Early Golden Park entry. *Bancroft Library*
210(t): *California Historical Society, Perkins*
210(b): Spreckels Bandshell
212: Electric Tower at the Midwinter Fair, 1894. *California Historical Society, Taber*
214: Midwinter Fair. *California Historical Society, Taber*
216: Early Park Presidio Drive. *Courtesy San Francisco Archives*
218: *Courtesy San Francisco Archives*
220(t): South pier Golden Gate Bridge rises above Fort Point. *Courtesy Redwood Empire Association*
220(b): Diver prepares for work on the pilings. *California Historical Society*
222(t): Raising the towers of the Bridge. *Courtesy Redwood Empire Association*
222(b): Spanning the bridge. *Courtesy Redwood Empire Association*
224: Opening Day, May 27, 1937. *San Francisco Examiner*

Land Use

204(t): *Bullet, 1968. Solar Productions*
204(b): Doelger houses
206: Promoting development in the Sunset. *California Historical Society, Bronstrup Poster*
208: Conservatory of Flowers. *California Historical Society*
212(t): Mary B. Connolly Children's Playground
212(b): Golden Gate Carousel. *Roy King*
214(t): *San Francisco Examiner*
214(b): End of the Embarcadero Freeway
218: The Presidio and Richmond District. *San Francisco Archives*

220: Traffic controller on bridge. *Courtesy Redwood Empire Association*
224(t): Painter on the Golden Gate Bridge. *Courtesy Redwood Empire Association*
224(t): Weygers' discopter port and harbor facilities, 1947 Reprinted with permission

Environment

203: Sunset District
205(t): Triad, *adapted from Corps illustration*
205(b): *Courtesy San Francisco Archives*
207: Benny Bufano's statue of Saint Francis
211: *Triad*
219: *Corps*
221: Reber's plan to dam San Francisco Bay. *Triad, adapted from 1942 rendering, San Francisco Examiner*
223: Path of Golden Gate channel. *Corps*
225: *Courtesy San Francisco Archives*

Roadside Attractions

203(b): Muni Metro in the Sunset
205(b): San Francisco State Student Union Building
207(t): Former Trocadero Inn, Stren Grove
207(b): Ocean Beach streetcar. *Courtesy San Francisco Archives*
209(t): *The Wizard of Oz, 1939. Universal Studios*
209(l): John McClaren. *Courtesy San Francisco Archives*
209(r): William Hammond Hall. *Courtesy San Francisco Archives*
211(b): California Academy of Sciences
221: "Double Exposure," from a Homer Ansley painting. *Courtesy Henri Lenoir, Smith Novelty*
223: Cover. *San Francisco Examiner, California Living Magazine*
225: Worker atop northern tower of the Golden Gate Bridge. *California Historical Society, Ted Huggins*

Resources

205: *Courtesy San Francisco Archives*
207: San Francisco Conservatory of Music
211: M. H. de Young Museum
213: San Francisco Mime Troup performs Patelin, 1968 in Golden Gate Park. *Courtesy Mime Troup, Charles Bigelow*
215: San Francisco Parks Department
219(l): Presidio housing
219(r): Fort Point, courtyard
221: View from the bridge: San Francisco
223: Runners in the Bay to Breakers Race. *San Francisco Examiner, Ken Lee, 5-19-85*

Marin County

226: Western Marin County. *Baron Wolman*

Origins

228: Construction of the Waldo Tunnel. *Redwood Empire Association*
230(t): *Bancroft Library*
230(b): Sausalito Ferry Passengers. *Bancroft Library*
232: Point Reyes. *National Parks Service, Ed Brady*
234: Marin Stage. *Bancroft Library*
236(t): Coast Road south of Stinson Beach. *Pat Hathaway Collection*
236(b): Upton's Beach. *Courtesy Jack Mason Collection*
238(t): Dipsea Inn. *Bancroft Library*
238(b): Early Auto Stage. *Bancroft Library*
240(t): Bolinas, 1904. *Pat Hathaway Collection*
240(b): Bolinas Stage, circa 1890. *Courtesy Jack Mason Collection*
242(t): Early Marin saloon. *Bancroft Library*
242(b): Early Olema. *Courtesy Jack Mason Collection*
244: North Pacific Coast Railroad. *Bancroft Library*

Land Use

228: Marin City Public Housing
232: Lady Bird Johnson at opening day, PRNSS. *National Parks Service*
234: Mount Tamalpais Gravity Train. *Bancroft Library*
238(b): Young egrets in nest. *National Parks Service.*
242: *Courtesy Trust for Public Land*

Environment

229(t): Osprey. *Audubon Canyon Ranch*
229(m): Marin Peninsula. *San Francisco Archives*
229(b): Marin Headlands looking toward San Francisco.

San Francisco Convention and Visitor's Bureau, Richard Frear
231: Sausalito from the Bay
233(t): Triad, *adapted from National Parks Service illustration*
233(m): Sandstone. *National Parks Service*
233(b): Granite. *National Parks Service*
237(t): Highway 1, looking toward Duxbury Reef
239: Bolinas Lagoon
241(b): *Corps*
243(t): *Corps*
247(t): Wild Iris. *National Parks Service*
247(b): Fallow deer. *National Parks Service, Laurie Dickson*

Roadside Attractions

231(b): Alan Watts. *Alan Watts Society for Comparative Philosophy*
237(b): Angela Beske
243(b): Bear Valley Visitor Center. *National Parks Service, Greg Gnesios*
243(t): Point Reyes Parade
245(b): Oyster mound along Highway 1

Resources

229(b): *Courtesy Pacific Publishers*
231: *Corps*
233: Muir Woods
235: Olema Inn staff and suppliers. *Art Rogers, Point Reyes Station*
237: *Point Reyes Light*
241: *Triad, Courtesy Point Reyes Bird Observatory*
241(b): *National Parks Service*
245(t): *Bill Majoue*

Sonoma County

248: Sonoma coastline, Jenner grade. *Baron Wolman*

Origins

250: Christo's Running Fence. *Courtesy Wolfgang Volz, Photo Volz*
252: Nikolai Rezanov. *Bancroft Library*
254(t): *California Historical Society*
254(b): *Bancroft Library*
256: North Pacific Coast Railroad, Brown's Canyon. *Bancroft Library*
258(t): Fort Ross, 1917. *Courtesy Pat Hathaway Collection*
258(b): Fort Ross, 1857. *California Historical Society*
260: Logging in the Sonoma redwoods, 1876. *California Historical Society*
264(t): Opening day, Russian River Bridge. *California Highways and Public Works*

Land Use

252: *Corps*
252(b): Bodega Head. *Corps*
258: *California Coastal Commission*
260(b): Site plan for Stillwater Cove accessway. *State Coastal Conservancy*

Environment

251: *National Parks Service*
253: Jetties at Bodega Harbor. *Corps*
255(t): Brown pelicans. *Courtesy San Francisco Archives*
255(b): *The Birds, 1963. Universal-International*
257(t): Russian River jetty and barrier sand spit. *Corps*
257(b): *Triad, adapted from Corps illustration*
261: *Triad*
263(t): Salt Point shoreline
263(b): Sea palm. *Corps*
265(t): *National Parks Service*

Roadside Attractions

253(t): Bodega
253(b): Bodega Bay
255: Fish market at Bodega Bay
257: Russian River
261(t): *National Parks Service/Richard Frear*
261(b): Bufano's totem pole, Timber Cove
263(t): Stewarts Point

Resources

253: Doran County Park

259: Fort Ross, 1985
261: Tidepool life. *National Parks Service*

Mendocino County

266: Little River Bridge. *Baron Wolman*

Origins

268: Gualala Sawmill. *California Historical Society*
270(t): Oxen logging teams. *Bancroft Library*
270(b): *Triad*
272: Loading chute, Point Arena. *California Historical Society*
274: Hauling ties, Navarro. *California Historical Society*
276(t): Schooner. *Bancroft Library*
276(b): Albion mill. *Bancroft Library*
278: Early auto in Gualala. *Bancroft Library*
280: Steam schooner. *Courtesy San Francisco Maritime Museum*
282: Schooners loading from chute. *Bancroft Library*
286(t): Main Street, Fort Bragg. *California Historical Society*
286(b): Georgia Pacific yard, Fort Bragg
288: Early coast road, Mendocino shore. *Courtesy Redwood Empire Association*

Land Use

270: *Corps*
274(t): Fresnel lens. *Corps*
274(b): Point Arena Lighthouse
278(t): Port of Albion
278(b): Fishing fleet at Noyo Harbor
282: Harry Meiggs. *California Historical Society*

Environment

269(t): *Courtesy Redwood Empire Association*
269(b): *Corps*
271(b): Jim Warger, *Redwoods, The World's Largest Trees, 1981*
273(t): *Triad, adapted from Corps illustration*
273(b): *National Parks Service*
275(t): Osprey and nest. *Courtesy Point Reyes Bird Observatory*
275(b): Whistling swans at Garcia River plain. *Corps*
277(t): *Triad, adapted from Corps illustration*
277(b): Sea stacks, Elk
281(b): Bush lupine
283(t): Gray whale head. *Lynn and Wick Ahern*
283(b): Whale sculpture. *Lynn and Wick Ahern*
285(t): Dungeness crab. *Corps*
285(b): Crab traps. *Corps*
287(t): Headlands at Jughandle State Reserve
287(b): *Triad, adapted from Corps illustration*
289: *Triad, adapted from Corps illustration*

Roadside Attractions

269: Gualala River
271(t): Gualala Hotel
271(b): Jack London. *Bancroft Library*
273: Anchor Bay Store
275(t): Downtown Point Arena
275(b): Road to Point Arena
277: Elk Market
279(t): Albion pocket beach
279(b): North of Albion
281(t): House on bluff
281(b): Mendocino bed and breakfast
283: Village of Mendocino
285(b): James Dean, publicity photo. *Memory Shop West*
287(t): Noyo Harbor. *Corps*
287(b): Daly's, Fort Bragg
289(t): North of Fort Bragg
289(b): Lost Coast. *Bureau of Land Management*

Resources

269: *Jon Goodchild/Triad*
271: Bucking crew slices log from fallen redwood. *National Parks Service*
279(t): Noyo Harbor
283: Whale sculptor Lynn Ahern. *Wick Ahern*
285: Kelly House Museum and Library

Index

Town and County Index

The Town and County Index refers only to listings in the Roadside Attractions column and the general county chapter pages.
See the main index for more detailed listing in all
columns.

The letter codes preceding
the page numbers indicate the
column in which the reference
is to be found: O = Origins,
L = Land Use, E = Environment, RA = Roadside Attractions, R = Resources.

A

Index